DISCOURSES IN AFRICAN MUSICOLOGY

J.H. KWABENA NKETIA FESTSCHRIFT

DISCOURSES IN AFRICAN MUSICOLOGY

J.H. KWABENA NKETIA FESTSCHRIFT

Edited by **Kwasi Ampene** (University of Michigan)
with
Akosua Adomako Ampofo (University of Ghana)
Godwin K. Adjei (University of Ghana)
Albert K. Awedoba (University of Ghana)

Co-Publishers **African Studies Center**
University of Michigan
Office of the Senior Vice Provost for Academic Affairs
University of Michigan
Institute of African Studies
University of Ghana, Legon

Copyright © by Kwasi Ampene 2015
Some rights reserved

This work is licensed under the Creative Commons Attribution-
Noncommercial-No Derivative Works 3.0
United States License. To view a copy of this license,
visit http://creativecommons.org/licenses/by-nc-nd/3.0/
or send a letter to Creative Commons, 171 Second Street,
Suite 300, San Francisco, California, 94105, USA.

Published in the United States of America by Michigan Publishing
Manufactured in the United States of America
Printed on acid-free paper
2018   2017   2016   2015   4   3   2   1

ISBN: 978-1-60785-347-3 (paper)

An imprint of Michigan Publishing, Maize Books serves
the publishing needs of the University of Michigan community
by making high-quality scholarship widely available in print
and online. It represents a new model for authors seeking
to share their work within and beyond the academy, offering
streamlined selection, production, and distribution processes.
Maize Books is intended as a complement to more formal
modes of publication in a wide range of disciplinary areas.

http://www.maizebooks.org

Copy Editor: Maria Phillips
Design: Franc Nunoo-Quarcoo

Contributors	Lester P. Monts
	Kwasi Ampene
	Akosua Adomako Ampofo
	Godwin K. Adjei
	Albert K. Awedoba
	M.E. Kropp Dakubu
	Joseph Kaminski
	Modesto Amegago
	David Locke
	Brenda Romero
	Ben Paulding
	Amy Unruh
	Alexis L. Danti
	Mawuli Adjei
	Jacqueline C. Djedje
	Nissio Fiagbedzi
	Bode Omojola
	George W.K. Dor
	Abena Kyere
	Bridget Chininouriri
	Craig Woodson
	George P. Hagan
	Patience A. Kwakwa
	Mitchel Strumpf
	Jesse D. Ruskin
	Paul W. Schauert
	Sylvanus K. Kuwor
	Kofi Asare Opoku
	Ruth M. Stone
	Kofi Agawu

Contents

10 **Preface**
Lester Monts

14 **Acknowledgments**
Akosua Adomako Ampofo,
Kwasi Ampene, Godwin K. Adjei, Albert K. Awedoba

16 **Introduction**
Kwasi Ampene,
Akosua Adomako Ampofo, Godwin K. Adjei, Albert K. Awedoba

Section 1 **EXPRESSING LANGUAGE, EXPRESSING MUSIC**

40 **Language and Music: Mind, Body, Meaning**
M.E. Kropp Dakubu

56 **Nketia's Influence in Ntahera Hocket and Surrogate Speech Analyses**
Joseph Kaminski

76 **The Textual Basis of African Drumming: The Interaction Between Spoken Language and Drumming**
Modesto Amegago

Section 2 **ANALYSIS OF TRADITIONAL MUSIC**

98 **Sweetness in Agbadza Music: Expressiveness in an Item of Agbadza Singing and Drumming**
David Locke

124 **A Theory of Infinite Variation**
Brenda Romero

156 **Kete for the International Percussion Community**
Ben Paulding

186 **Spontaneity, Improvisation, and Musical and Social Aesthetics in Ghanaian Kpanlogo Music and Dance**
Amy Unruh

Section 3 SINGING HISTORY

212 **Kasena Maiden Songs: A Genre on the Wane**
Albert K. Awedoba and Alexis L. Danti

236 **Documentation of Slavery in Ghanaian Folklore:
Anlo Ewe Slave Songs**
Mawuli Adjei

Section 4 DIASPORIC DIALOGUES AND CURRENTS

256 **Music and Diasporas Within West Africa:
The Pre-Colonial Era**
Jacqueline C. Djedje

276 **Give Me Silence, Space, and a Dance:
The Pianistic Style of Thelonious Monk**
Kwasi Ampene

Section 5 ANALYSIS OF WRITTEN COMPOSITIONS

306 **J.H. Kwabena Nketia's Republic Suite:
An Analytical Portrait of Movement I**
Nissio Fiagbedzi

330 **Representing Africa Through Creative Ethnomusicology:
Minimalism and Postcolonial Themes in the Music
of Samuel Akpabot**
Bode Omojola

350 **Exploring the Ontology and Application
of the "Nketia Dominant Seventh Chord"**
George W.K. Dor

Section 6 DISCOURSES OF GENDER

374 **Women Doing Music: The Lives and Songs
of Contemporary Ghanaian Women Musicians**
Abena Kyere and Akosua Adomako Ampofo

394 **Is A Woman Only Worth The Rib of A Man?:
The Place of Women in Zimbabwean Musical Arts,
Past and Present**
Bridget Chininouriri

Section 7 EMBRACING DONDOLOGY-ESTABLISHING A VISION

420 **Applied Ethnomusicology: My Lifelong Exploration and Expression as a Dondologist**
Craig Woodson

456 **Dondology: Music, Mind, and Matter**
George P. Hagan

Section 8 EXPERIENCING AND ARCHIVING THE VISION

480 **Kwabena Nketia and the Creative Arts: The Genesis of the School of Music and Drama, and the Formation of the Ghana Dance Ensemble**
Patience A. Kwakwa

508 **Professor J.H. Kwabena Nketia: Ethnomusicologist and Educator**
Mitchel Strumpf

520 **Biographical Writing and Individual Creativity in African Musicology**
Jesse D. Ruskin

538 **Kwabena Nketia and the Genesis of Archival Collections at the Institute of African Studies**
Godwin K. Adjei

552 **Nketia, Nationalism, and the Ghana Dance Ensemble**
Paul W. Schauert

574 **Representation: My Africanist Perspective**
Sylvanus K. Kuwor

MEMORIES
596 **The Two-Day International Conference University of Ghana, Institute of African Studies**
September 23–24, 2011

Preface

Lester P. Monts

Professor of Music
Arthur F. Thurnau Professor
University of Michigan
Ann Arbor

Discourses in African Musicology represents the results of a conference held at the University of Ghana in September 2011 in honor of Professor J.H. Kwabena Nketia on the occasion of his 90th birthday. The conference also served the purpose of exploring the many facets of African music studies by a broad array of scholars and performers. A number of junior and senior scholars presented papers representing a broad range of scholarship, much of it inspired by Professor Nketia. The conference provided a forum where those in attendance shared in the scholarly discourse on African music that has emerged over the last 60 years. At the center of these conversations, the influence of Professor Nketia was strongly pronounced. Prof, as he is affectionately known by many, not only helped shape the field of ethnomusicology, his scholarship in many ways formed the foundation for an African Musicology, comparable in scope and stature to the historical and cultural music studies conducted over the centuries in Europe and Asia.

Through various global initiatives, American universities have acquired a newfound interest in Africa. These global engagements have provided a strong set of connections for students and scholars that enhance their research and study while solidifying their connections with African institutions and colleagues. These recent initiatives bring Africa closer to the center of the modern global community, which in recent years has been dominated by connections between the United States, Europe, Asia, and Australia. It is noteworthy for us to recall the efforts of individuals like Professor Nketia who over many years played a pivotal role in the furtherance of the often forgotten arts and humanities as key focal points for educational connections in Africa.

Without question, Professor Nketia stands as one of the most prolific scholars focusing on the music of Africa; however, it would be quite limiting to relegate his contributions to a single sphere of musical scholarship and creativity. His career spans the birth and growth of the field of ethnomusicology, and at the age of 94, his writing on key topics continue and he remains a sought after lecturer around the world. Prof's career and contributions to music scholarship defy placing him in a specific category of composer, author, scholar, teacher, or performer. He is all of the above and much more. For the purposes of these brief remarks, I want readers of this collection of essays to consider him as the person around whom we have all gathered to engage in intellectual discourse, to establish enduring infrastructures, and to further our own scholarship and teaching.

Scholars of my generation will recall the many ways in which Professor Nketia served as the source of great inspiration for music researchers and for the creation of organizational structures to serve as gathering places for the further growth of African music scholarship. For many years, the major scholarly journals on Africa seldom published articles on music, and those pieces that found their way into these journals were widespread and often lacked the coherency of a particular theme. In the 1980s, Prof successfully encouraged the editors of the *Journal of African Studies* and *Selected Reports in Ethnomusicology* to devote special editions to studies on African music. Those Nketia-influenced publications, along with the volume co-edited by Jacqueline C. Djedje and William Carter *African Musicology: Current Trends*, constitute a substantial contribution to African music scholarship. These publications provided the stepping-stones for a number of young scholars, including myself, who were embarking on careers in ethnomusicology with major emphases on African music.

As the quintessential trailblazer for African music study, I should point out that Prof's reputation exceeds far beyond that of a scholar. For the Rockefeller Foundation in particular, he became known as a visionary on the frontlines of social change. For the Ford Foundation, Prof's work fell squarely within their mission to promote the well-being of humanity throughout the world. In 1992 and with major financial support from the Rockefeller Foundation, a group of music and dance scholars was convened at its Bellagio Center in Italy to engage in focused discussions on innovative ways to identify impact-oriented solutions to the study of African music and dance. From that successful gathering and with funding from the Ford and Rockefeller Foundations and the Swedish International Development Authority (SIDA), the International Centre for African Music and Dance (ICAMD), a semi-autonomous unit within the University of Ghana School of Performing Arts, was formed. The ICAMD established the Africa-based secretariats in South Africa at Walter Sisulu University, Mthatha; in Kenya at Maseno University; and in Nigeria at the University of Ibadan. The United States Secretariat was established and located for many years in the International Institute at the University of Michigan, Ann Arbor.

I want to thank and congratulate our colleagues, Kwasi Ampene, Akosua Adomako Ampofo, Godwin K. Adjei, and Albert K. Awedoba for organizing the symposium in honor of Professor Nketia and for serving as editors for this Festschrift. A special thanks is also due to the contributors to this volume who for their love and respect for Prof, many of whom traveled to Ghana to participate. Professor Nketia's long and productive career will forever shape our inquiries on the concepts, ideas, and values of African music. His work predates the establishment of the field of ethnomusicology and his contributions will continue to provide substantial strength to its theoretical base. He leaves to us a legacy of dedication and commitment to the growth and well being of African music scholarship now and in the future, and for that and much more, we sing his praises.

Acknowledgments

Akosua Adomako Ampofo
Kwasi Ampene
Godwin K. Adjei
Albert K. Awedoba

The project that you hold in your hands has had a long gestation period, however, it has been a labor of love. Collectively we would like to thank colleagues from the University of Ghana, Legon (UG), and the University of Michigan (UM), for their support and encouragement. Specifically, we are grateful to John Gyapong, Provost for the Office of Research, Innovation and Development (ORID), UG, for facilitating an ORID grant that helped support the the International African Studies Conference in honor of Emeritus Professor J. H. Kwabena Nketia, at which most of the papers in this volume were first presented. We also thank our corporate partner, Guinness Ghana Breweries Limited (GGBL), particularly the then corporate relations director Nana Yaa Ofiri-Atta, for working with us to support the conference which was the first event of the Intellectual and Cultural Heritage Festival series for the Institute of African Studies, UG. While many get excited about book projects and offer their support, subventions to carry the work forward are much harder to come by. Thus we greatly appreciate that Lester Monts, in his capacity as Senior Vice Provost for Academic Affairs, UM, provided a book subvention for the publication of this Festschrift. We are also grateful to Kelly Askew, Director of the African Studies Center at UM for supporting this publication.

There are many others we would like to thank: The Society for Ethnomusicology (SEM) for their spiritual and intellectual support; the African Music Section (AfMS) in the SEM for contributing to the planning, and participating in the conference and this Festschrift; the Nketia family for their presence and helpful musings; the Fellows and staff of the IAS for their ever-generous contributions of time and practical assistance; and of course, the many presenters at the conference, many of whom traveled long distances and at not insignificant personal cost, to share in the celebrations. Finally, our sincere gratitude to Professor Franc Nunoo-Quarcoo at the Penny W. Stamps School of Art & Design (UM) for the beautiful design of this book. We equally extend our sincere gratitude to Maria Phillips, for her skillful work as copy editor for this complex project.
    Ye ma mo nyina ayekoo!

Introduction

Kwasi Ampene
with
Akosua Adomako Ampofo
Godwin K. Adjei
Albert K. Awedoba

Praise Poetry
Mo, mo ne yɔ
Well done, well done
Wo na w'ayɛ asubɔnten a amasan nom mu nsuo
You are the river that provides sustenance for people all over the world
W'ayɛ aponkyerɛni a ɔma nsuo
You are the frog that gives water
W'ayɛ kokuromoti a yɛnsan wo ho mmɔ pɔ
You are the thumb without you we cannot tie a knot
W'ayɛ onyina kɛseɛ a yɛtena aseɛ gye mframa
You are a big silk cotton tree under which we sit for fresh air
Efiri tete barima atwa asuo
Mankind has been crossing rivers since the beginning of time
Mampong Kontonkyi Nana a
Grandchild of Mampong Kontonkyi
Yɛde akoboɔ gye wo taataa
We herald you with warrior stones
Asonaba ahoɔfɛ
Handsome child of Asona clan
Mo, mo ne yɔ!
Well done, Well done!

On September 23, 2011, twenty-two years after the two-volume Festschrift, *African Musicology: Current Trends,* was presented to Professor Emeritus J.H. Kwabena Nketia at the University of California, Los Angeles, a group of scholars from Africa, the United States and Europe gathered at the Institute of African Studies (IAS) at the University of Ghana to celebrate another milestone, his 90th birthday. By no means an ordinary gathering, it was a two day international conference from September 23-24, titled *The Life and Works of Emeritus Professor J.H. Kwabena Nketia.* The room in which the conference was held bore the name of our honoree, Nketia, having been so named by the Fellows of the Institute of African Studies (IAS) in recognition of his position as the first African director of the Institute as well as his contributions to African music.[1] In the months leading up to the conference and in the call for proposals, the Local Organizing Committee (LOC) involving Kwasi Ampene from the University of Michigan, and Akosua Adomako Ampofo, Albert Awedoba, and Godwin K. Adjei, all from from IAS, had encouraged Africanists from all disciplines to submit papers that could potentially be included in a proposed Festschrift.

The idea for a conference in Ghana to pay homage to Nketia on his 90th birthday began in 2009 during a business meeting of the African Music Section (AfMS) as part of the 54th Annual Conference of the Society for Ethnomusicology (SEM) in Mexico City. For the AfMS, the successful hosting of the SEM by nine local institutions in Mexico was unprecedented in the history of the SEM. Unlike the International Council for Traditional Music (ICTM) which is on record for holding annual meetings outside the United States, the SEM is a quintessential US-based organization that does not entertain the prospects of meeting outside its North American enclave of the US and Canada. Nevertheless, the meeting in Mexico City was an eye opener for the AfMS members that the SEM could be held in an African country as well. The urgency to advocate for a meeting of the society on African soil was stronger than ever. Essentially, this line of thought and growing sentiment in the AfMS stemmed from the extraordinary landmark contributions of Nketia in defining African Musicology and the larger field of ethnomusicology. Cage Averill, then president of the SEM, expressed in his congratulatory message published in the conference brochure that he "cannot even conceive of the field [of ethnomusicology] without considering the immense contributions of Professor Nketia." The AfMS membership were unanimous in proposing the University of Ghana as the conference venue, and Kwasi Ampene volunteered to coordinate this effort with the section chairs. Unknown to the AfMS, similar plans to celebrate Nketia's 90th birthday were in the works in Ghana at the Institute of African Studies.

For the director and fellows at the IAS, the impending 90th birthday provided the first impetus for a grand celebration that would be commensurate with the legacy of the first African director of the IAS. The second stimulus was the recognition of two cultural icons, Efua Sutherland and Ama Ata Aidoo, by their respective disciplines and professional bodies and the resultant publications dedicated to their legacies. Efua Sutherland's cultural activism and the development of modern drama in postcolonial Ghana are celebrated in the multi-authored book, *The Legacy of Efua* (Sutherland 2007). Similarly, *Essays in Honour of Ama Ata Aidoo at 70* (Adams 2012), celebrates Aidoo's cultural activism and her monumental contributions to the modern Ghanaian (and African) novel, poetry and children's stories. As is evident in Patience A. Kwakwa's contribution in this volume (see Section 8), it was Nketia who recruited Efua Sutherland and Ama Ata Aidoo to the drama section when he established the School of Music and Drama in 1962. Since Nketia was aware of both sets of plans, that of the AfMS and the IAS, he thought it would be helpful for us to combine our resources to jointly organize the program, and that set the stage for our international collaboration involving the AfMS in the US and the IAS in Ghana. The result is that a group of scholars from around the world with diverse disciplinary orientations came to pay tribute on this faithful day to a living legend. Sponsorship for the conference came from the University of Ghana, the IAS, the Office of Research and Development (ORID) at the University of Ghana, and our corporate partner, Guinness Ghana Breweries Limited (GGBL).

The opening ceremony began with members of the Ghana Dance Ensemble performing the Akan royal *Fontomfrom* drumming and dance as invited guests and participants made their way to the Kwabena Nketia Conference Hall. Like a royal procession among the Akan, the *ntahera* (ivory trumpets), performed by members of the ensemble, ushered Nketia and his family into their respective seats in the hall. In her welcome address, Akosua Adomako Ampofo, the director of the IAS and a member of the LOC, resounded the oft-cited multi-disciplinary nature of Nketia's work that reflects President Nkrumah's vision for the IAS when it was created and that remains central to the identity of the institute to date. According to Adomako Ampofo, it was Nketia who helped establish the institute's media archives when he donated the holdings of his International Center for African Music and Dance (ICAMD) to the institute in 2008, which currently contains over 3,000 copies of audio and video recordings in a variety of formats as well as over 8,000 photographs (see Godwin K. Adjei's paper in this volume). Chairing the opening ceremony, the vice-chancellor of the University of Ghana, Professor Ernest Aryeetey, extolled Nketia's manifold contributions to the University, Ghana, Africa, and the world at large. On behalf of our corporate sponsors, Nana Yaa Ofori-Atta, the then director of corporate relations, expressed her delight that GGBL had been invited to join in the celebration of such a foremost African intellectual. The Minister for Chieftaincy and Culture, the Honorable Alexander Asum-Ahensah, represented the government and Ghana's cultural institution. In his tribute, the minister highlighted Nketia's pioneering role in the curatorial aspects of Ghana's cultural heritage and in doing so, Nketia gained the reputation of being an ambassador of Ghanaian and African cultures. In her keynote address, Professor

Emerita M.E. Kropp-Dakubu delivered a thoughtful and stimulating speech titled, "Language and Music: Mind, Body, Meaning." In her bold attempt to establish the links between language and music, she examined the expressive, communicative, and aesthetic facets of this relationship that forms the core of Nketia's scholarship.

A revised version of her keynote address is published in this volume (see Section 1). A celebration of the life and works of Nketia would never be complete without a statement from the celebrant. As the Akan proverb goes, *twene anim da hɔ a, yɛnmɔ nkyɛn mu* (you do not play the wooden side of the drum when the membrane is there for that purpose). It was time to hear from the 'man' himself. As it turned out, the musical offering by the members of the Ghana Dance Ensemble, and Osei Korankye's praise singing accompanied by his *Seprewa* was an emotional moment for Nketia who was, momentarily, lost for words. There were several moist eyes in the room. Eventually, Nketia found his voice and in a characteristic fashion, took a trip down memory lane, providing a narrative that was as didactic as it was instructive, albeit overlaid with humor. The opening ceremony concluded, as it had begun, with live musical performances as the guests and participants made their way out of the hall.

The conference was structured to accommodate concurrent sessions, including roundtable discussions during the day and musical performances in the evenings, with the former taking place in the IAS' Kwame Nkrumah Complex, and the latter at the IAS' Yiri Lodge. Abibigromma, the resident drama group of the School of Performing Arts, and the Ghana Dance Ensemble, performed during the first night. As a founding member of the Ghana Dance Ensemble, Midawo Gideon Foli Alorwoyie, currently a tenured professor of music at the University of North Texas (US), performed with the ensemble as his tribute to Nketia and his contribution to the conference. On the second night, the Community Choir from Cape Coast University led by Kofi Ansah, and Nii Yartey's Noyam African Dance Institute performed for the conference dinner. As noted in our opening paragraph, a two-volume Festschrift was published in 1989 to honor Nketia. Indeed, Jacqueline C. Djedje, who was part of the earlier project was also a participant of the 2011 Legon conference (see Section 4 for her paper). In that sense, there is a discernible continuity between the two projects, though one might be tempted to question the need for a second Festschrift.

Although Nketia retired from the University of Ghana in 1979, in the over three decades following his retirement, he has been extremely busy, and some might argue these have been the busiest years of his career. In reality, he never retired! Following his own proclamation, he did not want to be like the "hoary haired retired professor...who work in seclusion in their homes and libraries." Rather, he wanted to continue to "share my knowledge, experience and reflections with others who might carry them forward" (ICAMD Newsletter, 1998: 1-3).[2] He took up a fulltime faculty appointment at the University of California, Los Angeles (UCLA) from 1979 to 1982, and from 1983-1991, he accepted the prestigious position as Andrew W. Mellon Professor of Music at the University of Pittsburgh, in addition to later serving as chair of the Department of Music in the same institution (Djedje and Carter, 1989; Eric A. Akrofi, 2002). He retired from the University of Pittsburgh in 1991, returned home to Ghana and by 1993, he established and became the founding director of the International Center for African Music and Dance (ICAMD) at the University of Ghana (Akrofi, 2002: 56-67; Trevor Wiggins 2005). The Rockefeller Foundation provided the initial seed money that was later augmented with funding from the Ford Foundation and the Swedish International Development Authority (SIDA). A proliferation of regional secretariats of the ICAMD were established at the University of Transkei-Umtata (Republic of South Africa in 2000), Maseno University in Kenya, the University of Ibadan in Nigeria, and the University of Michigan in the US (1997). As would be expected, all the landmark activities listed above were combined with an extensive list of keynote addresses, of which the 1989 Charles Seeger Memorial Lecture, delivered at the annual meeting of the SEM at Harvard University, stands out as the crowning glory of his illustrious career. In the mix of the above-named activities are Nkeia's residencies and visiting professorships at the China Conservatory of Music, Cornell University, Michigan State University, and Kansas University, to name a few. Nketia has also been the chancellor of Akrofi-Christaller Institute of Theology, Mission and Culture at Akropong Akwapim since 2006. Established by the Presbyterian Church of Ghana, it was at the Presbyterian Training College in the same town that Nketia studied in his formative years from 1937-1941 and where he was later appointed to teach music and Twi language (Djedje and Carter 1989: 6; Akrofi 2002: 5-11). During these years, his engagements with young and senior scholars from around the world continued at the ICAMD. Through the Fellows Program at the ICAMD, several scholars came from Nigeria, Uganda, Zimbabwe, and the Democratic Republic of Congo to study with him. Thus it seems to us that the imperative for a second Festschrift to mark the period since 1990 was obvious.

He has relentlessly published since 1979 and we will make reference to a particular example here. In 2005, Nketia published Volume I of his previously published journal articles and chapters in books from various sources with funds from his monetary award by the Prince Claus Foundation based in the Netherlands (1997).[3] Titled *Ethnomusicology and African Music: Modes of Inquiry and Interpretation,* he intended to publish five volumes grouped under a particular theme. A further three manuscripts are awaiting publication by Afram Press in Ghana. They are, *Sound Instruments of Ghana Volumes 1 and 2, The Poetry of Atumpan Drums,* and *Sankudwom.* Incredibly, he still travels all over the world to honor numerous invitations and consultations on various projects. In March 2013, he gave a keynote address at the University of Michigan for the China-Africa Symposium organized by the Center for World Performance Studies and the Confucius Institute (March 29-30, 2013). Prior to this symposium, he delivered a keynote address to the African Composers Summit at the University of Port Harcourt in Nigeria.

In the true sense of the word, Nketia did not retire and as a result, his honors and recognitions have not abated. At the 42nd Annual Meeting of the International Council for Traditional Music (ICTM) in Shanghai, China in 2013, he was elected an Honorary Member. He was elected Honorary Member of both the SEM in 2005 and the African Studies Association (ASA) in 1999. The AfMS has instituted the Kwabena Nketia Book Prize to recognize the most distinguished monograph on the topic of African and African diaspora music. Awarded every other year, Jacqueline C. Djedje won the prize in 2010 for her monograph, *Fiddling in West Africa: Touching the Spirit in Fulbe, Hausa, and Dagbamba Cultures* (2008), while Frank Gunderson won the award in 2012 for his book, *"We Never Sleep We Dream Farming: Sukuma Labor Songs From Western Tanzania."* Compared to his international awards and recognitions, relatively little is known to the outside world about his awards in Ghana and how Ghanaians view their illustrious son. We will highlight a few here. In 2013 and citing his extraordinary lifetime accomplishments, The Chartered Institute of Marketing Ghana (CIMG) recognized Nketia with the 25th National Marketing Performance Special Award. In 1956, a major Ghanaian newspaper, *The Daily Graphic*, gave him the Musician of the Year Award. He is also the recipient of the following awards: The Grand Medal of the Government of Ghana (Civil Division, 1968); Ghana Arts Award from the Arts Council of Ghana (1972); the Entertainment Critics and Reviewers Association of Ghana (ECRAG) Special Honor Award (1987); the Arts Critics and Reviewers Association of Ghana (ACRAG) Flagstar Award (1993); an Honorary Doctor of Literature from the University of Ghana (1993); the Companion of the Order of Star of Ghana from the government of Ghana (2000); the Ghana Gospel Music Special Award (2003); the Living Legends Award from the Ghana National Theatre (2003); and the Mampong Kontonkyi Award (2006) from the chiefs and people of Asante Mampong as part of the Kontonkyi Akwasidae Festival.[4] In 2009, the Nketia Music Foundation was established in Accra, Ghana to promote and preserve the intellectual legacy of Professor J.H. Kwabena Nketia. The directors of the foundation are Mr. Reindorf Baah Perbi and his daughter, Reverend Priscilla Naana Nketia.[5] On February 27, 2015, the Institute of African Studies (IAS) at the University of Ghana officially named its audio-visual archive the J.H. Kwabena Nketia Archives. Containing Nketia's field recordings since the 1950s and the transfer of his collections from the ICAMD in 2008 to the IAS, the audio-visual archive has a rich history and is an invaluable resource for teaching, learning, and research. In partnership with New York University's Audiovisual Preservation Exchange (APEX) Ghana and its parent unit, Moving Image Archiving & Preservation Program of the same institution, all the holdings of the archive are being digitized. The digitization project will ultimately lead to the creation of a database that will make it possible for storage and retrieval and make the metadata available to the wider public. Judith Opoku-Boateng, the archivist and her staff, have been working with experts from New York University's Making African Academic Resources Accessible (MAARA), the holdings of the J.H. Kwabena Nketia Archives will be the first materials to become part of the open access electronic archive at the University of Ghana and will be known as UGSpace. Yet another institutional recognition in Ghana is from the African University College of Communications (AUCC) in Accra. The Kwabena Nketia Center for Africana Studies will be officially commissioned at the AUCC in June 2015 to coincide with his ninety-fourth birthday.

Papers in This Volume

The framing concept and title of this volume, *Discourses in African Musicology,* provides continuity with the first Festschrift and recognizes African musicology as a viable discipline for Africanists. The multidisciplinary orientation of papers in this volume are indicative of diverse aspects of the broad academic field that has engaged the attention of Nketia for over half a century. Not entirely without potential flaws of compartmentalization, we have grouped the papers under thematic sections. **Section 1**, "Expressing Language, Expressing Music" examines the language-music nexus. The leading paper, "Language and Music: Mind, Body, Meaning" is a revised version of linguist M.E. Kropp-Dakubu's keynote address alluded to earlier. The downplay of language in African musicological studies in favor of the abstract concept of "rhythm" as the overriding musical expression on the vast continent of Africa has been the source of departure and frustration for scholars from postcolonial Africa (Agawu 2003 and Amegago's paper in this volume). As valuable as rhythm (melody and harmony included) analysis may be to our understanding of "meaning" in African musical expressions, Kropp-Dakubu asserts that, "...rhythm, as an abstract concept, does not have the inherent *emotion* (our emphasis) compared with language." Although several scholars have attempted to seriously engage with the linguistic dimension (Nketia 1963, 1971, 1974; Agawu 1995; Locke in this volume and several of his publications), but for a fixation on rhythm and getting to the bottom of the linguistic praxis has been nothing short of elusive for centuries. Based on two seminal articles by Nketia, "The Surrogate Languages of Africa" (1971), and "The Linguistic Aspect of Style in African Languages" (1971), Kropp-Dakubu explores the expressive, communicative, and aesthetic aspects of the relationship between language, music, and (oral) literature. Grounded in ethnomusicological analysis, and using one of Nketia's key articles, "The Hocket Technique in African Music" (1962) as his staging point, Joseph Kaminski expands on the analyzed repertoire of Ghanaian *ntahera* (ivory trumpet) surrogate speech. A great deal of emphasis is placed here on the intonation of speech while ensembles play hockets over which lead trumpets talk. Modesto Amegago's paper, "The Textual Basis of African Drumming" rounds out Section 1 by charging scholars to engage in dialogue with culture bearers in order to elicit their views on representing socially sensitive and repressed texts and themes in the public domain through musical codes. In that sense, *rhythm* can be an exemplar of a musical code.

David Locke's "Sweetness in Agbadza Music: Expressiveness in an Item of Agbadza Singing and Drumming," sets the stage for the four papers grouped under the *Analysis of Traditional Music*, the title and framing theme for **Section 2**. Based on aesthetics and prioritizing indigenous knowledge and systems of thought, Locke sets out to unravel the sources of *vivi* or *sweet[ness]* in Agbadza music as performed by Gideon Folie Alorwoyie for his *Agbadza Project*. In order to reconfigure old style Agbadza for contemporary relevance in his hometown Anlo-Afiadenyigba in the Volta Region of Ghana, Alorwoyie collected and performed twenty-five songs with new drum compositions with a selected cast of drummers, singers, and dancers. With his interest in the music of Anlo Ewe musical traditions, Locke has collaborated with Alorwoyie on several projects including the current one. As a scholar of Native and Latin American musical traditions, Brenda Romero's contribution in this volume, "A Theory of Infinite Variation," is indicative of the far reaches of Nketia's scholarship beyond the noted Africa and African Diaspora to the global academic space. Nketia's legacy of building interdisciplinary bridges and bridges between cultures is well noted (Djedje and Cater, 1989: 15). With her specialty, Romero is keenly aware of the multiple manifestations of African-based musics in the Americas. Deploying rhetoric to contest several assumptions, that, for instance, there is a type of "music theory," in Western classical music while labeling that of the *other* as ethnotheory, Romero advocates for a theory of variance (instead of non-variance) as a theoretical construct to capture the ever shifting "patterns and constant transformations of life everywhere." Although there are numerous references to Ampene (2005), Alan Merriam's tripartite model for the study of music as human behavior (1964) looms large in Romero's paper as a theoretical model. Additionally, Romero gives credit to a speech Susan McClary gave on the topic, "Africanization of World Music" (1998), for igniting her interest in the power of African musics to bring people from diverse cultures together. Prior to McClary's speech, Samuel A. Floyd Jr. had written, *The Power of Black Music: Interpreting Its History from Africa to the United* States (1995) to project the profound contribution of this music to American music and the world at large.[6] At times reflexive and in most instances prodding, Romero advocates for ethnomusicological studies that will create modules and concepts for the emerging field of world music theories that will transform traditional (Western) music theory to provide holistic analyses that are not limited to sound but will include the social and spiritual dimensions of music as well. As a percussionist, Ben Paulding's "Kete for the International Percussion Community" is geared toward providing a practical resource for fellow percussionists around the globe who, for various reasons, may not have the opportunity to travel to Kumase, the source of this royal orchestra. This "method book" approach is uncommon in percussion studies, as Paulding's paper follows a long list in the literature including that of his teachers and mentors. The list includes Royal Hartigan's *West African Rhythms for Drumset* (1995), to name one of several. Although Paulding references sources in ethnomusicology, his method of analysis and presentation is framed primarily in the language of modern percussionists. As in Hartigan's work cited above, Paulding explores the potential of transferring Kete rhythms to the drumset. Amy Unruh's, "Spontaneity, Improvisation, and Musical and Social Aesthetics in Ghanaian Kpanlogo Music and Dance," is a generalized discussion of the classic Ga recreational dance. During her field research in Ghana, Unruh studied and performed *kpanlogo* in one of the multiethnic cultural groups in Accra. Her dance and drum teacher was Habib Iddrisu, a Dagomba dancer, drummer and choreographer.[7] By implication, we should view Unruh's paper within the broader context of Nketia's visionary experiments in the 1960s when he established the multiethnic Ghana Dance Ensemble. Nketia's main goal was to create a national identity through the performing arts. The result is a proliferation of multiethnic "cultural groups" in urban areas and regional centers that perform dances from all over Ghana and in some cases from other regions in Africa. For Habib Iddrisu, a Dagomba musician, to perform *kpanlogo,* a Ga dance, at such a high level, is a positive development as Ghanaians continuously strive to construct a national identity from a diverse set of ethnic groups.

In Section 3, "Singing History," we turn our attention to the primacy of song genres and song texts in African cultures. In "Kasena Maiden Songs: A Genre on the Wane," authors Albert K. Awedoba and Alexis L. Danti examine the content and significance of *lenlâ,* a female song tradition among the Kasena-Nankana in the Upper East Region of Ghana. For the authors, it is not so much about privileging young women in a predominantly patriarchal society. What is of great concern is the waning status of *lenlâ* in a society that is experiencing rapid urbanization. The basis for comparison is the Akan *nnwonkorɔ,* which unlike the *lenlâ,* continues to grow in popularity despite the profusion of modern diversions such as television and the internet. After critically looking at the causes for the 'demise' we are informed that *lenlâ* is currently a central feature of Kassena-Nankana funerary rites. Some of us will see this as a positive development, since a ritual space such as funerary rites may, in the long-term, sustain *lenlâ* (though not in its entirety) and thus ensure its vitality. Given that musical change in any given society is a complex issue, there are no easy answers in Kassena-Nankana. We acknowledge that traditions are dynamic, and as such, cultural stagnation may not be desirable depending on who or how we view these issues. Both Awedoba and Danti identify a single cause to the apparent "demise" of *lenlâ*, but is it possible to cast the net wider to other areas in contemporary Kassena-Nankana? Because Akan *adowa* and *nnwonkorɔ* are referenced, it is helpful to remind readers that several Akan genres, *adakam, asaadua, Akosua Tuntum, Sikyi* were once popular, but for various reasons, the dances associated with the above genres have not enjoyed sustained interest in contemporary Akan societies. The above-listed popular dances are no longer performed, while some of the songs have been absorbed into contemporary groups. It may well be that *adowa* and, especially, *nnwonkorɔ* are still popular because they are performed during funerary celebrations (see Ampene 2005 and Nketia 1973). Nevertheless, there is a great deal of analysis of song texts providing a window into Kasena-Nankana culture and worldview. In his paper, "Documentation of Slavery in Ghanaian Folklore: Anlo Ewe Slave Songs," Mawuli Adjei examines song texts to engage scholars and the general public in a historical and literary dialogue about domestic and transatlantic slavery. The tenuous issue of slavery and its complex manifestations present unprecedented challenges for all societies around the world and Adjei's paper follows a long trail of scholars who are confronting the apparent issues. Akosua Perbi's, *A History of Indigenous Slavery in Ghana* (2004) is a comprehensive account of slavery and social systems in the pre-colonial era.[8] Adjei's contribution in this volume, however, stands out in his emphasis on song texts as the locus for historical data in a pre-literate society such as the Klikor.

Section 4, "Diasporic Dialogues and Currents," is particularly crucial in this volume as it speaks to Nketia's engagement at several levels with African diasporas in the Caribbean, the Americas, Europe and elsewhere (see Djedje and Carter, 1989:13). Interestingly, Jacqueline C. Djedje, an African American, writes on West African cultures while Ampene, a Ghanaian, writes on the phenomenal African American jazz pianist and composer, Thelonius Monk. Not surprisingly, Djedje's

"Music and Diasporas Within West Africa: The Pre-Colonial Era" sets out to engage the less trodden path of what might be seen as "internal diasporas" in West Africa. Framed around a set of questions, Djedje's literature review is essentially a *tour de force* that situates her topic in the appropriate context. Eventually, Djedje settles on three ethnic groups, the Fulbe, Mande, and the Hausa, in West Africa. These three groups have been the bedrock of her research for over three decades (see *Fiddling in West Africa*, 2008). Readers are enlightened on issues such as "multiple diasporas, changing diasporas, and diversity within diasporas," in order to better comprehend musical expressions in various African cultures in global terms. Ampene's paper, "Give Me Silence, Space, and a Dance: The Pianistic Style of Thelonious Monk," examines the causes for the rather belated recognition of Monk's foundational role in the jam sessions at Minton's Playhouse in Harlem that resulted in the birth of bebop. His paper is in two parts. In the first part, Ampene examines the perceived notions of jazz in the 1940s and 1950s in order to situate the bebop sound ideal in a larger context. In the second part, he examines the missing link in the scholarship around Monk by revealing Monk's relationship with Kofi Ghanaba, the self-acclaimed "Divine Drummer" and musical icon from Ghana, as the missing link in Monk criticism. Ghanaba is duly credited with introducing African drums and percussion into American jazz in addition to pioneering and recording his own brand of Afro jazz in the 1950s and 1960s.

In Section 5, "Analysis of Written Compositions," works by Nketia and the Nigerian composer and scholar, Samuel Akpabot, are the focus of musical analyses by our three authors. These compositions typify modern African music, broadly defined. In all its manifestations, modern African music is a complex and diffused terrain that includes Afropop, neo traditional music, written compositions (sometimes referred to with the problematic caption, "art music")[9] such as choral music in the African idiom, and chamber, orchestral and instrumental compositions, which yield a wide variety of combinations. In this sense, the subject area covered by our three contributors is just the tip of the iceberg. Admittedly, we have seen modest progress in the recognition given to African composers and their works in the literature in recent years, due, in large part, to sustained advocacy by the Nigerian composer and ethnomusicologist, Akin Euba; a new generation of African scholars; a cadre of African composers who continuously compose new music; and the pianist, William Chapman Nyaho.[10] As the Andrew Mellon

Professor at the University of Pittsburgh (1993-2011), Euba presided over proseminars with titles such as "Creative Ethnomusicology," and "Intercultural Musicology."[11] A pianist as well, he championed the concept of "African Pianism" (Euba 1999; Bode Omojola 2004 and his paper in this volume, as well as Ampene's paper in this volume). A positive outcome of Euba's advocacy is the recent publication in China, *Anthology of African Piano Music*. Published in 2009, the anthology is co-edited by Li Xin, professor of musicology at the Central Conservatory of Music in Beijing, and Akin Euba.[12] In 1993, the Iwalewa-Haus at the University of Bayreuth in Germany published *Modern African Music,* a catalogue of selected archival materials compiled by Euba. The five volume anthology of *Piano Music of Africa and the African Diaspora*, compiled and edited by the Ghanaian pianist, William Chapman Nyaho, and published by Oxford University Press in 2007, constitutes a crucial landmark. As a clinician in high demand, Nyaho uses his lecture-recitals and workshops as a platform to advocate for piano compositions by Africans and the African diaspora. Prior to publishing the anthology, he released the critically acclaimed and award winning CD compilation, *Senku,* and in 2008, another CD compilation, *ASA: Piano Music of African Descent.* Because African composers and their works are part of the curriculum in high schools and tertiary institutions in Sub-Saharan Africa, students are encouraged to produce theses based on these compositions. Some theses have been turned into books. Bode Omojola's *Nigerian Art Music: With an Introductory Study of Ghanaian Art Music* (1995), and Joshua Uzoigwe's *Akin Euba: An Introduction to the Life and Music of a Nigerian Composer* (1992) easily come to mind.

The leading article by Nissio Fiagbedzi, "J.H. Kwabena Nketia's Republic Suite: An Analytical Portrait of Movement I," explicates structure and African techniques of voice combination and separation to delineate moments of high and low points, sonic motion and the tonal implications of modal and cadential characteristics of traditional songs and instrumental music. As would be expected, West European harmonic and tonal procedures are inextricably woven into the fabric of the movement under discussion and Fiagbedzi relies heavily on analytical techniques of Euro-American theorists to make his analysis accessible to a wider readership. Minimalism and postcolonial representations of social and cultural values in Africa is the focus of Bode Omojola's paper, "Representing Africa Through Creative Ethnomusicology: Minimalism and Postcolonial Themes in the Music of Samuel Akpabot." Inspired by the issues raised in Kofi Agawu's *Representing African Music* (2003), Omojola's lucid analysis of selected works of the Nigerian composer and ethnomusicologist Samuel Akpabot is foregrounded in postcolonial discourse. According to Omojola, Akpabot's minimalism is a political statement whereby the composer "restores [Africa's] integrity and undermines Europe's "colonial hegemony." George W.K. Dor's, "Exploring the Ontology and Application of the 'Nketia Dominant Seventh Chord," rounds up Section 5. As a Ghanaian composer, ethnomusicologist, director of church choirs and the Ghana Symphony Orchestra, Dor has a long track record of performing Nketia's choral works in the African idiom, and also engaging these works at the scholarly level. Dor's goal in his paper is to outline "Nketia's idiomatic harmonic vocabulary," and his harmonization of a "characteristic Akan melodic structure of a falling fourth" at cadential points. Dor submits a "melody-driven" harmonic conception on the part of Nketia and his adoption of this in his own compositions to underscore the "idiom's appeal and popularity in Ghana."

Discourses of gender shape **Section 6**. In their paper, "Women Doing Music: The Lives and Songs of Contemporary Ghanaian Women Musicians," Abena Kyere and Akosua Adomako Ampofo join forces to contribute to the growing literature on women artists. Partly biographical and partly analytical, the authors engage the careers of three artists, Awura Ama Badu, Akosua Agyepong, and Nana Akua Amoah (popularly known by her stage name: Mzbel), and their relationships with the male-dominated music industry in Ghana. The narratives trace age-old practices of defining gendered spaces that ensures men and women grow up with clear expectations about appropriate gender roles. The authors show that as male hegemony comes to the fore, agency creates fluidity in gender relations and makes it possible for one gender to move into the space normally accorded the other, using the power of music to negotiate identity constructs. In the process, women musicians compose counter-narratives in their songs and live performances in order to resist cultural expectations of their prescribed role in society. In her paper, "Is A Woman Only Worth the Rib of A Man?: The Place of Women in Zimbabwean Musical Arts, Past and Present," Bridget Chininouriri uses "musical arts" as a launchpad to contest discourses of gender among the Shona in Zimbabwe. Chininouriri weaves a comparative narrative between past indigenous and contemporary practices of gendered roles in the musical arts and concludes that contrary to popular opinion, the modern woman in musical arts is much more disadvantaged and marginalized than her counterpart in indigenous pre-colonial Africa.

Sections 7 covers aspects of Nketia's vision we have mentioned in this introduction. "Embracing Dondology-Establishing a Vision" investigates various dimensions of Nketia's monumental legacy with the contributions of Craig Woodson and George P. Hagan. Created unofficially by students at the University of Ghana around 1962, *dondology* was considered a scholarly way to come to grips with the program of study that Nketia had set up at the School of Music and Drama (Djedje and Carter 1989; Akrofi 2002). In his quest to construct a national identity in post-independence Ghana through the performing arts, Nketia brought in traditional dancers and musicians as teachers, resource persons, and vitally, as founding members of the Ghana Dance Ensemble. With constant rehearsals and playing of instruments that could be heard beyond the confines of the institute, students ascribed *dondology* to the school. This ascription eased the discomfort felt by students due to the presence of "traditional arts on a campus where the curriculum and organization were dominated by a colonial heritage" (Trevor Wiggins 2005 and Akrofi 2002). While members of faculty in the School of Music, Dance and Drama did not take kindly to *dondology* as a label, Nketia deflected the perceived stigma associated with *dondology* by embracing it. For his inaugural professorial speech in 1973, Nketia titled his paper "Dondology Re-defined."[13] By embracing *dondology,* Nketia laid a solid foundation for African studies at the University of Ghana and within a decade, it became a recognized academic discipline. Following in his footsteps, both contributors to this section embraced *dondology* as "lived experience." Since his childhood in the United States, Craig Woodson has had a lifelong passion for musical instrument technology and he can be credited with being one of the pioneers of the now fashionable sub-discipline, applied ethnomusicology. In the 1970s, when Nketia attempted to transform traditional instruments from monolithic ethnic-based tunings and performance to national instruments with Ghanaian identity, he invited Woodson to join forces with local faculty and artisans at the Center for Cultural Studies at the then University of Science and Technology (now renamed to its original name, the Kwame Nkrumah University of Science and Technology),[14] to develop prototypes of "modern traditional instruments" for Ghanaian schools. This project later became known as the Musical Instrument Technology

Workshop (MITW). Although the MITW has been abandoned, Woodson returned to California in 1984 to continue his innovating work in the manufacturing of world musical instruments and educational materials for educators and professionals. In his auto-biographical portrait and reflexive paper, "Applied Ethnomusicology: My Lifelong Exploration and Expression as a Dondologist," Woodson chronicles his long but illustrious career in musical instrument technology as a tribute to his personal growth as a *dondologist,* and to those, like him, whose careers have been touched directly by the profound legacy of Nketia. Hagan, a Ghanaian scholar, taught at the Institute of African Studies from 1968 to 1998, and later became the director from 1997-1998, and the Chairman of the Ghana National Commission on Culture from 2000-2008. The goal of George Hagan's, "Dondology: Music, Mind, and Matter," is to examine the ontological and epistemological ideas in African cultures to access the intrinsic nature of sound and music and how music impacts all types of being. Theories of African philosophy loom large in Hagan's analysis of the Akan Ɔdomankoma Kyerɛma (the Divine Drummer), the materials used in constructing a pair of *Atumpan* drums, and *Ayan* (drum poetry and text).

Section 8 includes contributions from six authors and as a follow up to the preceding section, it is aptly titled, "Experiencing and Archiving the Vision." Patience A. Kwakwa's contribution is titled, "Kwabena Nketia and the Creative Arts: The Genesis of the School of Music and Drama, and the Formation of the Ghana Dance Ensemble." As one of the pioneering students who enrolled at the school in 1962, Kwakwa constructs the "insider's" narrative of Nketia's legacy in the creative arts and the experiments she conducted as extensions for her academic work in the school. It was in this school that Nketia sought to realize his own vision and that of the first President of Ghana, Dr. Kwame Nkrumah, "in practical terms." Nketia's vision was to "write and talk" about music and culture and to translate his research into performance programs by creating new forms of music, dance and drama based on traditional models that would be meaningful to contemporary reality and national identity. Kwakwa's insider account offers rare glimpses of Nketia's personal involvement in the school through his recruitment of and work with Ephraim Amu, Ben Anin, Simeon Asiamah and N.Z. Nayo for music; Efua Sutherland, Ama Atta Aidoo and Joe de Graft for drama; and for dance, he brought in his longtime friend, Mawere Opoku, the consummate dance choreographer, from the then Kumasi

Cultural Center (now the Center for National Culture). The natural progression of Nketia's experiments and vision at the School of Music and Drama culminated in the inauguration of the Ghana Dance Ensemble in 1967. Mitchel Strumpf follows Kwakwa's lead by shedding light on Nketia's interest in enculturation in music and on the music education of children in Africa in his paper, "Professor J.H. Kwabena Nketia: Ethnomusicologist and Educator." According to Strumpf, Nketia articulated in several of his writings the lack of experiential-based music pedagogy in Africa and set out to develop method books and instruments (as Woodson's paper in this volume reveals) that can be used in postcolonial educational institutions in Africa. With his longstanding research and publications in music education, Strumpf weaves a narrative based on his personal contacts and collaborations with Nketia and his work in the Department of Fine and Performing Arts at the University of Dar es Salaam in Tanzania.

Jesse D. Ruskin's "Biographical Writing and Individual Creativity in African Musicology," resulted from his review of the African musicological literature from the past two decades. Ruskin then traces the history of biographical writing in African musicology while identifying major contributions to the literature and situating them within the wider context of ethnomusicology. Ruskin's paper resonates with research paradigms in ethnomusicology and allied disciplines in the humanities and extends to the early 1970s. These paradigms foreground the people who make and experience music, since it is through individual experience that they express shared culture (Wade 2013). With this model, scholarship shifted from a preoccupation with culture (as in African culture or Bugandan culture) and the limits set by repertory studies to focus on the creative experience of an individual within a culture. Ruskin concludes with a discussion of the implications of biographical research for a socially engaged and creatively inclined African music scholarship. Godwin K. Adjei's paper, "Kwabena Nketia and the Genesis of Archival Collections at the Institute of African Studies" is timely and crucial to this volume for two reasons. First, this aspect of Nketia's legacy is low on the totem pole when his accomplishments are listed and second, the challenges and success of the J.H. Kwabena Nketia Archives at the IAS are instructive for educational institutions in Africa who are keenly aware of knowledge production and issues of representation in postcolonial Africa (Agawu 2003). As a research fellow and the coordinator of music and dance at the Institute of African Studies, Adjei's narrative is informed by his first hand knowledge of various strategies Nketia deployed in order to accomplish his vision of setting up an audio-visual archive at the University of Ghana. Established in 1952 in the Department of Sociology, local politics and unstable departmental focus led to trajectories of migrations of the archive from the Archeology Department to the ICAMD in the School of Performing Arts before arriving at its present location in the IAS. Paul Schauert's paper, "Nketia, Nationalism, and the Ghana Dance Ensemble," takes us to another area of Nketia's legacy that is less mentioned than his work as a scholar and educator. Schauert's aim is to demonstrate that the enduring legacy and relevance of the Ghana Dance Ensemble, at a time when most of the national dance troupes in other African countries are now defunct, is due in large part to Nketia's vision as a cultural activist in colonial and post-colonial Ghana. It is also due in part to his conviction that traditional arts should be mobilized to build a national consciousness and identity. Additionally, Nketia continues to weld considerable impact on the ensemble in terms of its direction. To his credit, Schauert includes the tenuous issues surrounding the relocation of the Ghana Dance Ensemble to the Ghana National Theatre in the early 1990s. In "Representation: My Africanist Perspective," Sylvanus K. Kuwor proposes a holistic approach to the study of African performing arts. For him, African dance needs a theoretical framework that its practitioners and scholars operate effectively. Kuwor advocates for collaborations between African scholars and their Western counterparts in forging his notion of a holistic theory for African dance.

Festschrifts do not necessarily imply a legacy frozen in time and place. In a moving introduction of Nketia that preceded his keynote address at the China-Africa Symposium at the University of Michigan in March 2013, the then Senior Vice Provost for Academic Affairs, Lester Monts, an ethnomusicologist and Africanist, stated that "Nketia's legacy is seen in the list of scholars he has trained." Indeed Professor Emeritus J.H. Kwabena Nketia lives on in the works of generations of students he has directly and indirectly mentored. He is the gift that keeps giving. As one of the *Abeɛ* in the Ntiribuoho Nyame Nkrabea Nnwonkorɔ repertoire goes, he is "the frog that gives water." Today we continue to benefit from Nketia's research, his scholarly writings, and his musical compositions, the J.H. Kwabena Nketia Archives, and the numerous performances of the Ghana Dance Ensemble and multiethnic cultural groups. His work contributes significantly to the varied terrain that encompasses the disciplines of African studies, African musicology, ethnomusicology, anthropology, linguistics and several disciplines in the humanities and social sciences to address wider questions of African knowledge systems and epistemology, and setting standards for scholarship for current and future generations. In this sense, this second Festschrift is both an honorific document and also a timeless resource of a rich array of scholarly essays that symbolically serve as an archive for the continuation of unending productivity for humanity. For all Africanists, Professor Kwabena Nketia is the embodiment of a true humanist scholar. We can never express our gratitude enough, well done! *Daasebre, mo, mo ne yɔ!*

Endnotes

1: Kwabena Nketia Conference Hall was commissioned on September 30, 2002.

2: *Sharing Knowledge and Experience* is the title of Nketia's biography published by Eric Akrofi in 2002.

3: Based in Amsterdam, the Prince Claus Fund's mission is to actively seek cultural collaborations founded on equality and trust …in spaces where resources and opportunities for cultural expression, creative production and research are limited and cultural heritage is threatened (www.princeclausfund.org).

4: Nketia's hometown is Asante Mampong.

5: Additional information on the Nketia Music Foundation can be found at www.nketiamusicfoundation.org

6: On the other end of the spectrum is *The Power of African Cultures* by Toyin Falola (2003) that examines ambiguous new identities of modern Africans as they come to terms with older traditions and new identities.

7: Habib obtained his PhD degree in Performance Studies from Northwestern University, Illinois in 2011 and is currently teaching at the University of Oregon-Eugene's School of Music and Dance and Folklore Studies.

8: Professor Akosua Adoma Perbi is the older daughter of Professor Nketia. She was once head of the History Department at the University of Ghana and the Chairperson of the Education Committee of the UNESCO Slave Route Project in Ghana.

9: Unless "art" is reserved for only Western European Classical music, there is no musical creation in the world that is not a piece of artistic creation.

10: Unlike African writers of fictional literature and poetry, Wole Soyinka (Nigeria/Nobel Laureate), Ngugi wa Thiong'o (Kenya), Ama Ata Aido (Ghana) to name just three, who are celebrated locally within Africa and in the broader international world of academia, modern African composers of written music have been sidelined in African musical studies. Just as African writers use the Western medium of the novel, African composers use the written (instead of oral) medium based on West European notation system. While the novels of African writers are accepted in the canon, most Western scholars dismiss works by African composers as cheap imitations of Euro-American forms.

11: In line with his advocacy, Akin Euba established a larger project, "A Bridge Across: Intercultural Composition, Performance, Musicology," that yielded symposia including, "Composition in Africa and the Diaspora," "Dialogue-Africa Meets Asia," "Dialogue-Africa Meets Latin America," and "From Folk Song to Art Song-Modern Traditions of Vocal Music in Africa and the Diaspora."

12: Ostensibly, our Chinese colleagues at the Central Conservatory of Music do not recognize Afro-Pop as a viable area for scholarly engagement.

13: The term 'Afrostats' is another designation for courses in African Studies that all students at the University of Ghana are required to pass in their First University Exams (FUE). In order to glorify those courses, the student body came up with their own label, Afrostats (African Studies).

14: The name "Kwame Nkrumah" was removed after the first president's overthrow in 1966. The university reverted to its original name in the early 2000s.

References

Adams, Anne V. 2012. *Essays in Honour of Ama Ata Aidoo at 70*. Oxfordshire, UK: Ayebia Clarke Publishing Limited.

Adams, Anne V., and Esi Sutherland-Addy. 2007. *The Legacy of Efua Sutherland*. Oxfordshire, UK: Ayebia Clarke Publishing Limited.

Agawu, Kofi. 2003. *Representing African Music: Postcolonial Notes, Queries, Positions*. New York: Routledge.

———. 1995. *African Rhythm: A Northern Ewe Perspective*. Cambridge: Cambridge University Press.

Akrofi, Eric A. 2002. *Sharing Knowledge and Experience: A Profile of Kwabena Nketia Scholar and Music Educator*. Accra, Ghana: Afram Publications Limited.

Ampene, Kwasi. 2005. *Female Song Tradition and the Akan of Ghana: The Creative Process in Nnwonkor*. Aldershot, England: Ashgate Publishing Limited.

Djedje, Jacqueline C. 2008. *Fiddling in West Africa: Touching the Spirit in Fulbe, Hausa, and Dagbamba Cultures*. Bloomington: Indiana University Press.

___. *African Musicology: Current Trends: A Festschrift Presented to J.H. Kwabena Nketia, Vol. II*. 1992. Atlanta, Georgia: Crossroads Press/African Studies Association.

Djedje, Jacqueline C. and William G. Carter, eds. 1989. *African Musicology: Current Trends: A Festschrift Presented to J.H. Kwabena Nketia, Vol I*. Atlanta, Ga: Crossroads Press/African Studies Association.

Euba, Akin. 1999. "Towards an African Pianism." In *Intercultural Musicology: The Bulletin of the Center for Intercultural Music Arts*. London, UK vol 1:9-12.

___. 1993. *Modern African Music: A Catalogue of Selected Archival Materials at Iwalewa-Haus, University Bayreuth, Germany*. Bayreuth, Germany: University of Bayreuth Press.

Falola, Toyin. 2003. *The Power of African Cultures*. Rochester, NY: The University of Rochester Press.

Floyd, Samuel A. 1995. *The Power of Black Music: Interpreting its History From Africa to the United States*. New York: Oxford University Press.

Gunderson, Frank D. 2010. *Sukuma Labor Songs From Western Tanzania: 'We Never Sleep, We Dream of Farming.'* Leiden, Boston: Brill Academic Publishing.

Hartigan, Royal. 1995. *West African Rhythms for Drumset*. Van Nuys, CA: Alfred Publishing Co. Inc.

Merriam, Alan P. 1964. *The Anthropology of Music*. Evanston, Ill.: Northwestern University Press.

Nketia, J.H. Kwabena. 1974. *The Music of Africa*. New York: W.W. Norton & Company Inc.

___. 1973. *Folksongs of Ghana*. Accra, Ghana: Ghana Universities Press.

___. 1971a. "The Linguistic Aspect of Style in African Languages," in *Current Trends in Linguistics: Linguistics in Sub-Saharan Africa*. Ed.by Thomas A. Sebeok. The Hague: Mouton, 733-758.

___. 1971b. "The Surrogate Languages of Africa," in *Current Trends in Linguistics: Linguistics of Sub-Saharan Africa, Vol 7*. Ed. by Thomas A. Sebeok. The Hague: Mouton., 699-732.

___. 1963. *Drumming in Akan Communities of Ghana*. Edinburgh and London: Thomas Nelson and Sons Limited.

Nyaho, William Chapman, ed. 2007. *Piano Music of Africa and the African Diaspora*. New York: Oxford University Press.

Omojola, Bode. 2004. *Studies in African Pianism*. Bayreuth, Germany: University of Bayreuth Press.

___. 1995. *Nigerian Art Music, With an Introductory Study of Ghanaian Art Music*. Ibadan, Nigeria: Institut Francais de Recherche.

Perbi, Akosua Adoma. 2004. *A History of Indigenous Slavery in Ghana: From the 15th to the 19th Centuries*. Accra, Ghana: Sub-Saharan Publishers.

Uzoigwe, Joshua. 1992. *Akin Euba: An Introduction to the Life and Music of a Nigerian Composer*. Bayreuth, Germany: University of Bayreuth Press.

Wade, Bonnie C. 2013. *Thinking Musically: Experiencing Music, Expressing Culture*. New York: Oxford University Press.

Wiggins, Trevor. 2005."An Interview with J.H. Kwabena Nketia: Perspectives on Tradition and Modernity." *Ethnomusicology Forum* 14 (6): 57-81.

Xin, Li and Akin Euba, eds. 2009. *Anthology of African Piano Music*. Shanghai, China: Shanghai Music Publishing House.

Discography
Nyaho, William Chapman. 2008. *Asa: Piano Music by Composers of African Descent*. Newtown, CT: MSR Classics.

___. 2008. *Senku: Piano Music by Composers of African Descent*.Newtown, CT: MSR Classics.

1

M.E. Kropp Dakubu
Joseph Kaminski
Modesto Amegago

EXPRESSING LANGUAGE, EXPRESSING MUSIC

Language and Music: Mind, Body, Meaning

M.E. Kropp Dakubu

Mary Esther Kropp Dakubu (BA Hons. Queen's University Canada, MA University of Pennsylvania, PhD School of Oriental and African Studies London) is emerita professor at the Institute of African Studies of the University of Ghana, with which she has been associated since 1964. She has published extensively in many areas of language in Ghana, including articles on phonology, syntax, historical linguistics and literary style, and has supervised the creation of dictionaries of Ga and of Gurene. Her current research concerns historical comparative linguistics, particularly the comparative study of the Kwa group and the history of the Ga-Dangme group.

I especially wish to address this essay to two papers by Professor J.H.K. Nketia that I have always considered both seminal and a personal source of guidance and inspiration, namely "The surrogate languages of Africa" and "The linguistic aspect of style in African languages", both published in 1971 in an important compendium entitled *Current Trends in Linguistics* Vol. 7: *Linguistics in Sub-Saharan Africa*. The late Professor Jack Berry (an associate editor of that particular volume) once said to me that although African musicology may have gained when Professor Nketia shifted his main focus to that field, African linguistics certainly lost. However, I prefer to think that in the long run they both gained, and to my mind those two papers constitute that demonstration. Here I do not refer to them frequently or directly, but they underlie much of what I have to say.

First I discuss various theories about language and music that I think are particularly interesting for illuminating the relations between these two modes of expression, and just how close they are, including in the ways they make meaning for their participants. Important among these ideas is the proposition that in the course of human evolution, music and language have developed from the same source, and are thus even more intimately linked than we might otherwise think. After one or two asides, I then discuss a very specific combination of musical and verbal text, to demonstrate one of the many ways in which these two communicative modes intertwine in performance on "surrogate" instruments to create layers of meaning that lie beyond the capabilities of either mode on its own.

Much of the theorizing about music and language, what they have in common and what differentiates them, hinges on information content. This discussion has been going on at least since the 18th century. For example, the German rationalist philosopher Immanuel Kant considered that music has no propositional content and is therefore unrelated to cognition. There is no "if X then Y" in music. To the English poet and critic Coleridge, on the other hand, strongly influenced by later German idealist thinking, music is an "empty sign", not tied to any referent, and for that very reason represents an abstract idea, in some sense a "perfect" idea (see discussion in Barry 1987: 135-6). Fast forwarding to the late 20th and early 21st centuries, modern linguistics tends to dwell heavily on a particular aspect of language, its function as an efficient instrument for conveying very complex factual

and conceptual information. It often seems to be taken for granted that this is its only function, or by far its most important function. This is understandable, because it does indeed seem to be what makes language different from music. It tends to be assumed, in contrast, that music is devoted to the expression of emotion. But we should bear in mind that both music and language express feeling, and that both are based in our physical beings, so that it is no accident that both language and music are frequently and perhaps universally spoken of as "voice". Furthermore, there is nothing necessarily or inherently "emotional" about music structure and musical thinking – musical structure is just as "abstract" as syntactic structure, although different to be sure. Another point is that we human beings are not just the only animals with language, we are also apparently the only animals that make music.
I think there can be no doubt that the physical basis of both music and language is in the human vocal tract, which we can think of as actually beginning with the lungs and extending through the vocal tract to the lips, involving most of the muscles of chest, throat and face. Verbal language calls on the resources of the vocal tract above the vocal chords to build the distinctions among vowels and consonants, which have no analogues in music, but before it ever reaches the mouth the air stream is acted upon to create the fundamental components of music which are also the features that in linguistics we class as prosody – pitch, tone, rhythm including the duration of a segment, intensity or amplitude and to some extent timbre. The mouth with the nasal cavity is among other things the original resonator, amplified through the skull. I suppose that humming is quite likely the original form of music, its proto- or *ur*-form – singing is not, because it already incorporates the extra dimension of articulated language.

All this is extremely fundamental, not just to what we know as music and language but to the constitution of the human being. It has been reported that on the basis of rhythm and intonation contours, infants less than a week old can distinguish between the normal language of their environment and another, strange language. It has even been suggested that this capability begins to develop in the womb before birth, through felt sensation of the mother's speech (Carroll 2004: 251). If infants recognize rhythm and intonation contour or melody virtually from birth, they also start producing them before they produce words, which require fine articulations at the upper end of the vocal tract – that is, consonants and vowels are distinguished mainly by the position of the tongue in relation to the various parts of the mouth. The syllable however, although we think of it as composed of a vowel and one or more consonants, is based on the pulse of air, in other words, on rhythm, which comes from the way we breathe, involving the lungs and also the heartbeat. As we all know, the "babbling" stage precedes recognizable speech, and it seems that this is the stage of development during which the basis for patterns of rhythm (and therefore syllabic organization) and intonation are practiced and perhaps established. An interesting side issue is how this characterization of the earliest stages of language acquisition as prosodic relates to acquisition of a language with contrastive tone on words. I do not know of any research on this topic. However the late Jawa Apronti, in a paper that describes the language of his daughter at the age of two, said that she had not yet acquired any tonal minimal pair, that is, any pair of words distinguished only by tone (Apronti 1971: 545). This is significant because the language she was acquiring, Dangme, has three tones, and lexical minimal pairs are not hard to find. It suggests that in such languages, despite the importance we tend to attach to it, lexical tone is actually a late development in terms of the acquisition of the phonological structure of a language and therefore, we would conclude, is not particularly high in communicative salience. The situation might be different for grammatical tone, which is what tends to give rise to characteristic intonation phrasing in tone languages, but Apronti did not mention it. As indicated above, human beings are the only animals that have language, but they are also the only ones with music. Furthermore, the two frequently combine – Barry (1987: 146) quotes Coleridge as writing that "Man is the only animal who can sing…" Furthermore, just as all human communities have language, all known human communities have something we can call music (Cross and Woodruff 2009: 77).

In view of all this, it has been proposed that language and music evolved together. Some have even proposed that language is an evolutionary offshoot of music, which in essence preceded the appearance of modern humans about 200,000 years ago. Here however we must make a distinction between what we modern humans would call music and what might have preceded it. There is a rather interesting discrepancy here between dictionary definitions of the English word "music." According to my copy of the Oxford English Dictionary (Compact Edition) it is that fine art concerned with combination of sounds "with a view to beauty of form and the expression of emotion." Obviously "beauty", or the aesthetic element, is essential, since emotion can be expressed by sounds that are not generally considered musical nor intended as such, for example screaming, or banging a pot lid on the floor. Webster's New Collegiate Dictionary (2nd edition), which is an American dictionary, defined music as the "pleasing, expressive or intelligible combination of tones." The term "tone" rather than "sound" seems to imply a fundamental aesthetic component, so that what is "pleasing" need not be pleasing to everybody, but what is interesting is the inclusion of "intelligible", which is not explicit in the Oxford definition. It suggests that contrary to Kant's opinion, some form of cognition is present, and it also implies system or organization. This latter idea is however implicit also in the Oxford definition, in the notions of "fine art" and "form." I return to this feature below. For the present however I want to stress that an aesthetic component rooted in form is fundamental to what we normally understand by "music", and that this is not necessarily implied by the claim that what we might call rudimentary music was present among pre-modern humans or hominins.

In an interesting article in a recent book on the prehistory of language, Steven Mithen distinguishes music in the usual sense from "musicality", by which he seems to mean the ingredients of prosody, what language and music have in common, and not necessarily "art." He proposes that "the musicality of language may be one of the most important clues to its evolutionary history" (Mithen 2009: 76). He also quotes Charles Darwin as proposing that "it is probable that the progenitors of man... endeavoured to charm each other with musical notes and rhythm" (Mithen 2009: 70), which in fact would grant at least our most recent precursors some degree of aesthetic appreciation. I do not think this is unreasonable, since many animals can be observed to prefer some sounds to others. If at a primitive stage communication was by what Mithen calls "holistic" utterances, that is, unsegmented utterances, utterances that cannot be divided into meaningful recombinable components, then (according to Mithen) the development of language would have been impelled by increasing social complexity. As societies expanded and the culture became more complex, melody, rhythm and variation in loudness would not give enough information, and there would simply be too much to talk about for a system limited to these features to handle. Therefore, on this reasoning, articulated language developed to enable the exchange of the greater volume of complex information required by changing circumstances. Such information need not have originally been what we think of as facts and propositions, but as language developed, so would its power of expression. Music, meanwhile, developed as an expressive art. Both served, and still do serve, to create social cohesion and express emotion, but they do it in different ways, and music serves these functions more immediately and intuitively. Such an account of the origins of language and music implies that they both start with the human voice. Figure 1 is my own interpretation of the figure given by Mithen (2009: 72).

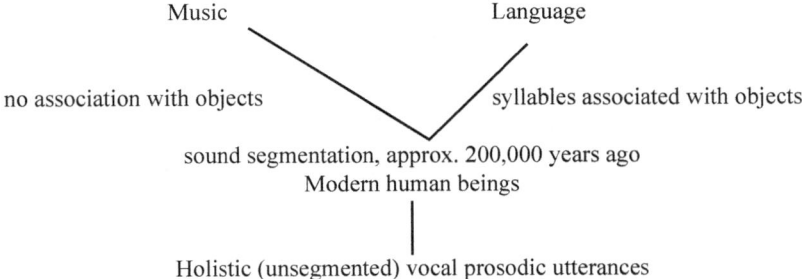

Figure 1

Note that segmentation, or recognition of recombinable parts, is necessary for music as well as for language, since this is what allows form and structure. All three modes of expression — holistic utterance (such as exclamation, 'oh!'), music and language, remain in use, and can be incorporated into each other if desired.

I see a problem in this scenario, however, not as it relates to the evolution of music and language but as they relate to each other. It is well known of course that the language met in musical texts is rarely if ever exactly the language of everyday discourse, and this needs to be taken account of. We have seen that the aesthetic component is essential to what we mean by music (even in a language which has no blanket term for the aesthetically expressive arts involving sound), but this is not true for language. When we add this component to language, we get a further development which we may refer to as literature. While Figure 1 proposes a historical schema, Figure 2 is strictly synchronic and does not say anything about development over time.

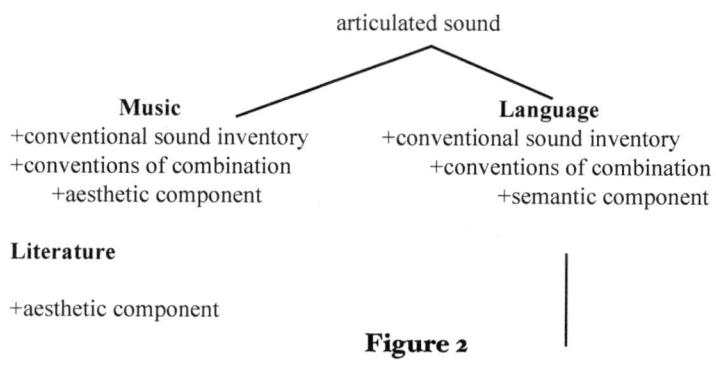

Figure 2

According to this scheme, the difference between music and language is that music already has an aesthetic dimension, which I think of as adjustments to the rules of combination intended to produce elevated and enhanced emotional and physical response. Aesthetics is not part of the definition of language, but language has a semantic component – that is, specific reference to things in the world. When the aesthetic dimension is added, language becomes literature. The difference is of course more complex, because the kinds of sounds in the inventory of each mode tend to be different, and the conventions of their combination are vastly different. However my main point here is that when we are talking about the relations between music and language, for example in some form of speech surrogate performance or a song, we are really talking about the relations that hold between music and the language of its associated literature.

Before further discussion of this topic, I would like to tell you about a really fascinating phenomenon I heard of very recently, that I think has significance for this topic, namely the whistled names of the Oyda people of south western Ethiopia, as recently discussed by Professor Azeb Amha of Leiden University. It seems that among the Oyda, the attitude to personal names is very different from what we know in West Africa. There is no formal naming ceremony. A child may be known by a nickname, such as "baby", until he or she goes to school or otherwise needs a name outside the home. It is not clear what governs the final choice, except that the person is eventually known by his or her own name, plus the father's name plus the grandfather's name, and it is considered a good thing if they alliterate.

In addition, almost everyone (it is not completely universal) gets a whistle name, often even before they get a 'real' name. This name is called *moyzé*, which is also the name of a side-blown horn, but names are played on this horn only at funerals. The names are in common everyday use, among both men and women, children and adults, and they are always whistled, using the hands held against the mouth to modify the airstream. People not only call to individuals this way over considerable distances, the person being called recognizes who it is that is calling. They say they recognize the whistler by 'the hand', just as we would recognize by the voice (Professor Amha has tested this).

These whistle names may be given by someone else or be self-chosen, and they are learned by a string of mnemonic nonsense syllables, which clearly bears no relation to the person's speech name, for example:

Speech Name	Vocalization of Whistled Name
Sas'ima S'andena	léeteléetetóom
Mamed Kalink'a	tiltéhmbéetetotóom
Matios Gigza	tóógirgidáarim

Figure 3

Oyda distinguishes two tones but Professor Amha informs me that it is best described as a pitch accent language, where the function of high tone is to give its syllable prominence. We might think therefore that pitch, perhaps in combination with intensity, would play an important part in the performance of these names, but when I looked at the vocalizations and whistled performances through a sound analyzer I found that the pitch contour of the vocalization in each case was quite flat, but that in the whistling there are one or two marked pitch spikes, while the intensity profile is not much different from the spoken version, also fairly flat. Thus the spoken mnemonic does not immediately tell you everything there is to know about the whistled phrase. Even note durations do not quite match syllable durations.

What is particularly interesting and makes them special is that the whistled names bear no relation to any spoken name or phrase at all in any language known to the Oyda or to the linguist who investigated. In other words, they are short musical phrases, and it is possible for a person to be known and identified by such a phrase.

It is common to think of language as founded on naming – witness the account in Genesis 3:19-23 of the origin of language through Adam's naming of things at God's behest. According to Dieterlen (1951: 2) Faro, the Supreme God of the Bambara, defined the world by naming, that is, he taught language, which is the basis of the constitution of the world. Even sophisticated scientific accounts such as Mithen's come very close to identifying language with naming, in speaking of human language being distinguished as tied to a referent, although it is true that the referent or "thing" can be an idea or an event, not necessarily something concrete or represented grammatically by a noun. Yet in Oyda whistled names we have a name that is definitely *not* spoken language, but a piece of music – which is identified with a unique referent in the external world.

One could argue that because the whistled name cannot be divided into signifying parts it should therefore be regarded as a holistic symbol of the person, but that is no solution because the same could be said of many spoken names. Perhaps this phenomenon indicates that information of the kind conveyed by language, including propositions, can perfectly well be conveyed by musically structured sound, except that to express more than a name, or a proposition about a name, would simply be too time consuming — unless perhaps musical tones were treated as a code, so that, say, a given pitch functioned like a letter of the alphabet. But then of course, if this were the prime consideration for composition it would lose its aesthetic component and not be music. This of course is exactly why theorists like Mithen think language developed in the first place – pitch, rhythm, intensity and timbre when modified by sequences of postures in the vocal tract and the oral cavity produce a more efficient means for expression of certain kinds of information than the prosodic components alone. One could (if very approximately) compare the difference between music and language to that between pictographs, which lend themselves to aesthetic elaboration, and an alphabet, which is more convenient but not so beautiful. When an alphabet is elaborated aesthetically, as in Islamic decorative art, it soon becomes impossible to read and so loses it function as a transmitter of language, although it may still function as a symbol of the language and even of the information it would transmit given a different material form. Similarly, when the aesthetic dimension of language is amplified by either emphasizing it for its own sake, as in some kinds of poetry, or combining it with music, it often ceases to convey what we think of as information.

Now to return to the relation between the types of artistic sound, namely music and literature; music is a very effective tool in creating sociality, not least because a group of listeners adjusts physically to the pulse (Cross and Woodruff 2009: 8-9). Since music and language both originate in the human voice, with its capacity for endless variation, it should not be surprising that they frequently interact in performance. Ever since Nketia's article on language-surrogate music (1971a), we are aware that in Africa, and specifically in Ghana, a large proportion of the music performed is related to verbal text at some level, and in many cases quite consciously and purposefully so (Nketia 1974: 177). I personally have been interested in the way "surrogate" instruments express linguistic features of a verbal text, and further, what the heard performance means to both audience and performer. I have been particularly interested in how expression is implemented on instruments with a potential pitch range that is greater than the number of contrastive tones in the language of the text, which is usually not more than two or three distinctive tones whose actual pitches are governed by several considerations, linguistic and physical. There are many such instruments, including in Ghana the one-string fiddle and the hourglass drum. I would like to illustrate here with an examination of how one performer brought together words and music in one piece for the fourteen-keyed Dagara xylophone.

A few introductory remarks on the instrument and the language: Dagara is spoken in the far north west of Ghana.[2] It has two contrastive tones, functioning both to distinguish lexical items and to indicate grammatical differences, with occasional downstepping, or lowering of the pitch of high tone, between adjacent high tones, probably induced in most cases by elision of a low tone syllable. More generally, it has downdrift, which means that over a succession of low-high intervals within a phrase the actual pitches of the tones, especially the high tones, are gradually lowered so that there is an overall descending intonation contour. This is said to be because as one speaks without taking a breath the air pressure below the glottis is gradually lowered, so that the vocal chords do not vibrate as fast.

There are many stories, customs and beliefs associated with the instrument, called *gyil*, which has very high prestige in this culture. It is considered spiritually dangerous, and other musicians are also dangerous to the player. One interesting associated custom is that when the player takes a medicine (*gyil ti͂ i͂*) to protect himself either against other players or against the force of the wood from which the keys are made he takes it with his left hand, itself a spiritually dangerous procedure. The tale widely associated with its acquisition from wilderness spirits associates it with supernatural powers (Seavoy 1982, Wiggins nd.),[3] and at least one folktale associates its power to attract with hunting (Bemile 1983: 33). Both of these traditions serve to consolidate the spiritual and physical dominance of human beings, specifically male human beings. During April and May of 1986 I worked with the late Joseph Chogring Kobom, who was a xylophone performer and teacher at the School of Performing Arts of the University of Ghana. He came from Nandom in the Upper West Region, and both the performance practice discussed and general information come from him. Adams Bodomo, at that time a graduate student in the Linguistics department, assisted with the interviewing and the transcribing of the texts.

For some purposes xylophones are played alone, but very frequently they are played in pairs. Although they are built and tuned alike, before performance the leader will 'test' the instruments to determine which should be the lead xylophone – it will be slightly sharper in tone – and exactly where the tonic should lie. The leading, more sharply pitched xylophone is called 'female', the other one 'male'. The verb for this 'testing' is *dam* , or in Central Dagaare dialect *d* , which means "stirring." This suggests a cooking metaphor, which is not inconsistent with the verb used for 'playing' which is literally "beating", *nmɛn*, although a verb meaning "put" (ıaŋ) may also be used. When it comes to the actual sound however the terminology refers to language: Kobom said that when he "stirred" the instrument he did it to *bɔŋ a gyil kɔkɔr* "know the xylophone's voice", and furthermore that playing was a form of speech: ...ma wa ŋmiɛra gyil ɛrʊ na ı ɛre a gyil pʊɔ "When I am playing xylophone I am speaking in the xylophone." (On playing technique and construction of the instrument see Strumpf 1970, also Wiggins.) Like most xylophonists he always hummed while playing, as if to express the player's physical identification with his instrument.

The piece I now examine belongs to the sub-genre known as "cool" Bawa, *báwà máárùŋ* or (in English) "slow" Bawa.[4] Unlike "hot" Bawa, *báwà tʊ´!lóŋ*, it is played for funerals, not recreational dancing. The musical difference is in rhythmic complexity, the "hot" version being more elaborate, and the cool type is also danced more slowly. The ensemble includes two xylophones, sticks, and two drums. With his right hand the lead xylophone plays the melody, which singers then maintain while the xylophone proceeds to improvise musical variations. The xylophonist was at pains to insist however that it is the left hand that really brings the words to the music, and is the sign of a master player. I interpret this to mean that the left hand makes the difference between music and mere imitation of speech. The second xylophone in cool *bawa* has no verbal text, and seems to be simpler than the second instrument in the hot variety, which does play a simple text.[5]

This is a good point at which to bring in dance, and its significance in relation to the music – language configuration. Many languages of the world do not have a word that precisely corresponds to the English word "music", which tends to contrast the non-verbal essence with speech. In Ghanaian languages the most general term is often either a word that primarily means "song", as in Akan, thus including the verbal, or "dance", which is the case in Dagaare (sɛrɪ), and seems to downplay the verbal in favour of the kinetic aspect. The language has another word for "song" (*yielu*), but "dance" can be generalized to cover all forms of musical expression. What is different about dance of course is that it develops the kinetic mode of expression far beyond what is found in the other modes, such as gesture and the kinds of limited kinetic expression indulged in by most musicians. We may speculate that non-musical language and literature repress the kinetic aspect of systematically organized expression in favour of the information aspect, and that dance downplays both information and the auditory to aim at physical transcendence of both.

To return to cool Bawa, I must emphasize that what I present here is based on a simplified version of the instrumental rendition. A notable shortcoming is that I was unable to take proper account of the left hand part. Nevertheless I think it is worth presenting, because although several authors have discussed the music better than I could (Godsey 1980, Strumpf 1970, Wiggin) none of them has paid more than cursory attention to the words. It seems to me that even in a "skeletal" rendition like this one, we can perceive a striking sensitivity and sophistication in the way words and notes are combined to produce a many-layered, meaningful whole.

In the text displayed I have spelled the first word of each verbal phrase, which also coincides with a musical phrase, with a capital letter simply to make it more visible. The notes indicated are those played by the right hand of the lead xylophone. Time and pitch values are very approximate, but I think they give a reasonable approximation to the way the piece moves. (I have not included the left hand because I do not sufficiently understand how it interacts with the right.) The literal English gloss is displayed above the text to make it easier to associate the words (and their tones) with the notes.[6]

                                        be.many PRT many
Yág mé kɔ̀lkɔ̀l
                                        ♪. ♪ ♪ ♪.
g' g' d' d'

witches PURP intervene PURP they finish them all
Sɔ́rbé tú !kpé à Bé báari bé zàa
♪(.) ♪ ♪ ♪(.) ♪ ♪. ♪ ♪ ♪.
a' a' a' g' e' e' e' d' d'
Nandom children FOC many PRT many
Nàndómé !bíirí Nà yág mé kɔ̀lkɔ̀l
♪ ♪ ♪ ♪ ♪ ♪. ♪ ♪ ♪.
g' b' b' a' a' f' g' g' b b

Sɔ́rbé tú !kpé à Bé báaré bé zàa
- ♪ ♪ ♪ ♪ ♪. ♪ ♪ ♪.
 a' a' a' g' e' e' e' d' d'

death oh death oh death oh
Kúũ wó ê Kúũ wó ê Kúú wó ê
♪ ♪ ♪. - ♪ ♪ ♪. - ♪ ♪ ♪. -
g' g' d' a' a' g' e' e' d'
(They) were many,
Witches intervened, they are all gone
The youth of Nandom were many
Witches intervened, they are all dead
Death alas, death alas, death alas.

The main body of the text has 5 beats to the phrase – it seems to play against 6 in the left hand. (And not, in my opinion, 3 against 2 see Strumpf 1970.) In most cases a long stroke (indicated as a dotted quarter above), counting as one and a half beats, corresponds to a long syllable – either CVC or CV: while a short stroke, counting as one beat, corresponds to a short, CV syllable. There are several exceptions, but there is no case where a long stroke corresponds to a short syllable, all these long syllables correspond to lexical roots, and all non-lexical roots are played with a short stroke. In other words, the syllables that correspond to words carrying the main semantic information get longer duration. The phrase *Nand me biiri* stands out rhythmically because it is played entirely in (five) short strokes, even though both its words begin in a long syllable, and it stands out linguistically as the only noun phrase among three clauses. It is also played only once, while a repetition of each of the others follows it. It is thus given special prominence both linguistically and musically. Brackets ( ) around the half-beat values in the second phrase indicate that they seemed to be lengthened very little, and the second occurrence of this phrase began in a very short rest. These shortened strokes seem to be partly compensated for in the left hand, which has the leading stroke. On the other hand, the second occurrence of the first phrase begins in an extra stroke, which is also the only occurrence of f'.

In this main portion, every verbal phrase has a High – Low tone contour, again excepting the phrase *Nànd´m´ !bíirí*, which is Low – High – downstepped High. The musical renditions all reflect this. The downstepped syllable *kp´*, which in speech would be followed by *à*, is treated as Low and the particle itself has no stroke. The downstepped word *bíirí* also gets a Low stroke, but it is not as low as the Low that begins this phrase. Note that this fourth phrase, which as we have already noted gets special treatment, has the highest note in the musical text, while the phrase that immediately follows it has the lowest, about an octave down – which, I suggest, serves to enhance the prominence of the high note.

The last part is entirely different. It is in a four beat rhythm, and the only lexical item in it, which also has a long vowel, gets one short stroke. There is nevertheless an exact match of the number of syllables to the number of beats, if we count the first (long) syllable as two – they just do not match the strokes, which are displaced by 1 to the right. I suggest that this change of rhythm and mismatch between syllables and strokes is a musical equivalent of syntactic focus, or literary change of tone, obviously related to its semantic content. Another feature is that in this phrase the rhythm of the left hand matches that of the right, which it does not in the preceding.

Nevertheless the last part, which musically we can call a coda, is not entirely disassociated from the rest, as Figure 4 shows.

	P1	P2	P3	P4	P1	P2	P3	Coda 1 2 3
1st notes	g'	a'	e' (g')	b' (f') g'	a'	e'		g' a' e'
Last notes	d'	g'	d'	a'	b	g'	d'	d' g' d'

Figure 4: Melodic Contour

Each time they occur, the first three phrases (P1, P2, P3) begin respectively on g', a' and e', and so do the repetitions of the coda. Again each time they occur the first three phrases end respectively on d', g' and again d', except P1 the second time – and so does each repetition of the coda. Thus the coda stands out rhythmically, but not melodically. On the other hand the 4th phrase stands out melodically, as does the phrase that immediately follows it, which is the repetition of phrase 1. Witches, death and the affected community are thus given prominence in the music, in a way that is at the same time musically driven and a satisfying expression the emotion of the text.

A final word on which comes first, the music or the text. In the case of this particular piece I do not know. Xylophone composers sometimes create their own text, but I don't think that was true in this case. In many minor texts, for example those for the second xylophone in hot *bawa*, it seems most likely that the melody came first and the words were suggested by it. Keil reports that composers of Tiv songs, who do create both words and music, report both – some say they create the words first, others the sounds, but some that they can come simultaneously (Keil 1979: 167-9). In the western tradition we are used to the idea of setting a poem to music, that is, the poem exists already, for example Schubert's many settings of poems by Goethe and others. On the other hand, composers of operas often exercise some degree of control over the lyrics. It seems to me it is basically a chicken-and-egg situation. Language and music go together, and it all started in Africa.

Endnotes

1: It may be objected that bird song is music. I am not familiar with the thinking in this area, but I provisionally adopt the view that the vocalizations of some kinds of birds may sound like music to humans, or be interpreted as music, but it is by no means certain that how and why birds make these sounds, apart from communicating with other birds, are in any way related to the hows and whys of human music making.

2: In Ghana, 'Dagara' refers to the northern varieties of the language generally referred to as 'Dagaare'. The term 'Dagara' is more generally used in Burkina Faso, where these varieties are also spoken.

3: Wiggins worked with Kobom shortly before I did, and collected essentially the same information on traditions.

4: Since this paper was delivered I have learned that the genre in fact originated in Nandom, and is performed mainly by the young (Wiggins 2010: 81).

5: See Wiggins (2010: 81-82) for a demonstration of how complex the 'hot' variety can be.

6: Abbreviations: FOC focus marker, PRT grammatical particle, PURP grammatical marker of purposeful action.

7: Dr. Wiggins (personal communication) recognizes most of the motifs as recurring in other music.

References

Amha, Azeb. 2011. "Methodological Problems in Documenting Interdisciplinary Topics in Endangered Languages: The Case of Whistling Names in Oyda (Omotic, Ethiopia)." Paper to Workshop. August 7-11.

Apronti, Jawa, 1971. "The Language of a Two-year Old Dangme." *Actes du 8e Congrès de la Société Linguistique de l'Afrique Occidentale*. Abidjan, 545-556.

Barry, Kevin. 1987. *Language, Music and the Sign: A Study in Aesthetics, Poetics and Poetic Practice from Collins to Coleridge*. Cambridge: Cambridge University Press.

Bemile, Sebastian K., ed. 1983. *Dàgàrà Stories*. Heidelberg: P. Kivouvou Verlag.

Carroll, David W. 2004. *Psychology of Language*. 4th edition. Belmont, Calif.: Wadsworth/ Thomson Learning.

Cross, Ian and Ghofur Eliot Woodruff. 2009. "Music as a Communicative Medium." In *The Prehistory of Language*. Ed. by Rudolph P. Botha and Chris Knight. Oxford, New York: Oxford University Press.

Dieterlen, Germaine. 1951. *Essai sur la Religion Bambara*. Paris: Presses Universitaires de France.

Godsey, Larry Dennis. 1980. *The Use of the Xylophone in the Funeral Ceremony of the Birifor of Northwest Ghana*. PhD dissertation, UCLA. University Microfilms International.

Keil, Charles. 1979. *Tiv Song*. Chicago & London: University of Chicago Press.

Mithen, Steven. 2009. "Holistic Communication and the Co-evolution of Language and Music: Resurrecting an Old Idea." In *The Prehistory of Language*. Ed. by Rudolph P. Botha and Chris Knight. Oxford, New York: Oxford University Press.

Nketia, J.H. Kwabena. 1986. *The Music of Africa*. London: Victor Gollancz Ltd.

___. 1971a. "Surrogate Languages of Africa." In *Current Trends in Linguistics*. Vol. 7: *Linguistics in Sub-Saharan Africa*. Ed. by Thomas A. Sebeok. The Hague, Paris: Mouton.

___. 1971b. The Linguistic Aspect of Style in African Languages. *Current Trends in Linguistics*. Vol. 7: *Linguistics in Sub-Saharan Africa*. Ed. by Thomas A. Sebeok. The Hague, Paris: Mouton.

Seavoy, Mary H. 1982. *The Sisaala Xylophone Tradition*. PhD dissertation, UCLA.

Strumpf, Mitchel. 1970. *Ghanaian Xylophone Studies*. Institute of African Studies: Legon.

Wiggins, Trevor. 2010. "Music Research in Northern Ghana: (Colonial) Mis-hearings and (European) Misconceptions." In *Readings in Ethnomusicology: A Collection of Papers Presented at Ethnomusicology Symposium*. Dar es Salaam: Department of Fine and Performing Arts, University of Dar es Salaam. Ed. by Mitchel Strumpf and Imani Sanga.

___. nd. *Xylophone Music from Ghana*. Wakefield, UK: Bretton Press.

Nketia's Influence in Ntahera Hocket and Surrogate Speech Analyses

Joseph S. Kaminski

Joseph S. Kaminski earned his PhD in ethnomusicology from Kent State University, and his M.A. from Hunter College. His journal articles on Asante ntahera (ivory trumpets) and his book publication, *Asante Ntahera Trumpets in Ghana: Culture, Tradition, and Sound Barrage* (2012) are the culmination of his field research among the royal Ntahera group at the Manhyia Palace in Kumase (Ghana). He has been freelancing in New York City as a college professor and trumpeter in jazz and ethnic musics, in addition to engaging in fieldwork in various avenues of transnationalization.

J.H. Kwabena Nketia was the first musicologist to research and publish musical analyses of an *ntahera* group in Ghana's Asante Region, in his article, "The Hocket Technique in African Music," which appeared in the *Journal of the International Folk Music Council*, Volume 14 (1962).[1] This research had a significant influence on UCLA graduate William Grandvil Carter,[2] and Joseph S. Kaminski, the author,[3] a Kent State University graduate. Both Carter and Kaminski, at different times, worked on Asante *ntahera* surrogate speech analyses, following in Nketia's direction. The *ntahera* is an ensemble of seven trumpet-like instruments that are made from elephant tusks. They have been classified as side-blown trumpets; however, they are commonly called horns because of their conical bore, although a tusk is a tooth and not a horn. The Twi word for the single instrument is *abɛn* and the plural *mmɛn*. The *ntahera* and the ivory horn ensembles have been used by court musicians for centuries to render surrogate praises to royal chiefs and their ancestral lines. The surrogate spoken eulogies played from a tusk are followed by horn songs (*nnwom*) in hockets, which are associated with that eulogy.

In Nketia's article, "The Hocket Technique in African Music," Nketia provides two transcriptions of hocketed trumpet songs. In his transcription 7a and 7b,[4] two hocketed parts are shown in treble and bass clefs in their approximate Western pitches. The treble clef also shows the tones and rhythms of the speaking trumpet preceding, and notated, above the treble hocket. Nketia explains how many Ghanaian languages are tonal, and trumpets with variable tones are used for reproducing verbal texts based on high and low tones in speech rhythms. This is surrogate speech.

Tone and Surrogate Speech
Surrogate speech is a phonological system by which word tones of a spoken language are represented in tones produced on a musical instrument. Ethnomusicologists regard this as a musical process. The language of the Asante is Twi, which is tonal, based on two tones, high and low. Ewe and Yoruba have three.[5] The tones produced on the talking trumpets outline the speech contours of the high and low spoken tones of Twi. Trumpet surrogate speech thus substitutes for spoken verse during rites, in performing eulogies to ancestor chiefs and tutelary spirits, as do "talking drums."

The flexibility of a trumpeter's vibrating lips produces tones through an elephant tusk and permits a player to glide tones more in common with the glides of speech. Rules of elision have evolved in the contraction of syllables, words, and phrases, resulting in silent, or omitted, syllables from the surrogate. However, lipped syllables do not correspond exactly to spoken syllables, and merely speaking the language does not give one the ability to understand the surrogate language. Surrogate speech therefore is ambiguous, unless the listener knows beforehand what the speaking trumpets will say. Kazadi wa Mukuna states that if a surrogate language's comprehension were commonplace, there would be no need for giving special attention to its training and preservation, or to its political and spiritual associations.[6]

Surrogate speech may substitute for spoken language when the latter is tonal, as Twi. However, some languages that are not tonal have speech surrogacy, such as Wolof in the *bàkks* played on the *sabar* drums.[7] Furthermore, not all tonal languages use speech surrogacy.

Chernoff stated, "In tonal languages, the pitch of the spoken word is important in determining its meaning, and the same sound pronounced at different pitches can mean entirely different things."[8] He says this in reference to Dagbani praise drumming among the Dagomba[9] (Dagbamba).[10]

Ladzekpo and Pantaleoni found that in *takada* drumming among the Ewe of Anyako, drum strokes suggest specific vowels and that when the timing of a pattern follows the long short values of these vowels in a sentence, as well as their pitch levels, language results.[11]

Hmong is a seven-toned language with two altered tones spoken in upland Southeast Asia and it has various speech surrogates that disguise voices through leafs, *guimbards*, free reeds, and a mouth organ called *qeej* (pronounced "*gaeng*"). Catlin states that originally, substitute words were more than for aesthetic purposes but to disguise communication to deceive listening evil spirits.[12] Today, Hmong surrogacy in secular use sets the speech apart, distinct from reality, marking it as a performance of a ritual.[13] For Hmong, there are four speech-distorting processes: 1) sung encrypting of words, 2) non-voiced speech modification, 3) instrumental abridgment of sung poetry, and 4) instrumental encoding of ritual texts.[14] Whereas the *qeej* provides instrumental encoding of ritual texts, the *ntahera* tusks provide an instrumental abridgement of poetry, as will be explained.

Theodore Sterns stated, "An abridging system, while preserving some phonic resemblance to the base utterance, represents only part of its phonemic qualities, so that it is frequently simpler than an encoding system."[15] He explained "encoding systems as having no essential physical similarity between sign and the sound feature it represents, as in Morse code," or *qeej* playing.[16] *Ntahera* surrogate speech abridgment thus is not the same as an encoding system, but based on contractions wherein lexical units are abbreviated in transmission.[17] Herein, *ntahera* surrogate speech may be classified and analyzed, for abridgments are made of contractions of syllables, as in the *ntahera* speech system.

Thus, *Ntahera* surrogate speech is not a syllable-to-syllable imitation of a spoken text but an abridgement of tonal syllables from the spoken equivalents. Certain syllables with tones are selected to be played, while others adjacent to them become contractions with them because they are not crucial to the overall tonal contour when making sense of words. If a syllable is adjacent to a syllable on the same tone, the two become a contraction. They bind, or one is elided.

While it is certain that the tones of a spoken language create the meaning in surrogate speech, they are not crucial for doing so in song melodies, as Kofi Agawu has shown.[18] Early thinking about speech tones' exact relations to melodic tones may be regarded as naïve.[19] Agawu proves that although variations of speech tones generate different meanings and that tones operate within the syntagmic chain, *intramusical*[20] procedures are not governed by speech tones.[21] Amegago reiterates that composers do not deliberately fit melodies to speech.[22] Agawu and Amegago both conclude that in Ewe songs, the relative durations of the melody reflect those of speech while the speech tones contradict them; therefore, rhythm really influences melodic structure.

This truth of melodic rhythm also holds for *ntahera* surrogate speech. The rhythms of the words are conveyed in the surrogacy to distinguish one word from another of the same pitch or tonal contour. Carrington has shown how rhythmic grouping operates in Lokele talking drums by taking a series of words with the same tonal pattern in the contexts of their phrases and grouping them into the rhythms of their component words.[23]

Fieldwork in talking drums in Africa has been intensive. Akin Euba thoroughly documented the speech style of the *ìyáàlù* talking drum of *dùndún* music of the Yorùbá-speaking people of Nigeria.[24] Amanda Villepastour has done the same for the Yorùbá *bàtá* drum.[25]

David Locke documented his lessons with the Dagbana musician Abubakari Lunna in *Drum Damba*,[26] wherein he describes the Damba festival and the two main drums, the *luna* and the *gun-gon*. The *luna* is the talking drum that produces implicit texts, particularly proverbs, or *salima*, and praises families. Abubakari believes that unless you speak Dagbani it is absurd to play lead *luna* since its every sound should have meaning not only as music but as language.[27] Abubakari explained this as *bansim*, which is the drummer's knowledge, learning, and understanding.[28] Baring this in mind, Locke addressed the concept of *golsigu*, which is the musical aspect of the drumming: the drummer's style, individuality, and creativity. Locke demonstrates the differences between the musical and musico-linguistic meanings and how drumming may be analyzed as absolute music, providing transcriptions of the *luna*, answer *luna*, and *gun-gon* parts that interlock in contrapuntal rhythms.

Chernoff states that drummers may be able to beat the rhythm without knowing the meaning,[29] for there is a high degree of specialization necessary to be able to render exact duplication of speech.[30]. Tang also found that among the Wolof drummers of Senegal, while rhythmic phrases played on the *sabar* drum where derived from the spoken word, in recent times new *bàkks* are no longer based on words but are more rhythmically complex to highlight the percussionists' virtuosity.[31] Furthermore, in Locke's work with Godwin Agbeli, *Kpegisu*, he states that in olden days, the lead drum literally spoke, and he suspects that most contemporary Ewe players think of the drum phrases as absolute music and not as a form of surrogate speech.[32]

Carrington stated that many of the words of the talking drums are old and have fallen into disuse in spoken language. Quoting a Lokele drummer, he said, "These words were given to use by our fathers and we do not understand what they mean."[33] Thus, in contemporary contexts, analyzing speech rhythms of drums can and should be studied musically, as also may be done with *ntahera* trumpet music. Nketia's first article on the hocket technique in African music[34] was as musical study.

In 1957, Laura C. Boulton recorded surrogate speeches recited on a war horn of the Kru people of Lagos.[35] She explained how the messages played on the instrument were not like a system of Morse code of dots and dashes but actually based on the musical elements of speech. In Africa, the signals of such horns thus are based on the tones and rhythm of the language. The structure of Asante ivory trumpet music is based on "surrogate speech," a horn blower constructing his performances on Twi tonal patterns.

In Liberia, Verlon and Ruth Stone recorded an ensemble of four wooden Kpelle horn blowers.[36] The horns are called *túru* and are performed in tonal language, used as voice disguisers. On a *túru*, a player also produces vibrations from his larynx through his mouth into the horn, making more words. Asante horns are not used in this way. They only make surrogate speech via their lips, not their larynx. These tusks are classified as lip-vibrated aerophones, or *cheilophones*.[37]

Surrogate speech can be studied linguistically and musically. Asante surrogate speech is made from an order of verses that develop into complex variations. The process involves players selecting phrases and their tone patterns from a spoken verse and imitating the tonal contours of the phrases. As stated earlier, the precise number of syllables in the imitation does not need to match the number of syllables in the spoken text; only the tonal contours match.

The hocket is built from a repetition of a catch-phrase from the verse, staggered by the ensemble in interlocking parts. An *ntahera* ensemble thus requires two parts to complete the transmission of a phrase or word: a high part and a low part. The entire structure of this music is based on words.

Peter Sarpong states that the horns "speak,"[38] and they sound like the human voice.[39] Nketia states that the Asante ivory trumpets' variable tones reproduce verbal texts that are used for communication in much the same manner as "talking drums."[40]

The basis for a theory of *ntahera* surrogate speech derives from the observation that neither a one-to-one correspondence of spoken syllable to surrogate tone need not occur. Carter states that the process utilizes only selected elements of verbal speech[41] and that the players stylize spoken language to fit their medium.⁴² The medium shapes this stylization, and the surrogate speech becomes not just *"l'imitation correcte du language parlé* [the correct imitation of language]," as Gansemans stated *ihembe* signaling *was not*.⁴³ Concerning this antelope horn of the Hutu,

> *Tenant compte de la composition des formules basées sur une répétition alternée de sol et de fa, nous supposons que la succession des tons hauts et des tons bas du langage parlé n'a pas été imitée dans la langage musical de l'ihembe. Nous avons l'impression que l' intelligibilité des "messages" est surtout basée sur une succession de formules stardardisées sur un des deux tons que produit l'instrument plutôt que sur un l'imitation correcte du language parlé.*

> Taking into account the composition of formulas based on an alternate repetition of the tones *G* and *F*, we found that the succession of high and low tones of the spoken language was not imitated in the musical language of the *ihembe* (antelope horn). We have the impression that the intelligibility of the "messages" is based more on a succession of standardized formulas on one or both tones that the instrument produces, rather than on a correct imitation of spoken language.⁴⁴

Surrogate speech uses selected tonal-rhythmic elements from spoken text. Thus, it is not the correct imitation of language.

George Herzog wrote that the four-tone horn-signal-melodies of the Jabo are not reflections of speech-melody but its "abstractions."⁴⁵ The four tonal registers are reproduced by an equal number of tones on a horn, some produced by the player stopping the end with his hand.⁴⁶ The variation in tones by instrument is comparable to the tonal variations in spoken language among different people. Thus, the horn tones are not reflections of exact tones, for spoken tones are not even static between different people or for the same person at different times.⁴⁷

A detailed accounting of Twi surrogate speech is found in Nketia's chapter "Surrogate Languages of Africa."⁴⁸ He lists two types of processes for surrogate speaking instruments: (a) signals that elicit specific behavior when interpreted as call signals, and (b) sounds that give the aural impression of speech when ordered in specific ways.⁴⁹

As visual signals, auditory signals cannot properly be regarded as functioning as surrogate languages, for they can be selected arbitrarily without reference to spoken language. However, there are cases in Africa in which the selection of signals is based on texts, and they are therefore intended to function as surrogate language.[50]

Clarifying this, Nketia makes specific references to two types of Asante ivory trumpets. This distinction is also maintained in the language of the trumpets. There are trumpets (*mmɛntia*) which play signals based on short texts, and talking trumpets (*asesebɛn*) with a much wider vocabulary.[51]

The surrogate speech process uses language as the raw material for creating a speech work.

Mukuna maintains that surrogate speech is a musical process, like the shaping of words to a melody for singing, or the carrying of extra-musical content in instrumental music. In the comparison of music associated with words to surrogate speech, Mukuna states. . . .

> it is relevant to point out that music does not blindly follow speech tonal inflection, nor its rhythmic structure, but accepts the raw material to work with. In other terms, regardless of the nature of the musical instrument upon which the surrogatelanguage is transmitted, patterns heard are not direct imitations of the consultant words, although general patterns (tonal and rhythmic) may be derived.[52]

Regarding the comparison of a music's extra-musical content to surrogate speech and further clarifying surrogate speech as a musical process, Mukuna adds,

> If it is a fact that there exist musical forces which do override their linguistic counterpart in melodic contour (tonal sequence) and rhythmic organization (as pointed out in vocal music and instrumental rendition in surrogate languages), then we must agree with the statement that the role of musical instruments in surrogate language is predominantly musical even though the basis for its structure may be derived from, or may carry, an extra-musical content.[53]

Surrogate speech thus is a musical process. From the point of view of John Blacking, surrogate speech *is* music, for music is "humanly organized sound."[54] *Ntahera* surrogate speech is an organized musical system based on, in Herzog's terms, the abstraction of speech-melody. Nketia has demonstrated how the abstractions are taken by bonding silent syllables to the played syllables.[55]

In light of the tonal and syllabic abstraction process, the creativity managing the process, and the ensuing musical phenomenon derived from the play of tones and rhythms, surrogate speech is a musical behavior. The creative ingenuities of the trumpeters resort to techniques that permit them to interpret melodic verbal phrases into abstractions. They then recite them as performances that demonstrate further creative variation in the course of a verse's repetition and elaboration.

Nketia's Influence in *Ntahera* Studies
Nketia published translations of surrogate speech for Asante drumming and trumpeting in his chapter, "Surrogate Languages of Africa." He states that two types of trumpet speech occur: signals eliciting specific behavior when interpreted as call signals, and sounds giving the aural impression of speech when ordered in specific ways. Such a signal may be seen in the first two bars of Nketia's transcriptions 7a and 7b, and the speech may be seen in the third and fourth bars of the transcriptions.[56]

William Carter later decoded a *ntahera* surrogate-speech system of bound words and rhythmical contractions.[57] He found and indicated syllables contained in the musical tones produced by the Juaben (Dwaben) horn blowers, and then he explained the rules for speaking the secret language. The important practice to be aware of is that there is not a one-to-one correspondence of syllable to tone. Carter showed how the system utilizes only selected elements of speech.[58] Some syllables require two tones while a combination of syllables may be contained in only one tone as a contraction. Players stylize the language to fit the medium.[59] Kaminski found that a player arranges lines liberally to make verses, and these vary when consecutively repeated with ornaments and rhythmical diversions. A line becomes more rhythmically and phonically complex with each repetition.[60]

Carter wrote

> The linear units are 'freely' drawn from a rather limited stock source; they are 'freely' inserted, deriving their ordering from the imagination of the soloist. This selection and inclusion is 'improvisatory' in nature and means that no two performances will be identical.[61]

The Kumase *ntahera* musicians refer to this creative process as player's "style." Some players learned their source materials from the same teacher and have similar styles. If they are young and eager to expand their conception, some adapt features of other styles. The most experienced players have distinct styles and maintain them as their specialty, improvising around them. Carter adds

> The principles at work here are the same as those we use in judging music or script-readings. The performer exhibits his talent by the way he realizes the relationship of words, lines, and thoughts. His insight is the tool with which he discovers the essence of the material; his creativity is measured by the skill with which he communicates that which his insight has discovered.[62]

Nketia in the "hocket" article" defines that the lead trumpet part with variable tones imitates falling intonations used in speech. I observed that the *ntahera* trumpeters loosened their lips to produce falling intonations, allowing tones to drop as though the *ntahera* trumpeters were speaking naturally with their voices. Trumpeters truly imitate speech tones because of their flexible lips, which are like vocal chords.

Viewing Nketia's transcription 7a,[63] trumpet ensembles are comprised mainly of seven instruments that play hockets over which lead trumpets talk. The lead trumpeter's surrogate speech is varied rhythmically from spoken texts but guided by textual considerations. Words are not indicated in the transcriptions 7a and 7b, for these are musical analyses. The speech rhythm and tones without words are indicated on the top staves.

Comparing Nketia's transcriptions to those of Carter from Dwaben[64] and Kaminski from Kumase,[65] 7a appears to be the standard *ntahera* song *Ɔkwan*, which means, "The Way," and 7b appears to be the *ntahera* song *Kankane Repɛ Etwie Ayɛ*, which translates into English as "the dog wants to be the leopard but cannot," connoting an envious person wanting to be a chief but cannot. It is an Asante proverb. The hockets in the transcription sets are the same, although notated differently by the three. Nketia's notation of the trumpet signal and opening phrase through bar 4 are tonally the same as Carter's, but the transcriptions of the speech phrases are rhythmically different because of the differences in the way the players paced their speech, the way they talk, and they way they interpret the contracted syllables to cloak the speech from outsiders. The first two bars of the surrogate speech here are *momma yeama yen ho so,* which means, "Lift it up! We have lifted ourselves." This phrase is the leader's call to the ensemble to get ready, an perceived as a signal. The third and fourth bar of *Ɔkwan* is the word itself, in two syllables, a high and then a low. As Nketia and Carter both have differently shown in the compared transcriptions, the individual players' interpretations of the surrogated word are elaborated, varied, and ornate.

The *ntahera* song *Ɔkwan* is played to repel evil spirits from the path on which the chief or king walks in procession, so thus, the word *Ɔkwan* shows "the way" to walk. This song is often preceded by a long surrogated speech of the eulogy to the river spirit Tano, the first line of which is *Ɔkwan atware asuo*, "The path has crossed the river." Nketia or Carter did not reveal this longer transcription in their work. Kaminski published it in "Surrogate Speech of Asante Ivory Trumpeters in Ghana," *Yearbook for Traditional Music* vol. 40 (2008).[66]

The hocketed tones of the ensemble indicated in all of the transcriptions of *Ɔkwan* are divided into two dissonant clusters, dissonant for the purpose of creating a harsh sound to scare evil spirits. Agyeman-Duah noted that "when anyone hears the sound of these horns, he runs away."[67] Nana Kwame Fofie Opoku, the Kumase Ntaherahene, revealed to me how the *ntahera's* power derived in its sacred origin. The fear it instills is not from the sound alone but rather from the *ntahera* spirit. The spirit is said to have descended from heaven with the Golden Stool in 1697, already placed in the horns. The sound of the *ntahera* is to protect the Golden Stool, the Asante throne.

By convention, seven trumpets make an *ntahera*. The six that blow the two clusters are divided into usually three *agyesoa*, two *afrẹ*, and one *bọsoọ*. The three *agyesoa* and the *bọsoọ* cluster together. The *agyesoa* and *bọsoọ* respond first in the hocket to the *seseẹ's*, or speaking trumpet's signal; *agyesoa* literally means "responder." The *bọsoọ*, usually the longest tusk, functions as the *agyesoa's* ground, sounding with it.

The hocketed *afrẹ* cluster is the lower cluster and blown rhythmically on the strong pulses of a song, after the *agyesoa*, to support the *seseẹ's* phrases. *Afrẹ* means "the one that calls,"[68] although it is the *seseẹ* that does the calling. The hocket in itself renders the catch phrase of the surrogate speech. In this song, the hocket pronounces a two syllable word, high to low, seemed to be interpreted differently in the field.[69]

Nketia's other transcription 7b[70] appears to be of the song *Ọkankane repẹ etwie ayẹ*, which translates into English as "the dog wants to be the leopard but cannot." Carter titled the song in his transcription *Ọkankane*.[71] In Nketia 7b, the introductory phrase is transcribed in bars 3 and 4, after the call *momma yeama yen ho so*, transcribed in bars 1 and 2. Nketia's *ntahera* speaker is shown here to have rendered the eleven-syllable phrase in just seven syllables, according to his style. In Carter's transcription Figure 6,[72] the call to get ready *momma yeama yen ho so* is shown on the third stave in the first seven tones, and the eleven syllable phrase *Ọkankane repẹ etwie ayẹ* follows in just nine tones, two more that what Nketia's trumpeter had rendered. Readers must remain aware that in this system, one-to-one correspondences of spoken syllable to surrogated tone are not what make a surrogate phrase comprehendible, but the contour of the speech tones in sequence does. These are contractions, or "abridgements." On a close look, the tones representing *Ọkankane repẹ etwie ayẹ* have the same contour of high and low, and this is what the chiefs understand in the tonal language. They are also grouped rhythmically to the phrase.

While the rhythmical variation between the two trumpeters' introductions is evident, once the ensemble hocket begins, the surrogated word *Ọkankane* played by the leading speaking trumpet is closely the same, with improvisation around the words of the phrase. Carter notates *Ọkankane* as an eighth-note and two sixteenth-notes, 3 syllables, while Nketia notates it as a quarter-note and two eighth-notes, also 3 syllables.

I attained *ntahera* surrogate speech texts from Kwame Boakye, the *seseɛ* of the Kumase *ntahera*, and Nana Owusu, the *seseɛ* of the *kwakwrannya* and grandson of Kwasi Kwarteng. I eventually performed with the *ntahera* twice at Akwasidae ancestor venerations at Manhyia Palace. Boakye and Owusu learned their surrogating technique from Kwasi Kwarteng, a former *seseɛ*. The surrogate speech technique in Kumase is unique for the Asantehene's *ntahera* and *kwakwrannya*, and it is most ornate. I did not find this style performed among trumpeters of other paramount chiefs. Since Kumase maintains the court of the Asantehene, the king of Asante, it may appear that this most ornate surrogate technique is the most highly stylized in the kingdom.

In Boakye's "*Ɔkankane Repɛ Etwie Ayɛ*,"[73] the Twi words surrogated in the introductory phrase are shown. He renders the eleven syllable phrase in eight tones. Different from the preceding *Ɔkankane* transcriptions, Boakye recites a lower tone before the first upper tone. He produces this tone to emphasize the beginning of the word *Ɔkankane* by accenting the second syllable *–kan* as the first and just attaching the preceding vowel Ɔ- as a prefix-contraction. This pre-syllable is a uniquely stylized feature of Kumase trumpeting and in Kwasi Kwarteng's style.

The next part of the phrase is almost similar to the phrases in Nketia's and Carter's transcriptions, but with two upper tones instead of three, followed by three lower tones. Boakye glides to the next upper tone, although not indicated in Nketia or Carter's works. This type of glide is characteristic of trumpet surrogate speech, making the surrogation very speech-like. The drastic difference in all three *Ɔkankane* transcriptions is that Boakye ends the phrase on a low tone,[74] whereas Nketia and Carter indicate the phrase ending on a high tone.

Two explanations of this last difference can be made. The first is that Boakye ends the phrase on the word *aye*, bound to the preceding syllable *–e* from the previous word. This practice creates a bound morpheme, and the last word is thus a low tone. The preceding transcriptions with the high tone ending evidently are indicating the surrogation of the shorter phrase, "*Ɔkankane Repɛ Etwie*," emphasizing that the dog wants to be the leopard without saying that it cannot. Perhaps the trumpeters did not need to pronounce the final word *aye*, understanding it to be presumed. The second explanation, the technical explanation, is that Boakye ends this phrase with a stylized clause marker, occurring after a bound morpheme and descending to mark the end of the phrase. I used Carter's linguistic model of the surrogate speech performance of the Dwaben *ntahera* to find linguistic occurrences. Such speech-trumpeting techniques involve bound morphemes and clause markers, as seen in Carter's dissertation page 265.[75] Carter's model for clause markers in the syllable *-e* explains why Boakye ends this phrase with the lower falling tone, also emphasizing the proverb's final word *aye*.

In *ntahera* surrogate speech, one-to-one correspondences of syllable to tone do not occur, but abridgements. Players utilize speech tones, but several syllables may be conveyed in a contraction to one tone, if they are on the same tone level. The system is thus a system of contractions, wherein the tonal contour and rhythmic grouping of words determine the textual meaning of the played tones.

Nevertheless, in Boakye's phrase "*Ɔkankane Repɛ Etwie Ayɛ,*"[76] eleven syllables are sounded in eight tones by way of abridgement, indicated by tied syllables. After this catch-phrase, the ensemble hocket begins its cycle, sounding a three-toned phrase, *(Ɔ)kan-kan-e*, dog.

In the transcription of the *ntahera* surrogate speech *Ɔkwan atware asuo* by Nana Owusu,[77] the first six tones represent a signal for getting people's attention. Owusu recites in surrogate speech the first ten lines of the poem, *Ɔkwan atware asuo*,[78] then continues with stylistic variation of the two beginning lines, *Ɔkwan atware asuo, Asuo atware Ɔkwan*. Here he adds a slurred tone to the bound morpheme and attached vowels of *-kwanˆat-* and *-suˆoˆat-*.

Owusu follows with a second, elongated, stylized, variation of just the first line, *Ɔkwan atware asuo,* and then his next line is an early signal, *Momma so!* ("Lift it up!"). He continues the poem with a third variation of the two opening lines, but this time with a slow lip bend that greatly exaggerates the two tones *via* the sound of the pitch bends. The entire speech concludes with the most standard strong name for Asantehene, *Asante Kɔtɔkɔhene* (Asante Porcupine king), followed by *Firi tete*, "from ancient time."

Summary

This paper was an attempt to 1) analyze a transcription from Nketia's work in *ntahera* music, and 2) how the transcription laid the groundwork for Carter and me, the author. The paper is meant to illuminate a fieldworker's need to study the work of those who came before. The same system of musicolinguistics prevails in Asante and throughout the Akan region. Similarities reveal shared repertoires and a history of the tradition, while differences reveal artistic means and creative idiosyncrasies. A close analysis of the three sets of transcriptions reveal they are of the same songs and that the creative genre is interpretive.

Endnotes

1: Nketia, J.H. Kwabena, "The Hocket-Technique in African Music." *Journal of the International Folk Music Council* 14 (1962) 44-52.

2: Carter, William Grandvil, "The Ntahera Horn Ensemble of the Dwaben Court: An AshantiSurrogating Medium," master's thesis, University of California-Los Angeles, 1971.
___. "Asante Music in Old and New Juaben." Ph.D. diss., University of California-Los Angeles, 1984.

3: Kaminski, Joseph S. "Asante Ivory Trumpets in Ghana: Traditions, Repertories, Histories, Metaphysics." Ph.D. diss., Kent State University, Kent, Ohio, 2006.
___. "Surrogate Speech of Asante Ivory Trumpeters in Ghana," *Yearbook for Traditional Music* vol. 40 (2008) 117-135.

4: Nketia, "The Hocket-Technique in African Music," p. 50

5: Agawu, Kofi. "The Rhythmic Structure of West African Music." *The Journal of Musicology* .5, no. 3, (Summer 1987) 400-18, p. 405.

6: Kazadi wa Mukuna, "Function of Musical Instruments in Surrogate Languages in Africa: A Clarification." *Africa: Revista do centro estudos Africanos* 10 (1987): 3-8, p. 4.

7: Tang, Patricia. *Masters of the Sabar: Wolof Griot Percussionists of Senegal*. Philadelphia: Temple University Press, 2007, p. 113.

8: Chernoff, John Miller. *African Rhythm and African Sensibility: Aesthetics and Social Action in African Musical Idioms*. University of Chicago Press, 1979, p. 75.

9: Ibid. p. 68.

10: See, Locke, David, and Abubakari Luna. *Drum Damba: Talking Drum Lessons*. Crown Point, IN: White Cliffs media Company, 1990.

11: Ladzekpo, S. Kobla, and Hewitt Pantaleoni. "Takada Drumming," *African Music* 4, no. 4 (1970), pp. 6-31, 18.

12: Catlin, Amy R. "Speech Surrogate Systems of the Hmong: From Singing Voices to Talking Reeds." *The Hmong in the West: Observations and Reports*. Edited by Bruce T. Downing and Douglas P. Olney. Papers of the 1981 Hmong Research Conference, University of Minnesota (1982): 170-200, p. 171.

13: Ibid. p. 193.

14: Ibid. p. 184.

15: Sterns, Theodore. "Drum and Whistle 'Languages:' An Analysis of Speech Surrogates." *American Anthropologist*. New series, Vol. 59, NO. 3 (June 1957), pp. 487-506, p. 488.

16: Ibid. p. 487.

17: Ibid. p. 489.

18: Ibid. p. 143.

19: See, Jones, A. M. *Studies in African Music*. 2 vols. London: Oxford University Press, 1959, p. 246.

20: Agawu, Kofi. "Tone and Tune: The Evidence for Northern Ewe Music." *Africa: The Journal of the International African Institute* 58, no. 2 (1988) 127-146, p. 127 (Agawu's emphasis).

21: Ibid. p. 132.

22: Amegago, Modesto. *An African Music and Dance Curriculum Model: Performing Arts in Education*. Durham, NC: Carolina Academic Press, 2011, p. 116.

23: Carrington, J. F. *Talking Drums of Africa*. New York: Negro Universities Press, 1969; reprint of London: Carey Kingsgate Press, 1949), pp. 33-34.

24: Euba, Akin. *Yoruba Drumming: The Dùndún Tradition*. Bayreuth: African Studies Series; Lagos: Elekoto Music Centre, 1990.

25: Villepastour, Amanda. *Ancient Text Messages of the Yorùbá Bàtá Drum: Cracking the Code*. Farnham: Ashgate, 2010.

26: Locke, David, and Abubakari Lunna. *Drum Damba: Talking Drum Lessons*. Crown Point Indiana: White Cliffs Media Company, 1990.

27: Ibid. p. 7.

28: Ibid. p. 85.

29: Chernoff, *African Rhythm and African Sensibility*, p. 76.

30: Ibid. p. 75.

31: Tang, *Masters of the Sabar: Wolof Griot Percussionists of Senegal*, p. 1.

32: Locke, David, and Godwin Agbeli. *Kpegisu: War Drum of the Ewe*. White Cliffs Media: Temple, Arizona, 1992, p. 117.

33: Carrington, *talking Drums of Africa*, p. 38.

34: Nketia, Kwabena. "The Hocket-Technique in African Music." *Journal of the International Folk Music Council* 14 (1962) 44-52.

35: Boulton, Laura C. "Notes" to *African Music: Recorded by Laura C. Boulton on the Straus West African Expedition of the Field Museum of Natural History*. Folkways. FW 8852, 1957.

36: Stone, Ruth. "Notes" to *Music of the Kpelle of Liberia*. Recorded by Verlon Stone and Ruth Stone. Ethnic Folkways. FE 4385, 1972.

37: From ζεῖλος, i.e., "lips."

38: Sarpong, Peter Kwasi. *Ceremonial Horns of the Ashanti*. Accra: Sedco, 1990, p. 1.

39: Ibid., p. 5

40: Nketia, "The Hocket Technique in African Music," p. 49.

41: Carter, "Asante Music in Old and New Juaben," p. 261.

42: Ibid. p. 265.

43: Gansemans, Jos. *Les instruments de musique du Rwanda: etude ethnomusicologique*. Tervuren: Museé royal de l'Afrique centrale, 1988, p. 106.

44: Gansemans, *Les instruments de musique du Rwanda*, p. 106.

45: Herzog, George. "Speech-Melody and Primitive Music," *Musical Quarterly* 20:4 (1934): 452-466, pp. 456-7.

46: Ibid. p. 455.

47: Ibid. p. 457.

48: J.H. Kwabena Nketia, "Surrogate Languages of Africa." In *Current Trends in Linguistics* 7: *Linguistics in Sub-Sahara Africa*, ed. Thomas A Sebeok, 669-732. The Hague: Mouton, 1971.

49: Ibid. p. 700.

50: Ibid. p. 701.

51: Ibid.

52: Mukuna, "Function of Musical Instruments in Surrogate Languages in Africa," p. 6.

53: Ibid. p. 7.

54: John Blacking, *How Musical is Man?* (Seattle: University of Washington Press, 1973), p. 3.

55: Nketia, "Surrogate Languages of Africa," p. 715.

56: Nketia, "The Hocket-Technique in African Music," p. 50.

57: Carter, "Asante Music in Old and New Juaben."

58: Ibid. p. 261.

59: Ibid. p. 265.

60: Kaminski, "Surrogate Speech of Asante Ivory Trumpeters in Ghana."

61: Carter, "Asante Music in Old and New Juaben," p. 270.

62: Ibid.

63: Nketia, "The Hocket-Technique in African Music."

64: Carter, "Asante Music in Old and New Juaben," pp. 284-5.

65: Kaminski, "Asante Ivory Trumpets in Ghana," pp. 149 and 153.

66: Kaminski, "Surrogate Speech of Asante Ivory Trumpeters in Ghana," p. 132.

67: Agyeman-Duah, *Ashanti Stool Histories,* Asante Stool 26.

68: Carter, "Asante Music in Old and New Juaben," p. 278.

69: Kaminski, "Asante Ivory Trumpets in Ghana," p. 149.

70: Nketia, "The Hocket-Technique in African Music."

71: Carter, "Asante Music in Old and New Juaben," p. 285.

72: Ibid.

73: Kaminski, "Asante Ivory Trumpets in Ghana," p. 53.

74: Ibid.

75: Carter, "Asante Music in Old and New Juaben," p. 265.

76: Kaminski, "Asante Ivory Trumpets in Ghana," p. 153.

77: Kaminski, "Surrogate Speech of Asante Ivory Trumpeters in Ghana," p. 132.

78: Cf.. J.H. Kwabena Nketia, *Ayan: The Poetry of the Atumpan drums of the Asantehene,* vol. 1. (Legon, Ghana: Institute of African Studies, University of Ghana, 1966), p. 15.

References

Agawu, Kofi. 1987. "The Rhythmic Structure of West African Music." *The Journal of Musicology.* 5 (3): 400-18 Summer.

____. 1988. "Tone and Tune: The Evidence for Northern Ewe Music." *Africa: The Journal of the International African Institute.* 58 (2): 127-146.

Agyeman-Duah, J. 1976. *Ashanti Stool Histories.* Legon: Institute of African Studies, University of Ghana.

Amegago, Modesto. 2011. *An African Music and Dance Curriculum Model: Performing Arts in Education.* Durham, NC: Carolina Academic Press.

Blacking, John. 1973. *How Musical is Man?* Seattle: University of Washington Press.

Boulton, Laura C. 1957. "Notes" to *African Music: Recorded by Laura C. Boulton on the Straus West African Expedition of the Field Museum of Natural History.* Folkways. FW 8852. LP.

Carrington, John F. 1969.*Talking Drums of Africa.* New York: Negro Universities Press.

Carter, William G. 1971. *The Ntahera Horn Ensemble of the Dwaben Court: An Ashanti Surrogating Medium.* Master's thesis, University of California, Los Angeles,.

____. 1984. *Asante Music in Old and New Juaben.* PhD. dissertation, University of California, Los Angeles.

Catlin, Amy R. 1982. "Speech Surrogate Systems of the Hmong: From Singing Voices to Talking Reeds." In *The Hmong in the West: Observations and Reports.* Ed. by Bruce T. Downing and Douglas P. Olney. Papers of the 1981 Hmong Research Conference, University of Minnesota, 170-200.

Chernoff, John Miller. 1979. *African Rhythm and African Sensibility: Aesthetics and Social Action in African Musical Idioms.* Chicago: University of Chicago Press.

Euba, Akin. 1990.*Yoruba Drumming: The Dùndún Tradition.* Bayreuth: Bayreuth African Studies Series.

Gansemans, Jos. 1988. *Les Instruments de Musique du Rwanda: Etude Ethnomusicologique.* Tervuren: Museé Royal de l'Afrique Centrale.

Herzog, George. 1934. "Speech-Melody and Primitive Music." *Musical Quarterly* 20 (4): 452-466.

Jones, A. M. 1959. *Studies in African Music.* Vol. 2. London: Oxford University Press.

Kaminski, Joseph S. 2006. *Asante Ivory Trumpets in Ghana.* PhD. dissertation, Kent State University.

____. 2008. "Surrogate Speech of Asante Ivory Trumpeters in Ghana." *Yearbook for Traditional Music.* 40.

Ladzekpo, S. Kobla and Hewitt Pantaleoni. 1970. "Takada Drumming." *African Music.* 4 (4): 6-31.

Locke, David and Abubakari Lunna. 1990. *Drum Damba: Talking Drum Lessons.* Crown Point Indiana: White Cliffs Media Company.

Locke, David and Godwin Agbeli. 1992. *Kpegisu: A War Drum of the Ewe.* Tempe, Arizona: White Cliffs Media.

Mukuna, Kazadi wa. 1987. "Function of Musical Instruments in Surrogate Languages in Africa: A Clarification." *Africa: Revista do centro estudos Africanos* 10: 3-8.

Nketia, J.H. Kwabena. 1962. "The Hocket-Technique in African Music." *Journal of the International Folk Music Council* 14: 44-52.

___. 1966. *Ayan: The Poetry of the Atumpan Drums of the Asantehene. Vol. 1.* Legon, Ghana: Institute of African Studies, University of Ghana.

___. 1971. "Surrogate Languages of Africa." In *Current Trends in Linguistics: Linguistics in Sub-Sahara Africa*. Ed. by Thomas A. Sebeok. The Hague: Mouton. 7: 669-732.

Sarpong, Peter Kwasi. 1990. *Ceremonial Horns of the Ashanti.* Accra: Sedco.

Sterns, Theodore. 1957. "Drum and Whistle 'Languages:' An Analysis of Speech Surrogates." *American Anthropologist.* New series. 59 (3): 487-506.

Stone, Ruth. 1972. "Notes" to *Music of the Kpelle of Liberia.* Recorded by Verlon Stone and Ruth Stone. Ethnic Folkways. FE 4385.

Tang, Patricia. 2007. *Masters of the Sabar: Wolof Griot Percussionists of Senegal.* Philadelphia: Temple University Press.

Villepastour, Amanda. 2010. *Ancient Text Messages of the Yorùbá Bàtá Drum: Cracking the Code.* Farnham: Ashgate.

The Textual Basis of African Drumming: The Interaction Between Spoken Language and Drumming

Modesto Amegago

Modesto Amegago is a professor of dance at York University in Canada. A consummate drummer and dancer, his research interests include historical and cultural context of African music and dance, creative and performance processes, and aesthetics and arts education. He has written several articles and his book publications are *African Drumming: The History and Continuity of African Drumming Tradition* (2014) and *An African Music and Dance Curriculum Model: Performing Arts in Education* (2011).

Included in the functions of African drumming is its use as a medium of communication on the basis of language or text. The speech or textual basis of African drumming has been investigated by scholars such as A. M. Jones, (1959), Kwabena Nketia (1963), Kwabla Ladzekpo and Hewitt Pantaleoni (1970), John Miller Chernoff (1979), David Locke and Godwin Agbeli (1980), David Locke (1990), Akin Euba (1990), Modesto Amegago (2007) and Patricia Tang (2007). This paper draws from my own experiences and research and the works of some of the previous scholars to pay tribute to an illustrious Professor Nketia and augment the prevailing knowledge.

Language is defined as a body of words and a system for their use, common to a community, nation, or people living within the same geographical area, or having a common cultural tradition. Language is also defined as a mode of communication by voice, using arbitrary auditory symbols in conventional ways with conventional meanings (*Random House College Dictionary*, revised edition, s.v. "language). However, the definition of language in the African context should include human movements, gestures and other environmental sounds that communicate something meaningful to group of people and individuals. The speech or textual mode of drumming is a deliberate attempt by drummers to "speak with their drums", or to articulate or imitate human utterances: speech tones and phrases and vocal melodies on the drums. As Nketia notes, words, phrases and sentences may be transformed into drums sounds, and reinterpreted in verbal terms by the drummer and listener (Nketia 1963). He further states that in considering drumming, one must recognize on one level, drum sounds which are organized into rhythms and tones patterns and on the other hand, the verbal correlates in terms of which the drum sounds may be produced or interpreted (ibid). In his book, *Drumming in Akan Communities*, Nketia refers to the signal mode of drumming, the speech mode of drumming and the dance mode of drumming. He also states that the association of drum sounds with texts finds its greatest expression in the speech mode of drumming where texts are used solely for their communicative value, but it is to be found in some measure in the other modes of drumming (ibid). Here, Nketia is referring to the use of the Akan male and female *atumpan* and other drums in communicating on textual basis in social, ceremonial and other performance contexts. The Akan male and female *atumpan* drums have been adopted by many Ghanaian groups and institutions for use in communication on speech basis and in music and dance performances. However, the various Ghanaian ethnic groups also use some of their instruments to communicate in speech modes. For example, the Ewe would employ the *atimevu*, lead drum (which has a relatively wider tonal range) and supporting drums such as *sogo, kidi, kloboto, totodzi* and *kagan* (in *agbekɔ*) and *vuga* and *vuvi* (in *bɔbɔɔbɔ*) to communicate using speech modes while the Dagbamba of northern Ghana would use the *donno* and *brekete* for the same purpose.

Although, the textual basis of drumming is no longer emphasized by drummers in many contemporary African societies, there is much empirical evidence on the use of drums in communication in the speech mode in many African traditional societies. For example, the speech mode of drumming is still practiced among the Wolof, Yoruba, Dagbamba, Akan, Ewe, Ga and some other African societies. Akin Euba notes that almost all the Yoruba drums may be used to communicate on textual basis, but *iyaalu* or *dundun* ensembles are mostly used in communicating on speech basis. The *iyaalu* functions both as a musical and speech instrument. He notes further that of the various parameters of human speech, only rhythm and intonation are produced on *iyaalu* (Euba 1991). The speech mode of drumming involves the playing of both rhythmic texts and melodies (or melo-rhythms), sometimes in combination with non-textual rhythms/patterns, especially in integrated music and dance performances. Thus in integrated performances, the drum texts, other instrumental sounds, songs and dance movements are interwoven. For example, an Ewe *adzogbo* lead drummer may be speaking, singing and articulating the dance/narratives on the drum at a given time.

Characteristics of African Drum Texts

Texts that are played on African drums may be short and form the main patterns of the supporting or signal drums, or constitute the introduction sections of lead drum patterns. There are also lengthy texts that form part of the lead and complementary drum patterns, and range from a few patterns or phrases to lengthy ones and highlight sub-divisions of patterns or phrases and statements. Drum texts are usually composed in languages and dialects spoken by particular drummers and communities; but some reflect a fusion of local dialects, languages, English and French. They are usually cast in ordinary or colloquial languages, proverbs and allusions. There may or may not be a one to one correspondence between speech syllables or phrases and drum strokes or phrases. For example, a single drum stroke may represent one or more speech syllables; and two or more drum strokes may represent one speech syllable. The drums texts do not exactly mimic human voices but their close association with human sounds enables people familiar with the performance and culture to understand them. The texts are usually played in a musical mode thus making them sound different from the way they are normal spoken.

Euba notes further that different sentences may have the same tonal structure and in order to be able to interpret any of the sentences played on the drum, it is necessary to have adequate knowledge of the context in which they are expressed and of the general train of thought preceding the expression, so that possible alternatives can be judged in term of their logicality, or relation to the context. Hence, colloquial usage often facilitates the interpretation of the drum texts. When two different sentences are otherwise undifferentiated in their rendition in the drumming, the more colloquial of the two could be the correct one (Euba 1991). For these reasons, proverbs and sayings already well known to people are more easily decipherable when played on drum than the totality of unfamiliar texts (Euba 1991). Variations occur when drummers in different localities continue to reinterpret the texts in their own ways (on the basis of their subjective experiences). Other performers and listeners may give their own interpretations to some of the texts (including drum patterns that were not originally intended to communicate on speech basis). Some of these interpretations/meanings may become collectively accepted over time. All these may lead to varied interpretations of some of the drum texts.

Drum Mnemonic, Vocables or Syllables

In addition to the textual basis of African drumming, the drummers may express their drum beats or patterns in mnemonics; or what some writers refer to as vocables or syllables, and what Nketia refers to as nonsense syllables (Nketia 1974). The Ewe generally refer to such sounds as *ʋugbe* while the Akan call them *wɔpɔtɔ*. For example, syllables such as *ga* (used to express a bouncing hand stroke at the centre of the drum head), *gi* (used to express a pressed hand stroke at the edge the drum head), *de,* (used to express a bouncing stroke near the edge of the drum head), and *to,* (used to express a high pitch stroke at the centre of the drum head while pressing the membrane with the other hand/

stick) may be heard in Ewe drumming. Similarly, the syllables such as *pe, de, te, pa, ta* may be heard in some Akan, Ga and Mande drumming. Some of these syllables may be closed or muted with m, n, sh, tsi sounds, for example, den, pem, krish, kidi kitsi (see also Nketia, p. 33). These vocables or syllables are shaped by the size and sounds/pitches of the drums, the weight, speed and rhythmic groupings of the drum beats and the languages and dialects spoken by particular drummers and listeners. They may be viewed as an abstraction of the drums' sounds, or the uttering of the drum strokes/beats according to the ways they resonate in the ears of the drummers/listeners. Nketia also notes that these expressions are an extension of the common phonoaesthetic habit of imitating non-speech sounds such as mechanical noises, animals' cries, and songs of birds by means of speech sounds. They are also used when one wishes to speak out the musical rhythms of a particular drum, or the integrated rhythms of a complete ensemble in such a way as to bring out the duration of the drum beats and the tone contrast on which the particular piece is built (Nketia 1963:33). Instead of giving the meaningful translation of a series of drum beats, the drummer may choose to speak the rhythm in vocables or syllables; s/he may speak them where a proper translation of a section of drum patterns is forgotten, or obscure, or where s/he is unwilling either to give out secrets or to say what is better conveyed by drums or by word of mouth (ibid).

Some drums had derived their names from their basic sounds/syllables. For example, the *gudugudu*, kettle drum and *dundun* hourglass drum of the Yoruba; the *donno*, hourglass drum of the Dagbamba; the *djundjun* and *kenkeni* drums of the Mande groups, the *gugutegu*, ritual drum of the Ewe of ŋɔtsie, Togo and the *kidi*, supporting drum of the Ewe, (also called *asivui* and *kpetsi*) are all named according to their basic sounds and vocables/syllables. These names in turn, provide clues for remembering their sounds. Nowadays, the drum vocables or syllables are gaining popularity among the drummers and listeners in many communities and institutions at the local and international settings and are fast replacing some of the drum texts. Nevertheless, some African drummers would readily express their drumming patterns on textual basis; while some would express them as both texts and syllables/vocables. Among the Ewe, almost every drum text would also be expressed in vocables or syllables. Due to the limited scope of this paper, I have focused on the texts that are communicated through African drumming but include some of the vocables to clarify the topic.

Drum Texts and Their Contextual References

Based upon the analysis of the empirical data that I have reviewed in both the oral and literary traditions, the texts that are featured in various contexts of African drumming express multifaceted themes such as tribute to the spirits of the trees and animals whose products are used in making the drums, the cock and clock bird that awake people at dawn and alert them during the day, and the ancestor drummers, divinities and God who are the originators and custodians of the performances. Some texts express greetings, appellations, praises, commendation of peoples. Others recount the genealogies and histories of states, chiefs, kings, queens, ordinary individuals and their activities while some relate to the experiences of the age, sex, and gender of military, occupational and religious groups. Texts that feature in traditional military contexts express themes of toughness, bravery, greatness, alertness, readiness to combat, communication with divinities and the Supreme Being for guidance and protection; perseverance, victory, defeat and psychological state of the militants, etc. The texts that are featured in religious contexts express themes such as a call to duty, a tribute to drummers, singers/cantors, ancestors, divinities and the Supreme Being; indigenous African, Moslem and Christian's prayer (some in the form of jubilation over happy occasions, such as marriage, the completion of apprenticeship; sympathy over misfortune, revelations; warning about imminent danger, desire for goodness, God's guidance and protection; love relations, sanctity, beauty, perseverance and hope).

In addition, the texts that are played in drumming associated with socialization express themes of patience, commendation, beauty, social relations, feelings of love, arrival of loved ones, jealousy, patience, social vices, punishment, forgiveness, hailing of leaders, advice and warning to community members, and topical themes.

Texts that are featured in youths' performances express the youths' yearning for the return of their mothers, their comparison of mothers to young ladies, physical appearances of peers, beauty, youths' desire for drink and food; the desire to compete with one another; youths cautioning of peers; experiences of pain in certain parts of the body, reference to political leaders, the consequences of certain social vices as well as some socially repressed themes. Within the context of funerals, some of the drum texts express a wish to be surrounded by family members in the after life, a wish to depart without leaving debt behind; sorrow, sympathy, condolences, a wish for the return of the deceased to life and the fate that awaits the body after life. Some of the drum texts express provocative and socially repressed or immoral themes because of the critical roles of African drummers. Such texts may reflect the social realism and may be aesthetically pleasing when played on the drums. Below are some of the drum texts and their contextual functions:

Examples of African Drum Texts in Cultural Contexts
The following texts are drawn from the Akan drumming ('awakening texts') as documented by Nketia (1963). In the first example, the drummer evokes the spirit of the tree which is used in making the drum as follows:

Tweneboa Akwa
Tweneboa Kodua
Kodua Tweneduro
Tweneduro, wokɔ, baabi a
Merefre wo, yese bra
Meresua, momma menhu.
Meaning
Wood of the drum Tweneboa Akwa,
Wood of the drum Tweneboa Kodua
Wood of the drum Tweneboa Kodua, tweneduro
Cedar wood if you have been away,
I am calling you, they say come,
I am learning, let me succeed (ibid:6).

In the second example, the drummer evokes the spirit of the drum pegs as follows:

Obua Maniampon Akyerema repoma no
Obua, wokɔ baabi a
Merefre wo; yese bra
Meresua, moma menhu
Meaning
Drum pegs knocked in by drummers,
Drum pegs if you have been away,
I am calling you; they say come,
I am learning, let me succeed (ibid:10).
In addition, a drummer addresses the string that is used in making the drum as follows:

Obofunu Ampasakyi,
Obofunu ɔkaa akyire
Obofunu ɔkɔ baabi a,
Merefre wo; yese bra
Meresua, momma menhu.
Meaning
Ampasakyi, drum string of the bark of obofunu,
Obofunu, the last born,
Drum string, if you have been away
I am calling you, they say come
I am learning let me succeed (ibid:11).

A drummer would also address the animal whose skin is used in making the drum as follows:

Kotomirefi Gyaa kɔtɔkɔ,
Kɔtɔkɔ so no me ne sono,
Esono wokɔ baabia
Merefre wo; yese bra
Dee ohunuu won nyinsene,
Wanhunu w'owosee,
Yen kɔ ye nim, yereko,
Yenkɔ ye nim yeredwane,
Dabere esono abefere,
Esono ebu akuma,
Okokuroko-bedi-atuo e,
Esono wokɔ baabi a,
Merefre wo; yese bra,
Meresua moma menhu
Meaning
Elephant Kotomrefi that frees Kɔtɔkɔ
Elephant that swallow other elephants
Elephant, if you have been away,
I am calling you they say come
He that saw your birth never apprehend your beginning
He that knew of your formation
Never saw how you were born.
Shall we go forward, we shall find men fighting
Shall we press on, we shall find men fleeing.
Let us go forward in great haste
Treading the path beaten by the elephant
The elephant that shatters the axe
The monstrous one, unmindful of bullets

Elephant, if you have been away,
I am calling you, they say come,
I am learning, let me succeed (ibid:11).

A drummer would address the sticks that are used in playing the drum as follows:

Ɔfema duo nkonta
Nkonta kɔtɔkɔrɔ
Woakɔ baabi a
Merefrewo; yese bra,
Meresua momma menhu.
Meaning
Drum stick of ɔfema wood
Curved drum stick,
Drum stick of ɔfema wood,
If you have been away,
I am calling you; they say come
I am learning, let me succeed (ibid:13).

A drummer would also pay tribute to the cock and clock-bird that awaken people at dawn as follows:

Aboa Kokokyinaka Asamoa,
Yegye wo Deeben?
Yegye wo Anyaado
Yegye wo kyerema ba
Kyerema ba da nanye anɔpatutuutu
Meresua moma menhu
Meaning
Kokokyinaka Asamoa the clock bird
How do we greet you?
We greet you with Anyaado.
We hail you as the drummer's child
The drummer's child sleeps and awakes with the dawn
I am learning, let me succeed (ibid:44).
Similarly, the "awakening texts" played by Yoruba *dundun* drummers for Timi (the king) of Ode include the following:
Ola ojire
       Man of prestige, you have woken well.

Timi Ojire
> Timi, you have woken well (Euba 1991).
> A dundun drummer would greet Shango (the divinity of thunder and lightening) with the following texts (as played to Euba by Ayankule):

N'Olukoso to to
> Olukoso I address you with great respect.
> S/he would also greet the female leader of Eleriko masquerade group (as played by Ayanbunmi) as follows:

Iya egbe oku oku
> Mother of the group, I greet you I greet you

Obinrin ju obinrin lo oku
> Women are greater than women (ibid).

An Ewe *atompani* drummer may play the following appellation of a chief:

Tameklo tsitsi xoxo
Ebe yemenya mi na ʋɔga ʋɔgawo o
Ne ʋɔga ʋɔgawo mi ye ha
Wo adzɔ ye de tavi ade to

Meaning
An aged riverine-turtle
That could not be swallowed by great pythons
Even if great pythons swallowed him
They would vomit him along a pond
(cited from the Ewe oral literature).

The texts played by *mpintin* drum ensemble to herald the procession of an Akan king/chief (towards a gathering) include the following:
Meso agya mesoagya mentumi: I carry father, he is too heavy for me:
To this the bass drum responds: Dwa ho enwa: Can't cut bits off him to make him lighter (Nketia 1963).

Similarly, the texts played by a royal *agbl ʋu* drummer to herald or announce the speech of an Ewe chief, Akaba include the following:
Kaba gbe de ge, Kaba gbe de ge: Akaba will command, Akaba will command
(cited from the Ewe oral literature).

In addition, the texts played by *mpintim* drummers during the closing ceremony of the Adae festival include the following:

Akwadaa mo: Well done young one
Yaa nua mo: Thank you brother: well done (Nketia, p. 40).

Examples of Texts that Feature in Political and Military Contexts

The following are examples of drum texts that are played in military and political contexts. They may be played by a master drummer, intermediary drummers or by the master drummer and accompanied drummers in dialogue or unison.

The first example is taken from the Ewe *agbek* music/dance:
Giden gidetega tegide gaden
Kaleawo aʋa dzɔ vɔ (aʋa gbɔ na) mitso ne miadzo
Gallants war has begun get up and go.

The second example which is taken from the texts of a signal drum of the (Akim Kotoku) *asafo* company is interpreted as follows:

Petepire woahyia petepire: Tough one you have met a tough one (Nketia, p. 36).

The third example which is taken from the Akan *Asafo* drumming (as documented by Nketia) is interpreted as follows:

Bodyguard as strong as iron
Fire that devours nations
Curved sticks of iron
We have leaped across the sea,
How much more the lagoon?
If any river is big, is it bigger than the sea?
Come bodyguard, come bodyguard
Come in thick numbers
Locust in myriads
When we climb a rock it gives way under our feet
Locust in myriads
When we climb a rock, it breaks into two
Come bodyguard, come bodyguard
In thick numbers (Nketia, p. 112).

The fourth example which is taken from the proverbial texts played by the heavy drums in the middle portion of fɔntɔmfrɔm, akantam is interpreted as follows:

Ɔsakani Akuampɔn
Eye dee na Ofusuo da homa mu?
Efiri n'ano,
Akyereko Kwagyan
ɔtware Nwabe Aduru Ohwinm,
Meaning
Wild bear Akuampɔn
How did it happen that the water buck got tied up in cords?
It is because he could not hold his tongue
Akyereko Kwagyan
He crosses the Nwabe river and gets to Ohwim (Nketia 1963:140).

Examples of Texts that Feature Within the Context of Religion
The following are examples of texts played in the Yoruba Ogun drumming (as narrated by a drummer Ayansola, 1990):

Ogun gbe rere ko mi-
    May Ogun bless me with goodness
Orisa gbe te mi ko mi
    Orisa bless me with what is my due (Euba 1991).

The ensuing texts are drawn from adzohu/adzogbo, a sacred/religious music/dance of the Fɔn-Ewe of southern Benin, Togo and Ghana.
The first example is usually played by a master drummer and sung by the dancers who would move across the performance setting while looking into mirrors held in their right hands to display their beauty:
Drum language: Gazete gide gazete gide gadetega zetega tedegide
               gadetega...
Eʋe: Ewɔ ze atsyiadosi wɔ zebodza, atsyiado legbasi wɔ
               zebodza
Meaning
The stylists are ready to display, yes, they are ready to display
(narrated by Foli Adade, 1997; 1999; played by Alorwoyi, 2003).

The second example is usually narrated by a lead dancer, played by the master drummer and executed by the dancers in tribute to the master drummer and cantor:

Lead drum:	Dzadza dzadza dzadza dzadza gadegi tegi krebe gi
Eʋe:	Dzadza dzadza dzadza dzadza avalu (avɔ lu) koe le kɔ na mi
Meaning:	Dzadza dzadza dzadza dzadza tribute lies on our neck
Lead Drum	gitsi kide gin gitsi kre gidegidega zegitegi krebegi
Eʋe:	Minye avalu ʋutɔ minya avalu hasinɔ, avalu koe le kɔ na mi
Meaning:	We pay tribute to the drummer and composer/cantor, tribute lies on our neck (narrated by Foli Adade, 1997; 1999; Emmanuel Agbeli, 2010).

In the third example, the lead drummer and dancers express tribute to the Supreme Being in the Moslem's way (the text reflects a fusion of the Fon, Ewe and Yoruba languages):

Drum language: (begins with toto dzadza dzadza dzadza...)
Gidegin tegi krebegin (to) dzadzadzin dzadzadzin,
Gide gin tegi krebe gin gagi krebegin tegi krebe gin
detegagin gagide gagin gagiden gin gagide gagi,
gi to to to ten, gi to to to ten, gidegin tegi krebe gin
Eʋe: Toto dzadza dzadza dzadza
Atsyiado megbɔna 'tsyia loloe
Dzadzadzin dzadzadzin
Atsyiado megbɔna 'tsyia loloe
Guze atsyiado megbɔna tsyia loloe
Mafa lomboe mafa lomboe
Ka fe len ji Oluwa
Oluwa da da ni,
Oluwa da da ni, Allah
Oluwa da da ni
Atsyiado megbɔna atsyia loloe.

Meaning
The stylist, I am coming to display (2x)
The stylist, I am coming to display
Guze, the stylist (says) I am coming to display,
I will (pay tribute) give the land) to God,
God is a good God
God is a good God, Allah
God is a good God
The stylist, I am coming to display (narrated by Emmanuel Agbeli, 2010).

In the following example, the lead drummer and dancers recount a revelation that the past performers claimed to have received as follows:

Drum language:
Gidegadegi tegin tegiden gin to
Dzadzadzin dzadzadzin (2x)
Gidegadegi tegi tegidengin
Vlo gadegi tegitegiden gin
Vlo dagegin tegintegiden gin
Ga to-to tegidega- ga to-to degidega
Gadegide gadento degide ga
Gagidegin- didegagin
Gatoto degidega gide(gren) gito- kren ga dzi tsi dzi tsi dzi.

Eʋe: Dzosohu zu vodu bo do asi na dawoe dzadzadzi dzadzadzin
Kpɔwoe zu vodu fo nu na gbetɔ hɔwoe zu vodu bo yɔ hubonɔ
Oyekple dɔ su nu mi, Oyekple dɔ su nu mi
Ata kudo vi woedɔ su nu mi,
Aoo legba masi kpele,
Oyekple dɔ su nu mi dzidahutɔ kplokplo adza 'xɔlu mi.

Meaning
Dzosohu became God and spoke to the brave ones,
Dzadzadzin dzadza dzin
Leopards became God and spoke to human,
Eagles became God and spoke to the priest
Oyekple revealed these to us, Oyekple revealed these to us
Ata and vi revealed all these to us
Our God would never fail us
Master drummer, play (loudly)
And make us strong (narrated by Foli Adade 1997; Locke and Agbeli, 1980, pp. 44-45).

In the past, performers of adzohu would be secluded in the forest for many months where they would undergo rigorous training in communication with the divine. While in seclusion, they would claim to have received revelations from the Supreme Being and divinities through their leaders such as Oyekple and Okplagada and neighboring creatures. Such revelations were composed into appropriate drum texts, songs and dance movements. (Ata and vi are special fruits that grow in Yorubaland: vi is a type of kolanut; they are used by the Yoruba and Ewe religious leaders in rituals).

In the following example, the master drummer, singers and dancers express and enact the actions of social deviants and the consequences:

Eʋe: Ye wonye looo ye wonye fiafitɔ ame bada ye wonye 2x
Wo fi fi tsya wom lɔ na gbe de o
Wowu ame tsya wom lɔ na gbe de o
Xoxoa lɔa? Devia ha nalɔa?
Wo kata ame dekae wonye
O ge mtuna xo na adaba o daba li xoxoxo ge va do (2x).
Fiafitɔ ku tsi agba ngɔ, oo ku tsi agba ngɔ oo (2x).

Meaning
Such are the people they are (2x)
They are thieves and bad people,
They steal and would not admit it
They kill and would not admit it
Would the elder one admit for the younger one to admit?
They are all the same people
Beard does not narrate an old story to the eye lash
The eye lash was living long before beard came into being
There lies the thief dead in front of the stolen good
Oh dead in front of the stolen good (narrated by Emmanuel Agbeli, 1999; 2010).

In the following example, the master drummer, complementary drummers and dancers narrate a story of an elderly man who was led by a young man into a dance circle, knowing that the elderly man did not know the dance routine, he left him there:

Drum: Ga gi den-ga gi den- gigi te dzi gadegren-gite
Dzadzadzadza dzadzadzadza dzadzadzadza gito
Gito gide gin de ga gito gito gide gidega gi to
Gito ga to to tegi krebe gin
Ga gi den ga gi den gigi tegren gadegren gi te
dzadzadzadza gito.
Eʋe: Ovitse Ovitse wo di mi va gu me
Bo zɔ hayahaya muyɔ o
Ete na sɔm sɔ wua muyɔ wo
Gbetɔ na sɔm sɔ wua muyɔ wo
Nku mɔ sude ma mɔ di di te 2x
Ovitse ovitse wo di mi va gume
Bo zɔ hayahaya hayahaya muyɔ wo.

Meaning
Oh young boy young boy
you have brought me into the dancing circle
and walk away roughly roughly I call you
Because of this would somebody kill me?
I call you,
A person to kill me, I call you
Remember what you have done to me
Young boy young boy
You brought me into the dancing circle
And walk away roughly roughly I call you
(narrated by Foli Adade 1997; Emmanuel Agbeli, 1999; 2010;
see also Locke and Agbeli, 1980).

In order for the dancers to conform to the performance ethics, they would be told that anyone who fell while dancing would die or be severely punished by God, hence, the fear and shivering of the old man who was left alone in the dance arena.

Examples of texts that feature in social music and dance performances
The following text and song are played by two or three lead drummers in gohu in dialogue with the chorus, to express a historical incident that led to the punishment of a citizen of Anexɔ or Little Popo (a town near the Benin border in Togo) by a Dahumean king called Kundo, also known as Gbehanzin (meaning life is like an egg), who reigned between 1889-1894 and people's desire for a good and healthy life.

Lead drum:	Gahrebegite gin dzadza (2x).
Eʋe:	Kpɔ gbale dzie Kundo la zɔ.
Chorus:	Dzawutɔ be mele tɔgbuiwo fe zikpuia dzi
	Wobe ame ade laxɔ miawo srɔ le Wɔkedzi, adze sɔ sɔ sɔe
	'Nexɔ tɔwoe wo nua Kundo wu ame le Wɔkedzi
	'Meawo na da kpe ne mianɔ sesie.

Meaning
          Gahrebegiten dzindzadza
          Kundo will walk on leopard skin
Dzawutɔ says, I am on the ancestral stool
          They say who will take our wife/husband at Wɔkedzi
          It is all lies
          The Anexɔ people have done it
Kundo murdered at Wɔkedzi.

People should give thanks for good health
(cited from the Aŋlɔga Dɔnɔgbɔ Gohu drumming; Amegago, 2011, p. 166).

The following is an excerpt from Wolof sabar drumming piece called Ceebujen (as played by Tala Faye). The text was composed in honor of Lenge, a woman who used to cook delicious rice and fish (a traditional Senegalese meal).

Drum; gin-gin (ta-ta) gi gi gi-gin tarata- tara
Wolof: Lenge, Ceebu Lenge, akadai sor ne…

Meaning
Lenge always prepares delicious rice and fish
The following is an excerpt from the dundun/iyaalu drum text which is usually played during the Yoruba Ikomo, child-naming ceremony:
Omo tuntun   New born baby
Enikan ii moro   No one fails to rejoice at the sight of
Tuntun ko ma yo A new born baby
Omo tuntun   New born baby (Euba 1990:412).

Examples of Texts that Feature in Youths' Performances
In the first example, the gota lead drummer expresses the youths' yearning for their mother as follows:
Lead drum: Gazegitetegi gazegitete gigiga.
Eʋe: Dada gbɔgbɔge dada gbɔgbɔge namea.
English: Mother will return, mother will return to me.

The following is an interpretation of a bɔbɔɔbɔ text played by the Ewe youths:
Ge metua xo na daba o, daba o, daba o (2x).
Daba li xoxo hafi ge va dzɔ,
Gake kpekpe le ge nu wu adaba
Meaning
Beard does not narrate an ancient story to the eye lash, eye lash.
The eye lash was living long before the beard was born
But the beard is heavier than the eyelash.

In the following example, a bɔbɔɔbɔ lead drummer refers to a West African leader and his country:
Lead drum: Gadagada gadenga gadegren gaden

English: Thomas Sankara, Burkina Faso
The following kpanlogo lead drum text compares a young lady to a mother:
Fine fine baby ino go fine pass your mother.

A student atumpan drummer in Ghanaian elementary and secondary schools in the Ewe area may play the following text to announce a change of lesson and during a drum recital and school performances:

Wɔ dɔ za dodo ge
Work for the night is falling
Kuviatɔ fe agbleme ye da dzia vi do
Snakes breed on a lazy person's farm
Kutrikuku dua nugawo dzi
Perseverance overcomes difficulties
Dikeke a*fe* gbegble
Unhealthy competition destroys households.

Examples of texts that are played in the Yoruba drumming associated with funerals (as played by Ayanbunmi, 1990) are as follows:

Airin ono ni no sun bi:
May God grant that when I die, I will sleep surrounded by my children.
Emi naao ni je:
May I also not leave behind unsettled debts (Euba, p. 208).
The texts played by the Akan atumpan, mpebi and nkwawiri drummers during funeral rites include the following:

Damirifua due damirifua due damirifua due.
Condolences, condolences, condolences.

Another text which is played on the kɔrabra signal drum of the Akan during the funerary rites of a chief of Akim Abuakwa (and which forms part of the lyrics of a dirge sung on the occasion) is interpreted as:
Kɔrabra: When you go, return (Nketia, p. 36).

Conclusion
In this paper, I have elucidated the use of drums in communicating on speech or textual basis and the social, historical, religious, ethical, political and educational values that are communicated through the drums. I have also shed light on the interconnection of human beings

and other environmental creatures and features. In view of the fact that much of the drum texts remain within oral traditions, a researcher has to establish rapport with the cultural bearers and cross examine the texts in order to check their veracity. It has also been noted that some of the drum texts express provocative and socially repressed themes because of the social realism and critical role of African drummers. However, a researcher who sets out to investigate such themes would have to engage in dialogue with the cultural custodians (leaders) in order to solicit their views about representing such themes within the public domain.

In this contemporary era, there has been a shift from textual to text-less basis of African drumming. As Nketia notes, knowledge of the drum texts is growing less and less widespread even among drummers themselves (Nketia 1963:42). This phenomenon is due to the emergence of new modes of documentation and communication, the generational gap and censorship of some of the texts that express socially repressed themes. However, there is much empirical evidence that most of the traditional forms of dance drumming which are now text free originally had verbal bases, which helped to preserve unwritten scores from generation to generation (ibid:42). Despite contemporary phenomenon, the prevailing texts form part of the African cultural heritage, and may be used to complement other modes of documentation, communication, creativity and education. A study of drum texts would contribute to the understanding of Africans' historical and cultural experiences. However, the preservation and dissemination of the drum texts require the training of new generations of drummers, drum educators and listeners and educating people about the cultural significance and meaning of the texts, as well as encouraging people to use the texts in creating, documenting, communicating and performing African music and dance. This may require the modification of some of the older instruments and the invention of new instruments that best express the indigenous African and foreign languages and sounds and facilitate the preservation and dissemination of this significant cultural heritage for the benefit of humanity.

References

Amegago, Modesto. 2011. *An African Music and Dance Curriculum Model: Performing Arts Education*. Durham, North Carolina: Carolina Academic Press.

___. 2007. "Dance Elements of Ewe Music and Dance." *African Journal for Physical, Health Education, Recreation and Dance* 13: 524-546.

Chernoff, John Miller 1979. *African Rhythm and African Sensibility: Aesthetics and Social Action in African Musical Idioms*. Chicago: The University of Chicago Press.

Euba, Akin. 1991. *Yoruba Drumming: The Dundun Tradition*. Lagos and Bayreuth: Elekoto Music Centre and Bayreuth African Studies Series.

___. 1988. *Essays on Music in Africa*. Bayreuth, West Germany: Iwalewa-Haus, Universität Bayreuth.

Jones A. M. 1959. *Studies in African Music*. London: Oxford University Press.

Ladzekpo, S. Kabloa and Hewitt Pantaleoni. 1970. "Takada Drumming." *African Music Society Journal* 4 (4):6-31.

Locke, David and Godwin Kwasi Agbeli. 1980. "A Study of the Drum Language in Adzogbo." *International Library of African Music* 6(1): 32-51.

Locke, David. 1987. *Drum Gahul: A Systematic Method for an African Percussion Piece*. Crown Point, IN: White Cliffs Media Company.

Nketia, J.H. Kwabena. 1974. *The Music of Africa*. New York: W.W. Norton.

___. 1963. *Drumming in Akan Communities of Ghana*. Edinburgh: Thomas Nelson and Sons Limited.

Tang, Patricia. 2007. *Masters of the Sabar: Wolof Griot Percussionists of Senegal*. Philadelphia, PA: Temple University Press.

2

David Locke
Brenda Romero
Ben Paulding
Amy Unruh

ANALYSIS OF TRADITIONAL MUSIC

Sweetness in Agbadza Music: Expressiveness in an Item of Agbadza Singing and Drumming

David Locke

David Locke is professor in the Music Department at Tufts University. As an ethnomusicologist, he specializes in the traditional music and dance of Africa especially the Anlo Ewe and the Dagomba in Ghana. He is the author of the African chapter in the textbook *Worlds of Music*, and three books, *Drum Gahu* (1988), *Drum Damba* (1990), and *Kpegisu* (1992). His study of Dagomba music with Abubakari Lunna and Ewe music, Agbadza, with Gideon Foli Alorwoyie are freely available as online monographs (http://sites.tufts.edu/davidlocke).

African musicians with whom I have studied often synesthetically use the English-language adjective "sweet" to characterize a positive musical experience. Ewe-speakers may characterize as *"vivi,"* or "sweet," singing and drumming that is performed expertly, generates strong feeling, and conveys a meaningful message. Not a quality of cloying sentimentality, "sweet music" has a presence that moves a listener, often in a profound way (see Armstrong 1971). This paper sets out to articulate the sources of sweetness in Agbadza music from Aŋlɔ-Afiadenyigba, Volta Region, Ghana by means of a close account of the song "Akpabli Hɔsu Woɖo Ɖae." My premise is that listeners feel musical beauty through the interplay of the "phenomenal surface" of musical sound and the "theoretical underneath" of musical syntax. I suggest that African musicians are aware of the expressive opportunities afforded by musical syntax and intentionally create music within known systems. I deploy the evaluative term "sweet" to open a path towards the scholarly articulation of musical syntax in Agbadza and culturally relevant statements about aesthetic judgment.

Overview of Agbadza Music

Agbadza music consists of singing and drumming. At the time of Agbadza's creation, Ewe poets sang of battle during a tumultuous era (circa 1600-1900) of migration, war, and imperialism that included the trans-Atlantic slave trade (see Fage, Agbodeka). Pentatonic tunes give song lyrics poignant musical settings. Call-and-response arrangements enrich the "melo-rhythmic" power of the drumming. Agbadza's instrumental music features two-part drum language compositions for the low-pitched lead drum (*sogo*) and medium-pitched response drum (*kidi*) that are played within a multi-part texture sounded by recurring phrases of bell (*gaŋkogui*), rattle (*axatsɛ*), clap (*asikpekpe*), and high-pitched support drum (*kagaŋ*). In contemporary Ewe communities, Agbadza occurs at wake-keepings and memorial services. People actively participate by singing, clapping hands, drumming, and/or dancing. Lovers of traditional music, the "audience" so to speak, may quietly participate through contemplation and critical observation.

Vocal music entails interchange between the song leader part (*henɔ*), which is sung by only a few voices, and the group part (*haxelawo*), which has the thicker louder sound of many voices. In the style of Agbadza discussed here, each item of music begins with the song leader freely lining out the tune and text. After this brief introduction, the instrumental ensemble's "time parts" start the phrases that they continue without variation for the duration of the item. When the song and the time parts are going nicely the lead drummer plays the drum language phrases on the sogo using his two bare hands. The kidi response drummer answers the leader's call, using two wooden sticks to fashion the medium-pitched drum's recurring phrase. The lead drummer's solo line complements the singers' tune and weaves around the response drum's phrase. Each song is sung many times with subtle musical variation in tune and harmony.

The Agbadza Project of Gideon Foli Alorwoyie

The Agbadza music discussed in this paper results from the effort of Gideon Foli Alorwoyie who researched, produced, arranged, rehearsed and performed a collection of twenty-five Agbadza songs and drum compositions in the style of Afiadenyigba, his hometown that lies in the heart of Aŋlɔ territory and in the center of southern Ewe culture (Alorwoyie 2007). Alorwoyie's Agbadza project revitalizes an old style of Agbadza by pairing songs and drumming together on the basis of the meaning of the song lyrics and drum language texts. A sound recording of Agbadza music performed by Alorwoyie and a group of Ewe singers and drummers whom he trained is the central media product of this project (Alorwoyie 2003). I have transcribed the sound recording into staff notation and have prepared an interpretation of the music that is available on the web (http://sites.tufts.edu/davidlocke/agbadza-items/).

The Sweetness of "Akpabli Hɔsu": General Features of Vocal and Instrumental Music
Song Lyrics and Drum Language
Unlike some Agbadza songs that address social issues of contemporaneous relevance, the lyrics of "Akpabli Hɔsu" make a narrowly focused historical reference to an Ewe military commander who has been sent on a mission to confront an enemy (see Table 1 in Appendix). As interpreted by Alorwoyie, the Ewe soldier challenges his opponents to emerge from their fortress to meet face-to-face. In the climax of the text (line 9), Akpabli Hɔsu commands his own troops to break the barricade so he can move forward towards his objective.

To go with this song, Alorwoyie chose a composition for lead sogo drum and response kidi drum that has the following drum language, which is performed in two slightly different musical settings (see A and B in Table 2).

When pairing the song with this drumming composition, Alorwoyie imagined that the drums express Akpabli Hɔsu's challenge to the enemy, "Come out so that we can settle things face-to-face." When I prompted Alorwoyie to consider whether today's singers would take this text as a metaphor applicable to their own social lives, he suggested that it could stand for a challenge between friends but asserted that most singers would prefer to regard it as an historical song. My hypothesis, nevertheless, is that the item's meaning lies primarily in the sonic realm rather than in the semantics of its song text and drum language. A listener who understands the expressiveness of its sound within the context of its musical structure will "get" its meaning.

Form of Text and Tune

"Akpabli Hɔsu" begins with three iterations of the same line of text, set on a tune that is characterized by rhythmic repetition and melodic sequence (see Table 1). After the intervention of one new phrase of text and tune, the familiar material returns a fourth time. The form of the text is AAABA, which becomes A1A2A3 B1 A4 when melody is factored. Because this formal pattern is unique among the twenty-five in Alorwoyie's arrangement of Agbadza, it attracts a listener's attention. Aesthetically, textual recurrence tempered with melodic sequence makes the form "sweet."

Call-and-Response

The song leaders and the singing group share lyrics and melody in a distinctive arrangement that blends typical and atypical features. The general plan of the call-and-response is standard to Agbadza songs: alternation between leader and group in the first section, followed by unity between leader and group in subsequent sections. However, in the opening A section the durations of the leader and group parts are somewhat unusual: in lines 1-6 the group's short responses that follow the leaders' longer calls would be expected in a middle B section of the typical Agbadza song. When call-and-response unifies into singing by lead and group together, the repeat in lines 5-6 of the same lyric before line 7's new text further deviates from most other songs. On the other hand, it is quite normal for the song to end with collective reprise of material that had been sung in alternation in the opening section. Thus, the distribution between leader and group of text and melody is "sweet" by being both reassuringly traditional and captivatingly special.

Blend of Voices and Timbre
Doubling at the octave, men and women render the song's text together in rhythmic unison. Singers manage to establish their individuality within the group through personalized timbre and temporal variance at the micro-timing level. The individualized blend of voices combines with a nasal and raspy vocal quality to produce a complex, energetic quality to the ensemble's overall sound. Thus, the singing group's manner of presentation and their very sound is another facet of the music's appeal.

The Sweetness of "Akpabli Hɔsu": Melody
Tune
To my ear, an important dimension of the tune's "sweetness" lies in the sequential shifts in tonal emphasis that are achieved as its five melodic phrases unfold over the course of the entire song (see Table 3 and Figure 1 in Appendix).

Tonality
The tune of "Akpabli Hɔsu" is fashioned from an anhemitonic pentatonic scale. Listeners familiar with Agbadza music would hear the tonal structure of "Akpabli Hɔsu" in the musical context of an overall tonal system that includes all five modes of the anhemitonic scale, as well as modes in two hemitonic pentatonic scales. Since melodic motion suggests G as the tonal center, the mode is G-A-C-D-F, 1-2-4-5-7b. To my ear, the song stays "in G" with the tonal gravity of F providing a sense of pleasant tonal contrast. However, if a listener perceives the phrase finals on F as a new tonic, in phrases two and four the song shifts to another mode of the scale, F-G-A-C-D, 1-2-3-5-6. In both cases, motion between centers of tonal gravity and the suggestion of bi-tonality are ingredients in the song's attractiveness. The character of its mode and its manner of articulation contribute to this song's sweetness.

Harmony and Sonority
Although "Akpabli Hɔsu" has a distinctive tune, listeners likely would consider a performance in unison to be simplistic and dull. The texture actually is performed with multiple simultaneous melodic lines (see Figure 2 in Appendix). Melodic variation not only is constrained by the intervals in scale and mode, but also is disciplined by the expectation of hearing the pitch classes that give each phrase its musical identity and function within the overall tune. In the recorded performance vertical

sonority is particularly noticeable in the call-and-response of the A section, when assistant song leaders sing in more drone-like fashion on pitches C and D while the song leader performs a more active melodic line (phrases 1.a-b and 2.a-b). The two lines converge to unison on the phrase final (phrases 1.c and 2.c). When everyone sings together (phrases 3-5), singers often take their own personal melodic path from the emphasized initial pitch to the phrase final, which always is sung in unison. The outcome is closely voiced chords, so to speak, that shift as each syllable of text is intoned. Significantly, the final phrase always is sung monophonically, showing that texture varies with position within the cyclic musical form. In other words, "harmony singing" is guided by well-established expectations of musical syntax. The thickened vertical sonority that emerges from melodic variation is another facet of Agbadza's musical sweetness.

Melodic Rhythm
The rhythmic motion of the melody adds to its sweetness. Heard on their own, phrases 1, 2, 3, and 5 share an identical sequence of long and short time values; this repetitive linear design confers a unique rhythmic identity on "Akpabli Hɔsu" in comparison to the other twenty-five songs in Alorwoyie's collection. Leader and group guide the tune through the syntax of Agbadza's meter: the lead part accentuates four-feel beats two, three, four, and one, thus creating motion towards ONE, the structurally embedded moment of cyclic cadence. The group reply simply moves from four-feel beats three to four. Listening to the tune's relationship to strokes in the bell phrase, on the other hand, the longer lead phrase moves from stroke two towards the next stroke one, which is an absolutely canonical way for adept Ewe listeners to feel the flow of the bell phrase's linear rhythm. The shorter group reply reinterprets the bell's motion as stopping on stroke six, which usually is felt as a moment of penultimate temporal cadence that moves on towards stroke one. These phrases generate a sweet sense of forward motion through elapsing time.

What about the rhythmic syntax of the different and special phrase four, marked B in the scheme of text and form (see Figure 3 in Appendix).In contrast to the "in-four" accentuation of the A phrases, the time values that set the words "Danyeviwo" shift to the flow of onbeat six-feel beats. Furthermore, because its final sustained note lands on time-point 1.2, the words "Miʋua 'gbo mayi hɛɛ" articulate the flow of upbeat six-feel beats. These contrasts in rhythm add to the pleasing relationship between the A and B sections of the song.

Summary
Unified by lyric form and call-and-response presentation, disciplined by gamut and texture, given momentum by its progression of tonicized pitches, stimulated by rhythmic contrast within repetition, this is a lovely melody. The tuneful surface details distinctively engage with enduring syntactic patterns characteristic of the Agbadza song style. The vocal music of "Akpabli Hɔsu" is sweet to my ear.

The Sweetness of "Akpabli Hɔsu": Ensemble Instrumental Music

Alorwoyie combined drumming and singing according to language-based meaning. The "sweetness" in the complementary reinforcement of song text and drum language was his guiding force. Nevertheless, he was definitely cognizant of the musical synergy generated by the interaction of vocal and instrumental music (personal communication). Agbadza's recurring phrases of bell, hand clap, rattle, and high-pitched support drum, inevitably align in exciting ways with all songs and compositions for lead drum and response drums; that is a given in Agbadza's musical design. Alorwoyie's specific choice of sogo-kidi composition to go with "Akpabli Hɔsu," on the other hand, set up a distinctive musical relationship to this particular song. Furthermore, he crafted his improvisation on the lead drum with close attention to the singing at the recording session. This paper will focus instead on the interaction of lead-response drums.

The implicit texts of the Agbadza time parts relate to the context of urgent action, which makes sense given Agbadza's first and original use in times of war. Listeners who understand drum language and empathize with these sentiments are likely to be impassioned by their meaning. Other listeners are likely to find sweetness in the sheer sound and musical design of these parts (see Table 4 in Appendix).

As the time parts recur over-and-over in performance, their capacity to have impact on each other increases. Repetition, in other words, is a central feature of the musical syntax of Agbadza's instrumental music. The music of these phrases likely is familiar to readers of this volume, but I would call attention to the handclapping theme that articulates what I term the six-feel beats. Since the four-feel beats are foundational to Ewe music that uses this bell phrase (see Agawu), the prominent articulation of six-in-the-time-of-four is a key attribute of the Afiadenyigba style of Agbadza discussed here (see Figure 4 in Appendix).

Kidi Response Drum

The kidi part that Alorwoyie chose to go with "Akpabli Hɔsu" has two themes A and B. (see Figure 5 in Appendix). Theme A has two bounce strokes that mark two three-feel beats (half-notes) that are in 3:4 relationship with the four-feel beats (dotted quarter-notes). This position of the three-feel is a favorite in many kinds of Ewe dance-drumming, indicating that Ewe listeners find it particularly sweet.

The bounces in kidi theme A project their pattern of offbeat accentuation onto all the other instruments in the ensemble and give them added polyrhythmic depth (see Hasty). For example, the kidi bounces align with the first and last strokes of a high-pitched kagaŋ drum motive, and are offset from handclaps five and six. The kidi bounces also set up a "sweet" contrast to the rhythm of the song, which is our primary concern here.

As shown in Figure 6, the bounces sound together with syllables that are relatively unstressed in the text and unemphasized in the tune. In the main line of text, "Akpabli Hɔsu woɖo ɖa hɛɛ. Miʋua 'gbo," kidi bounces match the "-su" of "Hɔsu", the "ɖo" of "woɖo," and the "-ʋua" of "miʋua" but dramatically are offset from the "'gbo" of "Miʋua 'gbo." Instead of adding weight to this key word, which matches with bell stroke six and four-feel beat four, the kidi bounce adds force to the short bell stroke seven and to time-point 4.3 that usually functions as a pickup to ONE. In the contrasting line of text, "Danyeviwo miʋua 'gbo mayi hɛɛ," the kidi bounces match with otherwise modestly placed elements, namely, the "-ʋua" of "miʋua" and the "ma-" of "mayi." My argument is that by injecting a counter-rhythm to the song, the kidi theme adds beauty to this item of Agbadza music.

Kidi theme B sets up different, but no less pleasing, interactions with the song and instruments of the ensemble. Here, I only mention the way kidi theme B serves to join adjacent bell strokes four-five into a two-note unit, thus highlighting a rhythmic nuance of protean musical force of the bell phrase.

The "Sweetness" of "Akpabli Hɔsu": Sogo Lead Drum

In addition to maintaining the excitement of the instrumental music and cueing dancers, the sogo player has other functions in the performance such as heralding individuals with praise names and helping to pace the overall performance event (see Burns 2012). Here, we engage only with the drummer's musical role in the instrumental ensemble, especially in relation to the song. Inspired by song lyrics, the lead drum always plays a pre-selected composition, albeit in many different ways, and interjects phrases to spice up the conversation with kidi and enliven its relationship to the song. As discussed below, the lead drum seldom repeats the same phrase more than a few times before making a change. The intense rate of invention in the sogo part contrasts with the recurrent iteration of the other instrumental parts.

Composed Drum Language Themes
Since both of the sogo-kidi themes set the same implicit drum language, "Do va ko, do va," it is not surprising that the sogo uses the same sequence of strokes and tones in each (see Figure 7). Mnemonic vocables, "ga dzi ga ga dzi," orally notate a drumming melody whose contour is low-high-low-low-high. In theme A, sogo's first three strokes have an even rhythmic flow, while in theme B sogo's second stroke has longer time value that gives its three-stroke figure an uneven temporal quality. On bell stroke five high-pitched dzi strokes of sogo, which function as musical cues to the kidi player, match first bounce strokes of kidi. I find that theme A has a punchy, aggressive quality in comparison to theme B, which feels more languid and flowing (see Figure 7 in Appendix).

"Episodic" may effectively characterize the musical form of the sogo part. Bursts of fast notes, usually called "rolls" by English-speaking Ewe drummers, periodically bracket longer passages in which the sogo player not only states the composition in various ways but also inserts improvised phrases that create excitement by interacting with the kidi theme. In the recorded performance, Alorwoyie times his drum rolls to fit with the song. Sogo rolls tend to occur toward as the song either nears its end or begins another iteration. Although rolls do occur during the lead singers' opening phrase in the last three iterations of the song, this is not a rigid formula, however. It appears that Alorwoyie flexibly uses the musical form of the sogo part to maintain the forward drive of the performance.

Sweetness in the lead drum part also lies in Alorwoyie's inventive statements of the drum language theme (see Figure 8), in relatively brief call-and-response gambits with the kidi response drum (see Figure 9), and the intricate details of linear flow and metric accentuation of the rolling passages (see Figure 10).

Variations on Drum Language Compositions
According to my transcription, Alorwoyie played the drum language in seven different ways from when the sogo first calls in measure 9 to when it rolls before calling for theme B in measure 43. The drum language for theme B gets eleven treatments over the span of sixty-one bell cycles (mm. 46-117). The variants on the basic drum language, which consist primarily of "creating space" by omitting strokes and or "filling space" by substituting a multi-stroke figure for a single stroke, are musically nuanced (see Locke 1988 and 1992). Many variations serve to accentuate either the onbeat or upbeat six-feel beats (for onbeat six, see A.1 and B.1; for upbeat six, see A.4 and B.8). Socially, variations on the drum language composition keep sogo in dynamic conversation with the kidi player and in constant musical contact with the singers; texturally, Alorwoyie's inventions are characterized by restraint and use of silence (see Figure 8 in Appendix).

Improvised Call-and-Response
Alorwoyie interjects intense motives of several beats' duration that not only enliven the call-and-response of sogo and kidi but also spur on the singers (see Figure 9 in Appendix). Fast stroking in these motives creates very quick interaction with strokes in the other parts and, by using eighth-note and sixteenth-note figures to accentuate the tacit eight-feel beats, make the music appear to double in tempo. Most of these improvisations come when kidi is playing quiet press strokes, but occasionally they are like short rolls that obliterate the kidi bounces (see A.3). Alorwoyie may design his improvisations to highlight a flow of beats with 3:2 relationships to the fundamental ternary-quadruple schema (see theme B.5 that accentuates the upbeat six-feel beats). Significantly, Alorwoyie does not overwhelm statements of the drum language composition with sogo improvisations. By playing them only occasionally, he establishes the presence of the sogo line alongside the song while also building the momentum of the instrumental music. His socially interactive playing is "sweet." (see Figure 9 in Appendix).

Rolling Passages

Not only capable of playing with tasteful restraint, Alorwoyie also is an experienced instrumental virtuoso whose expertise and talent explodes in the rolling passages. Over the period of two or three cycles of the bell, Alorwoyie invents self-referential, musically coherent lines that temporarily suspend the give-and-take between lead and response parts, substituting in its place a burst of high energy. Each of his thirteen rolling passages is unique.

Alorwoyie opens the recording with his most elementary version of the Agbadza roll, which moves through each four-feel beat with bounce strokes grouped in four-note, long-short-short-long figures that create 2:3 between the eight-feel and twelve-feel beats (two dotted eighths in-the-time-of three eighths). Never again in the recording is Alorwoyie content to play so repetitively in terms of time values and stroke timbre. Instead, he recombines short time values (sixteenths, eighths, and dotted eighths) to create motives that move in their own way through sets of two, three or four four-feel beats. The roll phrases are melodic, too, with contours that move among the sogo's three pitch classes and timbres (equivalent to the "bass," "tone," and "slap" of a conga). The roll in measures 104-106 of the full score is particularly gorgeous (see Figure 10 in Appendix). It begins with four motives of great technical difficulty that accentuate the upbeat six-feel--gaDET de KRE, gaDET de KRE, gaDEgi de KRE, gaJI de KRE--and then follows with two motives that push the eight-feel--gaGIdegiDE giDE, gaDEgi DE giDE giGA--before bringing back the drum language composition; capitals indicate accentuation (see Figure 10 in Appendix).

Factors that I would identify as "sweet" in the rolling passages include (1) eight-feel accentuation, (2) the sense of forward motion through time, and (3) the beautiful design not only of each motive but also the overall passage they combine to make. Of course, simply bearing witness to the performance of a classic musical idiom by an experienced and gifted artist surely is enjoyable! To my ear, Alorwoyie makes the right musical choice every time and executes his strokes with sure articulation and clear sound.

"Sweetness" in the Dynamic Relationship of Vocal and Instrumental Music

By arranging songs and drumming together on the basis of their texts, Alorwoyie intends his Agbadza music to make exhilarating impact on listeners. The power of the whole art form will transcend the force that the vocal or instrumental music would have on its own. As we have seen, the song lyrics tell of an historic Ewe warrior who confronted his enemies, challenging them to a direct encounter. At the same time, the language implicit to the drums advises, "Your only recourse is to come out and face me." The two messages combine synergistically to vividly re-enact the scene. The cooperation between song and drumming extends to realm of musical sound. The relevant question for music analysis is, "How do tune and drumming work together to become more than the sum of their parts?"

On its own, the song has many facets that elicit positive aesthetic and affective response (see Table 5 in Appendix).

The drum ensemble also operates as a self-contained musical domain that has its own musical power (see Table 6 in Appendix).

What are key aspects of how all this musical action combines to make the experience of listening to this item of Agbadza music artistically edifying? Although each part serves a well-defined musical function, everything is in dynamic interaction. The object of a listener's attention, therefore, always is capable of change depending on the set of elements occupying attention. For example, the entire figure-ground relationship between steady beats and the musical surface can easily shift from ternary-quadruple to binary-sextuple if the six-feel marked by the hand claps becomes the basis of temporal perception.

While the song is prominent to Ewe culture-bears, the drumming is not in a subservient role as accompaniment but instead is a co-equal dimension of the overall music. The lead drum listens to the form of the song, timing its intensifying passages in relation to the song's reiteration. Singers also respond to particularly exciting passages of drumming with exhortations. The two elements reverberate together, making sweet Agbadza music.

Endnotes

1: Nissio Fiagbedzi writes, "We also note that the native English speaker also describes a song or music as sweet or ravishing, etc. In the Ewe language, however, music . . . [is] usually not described as being beautiful. For the purpose, the Ewe appeals to the senses of hearing, taste, movement or motion and balance rather than to sight, the appropriate terms used being nya se or dze to (lit. pleasant or fitting to the ear), vivi (meaning sweet, tasty), tsɔ afɔ nyuie (walks well), le du dzi (running away or moving too fast), or mesɔ o (improperly balanced" (Fiagbedzi 2005: 9).

2: Simha Arom expresses reservations on syntax as a heuristic tool for analysis of African music (see Arom).

3: This paper engages only with the sonic dimension of Agbadza "music," thus intentionally and knowingly excluding other expressive media such as dance, rhetoric, costuming, and event drama. A comprehensive and culturally resonant approach would cross these boundaries.

4: "Melo-rhythm" is a term coined by Meki Nzewi to counter the irrelevant connotations of the Eurocentric term "percussion" (see Nzewi: 34-35). He writes, ". . . drum music playing is a process of deriving a rhythmic essence melodically, that is, a melorhythmic principal" (35). The term effectively emphasizes the inseparability of the musical features of melody and rhythm.

5: For me, the seminal account of traditional music in Ghana is Nketia's wonderfully titled book African Music in Ghana (1963).

6: "Eʋegbe" (literally "Ewe tongue") translates into English as the "Ewe language."

7: James Burns has told me that the sense of this phrase in the context of battle would be to bring whatever you have out in the open to fight, instead of relying on trickery or subterfuge. He mentions an Ewe praise name that expresses the same idea:"Beɖi menye ŋutsu. Do va nava wɔe, ŋkume kplẽ ŋkume. The person who hides is not a man. Bring it here and do it eye to eye" (Personal communication).

8: The Cantometrics project is an excellent resource for ways to hear timbre, vocal effects, and vocal blend (see Lomax).

9: Although singers vary their path through the tune according to the limits of Agbadza's musical style, I think it is reasonable to posit a stable melody. The complete score shows that the melody discussed here recurs rather consistently.

10: Many Agbadza songs use six pitch classes. Although this suggests hexatonic scales, I prefer to theorize these songs as using pentatonic scales with added pitches (see Dor). Pitch classes outside a song's primary pentatonic scale serve special melodic purposes, such as enabling melodic imitation or modulation to another tonal center or a different pentatonic mode. The distinction is more than an "academic issue" about terminology. I would argue that the melodic motion in Agbadza songs almost always is pentatonic in nature, a musical quality that is obscured by positing the presence of hexatonic scales.

11: An argument can be made for identifying a cadence point on bell stroke six, which also is four-feel beat four (see Lehmann).

12: James Burns theorizes Agbadza's rhythm as monometric. The meter is anchored by the metric accents of 12/8 meter around which interweave the six-feel beats (see Burns 2010). For early formulations of my theoretical ideas see Locke 1978 and 1982.

13: The twelve fast-moving pulses within one bell phrase can be identified by their position within each ternary four-feel beat as follows: 1.1, 1.2, 1.3, 2.1, 2.2 2.3, etc. This method enables clear designation of temporal position by slower moving beat and faster moving pulse.

14: When Alorwoyie starts the bell and rattle parts, he usually begins with a stroke on time-point 1.1, a style explained by the implicit text (see Figure 4). The drum language of the first notes--the bell's "do" and the rattle's "tsia"--change the sentence to a command: "Get up!" and "Go quickly!" The text of subsequent passes through the temporal cycle is phrased to end, not begin, on time-point 1.1.

15: The arithmetic formula is 4 x 3 = 3 x 4 = 12, that is, within a span of twelve fast pulses four shorter beats containing three fast pulses co-occur with three longer beats containing four fast pulses.

16: As I theorize Ewe music, there are four positions of 3:4 within the time span of one bell phrase. When the three-feel beats coincide with the four-feel beats on time-point 1.1 I designate this as "non-displaced." The three other positions of the three-feel beats are identified as being displaced from this "onbeat position" by one, two or three eighth-notes.

17: In an in situ performance of Agbadza the lead drum rolls cue participants to begin an episode of dance. The drummer's link to the song would be a secondary factor.

18: If the time values of the four notes in this figure are made equal, which could be notated with dotted sixteenth notes, 4:3 is created. If this rhythmic action becomes pervasive the overall musical feel morphs from ternary to quaternary, akin to switching from 12/8 to 4/4 time signatures (see Burns 2009).

19: Steven Friedson's study of a traditional Ewe religious system suggests a homology between musical shape-shifting, so to speak, and cultural practices like spirit possession (Friedson).

20: In conventional time signatures, this shift would be from 12/8 to 6/4.

References

Agawu, Kofi. 2006. "Structural Analysis or Cultural Analysis? Competing Perspectives on the 'Standard Pattern' of West African Rhythm." *Journal of the American Musicological Society* 59 (1) Spring.

Agbodeka, Francis, ed. 1997. *A Handbook of Eweland*. Accra: Woeli Publishing Services.

Alorwoyie, Gideon. 2007. *Agbadza Music. Edited, Transcribed and Introduced by David Locke*.

Armstrong, Robert Plant. 1971. *The Affecting Presence: An Essay in Humanistic Anthropology*. Urbana: University of Illinois Press.

Arom, Simha. 1991. *African Polyphony and Polyrhythm: Musical Structure and Methodology*. Translated from French by Martin Thom, Barbara Tuckett and Raymond Boyd. Cambridge: Cambridge University Press.

Burns, James. 2012. "'Doing It With Style': An Ethnopoetic Study of Improvisation and Variation in Southern Ewe Drum Language Conversations.'" *African Music* 9 (2).

___. 2010. "Rhythmic Archetypes in Instrumental Music from African and the Diaspora." *Music Theory Online* 16 (4) December.

Burns, James. 2009. *Female Voices from an Ewe Dance-Drumming Community in Ghana: Our Music Has Become a Divine Spirit*. Farnham: Ashgate Press.

Dor, George. 2000. *Tonal Resources and Compositional Processes of Ewe Traditional Vocal Music*. PhD. thesis, University of Pittsburgh.

Fage, J.D. 1969. *A History of West Africa: An Introductory Survey*. London: Cambridge University Press.

Fiagbedzi, Nissio. 2005. *An Essay on the Nature of the Aesthetic in the African Musical Arts*. Accra: s.n.

Friedson, Steven. 2009. *Remains of Ritual: Northern Gods in a Southern Land*. Chicago: University of Chicago Press.

Hasty, Christopher. 1997. *Meter as Rhythm*. Oxford: Oxford University Press.

Lehmann, Bertram. 2002. *Syntax of 'Clave': Perception and Analysis of Meter in Cuban and African Music*. Masters thesis, Tufts University.

Locke, David. 1982. "Principles of Offbeat Timing and Cross-Rhythm in Southern Ewe Dance Drumming." *Ethnomusicology* 26 (2).

___. 1988. *Drum Gahu*. Tempe, AZ: White Cliffs Media Company.

___. 1992. *Kpegisu: A War Drum of the Ewe*. Tempe, AZ: White Cliffs Media Company.

___. 1978. *The Music of Atsiagbekor*. PhD thesis, Wesleyan University.

___. *Agbadza*. Website: (http://sites.tufts.edu/davidlocke/agbadza-items/).

Lomax, Alan. 1976. *Cantometrics: An Approach to the Anthropology of Music* University of California Extension Media Center.

Nketia, J.H. Kwabena. 1963. *African Music in Ghana*. Evanston: Northwestern University Press.

Nzewi, Meki. 1997. *African Music: Theoretical Content and Creative Continuum: The Culture-Exponent's Definitions*. Olderhausen: Institut fur Diaktik Popularer Music.

Discography
Alorwoyie, Gideon. 2003. *Agbadza! Afrikania Cultural Troupe of Ghana West Africa*. CD.

Appendix

Table 1

Call-Response	Eʋegbe Lyrics	English Translation	Line
Henɔ (Leader)	Akpabli Hɔsu woɖo ɖa hεε	Akpabli Hɔsu has been sent.	1
Haxelawo (Group)	Miʋua 'gbo	Open the gate!	2
Henɔ	Akpabli Hɔsu woɖo ɖa hεε	Akpabli Hɔsu has been sent.	3
Haxelawo	Miʋua 'gbo	Open the gate!	4
Henɔ and Haxelawo	Akpabli Hɔsu woɖo ɖa hεε	Akpabli Hɔsu has been sent.	5
	Miʋua 'gbo	Open the gate!	6
	Danyeviwo Miʋua 'gbo mayi hεε	My mother's children, Open the gate for me to pass.	7
	Akpabli Hɔsu, woɖo ɖa hεε	Akpabli Hɔsu has been sent.	8
	Miʋua 'gbo	Open the gate!	9

Table 1 Song text and translation

Table 2

A.

sogo								
translation	Come out, come out.							
word-for-word	out	come	only	come out	out	come	only	come out
Eʋegbe	do	va	ko	do va	do	va	ko	do va
mnemonics	ga	dzi	ga	ga dzi	ga	dzi	ga	ga dzi
kidi								
mnemonics	i	kri	ga	i krin	i	kri	ga	i krin
Eʋegbe	do	va	ko	do va	do	va	ko	do va
word-for-word	out	come	only	come out	out	come	only	come out
translation	Come out, come out.							

B.

sogo								
translation	Come out, come out							
word-for-word	out	come	only	come out	out	come	only	come out
Eʋegbe	do	va	ko	do va	do	va	ko	do va
mnemonics	ga	dzi	ga	ga dzi	ga	dzi	ga	ga dzi
kidi								
mnemonics	ki	di	gi	i krin	ki	di	gi	i krin
Eʋegbe	do	va	ko	do va	do	va	ko	do va
word-for-word	out	come	only	come out	out	come	only	come out
translation	Come out, come out.							

Table 2 Drum language and vocables for lead-response drum composition

	Gamut	Emphasized pitches in temporal order	Tonicized pitch class
1	displaying entire range: d4-a5	f5-g5-c5-g4-d4-g4	G
2	only upper range: c5-a5	f5-g5-f5-c5-f5	F (upper)
3	shifting downward: d4-f5	f5-d5-c5-g4-d4-g4	G
4	shifting downward: d4-c5	c5-a4-g4-f4	F (lower)
5	centering on G: d4-d5	g4-d5-c5-d4-g4	G

Table 3 Table 3 Tonal patterns in tune

	Implicit Ewe Text	English Translation
gaŋkogui bell • first time • all other times	Do mayi makpo teƒe mava mayi! Mayi makpo teƒe mava mayi.	Get out and see for yourself. I will go to witness the thing and return.
axatsɛ rattle • first time • all other times	Tsia mayi makpo teƒe mava mayi! Mayi makpo teƒe mava mayi.	Get up quickly and see for yourself. I will go to witness the thing and return.
kagaŋ support drum	Míayi ava yia afia	We shall go and show (our bravery).

Table 4 Table 4 Supporting Instruments--Implicit Ewe Texts

Figure 1 Phrase analysis of melody

Figure 2 Part singing example

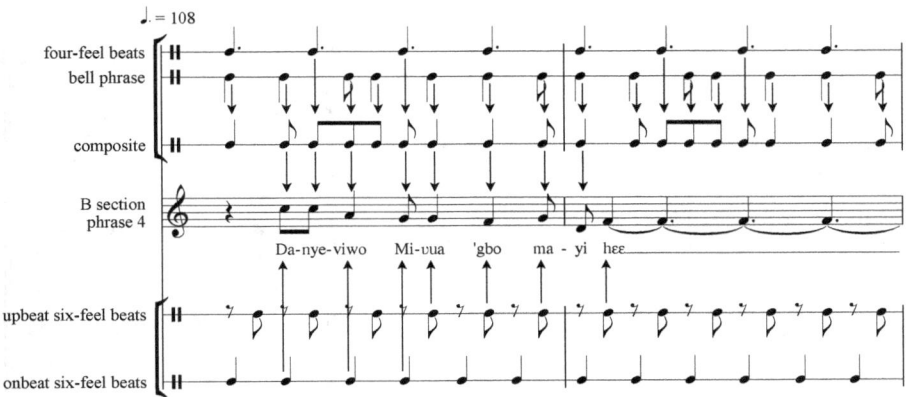

Figure 3
Analysis of rhythm of phrase 4

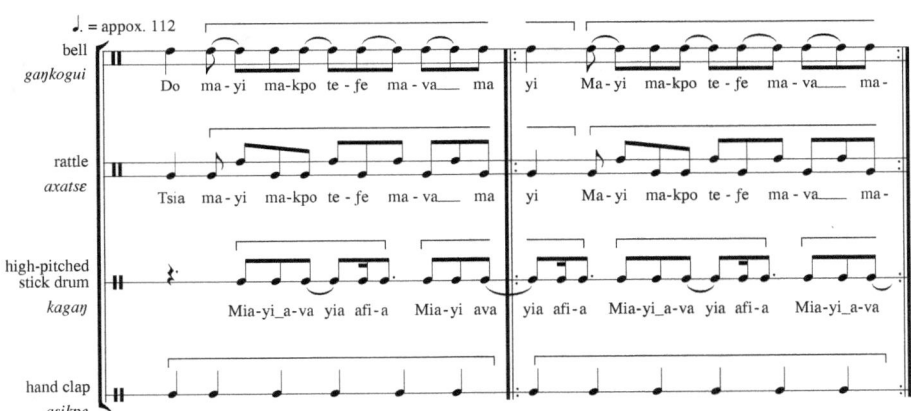

Figure 4
Musical setting of drum language of the time parts

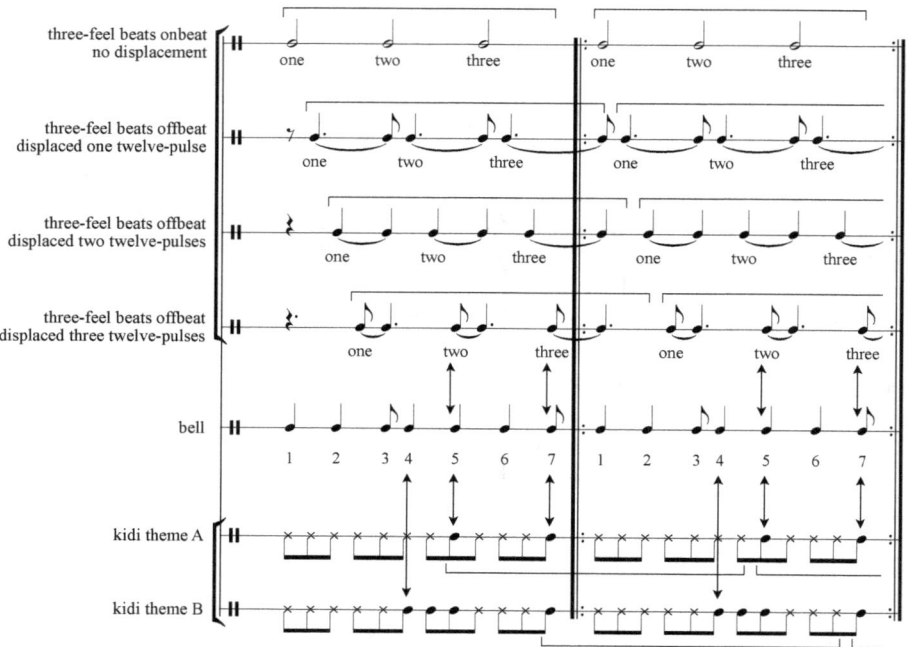

Figure 5
Kidi themes A and B with three-feel beats

Figure 6
Kidi theme A with melodic rhythm of song

Figure 7
Sogo-kidi themes A and B with bell

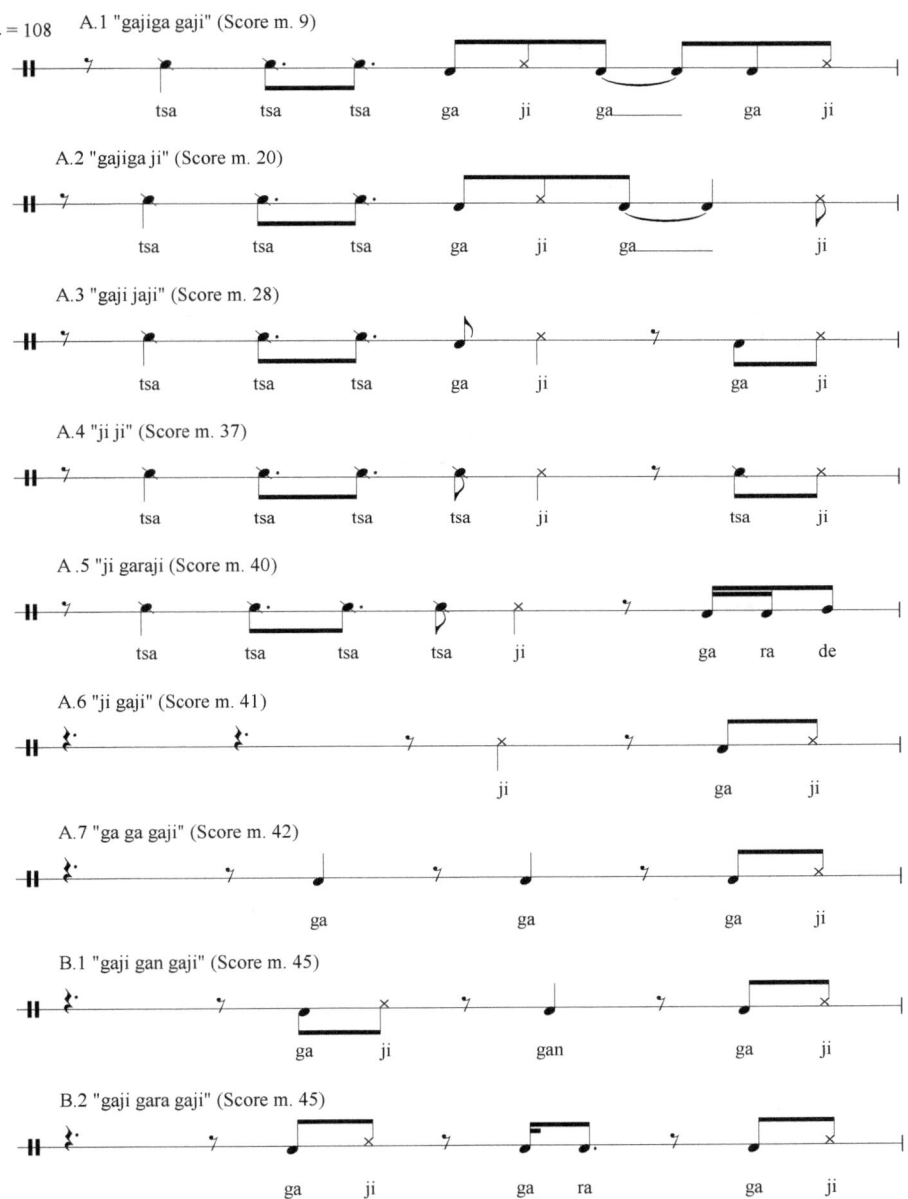

Figure 8
Sogo variations on themes A and B

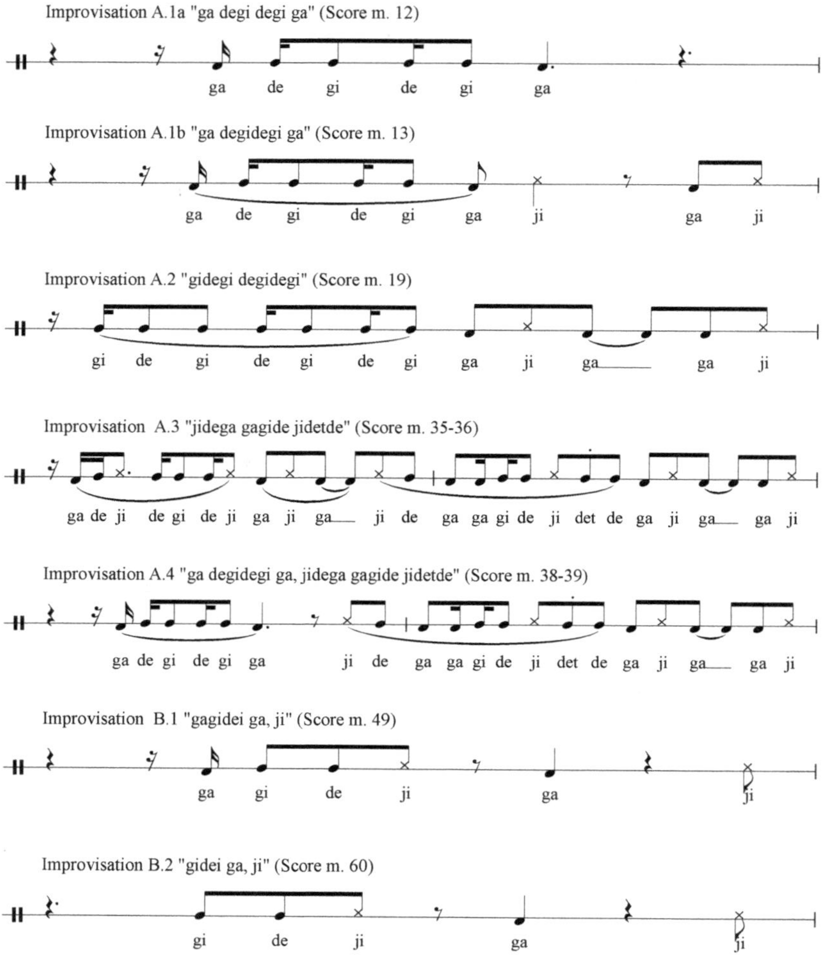

Figure 9
Sogo improvisations

Figure 10
Analysis of a rolling passage

A Theory of Infinite Variation

Brenda M. Romero

Brenda M. Romero is professor of ethnomusicology at the University of Colorado-Boulder. She holds a PhD from the University of California, Los Angeles, and Bachelors and Masters degrees in music theory and composition from the University of New Mexico. She worked extensively on the Matachines Danza in New Mexico as Fulbright García-Robles Scholar in 2000-01, and as Fulbright Colombia Scholar in 2011. She coedited *Dancing across Borders: Danzas y bailes mexicanos* (2009). Her forthcoming monograph is titled *The Transcultural Matachines, Creativity and Renewal in the Americas*.

It is a special honor to be able to dedicate this very personal and reflexive work to Professor Emeritus Dr. J. H. Kwabena Nketia on the occasion of his 90th birthday. It is exciting also, to reflect on the work of my dear friend and colleague, Ghanaian musicologist Dr. Kwasi Ampene, whose presence and Highlife Ensemble performances brought so much joy to the Boulder-Denver community in the years he lived in Colorado. I do not pretend to be a specialist in African music, but at some point we all synthesize vast amounts of the research our discipline has produced and come up with our own creative and respectful ideas and I am honored and privileged to share some here.

I believe that a paradigmatic shift is taking place in music studies, away from Eurocentrism to kaleidoscopic glimpses of music, that by virtue of their complex, colorful, and ever shifting patterns reveal the constant transformations of life everywhere. In this theoretical paper, I speak somewhat rhetorically in pursuing a discussion on the wonder of difference, the magic of exploring different cultural practices that we may one day understand. According to Colombian scholar Oscar Hernández Salgar, however, the "natural" status of Western art music has been maintained by continuing to see the Other as exotic and different (Hernández Salgar 2005:7), but this should not act as a deterrent to pursuing the significances of different intellectual trajectories.

Rather than search for universals, I am moved by the implications of music concepts that have developed in the very cradle of human existence, and imply that music is closely linked to processes of human survival. It is a paper that speaks to the sense that African music is a force in today's world.

It was Susan McClary whom I first heard voice the idea of the "Africanization of world music" and a power to gather people together (McClary 1998). I became intrigued by McClary's idea, as I understood it, that something inherent to African music gives it this power. This article attempts to theorize instances in which "intrinsic" musical meaning is a form of cultural practice, implying a "process of composition, performance, and listening as an integrated system of social action," as Kwasi Ampene alluded to the work of Hugh Tracey on Chopi xylophone music (Ampene 2005:13).

In order to contextualize this as a conceptual, world music theoretical study within the discipline of ethnomusicology, I will revisit and attempt to update Alan P. Merriam's foundational tri-partite "theory and methodology for the study of music as human behavior" (Merriam 1964:viii). I want to advocate also for the development of ethnomusicological studies of musical concepts into world music theories, adding to the tools of traditional music theory (microanalysis) through holistic analysis (macro analysis) applied not only to the sound itself, but also to the social implications of musical sounds, and to the spiritual dimensions of music with all they might imply.[2] Because this essay is based on a premise that survival is closely linked to collective agreements, I will offer two ethnomusicological axioms as the bases for a theory that music in general is essential to human survival. I will call on Kwasi Ampene's work to illuminate a participatory ethos in the social processes of vocal music composition among the Akan in Ghana. Using an example that Caucasian mbira performer, singer, and composer Chris Berry shared with me and my students in the late 1990s, I will argue that the musics of both the Ghanaian Akan *nnwonkoro* and the Zimbabwean Makorekore *engoma* ensembles codify communal ideas of human interdependence and demonstrate an innate human drive for maintenance as well as infinite variation, or renewal, features that characterize the Akan, Shona, the Makorekore and other African music cultures, among other world traditions.

Music and Survival

Motivated by anthropologist Nina Jablonski's beautiful book *Skin, A Natural History*, in which she argues that the scientific world hardly engaged research on skin color because they didn't see skin color as necessary for survival, I began to think about music's links to human survival, primarily based on my work with American Indian music and my interest in ideas of rhythmic cycles in Sub-Saharan Africa. The first developed in part out of an interest in music and spirituality, the latter came from a graduate seminar I took with French-Israeli ethnomusicologist Simha Arom when he was a visiting professor at the University of California, Los Angeles (UCLA) in the late 1980s. A lifelong arts advocate, I have hoped that a general understanding of music's links to human survival might help music survive socio-political purges of the arts and humanities spurred by a depressed economy, and in general be more valued in human societies.

For a moment, let me reflect on journalist Elizabeth Landau's musings in a recent news report prominently featuring a photograph of bassist Victor Wooten, who is quoted in the caption as saying "you don't need to start with the rules of music in order to play an instrument" (1). Landau also cites Daniel Levitin, a psychologist who studies the neuroscience of music at McGill University in Montreal, Quebec, "The structures that respond to music in the brain evolved earlier than the structures that respond to language" (2). It seems fair to suppose, however, that at some point music and language evolved at the same time for different purposes. Especially as people developed different languages, music was unbound by the same strict "rules" and could express emotive concerns conceived and perceived differently from language – what Victor Wooten may be alluding to. It is intriguing that African music has developed in close proximity to linguistic considerations, as Kwasi Ampene highlighted in his study of the prominent *nnwonkoro* female song tradition among the Akan in Ghana, submitting that there is "widespread understanding among Akans that words and music evolve within a single process, since there is no distinction between the poet who provides the lyrics and the musician who sets them to music" (Ampene 2005:79).

Neurologists like Robert Zatorre at the Montreal Neurological Institute affirm that music "is strongly associated with the brain's reward system," but apparently stop short of calling this a "direct biological survival value" (ibid.) That is, you can literally "live" without music, but this is only a definition of life that is based on the lowest common denominator of existence. Survival can imply more than the violence associated with the "survival of the fittest" and social Darwinism. Let us imagine that sage humans have contemplated these things in the past and over millennia have developed musical intellectual concepts big enough to save the humans from themselves, precisely because those sages have understood music as a force for surviving in the world. Others have apparently seen this as evolutionary or pre-modern behavior:

> "Some people have theorized that that was the original function of this behavior in evolution: It was a way of bonding people emotionally together in groups, through shared movement and shared experience" (Aniruddh Patel of the Neurosciences Institute in San Diego, California, cited in Landau 2012: 3).

They seem to fail to see the value of the immediacy of this behavior for basic survival in contemporary life: why should group behavior be less coded for survival now, than in the remote past?[3] Ampene draws a distinction between communal behavior, "the product of the whole community," and the behavior of a "distinct group within the society" (Ampene 2005:10). These are no doubt inextricably connected, as distinct groups vie for legitimacy and make an impact on the whole community. Forming distinct groups, many African musicians play specialized holistic roles, typically interactively, within their communities. For instance, in his analysis of Akan oral composition procedures, Ampene found, "By maintaining the fixed formulaic phrases, performers and audience in Akan are able to recognize the songs whenever they are performed. However, in order to situate the songs in a particular context, Akans expect *nnwonkoro* performer-composers to recompose some phrases in the song units" (ibid, 69). Ampene concludes that *nnwonkoro* musicians play specialized but critical roles in mediating the continuity of life and death by playing and singing polysemic phrases whose metaphorical connotations often reach beyond the surface in profound dimensions.[4] Ampene elaborates on the artistic dimensions of *nnwonkoro* performance: "In addition to archaic language, *nnwonkoro* performer-composers commonly appropriate the prosodic features of the Akan language, such as the repetition of their sound structures, making the words easier to memorize and thereby ensuring greater community participation by non-musicians" (ibid, 85).

This theoretical paper is founded on the scholarship of Dr. Nketia, as I read it in his classic book, *Music of Africa*, from which I quote the following:

> Organized games and sports (such as wrestling), beer parties and feasts, festivals, and social and religious ceremonies or rites that bring the members of a community together provide an important means of encouraging involvement in collective behavior, a means of strengthening the social bonds that bind them and the values that inspire their corporate life. The performance of music in such contexts, therefore, assumes a multiple role in relation to the community: it provides at once an opportunity for sharing in creative experience, for participating in music as a form of community experience, and for using music as an avenue for the expression of group sentiments (Nketia 1974:22).

In particular, Dr. Nketia's work identifying the emphasis on community in African music has surely been an impetus that has led many scholars to correlate communal and cooperative values with expressive forms that are interlocking in nature, and are represented in music, vocals instrumental accompaniment, dance, proverbs, textile designs, and so on. The signification of proverbs, repeated as patterns of musical sound, and the signification of designs and colors on Akan *adinkra*[5] and *kente* ceremonial cloth are well known, although improvisation is also highly prized.

Ruth Stone describes the sonic connection with power dating to ancient African empires: "The musical bow player communicates not only aesthetically pleasing sounds but sounds with lexical meanings, often based on proverbs. So word meanings layer upon tone color layers in a dynamic mixture – all coming from the deceptively simple looking one-string bow" (Stone 2005:55); and "The sonic symbols amplified the visual symbols of power displayed in cloth, as well as gold leaf on swords, stools, and staves" (ibid:12), as well as contemporary West Africans: "The audience that observed this spectacle had come to value the horn players who created a composition that required split-second timing and how the ensemble symbolized the ultimate in cooperation between multiple players. The most valued form of music was attached to the political leader who used these sounds to reinforce his status" (ibid:30). Idealized metaphors of community include the link of a chain as a symbol of the bond of human relationships and one Ghanaian *adinkra* pattern symbolizes the teeth and the tongue, reminding people of the need for friendliness and interdependence.

> Music and dance are similarly interdependent and interlocking, as Ampene emphasizes:
> Moreover the function of instrumental accompaniment is to provide an outlet for dance; the analysis of drum rhythms should ideally take into account the corresponding dance movements . . . (ibid:2).

In actuality, the visual symbols can also be represented in interlocking and interactive music and dance forms that promote a "participatory ethos." Ethnomusicologist Thomas Turino describes a participatory ethos in the Andean region, where interlock is also central to music making, in terms that resonate strongly with the African contexts:

> ... *participatory music* is defined by contexts where everyone is invited, and often expected, to participate musically or by dancing and where there are no clear-cut artist-audience distinctions, only participants and potential participants (xiii). Moreover, in this type of tradition, the quality of a performance is judged by the level of participation and the practices and style of the music are oriented toward inspiring maximum participation. Participatory music is for *doing* rather than *listening*... Participatory traditions usually include a variety of roles such that people at any skill level can find a balance between their abilities and the degree of challenge necessary to keep them engaged... (Turino 2008:21).

Stone describes the element of "social resonance" in Liberia:

> A good song ideally involves a large number of names, actors, and identities. These names through a single word often trigger a host of associations. Within a short period of time, a host of interactions are presented to the audience.... There is the idea of resonance in whatever is done. Resonance of... aural sensations, visual sensations, and social chaining (Stone 1975:115, cited in Stone, 2005:61).

In contrast, "in presentational ensembles, the members tend to be at a similar skill level and personnel are often chosen on the basis of musical ability"(Turino 2008:22).

As previously mentioned, my initial motivation for pursuing this subject further came from hearing Susan McClary speak a number of years ago. This was the first time I ever heard articulated the idea that African music is a force in the world beyond itself. Not long after hearing McClary, I met musician, composer, dancer Chris Berry, who began to study with a Congolese musician, Titos Sompa in San Francisco at the age of 13 and moved to Africa at age 18 to continue his studies with Sompa. Berry eventually became one of a few Westerners who is considered a master mbira player among the Shona; as such he is capable of calling the spirits for a *bira* (ceremony). He also became integral to the rock band Panjea, which has sold over a million recordings throughout Africa. In the 2000s, Berry's musical-political message was deemed an enemy of state and he became an outlaw in Zimbabwe,[6] but when

I met him in Boulder in the late 1990s he was full of enthusiasm and joy. I invited him to give a guest lecture in one of my ethnomusicology classes and the lecture was so powerful that I began to consider the ways that kinship has provided a basis for musical conceptualizations that have come with the "Africanization of world music," At the time he visited my class Berry was married to a Shona woman and was a valued member of Shona society in Zimbabwe.[7] He shared with the class (and I will share here) his example of how kinship and community ideals are embodied in Shona musical ideas. One of the questions I am pursuing here is to what extent the concepts have been built into musical structures (*intrinsic musical meaning as cultural practice*), such that African drumming, for example, has found a widespread global appeal. Outside of its generative contexts, music seems capable of translating directly as concept.

The Value of a Name
I am aligned with Kwasi Ampene, Kofi Agawu, and others in avoiding the term "ethnotheory" and its implications:

> The prominence of indigenous terminology . . . points to a body of theoretical knowledge in Akan; however, the category of *ethnotheory* does not convey the full implication of indigenous knowledge. I wish to state that, as a matter of principle, I do not subscribe to prefixes (*ethno*musicology included) since it places certain knowledge on the periphery of scholarship while privileging and centering another type of knowledge (Ampene 2005:4).

I am motivated by Malena Kuss's incisive view of colonial naming processes (Kuss 2004), which superimposed entire histories and histories of ideas with Western linguistic markers of conquest. As elsewhere, I recommend Malena Kuss's "Prologue" to *Music in Latin America and the Caribbean, An Encyclopedic History* (ibid 2004) for a succinct reading on the impact of colonialism through the re-naming of places and ideas.[8] Although there is nothing new in arguing that Western musical terminology does not always fit musical concepts that have developed over centuries among other peoples,[9] this discussion probes what is reflected by a name or term, in this case "polyrhythm" and "rhythmic cycle." Ampene deconstructs the Western values attached to the term "composition" in his study of female "compositions without written texts" in Ghana (Ampene 2005:14). Not only does Ampene address the Western assumption of literacy in music creative process, but also stereotypes:

> In musicology part of the reason for the more exuberant assertions made about oral composition arises from ignoring the integrity and autonomy of the cultural practices in which oral communication functions. For instance, the numerous researches in African musical traditions do not regard the manifold musical creations – songs, drum music, flute music, xylophone music, mbira music, string music and many more – as compositions. Rather the impression gained from reading the literature on African musical practices is that African musicians just improvise in the context of performance and that there are no fixed and authentic texts. We should ask, however, whether the African musician considers what he does as improvisation (ibid:13-14).

In this article I will focus on a different kind of "text" in order to demonstrate how non-Western musical time and concepts have been re-named in a general fashion, without a clear understanding of the depth of musical significance possible in a musical utterance. I seek to illuminate a conceptual space in which this difference and significance can be perceived and understood. In so doing I will also lean heavily on Simha Arom's work on indigenous rhythmic concepts in Central Africa and Ruth Stone's meaningful study in Liberia.

After studying with Simha Arom as visiting professor at UCLA in the late 1980s, I was forever "marked" by questions of meter versus rhythmic cycle. By now my understandings may have deviated from Arom's, as I use his work to form a foundation for arguing that "polyrhythm" does not suffice to describe the musical concepts I will discuss below, in spite of Arom's use of the term in his 1991 book title. I will conclude with Chris Berry's example of the *Engoma drum* ensemble found among the Makorekoro in Zimbabwe to illustrate some of the internal meanings that inform the ensemble and its music.

Updating Alan P. Merriam's Tri-partite Theoretical Research Model

Alan P. Merriam was to be the Distinguished Lecturer at the 25th Anniversary of the Society for Ethnomusicology, but instead Stephen A. Wild and Bruno Nettl delivered tributes in honor of Merriam after his untimely passing in a tragic airplane accident on his way to deliver a series of lectures at Warsaw University. Ruth Stone was the Program Committee Chair and Frank Gillis the Local Arrangements Chair for that meeting, held in Bloomington, Indiana, SEM's home institution.

As Stephen A. Wild wrote:

> In preparing for my task today I found it unexpectedly, but understandably, difficult to commit my thoughts to paper. This was for two reasons. Firstly, since that day when I learned of his death I have been unable to think about Alan Merriam without emotional turmoil. Secondly, my thoughts of him are a kaleidoscope of images of a complex, many-faceted individual, which seem to defy coherent organization. But in Western culture we try to repair our sense of loss on such an occasion by talking about it and by recalling the reasons why the person endeared himself to us; perhaps by remembering how much he gave us the loss seems less. And perhaps since, as Alan Merriam said not so long ago, ours is a culture characterized by an obsession with enumeration and typologizing of things, an accounting of the things he left us helps us to cope with our troubled emotions... (1982:91).

These words still ring true today, as we look to Merriam for "an accounting" that "helps us cope with our troubled emotions," but instead of looking back we look forward to where he might lead us today. Some things have not changed; in 1969, Merriam wrote:

> None of us needs reminding that ethnomusicology today is poised on the horns of a bifurcated dilemma. Under the rubric of "ethnomusicology" we group together an amazingly diverse set of studies, some of which are historical in nature, some technical and structural, some descriptive, some analytic, and even some which seem to be none of these. Where our studies differ so do our methodologies, our theories, techniques, ideas, approaches, and our concepts of what it is we are trying to

learn. Is ethnomusicology a discipline? And if it is, what is the nature of that discipline, what are the principles on which it is based, and what is it seeking to learn?

Through my work with the College Music Society, which is multidisciplinary for music professionals, I too have observed that people abstract knowledge on their own terms; whatever disciplinary elements might intervene, we all dominate domains of discourse depending on our training and backgrounds. To add to the confusion, by now the amount of information we are working with is so abundant that we need to formalize smaller categories in order to keep track of the rapid growth of musicology in general and ethnomusicology in particular. When we begin to talk about "theories" and "pedagogies" we refine our focus, as we did when we began to talk about "cultures" or, more recently, "musics." In so doing, we begin to discriminate among types of concerns. As Margaret Kartomi has proposed (1990), we create taxonomies in which we group like things for the sake of order versus chaos. I retain anthropologist Alan P. Merriam's theoretical research model as the basis for discriminating among types of studies, but ethnomusicology in the present day is a lot different than in 1964, when Merriam published *The Anthropology of Music*. Thus it will be necessary not only to revisit but also to update Alan Merriam's tripartite model in an attempt to provide an overarching frame that might serve to guide others in particular domains of discourse, or music sub-disciplines. Merriam wrote:

> Since all these factors must be considered in studying the music of any given people, the immediate problem is whether a theoretical research model can be constructed which will take all of them into account. *Such a model must consider folk and analytical evaluation, the cultural and social background, the relevant aspects of the social sciences and the humanities, and the multiple facets of music as symbolic, aesthetic, formal, psychological, physical, and so forth* (1964:32, emphasis mine).
> The model proposed here is a simple one and yet it seems to fulfill these requirements. It involves study on three analytic levels – conceptualization about music, behavior in relation to music, and music sound itself. The first [conceptualization] and third [musical sound itself] levels are connected to provide for the constantly changing, dynamic nature exhibited by all music systems" (ibid).

For the purposes of convenience, we can begin with the third level, that of the music sound itself. This sound has structure, and it may be a system, but it cannot exist independently of human beings; *music sound must be regarded as the product of the behavior that produces it* (ibid, emphasis mine).

John E. Kaemmer's geometrical rendition of Merriam's model – "A model of musical process (modified from Merriam 1964:32-33)" (1993:25), useful for this discussion, could be said to incorporate a hierarchy of high and low space, with "musical sound itself" at the top (ibid.) and Behavior and Concepts at two ends of the bottom line of a triangle. An arrow points up from Behavior to Musical sound, and down from Musical sound to Concepts. The arrow between Behavior and Concept goes both ways, but the connection from Concepts cannot go directly to Musical sound. That is, Behavior affects Musical sound, which can affect Concepts directly, but Concepts must first translate into the behavior needed for the sound to occur. Musical conceptions of sound can dictate behaviors, however. And, what if, as for Tibetan monks, the concept *is* the sound and thought music is a possibility? Updating Merriam first requires embracing concepts of spatial synergy and things that cannot be observed directly (spirituality). We can do this by altering Kaemmer's rendition of Merriam's tri-partite model to make all arrows go in both directions -- a cycle – as in Figure 1, that suggests a fluid, synergistic model, as in Figure 2. As Stone concluded, "Sound is multiplied and amplified just as social relationships are amplified in a kind of connection or social chaining (61). Synergy helps provide access to what Stone calls "inner time" or "a qualitative time" that becomes more important than "outer time" intermittently (89), as it does in ritualized performative activities.

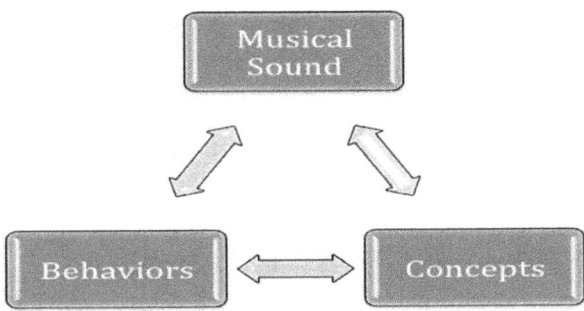

Figure 1: Kaemmer's configuration of Merriam's model, with arrows added in both directions

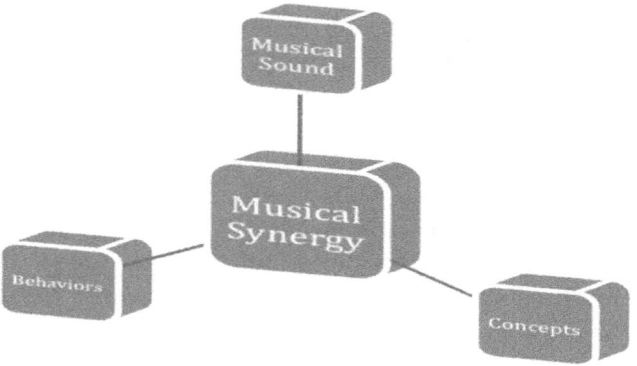

Figure 2: Romero "Model of Musical Synergy" (after Merriam and Kaemmer)

It is important to remember that each of Merriam's three categories is a world in itself that is largely informed from the inside of a culture. As Merriam concluded: "They are presented individually here in order to emphasize the parts of the whole; if we do not understand one we cannot properly understand the others; if we fail to take cognizance of the parts, then the whole is irretrievably lost" (ibid, 35). The concepts, behaviors, and sounds that combine to generate musical synergy can differ radically; thus this model is further modified below. But first, let us glimpse some of the activity since Merriam's final decades of the 1960s and 70s.

Ethnomusicologies

I would like to share with you with some of my own observations of how things have changed. For instance, today we can speak about ethnomusicologies in the plural. Let us contemplate a category called ethnomusicologies of musical sound. Surely this will include the systematic musicologists and ethnomusicologists who study sounds or musical sounds or cultural sounds or eco-sounds. This will include studies of organologies and acoustics, as much as studies on cognition, and perception. It will include the Western theorists whose work focuses on the analysis of sound structures, even within music-cultural frameworks like the Common Practice Era of the West. Although some of these terms go way back, other of these terminologies we can apply today were largely unheard of in the 1960s.

We can update Merriam's other parameters in a similar fashion. With regard to behavior in relation to music (behavioral ethnomusicologies?), we must consider more than the physical and social body required to perform, but add terms like "embodiment," "experience," "ontology," "phenomenology," "applied," "social agency," healing, dance, courtship, and so on. As an example, I quote Michelle Kisliuk:

> The location of the field, then, does not depend on geography, but on the self-constructed identity of the ethnographer in a given social landscape. Similarly, the emergent identity of a fieldworker depends not on a particular location or apparent resemblance to other investigators and interlopers, but on the quality and depth of research relationships and ultimately on the way we each intend to represent our experiences (Kisliuk 2008:192-93).

Finally, conceptualization about music (conceptual ethnomusicologies?) suggests that musical concepts are also communal ("cultural") expressions of being, and work together to document and preserve cultural understanding and in general create synergy: more than the sum of their parts and, I theorize, a door to extra-musical, spiritual experience. Kartomi identifies "culture-emerging" and "scholar-imposed" concepts and classifications (Kartomi 1990), and by extension one can name dominant and marginalized musicological narratives. In a talk that Philip Bohlman presented as an invited outsider for the UCLA Alumni Symposium in November 2010 he posed the possibilities of canonic and anti-canonic (among other) ethnomusicologies. My work, which is also motivated by a search for greater understanding of the spirituality and power of music, falls into Bohlman's anti-canonic category. "Sacredness," for instance, is rarely discussed in the West. I paraphrase a former student when I say that ethnomusicology courses are one of the rare contexts where students might explore what is sacred or "spiritual" in music or artistic expression.

Although it seems clear that there would be a great deal of overlap between categories, this article is primarily focused on this third category, focusing on concepts. As Hofstadter once wrote (with regard to Chopin):

> ...phenomena perceived to be magical are always the outcome of complex patterns of *nonmagical* activities taking place at a level below perception. More succinctly: the magic behind magic is pattern (174, cited in Taylor, n.p.).

Institutional Diversity Rhetoric

As I have been subject to the usual institutional rhetoric about diversifying course content (a rhetoric that was much stronger 10 years ago[10]), I once thought it could be possible to inject the usual music theory class with a shot of ethno, but it no longer seems feasible or desirable. Some have attempted a "repertory-nonspecific approach," but as YouYoung Kang puts it: "Music theory practiced in general, universal terms is often vague and unsatisfying, because it is the in-depth investigation of a musical culture that produces understanding and interested engagement" (49, 51).[11] Others have tried including non-Western examples to enhance a Western concept, "Although such inclusion can be well intended, this 'inclusive' approach gives Western music theory a 'universal' omnipotent status and subsumes all musics under the theoretical umbrella of Western art music" (ibid. 53). A student, who confided at a gathering of ethnomusicologists that although he loved his professor, he kept feeling that he was being indoctrinated into Christianity in that first semester of junior history, of Western Art Music.[12] But I seriously doubt that it is it possible to change that role without questioning and re-conceptualizing the conservatory model. In part, it is the hegemony of Western music theory that is objectionable, not the study of Western art music or theory per se. Although university music programs, particularly in state universities, continue to legitimize Western art music and undermine the music of world cultures and of the working-classes, it is still possible to focus on expanding the canon – or perhaps the "anti-canonic" (Bohlman 2010) by doing what ethnomusicologists do best: articulate difference, not impose it.

New Approaches to "Turf"

For some time now I have been thinking about new approaches to teaching that reconcile the gap between ethnomusicological method and Western music theory. Following discussions that occurred at College Music Society (CMS) meetings in the late 1990s and early 2000s, I founded, hosted, and facilitated the CMS Summer Institute on the Pedagogies of World Music Theories (a CMS Professional Development initiative), a five-day workshop that was held in the University of Colorado, Boulder (CU) College of Music in 2005, 2007, and 2010 (with planning underway for a future event). The Institute title developed in a move to decenter the idea that there exists only one "music theory," through scholarly dialogue primarily among the three founding faculty composer-ethnomusicologists: Paul Humphreys (Loyola Marymount University), Jonathon Grasse (California State University, Dominguez Hills), and myself. Professors from throughout the United States have come to the Institute to "tool up" when they have been asked to diversify their music course content. Participants include ethnomusicologists, composers, music theorists, and historical musicologists, an interdisciplinary music focus that is emblematic of CMS.

I initiated this project in part as a result of continuing frustrations with music institutional turf wars about who can and who cannot teach or address issues surrounding basic musicianship courses like Aural Skills and Basic Music Theory, and perhaps because I am an ethnomusicologist with a background in music theory and composition. I set out to find ethnomusicologically informed ways of teaching music theory as a potential fourth semester for students in our BA musicology program (a goal that became reality in spring of 2012 when the College of Music Curriculum Committee approved a World Music Theories course at both the undergraduate and graduate levels). Institute presenters have included a number of ethnomusicology or ethnomusicology-related scholars -- most of whom are also composers, one a systematic musicologist.[13] A recent reinforcing trend is seen in the emergence of the Analytical Approaches to World Musics (AAWM) biennial conference, held for the first time in 2010 at the University of Massachusetts at Amherst, and which Michael Tenzer, John Roeder, and their colleagues hosted at the University of British Colombia, Vancouver in May 2012. Founders also launched the AAWM online journal.[14] In his abstract for the AAWM 2010 conference, Kofi Agawu wrote,

> . . . the fullest views of structure and expression in African music, views that enhance appreciation not only of what African music is but of what it could enable creatively, come from looking beyond the comforting specifics that ethnotheory celebrates to a larger theory" (2009).

In contemplating the idea of "world music theories," I have embraced an ethnomusicological model that reflects the infinite uses and meanings of music, a theory of infinite variation, which this essay seeks to contextualize as "natural" to life processes and to music.

A Theory of Infinite Variation

Rather than turn our attention to music theories like Shenkerian analysis or set theory, then, I offer a new ethnomusicological theory, the theory of infinite variation based on my ethnomusicological observations over the past twenty-five years: *The nature of music, as of humanity, is to endlessly maintain and renew itself.* Closely correlated is the theory of interrelationship and interdependence: *Maintenance and renewal are achieved through the rituals of interrelationship and interdependence.* Both of these axioms are key to survival, and comprise processes that music and music-making represent and reinforce. The axiomatic value of the second correlated theory has emerged from my work with Native American music and musicians. *Mitakuye oyasin* is Lakota (Sioux) for "All my relations," meaning that everything on earth is interrelated. Societal definitions of the character of interdependence varies (variation is typically the rule). For instance, some societies condemn music's abilities to evoke the sensual; in contrast, African societies seem to utilize a holistic force of the body and all its energies in renewal. As synergistic processes that are not accessible to external observation, they were -- in the past -- easy to dismiss, but music could also be called the ultimate refuge, as music feeds the human spirit, and thus, arguably, aids biological survival itself. The Theory of Infinite Variation can be imagined via a model for infinite variation (see Figure 5) that is based on Merriam, Kaemmer, and especially on an interlocking multi-dimensional conception of anthropologist Johannes Wilbert.

A Model for Infinite Variation

As a graduate student at UCLA I was privileged and thrilled to hear UCLA anthropologist Johannes Wilbert speak in one of my seminars. He introduced to us his model for the study of enculturation in Latin America following his work with the Warao people of Venezuela (1979:22), which I have adapted in Figure 3 (below) as a model for infinite variation in combination with Merriam's and Kaemmer's ideas. After waiting many years to discover the significance of certain words in Warao songs and of the iconography on a Warao rattle he analyzed, Wilbert had conceived of a way to formulate ethnographic questions he might not have otherwise thought of, and that might have helped to inform his work earlier in the process. Wilbert wrote, "A full-scale study of enculturation is thought to consist of three dimensions: process, time, and space" (ibid.). Wilbert's top facet is devoted to the process dimension as "determined by the goals of enculturation, which entail the skill training, socialization, and moral education of the individual." They are listed from left to right in three *separate* intersecting categories: Skill-Training, Socialization, and Moral Education. The front facet of Wilbert's cube addresses the space dimensions of Environment, Society, and Culture *in each* intersecting category. Although Wilbert's model deserves more attention overall, that is beyond the scope of this essay. The categories of Johannes Wilbert's original model that I have retained here are those from his facet for time: they are weighed separately for infancy, childhood, and adulthood. I chose these because they trace the ways that people or their surroundings change over the course of a lifetime; other markers of development could be tied to specific events within those (or other designated) life phases. The same questions directed at people in each generation will likely result in different answers. Among Native North Americans in the U.S. this is important because, rather than entertainment, music is mostly valued for its role in spiritual *attainment* over the course of a person's lifetime[15] – and I suspect this resonates strongly with some African music values.

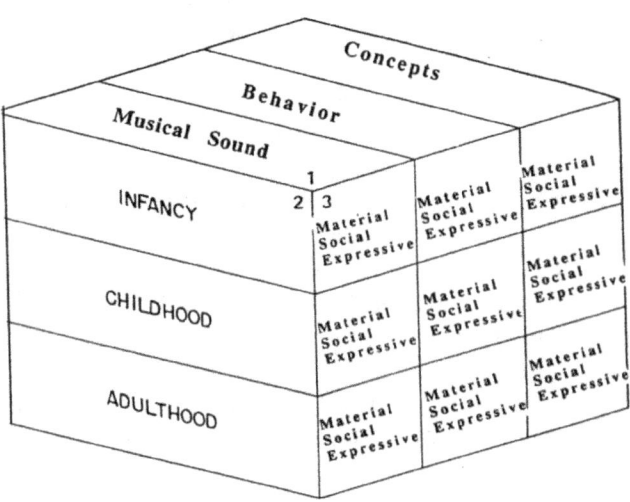

Figure 3: A Theory for Infinite Variation: Brenda M. Romero's "Synergy Cube," based on models by Alan P. Merriam (1964); Johannes Wilbert (1976); and John E. Kaemmer (1993).

The top facet of the Romero "Synergy Cube" (Figure 5) incorporates Merriam and Kaemmer's ideas as developed above, as separate intersecting categories with a model of musical synergy as the guiding concept. The third facet of the intersecting cube represents the socio-cultural system in its material, social and expressive dimensions *in each* intersecting category similar to Wilbert's model. One can systematically analyze musical sound, behavior, and concepts for different stages of life in the material, social, and expressive dimensions of the socio-cultural system (Kaemmer, 8), especially useful for formulating questions one might never have thought of otherwise – exactly what Johannes Wilbert suggested in the late 1980s, as previously mentioned. The model is open to infinite possibilities and variations, an aid with which to perceive processes of maintenance and renewal, and especially to accept difference.

The idea of infinite variation implies that this model can be adapted and readapted, interpreted and reinterpreted, in keeping with infinite domains of discourse and human variation. As Merriam wrote in 1964:

> Given the fact that the investigator cannot possibly consider every minute variation because of the simple limits of time, how can he ever know what is the "proper" or "correct" version of a song? The answer lies in the distinction to be made between an absolute correctness and an understanding that such an absolute probably does not exist. What is important is not the search for a single truth, but rather "the limits within which a culture recognizes and sanctions variations in a . . . given mode of behavior" (Herskovits 1948:570) (50).

and

> The ethnographic or ethnomusicological "truth," then, results from the gathering of the widest possible range of data concerning the given question, and then reporting of the consensus of behavior with equal attention given to the limits of variation within that consensus" (51).

In order to demonstrate how this model can be further adapted, consider a second version I developed as a source of integrating thinking skills and primary learning modes with musical / cultural activities. Although Howard Gardner's concept of multiple intelligences is now contested, his "Modalities" are still suitable for probing different aspects of human intelligence and their relationships to music. Consider the top facet to include Linguistic, Musical, Logical/Mathematical, Spatial, Bodily/Kinesthetic, Interpersonal, Intrapersonal, Naturalist, and perhaps other modalities that explore spatial synergy and things one cannot access visibly.

One facet of the cube could incorporate Bloom's taxonomy: Experience (Knowledge), Experience (Comprehension), Application, Analysis, Synthesis, and Evaluation. The front facet could incorporate Musical Concept, Behavior, and Sound, combined in each intersecting cube. These models are holistic because they consider how interrelationships are fluid and humans are endlessly creative and "original" through rituals of renewal, which typically incorporate music for musics' abilities to communicate in particular ways.

The following analysis is largely an intersection of music conceptualization in its material, social, and expressive dimensions during adulthood. The material dimension includes concepts behind the musical instruments, among others; the social dimension lies in the values assigned each of the instruments and their accompanying symbolic socio-musical discourses; the expressive dimension is represented by the actualization of musical sound and its desirable affect. As with the musical resultants that are formed within and between interlocking phrases in mbira music, working with discreet intersecting research categories illuminates other, less obvious, intersections.

Social Value of Concepts: Problematizing Terminologies

Simha Arom argues that "meter" is a specific term that carries cultural meaning and specific musical connotations. Taylor's definition, below, resonates with the understanding I took away from my graduate class with Arom at UCLA:

> According to Arom, African music (specifically, the music of the sub-Saharan Pygmy peoples) does not rely on the Western concept of meter. Classical European meter, he says, is nothing neither more nor less than a series of identical durations with regular accentuation--in other words, meter is a simple rhythm, spread out on a large scale. African rhythms are cyclical and repeating, but their lack of bar accentuation, as well as their

speed and complexity, distinguish them from European rhythms and meters (Taylor, n.p.).

The practice of using "meter" or "structured pulsation" as generic names equally for Western as for non-Western systems of counting musical time imposes a Western concept upon other music-cultural systems, renaming them as Western in the process. The term "meter" signifies a system of notating measured time that coincided with the invention of clocks during the Renaissance. Prior to clocks there were no bar lines in Western notation. The term "polyrhythm" is closely linked to meter as a way of implying interacting bar line groupings, or measures. The Western concept of "counterpoint" is based on a system of "meter." In contrast, African systems of counting time are really systems of signifying interlocking patterns that don't progress *through* time in a linear, goal-oriented fashion, but rather tend to exist *in* time and *not only in the music, but also in the dance and other expressive forms*. Important ideas are retained in embellished ways in this manner.

Interestingly, each world cultural system forges its own socio-musical identities in communal performances, but there are important differences. Among them, African musical time is closely linked to the body, dancing, and community, while Western musical time often eliminates references to the body. It can be argued that the community formed by symphony orchestras is meant to be elite and closed ("passive") in comparison to the communal awakenings that African musical forces invoke.

For want of a better term, I will use the term "rhythmic cycles" to refer to the Sub-Saharan African musical practices that depend on interlocking, interactive forms. According to what I remember from Arom's seminar, there is more to rhythmic cycles than Taylor's description above leads us to believe. Cycles require combinations of sounds: timbre (sound quality) and range (high, low, in-between), which Arom calls "markers" because sounds "mark" their place in the cycle. This is actually the resulting (repetitive) pattern – the *resultant* – that is formed. The concept of downbeat is absent and when it is consistently present may indicate Western musical influence from Christian missionaries, Western popular music, and so on.[16]

Expressive Culture: Embodiment of Community Ideals in Rhythmic Cycles

According to Chris Berry (1999), music may also express or reinforce gender roles, as among the Shona of Zimbabwe. Male and female musical concepts have long been identified for *mbira* playing. The *kushaura* represents the male *mbira;* it plows and breaks the earth *on the beat*. It begins the music. The *kutsinhira* represents the female principle, *off the beat*; it enters after the *kushaura* is established, in interlocking form. (One might argue that an ideal of male and female parity are thus established through the interlock.) Berry recounted an anecdote, that some of his Shona associates found Western popular music to be overly masculine as heard in the use of a deep and aggressive bass line. This suggests that the association of syncopation with African musical ideas may stem from African musical tendencies to place equal emphasis on and off the beat. Syncopation appears to be a borrowed element within the Western concept of meter. At this juncture these questions turn to the roles of social identity and musical behavior, which are often constrained by social norms and material status.

Berry recounted the story of the sacred *engoma* tone drums (played with sticks) assigned to the *Dare* ensemble of a rural people named Makorekore, in a place called Nyanewe in Zimbabwe.[17] The drums themselves may accompany mbira music but the ensemble itself does not travel. Although these are not the names given to the instruments (except for the *hosho*), most telling are the connotations of the instruments -- what they represent for the Makorekore:

> *Kagigiri* (1): Ancestors; hollowed wood block represents the sounds of their bones.
> *Va ambuya* (3): Grandmother is the lowest sounding drum; closest to the earth; most important. Three different sizes.
> *Va sekura* (2): Grandfathers.
> *Va bereke* (2): Parents. These drums do most of the work; they are the voice of the "family."
> *Va sikana* (2): Girls; daughters.
> *Va komana* (1): Boy; son.
> *Va zvarwa* (2): Spirit of unborn children. *Havasati,* or *Hosho* shaker.

There is no explanation for why there should be two daughter and only one son, or three *Va ambuya*, only that the lowest sounding one is called Grandmother; perhaps the other two are aunts. According to Isabel Mukonyora of the University of Zimbabwe, women are subordinates in Shona societies, and perhaps also among the Makorekore. "As the *vatorwa*, the ones from outside the lineage in a system of exogamy, women remained a stage removed from the religion of the ancestors, even if they sometimes fulfilled important roles. *Madzitete* (aunts) and *madzimbuya* (grandmothers), for example, brew the beer for drinking at ritual gatherings" (Mukonyora 277).

Interestingly, Berry revealed that women (and especially grandmothers) have a great deal of status in the Makorekore community, such that, in his experience, a term of respect for male elders is the equivalent of "Mrs." He calls this "the secret role of the drums," as outwardly women are not seen as important – "they don't call the drums that, but that is what they represent" (1999). Berry cited a well-known African proverb, "Man might be the head of household, but woman is the neck that turns the head." Berry believes that these levels of knowledge, specifically of this marginalized group, are not incorporated into the city scenes (2012). This suggests a pre-colonial nomenclature, and the possibility that women had greater authority prior to the imposition of male-dominated Western colonization, a process that affected indigenous societies throughout the Americas as well.

Most wondrous, is the literal correlation between the *hosho* and the unborn fetus (see Figure 4.) The shakers are made from the dried shells of Zimbabwean wild fruits. They are filled with stones, pebbles, or seeds, and they are played in pairs, one in each hand, full of symbolic male and female generative potential.[18] They typically accompany mbira music too.

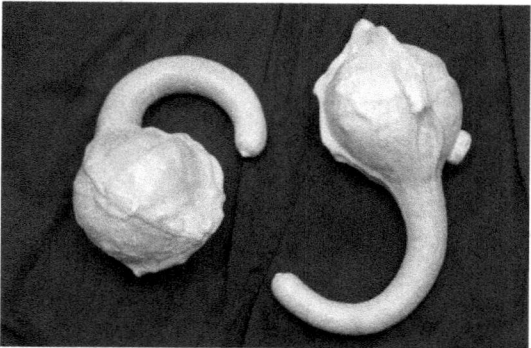

Figure 4: *Va zvarwa* (2): Spirit of unborn children. *Havasati*, or *Hosho*
Photograph courtesy of Janet Meyer, used with permission.

In contrast, the *Kagigiri* (ancestors) are sounded on the wood of a dead tree; the sound of the ancestor's bones. Berry suggested that this was the concept of reincarnation indirectly expressed (1999), but it could also represent a general concept of renewal and endless regeneration without naming it "reincarnation." Although speaking specifically about the Akan of Ghana, Ampene sheds light on the significance of the ancestors in Africa:

> It is noteworthy that the spirits and ancestors are not considered God, neither are they deified or considered a pantheon of gods and therefore, they are not worshiped. On the other hand, the ancestors are venerated and given the highest honor and respect (2005:127) ... They are supposed to be in close contact with the Supreme Being (Onyankopon), and to have the power to intervene between human beings and the Supreme Being. Ancestors are also considered the custodians of the laws of the society (ibid, 137.)

Other scholars of African musical traditions have found similar traditional nomenclatures (see, for instance, Stone, 2005.)

Polyvocality

A general controversy over the use of the term "polyrhythm" for African music is at the heart of Michael Bakan's term, "polyvocality" (2007) to imply a unified diversity of views and perspectives, or a "musical conversation" with lead musicians improvising – a source of infinite musical variation. With regard to his chapter, "Musical Conversations: Communication and Collective Expression in West African Musics," Bakan clarifies the terminology:

> This chapter explores the musical element of polyphony, music of "many sounds," of "many parts." It might be more accurate, however, to describe this as a chapter about **polyvocality,** "many *voices*. The music we will explore is not generally conceived of by its makers as music that exists solely for its own sake. Rather, it is a form of *conversation*, in which people alternately speak in turn and all at once. The ability of many voices to speak and be heard simultaneously, and in the process to express a unified diversity of views and perspectives is valued in many modes of social and conversational interaction in West

Africa. It resonates strongly in the social interaction of music making (Bakan 2007:188.)

Canadian ethnomusicologist Jeffrey Cupchik bases his understanding of the term "polyvocality" on the literature emerging from the University of Birmingham's Center for Contemporary Cultural Studies (CCCS), and the work of Paul Willis, Dick Hebdige, Stuart Hall, and Lawrence Grossberg. Cupchik states,

> The term, to my knowledge, is a discursive, literary and ethnographic strategy for inclusion implemented in the post-colonialist energetic swell of the oceanic tidal crisis in ethnographic representations within Cultural Anthropology in the mid-late 1990s. "Polyvocality," as Bakan uses it, is confusing... Rather, "polyvocality" is a strategic maneuver for inclusion of the disenfranchised from the margins, literally, the many voices and multiplicity of perspectives and agencies felt, heard, and experienced that are often omitted from ethnographic representations because we tend to simplify "many voices" in exclusionary tight narratives that do violence to more inclusive historiographical perspectives.[19]

As such, Cupchik provides yet another side of the naming issue discussed in this essay. Yet, even though Cupchik finds Bakan's use of the term confusing, it is particularly suitable insofar as a lot of Sub-Saharan music emerges from speech sounded on musical instruments. "Ivory trumpet surrogate speech with its ensemble hocket catch-phrases is an oral tradition filled with historical meaning, contained in the metaphors of the denotative word-tones" (Kaminski 2003). Sometimes the speech comprises instructions for musicians or dancers, or is part of the ritual (Ampene, 2011), but the rhythm conforms to the larger formal structures, and not necessarily to a system of counting musical time. Taking "polyvocality" a little further, the term can represent salience of different kinds. In Berry's example above, for instance, sound signification includes "markers" of family kinship, but also various markers of instrumental, spiritual, social, and artistic status. For instance, instrumental prominence follows communal values and makes the grandmother drum the most important; the master drummer (even though a man) thus honors grandmothers. The large drum carries spiritual, social, and artistic connotations. Other instruments honor the family and the spirits of the ancestors and those of the yet unborn, and the status of each is implied in a way that reinforces social practices.

If one applied the categories of Mantle Hood's Instrument Classification System to this analysis, one would no doubt find additional markers of signification. The intrinsic sound is an icon of cultural value and practice.

The concept of marking musical time in interlocking, interactive forms is intellectual property with a long historical trajectory. To reduce such rich ideas to "meter" and "polyrhythm" is to ignore the true depth and meaning of a culture's social-intellectual outpouring. More to the point are terms like "melorhythm," which is a rhythmic cycle that produces a melody from the various interlocking tones (Kaminski 2003, after Nzemi 1997.) Ampene uses the concept in describing the music of the instrument that accompanies *nnwonkoro* today: "The keys on the *apreprensua* provide a melo-rhythmic background that simulates the tones and rhythms of the *atumpan* drums, inspiring the singers and dancers" (2005:33.) In addition to sounding a complete cycle (the process of maintenance), resultants can also be melodies and figures that emerge between the different interlocking lines, keeping each listening fresh, along with improvisational procedures that contextualize the event (the process of renewal).

Summary

There are a number of problems inherent in analyzing world music sound structures without simultaneously seeking to understand the cultural contexts, meanings, and concepts. Here I put on my Applied Ethnomusicology hat and argue for social engagement in a world that appears to be on the brink of disaster. The works of Nketia, Ampene, Agawu, Stone, and others, lead us to consider how African music can in fact be a force in the world. In this article I have suggested that the colonial practice of assigning Western names to non-Western subjects has clouded our abilities to accurately perceive difference in non-Western cultural forms of musical expression. In finding an ethnomusicological context for this study, I explored the possibility of classifying differing categories of ethnomusicological research along the same basic categories that Merriam proposed in 1964, with the potential for new and more encompassing categories, such as Sound Ethnomusicology(ies), Behavioral Ethnomusicology(ies), and the focus of this article, Conceptual Ethnomusicology(ies). Then I offered a two-part theory that emphasizes music's connections to life in real time, in an effort to demonstrate music's essential role in human survival. Only by truly understanding others do we begin to find value in difference. I have discussed Simha Arom's contentions surrounding the use of the term "meter," articulating Arom's and other scholars' informed bases for describing rhythmic "cycles." I clarify the social values that inform the musical sound of a Makorekore ensemble and conclude that this constitutes an intellectual history and is foundational as an African concept of music and the music event, and that the strength of this intellectual conception had gained momentum beyond its rootedness in Africa, and everywhere it is "a force in the world." Again I cite Ampene, who brings us back to Nketia:

> In addition to references to individuals and musical events, Africans conceptualize the organization of musical sound and structures within ensembles or solo performance as play or game. The incidence of call-and-response play in African musical practices is highly interactive resulting in what have been termed interactive structures. According to Nketia, interactive structures are evident in the manner in which the iron idiophones or gourd rattles, supporting drums and the leading drum converse among themselves and with dancers and singers. It is also evident in the participatory call and response at various levels in musical ensembles including the interaction between the lead singer and the chorus and the interactive response of the audience (Nketia, 1995:7.) It remains to be said that interactive structures encourage a dynamic (or communal) approach to the musical process as opposed to a contemplative or passive approach. The indigenous conception of music-making as play or game takes into account the rules of procedure, norms of behavior, and the decision of who takes part as an audience or a participant. In addition this concept may provide a framework for scholars to study the structures and procedures in African musical practices, including the rhythmic organization, as interactive structures (2005:63).

I have argued that music is essential to human survival, although I am not the first to consider this possibility. I have suggested that there is much to be learned from indigenous African conceptions of music, and I have offered glimpses at dynamic musical systems through the eyes and ears of some who have been the closest. More than merely musical innovations, I have demonstrated the depth of socio-musical articulation possible in forming a web of significance[20] that integrates life and death (maintenance) and helps to bring a new day (renewal).

Acknowledgments

I would like to take the opportunity to thank Emeritus Professor J. H. Kwabena Nketia for his groundbreaking work in African ethnomusicology. I also wish to thank Professor Akosua Adomako Ampofo, (Director, Institute of African Studies, University of Ghana, Legon), Dr. Akunu Dake (Chief Executive Officer, Heritage Development in Accra, Ghana), Dr. Kwasi Ampene (Director of the Center of World Performance Studies at the University of Michigan, Ann Arbor), and Dr. Godwin Adjei (Research Fellow a the Institute of African Studies, University of Ghana, Legon) for all their work in organizing the International Conference titled "The Life and Works of Emeritus Professor J. H. Kwabena Nketia" at the Institute of African Studies at the University of Ghana in South Legon on September 23 – 24, 2011. Midaasi! I would also like to thank Daniel Sher, Dean of the College of Music, University of Colorado at Boulder, for funding to attend the conference. Thanks also to Susan McClary and to Chris Berry for their inspiring talks so many years ago.

Endnotes

1: I have presented versions of this paper at the Joint American Musicological Society/Society for Music Theory Annual Conference in Nashville, Tennessee in November 2008; Music Colloquium at Wesleyan University, Middlebury, Connecticut in April 2010; Southwest Chapter of the Society for Ethnomusicology Annual Meeting in Tucson, Arizona in April 2010; and at the Society for Ethnomusicology Annual Meeting in Los Angeles, November 2010.

2: The qualifiers "micro-" and "macro-" can be applied differently in different contexts. With regard to *nnwonkoro*, Kwasi Ampene uses the term "macro-level" to refer to "a surface interactive structure represented by [. . .] the overarching cyclic form . . ." and the "micro-level of an archetypal song unit" as its "interactive substructure . . " (Ampene 2005:63-64). I am using "microanalysis" to represent the process that music theorists typically engage in, which is the analysis of sound structures at both Ampene's macro- and micro-levels. I am using "macro analysis" to imply a holistic approach toward understanding the overall social significance of the music, including that of its interactive substructures.

3: On a more spiritual note, the *Baha'i* Faith practitioners believe that at this time in history redemption is only possible through horizontal, or group effort. *Johrei* practitioners also believe that although vertical (individual) development is important, group work is most needed now. (The Baha'i Faith originated in Iran in the 1840s; *Johrei* originated in Japan in the second half of the twentieth century.)

4: "I have already examined how nnwonkoro songs are sometimes modeled on the *nsui*. If *nsui* mediate the continuity between life and death, then it is safe to conclude that nnwonkoro songs, modeled on *nsui* mediate the continuity between life and death. In other words, during funerary celebrations, nnwonkoro songs become a metaphor for mediating the continuity between life and death" (Note 1, Ampene, 2005:179).

5: "Lit. 'farewell'; traditional mourning cloth of the Akan stamped with symbols denoting Akan philosophy and religious beliefs" (Ampene 2005:xix).

6: Berry now lives in the United States, with residences in New York City and Hawaii. He recounts his terrifying experiences leaving Zimbabwe:

About why I'm no longer allowed in the country [Zimbabwe], well, number one, at first the president was very well respected and we all supported him – [almost inaudibly] Mugabe, but as he slowly started to turn, our songs started talking about, his, you know, what was going wrong and stuff and he didn't like that. Basically all the radio, all the media is run by the state, so if you stepped out of line from that you were reprimanded in very violent ways. So that was number one, but number two, he also thought for some reason that was never really true, that I was maybe part of the CIA, he's a bit paranoid, that I was part of a CIA you know, sort of mission, to like, get him out. So they sent – twice they tried to execute me while I was there, and finally I got away. But it was, you know, politics in Africa, well I guess everywhere, but really in Africa it's really dangerous.

I never meant to get involved. We were just trying to sing about what we saw going on...but that's what happened (http://www.youtube.com/watch?v=78XWcTswkeU), accessed May 31, 2012.

7: I have Chris Berry's permission to cite him in this paper.

8: Evidence that an anti-hegemonic genie is aloft, in 2005 one of my indigenous dissertation fieldwork sites changed names by popular vote from San Juan Pueblo (New Mexico) – or St. John's Village – to their pre-Hispanic name Ohkay Owingeh, or "Place of the Strong People."

9: One recalls that after the ancient Arabic translations of Greek writings (including those of Aristotle, the founder of Western "logic" and Alexander the Great's mentor) were found in Toledo, Spain early in the twelfth century, many Arabic words entered the West in translations for which there were no equivalents in Latin (Burke 1986). Presumably there would have been such words in Aristotle's specialized Greek, unless Alexander the Great or his Arabic scribes included (glossed) West Asian concepts when they first made the translations (circa the mid-330s B.C.E.), in a reverse process from Greek to Arabic.

10: Mark Slobin's observations that the growing decline in the term "multiculturalism" might stem from "the growing distrust of the distinctiveness of minority groups. They can now be seen as possible threats rather than as colorful chips in the social 'mosaic'" (108).

11: See also Edna Aurora C. Culig's "A Content Analysis of Asian-Pacific Folk Songs in American Elementary Music Textbooks from 1967 to 2008," doctoral dissertation in Music Education, University of Colorado at Boulder, Spring 2012. Culig discusses studies that coincide with Kang's assertion that "it is the in-depth investigation of a musical culture that produces understanding and interested engagement" (Kang, 51).

12: I remember a similar feeling of feeling forced to follow a rigid template for music, until I realized I was only learning a style.

13: In addition to myself (an ethnomusicologist-composer who looks forward to a time when I can get back to my compositions), faculty for the CMS Summer Institute on the Pedagogies of World Music Theories has included composer-ethnomusicologists Paul Humphreys (Loyola Marymount University), Jonathon Grasse (California State University, Dominguez Hills), and Michael Tenzer (University of British Colombia); systematic musicologist John Hajda (University of California, Santa Barbara); ethnomusicologist-composer-performers Münir Beken (University of California, Los Angeles) and Kwasi Ampene (now at the University of Michigan, Ann Arbor); and ethnomusicologist-performers Jay Keister (University of Colorado, Boulder), Sarah Morelli (University of Denver); and Victoria Lindsay Levine (the Colorado College).

14: Perhaps prematurely, music theorist Lawrence Shuster submits that a historical trajectory for this line of inquiry "has already been well established since the work of [composers] Robert Cogan and Pozzi Escot and ethnomusicologist Jay Rahn going way back to the mid 70's." Email correspondence with author, October 31, 2011.

15: See Beck, Peggy V., Anna L. Walters, and Nia Francisco. *Sacred Ways of Knowledge, Sources of Life*. Tsaile, AZ: Navajo Community College Press, 1992.

16: Middle Eastern concepts of time appear to syncretize the idea of cycle and meter, since a downbeat is important, but high and low pitch markers form a pattern that signifies a rhythmic mode with extra-musical connotations – a kind of "metric cycle," a classificatory term I use.

17: The *Dare* is the "spirit house," the home of the Makorekore community's patron spirit. Telephone interview with Chris Berry, July 15, 2012.

18: This may suggest African roots for the South American/Caribbean tradition of paired, gendered shakers, with the *macho* (male) pitched slightly higher than the *hembra* (female), although rattles were also used among pre-Columbian indigenous peoples of the Americas. *Macho* and *hembra* are Spanish terms.

19: Email communication with author, June 5, 2012. See also Cupchik's "Polyvocality and Forgotten Proverbs (and Persons): George Harrison, Ravi Shankar and Shambhu Das" (forthcoming), and Laura B. Lengel's "Researching the 'Other,' Transforming Ourselves: Methodological Considerations of Feminist Ethnography," in the *Journal of Communication Inquiry*, July 1998 vol. 22 no. 3 229-250.

20: See Clifford Geertz. "Thick Description: Toward an Interpretive Theory of Culture" in *The Interpretation of Cultures*. New York: Basic Books, 2000 ed. (1973): 3-32.

References

Agawu, Kofi. 2009. "Against Ethnotheory." Abstract for the 2009 Analytical Approaches to World Music Conference. http://www.analysisworldmusic.com/images/agawuaawmabstract.pdf, accessed in April 2009.

Ampene, Kwasi. 2005. *Female Song Tradition and the Akan of Ghana*. Burlington, VT: Ashgate Publishing Company.

___.2011. Personal communications with the author, September.

Arom, Simha. 1991. "Book 4: Theoretical Tools, I: The Notion of Relevance." In *African Polyphony and Polyrhythm*. Cambridge: Cambridge University Press, 137-75.

Bakan, Michael. 2007. *World Musics, Traditions and Transformations*. Boston: McGraw-Hill.

Beck, Peggy V., Anna L. Walters, and Nia Francisco. 1992. *Sacred Ways of Knowledge, Sources of Life*. Tsaile, AZ: Navajo Community College Press.

Berry, Chris. 1999. Guest lecture. University of Colorado at Boulder.

___.2012. Telephone interview with author, July 15.

___.2009. "Chris Berry Live Performance, #1, October 15. Relix, Chris Berry of Panjea." http://www.youtube.com/watch?v=78XWcTswkeU, accessed May 31, 2012.

Bohlman, Philip. 2010. Guest keynote presentation at the UCLA 50th Anniversary of Ethnomusicology Alumni Symposium, Los Angeles, California, November 9.

Burke, James. 1986. *The Day the Universe Changed* (television series). "In the Light of the Above." Written and presented by James Burke (Medieval Conflict: Faith and Reason #2), co-produced by BBC and RKO. Los Angeles, CA: Churchill Films.

Cupchik, Jeffrey Dwayne. "Polyvocality and Forgotten Proverbs (and Persons): Ravi Shankar, George Harrison, and Shambhu Das," forthcoming.

___.2012. Email correspondence with the author, July 5.

Hernández Salgar, Oscar. 2005: "El sonido de lo otro: Nuevas configuraciones de lo étnico en la industria musical," *Cuadernos De Música, Artes Visuales Y Artes Escénicas* 1/1: 4 – 22.

Hofstadter, Douglas R. 1985. *Metamagical Themas: Questing for the Essence of Mind and Pattern*. New York: Basic Books.

Hood, Mantle. 1982. *Ethnomusicology*. Kent, Ohio: Kent State University Press.

Jablonski, Nina G. 2006. *Skin, A Natural History*. Berkeley, Los Angeles, and London: University of California Press.

Kaemmer, John P. 1993. *Music in Human Life*. Austin: University of Texas Press.

Kaminski, Joseph S. 2003. "Asante Ivory Trumpets in Time, Place, and Context: An Analysis of a Field Study." *Historic Brass Society Journal* 15: 259-290.

Kang, YouYoung. 2006. "Defending Music Theory in a Multicultural Curriculum." *College Music Symposium, Journal of the College Music Society* 46: 45-63.

Kartomi, Margaret. 1990. *On Concepts and Classifications of Musical Instruments*. Chicago: University of Chicago Press.

Kisliuk, Michelle. 2008. "(Un) doing Fieldwork, Sharing Songs, Sharing Lives." In *Shadows in the Field: New Perspectives for Fieldwork in Ethnomusicology*. Ed. by Gregory Barz and Timothy Cooley. New York: Oxford University Press.

Kuss, Malena. 2004. "Prologue" to *Music in Latin America and the Caribbean, An Encyclopedic History, Volume 1: Performing Beliefs: Indigenous Peoples of South America, Central America, and Mexico.* Ed. by Malena Kuss. Austin: University of Texas Press, ix – xxvi.

Landau, Elizabeth. 2012. "Music: It's in Your Head, Changing Your Brain."– CNN.com. http://www.cnn.com/2012/05/26/health/mental-health/music-brain-science/index.html?hpt=hp_c2 accessed May 28, 2012.

Lengel, Laura B. 1998. "Researching the 'Other,' Transforming Ourselves: Methodological Considerations of Feminist Ethnography." *Journal of Communication Inquiry* 22 (3): 229-250.

McClary, Susan. 1998. "Rap, Minimalism, and Structures of Time in Late Twentieth-Century Culture." Public lecture, Boulder, University of Colorado. October 9.

Merriam, Alan P. 1969. "Review of *Venda Children's Songs: A Study in Ethnomusicological Analysis,* by John Blacking." *American Anthropologist* 71 (5):935 -37.

___. 1964. *The Anthropology of Music.* Illinois: Northwestern University Press.

Mukonyora, Isabel. 1999. "Women and Ecology in Shona Religion." *Word and World* 19 (3): 276-284.

Nketia, J. H. Kwabena. 1974. *The Music of Africa.* New York: W. W. Norton and Company, Inc.

Nzewi, Meki. 1997. *African Music: Theoretical Content and Creative Continuum.* Germany: Institute für Didaktik Populärer Musik.

Shuster, Lawrence. 2011. Email communication with the author, October 31.

Slobin. Mark. 2007. "Musical Multiplicity: Emerging Thoughts." *Yearbook for Traditional Music.* 39: 108-116.

Stone, Ruth M. 2005. *Music in West Africa. Experiencing Music, Expressing Culture Series.* New York: Oxford University Press.

Taylor, Stephen A. 1997. "Chopin, Pygmies, and Tempo Fugue: Ligeti's Automne a Varsovie." *Music Theory Online*, The Online Journal of the Society for Music Theory, Volume 3.3. http://www.mtosmt.org/issues/mto.97.3.3/mto.97.3.3.taylor.html#Section4 accessed May 2007.

Turino, Thomas. 2008. *Music in the Andes: Experiencing Music, Expressing Culture.* New York: Oxford University Press.

Wilbert, Johannes, ed. 1976. *Enculturation in Latin America.* Los Angeles: UCLA Latin American Center Publications, University of California.

Wild, Stephen A. 1982. "In Memoriam, Alan P. Merriam (1923 – 1980)." *Ethnomusicology. 25th Anniversary Issue.* Illinois: University of Illinois Press on behalf of the Society for Ethnomusicology 26 (1). January: 91-98.

Kete for the International Percussion Community

Ben Paulding

As a percussionist, Ben Paulding studied Akan royal drumming with Attah Poku at the Center for National Culture (CNC) in Kumase, Ghana. With the Nsuase Kete Group, he has performed at national events in addition to performing with the royal Fɔntɔmfrɔm group as part of court ceremonies at the Manhyia Palace in Kumase. He is currently a graduate student at Tufts University where he is a lead drummer for Professor David Locke's Agbekor Drum and Dance Society and Attah Poku's Kete Ensemble.

Introduction

"Kete for the International Percussion Community" answers Emeritus Professor J.H. Kwabena Nketia's call for preservation of traditional Ghanaian culture by presenting Kete in Western notation for drummers around the world. The paper begins by briefly introducing the reader to Ashanti government, which is the original context of Kete drumming. Thorough musical analysis – including a musical overview, instrument construction, playing techniques, timeline analysis, extensive scores and transcriptions, and an explanation of lead drumming – makes up the majority of the paper. Encouraged by Professor Nketia's usage of traditional music as inspiration for musical creativity, the paper ends with an exploration of Kete rhythms adapted to the drumset.

The Importance of Archiving Traditional Ghanaian Culture

In 1998, Professor J.H. Kwabena Nketia delivered a paper entitled "The Challenge of Cultural Preservation in a Dynamic Social Environment," in which he outlines the need for traditional Ghanaian culture to be preserved and transferred into contemporary settings. He laments that the active approach towards African cultural revival, popular during the post-independence period, has been losing momentum in Ghana. As one of many methods of promoting traditional culture in modern society, Professor Nketia encourages archiving traditional music using modern technology, and making these resources available to composers, performers, and educators (Akrofi 2002: 136-139).

The Target Audience

This paper is written for the modern international percussion community, which is represented by organizations such as the Percussive Arts Society and publications such as *Modern Drummer* and *Drum!* magazine. This community centers around drumset, classical repertoire, and marching percussion performance. Increasingly, members of this community show interest in so-called "world percussion" traditions such as Afro-Cuban drumming, Brazilian samba, Indian percussion, and West African drumming. Although useful for percussionists with experience in Ghanaian drumming, this paper presents musical content in a way that any proficient percussionist from around the world – experienced in African music or not – could use it to learn to play a simple version of Kete. As a performing percussionist experienced in multiple genres of music from across the globe, I have found Kete one of the most exciting and challenging pieces I have yet to encounter in my musical career.

This paper serves as my contribution to help share the incredible drumming of this Ashanti masterpiece with percussionists who would otherwise not have the opportunity to hear, study, or perform this music. As it is written by a performing percussionist and directed towards performing percussionists, this paper utilizes the language of the modern international percussion community rather than the language of ethnomusicology.

Need for Information on Kete

Unfortunately, in the percussion performance world, there is still only modest literature on Ghanaian drumming, even less on Ashanti drumming, and in my search, none at all on Kete. However, there are a few valuable scholarly resources on Kete. Professor J.H. Kwabena Nketia's book *Drumming in Akan Communities* provides an excellent resource to understanding the history, cultural purpose, and drum language of Kete. James Koetting's Master's thesis, *An Analytical Study of Asante Kete Drumming*, thoroughly describes Kete from an ethnomusicologist's point of view. Still, there is nothing aimed to teach Kete, nothing with full scores in staff notation, and nothing that systematically "breaks down" the music for a percussionist interested in learning Kete. My paper will augment the aforementioned works by providing an educational "how-to" guide for performing percussionists throughout the world.

Methodology

The information in this paper is primarily based on my two study trips to the Ashanti region of Ghana. In January 2009, I traveled to Ashanti Mampong with a University of Massachusetts Dartmouth group led by Professors Royal Hartigan and Kwabena Boateng. I studied Kete drumming and dancing with Daniel Annan Sackey, Ernest Domfeh, and John Boame, all of the Centre for National Culture, Kumasi. In September 2011, I travelled to Kumasi to study Kete with Emmanuel Attah Poku. We worked primarily at the Centre for National Culture, Manhyia Palace, and with Attah's youth Kete group in Ampabame, Kumasi.

Ashanti Culture and Government

The Ashanti people (also spelled Asante) are a subgroup of a larger ethnic group known as the Akan. Within Ghana, the Akan are approximately forty-five percent of the total population, and primarily inhabit the Brong-Ahafo, Ashanti, Eastern, Central, and Western Regions (*Rhythms of Life* 1996:3). The Ashanti Region – home to the Ashanti people – is the fourth largest region in Ghana by land area, and has a population of 3,612,950 (Kyeremateng 2004). The origin of the Ashanti people is not universally agreed upon. Clear records of the Ashanti empire emerge around 1700 when the first Asantehene, Osei Tutu I, consolidated power over local states around Kumasi, which then became the capital of the Ashanti empire (Kwadwo 2004: 6-13). Since the rule of Osei Tutu I, the Ashantis have maintained a centralized government, led by the Asantehene from Manhyia Palace in Kumasi. The Asantehene, who rules for life once put into power, reigns over a hierarchy of rulers that includes subsidiary chiefs throughout his empire. His public appearances at important cultural events are always made grand and prestigious with the presence of traditional drumming, dancing, and singing. Because Ashanti inheritance is matrilineal, the Asantehene is chosen by the Queen Mother. Since Ghana's independence, the traditional Ashanti governing system remains, but is subservient to the national government created in 1957.

History of Kete

There are many stories on the origin on Kete. Some claim that Kete was originally played by super human creatures (*mmoatia*) and discovered by hunters in their trips to the bush. Others allege that Kete was captured in war from the Gyaman people of the Brong-Ahafo region. Some simply say the origin of Kete is unknown (*Asante Kete Drumming* 2004:4). One particularly interesting account of Kete's history is recalled in an interview with Nana Sarfo, Deputy Director of the Centre for National Culture, Kumasi. Sarfo explained that Kete was composed by a divine drummer named Kyrema Opong and was given to the Asantehene as a gift. The story begins:

He [Kyrema Opong] committed an unpardonable offense against the stool [a symbol of the Ashanti kingdom]. Because of that, he was summoned before the chiefs and the people, and he was found guilty. And he was condemned to death. But, because of his ingenuity in drumming, they decided that they should spare his life until he [trained] somebody to replace him (Sarfo 2011).

This divine drummer, ashamed to be seen in public, went to the bush to await his punishment. While there, he spent his days listening to the sounds of nature. The sound of water passing over rocks in the river led him to create the *kwadum*, and the high-pitched chirping of birds led him to create *aburukwa*. He joined these parts together with apentema and petia, and presented the music of Kete to the Asantehene as a gift for temporarily sparing his life. Opong covered the drums with red and black checkered fabric to symbolize his fate: black to represent sitting in darkness, waiting to die, and red to show that his blood would soon flow. These colors are still used on Kete drums inside of Manhyia palace. While some people use these colors throughout Ghana, my teachers used different color schemes, asserting that the red and black be reserved for the Asantehene.

Historical and Contemporary Usage of Kete

In his groundbreaking book, *Drumming in Akan Communities*, Professor J.H. Kwabena Nketia thoroughly describes the original cultural context of Kete. The chapter "State Drumming," which includes Kete, Fontomfrom, Apirede, and Mpintin, explicitly describes the purpose of Kete in Ashanti society. Professor Nketia begins by defining state drumming as "a comprehensive term for all forms of drumming which are directly associated with the chieftaincy" (Nketia:119). He then proceeds to describe the usage of state drumming within traditional government:

With the exception of village headmen who usually have no drums, every important chief has special music played for him on state occasions. Much of this music is provided by drums kept in his palace and regarded as part of the stool regalia. In the past many of the drums and drum ensembles of chiefs could not be privately owned or played without the permission of the chief; nor could they be played at any time other than that laid down by custom and tradition. No chief would attend a durbar or a festival without a retinue of drums and drummers (Nketia 1963: 119-122).

In his essay *The Protection of Choreographic Works in Ghana,* W. Ofotsu Adinku describes how Kete first left the walls of the Asantehene's palace. Ghana's first president, Kwame Nkrumah, formed the Ghana Dance Ensemble in 1962 to perform music from all over Ghana in order to foster a sense of national identity and discourage separation of Ghana's multiple ethnic groups. Professor Nketia was appointed Director of the new ensemble, and his friend Professor Mawere Opoku became Artistic Director. Opoku faced the challenge of adapting traditional cultural dances for the stage and trying to make them exciting for seated audiences. To use and choreograph Kete, Opoku asked Asantehene Sir Nana Osei Agyemang Prempeh II in 1963 for permission to use the court music in public. Permission was granted, and the Ghana Dance Ensemble helped spread Kete throughout Ghana, and eventually, worldwide (Adinku 200: 351-354). Today, Kete is still played in the palace of the Asantehene. In addition, it has taken on a central role at cultural ceremonies, such as funerals, throughout the Ashanti region. Kete is also common in the repertoire of cultural troupes throughout the nation such as the Kumasi Cultural Centre and the Ghana Dance Ensemble. In recent decades, Ghanaian teachers have taught Kete to students from many nations, adding it to the repertoire of African music ensembles worldwide.

Musical Overview of Kete
A full Kete performance consists of drumming and dancing. Performances of Kete in the Asantehene's palace utilize melodic pipes, however, most public performances use only drums. Professor Nketia writes about vocal interludes which are sung to help the listener understand the meaning of the language in the drumming (Nketia 1963:128). As pipes and vocals are no longer common in public performances of Kete, they will not be examined in this paper. It should be noted that the ultimate purpose of Kete drumming is to accompany dance. "The dancing ring," as it is called by Professor Nketia, allows Akan people the chance to express themselves publicly. Virtually all Ashanti drummers can dance, at least to a basic level. Understanding the dance is vital to understanding the feel of the drumming. Although this paper will make constant mention to elements of the dance (such as the rhythm of the dancers footsteps and the interaction with the lead drum) this paper is ultimately written for drummers and concerned primarily with the music of Kete, and will make no attempt to fully explain the dance.

There are eight instruments in Kete, each played by an individual drummer. The eight instruments, to be discussed in more detail in the next section, are *kwadum, apentema, aburukwa, petia, donno, ntrowa,* and two *dawuro*. The drummers play sitting side by side, sitting in individual chairs. Looking at the ensemble from the "audience" point of view, the arrangement of drums from left to right is as follows: *aburukwa, kwadum, apentema, petia*. The people playing *dawuro, ntrowa,* and *donno* sit or stand behind the drummers, in no particular arrangement.

Kete has at least seventeen different sections with their own distinct names, many of which share the same timekeeping rhythms, but each of which have their own unique support and lead drum parts. The seventeen sections of Kete, as taught by Emmanuel Attah Poku, are *Kwekwe Nisuo, Akwaduom, Adamrebua, Abofoo, Adabanka, Adowa Kete, Adaban, Wofa-Ata, Kyeretwie, Kyremateng, Apente, Akatape, Ohenko, Akokonobete, Akyakyakuntu, Sresrebidi*, and *Adinkra*. Each section can be played separately, or can be linked together at the master drummer's discretion. Kete performances can vary greatly in length and content. A contemporary cultural troupe such as the Centre For National Culture in Kumasi can play a choreographed arrangement of Kete that includes multiple sections in just five to ten minutes (see "Traditional Ashanti Dancers and Drummers" video for an example). At a funeral, on the other hand, it is common to play one section of Kete for fifteen minutes straight, then stop, then play another section for another fifteen minutes. To change from section to section, the master drummer simply plays the basic *kwadum* pattern for the new section he wants to change to, and the rest of the drummers follow. This is usually done without change in tempo or dynamics. In this paper, two sections of Kete will be examined: *Abofoo* and *Akwaduom*. These two sections are common in Kete performances, and are representative of standard Kete rhythms on *dawuro, ntrowa, donno,* and *petia*. They also offer variety by demonstrating a slow section (*Abofoo*) and a fast section (*Akwaduom*).

To start the drumming, the lead drummer cues the timeline instruments by playing the lead dawuro rhythm on the *kwadum*, starting on the second stroke of the measure. As soon as the *dawuro* player hears this, he begins to play his part, and the other timeline instruments join with their rhythms quickly. To cue the drums, the master drummer plays the basic *kwadum* phrase for any section of Kete (to be discussed in detail below), and the support drummers join with their parts as soon as they recognize which section the master drummer is playing. There is also an optional introduction that can be used to start any 12/8 section of Kete (see Figure 1 in Appendix). To stop the ensemble when he wants the drumming to finish, the master drummer can simply stop playing his rhythm, and start quietly making noise on the *kwadum,* telling the other drummers to stop. There is also a specific ending phrase that can be used to end any section of Kete, except for *Apente* or *Akonkonobete*, which are in 4/4 instead of 12/8. This phrase, started by the kwadum, is often played at a slower tempo than the preceding section of drumming.

As soon as the drummers hear the call, they adjust to the new tempo and play the unison ending phrase with the *kwadum* (see Figure 2 in Appendix).

In terms of tempo, it is common to start a Kete performance relatively slowly, then build up the speed gradually over time. For a general reference, a slow Kete performance would be around dotted quarter note = 90-100 BPM. A normal performance would be around dotted quarter note = 150-160 BPM. At its peak, a fast performance can reach slightly upwards of dotted quarter note = 200 BPM. Attah Poku told me that good Kete drummers intentionally start slow and relaxed, and build speed during the course of the performance. For example, every track on the Nsuase Kete CD (*Asante Kete Drumming*) significantly speeds up from the beginning to the end. In terms of dynamics, Kete is virtually always played loud. As the music gets faster, it is standard for volume to increase as well. The only limit on volume is often the drummer's physical strength and stamina; the goal (especially on *petia*) is often to play as loud as possible!

One aspect of Kete that will not be considered in this paper is the Twi poetry and proverbs embedded in the drumming. Many of the rhythms of Kete, particularly the *kwadum* phrases, are set with accompanying words in Twi. These poems can praise chiefs, insult rivals, and offer bits of ancient wisdom. As this paper is focused on the music of Kete, the meaning of the drumming will not be examined. Detailed explanation of seven poems embedded in Kete drumming can be found on pages 128-133 of *Drumming in Akan Communities* (Nketia 1963). For more valuable insight into the meaning in Akan court music, including Kete, see Kwasi Ampene's upcoming book *Experience and Values in Akan Court Music.*

Instruments

The *dawuro* is a boat-shaped iron bell, struck with a small metal beater. Its sound is loud and penetrating, which is appropriate for its role of being the main rhythmic point of reference for the dancers and the other drummers in the ensemble. There are three strokes on the *dawuro*: open, muted, and a buzz stroke that is in between open and muted (see Figure 3 in Appendix). The *dawuro* plays a repeating ostinato phrase that all of the other parts are based around. The Kete ensemble has two *dawuros*: a larger, lower-pitched lead dawuro that plays the main bell pattern, and a slightly smaller, higher-pitched support *dawuro* that plays a complimentary phrase. The *ntrowa* is a gourd rattle filled with seeds, shells, or pebbles. Normally, the *ntrowa* is held in the strong hand, and is quickly swished clockwise to create is signature sound, which has a relatively long duration and an attack that is not as defined as the drums of the Kete ensemble (see Figure 4 in Appendix). Its purpose is to embellish the timeline, as set by the two *dawuro* parts.

Donno is a double-headed hourglass shaped tension drum that is normally played while standing up. It is held in the left armpit, and played with a curved stick held in the right hand (opposite for left-handed people). The *donno* has many possible pitches that can be controlled by manipulating the strings on the side of the drum (see Figure 5 in Appendix). The *donno*, which is a relatively quiet instrument, has the most room for improvisation out of all the drums in the Kete ensemble. *Petia* is a short, medium-wide drum that is fairly loud and is the lowest pitched support drum. Because it is a single headed drum, the *petia* is tilted slightly away from the drummer by placing a stick or similar object underneath the side of the drum closest to the player. It is played with straight drumsticks and has two tones: open and attack stroke (see Figure 6 in Appendix). Throughout this paper, I use the term attack stroke to describe the stroke when one stick presses into the head, raising the pitch and muting the drum, and the other stick plays an open stroke. This sound, similar to an Ewe "*to*," is loud and highlights the attack of the stick hitting a muted head. *Petia* has two predominant patterns that it plays for many sections: one generally used for slow sections, and one generally used for fast. It has other unique patterns it plays for sections like *Apente* and *Adaban*, which have different timeline patterns as well.

Aburukwa is a high-pitched, single-headed drum. Like *petia*, it is also tilted away from the drummer by placing a stick or similar object underneath the drum. *Aburukwa* is played with two long, straight sticks that are almost flat when hitting the drum, just shy of a rimshot. Like *petia*, the *aburukwa* is played with sticks and utilizes the open and attack strokes (see Figure 7 in Appendix). *Aburukwa* significantly adds to the unique rhythmic design of each section of Kete, as it has a different part for almost every section, and is one of the loudest, most penetrating instruments in the ensemble. It interlocks tightly with the *kwadum*. The *apentema* is also a high-pitched single-headed drum. The drum rests on the ground and is held between the legs at an angle slightly tilted away from the player. It is struck with the hands and produces two main tones: open and mute. The mutes on the *apentema* are played loud for mutes: in practice, they often sound almost like closed slaps. There are two other tones occasionally used on the *apentema*: muted slap and bass tone (see Figure 7 in Appendix). The *apentema* plays highly syncopated ostinato figures that contribute to the rich polyrhythmic texture of the Kete ensemble.

The master drum is known as the *kwadum*. It is a wide drum that produces a thunderous, deep tone when struck with curved sticks, known in Twi as *nkonta*. It has three strokes: open, mute, and attack (see Figure 9 in Appendix). It should be noted that almost anywhere an attack stroke is notated for *kwadum*, it can be played at a range of dynamics. The standard dynamic is forte, and at that volume, an attack stroke functions exactly as described above. However, when the lead drummer wants to give more emphasis to the open strokes, or is simply getting tired, he can play a medium or soft stroke with the same technique as an attack stroke. A soft stroke with attack stroke technique yields a sound that functions more as a muted ghost note, in that it is used more to keep time than for its actual sound. Also on the notation key on Figure 10 (see Appendix) are flams, which are notated in traditional Western notation, but are always played with both hands at even volumes, which is almost always loud. The *kwadum* also utilizes ghost notes with open and mute strokes, which are in the notation as normal noteheads in parenthesis. Being the master drum, the *kwadum* is responsible for starting the music, transitioning between sections, setting the tempo, interacting with the dancers, and ending the music. Its parts are the most complex and change most often out of all the instruments in the ensemble. Playing the drum requires a thorough knowledge of the drum ensemble and the dance.

Timeline Analysis
The main body of Kete drumming is in 12/8, with an underlying pulse of four dotted quarter notes. Even though the Kete dance is beyond the scope of this paper, it is useful to consider the rhythm of the dancers footsteps in understanding the drumming. Through most of Kete, the dancers step to the pulse of two dotted half notes per measure. This half time feel is fundamentally important to feeling the groove of Kete. As Kete is often played at tempos up to 200 BPM, the fastest underlying

subdivision is the eighth note. There are two constantly underlying polyrhythms which are felt in relation to the dotted quarter note pulse: a layer of six quarter notes (6 over 4), and a layer of three half notes (3 over 4) (see Figure 9 in Appendix). For the unfamiliar listener learning to play Kete, it is important to always keep the dotted quarter note pulse in mind. 12/8 can easily be heard "in three" as 3/4, but this does not represent the groove of the music as expressed by the dancer's footsteps. In his article "It's Not A Waltz! Understanding the Triplet Feel in Afro-Centric Music," percussionist Michael Spiro explains that in virtually all 12/8 African-based music, the groove is felt as four beats, each with three subdivisions (triplets), as opposed to three beats, each with four sixteenth note subdivisions. Kete is no exception. The incorrect feel of 3/4 is shown in Figure 10 (see Appendix), and the correct feel of 12/8 is shown in Figure 11 (see Appendix).

According to Attah Poku, Kete is traditionally played in Manhyia Palace with only one *dawuro*. This phrase utilizes seven strokes, and is only one stroke different from the Standard 12/8 Bell (see Figure 12 in Appendix). It is comprised of all open strokes: four accented and three unaccented. In my two trips to the Ashanti region, however, every group I heard or performed with used two dawuros. In an attempt to convey how Kete is currently played, I will present the patterns for two basic interlocking *dawuro* patterns, as taught by Daniel Sackey and Ernest Domfeh (see Figure 13 in Appendix). Like the clave in Afro-Cuban music or the *gankogui* in Ewe music, the lead *dawuro* pattern is the main rhythmic point of reference for all musicians and dancers. The lead dawuro has four strokes: 1 – on beat one, 2 – on the 2nd partial of beat two, 3 – on the 2nd partial of beat three, and 4 – on beat four. It aligns with the dotted quarter notes on beats four and one, and plays with the basic ntrowa pattern on the second partial of beats two and three.

There is a secondary support *dawuro* pattern played on a higher pitched instrument that interlocks with the main pattern to fully set the time for the drumming ensemble. The two patterns connect to create a composite rhythm that is similar to the bell pattern of other Akan dances like *Adowa* and *Adenkum* (Hartigan 1995: 35, 51). In the composite melody created by the two tones, the support dawuro plays a high pitched "quarter note triplet" around the downbeat, and the lead dawuro plays on the second partial of beats two and three, resolving to beat four.

One approach to learning the Kete bell is to understand it in relation to the "Standard 12/8 Bell" used in many African traditions and specifically in Ghana for Ewe pieces such as Agbadza and Atsiagbekor. There is a reduced version of this pattern, used for pieces like *Fume Fume*, *Fofui*, and *Adzrowo*. The reduced pattern omits the 4th and 7th strokes of the Standard 12/8 Bell, leaving a pattern that is possible to play at a very fast tempo. This pattern is known in Afro-Cuban music as "Triple 3-2 Son Clave." By omitting the second stroke of the reduced 12/8 bell, it turns into the Kete bell (see Figure 14 in Appendix). There are three main *ntrowa* patterns for Kete (see Figure 15) in Appendix), but in the most basic pattern it plays off beats two, three, and four, specifically on the second partial of beats two, three, and four. The basic function of this rhythm is to reinforce the *dawuro* part, and to provide strong offbeat accents. It is possible to omit the second of the three rattle strokes, and also, to simply sound out the dancers' dotted half note pulse. The first *ntrowa* pattern described above is very common in Ashanti music. Some 4/4 Ashanti pieces like *Sikyi* and *Apente* use a binary version of this pattern which is on the "and" of beats two, three, and four.

Kete: Abofoo

Abofoo, which is traditionally used as hunters music, is often played first to start a Kete performance. Although it can be played at any tempo, Abofoo is often played slowly, although it does normally build to a medium tempo over time. *Abofoo* uses the standard Kete timekeeping rhythms described in the "Timeline Analysis" section. On top of this foundation, the *donno* improvises on a two-stroke phrase on the first and third of every three quarter notes. This pattern repeats every two beats and reinforces the dotted half note feel. The transcribed *donno* part is the most basic pattern played on the drum; in performance it is merely a springboard for traditional variations. Experienced players enjoy the freedom to play unique improvised phrases as long as they fit with the timeline and stay within the idiom of traditional Ashanti rhythmic vocabulary (see Figure 16 in Appendix). The *Abofoo petia* part is the standard petia rhythm for the slower sections of Kete. An attack stroke fills in the gap between the first two strokes of the lead bell, and then three open strokes lead up to beat four. Because it plays directly on beat on beats three and four, the petia is the easiest part for many Western percussionists to play in Kete.

The *aburukwa* repeats a two-beat phrase that also reinforces the half time feel. The part consists of four consecutive 8th notes that straddle the first and third dotted quarter notes. Specifically, the third *aburukwa* stroke lines up with beats one and three. The *apentema* part is challenging. It utilizes eight of the twelve possible 8th notes in 12/8, but not one of them is on the beat. It plays every offbeat partial, which is very common for the apentema in Kete. For *Abofoo*, it has open strokes off beats four and one, which are the beats where the dawuro aligns with the basic pulse. While its open strokes surround the downbeat, the *apentema* plays mute strokes off beats two and three, or directly around the second dotted half note of the measure (beat two of the half time feel).

The basic *kwadum* phrase is a repeating two-beat phrase with three strokes: an attack stroke on beat one, then a two open strokes leading up to beat two. This same three-stroke phrase repeats starting on beat three. The attack strokes of the basic *kwadum* pattern directly outline the half time feel of *Abofoo*. The open strokes of the lead drum phrase fall directly in the gaps of the *aburukwa* rhythm (see Figure 17 in Appendix). Together, the two parts utilize all twelve of the 8th notes in the measure. It is very common for the *kwadum* and *aburukwa*, the two instruments most responsible for creating the distinct rhythmic texture of each section of Kete, to tightly interlock with each other.

There are many set variations on the basic rhythm that the *kwadum* can play at will. To a large degree, the arrangement of these traditional variations makes up what is considered to be a drummer's improvisation. In performance, the arrangement of these variations is highly dependant on the movements of the dancer, which again, is beyond the scope of this paper. When learning Kete, it is best to play the variations as they are written. A highly experienced player, however, has the liberty to improvise and create unique variations on the basic, often inspired by drum language texts. Figure 18 (see Appendix) shows sixteen of the traditional variations for *Abofoo*. The first five, A-E, are one measure patterns that are essentially used as fills during the basic. For example, the *kwadum* could play two measures of basic, one measure of variation A, three measures of basic, one measure of variation D, two measures of basic, then one measure of variation B. These patterns are almost never repeated more than twice in a row, for they need to maintain their character as fills that are embellishments to the basic pattern. Variations

F, G, and H are two measure patterns that are used the same way as A-E: as fills played during the basic. Variation I is a three measure version of the same concept.

Variations J-P are often used when Abofoo starts to speed up. They heavily use mutes, which are less fatiguing to play than attack strokes, especially at lively tempos. Unlike A-I, variations J-L can be repeated. Variation J can provide something of a temporary B section during the basic. For example, the *kwadum* could play the basic (interspersed with variations A-H) for two minutes, variation J for thirty seconds, then the basic for another minute. As variation J contains mutes, it can also be used with variations K-P, to be discussed below. Variations K-P as a whole constitute a true B section for the *kwadum* in *Abofoo*. Once the kwadum plays any of these variations, it usually stays in the K-P category for at least a minute before returning to the basic. Variation K is the simplest, least physically demanding reduction of the basic. It can be used when the lead drummer needs to rest, or to provide contrast immediately after an intense section of drumming. Variation K can be repeated. Variation L is a two measure embellishment of K that can also be repeated. Variations M-P are two measure variations which are simply created by adding strokes from variations A, B, C, and E into a two measure template of variation K. Specifically, the third partial of beat two through the second partial of beat four from A, B, C, or E is added (literally copy and pasted in the notation) into the first measure of two bars of K. To save the reader from having to figure these out, I have transcribed these four rhythms. M=A, N=B, O=C, and P=E.

Kete: Akwaduom
Akwaduom is an energetic section of Kete which is often played at a fast tempo. Like *Abofoo*, it uses the standard timekeeping rhythms described in the "Timeline Analysis" section. It also has the same basic *donno* pattern described in the *Abofoo* section. The *petia* plays its standard phrase used for most of the fast sections of Kete. This phrase intensely drives the music forward, as it is played extremely loud and on top of the beat. It directly outlines the fundamental pulse of four dotted quarter notes by playing a dotted quarter note on beats one and three, and two consecutive eighth notes (followed by an eighth note rest) on beats two and four. This rhythm is common in the Ghanaian drumming repertoire: it is the *gankogui* pattern for the Ewe dance *Husago*, one of the hand drum support patterns for *Fume Fume*, and also the bell pattern

for the *Atopretia* section of *Fontomfrom*, to name a few (see Figure 19 in Appendix).

The *aburukwa* part for *Akwaduom* is hard to play and is virtually impossible to accurately capture in Western notation. The score offers two interpretations of the rhythm, although the actual rhythm lies in a gray area in between these two written rhythms. The first transcription is the closest possible way to quantize the *aburukwa* pattern into the grid of twelve eighth notes. In this interpretation, it plays open strokes on the first, third, sixth, eighth, ninth, and twelfth eighth notes. In reality, the second half of this phrase (breaking the phrase into two motifs, each made of three strokes), is slightly more evenly spread out. A way to represent this is to keep the first motif (twelfth, first, and third eighth notes) the same, but to stretch the second motif into three notes with even rhythmic value. The second motif consists of three dotted sixteenth note upbeats: the "a" of two, and the "e" and "a" of three. This is a slightly more accurate way to represent the rhythm, especially when played fast. Again, the actual aburukwa phrase lies somewhere in between these two transcribed rhythms. The last two strokes of the second motif are slightly more spread out than they appear in interpretation 1, but are slightly closer than they appear in interpretation 2. The *aburukwa* has a specific response for *ndwamu*, which will be discussed below. The *apentema* has two phrases for *Akwaduom* that are both played in response to specific calls from the *kwadum*. Response 1 is the same as the apentema part for *Abofoo*: open strokes off beats four and one, mute strokes off beats two and three. Whenever the *kwadum* changes to one of its other parts for *Akwaduom*, the *apentema* responds with a phrase that still utilizes all eight upbeats, but places the open strokes off of beats one and three.

Akwaduom is a complex and rich section for *kwadum*. There are three basic parts for *kwadum*, each with its own variations and each with its own corresponding *apentema* pattern. These parts are labeled 1, 2, and 3 on the transcription on Figure 20 (see Appendix). The structure of these lead drum rhythms is different than *Abofoo*. For parts 1 and 2, there is no basic rhythm that the *kwadum* constantly returns to. All of the variations within each part are used freely and interchangeably. Part 3 does have a basic, and functions similarly to the *kwadum* rhythms in *Abofoo*. The master drummer usually stays in each part (1, 2, or 3) for at least 8-10 measures before moving on to another part. It is normal play each part more than one time; for example, to play 1, 2, 1, 3, 1, 2. Part 1 is usually the starting point for *Akwaduom*, and therefore, is the part that is transcribed on the score on Figure 19 (see Appendix). Within all six variations on part 1 (separated by double bar lines in the transcription), the *kwadum* is active inside of beats two and three, but plays dotted quarter notes on beats four and one. These dotted quarter notes make room for the open strokes on the *apentema*, which are on the upbeats off of beats four and one (*Apentema* Response A). To change to part 2, the *kwadum* can play the three measure transition notated in Figure 20 (see Appendix) only when coming from part 1, (see Appendix) or can just move straight into figure (coming from any of the parts). The first variation on part 2 has a dotted quarter note attack stroke on beat one, three eighth notes on beat two, a dotted eighth note on beat three, and two eighth notes followed by an eighth note rest on beat four. The other three variations are created by adding a flam to this phrase, or substituting some of the open strokes for mutes. The *apentema* responds to part two by still playing all the eighth note upbeats, but playing its open strokes off beats one and three (Response B).

Part 3 normally follows the intensification or *ndwamu*, both to be discussed below. The first two-measure variation (with the dotted eighth notes) functions as the basic for part 3, as it is played the majority of the time in part 3. The second two-measure variation functions as a fill, similarly to how the transcribed variations for *Abofoo* function within the basic. The *apentema* also plays response B for part 3. In fact, the apentema plays response B for everything in *Akwaduom* except for part 1.

The *kwadum* has two other rhythms it can play during *Akwaduom*. One, called *ndwamu* (see Figure 21 in Appendix), directs the dancers to do an intensified movement which is called "pairing" at the Centre for National Culture in Kumasi. There are two versions of *ndwamu*, the first being the basic, and the second being a more spacious version of the basic that is twice as long. The master drummer first plays a one measure introduction, then can play either the basic or the two measure version, repeating the pattern for around 4-8 measures. Sometimes, the lead drummer will start with the two measure version, then go to the basic, but not the other way around. *Ndwamu* has a specific ending phrase which is played slightly differently by many players, but is transcribed as taught by Attah Poku. *Ndwamu* utilizes *apentema* response B, as well as a specific *aburukwa* phrase that is notated on the transcription.

During *Akwaduom*, the *kwadum* can play a phrase that is used in multiple sections of Kete, such as *Kwekwe Nisuo* and *Adowa Kete*. This phrase has no name in Twi, so for the purposes of this paper, it will be called the intensification. The intensification brings a notable change to the feel of the drumming, as it includes a highly syncopated rhythm based based out of a binary feel, which is represented in 12/8 as upbeat dotted sixteenths. Like *ndwamu,* there can be variation from player to player in the ending phrase of the intensification. The version I have transcribed is the version I learned from Attah Poku. The intensification also calls the *apentema* to play response B (see Figure 22 in Appendix). All Kete lead drumming, but especially phrases like *ndwamu* and the intensification, are directly related to the movement of the dancers. While these phrases can be learned at a basic level from my transcriptions, the ability to interact with dancers as a highly nuanced art that is best learned in person.

Kete for Drumset
I first met Professor Nketia in 2009 when I was traveling with the Kekeli West African Drum and Dance Ensemble from the University of Massachusetts Dartmouth. Speaking to a group of American music students who had just spent three weeks studying Kete in his hometown of Ashanti Mampong, Professor Nketia surprised me with his advice. He urged us to use the traditional Ghanaian music we had learned as inspiration for our own creative composing. When I got home, I took Professor Nketia's advice by trying to adapt Kete to my main instrument: drumset. I was delighted to find that Kete works quite nicely on drumset as many of its rhythms are complex yet sparse, in that there usually are no mutes in the support drum rhythms (except for *apentema*), so they are possible to play with one limb while playing drumset. There are many different ways to orchestrate Kete rhythms onto the drumset. I will explain and notate two approaches that have worked well in my playing: one uses Kete rhythms for world jazz (similar to how Latin rhythms have been adapted to drumset), the other tries to closely replicate the sound of an entire Kete drumming ensemble.

The first approach is to use Kete rhythms as an inspiration for creative drumming. A simple way to start is to take three rhythms from Kete and use them as ostinatos, then to improvise with one limb. In groove 1 (see Figure 23 in Appendix), the right hand plays the lead *dawuro* on the ride, the right foot plays the dotted half note pulse on the bass, and the left foot plays the basic *ntrowa* phrase on the hi hat. Groove 2 is the same, but with dotted quarter notes on the bass drum. After working out some basic independence (I recommend playing pages 61-69 from Horacio Hernandez' *Conversations In Clave* in the left hand over grooves 1 and 2), try playing support and lead rhythms from various sections of Kete in the left hand. Figure 23 shows a smapling of phrases from *Akwaduom* on the left hand. Groove 3 uses *petia*, groove 4 uses *aburukwa*, groove 5 uses the *aburukwa* response to *ndwamu,* groove 6 uses *apentema* response A, groove 7 uses *apentema* response B, groove 8 uses a simplified version of *kwadum* part 1, and 9 uses a slightly simplified version of *ndwamu*. Once these patterns are mastered, they can be used as a basis for creative improvisation.

Another approach to adapting these rhythms to drumset is to try to closely replicate the sound of a traditional Kete ensemble. In my experimentation, this has been best accomplished by having two percussionists: one drumset player, and one drummer playing *kwadum*. The drumset player can replicate almost the entire Kete support ensemble by playing lead *dawuro* with the right foot on a jam block or cowbell, *ntrowa* with the left foot on the hi hat (or the LP Hi Hat Shekere), *petia* with the right hand on the floor tom, and *aburukwa* with the left hand on the snare with the snares off. Another percussionist can then play *kwadum* on top of the dense and rich drumset part, creating a sound that is quite similar to an actual Kete ensemble. See Figure 24 (in Appendix) for notation of *Abofoo* and *Akwaduom* for drumset in this approach.

Conclusion

In my view, traditional Ghanaian drumming is among the most exciting, energetic, and rhythmically complicated styles of music on earth. Surprisingly, it is strangely absent from the literature in the international drumming community. By writing this paper for the modern percussionist, I seek to add Kete to the repertoire of drumming music that is respected, taught, practiced, and performed throughout the world. In response to Professor Nketia's call to action for cultural preservation, I humbly submit this paper as my effort to assist in the vast project of archiving and spreading traditional Ghanaian music.

Acknowledgments

I want to sincerely thank my teachers who have shared their knowledge of Kete with me: Emmanuel Attah Poku, Daniel Annan Sackey, Ernest Domfeh, and the rest of the staff at the Centre for National Culture in Kumasi. I would like to thank Professors Royal Hartigan and Kwabena Boateng for originally taking me to the Ashanti Region of Ghana to study Kete. Lastly, I would like to thank Professor David Locke for his editing, guidance, and encouragement with this paper.

References

Adinku, W. Ofotsu. 2000. "The Protection of Choreographic Works in Ghana." In *Fontomfrom: Contemporary Ghanaian Literature, Theater, and Film*. Ed. by Kofi Ayidoho and James Gibbs. Amsterdam-Atlanta Georgia: Rodopi. Accessed May 5 2009. On Google Books, pages 351-354: <http://books.google.com/>.

Akrofi, Eric A. 2002. *Sharing Knowledge and Experience: A Profile of Kwabena Nketia, Scholar and Music Educator*. Accra, Ghana: Afram Publications, Ltd.

Hartigan, Royal. 1995. *West African Rhythms for Drumset*. Van Nuys, CA: Alfred Publishing Co., Inc.

Hernandez, Horatio. 2000. *Conversations in Clave*. Miami, FL: Warner Bros. Publications.

Koetting, James. 1970. *An Analytical Study of Asante Kete Drumming*. Los Angeles, CA: University of California.

Kwadwo, Osei. 2004. *An Outline of Asante History: Part 1*. 3rd ed. Kumasi, Ghana: O. Kwadwo Enterprise.

Kyeremateng, K. Nkansa. 2004. *The Akans of Ghana: Their Customs, History, and Institutions*. Kumasi, Ghana: Sebewie De Ventures.

Nketia, J.H. Kwabena Nketia. 1963. *Drumming in Akan Communities of Ghana*. London, England: Thomas Nelson & Sons.

Sarfo, Nana. Personal interview. Centre for National Culture, Kumasi, Ghana. September 2011.

Spiro, Michael. 2011. "It's Not a Waltz: Understanding the Triplet Feel in Afro-Centric Music." *Percussive Notes* 49 (5) September: 42-43.

Discography

Asante Kete Drumming: Music of Ghana. 2007. Nsuase Kete group, recorded and produced by Joseph Kaminski. Lyricord Discs.

Rhythms of Life, Songs of Wisdom: Akan Music from Ghana, West Africa. 1996. Recorded, compiled, and annotated by Roger Vetter. Smithsonian/Folkways Records.

Videography

"Traditional Ashanti Dancers and Drummers." Online posting. Youtube. Uploaded 8 August, 2008. <http://www.youtube.com/watch?v=JeFtlcwuOZQ>.

Appendix

Figure 1: Introduction

Figure 2: Ending

Figure 3: Dawuro Notation

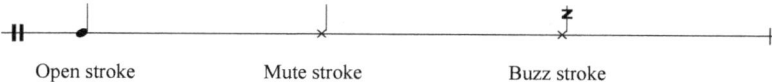

Figure 4: Ntrowa Notation

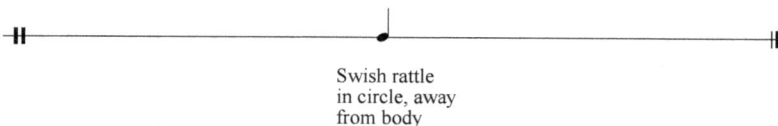

Figure 5: Donno Notation

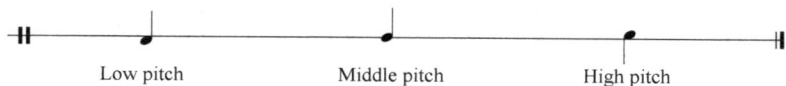

Figure 6: Petia & Aburukwa Notation

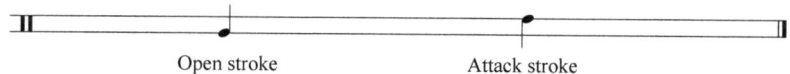

Figure 7: Apentema Notation

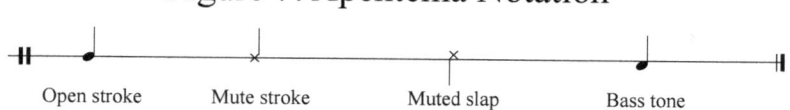

Figure 8: Kwadum Notation

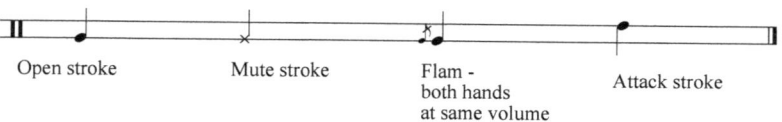

Figure 9: Metric Matrix

Figure 10: Kete in 3/4

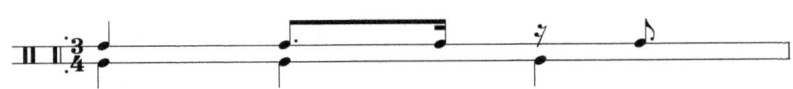

Figure 11: Kete in 12/8

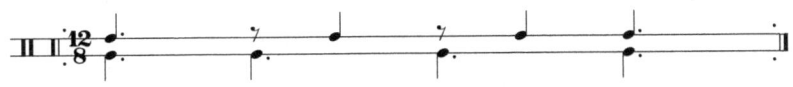

Figure 12: Traditional Dawuro Pattern

Figure 13: Dawuro Analysis

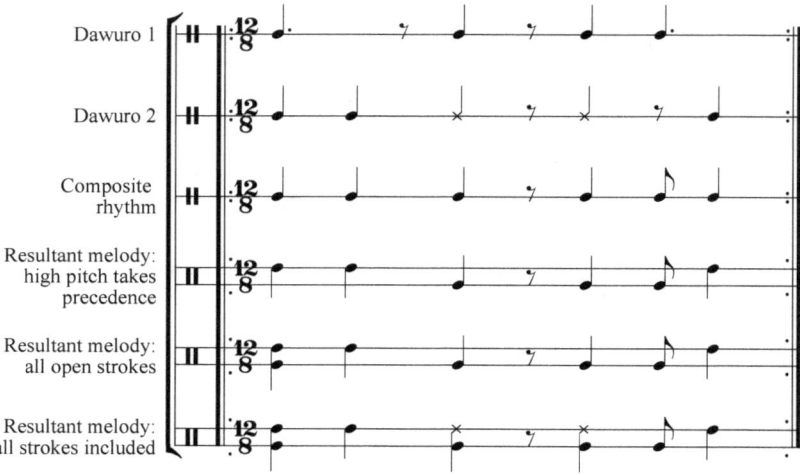

Figure 14: Relationship to Standard 12/8 Bell

Figure 15: Ntrowa Patterns

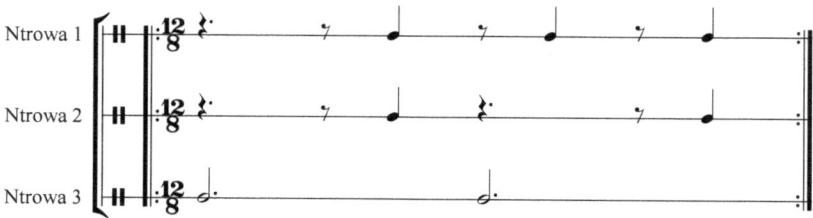

Figure 16: Abofoo Score

Figure 17: Kwadum & Aburukwa

*Written above line to show pitch relationship to kwadum

Figure 18: Abofoo Lead

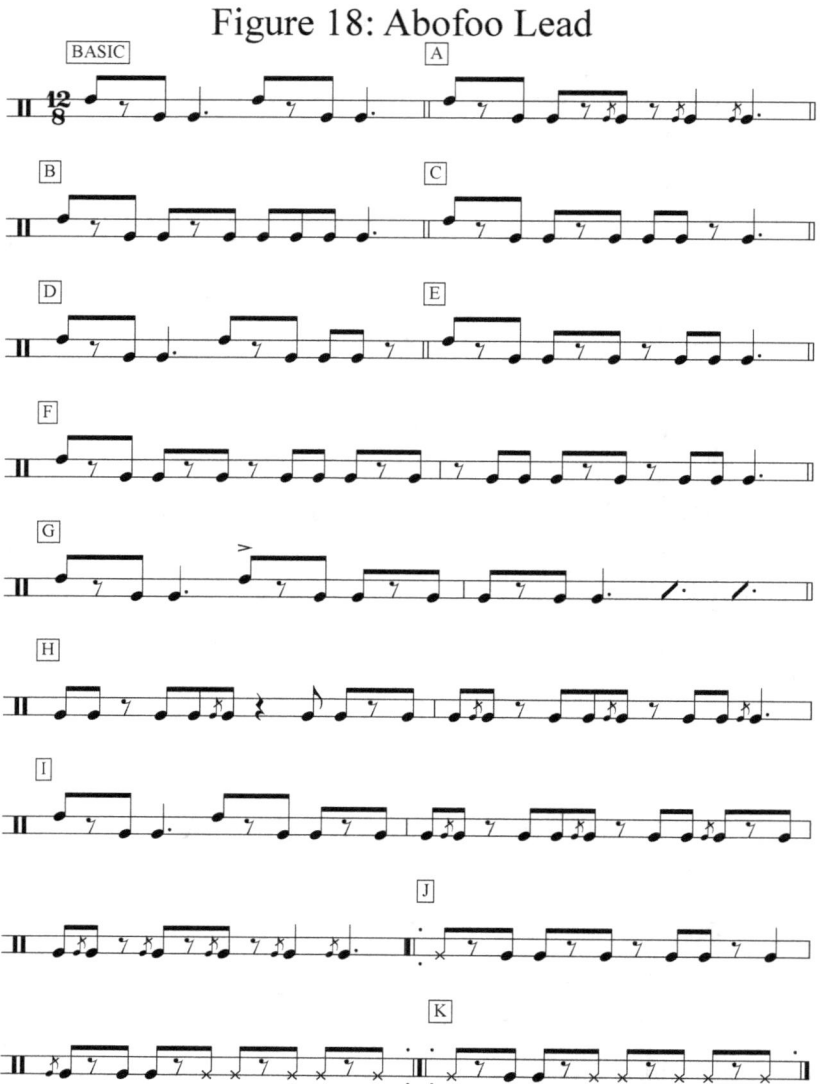

Figure 19: Akwaduom Score

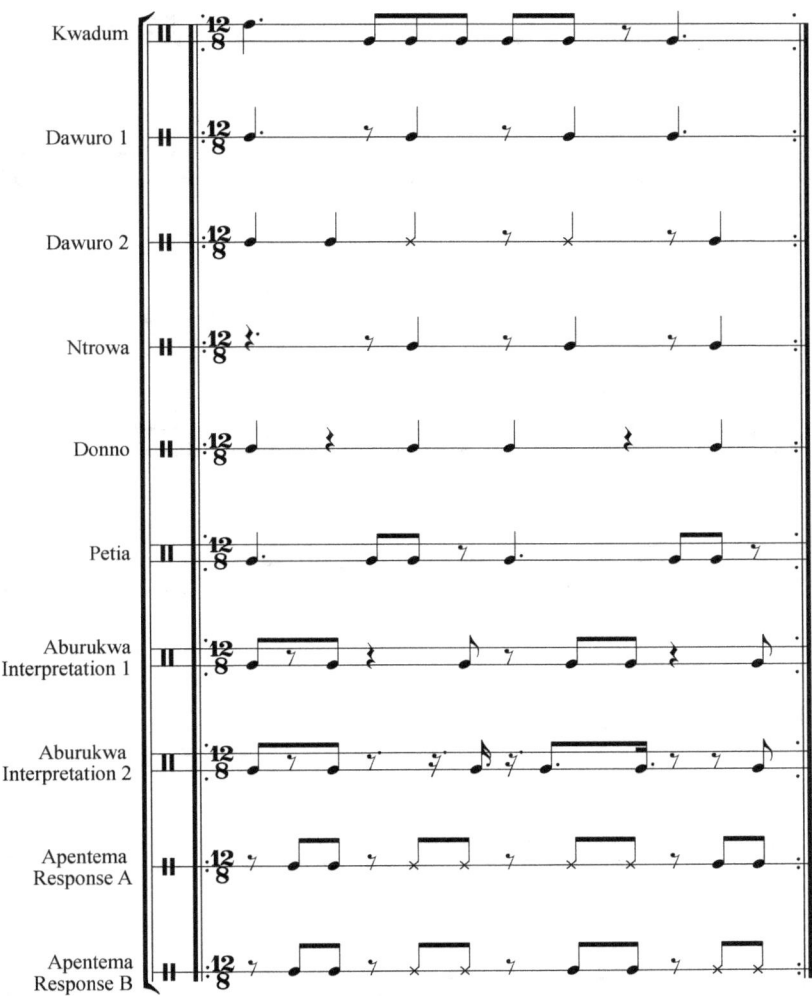

Figure 20: Akwaduom Lead

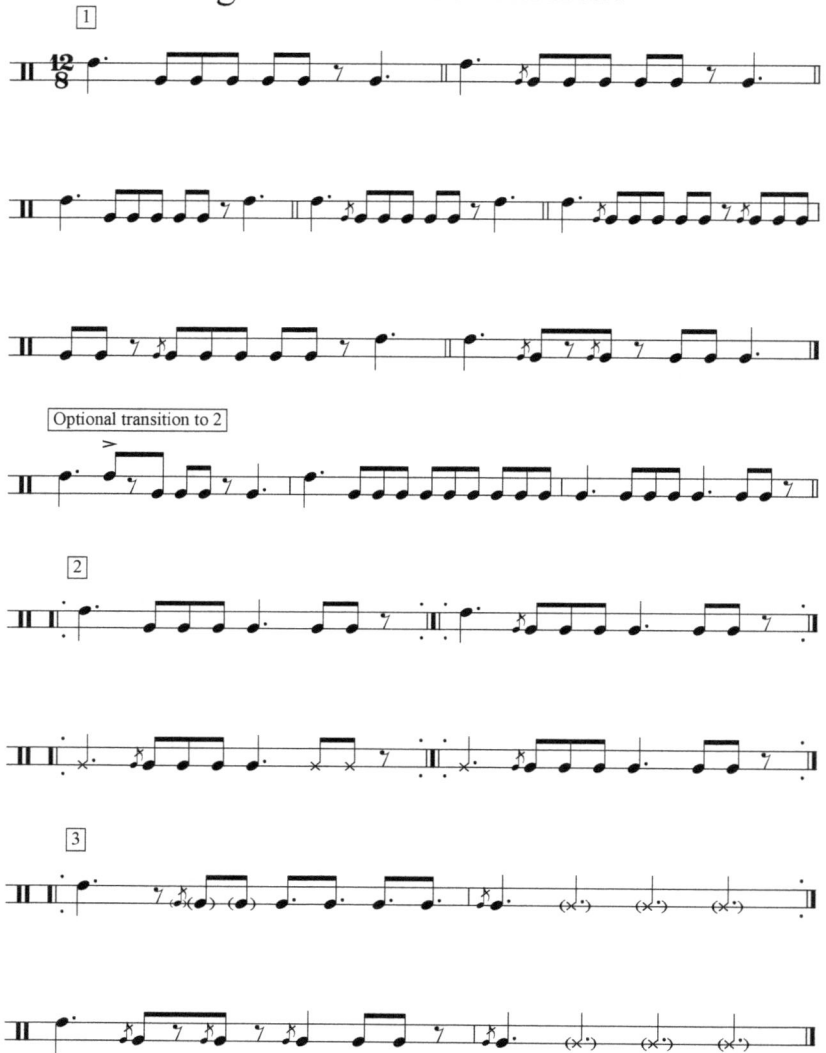

Figure 21: Ndwamu

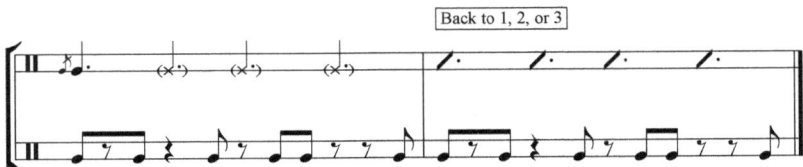

Figure 22: Intensification

Figure 23: Drumset Approach 1

Figure 24: Drumset Approach 2

Spontaneity, Improvisation, and Musical and Social Aesthetics in Ghanaian Kpanlogo Music and Dance

Amy Unruh

Amy Unruh specializes in West African musics, their influences on the development of African-European hybrid musics in the Caribbean and Americas, and in particular, how African-derived musics influenced American composer, Louis Moreau Gottschalk. Learning primarily from Godwin Agbeli, Steven Cornelius, Habib Iddrisu, and Bernard Woma, she has studied aspects of music and dance in Ghana for over twenty years. She is currently an assistant professor of music at Kent State University's Main and Stark Campuses, and performs regularly with Ka De Dunaa.

Kpanlogo is a relatively recent expressive music and dance genre of Ghana, West Africa. It originated in Ga communities along the ocean in the capital city of Accra and in the Greater Accra Region. Generally, Kpanlogo is believed to have developed in the 1950's because this is when it seems to have first received its name; however, some Ghanaians say Kpanlogo was thriving as early as the 1930's. Performances in Ga communities are generally lively and informal, offering participants opportunities for spontaneous creative interaction and social commentary. In comparison, arrangements of Kpanlogo for multi-ethnic professional dance troupes tend to be more organized and homogenous. Kpanlogo arrangements are not only found throughout Ghana, but are also becoming more common in other countries as well, especially in the United States. In both traditional Ga performances and professional arrangements, Kpanlogo is learned and created through oral tradition. Kpanlogo is especially popular today among Ga youth.

The Ga traditionally make their living as fishermen, and fishing played a key role in the genre's development; in particular, some Kpanlogo dance movements originated as choreographed fishing motions. The name "Kpanlogo" is a combination of three Ga words: *kpan* meaning fishing net or thread, *lo* meaning fish, and *logo* meaning something that is ticklish.

As with the Akan genre, *Adowa*, Kpanlogo exists in two forms. Its first form is played on indigenous Ghanaian instruments; the second continues to change and develop as a central component of Ghanaian High-life—popular music played on Ghanaian and Western instruments in combination. This paper will primarily focus on the first, more traditional form of Kpanlogo as it exists in Ga communities, as well as similar versions adopted by professional Ghanaian dance troupes. Understanding the importance of community and social context in Ghana is essential to understanding Kpanlogo. Unity is a central theme in Kpanlogo performances, and this is most immediately apparent in the genre's title. Kpanlogo is the name of the music, the dance steps, the drums used to play Kpanlogo, and the genre as a whole. As a researcher, it is difficult to draw a line between ideas such as music and dance, or music and language, because in Kpanlogo their boundaries overlap so much that they become almost indistinguishable. Not only is there traditionally little or no separation between Kpanlogo "performers" and "audience" members, but also among the Ga, individual identity is in reference to one's place within the community as a whole. Likewise, instrumental parts, vocal songs, proverbs, and dance steps are not isolated parts that can be extracted and analyzed independently but rather fully integrated concepts that form a continuous dialogue and are only understood in reference to each other. As Ghanaian ethnomusicologist J. H. Kwabena Nketia has so eloquently pointed out:

> ... a music tradition consists of 'intrinsic' and 'extrinsic' facts of some sort, of repertoire and the oral traditions associated with it. The analysis of scale, modes, melodic direction, intervals, harmony, etc., provides one type of meaning to those accustomed to thinking of music in those terms. To the African performer and his collaborators and "listeners" the music means much more than these, for it is part of a way of life. A theory of 'crossing the beats' or 'multiple main beats' based on analysis of procedure in drumming may help in bringing order into what appears to others as 'chaos'. It may demonstrate the African musical art of achieving complexity through the use of relatively simple elements. But drumming as a cultural activity has a meaning beyond structure and the ethnomusicologist enriches his understanding of meaning by going beyond formal analysis.[1]

Participation played a central role in my research and helped me to understand how each aspect of Kpanlogo, both musical and cultural, related to the others.

I primarily studied Kpanlogo with Ghanaian master musician and dancer, Habib Iddrisu. From Iddrisu, I learned to play the core instrumental parts of Kpanlogo, including numerous master drum rhythms. In addition, I learned several Kpanlogo songs, Ga proverbs associated with the genre, and various traditional dance patterns. I then augmented my knowledge of the genre by comparing what I had learned from Iddrisu with additional versions and performances of Kpanlogo in Ghana and the United States, adding to my vocabulary of Kpanlogo rhythms, proverbs, and dance steps. Whenever possible, I experienced Kpanlogo through both participation and observation. By interacting with musicians and dancers, I was able to synthesize the material at a deeper level than if I had merely observed other participants. Musically, Kpanlogo is not the sum of its parts but rather a collectively understood process, a balance between traditional structure and the ongoing relationships individual participants create. Therefore, Kpanlogo can have regional differences and immeasurable possibilities while simultaneously being clearly distinguishable from other Ghanaian music and dance genres. The instruments used to play Kpanlogo are as follows: a bell called *ngonngo*, single-headed hand drums called kpanlogos, and a rattle. Kpanlogo is polyrhythmic, and as is typical of many music and dance genres in Ghana, has three principle rhythmic components that form its characteristic rhythmic texture. When all of these rhythmic layers of Kpanlogo combine, they form a melody (a direct result of tuning the various kpanlogo drums to different pitches) that distinguishes Kpanlogo from other Ghanaian music and dance genres. This rhythmic melody, termed melorhythm by Nigerian ethnomusicologist Meki Nzewi, is not played by any single individual; rather it is the result of specific and accurately combined musical parts and relationships.[2]

The term polyrhythm could be used to describe Kpanlogo as well, but as a label, the term can be somewhat misleading. The Harvard Concise Dictionary of Music defines polyrhythm as "The simultaneous use of contrasted rhythms in different parts of the musical texture." The Kpanlogo bell pattern, support drum patterns, and master drum patterns do contain contrasting rhythmic ideas. The rhythmic structure of Kpanlogo, however, is far more complex than the label "polyrhythm" could suggest because of the way Kpanlogo's contrasting rhythms overlap and interlock. These patterns combine to form a texture that is constantly changing because the master drummer incorporates unending variety as he plays. Even when master drummers double a support drum pattern as part of the arrangement, they typically vary the pattern slightly with each cycle of the bell. To the Ga, the term polyrhythm is an academic idea, not one used by participants in Kpanlogo. While polyrhythm may loosely describe the rhythmic texture of Kpanlogo, it should not be taken to define the genre as a whole.

The aural center and primary rhythmic component of Kpanlogo is the bell (*ngonngo*) and its characteristic rhythm, something researchers such as J. H. Kwabena Nketia have referred to as a time-line pattern (see Figure 1 in Appendix).[3] The bell pattern repeats without variation, establishing a cyclic sense of time, and functioning in a similar way to how it is used in other Ghanaian genres such as those of the Ewe.[4] The bell is the principal aural reference point for all other musical occurrences and dance steps. The bell pattern is the most essential and consistent pattern within Kpanlogo, but on its own it does not begin to define the genre because it is not unique to Kpanlogo. Kpanlogo's bell cycle is familiar abroad as a 3-2 clave pattern. Although there are four beats to one bell cycle in Kpanlogo, performers play in relation to the rhythm rather than to a prescribed meter of 4 /4. Likewise, dancers align their steps with the musical cycle rather than counting them. An additional rhythm on the shaker is sometimes added to the bell cycle to embellish the beat. The bell pattern provides a stable foundation for all other relationships in Kpanlogo.

Just as individual identity is seen in reference to the community as a whole, everything that happens in Kpanlogo happens in reference to the bell pattern. When transcribing, I place beat one where players begin the bell pattern, with one complete bell cycle equaling one measure. It should be noted, however, that in Ghana the concept of "beat one" does not apply to performing Kpanlogo, and that "beat one" is only one of several points within the bell cycle that participants emphasize. Support drums add the next rhythmic layer to Kpanlogo. Kpanlogo has two standard support drum parts; one is highly syncopated, the other is not. Essential to each are bass tones that align with the second and fourth beat of each bell cycle. Like the bell pattern, the support drum patterns also consistently repeat with each cycle. In some performances, additional support drum patterns (such as one that emphasizes all the upbeats) as well as other percussion instruments may be included. Despite slight regional variations, support drum patterns often do not change within a performance, thereby contributing to the sense of stability established by the bell. The bell and support drum patterns provide a stable foundation that allows for more variety, creativity and spontaneity in the master drum part. Transcribed below are the two most common support drum patterns for Kpanlogo as they enter against and align with the bell pattern (see Figure 2 in Appendix). The variations shown below are transcribed as my primary Ghanaian teacher, Habib Iddrisu, plays them. The central components of these rhythms are consistent with slight variations I have learned and observed from several additional Ghanaian teachers, professional dance troupes, and communities in Ghana.[5] In both support drum patterns bass tones directly align with beats two and four. Open tones played between the bass tones give a feeling of lifting up and, in the case of syncopated portions of the Kpanlogo 1 part, moving away from the beat, only to return at the next bass tone. Syncopation in the Kpanlogo 1 pattern happens from the second sixteenth note of beat four through the bass tone on beat two. Here, sixteenth note pulses are grouped in threes through repetition of sixteenth notes followed by eighth notes, momentarily suggesting a pulse other than the beat. The more syncopated Kpanlogo 1 pattern can create a pull away from beat one because the more evenly divided Kpanlogo 2 pattern maintains a sense of the "downbeat." Interestingly, the bass tones where the two support drum parts are in unison occur on the "off-beats" within the bell cycle rather than on beat one.

Some especially common, or standard, Kpanlogo dance steps reflect a feeling of realigning or returning on beats two and four in Kpanlogo as well. Dancers may step and move their hips in a rhythm of one and two, three and four, ending a dance "motif" on beats two and four with a longer pause in movement. In other common dance steps, dancers step and extend their arms outward on beats one and three and step and pull their arms back in on beats two and four. One particularly fun and complex dance movement called *Logo Ligi* combines the common Kpanlogo hip movement with reaching out and pulling in. Duple divisions and balanced opposites are especially common in Kpanlogo. The bell pattern can be loosely divided in half. Beats four and one are played on the beat while more syncopated strokes fall around beats two and three. In the two support drum patterns, beats two and three (where the two parts are almost identical) are balanced against beats one and four where the two are quite different. Thus syncopation in the bell pattern and syncopation in the Kpanlogo 1 pattern happen on the opposite halves of the bell cycle. These duple divisions create and maintain balance and stability in Kpanlogo when the master drummer varies from them.

The single beat can also be a cycle. A third common support drum pattern, not included in Iddrisu's arrangements, consists of two sixteenth-note open tones or closed slaps played on the second half of every beat. This pattern is regularly used by other Ghanaians such as master musician Bernard Woma. Iddrisu recognizes this pattern from another Ga genre called Gome. Although he does not consider this pattern to be Kpanlogo, its frequent inclusion in Kpanlogo arrangements suggests that it resonates with the collective understanding of how Kpanlogo works. Each two-part cycle in

Kpanlogo has a regular flow similar to the feeling of gently breathing in and out or walking. One-beat, two-beat, and four-beat units create fully integrated and proportionately larger binary cycles. By emphasizing the upbeats, this third support drum pattern reinforces this aesthetic of balance between sound and the spaces between sounds. The final rhythmic layer in Kpanlogo is the master drum, or lead drum part, and it is at this level where the most spontaneity and improvisation occurs. While an ensemble can have several support drummers, only one person will play the master drum part at a time. Musically, the master drummer is allowed the most freedom. A master drummer is in charge of everything happening in Kpanlogo ranging from signaling changes in dance steps by playing patterns called "breaks" to communicating with participants by reciting proverbs on the drum. Even in arrangements of Kpanlogo where the master drummer has specific patterns to play for each dance step, he will often break away from a predetermined pattern after establishing it for the dancers. Individual creativity and communication skills are central to being an accomplished master drummer. Spontaneous creation and interaction in Kpanlogo often combines a variety of elements resulting from distinct musical processes. In order to understand these processes, it is necessary to understand how Kpanlogo is typically learned.

Learning music in Ghana could well be a process that begins before birth, and even infants become familiar with ways to feel basic rhythms as they spend countless hours strapped to their mother's back as she dances. Music is part of nearly all aspects of Ghanaian life and participation is always encouraged. Often there is little separation between performers and audience members because everyone present is part of the performance community. Children grow up immersed in a diverse musical and rhythmic environment. Musicians and dancers learn oral traditions such as Kpanlogo through listening and participation. When children show an interest in playing music, they continue learning within the context of performances. They begin imitating the bell pattern and support drum patterns. Once they can play them, they spend hours at performances repeating each pattern while continuing to listen to how the different rhythmic layers interrelate. Musicians learn to keep their part steady while focusing on others. They learn to hear and feel the basic rhythmic relationships of a genre, and begin to attain a rhythmic vocabulary. Only the most accomplished musicians will learn the lead drum or master drum patterns. Due to its complexity, the master drum is the most challenging part to learn to play. While learning to play the master drum, musicians continue to build their vocabulary of rhythmic patterns specific to a particular genre such as Kpanlogo. Because many master drum rhythms reference dance steps, a thorough familiarity with the dance is also necessary. Master drummers also become familiar with how to play well-known proverbs on the drum. A musician becomes fluent in a particular genre like Kpanlogo when he has learned enough material to understand the processes behind it and can now freely create his own new material within the genre from his established vocabulary. This process results from continually learning new ways to hear and feel the rhythmic texture of a particular genre.

Although Habib Iddrisu did not learn Kpanlogo growing up in a Ga community because he is Dagbamba, the way he learned Kpanlogo in a professional dance troupe in Accra echoes the traditional process. Although he had the playing technique to play more complex patterns, for the first two months that he participated in Kpanlogo, he only played the bell pattern. He used this opportunity to listen to how the rhythmic patterns interacted with the bell cycle and with each other. He became acquainted with the bell cycle's exactness and stability by learning to listen to each of the other parts while maintaining the strict rhythm of his own part. He observed how the drum patterns interlocked with the bell. He listened further until he understood the relationships between the support drum parts, and the relationship between the master drummer and the dancers. Before he began playing the individual support drum patterns, he knew how they worked within the context of the whole idea of Kpanlogo rather than as separate components. He figured out the degree to which other components of Kpanlogo could vary without changing the genre's characteristic feel. After learning the support drum patterns, he next found it necessary to learn the dance movements before finally learning the master drum because of the close association between the two. Iddrisu then added more dance steps, songs, and master drum ideas to his Kpanlogo vocabulary by participating in numerous traditional performances in Ga communities. Since he is also fluent in Ga, he could learn how to imitate spoken language and play Ga proverbs on the master drum. Because of his familiarity with the genre and the Ga language, Iddrisu can fluently improvise the master drum part for Kpanlogo.

The term improvisation can be somewhat ambiguous in definition. It can suggest a variety of processes ranging from an ability to manipulate certain musical perimeters, to composing while performing, to freedom to play anything. In Kpanlogo, three components contribute to master drummers' improvisations: rhythmic patterns, dance steps, and spoken proverbs. Rhythmic patterns are a central component of improvisation in Kpanlogo. A master drummer can manipulate existing rhythmic vocabulary in a variety of ways. Unlike some Ghanaian Ewe genres, where master drummers can play with different placements of the beat within one bell cycle, Kpanlogo always has four beats per bell cycle. Improvisation in Kpanlogo does, however, share some characteristics with other Ghanaian genres, including an emphasis on the space between notes, which is perceived as aesthetically pleasing. Just as a support drum part is sometimes added to Kpanlogo which fills in the spaces between the beats by playing only on the upbeats, a master drummer can make existing rhythmic patterns more complex by filling in the spaces within the patterns with more drum strokes, thereby increasing the rhythmic density. He can also fill in spaces within the overall rhythmic texture created by the bell cycle and the support drum parts. Likewise each component of Kpanlogo (drum patterns, dance steps, etc. . . .) contains empty spaces and places of momentarily suspended movement for others to fill in. It is said that the best master drummers will create patterns that allow participants to hear the various relationships between the other parts in new ways.

Kpanlogo master drummers will play with sonic proportions while improvising rhythms. For example, they may emphasize every third eighth or sixteenth note within a pattern. This shifting of emphasis as well as hearing, and filling in of spaces within the rhythmic texture can be combined to create a feeling of stretching away from, and eventually returning to points of stability. Points of stability can be found throughout the interlocking patterns within Kpanlogo's overall rhythmic texture. They can be as frequent as individual beats or as far apart as the downbeat of the bell pattern after several cycles. The bass tones in the two standard support drum patterns that align on beats two and four provide another choice. Master drummers often stretch away from the ensemble's stability for several bell cycles before returning. Throughout Kpanlogo, the master drummer must maintain a balance between the stability of the established rhythmic and melodic textures, and the changes he introduces to make the performance interesting and entertaining.

Improvisation in Kpanlogo is also closely associated with dance. Music and dance exist in constant dialogue. Communication can be between one or more individuals, or groups of participants, and can become simultaneously multi-directional. When dancers respond to signals from the master drum, they must place their steps correctly in relation to the bell cycle. Many dance moves are associated with specific rhythms the master drummer plays. In informal social performances of Kpanlogo, the master drummer will interact with individual dancers by playing patterns that fit their movements. This type of interaction establishes a dialog between performers that researchers have referred to as "call and response" although, in practice, the dialog is often much more complex than this label implies, especially when the specific immediate context of social relationships is considered. J. H. Kwabena Nketia elaborates on this complexity:

> The importance attached to the dance does not lie only in the scope it provides for the release of emotion stimulated by music. The dance can also be used as a social and artistic medium of communication. It can convey thoughts or matters of personal importance through the choice of movements, postures, and facial expressions. Through the dance, individuals and social groups can show their reactions to attitudes of hostility or cooperation and friendship held by others towards them. They can offer respect to their superiors, or appreciation and gratitude to well-wishers and benefactors. They can react to the presence of rivals, affirm their status to servants, subjects, and others, or express their beliefs through the choice of appropriate dance vocabulary or symbolic gestures.[6]

Just as master drummers select rhythms, dancers select their steps from a variety of established possibilities, and will on often feel inspired to create new variations or new movements. Likewise, the master drummer may be inspired by a particular dancer to create an entirely new rhythm that may later be regularly used within the genre. The meanings of certain dance movements can also be referenced by playing a rhythm that is specific to a particular step. Master drum patterns and dance steps are often the result of one idea realized through two mediums. As ethnomusicologist John Miller Chernoff who studied Ewe and Dagbamba music in Ghana has noted, "When you ask an African friend whether or not he 'understands' a certain type of music, he will say yes if he knows the dance that goes with it."[7] This idea applies to the Ga when they participate in Kpanlogo as well. What a master drummer plays loses some of its meaning without the dancing. In arrangements, dancers need the master drummer to signal when to change dance steps as well as which dance steps to change to. Likewise, the master drummer derives his patterns from the rhythmic movements of the dancers. When I recorded Iddrisu playing the master drum pattern for an arrangement of Kpanlogo, not only did he need someone to play the bell pattern as a reference point, but he also needed me to dance the steps while he played. His part was only accurate within the context of others. Even in instrumental arrangements of Kpanlogo, drummers will include arm motions derived from dance steps and performed choreographed movements while reciting and playing proverbs. Drummers sometimes move in ways that suggest dance steps while playing, suggesting that they feel them even in the absence of dancers.

Master drummers also improvise through direct references to spoken language. Music in Kpanlogo is integrally linked to language, communication, and social interaction. Not only do vocal songs interlock with the bell pattern and communicate messages, but spoken proverbs do as well. The master drummer can converse with the community by playing proverbs that have both literal and implied meanings. Spoken proverbs can be played on the drum through the replication of speech rhythms and tones. This technique is applied to tonal and non-tonal languages including English. Although Ga is not a tonal language, musicians can still imitate the inflections and rhythms of speech on the drum. Master drummers can therefore play spoken proverbs on the drum as a form of social commentary. Proverbs can have layers of meanings ranging from references to everyday life to direct comments on an individual's behavior. One proverb, "*Anagi lege lege, ton toro musu agbo,*" references the insatiable appetite of mosquitoes, stating "The mosquito has small legs but a big stomach."

Other proverbs can be more personal, for example:

> *Ayee sebe wonu*
> *Ayee Ayee sebe wonu*
> *Ayee yaa wo a anaago yo bi ho*
> *Ayee sebe wonu*

(see Figure 3 in Appendix)

This proverb literally associates Ayee (a person's name) with garden egg soup. Ayee is a common name for a young man. Sebe wonu is garden egg soup. A garden egg is a small, green, egg-shaped fruit grown in Ghana that is similar to an eggplant or tomato. This proverb implies that Ayee, who impregnated someone's daughter outside of wedlock, is not very intelligent. His brain is soft like a garden egg in soup. Note how the played proverb interlocks with the bell cycle.

Proverbs in Pidgin English can also be incorporated into master drummers' improvisations. One example states,

> *Fine, fine baby*
> *You know de fine, pass your mother*

(see Figure 4 in Appendix)

This proverb could be played to a young woman who thinks quite highly of herself. It complements her beauty, only to add that her mother's looks surpass hers. It serves as a way to remind the young woman that she is not as exceptional as she thinks. Rhythmically, this proverb aligns closely with the bell pattern. Depending on the current circumstances, master drummers can replicate any number of relevant proverbs while improvising social commentary. Language and communication also play a significant role in dance. Some dance steps have retained meanings from choreographed fishing movements, such as movements that imitate pulling in a fishing net, shaking a basket of fish to sort them, and rowing a boat. Other movements are intended to invite people to join in and to show excitement. In one movement, dance partners will place the tops of their heads and their hands together, and rotate their bodies 360 degrees in place, without separating. This movement is said to represent bringing members of opposite sexes together. On addition, dancers can "dance" social commentary by choosing movements with well-known general and/or specific meanings. While one set of steps may communicate a proverb with multiple layers of meaning, another set of moves, danced at a funeral for example, may reference part of the deceased's life.

Language can also facilitate learning dance steps and arrangements. When I studied Kpanlogo with Iddrisu, he did not teach me the dance by counting the steps, but by singing the bell pattern, singing the master drum parts and reciting the rhythms of the dance moves as rhythmic syllables. In this way, rhythm became a verbal language, as well as an aural and kinesthetic language. As I learned the rhythmic language of Kpanlogo, I learned the dance steps and drumming parts and their relationships to each other.

Improvisation in Kpanlogo is often a combination of all three spontaneous processes mentioned here: manipulation of rhythmic patterns, interaction with dancers and other participants, and social commentary through referencing spoken language. It is as if the master drummer is rearranging his rhythmic vocabulary into new sentences. It should also be mentioned that there are two things a master drummer cannot do while improvising. He cannot play something that sounds like another genre, and in arranged performances, he cannot play something that sounds similar to a signal for a change in the music or the dance. Therefore, the master drummer must not only be highly familiar with Kpanlogo, but with other local genres as well. In the hands of the most proficient master drummers, improvisation is an automatic and spontaneous process despite the complexities it can attain.

We can begin to move closer to understanding the aesthetics of Kpanlogo by discerning implied points of emphasis that result from layers of overlapping cycles. Each musical cycle in Kpanlogo, as established by the bell pattern, has four beats that can be emphasized in a variety of ways. This is different from some Ghanaian genres, such as those of the Ewe, where one bell cycle can be simultaneously felt in several different meters, creating complex cross-rhythms through the use of offbeat timing.[8] Overlapping cycles in Kpanlogo are not the result of overlapping meters but of overlapping points of emphasis. While bass tones in the support drum rhythms emphasize beats two and four, other components of Kpanlogo including song phrases, and master drummers' patterns frequently emphasize beat one, and dance steps can coincide with either. In combination, all of these components form a cyclic feel that builds up to and concludes or releases on beat one. Conceptually, beat one is often the end of a cycle in Kpanlogo, but it is also the beginning for some individual parts. In the bell pattern, beats four and one are on the beat, while the rest of the pattern is syncopated. Participants emphasize a push towards beat one by clapping with the bell on beats four and one. The second support drum pattern is often most rhythmically dense on beat one as well. Long notes at the end of vocal song phrases also frequently occur on or are held through beat one.

In Kpanlogo arrangements, master drummers often play a slap on beat four to alert dancers to a "break" (a call for a change in dance steps). The break consistently begins and ends on beat one, and can be realized in a number of ways. The rhythm on the first two beats of the break is seldom varied so that it will be clear to dancers when the master drummer is beginning the signal. The master drummer has more options for how he completes the break over beats three and four, emphasizing through variety the second half of the break pattern as he pushes through to its conclusion on beat one. Two popular dance steps illustrate an emphasis of moving towards beat one as well; Iddrisu refers to them as "Uniting People" and "The Kick." In the "Uniting People" movement, dancers extend their arms over their heads on beat four before immediately bending over at the waist on beat one, a move intended to encourage others to join in and participate in the dancing. Dancers remain in this bent over position while stepping and turning on beats two and three, until beat four where they straighten and extend their arms upward before bending over again on beat one. In "The Kick" dancers emphasize beats four and one by kicking forward on beat four and returning their leg to the ground on beat one. Master drum patterns that accompany these dance steps typically emphasize beats four and one too. When we look at how this feeling of moving towards beat one changes when outside sources have influenced Kpanlogo, it becomes even more obvious how it is a key part of Kpanlogo's structure. For example, one common vocal song found in Kpanlogo is a children's song that was used to teach Ghanaian children the letters of the English alphabet, here titled, "A, B, C, D...." In the first half of the song, where the text is the letters of the English alphabet, all singing is strictly on the beat, with phrases beginning on, and moving away from beat one. The second half of the song, where the text is in Ga, is very syncopated, and returns to feeling like Kpanlogo. Like other Ga Kpanlogo songs, such as "Tra La La Ye" the second half of "A, B, C, D..." emphasizes movement towards beat one with phrases that end in long notes on beat one, as well as with interjections from the song leader on beats four and one (see Figures 5 and 6 in Appendix).

Four beat phrases do not always begin on beat one though. Staggered points of entry are typical in Kpanlogo, as well as in other West-African music.⁹ Kpanlogo support drum players consistently begin their patterns on beat three, as in Figures 5 and 6 (in the Appendix). Yet as the master drummer, Iddrisu could take more liberty when he doubled the Kpanlogo 1 pattern after playing the introductory call. He entered the pattern on beat four, while the support drummers waited until the following beat three to enter. In a specific arrangement that Iddrisu created for Bowling Green State University's Afro-Caribbean Ensemble, specific master drum patterns began in a variety of places in relationship to the bell following breaks. The feel created by these varied entrances is difficult to represent in transcriptions because the bar-line only falls at the beginning of patterns that begin on beat one.

Finally, cycles can be extended over several repetitions of the bell pattern. The master drummer can stretch the feeling of moving from beat four to beat one over several measures through complex improvised patterns. Likewise, vocal songs, dance movements, improvised dance solos, and proverbs played on the drums by the master drummer can extend over two or more bell cycles. Master drummers can also improvise longer phrases that create pulses and "off-beat" pulls within and away from the established patterns. Especially common is an emphasis on groups of three sixteenth notes. Interestingly, Iddrisu would play some of his most offbeat improvised phrases while dancers were executing steps that required careful attention to balance. In a variation of the move called "Logo Ligi," dancers kick a high circle in the air with their left leg rather than just stepping to the side. Dancers are stretching furthest from the ground at the same time the master drummer is stretching furthest from the established beat. Yet this dance pattern repeats every four beat while the master drum pattern extends over four bell cycles. Layers of overlapping cycles reflect some of the simultaneous and complex relationships at work in Kpanlogo.
Each participant in Kpanlogo has a role to play. While the bell pattern is seen as the most essential part, the bell player does not conduct or lead a performance, but rather provides a stable foundation for overlapping cycles and relationships in the genre. Kpanlogo's stability, which is further established by standard patterns and balanced phrases, leaves room for individual contributions and creativity. Because they must maintain the stability necessary to balance a performance, the bell player and support drummers have the least opportunity for creative liberties. In unarranged performances, master drummers, song leaders, and solo dancers have the most freedom. Yet they do not play, sing or dance their

part to get individual attention, but rather to contribute in aesthetically pleasing ways to the whole. Participants will frequently switch roles as drummers get up to dance and different individuals take turns leading songs. This often-spontaneous role changing shows how Kpanlogo's structure allows for flexibility. In arranged versions, flexibility mostly occurs in the creation of the arrangement. Improvisation is limited to the master drummer and to individual dancers during sections where they perform solos.

Any performance of Kpanlogo is a shared creation. In Ga communities, there is no single composer or choreographer. Dance Troupes, on the other hand, may follow one individual's arrangement, but the nature of Kpanlogo still gives performers room for individual expression. Kpanlogo's structure does not dictate the details of the end result. Instead it provides the beginning for many possibilities. This is why every Kpanlogo is different, yet the same. Support drum patterns will vary slightly from one community or professional dance troupe to the next. What must remain consistent are the bass tones on beats two and four and the tendency for one part to be more syncopated than the other. This creates a feeling of "tension and release" or "separation and reunion" as they alternate between the bass and open tones. Master drum patterns that coincide with specific dance steps also vary. Iddrisu included slight changes in the master drum patterns as he repeated them, adding color to them in a way as unique as his own personality. As he varied what he played, the melodies that formed as the tones of all of the drums combined also varied. Everything that happens in Kpanlogo results from individuals playing with contextualized possibilities. As might be expected because of the importance of social context in Kpanlogo, changes in the genre are occurring as it continues to spread from Ga communities. Within Ga communities, social context has a continuous impact on which proverbs a master drummer chooses to play and the songs the song leader selects. In traditional Ga performances, the end result of a Kpanlogo performance is much less clearly specified than in stage adaptations.

Kpanlogo is now part of the standard repertoire of many professional dance troupes in Accra and elsewhere in Ghana. Adapting Kpanlogo for the stage means creating at least some separation between the performers and audience that doesn't happen in less formal performances. In stage arrangements, dancers all face the same direction (towards the audience). Specific songs, master drum patterns, and dance steps are chosen and arranged in rehearsals. A master drum break pattern will be specified as the signal for dancers to change movements. If this same break pattern were played in a performance in a Ga community, it would not necessarily signal anything because each dancer is doing their own movements. In arranged versions, all the dancers do the same steps at the same time. Professional troupes may determine ahead of time which foot to start movements on and what order to do the movements in. Dancers only retain creative freedom in how they each dance the same step in their own way, showcasing their individual personality.

Communication is also more structured, occurring more between groups of people rather than individuals. The characteristic spontaneity of Kpanlogo is reserved for interactions between the master drummer and individual dancers when they dance solos. But even in solo sections, dancers may choose to dance in groups of two or three and select their movements ahead of time. In stage arrangements, the emphasis in Kpanlogo leans more toward pre-determined structure.

Outside of Accra further changes in Kpanlogo may occur. Drummers may still play rhythms from Ga proverbs but the meanings will be lost in areas where people do not speak Ga. Without an understanding of Ga language the rhythms may be varied in ways that would not be possible in Ga-speaking areas. Similarly, performers might make aesthetic changes to dance steps, making their prior meaning now unrecognizable to the Ga. Dance movements and drum patterns can develop layers of new meanings, relative to their new contexts. As Kpanlogo becomes further removed from its original context in Ga communities, the participants may feel less connection and responsibility towards the tradition, and individuals may take creative liberties that would not have previously been possible. Changes that would not be accepted as Kpanlogo in a Ga community may be completely acceptable elsewhere, such as the addition of new instruments or rhythms. For example, as a member of an ensemble in Kent, Ohio, I learned an arrangement of Kpanlogo that included an atypical rhythm. One of the support drum patterns was quite different from the ones I had previously heard and studied (Figure 7). This support drum pattern included bass tones on the first two bell strokes as well as on beat three. When combined with the "Kpanlogo 2" pattern the result was an incessant repetition of bass tones on every beat. The more syncopated "Kpanlogo 1" support drum pattern, which I found essential for creating the feeling of Kpanlogo, was missing in the Kent arrangement. These differences made it difficult for me to dance the steps I knew to this resulting arrangement. The piece became heavy. The spaces between the bass tones, which had been as important as the bass tones themselves, were now thrown off balance as a direct result of the addition of more bass tones in this new support part.

When I played this different support drum pattern for Iddrisu, he replied that not only would he not consider the rhythm to be "Kpanlogo," but that he had never heard that particular pattern in Ghana. The ensemble in Kent had learned the rhythm several years previously from an American student who had studied with an acquaintance in Ghana. Iddrisu maintains that somewhere along the transition from Accra, to Kent, to the time I learned it, something changed. Iddrisu is especially concerned with how changes like this one to the structure of Kpanlogo can change the tradition, resulting in the creation of something entirely new. As a direct result of his years of experience with the genre, Iddrisu can easily distinguish what he accepts as Kpanlogo and what he does not.

If we want a consistent definition for Kpanlogo, we must look to the beginning rather than the end result. The bell pattern never varies. Timing is exact and all components of Kpanlogo have specific interlocking relationships with the bell cycle and consequently with each other. Support drum patterns and certain master drum patterns such as the introduction, break, and call to end the piece are also consistent once chosen from the possibilities for a performance. This stability allows the master drummer to improvise, vary, and stretch points of emphasis, and to engage in spontaneous dialogue with other participants without the ensemble falling apart. Stage arrangements are typically more structured than community performances in Ga districts. Iddrisu is not a typical Kpanlogo drummer or dancer because he has become highly skilled at both. He understands the language of Kpanlogo as it is created through complex relationships, and overlapping cycles and points of emphasis. It should come as no surprise that in addition to being fluent in countless Ghanaian drumming and dance genres Iddrisu fluently speaks eleven languages. All of this reflects his highly developed communication skills that are essential for successful participation in Kpanlogo.

When defining Kpanlogo, it makes sense to place the emphasis where Iddrisu chose to while learning it. He learned the "big picture" first, the structure established by the bell and the consequent ways other components could form relationships. This took precedent over learning technical details of individual dance steps and drumming rhythms, which he only learned to play after understanding the overall structure. He became part of the "Kpanlogo community" by learning the collectively understood possibilities of Kpanlogo. He understands Kpanlogo as a process and an idea. Kpanlogo is a vibrant genre full of variables that allow for continuous creativity and individual participation. Individuals like Iddrisu continue the tradition of Kpanlogo by filling in the framework in unique and spontaneous ways at each new performance.

In Kpanlogo, each part is meaningless until it is combined with the others. When Iddrisu is playing Kpanlogo, however, he is not thinking of how the total piece combines but from the perspective of how his part relates to each other part. If I ask Iddrisu to sing Kpanlogo he sings one individual part, usually the first support drum pattern, and dances a step to give a reference point. When he would sing Kpanlogo while teaching me dance steps he sang individual drum parts as well. He did not sing a rhythm that combined more than one percussion pattern. Kpanlogo is not one total rhythm. It is one idea. Habib Iddrisu understands Kpanlogo from individual interdependent viewpoints. Perhaps what master drummers do when they improvise is to explore the various possible perspectives within the community created at a given performance. Perhaps the most proficient master drummers are those who come up with the most creative and interesting viewpoints. As Kpanlogo continues to inspire High-life music in Ghana as well, musicians and participants are creating even more opportunities for new perspectives within the genre.

Endnotes

Special thanks to Habib Iddrisu, Steven Cornelius, and Bernard Woma for their support of this research.

1: See J. H. Kwabena Nketia. 1962. "The Problem of Meaning in African Music," *Ethnomusicology* (6)1: 3.

2: See Meki Nzewi. 1997. *African Music: Theoretical Content and Creative Continuum*. Olderhausen: Institut für Didaktik populärer Musik. pp. 34-5.

3: See J. H. Kwabena Nketia. 1974. The Music of Africa. New York: W.W. Norton, pp 131-2.

4: See David Locke. 1982. "Principles of Offbeat Timing and Cross-Rhythm in Southern Eve Dance Drumming," *Ethnomusicology* (26) 2, pp. 217-246.

5: Transcription Key:
B = a bass tone
O = an open tone
M = a muffled tone
S = an open slap
s = a closed slap
t or + = a touch
Tones indicated with capital letters are louder and more essential to the rhythms. They are written below the rhythms just as lyrics would be. Tones on the lower line are generally played with the stronger hand and tones on the upper line with the weaker.

6: See J. H. Kwabena Nketia. 1974. *The Music of Africa*. New York: W.W. Norton, pp. 207-8.

7: See John Miller Chernoff. 1979. *African Rhythm and African Sensibility: Aesthetics and Social Action in African Musical Idioms*. Chicago: University of Chicago Press, p. 23.

8: See David Locke. 1982. "Principles of Offbeat Timing and Cross-Rhythm in Southern Eve Dance Drumming," *Ethnomusicology* (26) 2, pp. 217-246.

9: See A. M. Jones. 1954. "African Rhythm," *Africa* (24)1, pp. 26-47.

References

Chernoff, John Miller. 1979. *African Rhythm and African Sensibility: Aesthetics and Social Action in African Musical Idioms*. Chicago: University of Chicago Press.

Iddrisu, Habib. 1999-2012. Personal communications.

Jones, A. M. 1954. "African Rhythm." *Africa* (24) 1: 26-47.

Locke, David. 1982. "Principles of Offbeat Timing and Cross-Rhythm in Southern Eve Dance Drumming." *Ethnomusicology* (26) 2: 217-246.

Nketia, J. H. Kwabena. 1974. *The Music of Africa*. New York: W. W. Norton.

___.1962. "The Problem of Meaning in African Music." *Ethnomusicology* (6) 1: 1-7.

Nzewi, Meki. 1997. *African Music: Theoretical Content and Creative Continuum*. Olderhausen: Institut für Didaktik Populärer Musik.

Woma, Bernard. 2000-2006. Personal communications.

Appendix

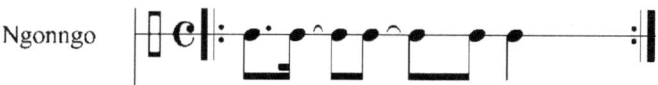

Figure 1: Kpanlogo bell pattern.

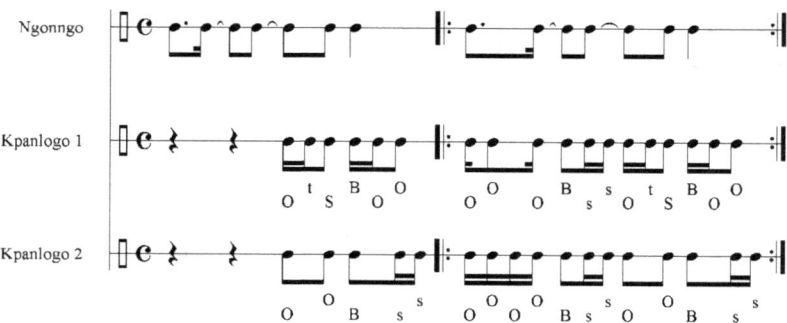

Figure 2: Kpanlogo support drum parts with bell pattern.

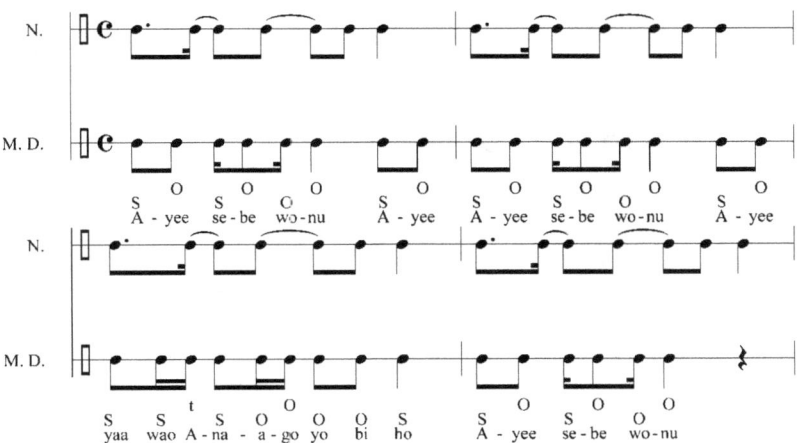

Figure 3: Kpanlogo master drum part for proverb "Ayee Sebe Wonu ..." with the bell pattern.

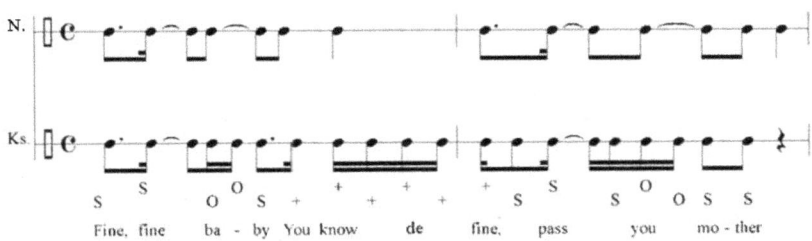

Figure 4: Kpanlogo master drum part for proverb "Fine, Fine Baby ..." with the bell pattern.

Figure 5: A, B, C, D . . . .

Figure 6: Tra La La Ye.

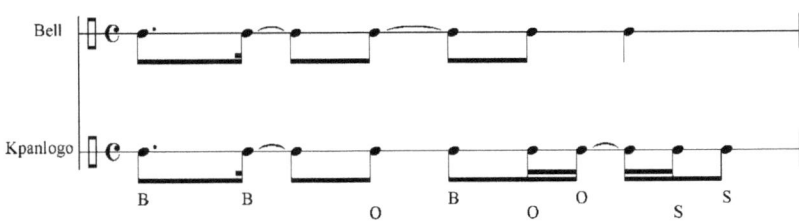

Figure 7: "Kpanlogo" rhythm from Kent with bell.

3

Albert K. Awedoba
and
Alexis L. Danti
Mawuli Adjei

SINGING HISTORY

Kasena Maiden Songs: A Genre on the Wane

Albert K. Awedoba and Alexis L. Danti

Albert K. Awedoba is a professor in the Institute of African Studies at the University of Ghana, Legon. His research interests include sanitation and health (acute respiratory infections, eye diseases, etc); oral literatures in Ghana; primary schooling; chieftaincy and development; understanding corruption; conflicts and response mechanisms; reproductive health; ethnic migration; grammar and phonology, and biographical studies of selected Ghanaians. He is the author of several books covering the above topics. He has previously consulted for WHO, OCP/APOC, UNFPA, UNIDIR and edited several journals including the *Contemporary Journal of African Studies*. He was president of the Pan African Anthropological Association from 2004-2005.

Alexis L. Danti is a lecturer in the Department of Gur-Gonja at the University of Education Winneba, Ghana. He specializes in Kasem, a language spoken in Northern Ghana. He holds an MA degree in Linguistics from the University of Ghana and a Bachelor of Education degree in English and Kasem from the University of Education, Winneba. Danti's publications include *The Kasem Adjective Phrase Structure*, *The Kasem Nominal Structure*, *Kasem Taamemɔɔnen Seina*, *Asuba*, *Di Nogo Kasem*, *Di Serepae Kasem*, and *Lei De Seina Taana*. He is the co-editor of the *Journal of African Cultures and Languages* and secretary of The Association of Teachers of Ghanaian Languages.

Preliminary Comment

Professor Kwabena Nketia's contribution to African musicology cannot be disputed; his influence on ethnomusicology pervades all dimensions of the subject. He educated a generation of scholars to appreciate, among other things, that in musicology cultural context and societal dynamics are just as significant as sound structure and function, and that the systematic study of the processes of music-making should be insisted upon (Wiggins 2005). Throughout his professional life Nketia appreciated musical art and artistry, its expression and performance, as well as the need for its preservation. He was concerned however that traditions should be made to be relevant to the needs of people and that by this those very traditions would be preserved. This last sentiment is indeed significant when we come to dying musical genres such as the Kasena *lenlâ*, the subject of this paper.

This paper, among other things, attempts to draw attention to *lenlâ* as a performative genre that combines music and dance. We discuss content and significance of a genre that privileges young women in a patrilineal and almost patriarchal society; and comment in the process on the status of the genre in a society which is urbanising at a rapid pace, with newly found tastes for things modern, such as television, internet, video etc. And finally we attempt to answer the question why this genre is losing popularity, while similar genres in other Ghanaian societies, like the Akan, are thriving.

In approaching the gender dimensions and implications of *lenlâ*, the genre under discussion, Nketia's leadership cannot be ignored, even if he did not study this Kasena genre. Long before gender was mainstreamed in academic endeavours Nketia had begun to charter the way to the appreciation of women's music. We are told that although his Presbyterian parents sang traditional songs, it was really his grandmother who influenced the young Nketia the most. In a sense many an accomplished musician is indebted, directly or indirectly, to the mater or a mother surrogate, such as the wet nurse. Arguably, the first songs a baby hears are the lullabies sung to sooth, calm or lull a restive child to sleep. Some might even argue that long before birth a foetus responds to external sounds, and this should include the music in the environment or what the mother hums to herself, and also sometimes to her unborn child. Music seems to come naturally to the lips of women who not only have frequent opportunities to sing their babies to sleep, but also to sing in self entertainment or to express joys and to relieve the sorrows and frustrations of life. It is common knowledge that Kasena women sang to motivate themselves to absorb the pain and drudgery of manual work in the days when grain had to be pounded in the mortar and ground into flour over slaps of granite (nɔŋɔ).

Brief Background on Kasena Society in the Past

A socio-cultural background of the Kasena is essential to an adequate appreciation of the *lenlâ* genre and its place. As space constraints do not permit for a detailed description, we refer the reader to the pertinent literature on the subject, such as Cassiman (2006), Awedoba (2000, 2010, 2011) and Fiedermutz-Laun (2005). Kasena are found in both Kasena-Nankana Districts of the Upper East Region of Ghana and in southern Burkina Faso. They were traditionally mixed farmers combining animal husbandry (cattle, sheep and goats), poultry and millet cultivation. Compound houses are reasonably interspaced to permit the surrounding land to serve as farms. The main crop was harvested in late October, the 'who-is-not-my-child' month (*wôndaabu chana*). Since the 1980s however maize and early maturing sorghum species have replaced the traditional varieties of guinea corn and piggery has become important. Drastic changes in the rainfall pattern accounted for these changes and alongside them the conversion of farmlands into residential plots. These changes have had serious societal implications. Also of significance for the culture and its traditional genres has been the impact of Christianity, Western education and urbanisation. Until Vatican II, Catholicism, as preached in the Kasena-Nankana area, kept local norms and practices at arm's length, but the vernacularisation of the church did not mean church acceptance of all Kasena practices.

The people are patrilineal and somewhat patriarchal in orientation. However, women enjoy liberties though nothing resembling remotely the licentiousness claimed by Cardinall (1921). In any case, though divorce is not a serious option for a well-constituted marriage conjugal separation has been common and estranged wives following their inclinations 'remarry' or live in what is seen as concubinage. Widow inheritance was a societal ideal: widows were expected to select a younger relative of the deceased husband to remarry. However, contrary to external perceptions, widows were not coerced into remarriage. Marriage is regulated by lineage exogamy and spouses should be selected from outside the clan-settlement. Until recently, men needing wives wooed young girls who had recently undergone the rites of female genital cutting (FGC or FGM); in the past every adolescence girl was expected to undergo these rites. As a pubescent girl attracted many suitors, elopement was sometimes inevitable, as parents either could not make up their minds whom to give a daughter's hand in marriage or were determined to marry her to a man she did not like. Wife capture occurred though this was never approved. Child betrothals were known, though not common. What was common was the practice of giving a niece to the father's sister in fosterage; there were ritual undertones to the practice. The paternal aunt through fosterage claimed the right to marry the fostered niece off to whomsoever she pleased, not discounting her own husband. Bridewealth applies in all cases, though it does not have to be presented in bulk (Awedoba 1991), and the inherited widow's family do not get a fresh bridewealth lot.

Kasena Musical Performances
Koetting (1980) provides a useful introduction to the music of the Kasena of Ghana and Burkina Faso, but regrettably his work has remained unavailable; consequently not much seems to be known about the musical traditions of the Kasena, even in Ghana. The Kasena (and we may include the Nankana) can be associated with a number of musical and dance performances and ensembles. These, including *jôåô*, a dance staged principally to welcome new brides and female visitors to the community, *nagela*, and *yɔŋɔ*, have been discussed by Koetting (passim) and the *mwanno* dance. There is the *lelara* or war dance staged on public occasions to exhibit the dancers' magical prowess and at funerals for the aged. The favourite musical instruments – the various categories of drums and flutes, have also been covered comprehensively by Koetting (1980) alongside the occasions when the specialised dances and musical instruments are played. It needs to be remarked that since the 1980s when Koetting carried out research in Nima and in Kasengo in the Upper East region much has changes and new generations of youth have come into existence for some of whom the musical types and performances investigated by Koetting would be unfamiliar.

Kasena Women's Musical Performances
Women's roles in Kasena musical performances seem less salient on the surface. Women dance to the music of *jôåô* but do not drum or accompany men as the latter sing the songs that go with *jôåô*; mostly men compose these songs, which are usually love songs and songs that narrate the concerns of the composer. Nevertheless *jôåô* is popular with

women who are not slow to seize the opportunity to show off dancing skills that are admired and acknowledge by dropping coins at the dancer's feet or by pinning currency notes to women's sweaty foreheads. Women however do more than dance, they ululate to encourage men who take the floor, especially when the male dancer is a significant individual.

A number of Kasena song types seem to have been of central importance to Kasena women, such as *luseiåa*, a dirge performed by both sexes in honour of elderly women at their final funeral rites; *sôlôlei* - performed when women stamp newly made gravelly floors, and *lenlâ*, the subject of this paper. The latter is not exactly a song type: more accurately, it is a performance in which a special type of song features (see Koetting's comment that linle (sic) is '. a generic form for several kinds of female genres or dances with music'). It could be said, as indeed Kasena would, that Kasena women 'own' *sôlôlei* and *lenlâ* in a sense not applicable to *luseiåa*. Given an elderly woman's position in the lineage, it falls to men (her sons) more than women (sons' wives or daughters) to eulogise the dead in funeral dirges that mourn the lineage's 'irreparable' loss with the demise of a 'mother'. Thus, while *lusei* [plural of *luseiåa*] honour women, they are composed presumably by men and performed by them. By contrast, *Nagoro* songs are composed by men, and performed only by them in honour of deceased 'heroes', men who killed in defence of the lineage.

In some respects *lenlâ* resemble *sôlôlei* (referred to above) and *biakwâåra lei* (children's play songs). *sôlôlei* fall within the category of female work songs and are associated with the stamping of the freshly surfaced floor; this is exclusively a women's task. Several women undertake this heavy chore, beating the floor rhythmically. Though not restricted to any age group, infirmed elderly women cannot be expected to have the energy for it. Some of the *lenlâ* songs can be mistaken for *sôlôlei*, given their close resemblances in lyrics and rhythm. In the case of *sôlôlei* the music is such that it should synchronises with the beating of the floor, not unlike the rhythmic clapping of hands in *lenlâ*. Some of the themes explored are also similar. In the case of *sôlôlei* we find women making statements, not about their love relations with men, but the regrets of life and the neglect that older housewives suffer when husbands have lost interest in them. A *sôlôleiåa* comments as follows:

When a woman's leaves dry and drop
She no longer will taste guinea fowl (meat)
Once the tail ends of the leaves drop
Where is the sense in woman

The genre *lenlâ* is different from the children's song games that Kasena children of various ages perform in the evenings. The latter are not exactly lullabies; they do not have a single lexemic reference label and are referred to as '*kwâára leî*' (lit. play songs, though they may include tongue twisters that are not songs at all). For lack of a better term they are sometimes referred to collectively as '*ameela meela saa*' songs. These so-called children's games are performed within the compound or in the outer courtyard where household members foregather. This differentiates them from *lenlâ* which are never performed inside the compound. *Lenlâ* involves far more physical activity than the more sedentary *ameela meela saa*. In addition to the types of songs performed and their accompanying sounds, other distinguishing features of *lenlâ* include their seasonality, the arena of performance, the composition and identity of the performers, and the objectives of the songs. These, among other particulars, will be discussed further. In summary, the three genres – *lenlâ*, *sôlôlei* and *kwââra lei* are similar to the extent that some of the songs may knowingly or unknowingly be performed out of context. For example a song belonging to the *sôlôlei* category may be performed at a *lenlâ* session.

Kasena *Lenlâ* and Akan *Nnwonkoro*

The word *lenlâ* is a lexeme that cannot be derived from any other; it comprises a reduplication of the root morpheme *-lâ*. As a noun it belongs to the *Kam –Sem* gender, since it collocates with the *sem* determiner. This makes it grammatically a plural noun, but it has no singular form. It is possible that its cognates are found in neighbouring Gur languages, but this is yet to be ascertained. From Danti's enquiries the Buli and Nankana lexical equivalents of the term are 'guna nichaala', and 'maale' respectively. The Dagaare term, 'ela' seems a closer cognate to the Kasem form.

It cannot be doubted that performances similar to *lenlâ* are found in other Ghanaian, and indeed African, societies. The question is whether there were/are differences, and what degree of similarity. The Asante *nnwonkoro*, as described in Amu (1999), Ampene (2005), and in Nketia

(1963) bears close resemblances to the Kasena *lenlâ*. Commenting on some features of Asante *nnwonkoro*, Amu remarks as follows:

> Nnwonkoro, as already mentioned, is a musical type performed by elderly women's groups in Asante, Brong Ahafo and the Eastern Regions of Ghana. Membership, which is voluntary, is open to any woman who is interested. Traditionally, it was performed by women on moonlight nights after a hard day's work to entertain themselves. The women gathered by going round houses calling each other to come out for a performance.

Ampene's evidence about the traditional performance of *nnwonkoro* is similar. He comments as follows:

> In the evenings after household chores, and especially when the moon was full, two or three women might gather in an open space in the village to sing nnwonkoro songs.. Gradually, other women would come to join the singing session and before long the entire group would form a large circle while taking turns in leading the songs. The women usually stood while singing and accompanied themselves with handclaps (Ampene 2005: 17).

From these scholars we get to appreciate that *nnwonkoro* was in the past purely a women's genre performed in the night, particularly on moonlit nights. It had an informal character, since it was not pre-arranged; the performance was usually begun with a few women of a village taking the initiative and then persuading other interested women to join them. Thus, from a small group a larger gathering resulted as the night wore on. The theatre of performance was, according to these accounts, an open space with the village, which implied that there was no specific venue designated for the performance.

It is also clear from Ampene's informative account that beyond the nightly performances middle-aged women staged the *nnwonkoro* at the funeral rites of a woman who in her time enjoyed the performance or was an active participant. This would not of course be surprising as it is customary in most societies to re-enact activities that a deceased person was associated with in life, as Goody (1965) illustrates for the Dagaba of the Upper West Region of Ghana. Ampene's account shows that in the past, *nnwonkoro* performances did not make use of instruments and that the handclap was distinctive of the genre. Ampene remarks as follows: 'drums and percussion instruments were noticeably absent ...' (Ampene 2005: 17-18).

Much of what is written about *nnwonkoro* in its traditional format is reminiscent of the Kasena *lenlâ*. There is however the difference that *nnwonkoro* songs praised male relations of the performers: brothers, husbands, lovers, and friends. Ampene justifies this by quoting a proverb that says 'If your uterine sister is a member of the *nnwonkoro* band, your name never gets lost' (Ampene, 2005: 29). This can hardly be said of the Kasena *lenlâ*. The point of the Akan proverb is that a sister would not fail to honour her brothers or relatives by using the medium of *nnwonkoro* to sing their praises. But it also means that if *nnwonkoro* was being used to praise, then it was subject to considerable customization of existing songs or else new songs were coined by the performers with the objective of praising relatives and individuals in their lives. If it is plausible to argue, and we do argue here, that *nnwonkoro* in its traditional form, i.e. in the form in which Ampene argues it was found in the 1880s or even before 1944, bore uncanny resemblances to *lenlâ*, then from the 1950s onwards *nnwonkoro* began to transform in ways that made it radically different from *lenlâ*.

Ampene says by 1944 both men and women had begun to be involved in *nnwonkoro* performances in mixed bands (Ampene, p. 19): 'It was only in 1944 that a group of women and men came together to formally constitute a *nnwonkoro* group in Kumase ..' with Nana Afua Abasa as their lead singer. He remarks also that by the 1950s there were several *nnwonkoro* groups and that they competed among themselves. Furthermore, the genre spread in popularity to others parts of the Ashanti Region and the Brong Ahafo taking inspiration from Nana Abasa. From Ampene's account the *nnwonkoro* moved out of the village square to the structured performance spaces of cities and towns. What is more, it enjoyed royal approval from Otumfoo Osei Prempeh II.

The Seasonality of Lenlâ

The Kasena *lenlâ*, as a cultural genre, is seasonal rather than perennial; it is usually performed in the evenings after the cooking was done and food had been eaten. That can be as late as nine o'clock in the evening in some households, though it could also be as early as seven o'clock. The domestic chores assigned to young teenage girls would first have to be completed if a girl in the appropriate category was to be permitted to go out in the evenings. Today, it might mean that homework from school might make it difficult for a school pupil to attend a *lenlâ* session. On moonlit nights young people [mainly teenage girls] would meet in an open space near the chief's compound or the compound of the community elder [*nakwe*]. Such meetings seemed unplanned and began with a couple of girls singing and calling to their mates. The invitation chants were often insults addressed at a named individual. She was told that she was ugly: 'They say your mouth has papules clustered together like snails and grains of sand stuck together by latex.'

In *lenlâ* the performers sing and dance primarily to entertain themselves. This is earned recreation for youth after the day's work, and it is expected that this would take place after the harvest season [*fani*], when food is available to all and sundry and there is joy and gaiety in the atmosphere, a replication, so to speak, of the sentiment of the white dove represented as saying in Kasem '*Puga na sua vona wuuri mo*' [to wit: when the belly is full the wings roar as they flap]. The *lenlâ* performance can be said to reflect the gaiety of a community which had made it through the difficulties of the year, with its uncertainties. In some respects it also recalls the *faao* celebrations, which like *lenlâ*, were never community level events until recent years. Referring to the seasonality of the genre Koetting (1980:62) expressed the view that *lenlâ* would not be performed in years when the harvest was poor. The typical time of year for the performance of *lenlâ* would be the period between late October and December. The rains would have ceased by then; the night skies would be cloudless and much of the harvest would have been gathered and stored; there would be less work in the evenings. At this time the eerie brightness of the full moon (*chan-cheiåa*, i.e. the moon that does not set but is eclipsed by the early morning sun) is said to light the night recalling a local composer's comment on his lover's beauty: *kayaga lam nye-de chan-cheiåa na peere yadâ tega* (Kayaga's beauty is reminiscent of the resplendence of the wet season's night as the full moon reigns supreme). It is unlikely that *lenlâ* performance would be relished in any other condition or time of the year. But according to some informants outside these times young women could stage *lenlâ* as a side show at the funeral of an older person. Koetting confirms this and adds that when a new compound is being found *lenlâ* may be staged.

Lenlâ is loud and is easily heard and noticed within the community where it is organised and in nearby communities. In some respects, it is meant to attract participants from within the vicinity and neighbouring clan-settlements. One *lenlâ* song alludes to this in the refrain, *ko yende ŋuuri yeim nwoo* (from where comes this deep loud sound?) followed by the name of the clan-settlement where the event is taking place. There is often considerable handclapping, as the refrain to *kon yende nguuri* interposes:

> *debam baåa baåa X bia mage mage wâ maa to,*
> *ko yaan ŋuuri yeim ywoo*
> (we the daughters/wives of X clansmen will clap/beat
> till sun down, do you ask where the noise issues from!).

Perhaps because of this, in the Kasem language *lenlâ* is described in the metaphor of 'beating' and 'clapping' – *ba mage lenlâ*. (lit. *lenlâ* is beaten/clapped). This is inevitable given that rhythm is required to keep the performance going. There is of course more than the handclap: the girls jostle each other and pairs take turns to hit each other as hard as possible with the buttocks. The vigour of the performance is suggested by a *lenlâ* song that exhorts performers to exhibit their strength by pushing down weaklings and whoever was not strong physically.

> Kwei n-de n-yare; Kwei n-de n-yare ywoo
> [Throw her down, throw her down]
> Nabwonu nabwonu, Kwei n-de n-yare
> [If weakling, spare her not, but throw her down]
> N *ná* wae n dwoŋi, Kwei n-de n-yare
> [If you are stronger, throw her down]

This is further confirmed by the song that literally invites a physical confrontation in the statement: 'my bones and my muscles are restless.'

A kuuro nye ywoo, Yaa yaa
> [my bones ache so]
A kuuruo nye zigzag kuna
> [my bones crack, *zag zag kuna*]
Nanbwona nye naa
> [How my flesh aches for action]
N laan nye nee
> [I ache for action]

In *lenlâ* performance no percussion instruments feature, as remarked above; that is to say no drums, sticks, whistles or flutes; not even the stick rattle (*senyaga*), which is commonly used by Kasena girls to entertain themselves, has a place in the genre. Women are known to play on small calabashes as they sing along, but instruments would be out of place in *lenlâ* for the simple reason that the performers need to be free to clap, hop, butt and jostle each other.

Youth and Lenlâ

From what has been remarked about *lenlâ*, it goes without saying that this is a young people's genre. Those who frequent *lenlâ* are young women and girls of various ages, often those in their teens and early twenties. This category comprises the unmarried girls and those recently married women yet to be shackled to babies. Girls below age thirteen would normally not be eligible, and if they attended they would be spectators, since they lack the physical strength to do the bottoms butting required. Indeed Danti (one of the authors) found that the participants are arranged in such a way that pairs of participants of comparable size and strength would face off for the butting. There are usually in any Kasena village community a number of young unmarried girls of the appropriate age: daughters of the community (*bukwa*), and girls living away from their natal homes. Within the latter category are betrothed girls who may or may not have begun conjugal life. There are also those girls who came into the community on fosterage. Kasena male siblings no longer practice the *boore* (see Awedoba 2003) but sisters continue to earn the right to foster that nieces born after they, the married paternal aunts, had performed the rites of engirdling the niece's mother when the latter became pregnant for the first time. Custom entitles such a father's sister (could be classificatory) to claim the niece born through her ritual intervention as it were, and to take the child to live with her and serve as domestic help. Fostering aunts invariably enjoy the right to select future husbands for the fostered nieces.

The *lenlâ* provides the pretext for the different categories of young women to meet outside the compound and socialise. In their midst may be found the odd young woman accompanied by her toddler child, but the demands of motherhood make it difficult for most young mothers to participate actively in the *lenlâ* event. In any case, some husbands object to a wife going off in the night to a *lenlâ* performance; parents might also have their misgivings. It would seem however that young women were not to be denied their right to participate in this nocturnal entertainment, prior to the advent of television. Girls wishing to attend a *lenlâ* session within the village would go in small groups comprising those from the same or adjacent compounds. This is to ensure safety and enable girls to keep each other's company and seek safety in numbers. Nevertheless, it is not unheard of for unmarried girls to elope or be abducted while out in the night attending a *lenlâ* session. The dangers of *lenlâ* are adequately captured in the folktale about the girl who never missed a *lenlâ* or *jôåô* dance event until one day she found herself in a dance staged by ghosts. It is not unreasonable to argue that myths such as these or those about trees assuming human guises at night aim to instil fear in those who leave the safety of the compound at night.

For want of something to do, young boys may accompany their sisters and cousins or go on their own to witness *lenlâ* performances. This is to be expected since culturally there is no male equivalent of *lenlâ*. When there is a group of such boys they engaged in their own sideshow alongside the girls staging *lenlâ*. While there seems to be no enthusiasm for male company during *lenlâ*, boys are nevertheless tolerated. Sometimes they receive the butt end of jokes when a *lenlâ* song is re-phrased to say something offensive about boys. The *Tia tia puuro* song for example actually alludes to male presence when the song tells Kamaana puuro (not clear if this is a real name or nickname) that he is a nonentity; he is short in stature and his male organ is unsightly like a log. The main point of the *lenlâ* then is to provide entertainment for those who engage in the performance, and if young men come to watch, that sits well with the girls. The singing, handclapping and the dancing around, pushing and shoving and bottoms butting seem to demonstrate physical strength. It is as if Kasena women emphasise that they are not necessarily the 'weaker' sex. It would be effeminate for a boy to engage in any of this, just as it would be to most Ghanaians effeminate behaviour for a boy to play *ampe*, which involves school girls hopping, clapping and trusting out the left and then the right leg. In *lenlâ* Kasena girls for a moment put aside their cares and worries.

Lenlâ is not without its socialization aspects. It is inevitable that young men should find the temptation to attend *lenlâ* irresistible, but it does not appeal to married men and older women. It is perhaps one of the few occasions when such young women, in a traditional Kasena setting, until the era of film shows and dances in the 1970s, could be together and enjoy each other's company. The life of a young woman in this culture was until recently not an easy one, as she accompanied her mother and other women to the farm, to the riverside to fetch water, to the bushlands to fetch firewood, or to forage for shea nut fruits and other wild products in the bushlands. If she was not doing any of these then she was in the kitchen or child-minding or working on the farm. In the past some teenage girls were herders taking care of the livestock – cattle, or sheep. Cattle herding is usually a boys' chore and girls naturally are resentful if required to herd livestock. In a *lenlâ* song the farmer is told point blank to tether his cattle. The lot of the maturing young girl, especially one living away from parents, was never likely to be an easy one. It was a life devoid of leisure, not to mention luxury and privilege. For such a young girl the *lenlâ* must serve as a special attraction, perhaps the only respite in her adolescent life. In the view of one informant, *lenlâ* brought together the teenage girls who would soon be genitally excised.

Themes Explored in *Lenlâ* Lyrics

As a mechanism that gave a collective voice to the voiceless teenage girl, *lenlâ* alluded to concerns such as opposite sex relationships; peer group relations and associations; the carefree life of a teenager; the daily chores of unmarried girls; as well as veiled criticisms of older women and husbands. There is also praise for hard work and achievement. Since authorship does not seem important, it can be argued that the themes fall within the domain of collective, rather than individual representations. Performers however could and did embellish and customize song texts. For young people the body remains the center of interest and attention and *lenlâ* songs contained a considerable amount of the erotic. The *Kamaana puuro* song is illustrative; the object of ridicule has an unsightly penis: *fwolo-zââ* (flaccid penis); a penis like a log (*fwolo ne dalôâô*); a circumcised penis (*fwol-manchiga tu*); penis with a bulgy tip (*fwol-yugula*). All this is sung accompanied by peals of laughter. Even the sexual act is alluded to when the butt of the sexual insults is told to bring corn in exchange for a purse (*ganlôge*).

We can talk of a 'love problematic' in a context where girls had little say in the choice of husbands. As pointed out, the traditional Kasena girl might be betrothed in infancy, fostered by a paternal aunt who will marry her to a man of the aunt's choice, or she remain with her parents until the clitoridectomy rites when she would be given to a man whom her parents and relatives considered suitable. However, girls could defy their parents by eloping with men of their choice. A song talks about the lurking boyfriend on whom kitchen water was accidentally poured. This is most likely the man in love whom the girl's parents do not approve; he is thus compelled to lurk about waiting perhaps for the right moment to talk his girl into eloping. The lyrics run as follows:

'I poured water on my boy friend, my boy friend, get me water so that I may rinse him.'

While the song that provokes and invites women to the performance arena does not flatter the invited individuals who are called out, however some *lenlâ* songs praise men – husbands, boyfriends and male siblings. A song invites participants to comment on the physical attributes of darling husbands (*n bala*) and boyfriends (*n bôôlo*) by describing how tall they are. The lyrics go as follows:

They ask, what size is your dear husband, [bis]
(*Ba we-n bala ma tɛ, ba we-n bala ma tɛ*)
Sure, your dear husband is a good-looking man
(*Ko da-n bala na mae wo-laao*)
They ask, what size is your lover, [bis]
(*Ba we-n bôôlo ma tɛ, ba we-n bôôlo ma tɛ*)
Sure, your lover is a good-looking man
(*Ko da-n bôôle na mae wo-laao*)

One song represents a lover praising his darling's beauty and instigating her to dress up in readiness for a flight. Miss Kamena is told she is – Kamena, the beauty (*kamen-laao*) and that she is like newly-made glass beads (*zon-doåo*); she is light-skinned without blemish (*Kamen-pwora*). Husbands, female affines, and paternal aunts have disciplinary roles vis-à-vis teenage girls. A person might be perceived as wicked if she was uncompromising in her disciplining of subordinates. A *lenlâ* song remarks about the old woman who was so wicked that on her death no one (presumably none of her daughters and daughters-in-law) would accept her ivory bangles. In the song the ivory armlets are displayed for whoever would like them, yet young women are warned by their parents (or those who know better) that the deceased owner was no good. She might have been a witch or a frustrated woman who bore people grudges. The implication seems to be that wearing her armlets could be dangerous for the wearer, as the spirit of the original owner might inhere in her treasures. Lenlâ does not spare the evil aunt.

Reference is made in the lyrics of *lenlâ* to the whining polygynous husband (*kan-baro wo-nyena*) who is advised that he should tether his cattle and give shepherd girls a break.

> Polygynous husband, forever whining, I am off
> Nakelakôgô bird reports that Agworayeri orders all artists be summoned
> Husband of women, tether your cattle
> We will dance the rhythmic *sinleinga* dance (in defiance)

The polygynous husband has considerable demands made on his resource by his numerous affines. The prime prestations (to use a phrase coined by Fortes 1972) are settled in cattle. Husbands must perforce take animal husbandry seriously, if they are to have the means to meet marriage prestations, but it has implications for domestic relationships — omelets cannot be made without breaking eggs. The very girls (betrothed) whose parents demand cattle must assist their husbands-to-be to raises the herd. The *lenlâ* participant is also a child miner, a job with its frustrations. A song comments on the marasmus fastidious child (*nena*) who rejects all foods and whose demands and attitudes are exasperating. You name it: *sworo* (muscilagenous stew), *kapwonnu* (porridge), *veo* (hibiscus sabdariffa stew), or what have you, but the child remains indifferent leaving the caretaker at her wits end. She is called names because of her lack of cooking skills, but who should she blame: her mother or her father, who placed her in this situation, perhaps by fostering her out? While polygynous husbands are criticised for being too hard, a song presents the opposite view: the case of the over-indulgent husband who would not allow his young bride to work. The song remarks:

> Anao says soil his wife will touch not
> If tomorrow a person should be lost
> Who will they blame

Kasena have the concept of *ka-yero*, the exquisite woman who is industrious and meticulous. She is clean and not messy. In a *sôlô* song the lyrics comment on the preparation of the *kayero*'s yard to enable her sweep it. (*A we-a per ka-yero diga mo se-o nwong-o zôre weeru*). The opposite is the *ka-pwogo*: the woman who is lazy and unkempt, and a disgrace to herself and her husband and family. The above *lenlâ* song warns protective husbands that over-indulgence spoils young brides; pampered wives grow into unskilled lazy and good-for-nothing wives. The point is that powerful old husbands can pamper the young wife, but they will not become *kayero* and moreover a hard life awaits them when the husband dies. Such a widow might be 'inherited' by a younger husband who might not dote on her, and then it might to be too late to learn the survival arts. Hard work, including farming chores, are seem as beneficial. This is reflected in the song which praises farm work. It remarks that the suffering associated with the farm (*kara* and *kaduga*) is the sweetest of all hardships, and that there is no other work that is so sweet.

The chief's huge herd of cattle are commented on positively. A song refers to the cattle of the chief of Manyoro, a chiefdom close to the Ghana-Burkina Faso border and the cattle of the chief of Koumbili in southern Burkina Faso. The lyrics go as follows:

Hay, I like to describe
    A laan maå' naa
Manyoro chief's cattle
    Manyara pâ naane
Let them be herded this way
    Ba kal' ba-jaa ba

Cattle were of critical importance in the domestic economy and made a difference. The greatness of a man was symbolized by the size of his kraal. A man of means in this traditional society was one who had cattle, and the colonial era chief had cattle, obtained as gifts and through sundry means, fair and foul. It used to be said that Navro-pio had over a hundred cattle.

Some songs, as pointed out, are insults. Where the remark is made in jest, a name is mentioned, and the insult is seen as a joke, comparable to nicknaming; but in a number of cases it is unclear who is being insulted. In the case of the Kamaana puuro song already referred to above, the subject is generic rather than specific — the detested suitor whose attentions are odious, yet the girl at whom they are addressed dare not make her feelings plain or public. Kasena say no unmarried woman should reject a suitor or let it be known that she detests the attentions of a particular suitor. There is a belief that rejected and disgraced suitors are capable of using magical means to harm disrespectful girls. The consequence of this is that when a girl is deemed to have come of age, numerous suitors converge at her parents' home to woo her. It can be argued that the medium of the *lenlâ* furnishes the opportunity to release punt up grievances.

Unlike war songs (*nagoro lei*) that target peoples from different chiefdoms and even ethnic groups associated with wars and slave raiding in the past, *lenlâ* songs are rarely negatively ethno-centric or offensive of non-Kasena people. However, a *lenlâ* song refers to attacks on the Moshie and goes on to describe them as lice-infested people whom it was a pleasure to see being assaulted and robbed of their money. It seems these attacks were very common in the late nineteenth century when Moshie traders came down south with their donkey caravans and merchandise. As members of a powerful chiefdom that in former times treated peoples like the Kasena as fodder there was no sympathy for these poor traders, in any case no one had the capacity to stop the attacks, until the British stationed a garrison in Navrongo around 1905.

Rhythm Without Much Meaning or Misunderstood Lyrics

Some songs, such as the 'Azunka weo' song, defy semantic interpretation. Its potential lexical items include: *zuŋa* – which could be translated as 'bird', but then it makes not much sense in the context. *Kabwolei* which occurs in the song is not a regular Kasem word. Items like *niyaa hee* and *hoyaa* are nothing more than rhythm carriers. Clearly then a song like this one has only one objective i.e. to generate a performance that can be danced to. Similar to this is the 'berese se se nyan gwoo' song which does not seem to lend itself to a Kasem interpretation. One is tempted to think that this is a song borrowed from another language or a different dialect of Kasem such as Nuni spoken in Burkina Faso. *Gwoo*, and *niyaa wei* are common rhythm carriers in Kasena music.

> Beere se se nyan gwo
> Niyaa wei
> A nu nyan sibiloo
> Niyaa wei
> Niyaa yaa kware

Some songs can be interpreted literally but they do not seem to say anything significant. It also seems that some of the songs are polythematic; they combine different themes, and this could be due to repeated improvisations and lexical substitutions. The song that invites performers to describe their loved ones begins with stanzas that do not seem to pre-empt the ultimate purpose of the song. It addresses the leech, asking it to show gratitude and then goes on to bid the leech farewell, and proceeds to make statements which seem to be unrelated:

> Bugani kasandi gwoo
>> River leech!
>
> Kasandi ke leilei
>> Leech make it quick
>
> Kwarajei ke leilei
>> Kwarajei, make it sooner
>
> A ma-n yein a kâ se-a ba
>> I am off

This song seems to relish rhyme and rhythm more than meaning. At least *bugani, kasandi kwarajei* seem to rhyme as the final syllable exemplifies the same vowel quality and bear high tone. The words are also trisyllabic. The song that comments on the attacks on the Moshie traders begins by talking of meals and a visit to Paga in two days times. It goes as follows:

> Aweoo aweoo, hanyaawei
>> Hear me, hear me
>
> A jwa yiga maa vei Paga, hanyaawei
>> I go to Paga tomorrow next
>
> Tentente gol-bia balei, hanyaawei
>> In the early morning, two slaps of thick porridge
>
> Dedaani gol-bia batô, hanyaawei
>> In the evening, three slaps of thick stiff porridge
>
> Ba mag-beilla pa sabia jaana, hanyaawei
>> The Moshie are assaulted, coins fly all over
>
> Beilla wora ba le karesa, hanyaawei
>> Moshie men picking lice

There seems to be thematic incoherence. What have meals to do with visits to Paga? The international boundary cuts through the Paga chiefdoms and it is reasonable to expect hostile encounters at Paga, and if traders are being attacked, their money and their goods would not be spared; but what has this to do with lice?

The Demise of Lenlâ

Death knell of *lenlâ* sounded over two decades ago. It no longer is performed in Central Navrongo except at funerals, and as the genre falls into disuse, it can be predicted that time will come when funeral rites will not include *lenlâ* performances. Some respondents say *lenlâ* is mandatory for every woman's funeral, regardless of whether she were ethnically Kasena or not. This can only remain true so long as there are women conversant with the performance of *lenlâ*. *Lenlâ* may persist in some remote rural areas. Rural electrification, extended to Navrongo and surrounding areas in the early 1990s, set in motion several irreversible processes: Akan and Nigerian TV dramas filled a yawning need for evening entertainment. Makeshift home entertainment theatres came into being showing African and Western movies and even village youths now have more exciting perennial sources of entertainment. But even before that, responding to the needs of youth in the 1990s individual disc jockeys began to tour the villages staging dances and charging gate fees. That began the demise of *lenlâ*. When it came to a choice, youth voted for the record dance and the tele-nouvellas.

Lenlâ's demise is due in no small measure to the genre's inflexibility and inability to change rhythm in tune with modern tastes. By contrast *nnwonkoro* survived because it was able to innovate and go public, and the accounts of Ampene and others show this. As one informant explained, the popularity of *lenlâ* was due to the nonexistence of other forms of entertainment in the community. In the pre-electrification days, youths and children told folktales in the evenings, but it was the same tales re-hashed and retold. Riddles, another feature of the evening's entertainment, were also repetitive and monotonous. Given this scenario *lenlâ* broke the monotony of village life, even if the songs were the same old ones that most people in the community were familiar with. Then TV and the video came and the record dance arrived.

A schematic comparison of Nnwonkoro and lenlâ shows why the former lives on while the latter had to go. Nnwonkoro was like lenlâ in the past, but it survives and thrives because it re-invented and meets the needs of its modern publics. The table below compares the two genres:

	Nnwonkoro	Lenlâ
Periodicity	All season	Very seasonal and occasional
Appeal	Universal	Parochial - a young women's issue
Innovation	Considerable	Minor and at the individual level
Royal Approval	Patronage by royalty	Lacked formal support from chiefs
Performance Domain	Went public	Remained in the local community

Conclusion

We began with Nketia's position that the traditional genres have to be made relevant to the needs of a changing public. The fates of *nnwonkoro* and *lenlâ* are instructive; *nnwonkoro* has adapted to changing times and demands, but *lenlâ* failed to do this and is now on the wane. But while we sing dirges to *lenlâ*, the spirit of *lenlâ* lives and manifests itself in many ways. Some of the post-Vatican II Catholic Church music in Navrongo is patterned on *lenlâ*, though no one admits this; *lenlâ* seem to recall the obscene and the profane. On festive occasions women's songs take after *lenlâ*, even if no one gives credit to *lenlâ*. In the future, older Kasena women's final funeral rites will not be complete without a ritual staging of *lenlâ*. And when *lenlâ* has been buried, along with it would be an important aspect of Kasena-Nankana culture. As the women's song text mourns: *'my old stick rattle hangs in the kitchen ceiling, but I have neither daughter nor younger sister to take it down and play.'*

Endnotes

1: The songs on which the paper is based were collected overtime. One of the authors, Awedoba, collected a number of these songs at Kakungu, central Paga, in 1989 with the support of Mr. Peter Aloa and his family. Danti, the other author, collected other songs at Pungu, one of the divisional chiefdoms of Navrongo. The authors are grateful to Christiana Akwozaga, a 28 year old woman from the Manyoro chiefdom who now lives in Accra, for shedding additional light on the interpretation of the song texts and the context of *lenlâ* performance.

2: Some of the important sources on the Kasena are in French and relate to the Kasena communities in the Burkina Faso side.

3: Introduced in 1906 or thereabout, Catholicism has been the predominant Christian denomination of the Kasena-Nankana area. The Church provided educational opportunities in an area where government did not sponsor educational institutions until recently. The first school in the north was set up by the Catholic White Fathers in Navrongo in 1907 or thereabout.

4: We have not been privileged to read any of his works. Koetting (1980) appears to be an unpublished dissertation, however we have had access to his list of Kasena musical terms covering instruments, types of songs and types of dances.

5: Floor stamping is a female chore usually undertaken by a group of women whose objective is to compact the floor surface by beating it with flat wooden mallets.

6: Koetting op cit. p69-70

7: The lyrics of *lusei* tell of the lineage's loss of a gorgeous maternal figure. She is described as a 'beautiful black bird moving gracefully within the tree leaves' (*teeini wone zonzwon-laao ko vei ka lea lea*), and as cloth that sparkles (gare-nyeŋo), etc. The death of an elderly person is however seen as more of a celebration of life than a mournful event.

8: To the extent that the composers of such folksongs are anonymous, ascribing authorship to men is no more than conjecture.

9: The word means literally, 'man-slaughter'; its themes reflect battle front exploits in the unsettled past when lineages fought each other and stood up to the slave raider — the *gwala* and the *kambonga* [foreigner] and the *'feila'* [white man] who exploded musketry that supposedly did not frighten or deter the deceased — *miatu* [the bow man] and his mates.

10: This is a complaint about male neglect of women past their prime: the song argues that women ought to know about male deceit, but in their youthful age they repeat the same mistake of permitting suitors to deceive them into elopement, contrary to parental advice.

11: The call phrase of one of the song games involved.

12: Reduplication is a common phonological process in Kasem from which new words are formed. In this case we can only guess at the meaning of the root morpheme: if related to the verb *lwâ* (to disparage), then *lenlâ* may well be interpreted as something that disparages. There is however no evidence that the associated songs aim to disparage, belittle or undermine anyone, even if a number are critical comments while some actually insult named persons.

13: See Awedoba (2007) for a discussion of Kasem genders and noun classification. The Kam-Sem gender by association is diminutive and can contain items that semantically have disparaging connotations.

14: Though most Kasem nouns have singular and plural forms a number do not inflect for number. Many liquids are plural, and the word for dance *sâ*, is a plural noun.

15: As praise and criticism [if not insult] tend to go together – Kipling's 'two imposters' - one may ask if *nnwonkoro* was not also used to criticize a 'bad' relative.

16: The juxtaposition of past and present tenses is justified since lenlâ is still being performed, though less frequently; at the same time some of its features are no longer application.

17: School homework and domestic chores are not alone in accounting for a school girl's rare appearance at *lenlâ*.

18: The Kasena *faao* was in former times a household event and there was no specific day on which the community held its faao. Indeed, not everybody observed faao, though this was the occasion when sacrifices were made to thank the ancestors and gods for their support over the past 'traditional' year. The same can be said of the Bulsa fiok. In years when the harvests were poor faao was not performed.

19: Koetting (op. cit: 62) suggests the period between late October and November, after the harvest of guinea corn.

20: Founding a new compound is an important rite of passage. The founder and his senior wife must leave the old compound and camp on the new site until the new compound is habitable. *Lenlâ* breaks the couple's solitude at this time. The time to found a new compound was anytime between January and March.

21: One respondent in an interview classified this song as belonging to the *sôlôlei* type. There is some justification in this, since the refrain talks of '... beating/ clapping till sun set', which suggests a daytime rather than a nighttime event. However, the rhythm is certainly one not suited to sɔlɔ, being too rapid for floor preparation.

22: It seemed reminiscent of shepherds establishing hierarchy by wrestling each other.

23: 'Engirdlement' is to safeguard the pregnancy and ensure successful childbirth. In this rite the pregnant woman should be kept in the dark about the enactment of the rite and should not know about the sister-in-law's presence in the compound. She should be taken by surprise and ashes blown at her by the husband's sister who tells her 'I have caught you red-handed'.

24: There is the belief that trees, the baobab especially, can transform and adopt human guises at night and frighten people. The spirits of the dead (*chira*) walk about, zombies (*kwogo*) prowl around and wicked persons change into cat-like creatures to harm others. In the past hyenas and predators (*kanyanchoro*) visited human settlements at night.

25: Feminine strength is a cultural ideal that should be demonstrated, as it should be in genital cuttings when immediately after the cutting girls should get up and execute a dance (*mage nampôle*).

26: See http://www.estcomp.ro/-cfg/ghana.html, retrieved on 20th September for a description of some Ghanaian children's games.

27: With the engendering of primary schools, boys now play Ampe, a thing that until recently would have been scandalous. Even the players of the national team, the Black Stars can occasionally be observed celebrating goals by dancing *Ampe*.

28: Traditionally male circumcision was culturally unknown.

29: This can be heard in the taped recording.

30: Clitoridectomy is the same as FGM or female genital cutting (FGC); Kasena did not regard the rite as 'mutilation'

References

Ampene, Kwasi. 2005. *Female Song Tradition and the Akan of Ghana*. Burlington, VT: Ashgate Publishing Company.

Amu, Misonu. 1999. "Creativity and Tradition in Nnwonkoro: The Contribution of Maame Afua Abasa." *Research Review* 15 (1).

Awedoba, A. K. 2000. *An Introduction to Kasena Society And Culture Through Their Proverbs*. Lanham, MD: University Press of America.

Awedoba A. K. 2001. "Matrimonial Prestations Among the Kasena of Navrongo." In *Regionalism and Public Policy in Northern Ghana*. Ed. by Yakubu Saaka. Frankfurt Am Main: Peter Lang, 92-117.

___. 2003. "The *Pepara* Hunt Among the Kasena-Nankana: A Way of Life or a Way of the Gods?" In *Ghana's North. Research on Culture, Religion, and Politics of Societies in Transition*. Ed. by Meier B. Gottinger Kulturwissenchafliche Schriften: Iko-Verlog Frankfurt am Main, 263-278.

———. 2007. "Gender and Kasena Classification of Things." In *Proceedings of the Colloquium the Annual Colloquium of the Legon-Trondheim Linguistics Project, Part 1: Nominal Constructions*. Ed. by M. E. Kropp Dakubu, G. Akanlig-Pare, E.K. Osam and K. K. Saah. Legon: Studies in the Languages of the Volta Basin, 28-42.

———. 2010. *Kasena Riddles: A Study of Kasena Literature and Culture*. Saarbrucken: Lambert Academic Publishing.

Bening R. B. 1990. *A History of Education in Northern Ghana, 1907-1976*. Accra: Ghana Universities Press.

Cardinall A. W. 1921. *Natives of the Northern Territories of the Gold Coast*. London: Routledge and Sons, Ltd.

Cassiman, Ann. 2008. "Home and Away: Mental Geographies of Young Migrant Workers and Their Belonging to the Family House in Northern Ghana." *Housing, Theory and Society* 25 (1): 14-30.

Cassiman, Ann 2006. *Stirring Life. Women's Paths and Places Among the Kasena of Northern Ghana. Uppsala Studies in Cultural Anthropology*. Uppsala: Uppsala Universitat.

Fiedermutz-Laun, Annemarie. 2005. "The House, the Hearth and the Granary—Symbols of Fertility Among the West African Kasena." *The Medieval History Journal* 8 (1): 247-265.

Fortes, Meyer. 1972. "Introduction." In *Marriage in Tribal Societies*. Cambridge Papers in Social Anthropology. Cambridge: Cambridge University Press

Goody, Jack. 1965. *Death Property and the Ancestors*. London: Tavistock Publications.

Koetting, J. T. 1980. *Continuity and Change in Ghanaian Kasena Flute and Drum Ensemble Music: A Comparative Study of the Homeland and Nima/Accra*. PhD dissertation. University of California, Los Angeles.

Lwanda, John. 2003. "Mother's Songs: Male Appropriation of Women's Music in Malawi and Southern Africa." *Journal of African Cultural Studies* 16 (2): 119-141.

Nketia J. H. K. 1963. *Folk Songs of Ghana*. Accra: Universities of Ghana Press.

Sutherland-Addy Esi and Diaw Aminata. 2005. *Women Writing Africa. Vol. 2: West Africa and the Sahel*. New York: The Feminist Press at the City University of New York.

Wiggins, Trevor. 1998. "Teaching Culture: Thoughts from Northern Ghana." *British Journal of Music Education* 15 (2): 201-9.

Documentation of Slavery in Ghanaian Folklore: Anlo Ewe Slave Songs

Mawuli Adjei

Mawuli Adjei is a senior lecturer in the Department of English at the University of Ghana. He specializes in African literature, oral literature, popular literature, creative writing, and literary criticism. He is currently engaged in research on the manifestations of slavery in African orature and film in West Africa. He is a novelist and poet with four publications to his credit. His publications are *The Jewel of Kabibi* (2011), *Taboo* (2012), *The Witch of Lagbati* (2014) and an anthology, *Testament of the Seasons* (2013).

Introduction

Slave songs remain invaluable sources of insight into slavery and yield much information about the past. They reveal certain aspects of slavery which are hard to come by in history textbooks. In Ghana, slavery continues to be treated as a taboo subject, yet it is an integral part of folk memory. It is only in dismantling the shroud of secrecy around the topic of slavery that the world can deal with it more appropriately. According to Ogude (1990:11), "the memory of the Slave Trade haunts the African imagination like a bad dream" and it must be confronted and exorcised from the African consciousness. Assimeng (1997:34), on the other hand, is of the view that although slavery has had "such a pervading attention in the historiography of Africa that it might appear overflogged …it appears not to have been sufficiently stressed, in searching for objects of African social theorizing." This present research into slave songs from the Anlo Ewe community was thus conceived as a challenge to engage the community in a historical and literary dialogue.

Methodology

The research was conducted mainly in the Klikor area in the Ketu District of the Volta Region. The researcher was personally involved in the recording, transcription and translation of the songs. This was facilitated by the now defunct Blakhud Research Centre based at Klikor which commissioned a group of singers to sing and perform the songs.

Slave Songs In Context

As indicated in the introduction, to fully appreciate the import and significance of slave songs, one needs to place them in the social, historical and religious contexts in which they were generated. As Akosua Perbi documents,

> The major sources of slave supply were warfare, the market, pawning, raiding, kidnapping and tribute. The minor sources included gifts, criminal conviction and personal transactions. The slaves were put to several uses, especially to labour in agriculture, trade and industry. They were also recruited into the administrative sectors of the state and enrolled in the military. Some performed domestic chores in palaces, shrines and individual households, while others were sacrificed from time to time in accordance with traditional beliefs and practices (2004).

Massiasta throws more light on the system:

> Simply put, slavery in Africa was originally a relatively mild, controlled and logical practice employed to rehabilitate or reform criminals, rebellious people and prisoners of war, especially in a nomadic society where there were no administrative and permanent penal mechanisms to enforce law and order. Unlike the modern form of slavery characterized by indignities and deprivations, in the original African slavery, the slave did not completely lose his personal freedoms...The slave, therefore, was not a commodity or a means of exchange to be traded on end or held permanently. In short, the slaver in the African system protected, cared for and even resettled the slave in return for his services and not for his labours (1994:4).

In both quotes above, central to the system of slavery are issues regarding displacement, deprivation, service, freedom, rights, privileges, punishment, warfare, shrines and households. Slave songs are thus woven around these major thematic areas, from the perspectives of slaves, relatives and communities. The songs must also be properly located in the song traditions of the Anlo Ewe. Above all, they must be seen as reflecting the worldview of the Anlo Ewe with regard to the thematic issues identified above.

Slave songs in the Anlo Ewe area derive essentially from the Anlo Ewe dirge tradition. Scholars such as Awoonor (1979), Anyidoho (1983) and Seshie (1973) who have researched extensively into Anlo Ewe dirge describe it as a song tradition noted for its expression of the human condition and the precariousness of life. There is a preponderance of a sense of fatalism and determinism, a sense in which the individual's life is seen as regulated and determined by 'Se' (Destiny or Fate)—equal to the Igbo 'chi'. However, antithetical to this sense of determinism and fatalism is a spirit of defiance. Thus, in most Anlo Ewe dirges, individuals may question and challenge their 'Se' for giving them a raw deal in life. The most obvious aspect of the Anlo Ewe dirge captured in slave songs relates to the former—fatalism and determinism. There is only a marginal propensity towards radicalism and defiance.

There are both public/secular and cultic slave songs in Ewe. Even though most of the popular songs are lost, the cultic and religious ones are still well documented in the divination repertory. This is due to the fact that shrines and traditional religious institutions played a vital role in the regulation and preservation of the institutions of slavery. For instance, in Eweland,

> The shrines, for a long time, remained as reformatories for the disadvantaged, the deviant or the criminal. A person who committed manslaughter and faced execution, for instance, might seek refuge in the shrine, where spiritual education, rituals, ordeals and confinement were intended to reform or give him spiritual and moral rebirth. He became an indemnified "slave" or servant of the god to be permanently replaced by his descendants – the origins of the FIASHIDI (TROKOSI) system (Massiasta 1994: 4).

Also, among the Anlo Ewe, the treatment of slaves in the house was governed by spiritual rules:

> Kindness to slaves, the fundamentals of these rules, was believed to bring blessings to the slaver or the household in which the slave lived. Such kindness, it was believed, saved the household from misfortunes. This belief was so strong in the past that slaves were actually given preferential treatment in matters of rights and privileges. Some slaves owned property and enjoyed liberties which free people did not have (ibid).

We must also be quick to point out that, sometimes, the distinction between a popular slave song and a cultic one can be very faint as most of the latter have found their way into popular usage.

Cultic And Secular Slave Songs
Song 1
Afe ade me o,
Donko megbe afe ade me o hee.
Afe ade me o,
Donko megbe añe ade me o hee.

No household
No household without a donko [slave]
No household
No household without a donko [slave].

Song 1 establishes emphatically a historical and social fact regarding the wide diffusion of slavery in times past. It seeks to remind society that, indeed, in the contemporary configuration of kinship in Eweland, there is no household without a descendant of a slave. It is a song that straddles the cultic and popular divide. The origin of this song is traced to the Krachi Dente cult and, till today, it is sung by the local devotees of Krachi Dente in Anloland. Song 1, whenever and wherever it is intoned, throws the searchlight on Kete Krachi, an important player in the Slave Trade. Kete Krachi served as a major slave market between the north and the coastal markets. Indeed, most of the slaves that fed the coastal markets were procured in Kete Krachi, Salaga, Bassari, Kadjebi, Chamba and other northern districts. Kete Krachi also happens to be the home of the famous deity, the Krachi Dente. The worship of the Krachi Dente spread to the coastal Eweland and its shrines harboured many slaves. Thus, the dictum "No household without a slave" finds its propriety both in the allusion to the large number of families in Anloland with connections to slavery and the many Dente shrines that served as sanctuaries for slaves. It also performs a social regulatory role by holding in check the use of slave identity as a social stigma.

Song 2
Togode be agbeme míele
Nogode be agbeme míele loo
Agbeme míele ee
Agbeme míele ee
Togode be agbeme míele loo
Nogode be agbeme míele ee

Fatherless we are, but we are in [this] life
Motherless we are, but we are in [this] life
We are in [this] life
We are in [this] life.
Fatherless we are
Motherless we are.

Song 2 depicts slaves as, literally, fatherless and motherless, or dislocated and displaced persons without relations. As noted earlier, most slaves were either captured in war, kidnapped or bought from elsewhere. However, by the tenor of the song, the slaves appear to have resigned to their fate. Life goes on: "We are in [this] life." By implication, wherever a slave finds himself/herself, he/she must accept the situation and adapt accordingly.

This song is recorded in the HUSAGO song tradition. HUSAGO is a dance music associated with the thunder divinity. HUSAGO provides the drama for the Ewe exodus from Notsie in present-day Republic of Togo. It also recaptures and dramatizes the horrors of the trans-Atlantic Slave Trade.

Song 3
Hanyeawo loo, hanyeawo loo
Meyina
Tovi be zado
Novi be nue ke
Enyo o, egble o
Meyina
Hanyeawo loo, hanyeawo loo

O my people, O my people
I am going
A brother said it's night
A sister said it's day
Whatever my fate
I am going
O my people, O my people.

Song 3 is sung from the perspective of an abducted or captured slave who does not know what lies ahead of him. It is a lament and, therefore, funerary in tenor, invoking pathos and collective empathy. The refrain "O, my people, O, my people" is an address to friends and relatives. As in Song 2, it underscores a sense of determinism and fatalism from the perspective of the slave. However, in the statement "Whatever my fate / I am going", one gleans an act of veiled defiance in the face of palpable danger. In that regard, the song draws on the Anlo Ewe war song tradition (particularly 'Atrikpui') in which the persona would normally express bravery and daring, almost eager to embrace death; for the death of the brave warrior is seen as victory worth celebrating. This song is recorded in the ADEKPETI song tradition and is closely related to Song 4 below.

Song 4
Vu la ho hee
Vu la ho loo
'M'ade yo Degesu nam'a
'M'ade yo Sakpaku nam'a
Be dzinye vudzo
Guda vua ho loo
'M'ade yo Degesu nam'a
'M'ade yo Sakpaku nam'a
Be ga dzodzo
Vu la ho ee
'M'ade yo Degesu nam'a
'M'ade yo Sakpaku nam'a
B'agbanye dze ta loo

The boat has weighed anchor
The boat has weighed anchor
Someone call Degesu for me
Someone call Sakpaku for me
My heart is burning
The white man's boat has weighed anchor
Someone call Degesu for me
Someone call Sakpaku for me
I say the metal is hot
The boat has weighed anchor
Someone call Degesu for me
Someone call Sakpaku for me
I say my luggage is on my head.

Song 4, like Song 3 above, is also a dirge-like lament from the ADEKPETI song tradition. The lament and its pathos are captured in the expression of loss and grief on the part of the singer. There is a clear reference to the trans-Atlantic Slave Trade in contradistinction to domestic slavery. This can be seen in the expression "white man's boat" and the word "anchor." The sense of determinism and fatalism we have established as a defining element in the songs we have discussed so far is present in this song. However, it is spiced with intense anger and pain, reflected in the metaphor "I say the metal is hot"—a more powerful rendition of the earlier expression "My heart is burning." There is ambivalence in the expression of pain, sorrow and separation.

On the one hand, it appears that the singer is grieving for "Degesu" and "Sakpaku" who are slaves being ferried away in the "white man's boat." On the other hand, the song may be from the angle of a slave who, with a final glace at the shore and with his ancestral homeland receding into oblivion as the boat "weighs anchor", invokes two names that are dear to his/her heart. The latter appears to be the case on the evidence in the last line of the song: "I say my luggage is on my head." This expression, in its original Ewe usage, is a figurative way of saying 'I am embarking on a journey'. Embedded in "luggage" are a series of references and allusions to the hypothetical traveller's personal belongings, his physical and spiritual baggage, his woes and travails as well as his destiny. It is in this connection that this particular song has become part of the ritual songs of many shrines in Klikor today, not necessarily in connection with slavery, but anything to do with a journey into the unknown, especially of a spiritual nature—induction into the Yewe cult or the Afa (Ifa). My suspicion that "Degesu" and "Sakpaku" may be real historical figures who could be traced to a particular family in the area could not be verified.

Song 5
Zizaglo be xedzrahosu meyoa xe tso xe dana o
Xe dzo vava vadze de wo dzi
Dzo bi gbe dzoxiawo tsi amlima
Me be xe kae amo 'yiza me do ha?
Kato gbogboe kpo agbo nugbe be yeawo
Zizaglo be hadzivodua de te
Hanyeawo mitso akaya
Kluvi wo do zamadui meli na gelesi o
Ame no agbe megbea dzesu o

If the master eagle calls the bird
It doesn't refuse to respond
The bird will flutter and perch in response
The bush is burnt but the sparks perform miracles
Who then knows the root of the earth?
The tethered little goat which wanted to imitate the ram
Zizaglo outdoored on the outer the divinity of songs
My chorus, take the rattles

> *No working slave works forever*
> A living person will definitely die

Zizaglo in this song is talking about death as a slave master personified by the eagle which is so powerful that any bird it calls must respond. Just as birds are prey to the eagle, human beings are also prey to death. In its extended metaphor, slaves are prey to the slave master. But in the master-slave relationship, death is a relief from pain and suffering, a benefactor who annuls all the suffering and misery of the slave. The main thrust of song is thus to be found in the opening and closing segments, especially the closing segment:

> My chorus, take the rattles
> *No working slave works forever*
> A living person will definitely die

It has to be stated that Song 5 does not fall in the category of the earlier songs. Zizaglo refers to Lumor Ahiakpote, a famous 'halo' (song of abuse) singer and performer in the Klikor area who died in 1978. Zizaglo is his 'hadzivodu' ('god of song') pseudonym. The song might have been composed to establish his superiority to his 'halo' rivals by depicting himself as the "master eagle" and his rival as an ordinary "bird." In that context, "No working slave works forever" becomes a statement of claim denoting his own 'immortality' and the 'mortality' of his rival—who will toil, like slaves, and eventually die.

Song 6
Yevuwoe do aho
Ava si afe na mi
Yevuwoe do aho
Ava si afe na mi
Be yevuwoe do aho
Ava si afe na mi hee...

The whites have laid siege
War has overrun our house
The whites have laid siege
War has overrun our house
I say the whites have laid siege
War has overrun our house

Song 7
Mewo nyo na mi
Sogbo be yewo nyui na mi
Aguda yevuawo
Sogbo be yewo nyui na mi

I have done you good
Sogbo says he has done you good
Aguda white men
Sogbo says he has done you good

Songs 6 and 7 are directed against the white slave dealers. In Song 6, an image of war is evoked: "The whites have laid siege / War has overrun our house." It is a cryptic statement establishing a state of affairs without hinting at what course of action the community intends to take. Modelled on the war song, it is atypical of Anlo-Ewe war song tradition, particularly 'atrikpui' songs, which exhibit exaggerated boastfulness and daring.

Song 7, on the other hand, is contemplative and introspective. Although there is no direct reference to slavery, the insinuation regarding the "good" done the white men can be extrapolated from idea that the white men are ungrateful. The community has lost many men and women to the slave trade, but the white men show or give nothing in return. This song, according to my informant, Godwin Azameti of Klikor, who is himself a cultural activist and researcher, is no longer employed in the service of remembering the Atlantic Slave trade but rather for other more mundane purposes. It is particularly invoked as an insinuating and allusive song used by any benefactor who feels aggrieved by a beneficiary of kindness who shows lack of appreciation or ingratitude. In polygamous relationships, it is often employed by wives who find it convenient to take a swipe at their rivals without mentioning names— "Aguda yevuwo" therefore becomes an abstract referent standing for the object of the singer's anger or criticism.

Slave Songs As Oral History
As Vansina (1965) points out, oral traditions are historical sources of a special nature deriving from unwritten sources couched in forms suitable for oral transmission. The preservation of these sources depends on the powers of memory of successive generations of human

beings. With particular reference to the Anlo Ewe, Dor (2004:31) notes that "songs narrating Ewe history continue to be performed irrespective of when they were composed, for the Ewe still celebrate their history, migration, victories in war, and powerful leaders through songs performed at festivals, installation of chiefs, and state burials." This point is buttressed by ethnomusicologist Kofi Gbolonyo who asserts that the Anlo Ewe, like most African societies, "used and relied extensively on music as one of the powerful tools in aid of memory and means of documentation of historical and other educational events and values." He further reveals that Anlo Ewe used music not just as repository but also as a reliable form of historical documentation, cultural transmission and moral education" (2005:4).

However, in appreciating songs as sources of oral history, one needs to be guided by questions relating to 'authenticity', 'reliability' and 'verifiability'. In other words, how much of historical 'truth' do songs retain when they become a cross-generational commodity? Can they be relied upon absolutely as truly reflective of particular historical events? These questions are addressed with regard to at least one of the songs in the study.

The two songs below (Songs 8 and 9) have direct linkages with specific historical events and were thus composed as commemorative pieces.

Song 8
Go ka nu dze gee woyina?
Go ka nu dze gee woyina?
Go ka nu?
Adose kple Afadina woe yina daa
Adose kple Afadina woe yina daa
Go ka nu dze gee woyina?

On which shores are they going to land?
On which shores are they going to land?
On which shores?
There go Adose and Afadina far away
There go Adose and Afadina far away
On which shores are they going to land?

Song 8, with its passionate rhetorical questions, is another lament demonstrating loss and the pain of separation. It is from the perspective of the relatives of Adose and Afadina who, like Degesu and Sakpaku in Song 4, may be real figures or imagery ones. The song imagines where slaves taken across the ocean would eventually land: it is a reflection on distance and separation, as in Song 4. However, this song is anchored on solid historical ground, unlike the others which appear to be lost in the miasma of myths, legends and conjectures. This is one of the most popular slave songs in Anloland due to the origin of the song. It is a classic example of the place of songs in oral history. According to Anlo oral tradition, the song was composed in connection with an incident at Atorkor, a coastal Anlo town noted for its active participation in the Slave Trade. As is common with oral tradition, there are many versions of this story. I reproduce below one of the versions captured in Anne Bailey's book *African Voices of the Atlantic Slave Trade: Beyond the Silence and the Shame* (2005):

> One day a group of drummers, famous drummers from the area, were playing their drums on the shores of Atorkor. The type of drum they were playing was called the *adekpetsi* drum. ...As the drummers played, the Europeans came to collect the slaves. As they were preparing to go, the captain of the ship invited these drummers to come aboard and play. He offered them barrels of drink, giving the same to the crowd that had begun to assemble on the Atorkor shore. An atmosphere of merriment ensued, and many became drunk. Thus were the drummers lured onto the European ship. Before they knew what was happening, the ship set sail, taking them away...They, too, joined the newly captured African slaves to be sold in the Americas (33-34).

Thus, Song 8 links us to a real and verifiable historical event. In a sub-heading titled 'Historical Confirmation of the Incident', Bailey traces the story to the American vessel *Jamestown,* commanded on that particular expedition by Captain James Ward, as recorded in Rev. Chas Thomas' *Adventures and Observations on the West coast of Africa and Its Islands* (1860) which suggests, based on log entries, that the incident happened in 1856.

The Atorkor incident is also recorded in other ethno-historical documents such as Kofi Awoonor's *The Breast of the Earth* (1975) and Charles Mammattah's *The Eves of West Africa* (1976). However, it must be emphasized that, in the Anlo folk consciousness, the song 'Go ka nu dze gee wo yina?' as an oral narrative based on the shameful Atorkor incident has become a more accessible—and more digestible—document of history, memory and silence than the incident from which it was generated. As song, this may be due to its lyrical and aesthetic appeal.

> **Song 9**
> Kundo yi yevuwode megbo o he
> Dada be mina mitso gbe de dzi
> Kundo yi yevowo de megbo o he
> Mitso gbe de dzi
> O! Miafe avafiaga do de aho me!
> Mieyina aho wo ge
> Miyi aho, miyi aho, miyi aho
> Mide so, mide so, mide so.
>
> Kundo has gone to the white man's land and hasn't returned
> Mother says let bet on it
> Kundo has gone to the white man's land
> Let's bet on it
> O! Our great king is perished in battle!
> We are going to fight
> Let's go to war, let's go to war!
> Let's fight and fight and fight!
> O! Our great king is perished in battle!
> Kundo has gone to the white man's land
> Let's bet on it

Again, like Song 8 above, Song 9 is based on a specific historical event and a popular historical figure in Anlo Ewe folklore and legend. Kundo, the protagonist declaimed in the song, refers to Togbui Kundo, a principal figure in the pantheon of Ewe culture heroes. How Togbui Kundo came to be celebrated in song is explained by Gbolonyo (2005: 61-62):

> Anlo Ewe use music in general and songs in particular as the primary forms in which the remarkable deeds of heroic ancestors are cast. Among the noted Anlo warriors and leaders

> are Kundo, Akplomada, Tsali, Wenya, Axolu, Sri, Tenge, and Adeladza. Togbui Kundo is regarded as one of the most revered of the above personalities. He is said to be the brain behind the Ewe's numerous victories over their enemies in Dahomey. Historical evidence points to the fact that *adzohu/adzogbo*, as one of the spiritual dance-drumming genres associated with the Ewe military institutions, emerged from [the] legendary struggles of Togbui Kundo against enemies and against European domination. Togbui Kundo, noted for being a great war commander, was also the last and the most famous king of ancient Dahomey prior to the Ewe's departure from that territory…According to history, Togbui Kundo was never really conquered by his enemies. One of the popular historical narratives indicates that he was kidnapped, probably by Europeans, while signing one of the numerous treaties which he made with them…Despite the perceived death of Kundo, some of his subjects still believed he was too strong and powerful to be kidnapped and killed, as later wishful-thinking rumors indicate through reports of Torgbui Kundo reappearing. Kundo was and is still an inspiration to only Anlo Ewe but all Ewe of West Africa. Ewes continue to perform musical activities that constantly remind them of this great king and warrior.

While Gbolonyo's account appears to be based on oral tradition, devoid of references to dates, Weduahlor's account (2006: 47) is composed as recorded history. He writes:

> In November 1874, the colonial Government passed laws to stop all slave-trading and to set all slaves free. By this proclamation, Anlo State, known to be the most notorious slave trading state, was stopped from trading in slaves. In 1892, the French fought Feddah [Whyddah?] and Dahome Kingdoms and in 1894, Kondo of Dahome, now Republic of Benin, was seized and taken to [sic] exile. As usual, a heroic folklore song was composed in remembrance of Kondo's predicament.

Song 9 demonstrates the oft-cited fluidity and imprecision of oral tradition and, by extension, oral history. Although Gbolonyo's account and that of Weduahlor appear to be similar and mutually corroborative and reinforcing, there is uncertainty as to whether Togbui Kundo in

Anlo Ewe folklore is the same as King Behanzin (1841-1906), King of Dahomey, who fiercely resisted French occupation of his kingdom. After a series of wars of resistance, he finally surrendered to the French in 1894. He was exiled to the island of Martinique in the West Indies and later transferred to Algeria where he died in 1906 (Amenumey 1986; Harris 1987).

Most of the old people I interviewed in Klikor insisted there was only one Togbui Kundo, popularly known as Dahume Kundo. None of them had ever heard of King Behanzin. Also, while some informants contended that Kundo was only a freedom fighter against colonialism and not necessarily an anti-slavery crusader, others insisted that he was, indeed, the latter. Thus, historically—at least in the domain of oral tradition—the phenomenon known as Kundo remains an enigmatic figure. What is important, for the purposes of this essay, is that Song 9, on the basis of its thematic concerns of resistance, freedom, exile, separation, kinship, loss and affection in the context of a journey across the oceans and encounters with white men, continues to be a popular song in the slave song repertory among the Anlo Ewe. It is also, on the basis of its imprecision, a classic example of the fluidity of songs as oral history.

Structural And Stylistic Features Of Anlo Ewe Slave Songs

A number of major stylistic features have been identified in the representative song texts discussed in this essay. These include: Brevity, Repetition, Allusion/Reference, and Lyricism. In terms of brevity, as we have noted earlier, most of the representative songs are short and cryptic. With the exception of Song 5 and Song 9, each song is built around one major thesis statement which is repeated over and over again, sometimes incrementally. Thus, repetition is a major structural and stylistic feature which derives from the cryptic nature of the songs. As in Anlo Ewe song tradition, this is also a mnemonic device which aids memorization. With regard to allusion, one notices that in a number of songs, allusions and references are made to individuals and events "Adose", "Afadina" "Sakpaku", "Degesu", "Kundo"," Zizaglo"). Significantly, with the exception of "Kundo" and "Zizaglo", none of the other referents are identifiable. It is also noticeable that, over all, the representative songs are overly lyrical in the sense that they draw on the emotions of listeners. For instance, in Songs 8, the rhetorical question, "Go ka nu dze ge woyi na?" ("On which shores will they land?") help us to place the songs in their proper context by drawing attention to loss and separation, as well as the horrors of slavery. Other rhetorical devices which characterize the songs include appeals to ethos through direct addressing of the audience as in "Hanyeawo loo..." ("O my people...") (Song 3), as well as the deployment of collective pronouns in a number of songs. As noted earlier, the philosophical undercurrents of fatalism and determinism further enhance the pathos and lyrical quality of the songs as statements that capture a phenomenon as disturbing as slavery.

Linkages Between Anlo Ewe Slave Songs And Negro Spirituals

Studying Anlo Ewe slave songs, one is tempted to ask whether they bear any affinity or antecedence to Negro spirituals in the New World. There appears to be enough evidence for a strong linkage. Chapter XIV of W.E.B. Du Bois' *The Souls of Black Folk* (1994) titled the "Sorrow Songs", lends some kind of fillip to the suspicion that Negro spirituals might have been inspired by ancient African song traditions, especially the Ewe, Akan and Kassena dirge traditions. In Du Bois' words, "They that walked in darkness sang songs in the olden days—Songs of Sorrow—for they were weary at heart" (155), songs which he rightly describes as a carry-over from "primitive African music" (158), He also notes that "In these songs...the slave spoke to the world" (158). But, perhaps, the strongest case in support of continuities is his assertion that:

> Through all the sorrow of Songs of Sorrow there breathes a hope—a faith in the ultimate justice of things. The minor cadences of despair change to triumph and calm confidence. Sometimes it is faith in life, sometimes a faith in death, sometimes assurance of boundless justice in some fair world beyond.

All these will stir the old debate regarding how much of the African artistic and song traditions were carried across the Middle Passage by slaves. Du Bois' answer is disarming: "Here we have brought our three gifts and mingled them with yours: a gift of story and song—soft, stirring melody in an ill-harmonized and unmelodious land..."

Conclusion

On the whole, these slave songs from Eweland, whether from the perspective of slaves, relatives of slaves or the community, are sober and funereal, demonstrating the emotions evoked by the slave experience. They view slavery as both a physical and spiritual journey into the unknown. They are also fatalistic and deterministic. This may be explained by the fact that in many cases the slaves "accepted" their situation as a fact of life.

References

Amenumey, D.E.K. 1986. *The Ewe in Pre-Colonial Times: A Political History with Special Emphasis on the Anlo, Ge, and Krepi.* Accra: Sedco.

Anyidoho, Kofi. 1983. *Oral Poetics and Traditions of Verbal Art in Africa.* PhD. dissertation, University of Texas at Austin.

___. 1997. "Ewe Verbal Art." In *A Handbook of Eweland Volume 1: The Ewe of Southeastern Ghana.* Ed. by Francis Agbodeka. Accra, Ghana: Woeli Publishing Services.

Assimeng, Max. 1997. *Foundations of African Social Thought.* Accra: Ghana Universities Press.

Awoonor, Kofi. 1975. *The Breast of the Earth: A Survey of the History, Culture and Literature Africa South of the Sahara.* Garden City, NY: Anchor Press.

___. 1979. *Guardians of the Sacred Word: Ewe Poetry.* New York: Nok Publishers.

Bailey, Anne C. 2005. *African Voices of the Atlantic Slave Trade.* Boston: Beacon Press.

Dor, George W.K. 2004. "Communal Creativity and Song Ownership in Anlo Ewe Musical Practice: The Case of Havolu." *Ethnomusicology* 48(1): 26-51.

Du Bois, W.E.B. 1994. *The Souls of Black Folk.* Mineola, New York: Dover Publications, Inc.

Gbolonyo, Stephen J.K. 2005. *Want the Music? Listen to the Music. Historical Evidence in Anlo Ewe Musical Practices: A Case Study of Traditional Song Texts.* Masters thesis, University of Pittsburgh.

Harris, Joseph. 1987. *Africans and Their History.* New York: Penguin Books.

Mamattah, Charles M.K. 1976. *The Eves of West Africa: Oral Traditions. Vol.1.* Accra: Advent Press.

Massiasta, Dale. 2006. *Slavery and Spiritual Reparation.* Akatsi: Falcon Printing Press.

Ogude, S.E. 1990. "Ideology and Aesthetics: The African Dilemma. In *Literature and Aesthetics.* Ed. by Ernest Emenyonu. Idadan: Heimeman Educational Publications: 3-14.

Perbi, Akosua. 2004. *A History of Indigenous Slavery in Ghana. From the 15th to the 19th Century.* Accra: Sub-Saharan Publishers.

Seshie, Klutsey L. 1973. *Akpalu Fe Hawo.* Accra: Bureau of Ghana Languages.

Vansina, Jan. 1985. *Oral Tradition as History.* London: James Currey.

Weduahlor, Korsiwor Amah. 2006. *Anlo Kotsoklolo: The Rise and Fall of Anlo State (Part One).* Accra: Frank Publishing Limited.

4

Jacqueline C. DjeDje
Kwasi Ampene

DIASPORIC DIALOGUES AND CURRENTS

Music and Diasporas within West Africa: The Pre-colonial Era

Jacqueline C. DjeDje

Jacqueline C. DjeDje is professor emerita, former chair of the Ethnomusicology Department, and former director of the Ethnomusicology Archive at the University of California, Los Angeles. Her research focuses on African and African American music, with specializations in religious music, West African fiddling traditions, and black music in California. In addition to numerous articles that have appeared in various scholarly journals and anthologies, DjeDje is the author and editor of several books, including *Black Music Research Journal Special Issue*, "Music of Black Los Angeles" (Spring 2011) and *Fiddling in West Africa: Touching the Spirit in Fulbe, Hausa, and Dagbamba Cultures* (2008).

Although much has been written on music in the African diaspora, most attention is given to peoples of African origin living *outside* the continent. Minimal music research has focused on diasporas *within* Africa, and even fewer studies have been concerned with pre-colonial, voluntary diasporic movements in Africa (Zeleza 2005:5).[1] Historian Oliver Bakewell's (2008:1) comments on this issue are noteworthy: "Ironically, within the growing volume of literature on African diasporas, very little of it is concerned with diasporas whose population is based on the continent. Africa is portrayed as a continent which generates diasporas rather than one in which diasporas can be found."

The paucity of music material on diasporas within Africa, especially migrations that occurred before the arrival of Europeans, raises several questions: Why do we ignore migrations or political and cultural constructs that developed on the continent during the pre-colonial era? Is it because of the lack of sources, the complexity of the topic, or the fact that we believe pre-colonial polities have little to offer the discussion of performance culture or issues (e.g., globalization, identity) of importance today? In my opinion, the problem lies partly in our perception of Africa. Many music researchers do not regard pre-colonial Africa as a continent with empires, nations, or societies with far-reaching extensions, but instead, as a place with insulated communities and few connections. Because of our focus on discrete, isolated African groups, we do not know why and how musical traditions were dispersed and maintained for hundreds of years, nor do we understand the processes that contributed to differences and similarities.

Continuing research on African music history begun by Klaus Wachsmann (1971), Kwabena Nketia (1971), and others, this essay explores music and diasporas (i.e., diasporic movements) in West Africa during the pre-colonial era. As Nketia states in his landmark essay, "History and the Organization of Music in West Africa," "the development of musical traditions in West Africa must be sought in the social history of the West African peoples" (1971:8). For this reason, history plays an important role in this discussion. Using print sources in history, anthropology, and music as well as data from fieldwork in West Africa, I will address the following: (1) If pre-colonial diasporic movements exist in West Africa, what are they and when and how did they form? What is distinctive about their music culture? (2) How has music (in the homeland and host communities) been affected by diasporic movements? (3) What can music in historic intra-African diasporas tell us about musicking in contemporary extra-African diasporas? Before tackling these questions, I will discuss how diaspora is both theorized and used in this essay.

Defining Diaspora, Diaspora Studies, and African Diasporas
When reviewing the literature, one will find many definitions for "diaspora." In a general sense, diaspora refers to the forced or voluntary movement of a group of individuals from one location to another involving some considerable distance. Webster and other dictionaries define diaspora, with a capital D, as "the settling of scattered colonies of Jews outside Palestine after the Babylonian exile; the area outside Palestine settled by Jews; or the Jews living outside Palestine or modern Israel" (Webster's 1974:315). Thus, the concept has several allocations: it can refer to the movement of a people, the place where people settle, as well as the people who moved. Yet, as anthropologist James Clifford (1997:251) reminds us, "Diaspora is different from travel . . . in that it is not temporary. It involves dwelling, maintaining communities, having collective homes away from home (and in this it is different from exile, with its frequently individualist focus)."

Because of his concern for diasporas *within* Africa, I use the four criteria that Bakewell proposes to satisfy the basic elements of a diaspora: (1) movement from an original homeland to more than one region, either through forced dispersal or voluntary expansion in search of improved livelihoods; (2) a collective myth of an ideal ancestral home; (3) a strong ethnic group consciousness sustained over a long time, based on a shared history, culture, and religion; and (4) a sustained network of social relationships with members of the group living in different settlement regions (Bakewell 2008).

During the twentieth century, many scholars in various disciplines have researched the topic diaspora.[2] Several reasons can be given for the fascination with the subject, but I believe some of the interest is a response to what is occurring globally. Although the reasons for travel in modern day may be the same as earlier times (e.g., work, environment, war, famine, disease, or a better life), the ease of travel and the short length of time to travel great distances have made movement more commonplace. As people move, the memory and nostalgia for home rarely disappears, but often increases. Thus, diasporic groups sometimes use symbols, objects, and ideas to lessen the pain and anxiety that accompanies displacement from home. And for many, it does not matter if home is imagined or real.

Other scholars provide similar but also different reasons for current research on diaspora. Joseph E. Harris, a historian and an authority on global African diasporas, states: "The study of diasporas is especially timely today because of the current fragmentation and displacement of people throughout the world.... These diaspora groups share characteristics of ethnic identity, marginality, and homeland linkage, and one can not understand them without an examination of their original homelands and the root causes and specific contexts within which they were dispersed" (Harris 1996:8). Clifford (1997:249) writes: "For better or worse, diaspora discourse is being widely appropriated. It is loose in the world, for reasons having to do with decolonization, increased immigration, global communications, and transport—a whole range of phenomena that encourage multilocale attachments, dwelling, and traveling within and across nations."

Most historians believe that the concept, "African diaspora," was first used in 1965 at the International Congress of African History at University College, Dar es Salaam, by George Shepperson, who drew parallels between the dispersal of Africans caused by slavery and imperialism to the experience of the Jews. Interestingly, Shepperson does not accept credit for the term's first usage and argues that the concept was "certainly established" in scholarly vocabulary before the 1965 Dar es Salaam conference. Nevertheless, Shepperson's work is important because he was among the first to introduce a broad definition of diaspora that included the movement of Africans to Europe before the Atlantic slave trade, the Islamic slave trade, and "the dispersal of Africans inside [Africa] both as a consequence of the slave trade and imperialism" (Shepperson cited in Alpers 2001:5; Edwards 2001:50-52). Since the 1960s, interest in African diasporas has surged. Commenting on this trend, Ingrid Monson (2000:1) states, "If the Jewish diaspora was the quintessential example of diaspora before the 1960s, the African diaspora has surely become the paradigmatic case for the closing years of the twentieth century."

The emergence of numerous case studies on diaspora during the latter half of the twentieth century has also given rise to critiques on the subject. A number of researchers are concerned that not only is our understanding of the concept limited, but also too much emphasis has been placed on the Americas. Historian Paul T. Zeleza (2005:36) explains:

The African diaspora, together with the Jewish diaspora ... enjoys pride of place in the pantheon of diaspora studies. Yet, despite the proliferation of the literature, our understanding of the African diaspora remains limited by both the conceptual difficulties of defining what we mean by the diaspora in general and the African diaspora in particular, and the analytical tendency to privilege the Atlantic, or rather the Anglophone, indeed the American branch of the African diaspora, as is so clear in Gilroy's seminal text.

To address this problem, some scholars began concentrating on issues that had been ignored or marginalized – for example, the global dimensions of African diasporas, overlapping diasporas, and intra- and extra-African diasporas (Alpers 2001). Researchers discovered that when examining African diasporas globally, it becomes apparent that "historic African diasporas can be divided into four categories in terms of their places of dispersal: the intra-Africa, Indian Ocean, Mediterranean, and Atlantic diasporas" (Zeleza 2005:44). Furthermore, intra-African diasporas, because of their variety, can be divided into five sub-groups: (1) trade (the Hausa and Dioula in western Africa); (2) slave (West Africans in North Africa and East Africans on the Indian Ocean islands); (3) conquest (the Nguni in southern Africa *and Mande in western Africa*)[3]; (4) refugee (the Yoruba wars of the early nineteenth century); and (5) pastoral (the Fulbe and Somali in the Sahelian zones of western and eastern Africa) (Zeleza 2005:45). Using a global perspective also makes it clear that while diasporas outside Africa are generally defined in racial terms – for example, "African diaspora" or "black diaspora" – diasporas within Africa are defined in terms of ethnicity, making them similar to diasporic groups in other parts of the world. Zeleza explains: "It is interesting that, whereas the other diasporas are defined in *national* or *ethnic* or even *ideological* terms, for Africa they are simply called African; whether the referent used is racial or spatial is not always clear. Also common are descriptions of African diasporas as 'black'; rarely are diasporas from other regions draped in colour" (40).
When researching African diasporas, music scholars tend to focus on peoples and idioms that developed as a result of the forced migration of

blacks across the Atlantic (Shapiro 1976[4]; Monson 2000; Alpers 2001). Only recently have more music researchers begun looking beyond the Atlantic to developments in the Indian Ocean and Mediterranean, including the Sahara and Arab Gulf (see Anderson 1971; Catlin 2002; Catlin-Jairazbhoy (2003), Catlin and Alpers 2003; Benachir (2005), Hamel 2008; Racy 1999). Studies on contemporary diasporas have also expanded the discourse and analysis of interconnections.[5] Hauke Dorsch (2004:105) explains:

> While African-American musicians appropriate the griots to connect their own work with ancestral West Africa, West Africans migrating to Europe or America quickly appropriate Afro-diasporan musical styles like reggae and rap. These musical forms transport messages of Blackness and exile reflecting the migrants' experiences in a strange and often racist environment. ... It forces African and Afro-Caribbean migrants to redefine their identity not only along lines of local belonging but also through their common Blackness.

Diasporas in West Africa

Now I will discuss each of the three questions raised at the beginning of this essay:

(1) If pre-colonial diasporic movements exist within West Africa, what are they and when and how did they form? What is distinctive about their music culture?

In a sense, the first part of this question is somewhat naïve because most researchers know that movement has always been an important feature of many African societies. Rather, it has been primarily Western laypersons and perhaps some individuals in other world cultures that view the continent as a place with little or no change and, as a result, serves as an ideal laboratory for studying ancient and primitive culture. Unfortunately, this thinking portrays the continent's many ethnic groups as unchanging and static societies with little differentiation. Yet, as Gerhard Kubik (1998:294) explains: "Over the centuries ... African societies have changed; in that respect they resemble the other societies of the world. Thinking of precolonial Africa as a mosaic of rigidly traditional, tightly knit autonomous, ethnic-linguistic units overlooked what might well have been the only stable trait in Africa cultural history, as it probably was elsewhere: continuous change."

While arguments can be made for any number of diasporic movements in West Africa, I limit my discussion to three -- the Fulbe, Mande, and Hausa -- because they are among the oldest, the most widely dispersed, and probably the largest (in terms of the number of people involved). Recognizing that caution should be employed when attempting to link the ethnicity or language of a people with music or other cultural traits, it is important to note that I am interested in ethnicity on the individual level; that is, the sense on the part of the individuals that they belong to a particular cultural community. While many definitions for cultural community or ethnic group exist, the one proposed by John Hutchinson and Anthony A. Smith in their work, *Ethnicity*, is a good working one for our purposes: "a named human population with myths of common ancestry, shared historical memories, one or more elements of common culture, a link with a homeland and a sense of solidarity among at least some of its members" (Hutchinson and Smith 1996:5; DjeDje 2008:54-56).

Since most historians trace the origins of the Fulbe, Mande, and Hausa to savannah West Africa, it is not surprising that these groups are culturally similar. Not only have they had ongoing contacts with each other through the development of empires and the movement of populations, all have experienced influence(s) from North Africa, and to various degrees have adopted Islam. While some are agriculturalists, others participate in cattle herding and trade. The social organization of each follows a stratified system that includes "a landed aristocracy, a hereditary military class, members of craft guilds, free peasants, hereditary house servants, and slaves" (Mabogunje 1976:19). The social organization of professional musicians among the three groups is also similar in that each is based on a socio-occupational structure that probably dates to the first millennium BCE or earlier. Musicians who belong to an endogamous family are born into the profession and receive training from kinsmen. Because musicians are attached to specific patrons, they are expected to know details of the history and genealogy of their patrons, which is transmitted orally from one generation to another (DjeDje 1998:444).

Fulbe. Oral tradition and most scholars link the Fulbe and Tukulor to Takrur, an eleventh-century state located in the middle of the Senegal valley that rose to power when the ancient kingdom of Wagadu (also known as Ghana) declined. The people of Takrur and their descendants are considered to be Halpulaaren (speakers of the Pulaar or Fulfulde language). During the colonial period, scholars began representing the Halpulaaren as two distinct groups – the Tukulor (sedentary agriculturalists) and the Fulbe (nomadic pastoralists). Although the two have some customs that differ, researchers believe they are the same culturally (DjeDje 2008:48).

At present, the Fulbe (also known as Fula, Foulah, Fulani, Ful, Foulbé, Fellani, Filani, Fallataa, Peul, Pullo) live in the midst of other populations throughout West Africa, extending from the Atlantic coast to the country Sudan. The migration of the pastoral Fulbe began in the twelfth and thirteenth centuries when they spread southward and eastward across the savannah, taking over at first only lands ill suited to agriculture. For this reason, their expansion caused no alarm. Their neighbors, in fact, welcomed the manure the Fulbe cattle provided for the fields and the milk and butter that they exchanged for agricultural products. Few of the pastoral Fulbe were Muslim; thus, religion was not a point of difference with their neighbors. Even when they were Muslim, the pastoral Fulbe were generally tolerant in disposition. However, they were often accompanied in their movements by some of their sedentary kinsmen, who were usually better educated, more sophisticated in political matters, and less tolerant of non-Muslims. It was the sedentary Fulbe who fostered the political influence of the whole group through military aggression, often in the form of jihads that began in the eighteenth and nineteenth centuries. In this way, the Fulbe became politically dominant in areas such as Futa Jalon, Bundu, Masina, Hausaland, and the Nupe country.

Fulbe who did not migrate eastward remained in Senegambia and lived among the Wolof, Serer, and other groups. During the fourteenth century, another wave of Fulbe migrants arrived in Mali and established communities in Masina. By the mid-fifteenth century, the Fulbe had reached Hausaland, beginning an infiltration in Hausa country that continued through the sixteenth century. In the mid-fifteenth century, a group of Fulbe also settled in Futa Jalon in present-day Guinea. The Fulbe began arriving in Adamawa in present-day Cameroon, and other regions of the savannah, east and north of Cameroon, during the eighteenth and nineteenth centuries.

For the Fulbe, the central markers of ethnic identity are code of behavior or way of life (*pulaaku* or *pulaagu*) and Fulfulde, the Fulbe language. Regardless of location, these two characteristics "not only distinguish the Fulbe from other ethnic groups, but also color Fulbe perceptions of themselves, as a sort of moral code" (Azarya, Eguchi, and VerEecke 1993:3; DjeDje 2008:56-57).

Due to their dispersions, generalizing about Fulbe music is difficult. But two important distinctions can be made between (1) the music in which the Fulbe themselves participate and that of the professional musicians who sing and play for them; and (2) between the hymns and songs (both sacred and secular) that have developed from Islamic tradition and everyday songs which are integral to the tradition of Fulbe herdsmen. Fulbe musicians can be divided into three groups: musicians who are weavers and singers; musicians who play musical instruments such as the plucked and bowed lute; and singers who play drums. Although a variety of instruments are identified with the Fulbe, depending on where they have settled, those that seem to be the most common include the flute, fiddle, and half calabash (Arnott 2007-2011; DjeDje 2008:61-63).
Mande. The legendary warrior and hero, Sunjata, and his allies established the West African Mande Empire in the thirteenth century. The homeland for the Mali Empire, situated along the Upper Niger River roughly between Bamako in southwestern Mali and Kouroussa in northeastern Guinea, became the center of one of the largest and wealthiest empires in West Africa. At its height in the fourteenth to the sixteenth century, the Mande Empire extended from Gao in the east and Timbuktu in the north to the Atlantic coast in the west. Their descendants today make up significant parts of the population of many West African countries: in Mali and Guinea they are known as Maninka (or Malinke in French writing); in Senegal, The Gambia, and Guinea-Bissau they are known as Mandinka (or Mandingo in British writing) (Charry 2000:1). Due to dispersions further east and south, Mande speakers can also be found in Côte d'Ivoire, Burkina Faso, Sierra Leone, and Liberia.

A class of hereditary professional artisans called *nyamakala* marks most Mande societies. Although specific professions vary according to the ethnic group and geographic location, among Maninka and Mandinka society four are generally recognized: "blacksmiths-sculptors (*numu*); leatherworkers and potters (*garanke* or *karanke*); musical-verbal artisans (Mn: *jeli*, pl. *jelilu*; Md: *jali* or *jalo,* pl. *jalolu*); and orators, expert in the Koran, specializing in genealogies (Bn: *fune*; Mn, Md: *fina* or *fino*)[6]" (Charry 2000:1). During pre-colonial times, Mande music culture encompassed three distinct traditions: (1) music related to hunters' societies and their hunter heroes sung to the accompaniment of the *simbi*, a seven-stringed calabash (gourd) harp; (2) music of the *jelis* (called *jeliya*), played on the *bala* (xylophone), *koni* (lute), and *kora* (harp), which is associated with rulers, warriors, traders, and other patrons; and (3) drumming music related to various life-cycle, agricultural, and recreational events played on the *jembe* (struck with the bare hands) and *dundun* (struck with a stick) in Mali and Guinea or the *tangtango* (struck with one hand and one stick) in the Senegambia. While drumming, which is associated with blacksmiths, and hunter's music predate the rise of the Mali Empire, *jeliya* dates to the beginning of the Mali Empire (Charry 2000:3).

Hausa. Of the many oral narratives that exist on Hausa origins, one that highlights the indigenous aspects of tradition suggests that the original home of Hausa speakers included parts of the Sahara, particularly Aïr (Azbin) in present-day Niger, and it was not until the Tuareg Berbers conquered them in the fourteenth and fifteenth centuries that they were pushed south toward their present location. Thus, most Hausa regard present-day northern Nigeria and southern Niger as their ancestral homeland. This is the area in which the majority of people speak Hausa as their first and only language, and the cultural and social traits often associated with the Hausa people predominates (Adamu 1978:1). The term, "Hausa," which does not appear until the sixteenth century, was primarily linguistic – rather than a religious or cultural – category (DjeDje 2008:114).

Through the late eighteenth century, Hausaland consisted of several distinct rival kingdoms that were involved in constant warfare either with each other, with groups in neighboring areas, or with foreign powers that tried to claim sovereignty over the Hausa. Thus, Hausaland never had one government until the early nineteenth century when the Sokoto Caliphate was created as a result of the jihad led by Fulbe scholar and teacher Uthman dan Fodio. This multi-centered state system in Hausaland, in contrast to the uni-centered system of other West African kingdoms, was of major social and economic benefit because it gave rise to more centers of commerce, thereby generating faster development through competition (Adamu 1978:14).

Diasporic movements among the Hausa started during the fourteenth century when they began trading in gold, kola nuts, and textiles with peoples south and west of them. Hausa culture spread to its widest extent during the nineteenth century, after the establishment of the Sokoto Caliphate. Adamu (1978:91) explains: "The vehicle in the expansion was the Sokoto Jihad, and the classes of Hausa emigrants involved included warriors and administrators, Qur'anic teachers (malams), traders and stock-keepers, craftsmen (particularly blacksmiths, and textile and leather workers), drummers and musicians, farmers, elephant hunters, rubber tappers, and refugees." As a result, the Hausa created a complex diaspora of interlinked communities throughout much of the west and northern half of Africa, including those in central and southern Nigeria, Benin, Togo, Ghana, Côte d'Ivoire, Cameroon, Chad, Sudan, Morocco, Tunisia, and Libya (Youngstedt 2004:95). Hausa traders also migrated west to Mali and Burkina Faso, but their settlements in these areas were not extensive (Adamu 1978:3).[7]
Before and after the jihad, the Hausa saw their society as an association of rulers and rule, nobles and commoners, or in ethnic terms, Fulani and Hausa. There existed a social stratification based on occupational specialization within these dichotomies. *Sarautu* (ruling) was an occupation that outranked all others. *Mallanci* (Qur'anic learning) and *kasuwanci* (successful trading), which had universalistic emphases, ranked next. Below these came the majority of Hausa occupations; ranking lowest of all were butchers, praise singers, drummers, blacksmiths, house servants, and hunters (Smith 1965:139; DjeDje 2008:117).

Hausaland's location at a crossroads with numerous contacts, borrowings, and cultural fusions not only helped the Hausa to become a powerful political, commercial, and religious force, it also produced one of the richest music cultures in West Africa. The closest term for "music" – *rok'o* (begging) – reflects social attitudes towards musicians rather than their occupation or product. A man participating in music is known as *marok'i* in Hausa, while a woman is called *marok'iya* or *zabiya* (Ames and King 1971:ix, 62, 76; Besmer 1998:519). At present, five major categories of professional musicians exist, which I believe date to pre-colonial times: (1) musicians attached to butchers, blacksmiths, hunters, farmers, and other socio-occupational groups; (2) court musicians of rulers and high officials; (3) freelance musicians of recreational music who play for the general public (including titled nobility, high officeholders, wealthy merchants) at dances, boxing and wrestling matches, and youth recreation; (4) musician entertainers and comedians who perform at markets and other large public gatherings; and (5) Bori musicians who play for spirit possessions and as entertainment for naming and marriage ceremonies (Ames 1973:134-141; DjeDje 1982:117, 2008:125). The Hausa categorize instruments using "terms such as *bushe-bushe* (singular, *busa*; blowing), *ka'de-ka'de* (singular, *ki'da*; beating, shaking, plucking, or bowing), and *wak'e-wak'e* (singular, *wak'a*; singing)," which refer to performance technique rather than sound (Ames and King 1971:ix; DjeDje 2008:125; King 2007-2011). Instruments that are blown and beaten, which tend to be associated with royalty, have a higher status than those shaken, plucked, or bowed. Similarly, instruments identified with recreation, entertainment, and Bori are ranked lower (DjeDje 2008:125).

(2) How has music (in homeland and host communities) been affected by diasporic movements?
Because of the uneven and limited amount information available for each group, it is difficult to address this question generally. However, evidence demonstrates that when diasporic groups move to different locations, the response varies. While the first inclination of some may be to maintain and re-create what existed in the homeland, others might decide to initiate change. The degree to which diasporic groups maintain or change traditions depends upon the situation and relationship with the host community. Even when individuals attempt to maintain traditions, over time minor changes will take place for various reasons: memory lapses, lack of resources, a new environment, new contexts and functions, generational differences, a desire to create a new identity, etc. Therefore, I argue that change is one of the primary factors affecting homeland and host communities, and transformation can occur in one or more ways: (1) the music repertory of communities may be enriched or enlarged; (2) the function, meaning, and status of musicians, music idioms, and instruments are modified, re-aligned, or altered; (3) some musical traditions are displaced or lost; or (4) the blurring of distinctions between groups over time can lead to the emergence of a new music culture that differs from both the indigenous host and homeland communities.

Hausa diasporic movements of the nineteenth century provide an excellent example of efforts to maintain homeland traditions in the host community. As the Hausa established settlements (called *zangos*[8] or *zongos*) in different locations throughout West Africa, many tried to duplicate Hausa society as they remembered it politically, culturally, and economically. Adamu (1978:16) states, "The moment a Hausa migrant settled down in a *zango* he ceased to be a foreigner socially; most of the non-Hausa incomers who settled in Hausa *zangos* became Hausa subsequently." Even when they were not in the majority, Hausa "often had a disproportionate influence on the others in religion and learning, economic affairs, roles and offices, dress, and language" (Pellow 2001:64). Because musicking was an essential part of Hausa life, "musicians and drummers kept the migrants entertained both during the journeys and in the zango settlements" (Adamu 1978:16). Thus, "it was natural that drummers and musicians from Hausaland were welcome wherever they went and even encouraged to settle" (100). In addition to "classical" music associated with Hausa royalty (e.g., *kotso, taushi, jauje* and *ganga* drums as well as the *algaita* reed pipe), *kalangu* drumming was popular "for the dancing pleasure of boys and girls" (100). Even praise singers (*kwando*) who use no musical instruments traveled and settled with migrants (99-101).

Pellow's late twentieth-century[9] research among Hausa in Ghana is noteworthy because it alludes to features that have been both maintained and changed, particularly in religious practices and gender roles at performance events. On religion, Pellow (1997:585) discusses change: "Just as Islam is diluted in this coastal city (i.e. Accra), so too is 'Hausa-ness.' Distance from home towns in northern Nigeria, with little opportunity to visit, inter-ethnic mixing and marriage within the *zongo*, and the location of the *zongo* within the larger context of a Christian, outward-looking, Western-oriented have led to acculturation." On the subject of gender, Pellow states, "In Accra's *zongo* areas, male-female lines of division, while present, are less well reinforced than in northern Nigeria or in the early days" (585-586) in Accra, indicating change. "But at life-cycle events like weddings and funerals[10] men and women celebrate separately" (586), demonstrating maintenance of tradition. At Hausa weddings in Accra, "both male and female *maroka* perform. The men's feast takes place in the forecourt and entrance hut, the women's in the women's quarters. At the men's gathering the celebrants are entertained by *roko* and drumming. At the women's, there is drumming, followed by bori dancing, and singing by the female *maroka*" (587). In some instances, however, some modifications have occurred in Hausa gender roles during performances. Because divisions between males and females have become more relaxed in Accra, so are restrictions regarding who can perform at women's events. In northern Nigeria, "the presence of a male 'doing maleness' (performing the male role) among secluded women would be dangerous and scandalous" (597). Yet, in Accra "where male-female interaction does not carry social opprobrium [disgrace], the male praise-singer, the *maroki*, can perform his traditional role ('doing praise-singing') among women. In so doing he bridges the male and female domains and in effect helps to maintain social order" (597).

For diasporic movements in other parts of West Africa, the contexts and dynamics stimulated other results. If we take the Mande, for example, interactions between those in the homeland (the Maninka) and host communities (e.g., Mandinka in Senegambia and Bamana in Mali) have led to cross-fertilizations that enlarged the musical vocabulary for all. Eric Charry explains: "The three traditional *jeli* instruments (*koni, bala,* and *kora*) are associated with different eras and different geographical regions of the Mande diaspora: the northernmost Mande regions (or the sahel in general) for the *koni*; old Mande, particularly the southern reaches in Guinea, for the *bala*; and Kabu (the western Mande territories) for the *kora*. The meeting of these three distinct musical instrument cultures (harps, lutes, and xylophones) in the hands of *jelis* accounts for the unusual breadth of Mande music" (Charry 2000:10). In the case of the Fulbe, the repercussions have varied. For example, although the fiddle, an instrument the Fulbe are believed to have dispersed in much of savannah West Africa, continues to be a symbol of their identity in both homeland and host communities, the Fulbe have embraced the music cultures in which they have settled (DjeDje 2008). In some cases, they have accepted the traditions of the host in their entirety, resulting in a loss of Fulbe traditions, similar to what occurred in Hausaland when Fulbe emirs controlled the Sokoto Caliphate and adopted what was already in place for Hausa rulers. In other cases, the Fulbe combined indigenous traditions with those of the host community to create something new; similar to what occurred among Fulbe rulers and nobility in Cameroon (Erlmann 1983).

Borrowing among groups in Senegambia (Mande, Wolof, Fulbe, and others) has made the entire region musically similar to such a degree that investigators such as Roderic Knight often discuss musicking there generally without specifying what is unique among the different ethnic groups. Knight (1983:45) writes, "It is clear that Fula-Mandinka relations have encompassed a wide range of situations. . . . The fruitful situation for both parties concerned, that of intermarriage, doubtless went hand in hand with most of the others, and continues to this day, making clear-cut distinctions between the two peoples less and less meaningful."

(3) What can the musicking in "historic" intra-African diasporas tell us about what is taking place in "contemporary" extra-African diasporas?
Because of the complexity of the issue, fully addressing this question is difficult. Therefore, my comments will be concise. First, studying "historic" (i.e., pre-colonial) intra-African diasporas makes us more keenly aware of the diversity of musicking in Africa – not only diversity between different ethnic groups but variation within the same cultural community. This was an issue in ancient times and the situation has not changed today. Therefore, instead of trying to identify the pureness of a cultural tradition, which is futile and nearly impossible (especially with extra-African diasporas, because the location of the homeland usually cannot be specified below the level of the continent), it may be more useful to compare the development of traditions within the same group in different host communities to determine both how features are similar or different and why varying features exist.

In addition, we must be cognizant that diasporic movements are constantly influx, shifting, and changing. The cultural identity that results from a diasporic movement is never complete, but is always in process or production (Hall 1993:222). As Edward Alpers (2001:24) has suggested, we need to adopt a definition of multiple and overlapping African diasporas that would allow us to address differences. For example, the movements that began in the twelfth and thirteenth centuries among the Fulbe continue today as Fulbe continue to migrate to other parts of Africa and the world. The same is happening in the Americas with Africans leaving homelands they established when they first arrived for other locations. The only thing that unifies them is that they may share a collective memory of the homeland. Therefore, it is important to document, examine, and compare traditions that are distinct to groups in specific locations at particular moments in time because they will certainly change over time. It is only when we are aware of issues such as multiple diasporas, changing diasporas, and diversity within diasporas will they help us to understand better musical traditions in various African cultures globally.

Now the larger question: what can a study of diasporas *within* Africa inform us about performance culture? Examining intra-African diasporas will, hopefully, remind us that there is not one African diaspora, but many. Because people in global culture, including Africans, respond to new ideas in different ways, comparative research (as I have noted in the foregoing) is critical to have a fuller understanding of the complexity of multiple creations. Just as we have focused on the numerous and varied musical traditions developed by African-derived groups *outside* the continent, a comparable amount of research and effort needs to be given to groups *within* Africa.

Endnotes

1: Zeleza (2005) states that the word, diaspora, can be used in several ways. "Extra-African" diaspora refers to the movement of blacks outside Africa (for example, peoples of African descent who have permanently settled in the Americas), while "intra-African" diaspora refers to migration within Africa. In addition, "historic" diasporas (those taking place during the pre-colonial era) are distinct from "contemporary" diasporas. Contemporary diasporas, according to Zeleza, are distinguished by three main waves: the diasporas of colonization, decolonization, and the era of structural adjustment, which emerged out of the disruptions and dispositions of colonial conquest, the struggles for independence, and structural adjustment programmes (SAPs), respectively. The diasporas of colonization include the students who went to study abroad and stayed, seamen who became settlers, and many others who migrated and became citizens according to the prevailing immigration regimes of the host countries. . . . The diasporas of decolonization include "indigenous" Africans as well as European and Asian settlers, such as the 32,000 Asians who were driven out of Uganda and the tens of thousands of former Portuguese settlers from Mozambique, who relocated overseas during the struggles for independence and immediately afterwards. "The diasporas of structural adjustment have been formed since the 1980s, out of the migrations engendered by economic, political, and social crises and the destabilizations of SAPs. They include professional elites, traders (such as the Senegalese vendors who trade the monolithic Africa of Afrocentricity on the streets of New York), refugees (such as the Somalis . . .), and many others" (Zeleza 2001:55).

2: Since 1999, I have personally been involved in several projects focusing on diaspora and global studies: (1) a year-long celebration of African music, entitled "The Globalization of African Music," organized by the UCLA Department of Ethnomusicology with concerts, lectures, and a symposium in 1999-2000; (2) the annual meeting of the African Studies Association in November 2001 in Houston, Texas, with the theme, "Africa and the African Diaspora: Past, Present, Future"; (3) a Global African Music and Arts Festival/Symposium organized by Karlton Hester at the University of California, Santa Cruz, in February 2003; (4) a symposium and festival on "Composition in Africa and the Diaspora" organized by Akin Euba at the University of Cambridge in England, in August 2005; and (5) the annual meeting of the Society for Ethnomusicology in Honolulu, Hawai'i, in November 2006 with the themes, "Diaspora Studies" and "Migration and Movement, with special references to Asia and the Pacific." Recent publications on music and diaspora include works by Aparicio, Jáquez, and Cepeda (2003); Catlin-Jairazbhoy (2003); Monson (2000); and Turino and Lea (2004).

3: Words in italics do not appear in the original publication; I inserted them for the purposes of this discussion.

4: From my cursory review of the literature, *Black People and Their Culture: Selected Writings from the African Diaspora* (Shapiro 1976) may be the first publication (or one of the first) in which researchers in the arts and folklore use the concept, "African Diaspora," in reference to the artistic creations of black people in Africa and the Americas (i.e. the Caribbean, North America, and South America). Published as part of the Smithsonian Institution's Bicentennial celebration, the work includes essays on music, dance, photography, woodcarving, hairstyling, weaving, booking, and other expressive arts.

5: Horton (1999) is noteworthy because he documents the return of the *gumbe* drum, the first evidence of feedback, to Sierra Leone. African popular music also represents contemporary interchanges; see wa Mukuna (1992) and Erlmann (1991).

6: Here, I have used abbreviations included in Charry (2000:1): Mn (Maninka), Md (Mandinka), and Bn (Bamana).

7: Some Hausa also migrated east; Hausa communities can be found in different parts of Central Africa, including the Central African Republic, Gabon, Congo, and the Democratic Republic of Congo (Works 1976:2).

8: Adamu describes *zango* as a voluntary settlement of Hausa migrants united by two factors: "their common desire to better themselves through their own professions and their membership of one cultural entity, the Hausa ethnic group" (1978:16). *Zongo*, according to Deborah Pellow, whose findings are based on research in Ghana, means "stranger quarter" (i.e. a settlement for foreigners). Established in the nineteenth century, many of the *zongos* (in Kumasi and Accra) became multi-ethnic enclaves, including Muslim Hausa, Yoruba, and Mossi traders, soldiers, and labor migrants as well as Frafra, Grusi, Dagbamba or Kusasi who were born and raised in the Islamic north. Within *zongos*, "the Hausa were always influential beyond their numbers, providing a model for the other Muslim groups in manner and behaviour [sic]. Thus many of the zongo dwellers self-identified as Hausa despite their true ethnicity, and their children perpetuated the fiction" (Pellow 1997:584).

9: Interestingly, Pellow conducted her fieldwork between the 1980s and early 2000s roughly one hundred years after the initial establishment of *zongos* in Kumasi and Accra, Ghana's two largest cities.

10: I find it noteworthy that funerals are mentioned here because a funeral for many Muslims is not a time for music making or celebration. Funerals are important events for musicking among most peoples in Ghana, including those in the Islamic North, probably due to influence from the South. However, funerals are rarely used as contexts for musicking in northern Nigeria. The fact that Pellow mentions the celebration of funerals by Hausa in Accra suggests that this is another area in which Hausa practices have changed due to interactions with the host community.

References

Adamu, Mahdi. 1978. *The Hausa Factor in West African History*. Nigeria: Zaria and Ibadan: Ahmadu Bello University Press and Oxford University Press.

Alpers, Edward A. 2001. "Defining the African Diaspora." Paper presented at the Center for Comparative Social Analysis Workshop. University of California, Los Angeles.

Ames, David W. 1973. "A Sociocultural View of Hausa Musical Activity." In *The Traditional Artist in African Societies*. Ed. by Warren L. d'Azevedo. Bloomington: Indiana University Press, 128-161.

Ames, David W., and Anthony V. King. 1971. *Glossary of Hausa Music and Its Social Context*. Evanston, IL: Northwestern University Press.

Anderson, Lois. 1971. "The Interrelation of African and Arab Musics: Some Preliminary Considerations." In *Essays in Music and History in Africa*. Ed. by Klaus P. Wachsmann. Evanston, IL: Northwestern University Press, 143-169.

Aparicio, Frances R., Cándida Jáquez, and María Elena Cepeda, Eds. 2003. *Musical Migrations: Transnationalism and Cultural Hybridity in Latin/o America*. New York: Palgrave Macmillan.

Arnott, D. W. 2007-2011. "Fulbe Music." Grove Music Online. http://www.oxfordmusiconline.com:80/subscriber/article/grove/music/10365 (Accessed August 16, 2011).

Azarya, Victor, Paul Kazuhisa Eguchi, and Catherine VerEecke. 1993. "Introduction." In *Unity and Diversity of a People: The Search for Fulbe Identity*. Ed. by Paul Kazuhisa Eguchi and Victor Azarya. Osaka, Japan: National Museum of Ethnology, 1-9.

Bakewell, Oliver. 2008. "In Search of Diasporas within Africa." *African Diaspora* 1(1-2): 5-27.

Benachir, Bouazza. 2005. *Esclavage, Diaspora Africaine et Communautés Noire du Maroc*. Paris: l'Harmattan.

Besmer, Fremont. 1998. "Hausa Performance." In *Africa: The Garland Encyclopedia of World Music*. Ed. by Ruth Stone. New York: Garland, 515-529.

Catlin, Amy. 2002. *Sidi Sufis: African Indian Mystics of Gujarat*. 79-minute CD. Van Huys: Aspara Media.

Catlin-Jairazbhoy, Amy. 2003. *From Africa to India. Sidi Music in the Indian Ocean Diaspora: A Video*. Van Nuys, CA: Aspara Media for Intercultural Education.

Catlin, Amy, and Edward Alpers, eds. 2003. *Sidis and Scholars: Essays on African Indians*. New Delhi: Rainbow Publications; New Jersey: Africa World Press.

Charry, Eric. 2000. *Mande Music: Traditional and Modern Music of the Maninka and Mandinka of Western Africa*. Chicago and London: The University of Chicago Press.

Clifford, James. 1997. *Routes: Travel and Translation in the Late Twentieth Century*. Cambridge, MA: Harvard University Press.

DjeDje, Jacqueline Cogdell. 1982. "The Concept of Patronage: An Examination of Hausa and Dagomba One-String Fiddle Traditions." *Journal of African Studies* 9(3):116-127, Fall.

___. 1998. "West Africa: An Introduction." In *Africa: The Garland Encyclopedia of World Music*. Ed. by Ruth Stone. New York: Routledge, 442-470.

___. 2008. *Fiddling in West Africa: Touching the Spirit in Fulbe, Hausa, and Dagbamba Cultures*. Bloomington: Indiana University Press.

Dorsch, Hauke. 2004. "Griots, Roots and Identity in the African Diaspora." In *Diaspora, Identity and Religion: New Directions in Theory and Research*. Ed. by Waltraud Kokot, Khachig Tölölyan and Carolin Alfonso. London: Routledge, 102-116.

Edwards, Brent Hayes. 2001. "The Uses of Diaspora." *Social Text* 19(1):45-73.

Erlmann, Veit. 1983. "Notes on Musical Instruments Among the Fulani of Diamare (North Cameroon)." *African Music* 6(3):16-41.

___. 1991. *African Stars: Studies in Black South African Performance*. Chicago: University of Chicago Press.

Gilroy, Paul. 1993. *The Black Atlantic: Modernity and Double Consciousness*. Cambridge, MA: Harvard University Press.

Hall, Stuart. 1990. "Cultural Identity and Diaspora." In *Identity: Community, Culture, Difference*. Ed. by Jonathan Rutherford. London: Lawrence and Wishart, 222-237.

Hamel, Chouki El. 2008. "Constructing a Diasporic Identity: Tracing the Origins of the Gnawa Spiritual Group in Morocco." *Journal of African History* 49:241-260.

Harris, Joseph E. 1996. "The Dynamics of the Global African Diaspora." In *The African Diaspora*. Ed. by Alusine Jalloh and Stephen E. Maizlish. Arlington, Texas: The University of Texas at Arlington, 7-21.

Horton, Christian Dowu Jayeola. 1999. "The Role of the Gumbe in Popular Music and Dance Styles in Sierra Leone." In *Turn Up the Volume! A Celebration of African Music*. Ed. by Jacqueline Cogdell DjeDje. Los Angeles: UCLA Fowler Museum of Cultural History, 230-235.

Hutchinson, John, and Anthony A. Smith. 1996. "Introduction." In *Ethnicity*. Ed. by John Hutchinson and Anthony A. Smith. Oxford: Oxford University Press, 3-16.

King, Anthony. 2007-2011. "Hausa Music." *Grove Music Online*. http://www.oxfordmusiconline.com:80/subscriber/article/grove/music/12561 (Accessed August 16, 2011).

Knight, Roderic. 1983. "Manding/Fula Relations as Reflected in the Manding Song Repertoire." *African Music* 6(2):37-47.

Kubik, Gerhard. 1998. "Intra-African Streams of Influence." In *Garland Encyclopedia of World Music*. Ed. by Ruth Stone. New York: Routledge, 3-16.

Mabogunje, Akin L. 1976. "The Land and Peoples of West Africa." In *History of West Africa, Vol. 1, 2nd ed*. Ed. by J. F. A. Ajayi and Michael Crowder. London: Longman, 1-32.

Monson, Ingrid. 2000. "Introduction." In *African Diaspora: A Musical Perspective*, Ed. by Ingrid Monson. New York: Routledge, 1-19.

Nketia, 1971. "History and the Organization of Music in West Africa." In *Essays on Music and History in Africa*. Ed. by Klaus P. Wachsmann. Evanston: Northwestern University Press, 3-25.

Pellow, Deborah. 1997. "Male Praise-Singers in Accra: In the Company of Women." In *Africa: Journal of the International African Institute* 67(4):582-601.

___. 2001. "Cultural Differences and Urban Spatial Forms: Elements of Boundedness in an Accra Community." *American Anthropologist* 103(1):59-75, March.

Racy, Ali Jihad. 1999. "The Lyre of the Arab Gulf: Historical Roots, Geographical Links, and the Local Context." In *Turn Up the Volume! A Celebration of African Music*. Ed. by Jacqueline Cogdell DjeDje. Los Angeles: UCLA Fowler Museum of Cultural History, 134-139.

Shapiro, Linn, ed. 1976. *Black People and Their Culture: Selected Writings from the African Diaspora*. Washington, DC: Smithsonian Institution.

Smith, Michael G. 1965. "The Hausa of Northern Nigeria." In *Peoples of Africa*. Ed. by James L. Gibbs, Jr. New York: Holt, Rinehart and Winston, 119-155.

Sulemana, Alhassan Iddi. 2003. Personal interview with the author, August 4.

Turino, Thomas, and James Lea. 2004. *Identity and the Arts in Diaspora Communities*. Warren, MI: Harmonie Park Press.

Wachsmann, Klaus P. 1971. *Essays on Music and History in Africa*. Evanston, IL: Northwestern University Press.

wa Mukuna, Kazadi. 1992. "The Genesis of Urban Music in Zaire." *African Music* 7(2):72-84.

Webster's New Collegiate Dictionary. 1974. Springfield, MA: G. & C. Merriam Co.

Works, John Arthur, Jr. 1976. *Pilgrims in a Strange Land: The Hausa in Chad*. New York: Columbia University Press.

Youngstedt, Scott M. 2004. "Creating Modernities Through Conversation Groups: The Everyday Worlds of Hausa Migrants in Niamey, Niger." *African Studies Review* 47(3):91-118, December.

Zeleza, Paul Tiyambe. 2005. "Rewriting the African Diaspora: Beyond the Black Atlantic." *African Affairs* 104(414):35-68.

Give Me Silence, Space, and a Dance: The Pianistic Style of Thelonious Monk

Kwasi Ampene

Kwasi Ampene is professor and the director of the Center for World Performance Studies (CWPS) at the University of Michigan. He specializes in the rich musical traditions of the Akan of Ghana. His book publications include *Female Song Tradition and the Akan of Ghana: The Creative Process in Nnwonkorɔ* (2005); and *Engaging Modernity: Asante in the Twenty-First Century* (2014). He has published in the *American Music Research Center Journal* (2012) and contributed an entry on the renowned Ghanaian dance band highlife musician, E.T. Mensah, in the *New Encyclopedia of Africa* (2007). His book reviews appear in the *American Ethnologist* (2009) and *Ethnomusicology* (2007).

Thelonious Sphere Monk (1917-1982) was the most distinctive modern pianist during the bebop and post bebop era. His influence extends beyond pianists Mal Waldron, Horace Silver, Cecil Taylor, Randy Weston, and Denny Drew, to horn players including soprano saxophonist Steve Lacy and others. In the early 1940s, he was the House Pianist at Minton's Playhouse in Harlem, New York, where jazz musicians converged for jam sessions (Fitterling 1997: 27-40). These jam sessions resulted in the birth of bebop or what Scot DeVeaux describes as "the bebop revolution" (DeVeaux 1997: 4). The spirit of experimentation and the search for new techniques that characterized the bebop revolution paved the way for future developments in jazz including cool, avant-garde, free jazz and others.[1]

Although Monk's compositions, including "'Round Midnight" (Blue Note BLP 1510) and "Straight No Chaser" (Blue Note BLP 1510), became part of the standard bebop repertoire and were performed by Dizzy Gillespie, Miles Davis, and John Coltrane, among a host of jazz luminaries, his contribution as a pianist to the early bebop was not recognized until the late 1950s when he played at the Five Spot with his quartet and more permanently after his death in 1982[2]. Two notable publications since 1982 are Robin Kelley's *Thelonious Monk: The Life and Times of an American Original* (2009), and Gabriel Solis' *Monk's Music: Thelonious Monk and Jazz History in the Making* (2008). What were the causes for the rather belated recognition? Why was it hard for his fellow jazz musicians, critics and the general public to understand his pianistic style?

This paper is in two parts. In the first part, I will examine the perceived notions of jazz in the 1940s and 1950s and describe the bebop sound ideal that the critics, jazz musicians, and the general public had come to expect. Following that, I will argue that these two perspectives represent an evaluation of Monk's pianistic style by the tradition-conditioned ears of the time, which did not consider a crucial aspect of performance practice in jazz; that is the "interactive, collaborative context of musical invention as a point of departure" (Ingrid Monson 1996: 75). The noted American musicologist, Richard Crawford, refers to this hallmark of jazz performance as "creative interaction", however, he expressed great concern that it is missing in jazz history and criticism (Crawford 2001: 838-844). It is worth noting that the collaborative context or the creative interaction should not be limited to what goes on between musicians in the course of performance, but also the relationship between the jazz musician and his or her instrument. As a result of this misunderstanding, Monk and his music were incompletely appreciated by his listeners. I shall therefore offer a new perspective that grounds Monk's pianistic style within the broader framework of African Pianism, a concept that embraces techniques, approaches, and resources of African roots to the piano. For, it is only when Monk's style of playing the piano is viewed in the context of African pianism can we truly appreciate him as an influential pianist of all time.

There is no doubt that Monk avoided familiar runs, chord changes, and used his flat-fingered technique in order to creatively open new doors for the jazz world. But, as Robert Doerschuk reports in the *Giants of Jazz Piano,* "to get inside new doors, a new key had to be forged" (Doerschuk 2001: 112). To this day, this new key has remained elusive or at best unattainable. Doerschuk's statement is revealing especially when it is apparent that less documented, and missing in Monk scholarship is his avid interest in the African roots of his music and his relationship with African drummers/percussionists. Consequently, in the second part, I will take a closer look at Monk's relationship with Kofi Ghanaba (formerly Guy Warren), the self-proclaimed Divine Drummer and a musical icon from Ghana as the new key or the missing link in Monk criticism. Ghanaba (May 4, 1923-December 22, 2008) is credited with introducing African drums and percussion into American jazz in addition to pioneering and recording his own brand of Afro jazz in the 1950s and 1960s.

Notions of Jazz in the 1940s and 1950s
By the 1940s and the 1950s, the use of fixed harmonic patterns defined the normal boundaries of jazz improvisation. In other words, chords with their particular tunes were a given. The role of a pianist in particular was to "comp" (accompany) behind soloists or the frontline men by providing specified chord structures (or chord changes). Furthermore, piano solos themselves were generally marked by long runs in a linear scalar fashion. However, Monk's idiosyncrasy and eccentric style would not permit him to conform to these expectations, because he took an entirely different approach to playing the piano. He purposefully avoided structured chord changes. With his flat-fingered technique, Monk's pianistic style was percussive (or drum-like), non-linear, and full of twists and turns and surprises with silence,

space, and body movements. When performing with Monk, one had to be able to improvise with the structured chord changes in mind without necessarily hearing them played on the piano.

It should be noted that silences due to the absence of sound as well as single notes and minimal chords were in contrast to the prevalent goal of harmonically oriented styles of the 1940s and therefore posed enormous difficulty for those not accustomed to Monk's pianistic style. Bandleader Dizzy Gillespie had the following piece of advice for jazz musicians: "If you want to play with Monk, you have to have the composition down cold, otherwise you turn around and suddenly are faced with the greatest difficulties" (Fitterling 1997: 101). Some of Monk's contemporaries were not privy to Dizzy's advice and had to go through the "ordeal" of playing with Monk for the first time. A case in point is James Moody's account of his initial encounter with Monk.

Moody had joined Dizzy Gillespie's band in 1947 for an engagement at the Spotlight Club on 52nd street in New York City. During one of the numbers, Moody stood up to take a solo; to his surprise, instead of the structured chord changes usually associated with that particular composition, he heard only one note. It was Monk, who was seated at the piano. The other members of the rhythm section kept playing without missing a beat. At that point, Moody said "I knew I was on my own, so I just closed my eyes and kept on wailing (Davis 1996: 69).

Moody's account of his initiation into Monk's style gives us an idea of what the unaccustomed ears of musicians, the audience, and critics had to contend with in the 1940s and 1950s. In fact, most critics viewed Monk's attitude as a mark of limited technical ability, but the idea of silence and space in music was very important to Monk. According to the pianist Randy Weston (1991), Monk was familiar with Oriental philosophy where ancient masters communicate without words[3]. Like many of the myths surrounding Monk, it is hard to prove this statement. At the same time, we cannot rule it out entirely since Monk appeared in public and performed on several occasions in a Chinese cap, probably in homage to his first name and his sage-like demeanor on other occasions.

The Bebop Sound Ideal
An examination of the unique sound of bebop may also explain the belated recognition of Monk's pianistic style. Explosive solos, altered

and extended chords, and bright but aggressive and dissonant harmony characterized bebop. Many of the beboppers, including pianists, expressed themselves by filling their musical space with several notes. In fact, most of the pianists at the time saw space as void and meaningless without sound. One need only compare the fast, brilliant playing and the rapid blowing lines of Bud Powell on *The Genius of Bud Powell* (Verve CD 827 901-2) with that of Monk's angular and percussive approach to comprehend the difference[4]. Monk's aggressive embrace of silence was so unique at the time leading to Orin Keepnews' remark that, Monk was "engaged in developing an essentially original piano style" (Tucker 1999: 232).

Conversely, some scholars invoke the fundamental tenets of the bebop revolution to explain the idiosyncrasy and eccentrics of Monk. According to Scott DeVeaux, bebop musicians initially sought to assert "their creative independence from the marketplace" (DeVeaux 1997: 4). That is, bebopers wanted to play from their hearts instead of playing to the demands of the recording industry or merely for economic benefits. In fact, the artistic freedom sought by bebopers was, in Mark Tucker's own words, a rejection of the "accommodating entertainer persona of swing musicians who were willing and, in most cases, expected to put the public's wishes before their own" (Tucker 1999: 234). If ever one man represented this ideal of the bebop revolution, it was Monk since he was less concerned with record sales than with developing a unique and a coherent pianistic style. Keepnews (1991) sums it all up when he remarked that the critics and musicians were not on the same wavelength with Monk; suggesting that Monk was ahead of his time and enjoyed his status as an avant-garde icon[5]. Having examined jazz in the 1940s and 1950s, and the bebop sound ideal, I will now examine Monk's pianistic style in the broader framework of African Pianism.

Since the late 1960s, the Nigerian composer, Akin Euba, has been working on a concept of African Pianism to describe the keyboard music of African composers trained in Western compositional idioms but whose piano works reflect African identity. According to Euba, the style arose from the "percussive treatment of the piano and making the piano 'behave' like African musical instruments" (Euba 1993: 8). The percussive treatment of the piano is exemplified in the use of a variety of bell patterns, drumming styles, xylophone and *mbira* music. Additionally, the tonal, melodic, harmonic, the modal orientation and formal conventions of traditional songs and African popular music (Afro-Pop) are the foundations of African Pianism (Kwabena Nketia, 1994: iii). Implicit in this definition is the notion of a functional substitute. That is, the piano becomes a substitute for all the numerous variety of African musical instruments. In this process, all kinds of performance practices and mannerisms associated with African instruments are brought to bear on the piano. These features are present in varying degrees in the piano music of the following composers: Halim El-Dabh, *Mekta' in the Art of Kita'* for piano (Egypt); Kwabena Nketia, *Volta Fantasy* (Ghana); and Akin Euba *Scenes from Traditional Life* (Nigeria).[6] In the *Volta Fantasy*, for instance, Nketia absorbed and transformed the concept of timeline in the traditional music of the *Anlo* (the Southern group of Ewe in Ghana). *Atrikpui, Atsiagbekor,* and *Agbadza* are dances performed by the Anlo with the same timeline pattern as the one used by Nketia in this piece. These dances invariably consist of a drum ensemble, a chorus with a lead singer, as well as dancers. Nketia captured the essence of the performance procedures by placing melodic phrases in relation to the recurring timeline or the handclap patterns, which are characteristically Anlo. The tonal pattern and the modal orientation are inevitably Anlo and as a result, is indicative of how Nketia transferred the distinctive features of these dances to the 19th century European character pieces for piano. Unlike European character pieces, the melodies are angular, cyclical, and the harmonies are not goal orientated while the pre-final and final cadences are archetypes of Anlo.

By suggesting African Pianism as the basis for understanding Monk's piano style, I am by no means implying that American jazz and African pianism are the same, for the idioms are different. With the exception of a few pieces by Halim El-Dabh, African piano pieces are written in its entirety with no room for improvisation while Monk's music is fundamentally based on improvisation. These two idioms developed independently from each other but the common bond between them seem to rest in the search for an identity. In Africa, colonial music education introduced Africans to Western music and Western harmony and not the multi-level music of Africa, which was unknown to the educators (Nketia, 1982: 90). As a result, there is a conscious search among African composers of written music (also referred to as 'art' music'), to compose music that will not only link them to international audiences but most importantly, their African roots.[7] For most African American jazzmen and women, there is a constant or conscious effort to keep jazz to its African origins with various levels of success and it is no surprising that Monk was pre-occupied with doing the same. The often-cited percussive technique, elbow clusters, flat-fingered playing, angular melodies, dissonances, the use of space and dance, are ample illustrations of Monk playing the piano as a functional substitute of an African drum.

Furthermore, the concept of African pianism is grounded in the fundamental approach to music making in African world traditions: that is, the concept of music making as *play* which Crawford refers to as *creative interaction*[8]. The word "play" comes up in several writings on Monk, scholarly or otherwise, but no single writer seems to go beyond the word. For instance, Gene Santoro's brief article, "Master of Space," first published in *The Nation* in 1994, describes Monk's pianistic style as a "playful, satiric concept of space."[9] Although play understood to mean prescribed but unfettered and spontaneous activity associated with children as opposed to "work" is a universal aspect of human behavior, the concept is emphasized more in African world cultures than elsewhere and is more integral to them. The *play* element most familiar to Western listeners is commonly referred to as *call and response* (an evidently communal approach to music-making) is highly interactive and can be referred to as the act of dialoguing. By incorporating dialogue into the structure of drum ensembles (which invariably includes a chorus, dancers, and an audience), African musicians are able to create silence and space. For instance, if an instrument or a lead singer calls, they have to *wait* for a response, while the response in turn will have to *wait* for the call. The wait in the previous sentence represents *silence* and *space* in time. Silence, as Kofi Agawu affirms, is not "absence of sound but an intentional placement of silence as a substitute for sound" (Agawu, 2003: 77). Agawu goes on to declare that knowing where the beat is but articulating it as a silence is "part of an aesthetic of play" common in the musical expressions in the African world. Similarly, the concept of silence and space is the basis of discussion in chapter one of *West African Pop Roots,* by John Collins (1992). In this book, Collins traces the transformations of African music throughout the twentieth century by concentrating on West African pop music. Collins further claim that the "hot rhythms of Africa make space and bend time, releasing an almost infinite permutation of spaces and times" (Collins, 1992:6). He then resorted to the analogy of the wood carver in Africa. According to Collins, the wood carver "chips away matter to produce space and inner form," just as "the African musician gives music an inner stability or shape by cutting holes in sound and being able to hear the silence (Collins ibid). The concept of chipping away matter to produce space is of particular interest to my discussion of silence and space in Monk's pianistic style.

The basis of *play* elements in African world cultures can be traced to the manifold occurrences of call and response in verbal discourses in formal and informal situations. For instance, when the King of Asante speaks direct to his people, the King's diplomats and orators punctuate his speech with responses.[10] Similarly, it is not uncommon for the deacons and members of the congregation of an African American Baptist Church to respond to the preacher with such phrases as "yes Lord," "amen," "preach it" and other responses. The incidence of call and response play in verbal discourses in African world traditions is readily transferred to the musical process. Kwabena Nketia, on his part, refers to the play-concept in African world traditions as being expressed in "interactive structures" (Nketia 1991: 71). For instance, interactive structures are evident in the manner in which the bells, supporting drums, and the leading drums converse among themselves and with dancers and singers. It is also evident in the participatory call and response at various levels in African world ensembles including the interaction between the lead singer and the chorus, and the interactive response of the audience. In recent times, the concept of "interaction" has found favor with musicologists. For instance, it forms the basis of Ingrid Monson's seminal book *Saying Something* (1996), which investigates the improvisational interplay among the rhythm section (drums, bass, and piano) in jazz ensembles. It remains to be said that interactive structures encourage a dynamic (or a communal) approach to the musical process as opposed to a contemplative or a passive approach.

In addition to African world ensembles, the concept of interactive structures are present in performances involving solo musicians and their instruments. Instrumentalists or solo performers incorporate interactive structures in their performance in several ways. For instance, Kakraba Lobi (1939-2007) was an accomplished xylophonist from the Lobi ethnic group in Northwestern Ghana. He interacts with his instrument by incorporating vocal grunts and other forms of "noise" when performing solo on his *gyil* (xylophone).[11] On the other hand, jazz pianists including Mary Lou Williams, Duke Ellington, Count Basie, and Bud Powell, to name just a few, are noted for interacting with their instruments by patting their feet in addition to making vocal grunts, and other forms of "noise" while playing the piano. What is unique about Monk is that, he took it a step further by adding the dance to his interactive approach.

In the course of a performance, Monk will suddenly jump from the piano and begin to dance to the music. To dance, according to the third edition of *The American Heritage Concise Dictionary,* is "to move rhythmically, usually, to music, and to leap or to skip about."[12] A typical occasion for Monk's gyrations is captured on the video documentary *Thelonious Monk: American Composer.* In the clip that featured "Bolivar's Blues," Monk plays the piano in his usual drum-like fashion and after a brief spell stands up, walks away from the piano and begins to dance. Why the dance? Why did Monk not "comp" behind Charlie Rouse? Certainly, the most favorable answer that comes to mind is that from the very beginning, dance has been an integral aspect of jazz. In addition to the above explanation, I would like to offer another view, a crucial one that can be linked to the concept of African Pianism.

Just as Kakraba Lobi interacts with his xylophone by using vocal grunts, dancing around the piano was Monk's technique of interacting with the piano. Further, Monk was aware that in order to make his simple musical structures consisting of single notes and minimal chords exciting and meaningful to members of his band and the audience, he had to approach piano playing as *play* in order to increase the level of interaction. According to the ethnomusicologist, Brenda Romero, a vital aspect of the African concept of play is an appreciation of the multi-dimensionality of musical sound, its acoustical, spiritual, emotional, and kinesthetic scope or impact[13]. She goes on to say that musical sound does not simply move in a linear fashion but radiates as a "splash" in all directions. Secondly, musical sound is not simply a chronological and mathematically proportional progression, but an affective event requiring some form of response. As a result, the African concept of *play* in music embraces an intellectual understanding of the multi-dimensionality of musical sound, which is evident in the dance steps of Monk.

Monk's consciousness and use of silence, space, and dance stand in contrast to the understood framework of structured chord changes that audiences and critics were accustomed to in the 1940s and 1950s. It also stood in contrast to the bebop sound ideal- a plethora of virtuosic notes. Bebop was first realized for speed and fluency and not the harsh percussive tone production and elbow clusters of Monk. As stated earlier, Monk was preoccupied with developing an essentially original piano style with African pianism as the foundation in order to connect jazz to its African roots. He needed the artistic freedom sought by bebopers to achieve his goal. Seen in this light, we can safely conclude that Monk is a true and genuine representative of the bebop revolution. He did not play to the wishes of the listening public or the demands of the recording industry and the promise of huge financial rewards despite his superficial differences from Parker and Dizzy Gillepsie's style. Monk's technique requires a broader analytical framework that takes into account the concept of *creative interaction* or the *playful* approach to music making in African world cultures. Consequently, I examined Monk's pianistic style within the broader framework of African pianism for the African concept of music as *play* recognizes the multi-dimensional property of sound and as a result, requires multi-dimensional affective response in the form of a dance. Embedded in this concept is the notion that the piano can be used as a functional substitute of African drums. Monk played single notes or no notes at all and sometimes he danced around the piano instead of compin' behind the soloist in order to increase the level of interaction or to re-introduce dynamism in jazz performance. In doing so, he was acutely aware that in order to make his simple musical structures consisting of single notes and minimal chords exciting and meaningful to members of his band and the audience, he had to approach music making by means of physical gestures not directly connected to the production of sounds. No wonder Charles Keil described the concept of play, which is an essential aspect of Monk's pianistic style as "sophisticated childishness"(Kiel 1994: 75).

The Talking Drum Looks Ahead: The Missing Link in Monk Research

Obviously, the theoretical framework of African pianism as an analytical tool in understanding Monk's pianistic style raises some pertinent questions. For instance, to what extent can one say absolutely that Monk was acting in response to African cultures? Was Monk aware of

African cultures and traditions or had these traditions worked their way into his piano playing? Did Monk ever write or speak about the effects of African traditions in his music? Monk seldom verbalizes about his music for he believed that whatever communication there is in his music could be obtained only by listening. For instance, Nat Hentoff and Ira Gitler are two jazz critics who interviewed Monk for the *Down Beat* and *Metronome Magazines* respectively. Nat Hentoff's article appeared on July 25, 1956 while Ira Gitler's appeared the following year in March 1957.[14] Both critics wanted to know the single source of influence in Monk's music. His response to this poignant question was that he did not pick a single musician to follow. According to him, there is practically something worth learning from nearly every musician he had heard. It is worth noting that, no matter how Hentoff and Gitler framed the same question, Monk responded in the same manner. However, I am of the firm conviction that although Monk may not have articulated the effects of African traditions in his music that does not mean he was not cognizance of it. I will proceed to examine Monk's relationship with Kofi Ghanaba as the missing link and the much-needed missing key in Monk scholarship.[15]

While working on this paper, I came upon a piece of information that was as startling as it was revealing. I was invited to a party at a friend's house in Boulder, Colorado. When we went to the basement, my gaze shifted to a particular LP on the shelf because the picture on the cover looked familiar. After a brief hesitation, I gathered courage and picked the LP from the shelf. Then I realized that the LP was recorded by one of the greatest jazz drummers from Ghana, Kofi Ghanaba, who was then known as Guy Warren. The title of the LP is *Themes For African Drums,* and it was recorded at Webster Hall in New York on May 22 and 23, 1958 and produced by Lee Schapiro for RCA records. Band 5 on Side One of the LP is titled *The Talking Drum Looks Ahead* and this is what Ghanaba had to say:

Here is that drum again. This time it is playing jazz and it is playing a melodic line just like any other melody instrument. If it's played well, this amazing drum fits comfortably into the idiom just like that! I use a typical traditional American blues form as a take-off. To me, jazz IS the blues and the blues IS jazz. What you hear here is one of the things Africa has to offer jazz. Matter of fact, this is JAZZ AS I SEE IT. I am dedicating the tune to my idol and friend, Thelonious Monk.

The bassist was James Styles and the vibist, Earl Griffin. They sure laid it down, didn't they?

In order to ascertain why Ghanaba dedicated this particular track to his friend and idol, Thelonious Monk, a brief discussion of the talking drum is in order. Although there are numerous types of drums in Africa, the idea of a "talking drum" dates back to the early days of European explorers and their fascination with a family of hourglass shaped drums mostly common in West Africa. This particular type of drum is prominent among the Yoruba and Hausa in Nigeria, the Dagbon and Akan in Ghana, and in Senegal and Gambia. A distinctive feature of this drum is its ability to closely imitate the rhythms and intonations of spoken language. Since Ghanaba is from Ghana and the drum features prominently in Dagbon in the North, than their southern neighbors, the Akan, I will provide the attributes of this drum in Dagbon. The *luna,* as it is called in Dagbon, is the main instrument of the *Lunsi,* hereditary drummers who are recognized as verbal artists, genealogists, counselors to royalty, cultural experts and entertainers. The *lunsi* may also use the *luna* to drum the praise appellations to honor ancestor chiefs and the incumbent chief. Vitally, drumming the history of the Dagbon and their migration from Northern Nigeria to their present location in Ghana is a major undertaken of the *lunsi.*[16] All the activities above involve recalling the past, to learn about the past, in order to understand the present and go forth into the future. As a result, the *luna* symbolizes the past, the present, and the future. That is why the *lunsi* (the drummers of *luna*) are highly respected in Dagbon society. Did Ghanaba recognize these attributes in the music and performance of Monk?

By 1999, and with hindsight, some scholars have, gradually, come to recognize the above attributes of the Dagbon *luna* in Monk's music. A case in point is Robin Kelley who noted in his contributing essay in the *Black Music Research Journal* (BMRJ) that a few critics and musicians recognize in Monk "a startling modernism as well as a direct link to the rich traditions of Black music making" (Kelley, 1999: 139). While Kelley's declaration resonates with similar pronouncements by other scholars, it falls short of linking Monk's music and performance mannerisms further to Africa. As it turned out, Ghanaba recognized these traits that Monk did not stop at the Black music traditions in the US but extended his search to the African origins of Black music four decades earlier. In all likelihood, there is the possibility that Ghanaba and Monk might have met when the former came to the United States in the 1950s. What is intriguing is the apparent lack of documentation of any kind that might suggest a connection between these two great musicians. As I read Ghanaba's album notes for the tenth time, it dawned on me that the answers to the questions posed at the beginning of this paper are in my homeland, Ghana! All of a sudden, my premise of examining Monk's pianistic style in the context of African pianism assumed a new meaning.

I borrowed Ghanaba's LP, took it to my office the next morning, made copies on two cassettes and returned the LP and a cassette tape to my friend. I went to Ghana in the summer of 2002, and did not waste time in contacting Ghanaba. I knew someone, who knew someone, who knew Ghanaba. I went to Ghanaba's village to arrange a meeting to see what I could obtain from him. I met with Ghanaba a week later and he told me a lot about his relationship with Monk. He refers to Monk as His Highness, and Mrs. Monk, Nelly O. He pointed to an autographed post card signed by Monk and hand delivered to him on September 24th, 1964 and hanging on a wall as part of the collection in his personal archive. It reads: "keep on playing those Drums, Guy Warren." Below the card, Ghanaba has provided a description of how he got the card. I have reproduced the original description by Ghanaba without altering or editing the text. Plates 1 and 2 are reproductions of the autograph, description, and Monk's picture (see Appendix).

On another wall in the archive is yet another historical picture featuring Ghanaba, Charlie Parker, some jazz musicians, and a female reporter for the *Down Beat* who, I understand, was doing a story on Parker. Taken in a Chicago nightclub, Parker is seen wearing Ghanaba's *kente* cloth while Ghanaba poses in Parker's jacket (1955). After our brief but rewarding meeting, I wanted to go back and search through the numerous memorabilia in his archive but without the benefit of a research grant, I could not do much so I informed him that I would like to meet with him the following summer for a detailed field research that shall include copying materials from his archive and a series of conversations. I went back the following year in June 2003, this time, armed with a research grant from my university. Who is Kofi Ghanaba?

A Brief Note on Kofi Ghanaba

Born in 1923 in Accra, Ghana, Ghanaba is described variously as a genius, a living legend, an enigma, a unique and a radical figure in African music.[17] He is credited with introducing African drums and percussion into American jazz in the 1950s. Ghanaba was uncompromising when he came to the US, and succeeded against all odds by introducing and recording his own brand of *Afro jazz*. In 1955, Decca released his LP, "Africa Speaks! America Answers," (Decca DL-8446). Although I do not have the facts, it has been said that Max Roach stated that "Africa Speaks" sold over a million copies (Roach, 1974). It is still considered a classic to this day. In 1958, Lee Schapiro produced "Themes for African Drums" for RCA (LSP-1864). Columbia followed in 1969 with his LP, "Afro Jazz" (SX6340). Over the years, and indicative of the far-reaching effect of his music, various musicians have covered different tracks from these LPs. For instance, the hard bop drummer well known for his leadership role in the Jazz Messengers, Art Blakey and the Afro-Drum Ensemble have a cover version of Ghanaba's piece "Love, The Mystery of" on the 1962 recording, "The African Beat." The jazz pianist, Randy Weston's *Khepera* CD also features a cover of the same piece. Of particular interest is Bert Kaempfert's arrangement of "Eyi Wala Dong" (My Thanks to God) from *Africa Speaks,* which Bert re-titled "That Happy Feeling." Released in 1962, "That Happy Feeling" was an instant hit and has since been covered by several artists.

Ghanaba was the first African musician to be elected to the membership of the American Society of Composers, Authors, and Publishers (ASCAP) in 1958. Originally he was known as Guy Warren until his spiritual transformation in the early 1960s when he officially changed his name to Kofi Ghanaba. He came to national attention in Ghana when in the early 1940s he played the drum set in the Accra Rhythmic Orchestra led by Joe Lamptey. In 1947, he played the drum set and backing vocals in the reconstituted E. T. Mensah and His Tempos Band. Before traveling to the US in 1953, he worked as a disc jockey (a DJ) in Liberia, and also lived in London where he was a member of Kenny Graham's Afro-Cubist band. In the US, he settled in Chicago and worked on the periphery of the jazz business. While in Chicago, he sometimes appeared in small combos or sometimes went without playing jobs for months. Now and then, he performed with some big names including Duke Ellington's band for several weeks in July 1957, at the Blue Note. He also appeared on the same program with Billie Holiday. He later relocated to New York City in 1957 (the big village he calls it) after going through extremely difficult times in Chicago. He was hired in the African Room on 3rd Avenue (Harod Kanter, owner) where he not only performed his own brand of Afro jazz for over a year, but he also led his own jazz group, the Guy Warren Soundz.

Although Ghanaba passed away in 2008, his music is still way ahead of its time as exemplified by a recent review of his newly released CD by the Retroafrica label. Over the years, he developed his idiosyncratic style of playing drums in Ghana to the extent that he is without peers or contemporaries. Personally, I have never come across a single drummer on the continent whose body is coated from head to toe with white clay or powder as part of his costume like Ghanaba. The *fontomfrom* court drums of Akan in Ghana feature prominently in his performances but these drums are either played standing or carried on the head in processions during traditional ceremonies. For Ghanaba's set up, the two drums lie on their sides on the ground. He has attached foot pedals to the head of these drums and plays with his feet while playing a set of five drums around him with sticks. Ghanaba occasionally performs in Ghana and has received several national awards including the Life Time Achievement Award by the Entertainers and Critics Reviewers Association of Ghana (ECRAG). Like Monk, those familiar with Ghanaba's music and his lifestyle can attest to his eccentric style of playing drums and his somewhat odd behavior. It took several decades for his countrymen to accommodate his music and his lifestyle on limited basis. For instance, while on a government scholarship at the Achimota College in Accra, he was considered either a genius or a damn fool. After several clashes with the school's authorities and when his housemaster became convinced that he must be a genius and that his lifestyle and music should be tolerated, he was given his own private room where he could play his "crazy music" anytime. Despite this arrangement, he left the school in his final year for according to him; he could not deal with the regimented ways of the school or society in general. He wanted to have his own way in whatever he chooses to do. Ghanaba returned to his native Ghana in 1962, after experiencing profound hardships in New York. Until his death, he lived in Medie where he managed his personal archive, The African Heritage Library. Since September 2005, New York University has partnered with Ghanaba to manage the library.

His collection includes several books, records, audio-visual materials, pictures, newspapers and magazines, and as we can imagine, drums of all sizes and shapes. Ghanaba is featured in the 1994 movie, *Sankofa* by the Ethiopian film director, Haile Gerima.[18] He was in Washington DC and New York in the same year during the premier of the movie in the US. Although Ghanaba first met Monk in the Chicago days, it was when he moved to New York and was playing in the African Room that they really became close friends.

Ghanaba's First Encounter With Monk
Ghanaba describes his first meeting with Monk as a "strange meeting" in Chicago. He was at the Roosevelt University to perform his brand of African jazz and Monk was in town to play at the Blue Note. According to Ghanaba, Monk came and sat in front of him motionless and stared seriously at him, paying attention to everything he did. At the end of the concert, Monk left without uttering a word. Despite a strong encouragement from a friend, Ghanaba in turn could not say a word to Monk either and they both went their separate ways. Eventually, when Ghanaba relocated to New York, he got in touch with Orin Keepnews (Riverside Records) who readily arranged a meeting between the two. Upon his arrival at Monk's apartment on 63rd Street, Ghanaba presented Monk with his album *African Speaks! America Answers*. Monk read the album notes and when he came across a phrase that described Ghanaba's music as "unconventional as they come," he asked Ghanaba what they mean by such a phrase. Ghanaba responded, "They mean unconventional." After this initial meeting, Monk made several trips to Ghanaba's apartment. According to Ghanaba, he would get a call from Nellie O, Monk's wife, and she would inform him that "your friend has just left home and he is on his way to see you."

A remarkable aspect of Monk's visit to Ghanaba's apartment is that, Ghanaba's bold attempt to reintroduce what he calls the "African accent" in American jazz brought resentment and while several of the important figures in jazz stayed away from him, it was only Monk who really took a particular interest in Ghanaba's ideas about Afro jazz. What is Afro jazz? Ghanaba's definition of Afro jazz is: jazz music with African melodies, African rhythms, and African harmonies. On the surface, this definition is really simple so why would jazz musicians avoid him? Upon close scrutiny however, we realize that what Ghanaba wanted to introduce in the 1950s was nothing short of a revolution. I stated in the first part of this paper that the foundations of chord changes in the 1940s and 1950s were based on Western European tonal harmonic practices. Just like the concept of

African pianism, the re-introduction of African melodies and harmonies will have reduced the dependence of jazz on tonal harmony and chord progressions. The critics, audience, jazzmen and women have come to rely on these chord changes in order to assess jazz musicians and their music. The re-introduction of African melodies and harmonies will have displaced these expectations especially, for those with limited knowledge of African music. When we move on to rhythm, we have to look at the jazz ensemble. The organization of jazz ensembles by this time had settled comfortably into the frontline and the rhythm sections. Up until the beboppers partially elevated the function of the drum set, the drum set has been domesticated and reduced to keeping a four-four time in the background. The disciplining of the drums set in jazz ensembles has been the source of disappointment for Ghanaba who is deeply aware of the role of drums in West African ensembles. He could not imagine the *luna,* or the *atumpan* and *fontomfrom* drums of the Akan playing a subordinate role in an ensemble. Ghanaba's idea of re-introducing African rhythms into jazz would have meant that the drum set would be giving a leading role in the jazz ensemble. Additional percussion (or auxiliary percussion) could be added to perform the role of keeping the time or the drum set could perform that role and at the same time, a leading role by sometimes playing the melody as he aptly demonstrates on his LP *Themes for African Drums.* Can you imagine reducing the pre-eminence of the Coltranes, Miles Davis', Guillespies, Parkers, or the Bud Powel's as soloists? It would have required these top-notch soloists to re-orient their melodies to accommodate African melodies and harmonies that are cyclical in several respects. It would have required a new training for jazz drummers including Kenny Clark, Max Roach, Art Blakey, Alvin Jones, Cozy Cole, Chick Webb, Sid Catlett and Buddy Rich and others. All these features of Ghanaba's Afro jazz are present in his music including "the talking drum looks ahead." Interestingly, Ghanaba and Monk were operating on different levels. Ghanaba wanted to free the drum and assign melodic and leading role to it. Seen in this light, it could be argued that Monk saw those ideals in his quest for creating a new style by transferring percussion and drum styles to the piano. In several respects, Ghanaba's conception of *Afro jazz* preceded the musical conception of the avant-garde of the 1960s and the free jazz of the 1970s. Here are some of the features of free jazz:

—A move away from standard chord progressions
—A move away from tonal harmonic practice
—A move away from traditional sixteen-and thirty-two bar song structures
—New possibilities for improvisation by drawing on non-Western music
—Developed forms of collective improvisation based on linear rather than vertical relationships (Kelley, 1999: 137)

Why was Monk interested in these ideas? Monk's numerous visits to Ghanaba's apartment are indicative of his awareness of African cultures and his conscious search for ways of incorporating African musical elements into his music and his approach to the piano. Monk the proverbial "talking drum" was the only jazzman at the time that saw the future of jazz in Ghanaba's Afro jazz. As Ghanaba succinctly maintain, none of those who shun away his company really understood what he was saying. This statement of Ghanaba in the 1950s has been collaborated, twenty- seven years later in 1974, by Max Roach when he traveled to Ghana in search of Ghanaba and the African roots of Black music in the US.

Max Roach is considered the greatest jazz drummer of the modern age and one of the original innovators of bebop. He first met Ghanaba in Chicago in 1956 when the former was playing at the Beehive Club. As a jazz drummer, Max Roach was interested in Ghanaba's idea of Afro jazz but like many others, he could not understand him. Although he advised Ghanaba to move to New York, he really did not collaborate with Ghanaba besides occasionally showing up in the African Room to see Ghanaba play with his band and jamming with him once in a while. In 1974, Ghanaba hosted Max Roach for two weeks in Ghana and during his stay, he was reeducated in Ghanaba's concept of Afro jazz and upon his return to the US, he wrote a letter to the Ghanaian newspaper, *The Daily Graphic* referring to Ghanaba variously as "the giant creator of music" and "the god of the drums."[19] The letter from Max Roach was published on Friday August 30, 1974 and below is an excerpt of that letter:

In this letter, I will like to record that Ghanaba was so far ahead of what we were all doing, that none of us understood what he was saying, that in order for Afro-American music to be stronger, it must cross-fertilize with its African origins. Ghanaba's conception, like that of Marcus Garvey, George Washington Carver, etc., was beyond our grasp. We ignored him. Seventeen years later, Black Music in America has turned to Africa for inspiration and rejuvenation, and the African soundz of Ghanaba is now being imitated all over the United States wherever Afro-American music is played.[20]

When Max Roach stated that all forms of African American music have turned to the African soundz of Ghanaba for inspiration, he meant every single word of that statement. It seems Ghanaba has been ignored and written out of jazz history. Yet, his conception of Afro jazz looms over developments in modern jazz from the late 1950s to the present. He is the spiritual father of all the modernisms in jazz. His lingering presence is felt in Max Roach's "Freedom Now Suite" recorded in 1958 and the 1961 recording of John Coltrane's *Africa/Brass*. Along the same lines, the free jazz of Ornette Coleman and Cecil Taylor, which is said to have extended Monk's celebration of the piano as a giant tuned drum with manifold possibilities owes a debt of gratitude to Ghanaba (Ted Gioia, 1997: 248). Certainly, we cannot leave out Sun Ra's Arkestra and their references to African music and instruments in their music. Similarly, the costumes, face painting, mask wearing and the music of the post-modernist group, The Art Ensemble of Chicago, and the African orientation in the music of The World Saxophone Quartet (WSQ, Metamorphosis 1991; Moving Right Along 1994, include African drums played by Senegalese drummer Chief Bey) all owe allegiance to Ghanaba. In recent years, Ghanaba's contribution to modernisms in jazz is gradually being recognized in academia. In his most extensive biography of Monk and recent publication, the American historian, Robin Kelley was the first to write about the relationship between Monk and Ghana (Kelley, 2012 and 2009). Those familiar with Ghanaba's classic album cannot miss the source of inspiration for Kelley's latest book, *Africa Speaks, America Answers: Modern Jazz in Revolutionary Times* (2012). Like Max Roach before him, Kelley traveled to Ghana to meet with Ghanaba and had several conversations with him.

In a related development, John Collins (1992) reports in his general introductory book to Afropop titled *West African Pop Roots*, that Thelonious Monk was an acquaintance of Kwesi Asare, another Ghanaian drummer. Kwesi lived for a long time in Britain and according to Collins, in 1958 he met and performed with Duke Ellington, had a long relationship with Count Basie and in the 1960s played percussion with a number of African American musicians including Sarah Vaughan. According to Collins, Monk stayed with Asare whenever he performed in Manchester (John Collins 1992: 294-297). It is worth noting that, by citing relationships between these two notable percussionists from Ghana and Monk, there is the possibility, and typical of Monk, that there is something, however minimal, that he liked about these two Ghanaian drummers or by extension, the African roots of his music. Why is it that critics have avoided discussing Monk's music in relation to his interest in African musical practices?

Conclusion

I have examined Monk's relationship with Kofi Ghanaba as the missing link in the criticism of his music and his approach to the piano. I have also touched briefly on similar connections with another Ghanaian percussionist, Kwesi Asare. For those looking for one-to-one correspondence between the music of Monk and Ghanaba, this seems far-fetched at this point. My approach is quite different from Joseph Patel, who has written a compelling paper tracing the sources of inspiration and sampling in the hip hop music of Missy Elliott, Mos Def, Nas, Common, Blackalicious and electronic dance music to the Afro Beat music of Fela Kuti (Joseph Patel, 2003: 25-34). Fela is another musical icon, a revolutionary and a visionary from Nigeria whose music is infused with biting sociopolitical critique of African governments, foreign political interference in Africa, biased global economic policies and corruption in Nigeria. As a music critic in the New York area, Patel was physically present and had access to a lot of the happenings in the hip-hop world. Subsequently, Patel was able to trace the sampling of these hip-hop stars to Fela's music. Unlike Patel, I was not in Chicago or New York in the 1950s and 1960s. I had to rely on secondary sources and interpret available data in print in addition to my personal conversations with Ghanaba.

Although I have made all these connections, I am by no means suggesting that Monk got his style from Ghanaba. By the 1950s when Monk met Ghanaba, Monk was far advanced in his compositional methods and piano style. However, we can assume that in meeting and knowing Ghanaba, who was forever vocal, and would not hesitate to share his ideas of Afro jazz with whoever will listen to him, proved to be the needed assurance that he, Monk, was on the right path with the African roots of his music. At least we know that Monk was not dancing around the piano in the 1940s and 1950s and that his elbow clusters and flat finger techniques became more pronounced in the 1960s and after. Ghanaba was concerned with elevating the drum set from just keeping a four-four time in the rhythm section to a more prominent and leading role in addition to introducing additional percussion instruments from Africa. Monk was less concerned with changing the role of the drum set than transferring African drum techniques to the piano.

Truly, Monk was occupied with developing an essentially original piano style with African musical expressions of play and interaction as the foundation in order to connect jazz to its African roots. Consequently, we can definitively say that in Ghanaba's music and his conception of Afro jazz, Monk found an icon from West Africa whose music and ideas assured him that he was on the right path with the African roots of his music. His interest in the African roots of jazz is evidenced in his first meeting with Ghanaba. Having arrived in Chicago to perform, how did he find out that Ghanaba was in town? He sat in the front row, motionless throughout Ghanaba's performance at Roosevelt University. At a time when most jazzmen stayed away from Ghanaba, it was Monk, who welcomed Ghanaba to his apartment and subsequently, continued their friendship with several visits to Ghanaba's apartment. My answer to the initial questions generated at the beginning of this section is in the affirmative. Yes, Monk was deeply aware of African musical practices and consciously sought to incorporate these techniques, approaches, and resources of African origins to the piano. Like the African wood carvers and musicians, Monk created silence and space in order to provide inner stability to his music. He creatively interacted with the piano by dancing around it in order to introduce dynamism and multi-dimensional affective response to his music. Consequently, Monk may not have articulated the African elements in his music but that does not mean he was not cognizance of it. Cognition and consciousness of the African roots would have been incorporated into his music without articulation.

In 1958, Ghanaba, a visionary himself, labeled Monk as the proverbial African "talking drum" when he dedicated a track on his LP *Themes for African Drums* to him. It is worth noting that all the critics who dismissed Monk's style of playing the piano as a mark of technical deficiency, failed to recognize the African roots of his music. As I have noted previously, jazz history and criticism does not consider creative interaction as a distinctive feature of jazz performance leading to the belated recognition of Monk. Similarly, those who wrote Monk out of the bebop revolution failed to recognize the future of jazz. His performance technique lived beyond the bebop era for his elbow clusters became the foundation for the later developments in free jazz, modern jazz, or post-modern jazz. Additionally, those who finally recognize the genius of Monk in the late 1950s during his Five Spot days with his quartet, the favorable criticisms after his death in 1982, and the numerous criticisms, and biographies all missed an important source of inspiration for his music. Making a declaration after his trip to Ghana in 1974, Max Roach's statement stands as a testimony and a challenge for critics and historians to take a second look at their assessment of Monk. Yes, Thelonious Monk is the proverbial African "talking drum." And like the "talking drum," his music will always connect us to the past in Africa, in order to inform us of the present, and in the process, link us to the future.

Plate 1:
A close up shot of Monk's 1964 autograph with his picture hanging on the wall in Ghanaba's African Heritage Library.

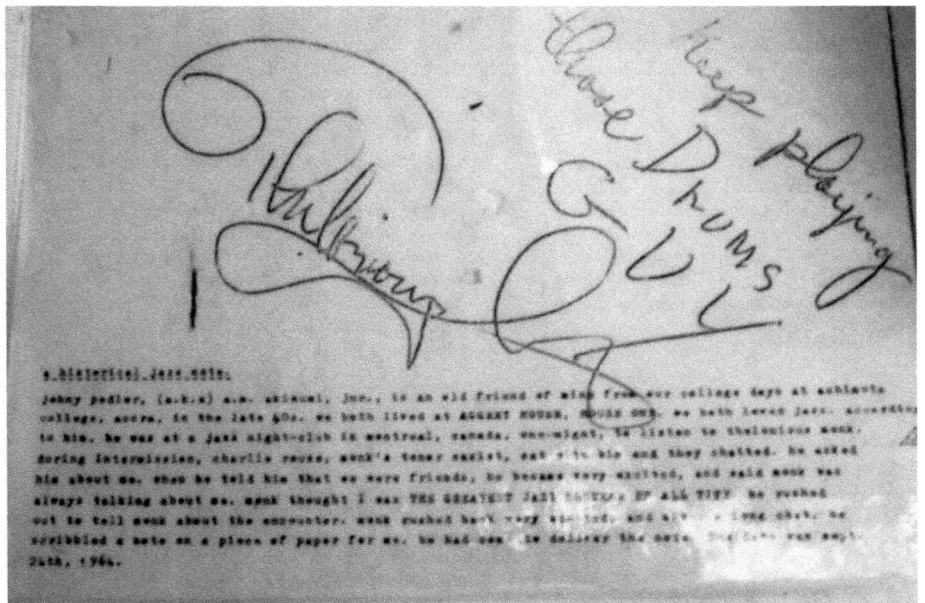

Plate 2:
Monk's autograph with the words, "keep playing those Drums Guy." Note the spelling of drums with a capital "D."

historical jazz note
johnny peddler, (a.k.a.) a.n. Akinwemi jr., is an old friend of mine from our college days at achimota college, Accra in the late 40s. we both live at AGGREY HOUSE, HOUSE ONE. we both loved jazz. according to him, he was at a jazz nite club in montreal, canada one night to listen to thelonious monk. during intermission, charlie rouse, monk's tenor saxist sat with him and they chatted. he asked him about me and when I told him that we were friends, he became very excited and said monk was always talking about me. monk thought I was THE GREATEST JAZZ DRUMMER OF ALL TIME. he rushed out to tell monk about the encounter. monk rushed back very excited and after a long chat, he scribbled a note on a piece of paper for me. he had come to deliver the note. the date was sept. 24th, 1964.

Acknowledgments

My field research in Ghana was funded with grants from the Graduate Council on the Arts and Humanities (GCAH) and the Office of Diversity's Implementation of Multicultural Perspectives and Approaches in Research and Teaching (IMPART) Award at the University of Colorado-Boulder.

I would like to thank Professor Tom Riis for reading the initial draft of this article and his valuable suggestions, Professor Brenda Romero for sharing with me her notion of the "multi-dimensionality of sound," and Professor John Galm for his helpful comments about Monk's flat-fingered technique.

Endnotes

1: Miles Davis (trumpet) was the chief exponent of cool and modal jazz, John Coltrane (tenor saxophone) that of avant-garde, and Ornette Coleman (alto saxophone) and Cecil Taylor (piano) that of free jazz.

2: Monk and his Quartet performed at The Five Spot in the Spring and Summer of 1957. Members of his Quartet at the time included John Coltrane on ternor sax (he was later replaced by Johnny Grifin), Wilbur Ware on Bass, and Shadow Wilson on Drums. There were several changes in personnel however, the famous Monk Quartet after the engagement at The Five Spot included Charlie Rouse on tenor sax, Larry Gales on bass, and Ben Riley on drums (Fitterling 1997: 63-71).

3: From the 1991 Video Documentary, *Thelonious Monk: American Composer*, Producer, Toby Byron and Richard Saylor.

4: Bud Powell was one of Monk's closest friends and it was Monk who convinced his colleagues at the Minton's Playhouse to admit Powell to the jam sessions (Fitterling 1997: 34).

5: From the 1991 Video Documentary, *Thelonious Monk: American Composer*, Producer, Toby and Richard Saylor.

6: Other examples include Gyimah Labi: Dialects 2; Kenn Kafui *Pentanata* (both from Ghana); Gamal Abdel-Rahim: *Variations on an Egyptian Folk Song* (Egypt); and Joshua Uzoigwe: *Four Igbo Songs* (for female voice and piano, Nigeria). Euba has since broadened his definition to embrace the keyboard music of non-Africans (see for instance Ebua, 1993: 8). There are several publications dealing with African pianism. Readers are referred to my Master's thesis, the *Artistic and Compositional Analysis of J.H. Kwabena Nketia's Volta Fantasy* (Kwasi Ampene, 1994); Joshua Uzoigwe, *Akin Euba: An Introduction to the Life and Music of a Nigerian Composer* (1992). The Iwalewa-Haus at the University of Bayreuth in Germany has an archive of modern African music with a substantial collection of wriiten African music including solo piano pieces, choral and symphonic music by African composers.

7: There is a parallel between written composition in Africa and neo-African literature in the works of Africa's foremost Nobel Laureate, Wole Soyinka, Ngugi wa Thiong'o, Ama Atta Aidoo, Ayi Kwei Armah, and the numerous modern writers. These writers use the European idiom of the written novel, as against the orally based literature in Africa, but write literature that can be referred to as African.

8: African world refers to people of African descent including the African continent and those in the Americas, the Caribbean, and Europe or wherever they might be.

9: See *The Thelonious Monk Reader*, pages 241-245.

10: *Okyeame* is the indigenous Akan term for Royal Diplomats and Orators who are wrongly referred to as linguists due to their oratorical skills. For a detailed discussion of this subject and the politics of Akan royal oratory, readers may refer to Kwesi Yankah, 1995.

11: One of the greatest virtuosos of the *gyil*, Kakraba Lobi passed away on July 20th, 2006 after a short illness in Ghana.

12: *The American Heritage Concise Dictionary*, 3rd ed., s.v. "Dance."

13: Personal communication in 2001.

14: Both interviews are reprinted in *The Thelonious Monk Reader* edited by Rob van der Bliek, from page 71 to 83.

15: See for instance The *Monk Reader* edited by Rob van der Bliek, or Monk's biography by Thomas Fitterling (1997) and Leslie Gourse (1997).

16: See *Drum Damba* (1990) by David Locke and the Dagbamba entry by the same author in the *Worlds of Music* 4th edition (2002)

17: Readers are referred to Ghanaba's Autobiography; *I Have a Story to Tell*. Royal Hartigan's article in the *Annual Review of Jazz Studies* goes beyond what I present here.

18: *Sankofa* is an Akan word meaning, one must return to the past in order to move forward. It is represented in *Adinkra* cloths and wooden carvings by a bird picking an egg on its back with its beak.

19: Max Roach's trip to Ghana in 1974 was partly inspired by the socio-political climate in the 1970s when African Americans, more than ever, aligned themselves with post-colonial Africa.

20: John Collins (1992: 289-290) is a brief entry on Ghanaba including this same quote from Max Roach.

References

Agawu, Kofi. 2003. *Representing African Music: Postcolonial Notes, Queries, Positions.* New York and London: Routledge.

Ampene, Kwasi. 2012. "One on One: Max Roach in Conversation With Kofi Ghanaba." *American Music Research Journal* 20 Summer.

___. 1994. *Artistic and Compositional Analysis of J. H. Kwabena Nketia's Volta Fantasy.* Master's thesis, West Virginia University.

Brown, Frank London. 1958. "Thelonious Monk: More Man Than Myth, Monk Has Emerged From the Shadows." *Down Beat* .

Collins, John. 1992. *West African Pop Roots.* Philadelphia: Temple University Press.

___. 2009. *Thelonious Monk: The Life and Times of an American Original.* New York: Free Press.

___. 1999. "New Monastery: Monk and the Jazz Avant-Garde." *Black Music Research Journal* 19 (2): 135-165.

Locke, David. 1990. *Drum Damba: Talking Drum Lessons.* Crown Point, IN: White Cliffs Media Co.

___. 2002. "Dagbamba" In *Worlds of Music: An Introduction to The Music of the World's Peoples.* Gen. ed. Jeff Todd Titon, Belmong, Calif: Schirmer/Thomson Learning.

Monson, Ingrid. 1996. *Saying Something: Jazz Improvisation and Interaction.* Chicago: The University of Chicago Press.

Nketia, J.H.K. 1991. "The Play Concept in African Musical Traditions," In *Laura Boulton Lectures.* Ed. by Tom Vennum Tempe, Arizona: Hurd Museum.

___. 1982. "Developing Contemporary Idioms Out of Traditional Music." *Studia Musicologica Academiae Scientiarum Hungaricae* XXVI: 81-97.

Patel, Joseph. 2003. "Power Music, Electric Revival: Fela Kuti and the Influence of His Afrobeat on Hip-Hop and Dance Music." In *Fela: From West Africa To West Broadway.* Ed. by Trevor Schoonmaker. New York: Palgrave Macmillan Publishers.

Tucker, Mark. 1999. "Mainstreaming Monk: The Ellington Album," in *Black Music Research Journal* 19 (2): 227 224.

Roach, Max. 1974. "Ghanaba is a Genius." In the *Daily Graphic.* p. 7.

Santoro, Gene. 1994. "Master of Space." *The Nation* 258 (14): 498-500.

Solis, Gabriel. 2008. *Monk's Music: Thelonious Monk and Jazz History in the Making.* Los Angeles: University of California Press.

Uzoigwe, Joshua. 1992. *Akin Euba: An Introduction to the Life and Music of a Nigerian Composer.* Bayreuth: University of Bayreuth, Germany.

Van der Bliek, Rob. 2001. *The Thelonious Monk Reader*. Oxford: Oxford University Press.

Warren, Guy. 1966. *I Have a Story to Tell*. Accra, Ghana: Guinea Press.

Yankah, Kwesi.1995. *Speaking for the Chief: Okyeame and the Politics of Akan Royal Oratory*. Bloomington: Indiana University Press.

Discography
Blakey, Art and the Afro-Drum Ensemble. 1962. *The African Beat*. Blue Note 22666.

Coltrane, John. 1961. *Africa/Brass*. Impulse Kaempfert, Bert and his Orchestra. 1962.

That Happy Feeling. Decca LP 74305. Released on CD in 1996 by Taragon 1021.

___. 1996. *The Very Best of Bert Kaempfert* Taragon 1014.

___. 1998. *A Swingin' Safari*. Polygram International 825494

Monk, Thelonious. 1947. "'Round Midnight," From *The Genius of Modern Music: Volume 1,* Blue Note BLP 1510.

___. 1948. "Straight No Chaser," From *The Genius of Modern Music: Volume 2,* Blue Note BLP 1511.

Powell, Bud. 1950. The *Genius of Bud Powell,* Verve CD 827 901-2.

Roach, Max. 1958. *Freedom Now Suite*. Candid Records.

Warren, Guy. 1956. *Africa Speaks! America Answers*. Decca DL 8446.

___. 1958. *Themes for African Drums*. RCA Victor LPM 1864.

___. 1963. *Emergent Drums*. Columbia 33SX 1584.

___. 1969. *Afro Jazz,* Columbia SCX 6340 Weston, Randy. 1998. *Khepera,* Verve 314 557 821-2.

World Saxophone Quartet. 1991. *Metamorphosis*. Nonesuch 79258.

___. 1994. *Moving Right Along*. Black Saint 120127.

___. 1996. *Four Now*. Justin Time.

Videography
1991 *Thelonious Monk: American Composer.* Producer, Toby Byron, Richard Saylor. Director, Matthew Seig, East Stinson Inc.

Gerima, Haile. 1994. *Sankofa*. Washington, D.C.: Mypheduh Films, Inc.

5

Nissio Fiabgedzi
Bode Omojola
George W. K. Dor

ANALYSIS OF WRITTEN COMPOSITIONS

J. H. Kwabena Nketia's Republic Suite: An Analytical Portrait of Movement 1

Nissio Fiagbedzi

Nissio Fiagbedzi recently retired from the Music Department at the School of Performing Arts (University of Ghana-Legon). Specializing in the areas of aesthetics, philosophy, and theory, his numerous publications include, *Form and Meaning in Ewe Song: A Critical Review* (2009); *An Essay on the Nature of the Aesthetic in the African Musical Arts* (2005); *Toward Philosphy of Theory in Ethnomusicological Research* (1989); *On Signing and Symbolism in Music: the Evidence from Among the Anlo-Ewe* (1985); *Observations on the Study of African Musical Cultures* (1980); and *Religious Music Traditions in Africa: A Critical Evaluation of Contemporary Problems and Challenges* (1978).

The purpose of this analysis[1] is twofold: to delineate as far as possible (1) the important compositional techniques that make the *Republic Suite* well-formed in general – in particular the relevant Africanisms that possibly enter into its style, and (2) to encourage others also to engage in similar analyses of both contemporary African and traditional forms for the further benefit of those who wish to gain a more explicit understanding of the forms and/or engage in similar applications of technique and style.

The *Republic Suite* is one of six other instrumental works of various kinds by Nketia comprising: (1) Three Piano Pieces; (2) Six Piano Pieces in African Rhythm for the Young Musician; (3) Four Flute Pieces; (4) Bolga Sonata for Violin and Piano; (5) Antubam, dirge for cello and piano and (6) Quartet nos. 1 and 2 for Atenteben (i.e bamboo flutes). Originally named simply as *Suite for Flute and Piano*, the new title, *Republic Suite*, was given by Seth Cudjoe[2], who, hearing the work performed, became so delighted with it that he, as the chairman of an Interim Arts Council appointed by Osagyefo Dr. Kwame Nkrumah to oversee the development of Culture and the Arts promptly commended it for performance at an official concert scheduled to be staged on the evening of the 1st of July, 1960 to round off the celebration of Ghana becoming a Republic, thus in a way associating the work with the occasion of Ghana's transformation into a republic.

Yet even before Cudjoe's recommendation, it was remarkable that Nketia[3] had composed the first two [g¹-f#¹] and [g-d¹] motifs that began the first movement of the suite to musically reflect *Kofi*, the first name of Dr. K. A. Busia called loudly as though from a distance, and *Abrefa-Mmore*, his middle name, respectively. (personal communication). See fig. 1 below and/or bar 1 to 2¹ of the score on page 309.

Figure 1

As history informs us, in 1958 when the National Liberation Movement (NLM) and other political parties in opposition to Nkrumah's government and the Convention Peoples Party joined together in independent Ghana to form a United Party, Professor Busia, under whom and with whose guidance Nketia worked in the department of sociology in the then University College of Ghana, decided to and did abandon a brilliant career as an academic in sociology to lead a new United Party and the opposition in parliament. Indeed the United Party was formed from Busia's Ghana Congress Party and the then National Liberation Movement. Note here that by deriving the motifs from Busia's name, the composer was, of course, deliberately exercising his prerogative as a composer to construct a musical abstraction of Busia's names as a thematic resource; for, by 1959 when the first movement of the suite was completed, Nketia must have had the opportunity to observe and ponder the intellectual positions and political decisions of Busia, the academic, vis-à-vis the troubled condition of Ghana as characterized by the cultural and sociopolitical events and issues relating to the question of welding independent Ghana's ethnic cultures into a nation with a common destiny. Indeed, from this perspective, the first movement of the suite might be interpreted conceptually and in theme as a musical picture or comment on the contrasting and potentially tension-perpetuating conditions and situations in Ghana and Africa at the time. Notice that besides the two motifs that began and largely characterized the first movement, the entire [g^1-f#] (bar 1-10) and the [e-a] question and answer themes of the flute and piano (bar 11-20) also present such other structural units (see fig. 2 below) as (1) [g^1-f#^{1}] in semiquavers (bar 2^1-3^1), (2) [b/g-a/f] accompanying semiquavers in bar 6, (3) [c^1-f#] triplet (bar 9-10) and (4) [a-e] semiquaver figures in bar 10 and (5) [e-b] dotted-note figure and semiquaver sequences in bar 11-12 that later became significant as building blocks that severally and jointly determined the overall style of the movement.

Figure 2

Seven movements in all make up the suite. Thus, while at a more restricted level, movement 1 might be seen to have musically depicted tensions vis-à-vis putative resolutions in Ghana as perceived by the composer, the subsequent six movements focus individually on and reflect conceptually one or the other of the contrasting conditions and situations in Ghana and Africa. For example, the theme of movement 2 (N.B: bar 1-18 of its score refers) was based on the first phrase of a Ghanaian popular/street song taken to symbolize popular culture of the Ghanaian non-elite. Compared with movement 1, the movement, essentially modeled on traditional song form, was, we understand, an insertion, included in the suite to provide a "break" (personal communication) that contrasts musically indigenous musical forms and practices of the ordinary largely illiterate Ghanaian with the 'high' Western-oriented modes of cultural expression as manifesting at the time among the Ghanaian elite in the phenomenon of 'high class' ballroom music and dance and the evolution of high life, brass band and Ghanaian church and art music. Indeed the suite is a species of contemporary Ghanaian art music tradition.

Furthermore, while movement 3 was meant to reflect francophone cultural phenomenon and presence in West Africa and the contrasts this presence manifested relative to independent Ghana, movement 5 was inspired by the persistent challenges stemming from the uneasy unification at independence of former mandated Togoland with Ghana and the continuing alignment of some Ewes from the Volta Region with the breaking-away sympathies of the United Party and the opposition in parliament. The incorporation of the Ewe gakogui or 'standard' time line in the piano accompaniment (bar 46 of the movement onward) represents the Ewe unification issue as a factor of the Ghanaian cultural and political equation (personal communication). On the other hand, movement 4, slow and dirge-like, was motivated by the unsuccessful result of the Ashanti NLM's bid to secede and become an independent nation within Ghana.

Again, while movement 6, also an insertion, was based on an original bamboo flute tune from northern Ghana (personal communication) adding to the image of diversity that characterize Ghana, movement 7 was pan-African in conception – based on tunes from the Congo taken from (1) Alan Merriam's recordings[4] of Congo music and (2) women's play song from Ghana (personal communication). It was to ponder musically over the challenge posed by the Danquah/Busia-led cautious, 'step by step' tradition of cultural and political development as opposed to the pan-African vision that sustained Nkrumah's radically socialist and Africa unite agenda.

Before plunging into the analysis of the first movement, a number of preliminary submissions may further help to put the work into perspective. First, the work was composed for the 'Western' concert flute as a solo instrument and for the piano performing the dual roles of accompanying and of taking solo lead. Thus, while the instruments for which the work was intended are culturally essentially 'Western' in origin, musically, their mutual function as solo versus accompanying sound sources are not necessarily only European in conception. They are African as well. Secondly, the work draws on multipart voice combination and separation techniques in both Western and African styles, such as are popularly identifiable as harmony and parallelisms of various sort. Here, the work exhibits forms of both Western and African multipart structuring that allows for thinking of harmonic progressions in terms of textures that can be vertically as well as horizontally construed. Thirdly, Nketia was encouraged to compose the work because a competent Ghanaian flautist, the late Charles Simmons[5], could at the time perform the suite.

Movement 1

In general, the 67-bar unfolding of the first movement encompasses contrasting thematic, structural and harmonic or multipart processes of various kinds and complexities, levels of dynamic intensity and tension beside successions of high climactic points that either introduce, help constitute, delimit, expand or reconfigure individual motifs, phrases and sections. Individual phrases tend to exploit call and response structure, discord/tension and resolution, musical debate and/or contrasting situations musically such as, in the composer's view, comprised opposing versus complementary phenomena that manifested *culturally, socially and/or politically* for Kofi in pre-Republican independent Ghana. For example, since, as already deduced, the signifying, [g¹-f#¹] motif (bar 1) of the flute captures for the composer what Kofi might have stood for, the subsequent, much longer [g¹-b] flute sub-phrase (bar 2 to 4) could also interpret (though not correspondingly on a one-to-one basis) as lining out loud the composer's musical abstraction of the condition of independent Ghana – ruminating on it -- the subsequent unfolding of [a-f#] (bar 5 to 10) extending the sub-phrase call, rising musically pitch-wise and hence in intensity to semiquaver pitch [a¹] (bar 8), the very first significant high point of tension in the work from which the unfolding quickly modulates decrescendo into truncated [f#] quaver-triplet motion (bar 10). (For illustration, refer back to fig. 2).

Notice the complementarily suggestive way in which the [f#] quaver-triplet motion in bar 10^1 reverberates its earlier two semiquaver-quaver iterative counterpart in bar 4 as being of idiomatically stylistic significance. Notice also how the intensity of the high point of bar 8 was preceded by pitches [b^1 and a^1] of bar 2; and how, like the [g^1-f#^{1}] progression, the expanded [g^1-f#] phrase (bar 2-10) also remains tensed, resolving on to [f#], an unsettling, leading-note cadence.

Likewise, imagine how, owing to its high register, its mezzo-forte dynamic level placement and relatively prolonged landing on the leading note, the [g^1-f#^{1}] flute phrase (bar 1) exudes a restlessly impatient pathos in its unfolding; and how in confirmation, the piano also passionately repeats the [g^1-f#^{1}] motif forte in bar 5 of the accompaniment and in parallel octave and varied voice-separation or harmonic contexts, reverting stylistically to Kofi to reinforce the listener's attention to the originating [g^1-f#^{1}] symbolizing abstraction!

As may be noted, it is also important that as an unaccompanied, contextually keyless monody that prolongs on a leading note, the selfsame [g^1-f#^{1}] motif should also be ordered in dotted-note rhythm. For, not only does the dotted-note format, transformed as below into the rhythm of the [e-b] parallel octave progression in bars 11 and 45 for instance, serve to introduce two phrases in bars 11-17 and 45-51 of the score respectively that ascend in bar 15 and in bar 49 to [b^2] flat and [e^2] flat strategically-placed climactic points of tension, it also enables the composer to effect the climactic rise in tension by simply pitching accompanying semiquaver progressions against semiquaver-dotted-quaver (i.e reversed) or un-reversed dotted note motions with the double octave parallel format pitched either a perfect 4th higher or a perfect 5th lower respectively in the piano part. Compare fig. 3 with bars 11 to 17 and bars 45 to 51 of the score.

Figure 3

Likewise even more important the [g¹-f#¹] motif itself recurs as below in several transformations such as occur as (1) motif [f¹-e¹] on IV7-V7d accompaniment chords in F major (see bar 2 of fig. 4 below/ bar 21 of the score); (2) [e¹-d#¹] on added-note II9c-VII7d chords in E major (bar 5/24); (3) [g#¹-f#¹] melodic progression (bar 6/25); (4) [a/f#-g#/e] of IVb-V7 and (5-6) VII-IV9b parallel thirds chords in A major and D major (bars 8/27 and 10-11/29-30 respectively); and (7-8) [c-b] in C major (bars 15/34 and 16/35). See figure 4 below.

Figure 4

Further, notice (1) that, as illustrated above here and there, multipart progressions differentiate as vertically structured harmonies and into horizontally construed parallelisms as well; and that modulations are not always prepared.

(2) likewise, the [g¹-f#¹] leading note motif contrasts in its keyless neutrality with its subsequent transformations in key-based multipart contexts. Compare the examples in figure 5 below or in bar 1, bars 4²-5, 21, 24, and 35 of the score.

Figure 5

And (iv), structurally as well, the points of tension and intensity introduced by the [g¹-f#¹] motif also recur successively at higher and higher pitch-levels as at [b flat²] (bar 15), [c²] (bar 22) and [g#²] (bar 32²) until at bar 34 yet another [c¹-b] dotted-note motif marks the end of the first half (or section 1) of the movement. Immediately thereafter, a structural role-change is introduced that enables the piano hitherto essentially performing an accompaniment role to also incorporate in bar 35 to 44 the solo part of the just closed first section (bar 1 to 20) a perfect 5th down in its new role as a multipart lead instrument with the flute providing bits of quaver-triplet, whole-bar triplet and dotted-note melody in counterpoint. The points of tension anticipate and lead to the structural role change of bar 35.

After bar 32, the flautist scales down climactically from the fleeting but obtrusively piercing [g#²], the highest point of tension (bar 32²), to [e²] (bar 40) and down again to [e flat²] (bar 49) which at fortissimo appears to have superceded the [g#²] high point in its intensity, thereby asserting a claim to being a legitimate climax and turning point of the 67-bar unfolding until at [e²] in bar 56, still at fortissimo, the [e²] is duplicated vertically two octaves apart in the piano accompaniment. Apart from the rising two-octave [g#-g#²] high point interval (bar 32), the [g¹-e²] major sixth interval in bar 56 is the second smaller in point of size. Thus, by virtue of its positioning at least two-thirds into the piece i.e five bars into the final coda, the [e²] (bar 56) could also mark a point of great consequence, prioritizing and legitimizing itself as the most effective climactic high point. The inference is examined below. Further, the piano's assumption and articulation of its lead role in bar 35 as the octave parallel [c-b] motif harmonized in II7c-VII7c dissonant chord progression marks the beginning of the second section, subdividing the piece into two sections. Like the initial [g¹-f#¹] motif (bar 1), the articulation at bar 35 not only more than echo the initial call on Kofi fortissimo but also launches the second section of the work conspicuously in key C major, firmly establishing the key in which final closure takes place.

We revert at this point to the beginning of the movement where we recall that the initially unaccompanied [g¹-f#¹] leading note motif is immediately answered in bar 1² to 2¹ by the piano playing an ascending and interlocking [g-d¹] progression reminiscent of Abrefa-Mmore. Note that the progression recurs in bars 10 and 20 also in contextually modified descending and ascending forms respectively (see below); and that, in all three instances, the progression is cast in parallel octave format serving to connect the initial monody to its subsequent unfolding (see bar 1 to 10) as well as the entire [g¹-f#] call to the [e-a] response phrase (bar 11-20), besides introducing the [f¹-e¹-c²] motif harmonized forte in bar 21-22. Here the motif performs a purely musical than a symbolic function linking the sub-phrases of section A (bars 1-10 and 11-20) and the inner coda of bar 22-34/35. Examine figure 6a in the context of the section and the inner coda.

Figure 6

Of greater structural import, however, is the *semiquaver* motif in bar 2¹ to 3¹ which like the monody unit also occurs in several modulated parallel thirds versus uni-linear transformations (e.g in bar 28-29, 30-31, and 36-37 respectively) that either connect or accompany and propel the motion of individual motifs of sections A and the initial phrase of section A1.

Figure 7

Between the first and second sections in bars 1 to 22 and 35 to 51 respectively lie a 13-bar passage (bar 22–34). Thus wedged as it were, the passage carries features that characterize it as a short inner coda that concludes the first section and introduces the second section. First, beginning with an ascending, interlocking and accompanying [f-b flat] parallel octave figure (bar 20) based on that of bar 1^2-2^1, the [f^1-c^2] motif (bar 21-22^1) recast from previous [g^1-$f\#^1$] monody (bar 1) is now harmonized forte by a $II9b$-$V7$ dissonant chord resolving into yet another [I^9b] dissonant first inversion F minor ninth chord to introduce a stretto-like passage that exploits the monody motif in the flute and piano accompaniment parts from bar 24 through to bar 35 to lead into the second section. Note that the dissonant chords reinforce the tensions that had begun with the [g^1-$f\#^1$] monody and characterized the subsequent interactive gestures of the flute and piano. In particular, so does the dissonant $II9c$-$VII7c$ progression of bar 24 as well as the semiquaver figures of bars 26, 28 and 30 propel the stretto-like progressions in variously vertically formed, octave parallel and parallel 3rds motions that introduce excitingly agitating atmosphere into the sonic proceeding.

Figure 8

At bar 52, the final coda enters, beginning with gradually ascending [d-f] interlocking and generally broadening quaver-triplet figure in parallel octave motion yielding place to vertically structured harmonies that accompany equally ascending and interlocking melody-bits also in quaver-triplet motion as below:

Figure 9

In effect, the general dominance of whole and half bar triplet rhythm enforces an enabling slow-down action that counteracts the hitherto agile sonic feel. From bar 53, the flute passage rises expressively in four bars to high pitch [e²] in bar 56, anticipated earlier in two and one octaves respectively in bars 54 and 55 and vertically duplicated at mezzo forte on a sub-mediant chord in bar 56. Notice how between bars 54²-56¹ the V-VI progression strikingly combines parallel octave, fifth and third motions in vertical cum simultaneous multipart structure!

Structurally considered then, the 1st movement is thus in a two-section, [A+x] +[A¹+x¹], form. Section A1 is a virtually identical repetition of section A. Both the A (bar 1-20) and A¹ (bar 35-51) sections sub divide into shorter and unequally outlined sub-phrases that still maintain easily perceptible measures of continuity. The sub-phrases are: [a (bar 1-4)+ b (bar 5-10) + c (bar 11-20)] and [a¹ (bar 35-38)+ b¹ (bar 39-44) + c¹ (bar 44-51)] respectively. The [x] and the [x¹] stand for the inner and final codas of bars 20-34 and 52-67 respectively.

From the point of view of style, a number of observations should be of help in guaranteeing our further appreciative understanding of what the unfolding of section A for instance could signify. First, we note that by articulating the very first note of the movement at [g¹] more than an octave above middle C, the composer could be said to have deliberately aimed at exploiting the naturally piercing and penetrating sound quality of the flute. He generates tension by articulating at that level. Also, by tonguing the dotted-note as a quaver plus a semiquaver rest, it enables the flautist to successfully transfer the intensity hitherto generated across the semiquaver pitch [a] to the subsequent [f#¹] leading note that sustains the momentum of the [g¹-f#¹] motif at mezzo forte, betraying, together with the subsequent interlocking [g-d] as well as [g¹-f#¹] semiquaver motif (bar 2-3) a sense of restlessness which, in effect, becomes more conspicuous in retrospect in the general harmonized quaver-triplet pace-slackening of the next three bars (bar 3-4). Thus stylistically, musically agitating tension gives way to a broadening effect as bar 3-4 succeeds restive bar 1-2, and bar 5-9¹ yields place to quaver-triplet figures in bars 9²-10¹. Thus, from bar 1c onward, the agitated tension-radiating sense carries further into virtually all the semiquaver-based progressions, especially such as occur in the piano accompaniment in bars 10-11, 12-18 and then again in bars 27-32 including the corresponding flute passages. Consequently, tension build-ups/curves of various lengths and intensities become discernible as motifs, sub-phrases, phrases, unaccompanied vrs accompanied, vertically-structured or parallel octave, sixths and thirds simultaneities succeed one another at various dynamic levels. Thus, for example, crescendo and poco a poco leggiero progressions of ascending dotted-note and semiquaver parallelisms of bar 11 unfold through to dissonances in arpeggio (bar 15-18) that underscore equally agitated and ascending flute phrases to define an intensity curve that rises to fortissimo at bar 15 and falls mezzo-forte to iterated [a] at bar 20. From the rising and interlocking mezzo piano figure through to the emphatic dotted note [f¹-c²] outburst landing forte in F minor in bar 22, yet another curve begins, launching the inner coda passage in stretto in which a debate-like mode of articulation seems to prevail (see bar 22-27), leading dolce but argumentatively as well to the vehemently expressive [g#²-b] outcry [bars 32-34] that brings back a transformed repeat of the [g¹-f#¹] motif as [c¹-b] to end the first section of the piece and introduce the second.

Effectively thus, contrasts involving fast moving semiquaver progressions and pace-slackening, quaver-triplet-based multipart simultaneities show not only in the internal unfolding of section A, but even more tellingly between the internal structuring of the second section (A1) and of the final coda and between the inner and final codas. As the successive distribution of the dotted quaver-semiquaver versus the quaver-triplet structures indicates, the contrasts are mainly rhythmical. Viewed in terms of the strategic balancing of parallelisms with vertical harmonies, however, changes in resulting harmonic rhythm show in the respect and degree to which individual phrases reveal or not bear traces of concord versus discord progressions. The latter tend to predominate strategically. See for instance bar 20-22 where a parallel F major interlocking motif followed by a IV7-VIIb-IV9b discordant progression could easily have replaced [g¹] with [f¹] to make the closure in bar 22¹ concordant in F minor. Notice also how the discord becomes more marked as the hint at bar 20-22 gives way to a more pronounced effect in bar 23-24. Besides, we already noted how the keyless, neutrally marked opening versus the final closure of the movement in C-major tonality, the generally descending versus ascending trajectories of the first and second subject themes of the sections as well as the overall global descent from the [g¹-f#¹] beginning to the closure on [f-e] finally more than an octave below equally bear testimony to deliberately designed stylization.

Further, and purely in respect of musical antecedents, sonic motion and tonal succession, the piece may be understood as a journey experienced in musical sound, rhythm and dynamic intensities that begins at a point in time, continues from that moment and comes to end one way or the other. Like a narrative, the experience unfolds in a given musical plot leading to a moment of tremendous consequence from which point the unfolding is quickly brought to a close. As may be recalled, the Ist movement ends with an [f-e], I9c-V7-I perfect cadence in C major. It begins with the by now very familiar, tensed and un-harmonized [g¹-f#¹] motif expanded into [g¹-f#] (bar 1-10) to make up the very first thematic sub-phrase, landing on the truncated, rhythmically static [f#] quaver-triplet. As a prolongation of the tensed build-up, the [g¹-f#¹] to [f-e] or I-VII to V-I unfolding embracing the entire span of the movement constitutes a resolution, a calming of restless agitation with which the prolongation started. Expectations with regard to the progression of the motifs, the phrase and its supporting multipart successions have in the larger span been thus fulfilled. One may however ask: what within this sonic trajectory constitutes the moment of supreme consequence? Wherein does it lie? What form(s) does it take?

We recall from previous experiences that, structurally, such super-moments quite often occur as far removed from the beginning and as close to the end of a piece as are necessary for them to produce their maximum intensifying effect. On the other hand, such moments of intensity could also be brought about quite close to the beginning with their effect carried forward as the piece unfolds. Further, the moment normally takes the form of the most momentous musical utterance or act in the chain of events; and there could be a single moment or a chain of moments of varied hierarchical importance distributed across a musical narrative. Thus as already hinted, the first point of climax beginning from the end of the piece backwards is [e^2] in bar 56. It was preceded by [e flat^2] in bar 49 and by [e^2] again in bar 40. Before that, [$g\#^2$] (bar 32^2) registers as the highest and most expressive semiquaver towards which the movement unfolds and from which it moves away. And before that, all other instances (e.g [a^1] bars 1, 5 and 8, [b flat^1] (bar 15), [c^2] (bar 22) all lead towards [$g\#^2$] at progressively higher and higher levels. However, considered hierarchically, [$g\#^2$] and [e^2] would thus appear among the seven candidates to be the two most eligible high moments. Notice that the two high points embed relatively close to the end/beginning of their respective inner (i.e [x]) and final (i.e [x^1]) codas; that whereas [$g\#^2$] precipitates the beginning of section two (i.e end the inner coda) from an upper end of an ascending interval of two octaves (bar 32^2), [e^2] marks an upper end of a rising major 6th interval (bar 55-56) in the final coda; and that although the two equally represent turning points in their respective sections, in terms of intensity, the former is to be performed mezzo forte, the latter fortissimo just as the previous passages (bars 18-32 and 49-55 respectively) leading to the high points were.

Thus characterized, two choices would seem to compete for recognition: (i) either one assigns supremacy to [g#²] because it occurs at the top of a two-octave interval that confers the very high though rather short-lived intensity; or, one overrules its importance in favor of the major sixth [e²] high point because, in spite of the highly suggestive interval-size, the former occurs too early structurally (i.e even before section A¹ begins) to make its effect conclusive relative to the other high points.

Since, however, of the two alternatives, the [g#²] supreme moment of semiquaver intensity was clearly intended to and did expand contextually beyond itself to embrace [g#²–b] (bar 32-34) -- the descending three-bar phrase ending the inner coda -- the first alternative would appear to be preferable, the composer apparently deliberately making [c¹-b¹] (bar 34) prepare the listener for the evocative onslaught on section A1 -- the expansion thus implying that, by ending on a [c¹-b] transformation of the first bar motif, the extended [g#²–b] moment would naturally forcefully return the listener to an emphatic recall of the initial motif. Significantly, the initial theme (bar 35-43) of the piece now re-assigned to the piano in section A1 categorically begins with a [c²-b²] motif played fortissimo and supported by a II7b-VIIc discord progression!

The delineation of moments of supreme high points quite often derives its justification from tendencies in melodic and chordal progressions showing the way(s) in which the tendencies support and direct the progressions and vice versa for generating intrinsic as well as extrinsic meaning in the tonal span of a piece. To illustrate the tendencies, certain melodic and chordal progressions are hereby highlighted as a way of indicating tonal meaning. For the purpose, let us examine for instance the general unfolding of the first theme of section A (bar 1-10) repeated in Section A1 (bar 35 to 43). The subsequent themes of the two sections (bars 11-20 and 45-51) will also follow.

First, by initiating the [g¹-f#¹] motif *on the beat* (my emphasis) and at mezzo forte it would seem logical to expect that an emphatic tendency becomes generated which by virtue of its ordinal placement would have routinely resulted in a stress on [g¹]. However, owing to the need for musically extending the

[g¹-f#¹] motif/Kofi loudly articulated to 'Koofi-ee' – this would seem to require that a prolongation of the [f#¹] leading-note crotchet reflect the linguistic change as well as the concomitant functional transfer of the putative stress to end the motif.
Of interest here, of course, is the probably equivalent adoption of a local 'strong-name-exchange' format in which Busia's names are musically abstracted and dialogued. For, as can be attested, no sooner has the 'Koofiee' motif been enunciated than the piano enters in dialogue and at piano-crescendo the rising, interlocking semiquaver figure representing 'Abrefa Mmore', Busia's complementary name! And when the flautist next took up the incipient dialogue expanding the initial motif into the [g¹-b] sub-phrase of bar 1-4, the pianist took on an accompaniment role in concurrent support and no longer in dialogue as before. That is to say that with both the flautist and the pianist having completely finished with calling on Busia musically in incipient dialoguing format, the tendency to continue in the same fashion had to give way to the two protagonists relating in contrastive format, the absolute dialoguing format initiated having seemed to have exhausted its unique charm! To clinch home the individualistic attribute, a general broadening thus ensues within which the protagonists function as solo and multipart communication media. That is, in lieu of the pianist's rising [g-d] parallelism in interlocking semiquaver motion (bar 1²-2¹) – this gives way to a vertically structured III-VI7c-II13-VIb progression harmonizing a slower-paced and differentiated melody ending on iterated [b] in bar 4². (Notice incidentally, the semiquaver-quaver iteration that recurs at the end of the second sub-phrase [b¹-f#] (bar 4²-10¹) as a truncated, all-quaver [f#] iteration. Notice also the other assorted types – the semiquaver-quaver (bars 20 and 40), whole bar crotchet-triplet (bars 27, 33, 57) and half-bar all-quaver iterations (bars 3, 9, 18 etc) – that occur either at the end, middle or beginnings of other flute and piano passages. They give character to the passages they feature in).

It is important to also notice that the bar 4²-10¹ accompanying complement to the initial sub-phrase in bar 1-4 also begins with a harmonized repetition of the [g¹-f#¹] motif in the piano accompaniment – beginning off-beat, this time around. Unlike its original monody-like articulation, the repeat at fortissimo combines the attribute of vertical harmony with parallelism at the octave in multipart structure for the benefit of the discriminating listener; for, over and above the newly introduced texture, the flute proceeds to cultivate the melodic independence it arrogates itself from bar 2 which it maintains up until the onslaught of section A1. Notice that the parallelism in octaves (bar 5) differentiates into thirds in bar 6 and that discord harmonies balance regular triad-based progressions in bars 7-10.

Further, a comparison of sections A and A1 reveals that the melody assigned to the piano (bar 35-43) is the same as the former in bar 1-10 initiated by the flautist. The latter is thus a transposed version and hence a modified repetition of bar 1-10, having been completely harmonized and varying from fortissimo through dolce forte and mezzo forte. The former (bar 1-10) is, of course, partly un-harmonized, beginning at mezzo-forte. Where, as in the first two bars of section A, the [g^1-$f\#^1$] motif of the flautist is linked to its continued [g^1-$f\#^1$] phrasing in semiquavers (bar 2) by a rising interlocking [g-d^1] motif played piano-crescendo, the [g-d^1] linkage presents the listener with his very first experience not of vertically structured harmony but of parallelism at the octave. On the other hand, in the first two bars of section A1, the composer offers the listener a taste of the selfsame melody transposed as [c^2-b^1] in bar 35 and harmonized with a II7c-VII dissonant chord that virtually wakes the listener up at fortissimo, virtually thrusting the motif at him, calling on Kofi once more. Thus in spite of their identity, the two bars of original versus transposed melodies differ in their melo-dynamic versus chordal tendencies – the directions the two types of sonic motion take and lead each other. Notice that the [g^1-$f\#^1$] unaccompanied motif in bar 1 has been subtly replaced with intriguingly direct harmonization of [c^2-b^1] in bar 35!

Also, by making the piano to assume responsibility for the theme now transposed a perfect 5th down and harmonized within a C major diatonic framework, the composer now treats the listener to an en-clothing mantle of multipart progressions with a difference. The tendency to repeat the theme enforces a need to present the transposed melody differently in piano sound, delivered within a plenum of varied dynamics ranging from fortissimo through sweet forte to mezzo forte in but three bars (bars 35-37) and subsequently in vertical harmonies that range from simple diatonic to dissonant added-note progressions and iterated, virtually static parallel 3rds, 4ths, 5ths and octaves or combinations thereof (bar 37-51). With the assignment of the transposed melody to the piano, the flute is invested with a new opportunity of enthralling the listener with its comments in counterpoint on the transposed melody unfolding over the progressing versus static harmonies of the piano.

What other insights can be afforded to the listener experiencing bars 11-20 and 45-51 of sections A and A1 respectively? To begin with, just as was previously the case with bars 35-43 and 1-10, the listener will note that the flute melody in bars 45-51 is also a transposition of bars 11-20, except that the former falls short by three bars in order, presumably, to allow for moving on directly into the final coda.

We notice in bars 11-20 of section A that the flute and right hand of the pianist play bars 11-12 in unison, the left hand of the piano also performing the selfsame melody an octave lower down. The two instruments thus play partly in unison with the piano playing an octave below the unisonous part. From bar 12 through to 15, the flute ascends to a [b^1] flat moment of intensity from whence it gradually descends through a concluding sub-phrase made up essentially of quaver triplets to end on iterated two semiquavers and a quaver in bar 20. Notice that the flute draws on dotted note rhythm and the Abrefa Mmore motif and that by way of accompaniment, the piano exploits parallelisms in bars 12 to 14 ordered partly in octaves, compound thirds and compound sixths followed by vertically structured harmonies organized in arpeggios.

Likewise, in its transposed format in bar 45-51, the flute and the two piano parts in section A1 initially line up in one octave parallelisms that subsequently allow the flute to rise and attain an [e^2] flat high point in bar 49. In effect, this means that the flute rises a perfect 4th above the previous [b flat] point (bar 15) in section A. Thus, intensity-wise, bars 45-51 was also modeled on the pattern of bars 11-20. Notably, beginning in dotted-note rhythm in bar 45, the flute proceeds to develop its melody exploiting the Abrefa Mmore motif in bars 46-47, rising in leaps to [e^2] flat from whence it negotiates a gradually undulating fall into bar 51. And by way of harmony, the composer draws on the high point semiquaver motif in bar 8 and discordant arpeggios that propel and intensify the sonic motion of bars 46-51 just as they did in bars 11-17. Notice how doing so at a higher pitch confers additional tension that re-enforces the echo of the motion in arpeggio.

In particular, notice in bars 12 to 14, the abrupt chord variation and modulation which mediant 9th to supertonic second inversion (III9-IIc) chord progression achieved by simply converting [f#] (bar 12) to [f] natural (bar 13) and entering [b flat] in bar 14 respectively to modulate directly (i. e. without prior preparation) and in quick succession from G to C major and to F major. Similarly, in bars 46-51 of section A1, modulating in this way shows in the varied background harmonic progressions that underscore the changing high point semiquaver motifs (bars 46-48) and arpeggio figures (bars 49-51) that constitute the surface structures in A and C minor, and F and B flat major. The chord progressions may be schematized as follows:

Bar 46-47 = V9 in A min-V9 in C min
Bar 48 = V13e in F
Bar 49 = VII11e in B flat
Bar 50 = V13 in B flat
Bar 51 = V7c-V9b in B flat

as against

Bar 12-13 = III9 in G-II9 in C
Bar 14 = IVb-III7b in F
Bar 15 = VII11 in F
Bar 16 = VI7c-IV7 in F
Bar 17 = IV11c in F
Bar 18 = II7 in F
Bar 19-20 = Ic-V-I in F

From the two sets of progressions, it can be seen that modulation takes place into related keys where it occurs. While this fact may not as readily be obvious in just listening, the swiftness with which the affected chords change to differentiate the ascending modulations cannot be entirely as unnoticed. More so, the rate at which the dissonant 7ths to 13ths dominate progressions in general testifies to the deliberate ways in which they have been made to project tension, intensity and forward motion. Bye and large, the exploitation in the final coda of the broadening, pace-slowing motion first applied in bar 3 to 4 affords the listener a sense of ease in the harmonized closure of the movement in C.

Endnotes

1: The analysis was based on a 2008 copyrighted edition of the suite. CDs can be accessed online @ http://africanchorus.org

2: Dr. Seth Cudjoe was a medical doctor with passionate interests in the fine arts and music. He published in the field of African music.

3: Emeritus Professor J. H. Kwabena Nketia has been rated in 1974 as 'a most prominent scholar in the field of African music', and in 1987 as 'unquestionably the doyen of African musical scholars and educators'. For a most recent profile on his life and contributions, see Eric Akrofi's article . "Profiles of Educators: Kwabena Nketia (1921--)" published in *Prospects*: *Quarterly Review of Comparative Education, No. 139 Open File. Vol .36, no. 3, September 2006. pp. 375-386*. For a comprehensive bio-bibliographical portrait on him, see *African Musicology: Current Trends. A Festschrift* edited by Jacqueline Cogdell Djedje and William G. Carter. Vol. 1. 1989. Co-publishers: African Studies Center and African Arts Magazine (UCLA), Cross Roads Press/African Studies Association.

4: Merriam, Alan was professor of anthropology at Indiana University in the U.S.A. He wrote extensively on African music. Among his numerous and notable publications are: (i) *Anthropology of Music* and (ii) *African Music on LP*: *an Annotated Bibliography* published at Evanston, IL.: Northwestern University Press, 1964 and 1970 respectively.

5: Simmons, Charles trained in Ghana as a concert flautist and was accredited a Licentiate of the Royal Schools of Music, United Kingdom, in the area of performance.

Representing Africa Through Creative Ethnomusicology: Minimalism and Postcolonial Themes in the Music of Samuel Akpabot

Bode Omojola

Bode Omojola is a professor of music at Mount Holyoke College and the Five College Consortium at Amherst College, Hampshire College, Smith College, and the University of Massachusetts-Amherst. A former Radcliffe Fellow in Musicology at Harvard University, Omojola's research focuses on the indigenous and modern music traditions in Nigeria. His publications include *Popular Music in Western Nigeria: Theme, Style, and Patronage System* (2014); *Yorùbá Music in the Twentieth Century: Identity, Agency, and Performance Practice* (2012); *Music of Fela Sowande: Encounters, African Identity, and Creative Ethnomusicology* (2009). He is co-editor, with George W. K. Dor, of *Multiple Interpretations of Dynamics of Creativity and Knowledge in African Music Traditions: A Festschrift in Honor of Akin Euba on the Occasion of his 70th Birthday* (2005).

Introduction

African ethnomusicologists often combine academic research with compositional activity, a dual approach to professional engagement that is well illustrated in the career of Kwabena Nketia. Nketia's own work as a composer-ethnomusicologist is modeled on the works of an earlier generation of West African musicians, notably Ephraim Amu (in Ghana), Ekundayo Phillips and Fela Sowande (in Nigeria). Although Amu, Phillips and Sowande are now more widely known for their work as composers, they all engaged in one form of field research or another, and incorporated musical material deriving from their research into their musical compositions. The titles of Nketia's compositions often reveal their connections with the musical cultures that he had investigated as an ethnomusicologist. For example, His "Builsa Work Song" (for piano, 1968) is, as Kofi Agawu (2011: 57) has observed, based on a traditional song of the Builsa people; while his "Volta Fantasy" (piano, 1961) is a creative exploration of the West African "standard pattern," an important component of African drumming that has featured prominently in his academic writings. Similar to the Nketia model, West African musician-scholars like N.Z. Nayo, George Dor, Kennet Kafui (from Ghana), Akin Euba, Samuel Akpabot, Lazarus Ekwueme, Meki Nzewi, Joshua Uzoigwe, Christian Onyeji, and this writer (from Nigeria) have at one point or another combined compositional activity with research work. In paying tribute to Nketia for his pioneering work in the field of African music, this paper discusses the creative ethnomusicology of the late Nigerian composer-ethnomusicologist Samuel Akpabot (1932-2000). As a prelude to my discussion of Akpabot's music, it is instructive to briefly describe how creative ethnomusicology has been practiced in Nigeria.

The close relationship between research and composition is well illustrated in the works of Akin Euba, the man who coined the phrases "creative ethnomusicology" and "creative musicology." Euba has also articulated a number of conceptual approaches that informed his own work as a composer-scholar. For example, he developed the concept of *African pianism* as a theoretical framework for creating piano compositions that evoke indigenous Yoruba drumming, the focus of his ethnomusicological research. Euba's works in this category include "Igi Nla So" (Yoruba drums and piano, 1953) and "Scenes from Traditional Life" (piano, 1977), to mention just two.

Euba's African pianism concept has inspired many piano works by other composers, including those of Uzoigwe, which I discuss below, and my own *Studies in African Pianism* (Omojola 2004). Regarding creative ethnomusicology, Euba explained that: "composers around the world (especially those from non-Western countries) are producing music in which resources derived from traditional and folk music (normally the province of ethnomusicology) are combined with Western techniques of composition (normally the area of specialization of historical musicologists and music theorists)... ."[1] It is important to note that the concept of "creative ethnomusicology," although coined by Akin Euba, is reminiscent of the folk-inspired compositions of European composers like Bela Bartok, Modest Mussorgsky, and Kodály Kodaly. Meki Nzewi's approach to musical composition also reflects a strong interaction between research and composition. Although he had initially composed for Western instruments, he has recently been more interested in re-configuring Igbo traditional music, the primary focus of his research work, for modern concert performances (see Nzewi, 1992).[2] Joshua Uzoigwe, who devoted considerable time studying Euba's creative ethnomusicology, was also active as a creative ethnomusicologist. His works include "Lustra Variations" (for piano, 1976), which was conceived to evoke the *uli*, a form of painting and drawing that is associated with Igbo women; and "Masquerade" (for piano and the *iyaalu*, 1980), which evokes Yoruba drumming ethnomusicology)[3]. Christian Onyeji, another Nigerian ethnomusicologist-composer, coined the term "drummistic piano composition" to draw attention to the relationship between Igbo traditional drumming, the focus of his ethnomusicological research, and his piano compositions (Onyeji, 2008).

Creative Ethnomusicology as a Form of Representation
Composing music and publishing academic works represent two related modes of representation. The writing of musical compositions based on indigenous oral traditions has been described by Agawu as "music-on-music exploration" (Agawu 2011: 51) and a "metamusical" representation of "existing traditional musics" (Agawu 1992: 1). Agawu, whose groundbreaking book on the themes of representation and postcolonial discourse inspired the title of this essay, also commented about the unique significance of creative activity as a means of generating knowledge about Africa.[4] He observes that the "high valuation of African traditional music by ethnographers often overlooks the fact that its potentialities are best revealed not by gathering and confining

samples of the music to sound archives and museums, but by probing the music compositionally, engaging it through creative violation. It is impossible to overestimate the quality and quantity of the kinds of knowledge that are produced from self-conscious manipulation of traditional music's materials and procedures..." (Agawu, 2011: 50-51). Compared with those of Akin Euba, Nzewi and Uzoigwe, Akpabot's works are marked by a relatively populist style and a strikingly minimalist form, designed for a more inclusive patronage. Although he wrote choral compositions that feature relatively sophisticated techniques, as found, for example, in his "Verba Christi" (a cantata for solo, chorus and European orchestra), most of Akpabot's compositions are instrumental works with simple, and often minimalist forms. Focusing on selections from his works, I examine the nature of the relationship between Akpabot's research activity and creative work, and discuss the process and the dynamics of translating an oral tradition into a written form. As a background to my discussion of his music, I begin with a short biography.

Samuel Akpabot: A Short Biography

Akpabot was born on October 3, 1932 in Uyo in the present Akwa Ibom State of Nigeria. He however spent a considerable part of his life in Lagos, the former Nigerian capital that provided the setting for most of the political, social, and cultural developments that engendered the birth of new musical practices in the country. Akpabot's educational and cultural life was shaped similarly to that of his colleagues: he was introduced to European classical and Christian music in the church and at mission schools. He attended King's College, Lagos, and was a chorister at the Christ Church Cathedral in Lagos, under Nigeria's most important church musician of the period, Ekundayo Phillips. Commenting on his childhood experience under Phillips, he explained to me in an interview thus: "It was in Christ Church that I was introduced to a great deal of European masterpieces; I sang all of them before going to England and that turned out to be a very great challenge."

Those masterpieces included Handel's "Messiah" and Mendelssohn's "Elijah." Unlike most of his colleagues, however, Akpabot was also a prominent performer of popular music, especially *highlife*. Thus, as well as being a chorister, he found time to play in popular music bands, the most notable of which was the Chocolate Dandies, which was formed and led by a man named Soji Lijadu. In 1949, he formed his own group, The Akpabot Players (TAP), and later combined his work as a bandleader with the position of organist at the St. Savior's Church in Lagos. He described this dual experience thus:

> "I would come back very late in the night from nightclub and steal into the Bishop's Court where I lived (with Bishop Vining, then, of Lagos) and the following morning go to play for both the Holy Communion Service and the Sunday Mass."[5]

By the time Akpabot went to the Royal College of Music in London in the late 1950s to study, he had become quite proficient in the theory and practice of European music. It was while he was in England that he began composing. His first work from this period was initially entitled "Nigeriana" (Orchestra, 1959), but was later reworked and renamed "Overture for a Nigerian Ballet," a title that reveals the work's conceptual relationship with the European 19th century concert overture tradition. On his return to Nigeria in the early 1960s, he worked with the Nigerian Broadcasting Corporation (NBC) before transferring to the University of Nigeria, Nsukka to become one of the pioneering faculty members of the music department. As a music lecturer, Akpabot combined teaching with field research, and traveled occasionally to Etinan (his hometown), Lagos, and Onitsha to collect and study the musical traditions of the Ibibio, Yoruba and Igbo ethnic groups respectively. A considerable portion of the material that would later go into his doctoral thesis at Michigan State University was collected around this time. His other compositions include "Scenes from Nigeria" (orchestra, 1962); "Three Nigerian Dances" (string orchestra and percussion, 1962); "Ofala" (tone poem for wind orchestra and five African instruments, 1963); and "Cynthia's Lament" (tone poem for soloist, wind orchestra and six African instruments, 1965). Akpabot taught at the Institute of African Studies, University of Ibadan from 1976 to 1988, and the University of Uyo, where he served as a professor of music until his death in 2000.

As I explain below, Akpabot's compositions often display many of the features of Ibibio music, including ostinato patterns, word-borne melodies and harmonies, a strong element of dance, and folk-tunes or their adaptations.[6] In order to understand how his music reconfigures Nigerian musical and cultural elements, I have grouped his compositions into three categories, as informed by some specific themes. They are: evocation of real life events ("Ofala," and "Cynthia's Lament"); instrumental imitations of traditional Ibibio and modern Nigerian popular music ("Scenes from Nigeria" and "Three Nigerian Dances"); and sacred choral works ("Verba Christi;" and "Te Deum Laudamus" (church anthem, choir and organ 1975). I must mention however that these thematic categories are by no means mutually exclusive, as I shall make clear in my discussion.

Cynthia's Lament

"Cynthia's Lament" is conceived as a tone poem, as described fully by Akpabot in the preface to the unpublished score:

"Cynthia Avery was the 16 year-old daughter of the white American Vice Chairman of the American Wind Symphony Orchestra of Pittsburgh with whom I stayed during a visit in 1963 for the premiere of "Ofala". After the performance, we went to the Conrad Hilton to have coffee with Mr. Boudreau. The rather silly waiters deliberately avoided serving Miss Avery and myself (we were seated together a short distance from the girl's parents and Mr. Boudreau, who were served). This so distressed Miss Avery that she stormed out into the foyer, sobbing, "I don't know what has become of my people!" I decided to write a short piece for her, and on my next commission two years later, I produced Cynthia's Lament."

In the work, Cynthia Avery's lament is reinterpreted in Igbo and Ibibio musico-dramatic terms. The harmonic vocabulary of the work is almost entirely diatonic as found in traditional Ibibio, and Igbo music. Apart from the occasional use of chromatic paragraphs to enhance the agitation of the voice, the piece remains predominantly diatonic and marked by parts that move in parallel movements. The lack of tonality-generated tension in the work is compensated for by the use of a vocal line that has its own built-in agitation (see Figure 1 in Appendix). As can be observed in table 1, which summaries the structural procedures employed in the work, the development lacks any substantial key changes. The lament in "Cynthia's Lament," is conveyed through a repetitive singing of two words, *ewo* and *waiyo*, Igbo expressions for emotions ranging from anger, sympathy and surprise (see Figure 1 in Appendix).

In addition, the work is marked by the use of motivic fragments that are derived from the two main ideas of the piece to create repetitive layered rhythmic textures that are evocative of Ibibio traditional music. As illustrated in figures 1 and 2, style elements that are reminiscent of Ibibio and Igbo music (and indeed much of West African music) abound in the work. They include repetitive rhythmic patterns, parallel harmonies, as well as fragmentary and declamatory vocal phrases typified by constant change in dynamics. Although the form of the work hints at the European sonata form, it rejects the dynamic tonal and harmonic progressions that typify that form. It is mainly through the repetition of the words *ewo* and *waiyo* (and the emotive, fragmentary, and angular lines to which they are set) that the piece articulates the dramatic content of its background program--the lamentation of Cynthia Avery.

Ofala

Ofala is a tone poem based on the annual yam-eating festival of the Igbo people of Onitsha, Eastern Nigeria.[7] The formal outline of the work (see Table 2 in Appendix) is suggested by the format of the festival, which is described by Akpabot in the introduction to the unpublished score of the work thus:

> "During the festival, the Igwe (the king) comes from his palace to give an annual account of his stewardship to his people. On the first day, the Igwe emerges a few yards from his palace and then returns home, while on the second day he walks as far as the gates of the palace and returns. On the third day he walks out of his palace into the town to meet his subjects amidst scenes of great jubilation and dancing."

The third day is the grand finale when the main events of the festival take place. The work is scored for European wind instruments as well as Nigerian (Igbo, Yoruba and Ibibio) percussion. The percussion instruments are *ogene* (Igbo twin gong), *sekere* (Yoruba shaker), *obodom* (Ibibio wooden gong), and *tom-tom* (hand skin drums). These are often deployed to create a repetitive multilayered ostinato-driven material (see Figure 3 in Appendix). Akpabot explains that Western wind instruments featured in the work are conceived to resemble their Nigerian counterparts: Western horns to imitate the Ibibio elephant tusk horns (*uta*), Western flutes to imitate the Igbo five stop flute (*oja*), and Western trumpets to imitate Ibibio valve-less trumpets. In developing the thematic material of the song, Akpabot relies on stylistic devices common in Ibibio music. For example, the first section of the piece presents the main theme in a call and response pattern, while in the remaining part of the section, the theme is broken into smaller call and response fragments. This procedure later develops into a much longer call and response traditional fanfare (figure 4) that depicts the arrival of the *Igwe* (king) to the scene of the festival. It is important to note that Akpabot's tone poem, though apparently recalls a European romantic-era tone poems, does not paint in musical terms. Akpabot's work relies on Igbo- and Ibibio-derived musical material, instrumentation, and vocal resources in evoking the atmosphere, protocols and rituals of the Ofala festival.

Nigeria in Conflict
Similar features are observable in another work, "Nigerian in Conflict", which is also conceived as a miniature tone poem, this time, on the Nigerian civil war that lasted from 1967-1970. Like the "Ofala" and "Cynthia's Lament," the work makes use of a wind orchestra and Ibibio-type percussion (see Figure 5 in Appendix). Unlike the "Ofala," however, the different sections of the work are not referential of specific extra-musical procedures. Apart from its often agitated character, references to the civil war exist mainly in the setting of traditional tunes from the Eastern part of Nigeria (the Secessionist Camp) against a fragment of the then) Nigerian National Anthem. As can be observed in Figure 5 and Table 3, the work explores traditional Ibo and Ibibio music in the same manner as done in "Ofala" and "Cynthia's Lament." Features attesting to this similarity exist in the use of a layered melo-rhythmic texture defined by the use of ostinato, the mere juxtaposition of tonal areas rather than an organically evolved tonal movement, and a relatively free form.[8]

Akpabot's choice of instrumentation is in this work conditioned by the need to project the qualities of traditional Ibibio instruments that include gong, rattle, wooden drum, and xylophone. They are combined with Western woodwind and brass instruments, namely, flute, trumpet, horn, bass trombone, tuba and the timpani. European wind instruments are used to provide melo-rhythmic phrases that are idiomatic of the traditional Ibibio *uta* orchestra of elephant tusks.

Akpabot's next set of compositions, "Scenes from Nigeria" and "Three Nigerian Dances," reveal further interesting perspectives about his representation of indigenous Ibibio and modern *highlife* music. The *highlife* character of these works is conveyed through very simple diatonic harmonies, a ternary form, limited modulation, and a variation process that mildly simulates *highlife* improvisation. In the second movement of the "Three Nigerian Dances," for example, Akpabot adopts an open-ended form in which the main melody undergoes a continuous process of variation within a generally unchanging F major tonality. As in "Cynthia's Lament," motivic materials derived from the main melody are developed into ostinato phrases that help to accentuate the tonic-dominant punctuation of the cello, double bass and timpani. It is also important to note that key changes, when they exist—as in "Scenes from Nigeria"—are merely juxtaposed rather than organically evolved. The evocation of improvisation in these works recalls the oral form of Nigerian music, and underlines their populist orientation.

Verba Christi

The "Verba Christi" is a cantata for three soloists, chorus, and orchestra. The Nigerian Broadcasting Corporation (NBC) commissioned it for the World Black Festival of Arts and Culture (FESTAC), in Lagos, in 1977. This work departs from all the works discussed above in its use of atonality, the abandonment of highlife-Ibibio melodies and Nigerian instruments, and in the fact that it is a religious choral work. "Verba Christi" is modeled on the European baroque cantata, and the rhetoric to Nigerian music is significantly curtailed in it. Nevertheless, the work, like the ones discussed above, bears the imprint of Akpabot's inclusive approach to musical composition. Akpabot, in this composition, re-works European elements in African terms in a manner that demonstrates cross-cultural permeability of forms. For example, the 12-tones of the rows used in the music often do not appear intact because atonal passages are often marked by multi-layered and cyclically conceived material, a deliberate attempt to imitate Ibibio instrumental procedures. This technique is well illustrated in the chorus of the Pharisees where the use of a multilayered rhythmic texture (typified by loud dynamics) gives the hostility of the Pharisees a dramatic exclamation. Akpabot's instrumentation, in its percussive and often polyrhythmic character as well as its cultivation of instrumental lines with a limited melodic ambit, reveals an attempt to simulate the minimalist melo-rhythmic sounds of an Ibibio ensemble.

Conclusion

The popularity of creative ethnomusicology among African composers derives from a number of factors. Firstly, most African ethnomusicologists studied Western music during their undergraduate years, and were choristers singing European hymns in the church and in the high school prior to going to the university. The choice to study ethnomusicology often begins at the graduate level, when it becomes clear that the field of ethnomusicology would bring their scholarship closer to their indigenous musical traditions. By linking musical composition and performance to ethnomusicological work later in their career, African scholar-musicians are able to develop a vocation that is more sensitive to their African identity.

As illustrated in the works of Akpabot, creative ethnomusicology provides a means for retrieving ancient African musical practices, and reconfiguring them within cosmopolitan musical forms for the attention of an international audience. This form of identity representation has been discussed by George Dor, who, assessing the significance of his works and those of other Ghanaian composers, explained that they are often written to "share a creative experience" and "revitalize an indigenous music genre" (Dor, 2005: 441). Kofi Agawu has identified African "precompositional" elements and models that creative ethnomusicologists often employ in their works to include "the structure of drum language, various dance forms, the musico-dramatic genre of storytelling, and most important of all, the structures that make up the spoken languages ... ." (Agawu 1984: 37).

It is important to note that the compositional retrieval of traditional music as I have shown in the works of Akpabot is linked to the issue of power and the need to reaffirm a sense of identity that was stifled during colonial rule. Commenting on this, Dor explains that such a mode of representation often constitutes " a conscious attempt to revitalize the past," an activity that is "best captured in a cultural concept dubbed "Sankofa," a Twi word meaning "go back and retrieve it" (Dor 2005:448).

Akpabot's evocation of the African festival tradition within European-type concert music is particularly significant because the elitism of the European concert tradition contrasts with the communal nature of African festival performance in which kings, chiefs, and the general populace interact and assert a sense of group solidarity as they revitalize key features of their history and culture. The infusing of a European concert tradition with an African communal festival performance represents an important strategy for subverting European cultural hegemony that colonial domination engendered in Africa. In evoking a traditional festival in "Ofala," Akpabot engages in a second-tier retrieval project, while simultaneously re-interpreting, localizing and appropriating well-known European musical elements: European harmony, for example, is used rather rudimentarily, while the sonata form is used in a minimal form. It must be noted that Akpabot's knowledge of Western music theory, harmony and counterpoint, and composition was quite profound, having studied at the Royal College of Music, London, the University of Chicago, and Michigan State University in the United States. His evocation of communal music practices through a minimalist approach to musical form is thus not due to lack of knowledge of European compositional techniques. Akpabot's embracement of minimalism is informed by an appropriation strategy that is adopted to enhance the significance of the musical materials and styles derived from Ibibio and Ibo traditions. For example, the cultivation of Western harmony in a cyclic and somehow tokenistic form is structurally acknowledging of the equally minimalist character of Ibibio-derived ostinato-driven phrases that dominate Akpabot's compositions. Also, as I explained above, the choice of and use of Western instruments was often made with a view to making them function as surrogate African instruments. It is however important to note that the use of these features is crucially linked to Akpabot's vision about the societal role of modern African composers. His adoption of minimalism as a compositional strategy is designed to court popularity and generate a more inclusive patronage for modern African art music. Explaining this position, he stated that "it is for this reason that I often ignore European standard forms, in favor of formal elements commonly employed in traditional African music."[9]

Akpabot's domestication of European musical forms hints at a postmodernist strategy conceived towards narrowing the often taken-for-granted cultural and social gap between Western art music and indigenous African music. The presentation of easily accessible and orally conceived musical material within an elite, notation-based, European-influenced musical composition indeed amounts to a significant bridging of the social and the cultural. But the importance of Akpabot's work goes beyond the narrowing of social and cultural gap. Akpabot's creative ethnomusicology simultaneously acknowledges and demystifies the canonic status of Western art music. The apparent embracement of Western art music through its adoption, and its neutralization through the incorporation of African elements is paradoxical in a politically significant manner. This paradox speaks to an identity strategy that is politically important when viewed as a form of postcolonial discourse. Akpabot's works in their conception and syntax speak to the unequal power relations that defined colonial domination of Africa. The juxtaposition of African and European musical syntaxes in a manner that symbolically restores the integrity of one and undermines the hegemony of the other carries a strong message. Akpabot's statement about why he combines Western and African instruments in his work is particularly noteworthy in this regard, and I would like to give him the last word in this essay. Commenting on why he wrote short, repetitive, fragmentary phrases for both Ibibio and Western instruments, Akpabot explained that it was motivated by the need to achieve an orchestral effect in which "African instruments are treated on an equal footing with Western instruments and not as exotic instruments, which they are not."[10]

Endnotes

1: http://cimacc.org/ (Center for Intercultural Musicology at Churchill College), accessed on December 27.

2: Further discussions on the works of Nigerian composers, see the following: Euba, Akin. 1993. *Modern African Music: A Catalogue of Selected Archival Materials at Iwalewa-Haus, University of Bayreuth, Germany* Bayreuth: Iwalewa-Haus; Euba, Akin. 1999. "Towards an African Pianism." *Intercultural Musicology: The Bulletin of the Centre for Intercultural Music Arts, London, UK* (1): 9-12.; Irele, Abiola. 1993. "Is African Music Possible?" *Transition* (61): 56-71; Konye, Paul. 2007. *African Art Music: Political, Social, and Cultural Factors Behind Its Development and Practice in Nigeria* New York: The Edwin Mellen Press; Omojola, Olabode. 1994. "Contemporary Art Music in Nigeria: An Introductory Note on the Works of Ayo Bankole." *Africa: Journal of the International African Institute* (64):533-43; Omojola, Olabode. 1995. *Nigerian Art Music, with an Introductory Study of Ghanaian Art Music* Ibadan, Institut Francais de Recherche; Omojola, Olabode. 2009. *The Music of Fela Sowande: Encounters, African Identity and Creative Ethnomusicology* Point Richmond: MRI Press; Sadoh, Godwin. 2004. "Intercultural Creativity in Joshua Uzoigwe's Music." *Africa* (74):633-661.

3: See Joshua Uzoigwe. 1992. *Akin Euba: An Introduction to the Life and Music of a Nigerian Composer* Bayreuth, E. Breitinger, University of Bayreuth.

4: See Kofi. Agawu. 2003. *Representing African Music: Postcolonial Notes, Queries, Positions* New York and London: Routledge.

5: This was expressed in an interview with me in Ibadan, Nigeria in 1985.

6: For a discussion of Akpabot's research, see the following: Akpabot, Samuel. 1975. *Ibibio Music in Nigerian Culture* East Lansing: Michigan State University Press; Akpabot, Samuel. 1977. "Anthropology of African." *Africa: Journal of the International African Institute* 47 (2): 2-3.

7: This festival holds during the harvest season, usually between in July and August.

8: The term "melo-rhythm" was coined by Meki Nzewi to capture the percussive character of indigenous Nigerian melodies. For a discussion of this, see Meki Nzewi. "Melo-rhythmic Essence and Hot Rhythm in Nigerian Folk Music." *The Black Perspective in Music* 2(1) (1974): 23-28.

9: This statement was expressed in an interview that I conducted with Professor Samuel Akpbot in Ibadan, Nigeria in 1985.

10: This statement was expressed in an interview that I conducted with Professor Samuel Akpbot in Ibadan, Nigeria in 1985.

References

Agawu, Kofi. 1984. "The Impact of Language on Musical Composition in Ghana: An Introduction to the Musical Style of Ephraim Amu." *Ethnomusicology* 28 (1): 37-73.

Agawu, Kofi. 1992. "Representing African Music." *Critical Inquiry* 18 (2): 245-266.

Agawu, Kofi. 2003. *Representing African Music: Postcolonial Notes, Queries, Positions.* New York and London: Routledge.

Agawu, Kofi. 2011. "The Challenge of African Art Music." *Circuit : musiques contemporaines* 21 (2): 49-64.

Akpabot, Samuel. 1975. *Ibibio Music in Nigerian Culture.* East Lansing: Michigan State University Press.

____. 1977. *Three Nigerian Dances* (for Strings and Timpani). New York: Oxford University Press.

____. 1977. "Anthropology of African Music." *Africa: Journal of the International African Institute* 47 (2): 2-3.

Dor, George. 2005. "Uses of Indigenous Music Genres in Ghanaian Choral Art Music: Perspectives from the Works of Amu, Blege, and Dor." *Ethnomusicology* 49 (3): 441-475.

Euba, Akin. 2010. "Center for Intercultural Musicology at Churchill College." http://cimacc.org/ accessed on December 27, 2012.

Euba, Akin. 1993. *Modern African Music: A Catalogue of Selected Archival Materials at Iwalewa-Haus, University of Bayreuth Germany*. Bayreuth: Iwalewa-Haus.

Euba, Akin. 1999. "Towards an African Pianism." *Intercultural Musicology: The Bulletin of the Centre for Intercultural Music Arts*. London, UK (1):9-12.

Irele, Abiola. 1993. "Is African Music Possible?" *Transition* (61):56-71.

Konye, Paul. 2007. *African Art Music: Political, Social, and Cultural Factors Behind Its Development and Practice in Nigeria*. New York: The Edwin Mellen Press.

Omojola, Olabode. 1994. "Contemporary Art Music in Nigeria: An Introductory Note on the Works of Ayo Bankole." *Africa: Journal of the International African Institute* (64):533-43.

___. 1995. *Nigerian Art Music, with an Introductory Study of Ghanaian Art Music*. Ibadan: Institut Francais de Recherche.

___. 2004. *Studies in African Pianism*. Bayreuth: Bayreuth African Studies.

___. 2009. *The Music of Fela Sowande: Encounters, African Identity and Creative Ethnomusicology*. Point Richmond: MRI Press.

Onyeji, Christian. 2008. "Drummistic Piano Composition: An Approach to Teaching Piano Composition from a Nigerian Cultural Perspective." *International Journal of Music Education* 26 (2): 161-175.

Nzewi, Meki. "Melo-Rhythmic Essence and Hot Rhythm in Nigerian Folk Music." *The Black Perspective in Music* 2(1) (1974): 23-28.

___. 1992. *Ese Music: Notation and Modern Concept/concert Presentation*. Iwalewa-Haus, University of Bayreuth.

Sadoh, Godwin. 2004. "Intercultural Creativity in Joshua Uzoigwe's Music." *Africa* (74):633-661.

Uzoigwe, Joshua. 1992. *Akin Euba: An Introduction to the Life and Music of a Nigerian Composer*. Bayreuth: E. Breitinger, University of Bayreuth.

Appendix

Figure 1: Cynthia's Lament
Vocal Part

Sam Akpabot

Figure 2: Cynthia's Lament
Showing wind and percussion parts

Sam Akpabot

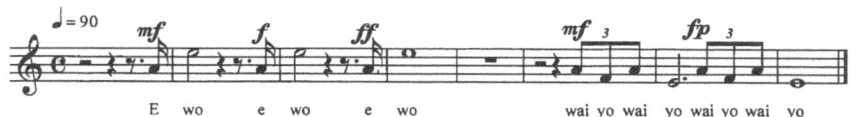

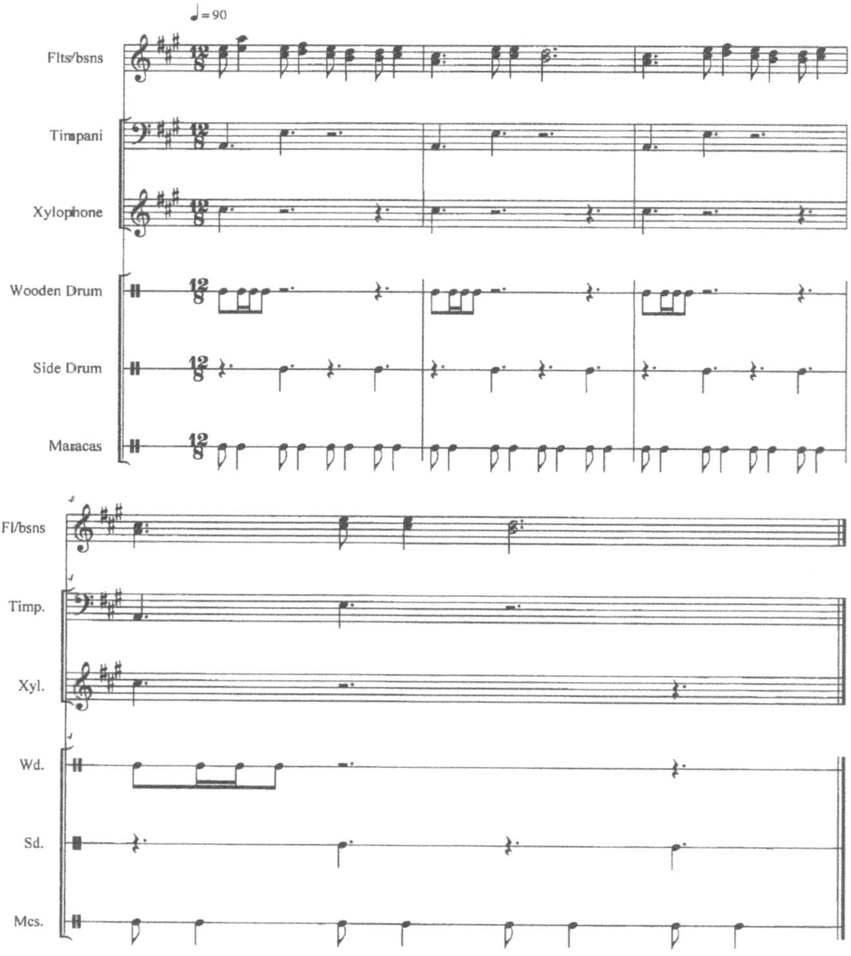

Figure 3: Ofala
Showing indigenous percussion instruments

Sam Akpabot

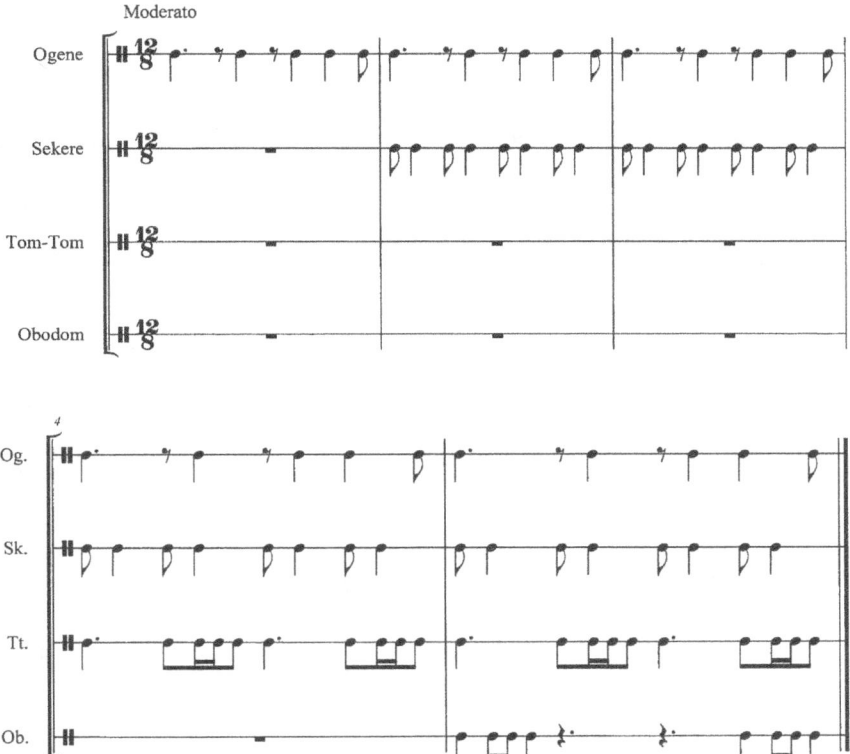

Figure 4: Ofala
Igwe's Fanfare

Sam Akpabot

Figure 5: Nigeria in Conflict

Sam Akpabot

Sections	Keys	Theme	Measures	Tempo
Exposition:	A minor	A	1-41	Grave
Short Link			37-41	
	A major	B	42-57	Tempo Giusto
Development	A major	A & B	58-99	Animato
			(65 ff)	Andante con moto
Link to recapitulation	C	A & B	90-99	
Recapitulation	C	B	100-107	
Short Link			108-111	Calando
	A minor (A major)	A	111-130	Andante con moto

Table 1: Outline of Form: Cynthia's Lament

Main Section	Measures	Key	Sub-Sections	Programmatic Connection
Exposition	1-10	Bb	Rhythmic Prelude	Pre-festival entertainment
	11-29		1st theme	
	30-43		2nd theme (Fanfare Section)	Arrival of Royalty
Development	44-87		1st development a) Wedge-like theme b) Vocal melody (both variants of 1st theme)	Ritual Ceremony
	88-99		Bridge passage	
	100-118	F	2nd development	
	119-120		Bridge passage	Post-ritual Entertainment
Recapitulation	121-133	Bb	2nd theme (Fanfare Section)	Departure of Royalty
	133-143		Rhythmic postlude	Post-Festival Entertainment

Table 2: Ofala: Outline of Form

Bars	Section	Tonality
1-61	Introduction	F
17-30	Rhythmic prelude	F
31-48	Sparse (quasi-pointillist)	Chromatic
49-70	Polyrhythmic ostinati	Eb
71-79	Polyrhythmic ostinati	Chromatic
80-83	Short link	Eb
84-107	Main theme and it variants	Eb main theme
108-116	Ostinato/poly-rhythmic	Ab
117-144	Fanfare passage	F
(138-144	- Bridge passage)	
145-172	Polyrhythmic; tutti (finally, homophonic, rhythmic)	F

Table 3: Nigeria in Conflict: Outline of Form

Exploring the Ontology and Application of the "Nketia Dominant Seventh Chord"

George W. K. Dor

George W. K. Dor is a teacher, composer, performer, researcher, and the McDonnell Barksdale Chair of Ethnomusicology at the University of Mississippi. His publications include *West African Drumming in North American Universities: An Ethnomusicological Perspective* (2014); "Multiple Interpretations of Dynamics of Creativity and Knowledge in African Music Traditions" in *A Festschrift in Honor of Akin Euba*, which he co-edited with Bode Omojola (2005); journal articles, book chapters, and an encyclopedia entry.

Foregrounding the Compositional Component of Nketia's Legacy

The scope, depth, and richness of Nketia's scholarship and creative work may metaphorically be compared to the *adwineasa* prestigious *kente* cloth. Only exceptional master kente weavers could produce this artistic nexus of several intricate motives that comprise adwineasa. The weavers not only employ the exhaustive use of all the beautiful motifs as the cloth's name literally suggests, but they also are, by conception, articulating the acme of creativity, innovative perfectionism, artistic expressivity and application of rare traditional knowledge embodied in both the process and product of the adwineasa. By extension, and still speaking figuratively, I will not be overly ambitious in attempting to describe even a single design of this cloth that may be regarded as the sublime of African creativity. Rather, I choose to describe the color of a single thread of the fabric. Accordingly, the subject matter of this essay is a single chord, which to me is an engaging novelty and a source of profound musical affect. I am confident that the preceding conceptual metaphor can stimulate readers' imagination and curiosity, and prepare them for the discussion or the "tale of a single chord." But for those who may not understand the salience of discussing a single chord as my contribution to this second and present Festschrift (after DjeDje and Carter 1989, DjeDje 1992) on Kwabena Nketia's titanic legacy—life and works, I explain my decision in the following paragraphs.

Most ethnomusicologists and Africanists are well informed about Emeritus Professor Nketia's phenomenal contribution to the field of ethnomusicology, in general, and African musicology (Wachsmann 1966, 1967, 1969, 1970; Nketia 1970, 1998; Nketia and DjeDje 1984; DjeDje 1992, 2005; DjeDje and Cater 1989; and Euba 2001), in particular. While Akrofi (2003) provides a profile on Nketia's accomplishments that readers often consult, I would like to mention only three of his pivotal landmarks in the Society for Ethnomusicology in order to further situate my discussion. Nketia gave the Charles Seeger Memorial Lecture to the Society for Ethnomusicology in 1989, and as we may all know, only very distinguished scholars are given this rare opportunity to share their rich experiences (Nketia 1990: 75-97). More recently in 2005 at Atlanta, Nketia became an Honorary Member of the Society of Ethnomusicology (the 50th Anniversary of SEM), an event that the younger generation of scholars had the privilege to witness.

Furthermore, SEM's African Music Section has institutionalized the Kwabena Nketia Book Prize to honor and perpetuate the excellence and rigor that his scholarship epitomizes. Then, I may be right to think that the preceding and other similar considerations motivated Professor Gave Averill, President of the Society of Ethnomusicology, and Dean of Arts, University of British Columbia, to have written and sent a congratulatory Message to Nketia on behalf of the entire Society (Conference Program 2011: 17). The number of ethnomusicologists who participated in the Nketia 90 Conference at the University of Ghana, Legon, affirms the extent of his seemingly unbeatable impact and legacy (Conference Program 2011: 17-18).[2]

In spite of the global academic community's awareness and acknowledgement of Nketia's exceptional scholarship, his legacy as a composer is not very well known in many parts of the world. Partly though, the global community is slow in its awareness of African art music. Appreciatively, through the concept and advocacy of/for "African Pianism" by Euba and Nketia (Euba 1989: 151-152; Nketia 1994; Kimberlin and Euba 2005; Labi 1997, 1994; Omojola 2001; Dor 2005: 18-21; Nyaho 2009), Nketia's piano pieces are now more frequently performed in America, Europe, Asia, and beyond. Further, seminars on African music that include the discussion of African art music have been given at the University of Pittsburgh (by Euba), Ohio State University (by Avorgbedor), University of California at Los Angeles (by DjeDje), and University of South Florida (by John Robinson), and their course discussions include works and creative lives of Nketia, Amu, Euba, Bankole, Sowande, Nayo, ElDabh, Uzoigwe, and other prominent African composers. Jesse Ruskin's essay, which is published in this Festschrift, is an outgrowth of such a course. Also, computer-aided translations of Nketia's handwritten scores of piano pieces, art songs, and chamber works by Andrew K. Agyemfra-Tettey, Nketia's special assistant, not only facilitated the accessibility of these scores to the larger art music community, but also provided handy visual and sonic illustrations that Nketia used during presentations of his compositions at international conferences.[3] Additionally, Nketia's publication of his *Sankudwom*, his original art songs, and *African Pianism: Twelve Pedagogical Pieces* enhanced the much needed global awareness to some extent. Ghanaians' recognition of Nketia as one of their great national art music composers presents an antithesis to the preceding international picture. Most Ghanaians are familiar with his compositions, some of which are very popular, especially the choral works performed mainly by church choirs. His art songs are among favorite test pieces often performed by voice students at the music departments of the University of Ghana, University of Cape Coast, University of Education, Winneba, as well as music candidates for the West African Examination Council's examinations.[4] As I will later discuss in this essay, younger Ghanaian composers have revitalized some of Nketia's compositions. While I have arranged the piano accompaniment part of *Wonya Amane*, an art song, with an orchestral version that includes Ghanaian drums and drumming, Ato Quayson has more recently expanded Nketia's *Monkanfo No*, a choral piece, by adding a voice solo introduction, an orchestral introduction, Ghanaian drums, and outlining of the choral parts by instruments, thereby providing new sonic and textural variety, or a transformed lighter choral musical sound into an intensified sonic grandeur of three combined ensembles—choir, drum, and orchestra[5]. Lahnor Adjetey Adjei conducted this revitalized version of the choral piece, which has been performed by the Harmonious Chorale and the Ghana National Symphony Orchestra as part of the "Ghana Arts Music Concert," organized under the auspices of the Salt and Light Ministries, directed by Joyce Aryee.[6] Additionally, I hope those who traveled to Ghana for the Nketia 90 Conference discovered this creativity legacy of which they were most likely hitherto not fully aware. During the conference, the Community Choir of the University of Cape Coast, directed by Kofi Ansah, performed more than two dozens of Nketia's art songs and choral pieces for the participants, and I hope some international participants have acquired CD recordings of the art songs. In any case, the fact remains that the global community's awareness of his creative legacy is still limited.

That Nketia's creativity legacy is disproportionate to his scholarly input is a result of a shift in focus. For, Nketia who was a very prolific composer and scholar, especially in the 1940s into the 1960s with a balanced productivity level for both activities, he later concentrated more on writing of scholarly texts than compositions, a focus that has spanned more than four decades of the latter phase of his career. Certainly, this focus on scholarship is reflected in the phenomenal volume of critical texts he had authored. Understandably, to his many students that he mentored in North America, especially at UCLA and Pittsburgh, he was first and foremost a scholar.

Although Nketia was composing less as his career progressed, he rechanneled his creative abilities, passion, and experiences into part of his ethnomusicological writings (Nketia 1982; Wiggins 2005). He had thus gradually laid the foundation for written discourse that foreground the intersection between research and composition, a tradition that Euba, his student, and others would inherit and develop. It is not surprising that themes relating to creativity became a hallmark research subject of a generation of scholars that received their influences from the University of Ghana and the University of Pittsburgh. Yet creativity remains a natural and passionate theme for all composers who are also ethnomusicologists.

I certainly corroborate the position that his compositional legacy is a very important facet of his life and works that need foregrounding.[7] It was therefore gratifying to note that Nissio Fiagbedzi, Eric Beeko, and Emmanuel Boamah, Ghanaian musicians and scholars, gave papers that themathized Nketia's selected art music compositions during the 2011 conference. I remain thankful to the University of Mississippi for empowering me to be present at the conference to present my paper also as a composer of Ghanaian art music,[8] as I joined others in celebrating the legacy of this industrious forebear and composer.

Discovering and Explaining the Nketia Dominant Seventh Chord

In the early 1990s, I had the privilege of studying the works of three path-finding composers of Ghanaian art music for my MPhil thesis and degree in music at the University of Ghana.[9] Indeed, Ephraim Amu, Nicholas Zinzendorf Nayo, and Kwabena Nketia epitomize a golden age of renaissance in Ghana's intercultural art music history. Beyond the commonplace knowledge that all three composers drew on various forms of Ghanaian traditional music as their pre-compositional resources, these forebears were also problem solvers, as Nketia once told me in a personal conversation. In addition to their assiduous efforts at configuring the best notational representations of Ghanaian and other African rhythms, they were also in their various creative moments confronted with the challenge of synchronizing the seemingly incompatible African and Western tonal systems. And yet these composers ingeniously drew on their bi-musicality, talent, and creative imagination in crafting their own individual stylistic idiosyncrasies as well as models that the younger generation of composers would later draw upon.

This discussion draws on data, experiences, and knowledge relating to a harmonic idiom, which I accessed during (1) my study of Nketia's works (Dor 1992), (2) teaching of the idiom to my students at Winneba (1992-1996), and (3) the use of the idiom in some of my orchestral and choral works. Accordingly, I use excerpts from Nketia's scores and recordings or live performances of relevant works to indicate the originality of this chord to him.[10] Further, as I explain the application of this chord, examples from my own works suggest Nketia's partial influence on my harmonic language and my appreciation for his path-finding agency as an imaginative Ghanaian art music composer. Additionally, my discussion reaffirms the extent to which the similarities between Akan and Northern Ewe melodic systems partly enabled my use of and interest in the Nketia dominant seventh chord.

From a body of stylistic personalities that I discussed in my MPhil thesis, I now focus on one idiomatic expression that is synonymous with Kwabena Nketia. In my study of Nketia's art songs I noted his taste for the falling melodic fourths that end some of his phrases. A classic example can be found in the two opening phrases of *Yaanon Montie!* (Statesmen, Listen!), a song that most Ghanaians may know very well because the Ghana Broadcasting Corporation (GBC) recorded and popularized Geoffrey Boateng's rendition of it. To a generation of Ghanaian listeners the mere mention of the song's title silently reechoes Boateng's beautiful tenor voice, which was accompanied on the piano by the composer himself. Yet I received one of the greatest affirmations from the composer himself when during my presentation of this paper at the Nektia 90 Conference I started to sing the preceding melodic excerpt in solfage. Pleasantly, Professor Nketia voluntarily joined me in singing the two phrases thus: (a) $^3_4$ t.d: d: d I d:. td I r: r: l I l:, and (b) s.l: 1: 1 I1:. sl taw: taw: f If:. While the first phrase ends with a drop from "re" to "la" (supertonic to submediant), the second closes with a sequential melodic progression from the lowered seventh "taw" to "fah," the subdominant. In Figure 1 (see Appendix), the staff notation of the two phrases may provide an additional perceptual dimension of the falling fourth melodic interval under review here.

As can be seen in Figure 2 (see Appendix) the opening phrases of *Onipa Beyee Bioo*, another of Nketia art songs, similarly end with falling fourths. The fall of a fourth in melodic progression can be found on numerous occasions in Nketia's choral works also, normally in the tenor or another inner part. In the coda of *Monkamfo No* ("Lets Praise Him" [God]), for example, specifically in the tenor and bass parts/tones on the penultimate statement of the text, *Nnipa mma nyina gye,* in measures 75 into 76, the tenor moves from lowered leading-tone to the subdominant ("taw" to "fah") as the bass shades the tenor in parallel thirds, thus descending with a fourth, from the domiant to supertonic ("soh" to "re"). The preceding is excerpted in Figure 3 (see Appendix).

Also, I have paid close attention to the characteristic manner in which Nketia stylistically harmonizes these falling melodic fourths and have observed that they vary according to the modal or tonal shifts. However, the consistency with which he harmonizes the falling subdominant to the tonic or "fah" to "doh" is the focus of this essay. And as I noted in my thesis about *Onipa Beyee Bio,*

> Bars 2 into 3 with an interrupted (deceptive) cadence speaks loudly of an Nketia idiomatic harmonic vocabulary. He is fond of harmonizing the melodic progression of the subdominant to the tonic with a dominant seventh chord resolving to the tonic or its substitute chord, submediant....Nketia omits the fifth of the dominant seventh chord and doubles the seventh since one should resolve onto the mediant and the other in the melody falling a fourth onto tonic (Dor 1992: 202).

After providing this visual illustration from the song "Onipa beyee bi" ("Man cannot accomplish everything in life)," I played an excerpt from "Wonya Amane" which is more lively and suitable for the celebratory occasion (Nketia 90 Conference).

In the penultimate and final phrases of this art song, Nketia again uses the falling melodic fourth idiom and characteristically harmonizes them with his dominant seventh chord at interrupted (deceptive) and perfect (full) cadences, respectively. It was performed by the Ghana National Symphony Orchestra with Kweku Yeboah (bass), and conducted by Isaac Annoh.[11] I did the orchestral arrangement to this Nketia art song in 1996.[12]

Personally, *Wonya Amane* is a powerfully moving song. It was its appeal that inspired me to arrange it for the symphony orchestra, and I thought my decision to add the Akan *sikyi* dance rhythm played by the percussion adds to its beauty. Further, when I played the excerpt from the DVD to illustrate my presentation, I was very happy that the Ghana National Symphony Orchestra could perform and record Nketia's composition for me just days before the September 2011 conference. To me, their gesture could be regarded as their contribution to the celebration of a very reputable Ghanaian. Yet, recapturing the atmosphere of the presentation, I was overjoyed by the presence of Emeritus Professor Nketia himself to listen to my paper on his idiomatic chord. Moreover, the orchestral version of the art song constituted a novelty to the many informed listeners present at the session, as some of them could not hide their affective responses. They included Akosua Perbi (Professor Nketia's daughter),[13] Mary Esther Kropp Dakubu, Nissio Fiagbedzi, Misonu Amu, Jacqueline DjeDje, Kofi Anyidoho, Patience Kwakwa, Patricia Opondo, Trevor Wiggens, James Makubuya, Eric Beeko, T. E. Andoh, and Godwin Agyei. More telling however, each time I hear the falling melodic fourth at cadences such as in *Wonya Amane*, it evokes a special Akan and Ewedome folksy sentiment in me. But what is the ontological source of this melodic idiom?

Exploring the Ontology of the Nketia Dominant Seventh Chord

Although the regular dominant seventh chord and the processes involved in Nketia's understanding and use of it are *a priori* to his transformation and use of his version of the chord, my intent here is not to go back to Hugo Riemann or Jean-Philippe Rameau with regard to detailed theoretical discourse on chords and harmony. Thousands of art, jazz, and popular musicians—professionals, amateurs, and students--use the dominant seventh chord without even questioning its origins. Of course, theorists do, and music historians may want to find out whether it was really Monteverdi or somebody else who first used the dominant seventh chord in his compositions. For me, what aroused my curiosity was the factors that motivated or compelled Nketia to have transformed the dominant seventh chord into his own stylistic idiom. Also, I consider it rudimentary to be spending time on questions on how did Nketia know about and could apply the dominant seventh chord. Though it may be important for some, a substantial body of literature exists on the effects and legacies of colonialism, Westernization, Christianization, globalization on many music cultures of the world. To be sure, specific biographical information on Nketia's enculturation is also available in other sources that I have cited earlier in this essay. What is important to address is to seek an understanding of the reasons for which I have not seen this chord in the works of Amu or Nayo, the other Ghanaian composers whose works I studied, though they have their own idiosyncrasies. Moreover, no Western (European, American) composer, to the best of my knowledge, used this version of the chord before Nketia, a consideration that dismisses the presupposition of a possible appropriation, and rather affirms innovative originality.

Thus in response to the ontological question of which factors including processes provoked the Nketia dominant seventh chord into existence, I argue that it was his innovative effort at harmonizing a typical Akan melodic structure involving a falling melodic fourth at a cadence, within the creative framework of a synthesized intercultural idiom. For, I argue that there would not have been any Nketia dominant seventh chord without this falling fourth at a cadence. Yet in retrospect, another question concerns the source of the falling melodic fourth as an idiomatic nuance in Nketia's works. To answer this question, I deem it appropriate to quote Nketia himself from a 1990 letter regarding his compositional resources, training, and style, and it reads:

> Dear Mr. Dor, Thank you for your letter of April 27 delivered to me in London by Dr. Willie Anku. . . The Festschrift you have been reading naturally puts a greater emphasis on my scholarly work than my creative output, although there is some correlations between the two. Indeed it was my interest in composition and poetry that led me to collect Akan songs in 1942-44 and then proceed from my creative understanding of the materials to their scholarly study almost a decade later when I became a Research Fellow in the Department of Sociology at the University of Ghana. The experiences of consciously collecting and learning Akan songs not only reinforced the models I knew from childhood but also enlarged my awareness of certain principles of construction in the areas of melody, rhythm, multipart organization and form in traditional music, something I explore in all my compositions (Dor 1992: 396).[14]

The preceding quotation also explains the strong reflexivity of Nketia's cumulative cultural consciousness in his creative works. During the Nketia 90 Conference, I vividly remember a session during which Nketia himself reinforced or even clarified his enculturation, sources of pre-compositional materials, and creative techniques after presentations by Beeko and Peebi on his works. He emphasized the importance of folk tales and other narratives forms, folk songs, poetic devices in traditional poetry, and related aspects of his enculturation and mastery of his culture. Also, in his article on "Developing Contemporary Idioms out of Traditional Music," Nketia provides composers' construction of "originality, authenticity, and identity" (1982:84) as motivating factors that derive from an Africanist art music composer's creative philosophy when drawing on his/his traditional music. It is really difficult for a musician who is well informed and familiar with Akan musical traditions and Western art music to fail to recognize and acknowledge Nketia's ability and success at achieving a homogeneous synthesis, in Hegelian terms, in his intercultural art compositions. During various conversations I had with Geoffrey Boateng and Gyima Labi in the 1990s, when we were all then at the University of Ghana's Music Department, we had remarked about and admired this Nketia's masterful strength. Certainly, the falling fourth is part of the "principles of construction in the areas of melody" that he wrote about in his letter that I have referenced above. But do other music cultures or composers use the falling melodic forth at the cadence?

Although it must be noted that Stravinsky used a falling fourth melodic interval to end some phrases in his "Rite of Springs" and "Petruska" in the minor key, involving the melodic progression of "m-r-l" (dominant, subdominant, and tonic). It is believed that this melodic idiom is a trait of Russian folk music's influence on Stravinsky. Some popular music singers also end a few of their songs in a falling melodic fourth. However, any listener with an informed knowledge about Akan music will readily recognize the source of this melodic idiom as part of the broader Akanness of Nketia's art compositions. While it will be too challenging for me to propose any explanation of how all fourths in the Akan melodic system came into being, I can at least share my observations on how a procedure of melodic variation can generate wider melodic intervals.

Published in 1995, Nketia wrote the article "Generative Processes in *Seprewa*[15] Music" as his contribution to the Festschrift that honors Rose Brandel. Two subject themes in this essay relate to this presentation and my other research. These are:

(1) the vertical relatedness of tones and (2) the substitution of melodic tones. In certain traditional African musical practices, specific tones within the set are harmonically related to each other. While Nketia (1995) calls them "related tones," John Blacking similarly notes the prevalence of "companion tones" in Venda vocal music (1970), and further, Gerhard Kubik (1994) calls the same phenomenon "counter-harmonic tones" as evident in many East African ethnic musical genres. Also, I have corroborated the preceding findings in my own research on the generation of concurrent pitch sonorities in the vocal musical systems of both the Anlo and Ewedome of Ghana (Dor 2000; 2005).

I have defined melodic commutation elsewhere as "a process of melodic variation in which certain tones are substituted by functionally related ones" (Dor 2005: 227). Drawing on perspectives from Nketia (1994) and also Simha Arom (1991: 222), who both have discussed melodic commutation, I have explored the salience of the process in my dissertation and later published an essay on this theme in the Akin Euba Festschrift (Dor 2000: 226-233, 2005: 227-246). In that essay I focused on the extent to which melodic commutation not only has implications for the generation of concurrent pitch sonorities, but also for the tone-tune debate, and in a more recent presentation at SEM 2010 in Los Angeles, I pointed out that analysts that abstract scales from melodies need to take melodic commutation into account before reaching their conclusions on the number of tones used in a particular melody. But specifically related to this essay, I focus on the wider melodic intervals that melodic commutation generates. Operating within the framework of the heptatonic tonal set, for example, Akan, Ga, and Northern Ewe singers may draw on their awareness of the relatedness of the tone "me" to "doh" and thus substitute "me" with "doh" when descending from "fa" upon the return or repeat of the same melodic phrase, thereby varying the progression of "fa" to "me" to become "fa" to "do." Similarly, the lowered leading tone "taw" may resolve to "fa" instead of going to a stepwise "la," or "re" to "la" in the place of "doh," and "soh" to "re" rather than "soh" preceding to "fa". These falling melodic fourths have become so common a feature of Akan, Ga, and Ewedome melodies that a formalist may simply observe and describe their pertinence without spending any time on the processes that bring them into being. Admittedly, a composer may place a premium on other creative concerns of phonemic tone, melodic goal, melodic beauty and affect in opting for a wider melodic interval, factors that I have discussed elsewhere.

Affect and My Application of the Chord

I recall how on one afternoon in the mid 1990s I met Emeritus Professor Nketia coming out of his International Center for African Music and Dance (ICAMD) office at the School of Performing Arts, University of Ghana, Legon, and as he wanted to know whether I was a Northern or Southern Ewe he asked me a question that I always remember. For, he framed the question in a humorous way as he asked, Dor, are you also *a borborbor* man? I answered "Yes Prof." However, it was rather my knowledge of the tonal resources and procedures of the *aviha,* female laments, *gabada* social dance, and *akpi,* war dance that provided me with the Ewedome (inland Ewe) source of the melodic fourth (Agawu 1990, 1995; Dor 2000: 2005: 234-240), similar to the Akan melodic feature that Nketia harmonized with this unique chord. It follows that the preceding is simply a reaffirmation of the commonplace parallels between the tonal resources of the Akan and Ewedome. Yet beyond my familiarity with such commonalities, it is the appeal of the chord or its affective impact on me that inspired the impulse in me to use it in some of my orchestral and art choral works. For, as the Ewe metaphor goes "it is the sumptuous soup that draws the stool *Detsivivi yehea zikpui.* Accordingly, whenever I have drawn on an extant Ewedome melody or I have composed a new one in the veins of the *aviha* or *gabada* genres including the characteristic cadential melodic idiom, the Nketia dominant seventh chord was one of my best choices.

Classic examples of my original compositions in which I used this chord include a simple one movement orchestral piece I composed in the stylistic streak of Kwabena Nketia and Seth Dor, my father, and which I have named "Echoes from Kwabena Nketia and Seth Dor." The Nketia dominant seventh chord abounds in the second half of the A Section of the piece, which is in ternary form. In Figure 6 (see Appendix) is the melody and examples of the Nketia Dominant Seventh Chord used in the piece. I cannot forget how this piece moved Professor Akosua Perbi and as I turned she stood up and was dancing to the highlife rhythm of this example. Similarly, I decided to make my presentation a celebratory one in which I expressed myself more in a free Ghanaian presentation mode than a rigid formal paper, and it was perhaps my swinging to the beat that partly encouraged others to express their reception outwardly. Further, my employment of this chord in my choral works is exemplified in an excerpt: "//: Afeto Yesu, Akpe na wo :// Woe kpefu de tanye ı'a `titsoga nuti, Afeto Yesue, Akpe na wo" (//: Lord Jesus, thank You :// You suffered on my behalf on the cross. Lord Jesus, thank you!) (See Figure 7 in Appendix).

As can be seen, the first melodic phrase ends with a falling fourth involving the supertonic to submediant, (r – l), for which there is no use of the Nketia Dominant Seventh chord. But upon a sequential repeat in the second phrase that ends in "doh" to "soh," another falling fourth, this interval becomes "fah" to "doh" in the dominant key. Accordingly, I decided to harmonize this second cadence in Nketian Dominant Seventh to Tonic in D major (Nk^v/v to $^1/v$) because the home key is G. Further, when the longer melodic phrase returns into the home key, and the melody gets into a higher registral field, I once again used the NkV_7 which harmonizes the idiomatic falling fourth. When one combines the effects of all three melodic phrases concluding in falling fourths, with the lyrics that speak about gratitude for Christ's suffering on the cross, this portion of the part-song invokes, and at the same time, is inspired by the *aviha*, Ewedome female laments that I mentioned earlier.

Also, in the episode of the Second Movement of my "Fraternity Suite," I have a few instances of this chord because I based the section on a popular Ewedome *aviha* song, **Wonutia dome, nye meyie wonutia dome o** (The traditional arbitration, I am not going to the arbitration).
The best example of this chord can be located toward the end of the episode or the B Section in F major, and it occurs just before the return to the A section in B flat major, and as in Figure 8 (see Appendix).

Something special happened during all my musical illustrations and I am deliberately adding these narratives, which I believe will enhance the paper and suggest the excitement with which people received my advocacy for the chord. When I was singing the preceding Northern Ewe folksong, Misonu Amu, Kofi Anyidoho, and Bertha Adom, who are all Ewe and know this song very well volitionally joined me with one of them even harmonizing in a parallel third. The paper was different from the several scholarly papers I have given. The audience was very receptive, joined in as though it was a story telling context, and it was indeed a celebratory tribute to the innovative composer who graced the presentation with his presence and participation.

Advocacy and Conclusion

From 1992 to 1996 when I taught harmony and compositional techniques at the Music Department of the then University College of Education, Winneba, I made it a point to train my students to learn to compose in the stylistic veins of Amu, Nketia, and Nayo. After teaching the dominant seventh chord, I would continue to teach the dominant thirteenth and then conclude with the Nketia dominant seventh chord as one of his idiosyncrasies. While I believe Bright Amankwa, George Essilfie, Eric Beeko, Joshua Amuah, Divine Gbagbo, among several of my students still remember our discussion of this chord, I can only believe that they continue to use it in their original compositions or arrangements. Furthermore, I recommend the appropriate usage of this chord when re-harmonizing even extant Ghanaian highlife tunes including *Yema mua Afrihyia Pa*. Specifically, on *Papa ne yeo, Bone ko o*, one could harmonize the first *kó o* with a subdominant to tonic progression in the original key, and then when the melodic phrase is repeated, the doh-soh in the melody on *kó o* could be harmonized as "fah" to "doh" in the dominant key, thus offering a good opportunity to use the Nketia Dominant Seventh Chord. I am advocating the relevance of teaching this chord to our students, not only because it is associated with Nketia, but also it harmonizes a melodic progression that is typically idiomatic of some Ghanaian ethnic music traditions. Further, let us popularize this chord to the awareness of the larger global community of art music. I have already done so at the invitation of John Latartara, my colleague, to share about the chord with his sophomore music theory class at my university, after I returned to the US from the Nketia 90 Conference. I am looking forward to other opportunities to discuss this stylistic nuance. To me, it does not matter when skeptics undermine my advocacy with the excuse of a probable insignificance of a single added tone. I am encouraged by the fact that only a single tone differentiates the Italian, French, and German augmented sixth chords from each other. If we can have these chords as well as the Neapolitan sixth, why not popularize the Nketia Dominant Seventh Chord into the Ghanaian Dominant Seventh Chord.

Endnotes

1: I thank the University of Mississippi, especially the Department of Music, and Office of Multicultural Affairs, for support that in part sponsored my trip to Ghana for the Nketia90 Conference.

2: My personal background as a Ghanaian, a Pitt alumnus who was mentored by Emeritus Professor Akin Euba--one of Nketia's doctoral students, as a teacher and researcher of African music, as well as a past Co-Chair of the African Music Section [AfMS] of the Society for Ethnomusicology, makes the importance of Nketia's scholarly legacy to my career, just as to hundreds of other Africanists', implicitly evident.

3: A classic example was during the Africa Meets North America Symposium held in 2009 at UCLA, which I also attended.

4: African art music compositions are now routinely part of such test pieces. In the late 1990s into early 1990s I accompanied candidates at Mawuli Secondary, Ho, Accra Girls Secondary School, among others. I was for more than a decade an Examiner for music on behalf of the West African Examination Council.

5: These two pieces have been recorded by TrinityDigitalGhana and posted on YouTube.

6: Rev. Dr. Joyce Aryee is one of Ghana's accomplished politicians who had served as the country's Minister of Information, Education, Local Government, and Democracy at various times from 1982 to 2001. She was also a Member of the National Defense Council, and Chief Executive of the Ghana Chamber of Mines. But her leadership in the promotion of Ghanaian Choral art music resides in the fact that she is now a Reverend Minister and leads a Ministry that is projecting Ghanaian art music in a phenomenal way.

7: He expresses this wish in the 1990 letter he wrote to me and it is in this essay. (See Appendix of this essay also).

8: I was disappointed that other established Ghanaian art music composers could not attend this conference. My consolation is that they should have legitimate reasons and excuses.

9: Supervisors of this thesis were Dr. A. A. R. Turkson and Professor Atta Annan Mensah. Dr. Asante Darkwa was then the department chair.

10: Although I performed illustrative examples during the presentation in September 2011, I use only sketchy scores to prove my points in this essay.

11: This recording was done in September 2011 purposely for this presentation. Isaac Annoh is the current Director of the National Symphony Orchestra.

12: It was first performed along with works of Amu, Nayo, Dosoo, Gbeho, Blege, and my original compositions during the First African Composers Series at the National Theatre.

13: Professor Nketia's daughter is a Professor of History at the University of Ghana.

14: He wrote this letter when he was the Mellon Professor of Music at the University of Pittsburgh, PA.

15: Professor Kwabena Nektia loves the music of the Akan *Seperewa*. Befittingly, Osei Korankye of the Ghana Dance Ensemble during the Conference sang a praise poetry and accompanied himself on the *seperewa* to honor Professor Kwabena Nketia.

References

Agawu, Kofi. 1990. "Variation Procedures in Northern Ewe Music." *Ethnomusicology* 34(2): 221-143.

Akrofi, Eric. 2003. *Sharing Knowledge and Experience: A Profile of Kwabena Nketia.* Accra: Afram Publications.

Arom, Simha. 1991 (1985). *African Polyphony and Polyrhythm: Musical Structure and Methodology.* Translated by Martin Thom,

Barbara Tuckett and Raymond Boyd. Cambridge: Cambridge University Press.

Blacking, John. 1970. "Tonal Organization in Venda Music." *Ethnomusicology* 14(1): 1-56.

DjeDje, Jacqueline Cogdell, ed. 1992. *African Musicology: Current Trends. Volume II. A Festschrift Presented to J. H. Kwabena Nketia.* Los Angeles: UCLA International Studies and Overseas Program/The James Coleman African Studies Center and Crossroads Press/African Studies Association.

DjeDje, Jacqueline Cogdell, and William G. Carter, eds. 1989. *African Musicology: Current Trends. Volume I. A Festschrift Presented to .J. H. Kwabena Nketia.* Los Angeles: UCLA African Studies Center and African Arts Magazine and Crossroads Press/African Studies Association.

Dor, George Worlasi Kwasi. 1991. "Trends and Stylistic Traits in the Art Compositions of E. Amu, N.Z. Nayo, and J.H.K. Nketia: A Theoretical Perspective." M.Phil. thesis, University of Ghana, Legon.

___. 1991. "Fraternity Symphonic Suite." Unpublished Handwritten Score.

___. 1994 ."Echoes from Nketia and Seth Dor." Unpublished Orchestra score

___. 1994. "Afeto Yesu, Akpe na Mo." Unpublished Handwritten Choral Score.

___. 2000. "Tonal Resources and Compositional Processes in Ewe Traditional Vocal Music." PhD. dissertation, University of Pittsburgh.

___. 2004. "Communal Creativity and Song Ownership in Anlo Ewe Musical Practice: The Case of *Havorlu.*" *Ethnomusicology* 48 (1): 26-51.

___. 2005. "Empowering the Neglected Voices in Ethnomusicology: Euba's Contribution." In *Multiple Interpretations of Dynamics of Creativity and Knowledge in African Music Traditions: A Festschrift in Honor of Akin Euba on The Occasion of His 70th Birthday.* Ed. by Bode Omojola and George Dor. Point Richmond, CA: Music Research Institute.

___. 2005. "Melodic Commutation and Concurrent Pitch Sonorities in Ewe Songs: A Pre-Compositional Resource for African Art Music." In *Multiple Interpretations of Dynamics of Creativity and Knowledge in African Music Traditions: A Festschrift in Honor of Akin Euba on The Occasion of His 70th Birthday.* Ed. by Bode Omojola and George Dor. Point Richmond, CA: Music Research Institute Press.

___. 2005. "African Musicology: Current Research and Future Directions." In *Multiple Interpretations of Dynamics of Creativity and Knowledge in African Music Traditions: A Festschrift in Honor of Akin Euba on The Occasion of His 70th Birthday.* Ed. by Bode Omojola and George Dor. Point Richmond, CA: Music Research Institute Press.

Euba, Akin. 1989. *Essays on Music in Africa 2: Intercultural Perspectives.* Bayreuth: Bayreuth African Studies.

___. 2001. "Issues in Africanist Musicology: Do We Need Ethnomusicology in Africa?" In *Proceedings of the Forum for Revitalizing African Music Studies in Higher Education.* Ed. by Frank Gunderson. Ann Arbor, Michigan: The U. S. Secretariat of the International Center for African Music and Dance, The International Institute, University of Michigan.

Kimberlin, Cynthia Tse and Akin Euba, eds. 2005. *Towards An African Pianism: Keyboard Music of Africa and the Diaspora.* 2 vols. Point Richmond, CA.: Music Research Institute (MRI).

Kubik, Gerhard. 1994. *Theory of African Music. Vol 1.* Wilhelmshaven: Florian Moetzal Verlag.

Labi, Gyima.1997. *Dialects in African Pianism.* Legon, Ghana: University of Ghana Press.

Nketia, Kwabena J. H. 1994. *African Pianism.* Legon, Ghana: ICAMD (International Center for African Music and Dance).

___. 1982. "Developing Contemporary Idioms out of Traditional Music." *Studio Musicologica Academiae,* T.

24, Supplementum: Report of the Musicological Congress of the International Music Council, 81-97.

____. 1990. "Contextual Strategies of Inquiry and Systematization." Charles Seeger Memorial Lecture, 1989. *Ethnomusicology* 34(1): 75-97.

____. 1994. *African Pianism: Twelve Pedagogical Pieces.* Accra: Afram Publications.

____. 1995. "Generative Processes in *Seperewa* Music." In *The Four Corners: A Festschrift in Honor of* Rose Brandel. Ed. by Ellen Leichtman. Warren, Mich.: Harmonie Park Press.

____. 1998. "The Scholarly Study of African Music: A Historical Review." In *Garland Encyclopedia of World Music, Volume 1: Africa.* Ed. by Ruth Stone. New York: Garland Publishing, 13-73.

Nketia, J.H.K. and Jacqueline Cogdell DjeDje. 2004. *African Art Music.* Accra: Afram Publications.

____. 1984. "Introduction: Trends in African Ethnomusicology." In *Selected Reports in Ethnomusicology. Vol. 5. Studies in African Music.* Los Angeles: UCLA Program in Ethnomusicology, Department of Music.

Nyaho, William Chapman, ed. 2009. *Piano Music of Africa and the African Diaspora.* New York: Oxford University Press.

Omojola, Bode. 2001. "African Pianism as an Intercultural Compositional Framework: A Study of the Piano Works of Akin Euba." *Research in African Literatures* 32(2): 153-174.

Wachsmann, Klaus. 1966. "The Trend of Musicology in Africa." *Selected Reports* 1(1): 61-65.

____. 1967. "The State of African Musicology." In *African Studies of Makerere 1961-66. A Report.* Kampala: Makerere University College, 82-93.

____. 1969. "Ethnomusicology in African Studies: The Next Twenty Years." In *Expanding Horizons.* Ed. by Gwendolen M. Carter and Ann Paden. Evanston: Northwestern University Press, 131-142.

____. 1970. "Ethnomusicology in Africa." In *The African Experience, Volume I. Essays.* Ed. by John N. Paden and Edward Soja. Evanston: Northwestern University Press, 128-151.

Wiggins, Trevor and J. H. Kwabena Nketia. 2005. "An Interview with J. H. Kwabena Nketia: Perspectives on Tradition and Modernity." *Ethnomusicology Forum* 14(1): 57-81.

Appendix

Figure 1: Falling Fourths in the Two Opening Phrases of "Yaanom Montie"

Figure 2: Falling Fourths in the Two Opening Phrases of "Onipa Beyee Bioo"

Figure 3: Falling Fourths in the Tenor and Bass at the Coda of "Monkamfo Mo"

Nketia Dominat Seventh Chord in Onipa Beyee Bi

Figure 4: Nketia Dominant Seventh Chord and Medolic Fourth in "Onipa Beyee Bio"

Wonya Amane

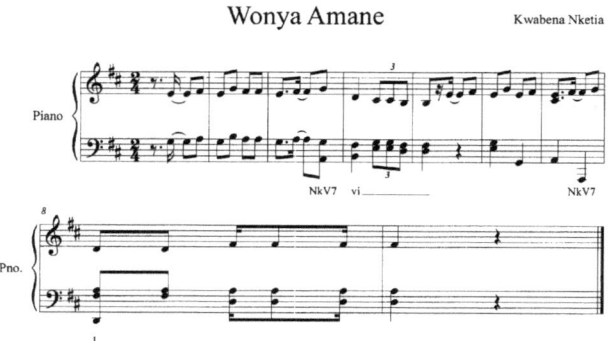

Figure 5: Piano Introduction to "Wonya Amane"

Excerpts from Echoes

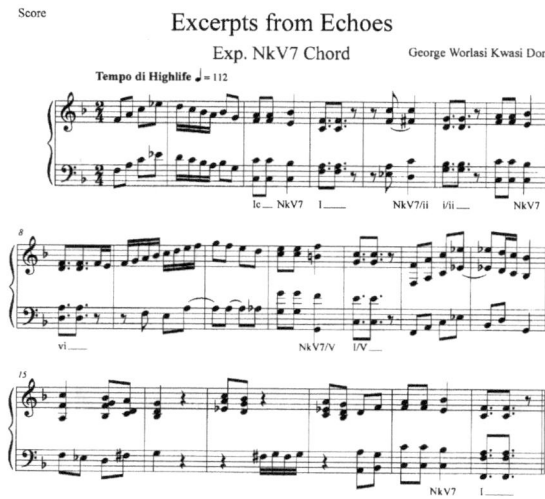

Figure 6: Nketia Dominant Chord in Excerpt from "Echoes"

Afeto Yesu Akpe Na Wo
Lord Jesus, Thank You!

George Worlasi Kwasi Dor

Figure 7: "Afeto Yesu Akpe Na Wo"

Excerpt from "Fraternity Suite," 2nd Movt.

George Worlasi Kwasi Dor

Figure 8: Excerpt from "Fraternity Suite," 2nd Movement

6

Abena Kyere and
Akosua Adomako Ampofo
Bridget Chinouriri

DISCOURSES OF GENDER

J.H. Kwabena Nketia Festschrift

Women Doing Music: The Lives and Songs of Contemporary Ghanaian Women Musicians

Abena Kyere and Akosua Adomako Ampofo

Abena Kyere is a teaching assistant in the Centre for Gender Studies and Advocacy at the University of Ghana, Legon. She has an MPhil degree in African Studies from the University of Ghana and serves as the research assistant for the Changing Representations of Women in Popular Music in Ghana project. Her research interests include gender and popular culture, gender and development, gender and religion as well as children's literature.

Akosua Adomako Ampofo is professor of African and Gender Studies, and the director of the Institute of African Studies at the University of Ghana, Legon. An activist-scholar, her work addresses African knowledge systems, higher education, reproductive health, identity politics, gender-based violence, women's work, masculinities, and popular culture. With Signe Arnfred she co-edited *African Feminist Research and Activism - Tensions, Challenges and Possibilities* (2009). She is founding vice president of The African Studies Association of Africa (ASAA), and co-president of the Research Committee on Women and Society of the International Sociological Association. In 2014, Professor Akosua Ampofo was a Mellon Fellow in the Centre for African Studies at the University of Cape Town. In 2010, she won the prestigious Sociologists for Women in Society Feminist Activism award.

Introduction

This Festschrift is about honoring a man who has made enormous contributions to music, about an intrinsic thread that weaves together the various facets of our very lives, as individuals and as communities—for as Nketia himself notes (1974), for us Africans music is a communal affair. Our societies have a strong tradition of music making and it is considered as a "site of memory" (Vambe, 2011). Family genealogies, state histories as well as happenings for so-called ordinary people were, and still are recorded in music. The enduring nature of Ghanaian music traditions bears repeating for the lay reader; it lies in the fact that all members of the societal fabric have the opportunity to create and perform music that is meaningful to their contexts (Kyere 2013). There is no social event, no rite of passage, no celebration of the joyous or marker of pain that is not accompanied by music among Ghanaian societies. According to Asiedu and Adomako Ampofo (2011) the ability of cultural products and popular culture to reflect and influence society therefore means that "these products cannot be taken for granted as they potentially have the power to shape the consciousness of society" (2011:1). Music thus provides a platform for us to be a part of each other's existence.

In the creation and performance of music and its traditions, typically different spaces were created for men and women, the old and young, initiated and not-yet-initiated, the ritual and secular, although there were instances when these groups performed music together in a communal spirit. Engaging in any discussion about Ghanaian music without examining the role of women would provide an incomplete picture, and yet much of the discourse focuses on men and the full participation of women in popular music in Ghana remains untold. It is true that although popular musicians are both male and female, the industry is male dominated. Indeed, the few women that initially found their way into the popular music arena were typically members of male dominated bands, mentored by male musicians and with male managers (Asante-Darko & Van der Geest 1983). However, the gap in the literature on women in popular music cannot simply be due to the limited number of women musicians in the secular arena, but the lack of attention given to their lives and work as artistic or worth studying. When women have been mentioned it has often been as a footnote, or else their roles in traditional or gospel music has been the focus (Sutherland-Addy, 2006).

And yet, women have been and continue to be active participants in the creation and performance of songs in Ghana. In this chapter, we turn the searchlight on contemporary women popular musicians, examining their careers and relationship to their music. For the purpose of this study popular music will be limited to highlife and hip-life. This type of music is patronized across generations, sex and class in Ghana. We argue that Ghanaian women's approach to song making, the songs they sing, and their lives and trajectories as musicians differ from those of men. Because music and musicians are powerful, reflecting on society's experiences, but also influencing the way people see and experience the world, including expectations for appropriate gendered behaviors and gender relations (Adomako Ampofo and Asiedu 2012),
we argue that women's place in this project is significant.

Women and Music

Traditionally there are many spaces available for the creation and performance of music in Ghanaian society, typically with different spaces accorded by social location—for men and women, the old and young, initiated and not-yet-initiated, the ritual and secular. For example, *Momome* songs, *Nwonkoro, Adenkum, nsuie, nmane tora,* and *avihe,* are some of the song types that have been strictly in the domain of women (Adjei, 2011). *Momome* songs are an example of how women participated in the Ghanaian political space through song. Among the Asante, women performed these songs to encourage male soldiers on the battlefield (Aidoo, 1985; Arhin, 1983). Women were also known for their praise songs that supported political office holders in their quest to win or retain power, a tradition which several contemporary African politicians have appropriated to their political advantage (Gilman, 2001). In the religious arena, women have performed songs for deities and ancestors—songs of praise, supplication and appreciation. Women have, and continue to sing to mark life stages. They have performed lullabies for their babies and also used songs to vent their frustrations against husbands, in-laws, co-wives and life's challenges in general (Allan et al. 2005). The composition and performance of songs associated with nubility rites among the Akan of Ghana is strictly the domain of women (Sarpong, 1977). Songs for these rites served as a form of education for the neophytes, preparing them for their duties as mothers, wives and adult lineage members. Most of these nubility songs can be characterized by their explicit description of sexual relations. Even in death women are central. They perform dirges, which are performances honoring the dead, messages of condolences for the family of the deceased, as well as historical chronicles tracing the deeds of the deceased and her or his family for the benefit of the living.

Beyond the communal social space that Ghanaian women occupy when it comes to musical performance, women have also sung to entertain themselves. Such recreational songs include *Nwonkoro, Adenkum* and those songs that accompany work (Evans, 1981). Recreational songs such as the *Nwonkoro* often centered on relations with loved ones and prominent citizens. In recent times this genre has been adopted into Christian church music in praise hymns to God. *Lɛnlɛ* is a song type produced and performed by young women purely for their own entertainment. The various themes raised by these young women opens a window for us into their lives and their society. *Lɛnlɛ* songs allude to concerns such as "sexual relationships between men and women; peer group relations and associations; the carefree life of the teenager, the daily chores of the unmarried." The authors also find that the songs contain eroticism. The songs hint at tensions between the younger and older generations expressed in veiled criticisms of older women and husbands. What these young women are doing is to appropriate a long tradition of songs of abuse which the less privileged such as the youth, daughters-in-law, and women more generally, have used to make their feelings and concerns known to the more powerful in society (Allan et al., 2005; Agovi 1995). Interestingly, there is also praise for hard work and achievement. Some of the songs performed by women in the 1950s and 1960s reflect Ghana's political climate at the time. There were many songs praising Kwame Nkrumah, who would later become Ghana's first president. Contrary to the silences in writings of political scientists and historians, a study of women's music reveals that women were not only politically conscious, or merely involved in local community politics, but they were also active participants in national politics.

Through these diverse genres and song types, Ghanaian women have expressed their concerns and their pains, and announced their triumphs and survival to the world. This long tradition of singing has been carried over into today's commercial music scene, and in this chapter we examine women's roles in the contemporary song-making industry via three perspectives: music consumers' perceptions of women musicians, themes that women sing about, and finally women musicians' trajectories in, and relationships with, the music industry.

Although traditionally women played important roles as musicians and performers, until around 1960, modern highlife in West Africa was predominantly a male affair (Asante-Darko & Van der Geest, 1983; Collins 2003). In much of Africa, as in the rest of the world, not only did men dominate the contemporary popular music scene, as musicians and managers, but women, where they did participate, were typically portrayed as being incapable of holding a regular profession, and as sexually loose. Writing of his native Côte d'Ivoire, Aicha Kone states, "not all families will accept a woman to be an artist and embrace her as a bride..." (Harvey, 1992 cited in Collins 2003: 1). In his own work titled *Ghanaian Women Enter into Popular Entertainment,* Collins (2003) provides a trajectory of the hurdles that women have had to overcome to find their space in the contemporary world of music and acting. Women's entrance into the music arena in Ghana started with their involvement in the concert party in the 1950s, where they were first recruited to perform on the stage. This gave them the exposure that had hitherto been denied them. However, when we take a closer look at the songs performed by men and women this reveals differences in the themes and issues that they are concerned with. In his work on the music industry in Ghana, Wright (1995) notes that popular songs by women normally revolved around "common feminine identifiable ideas (community and family for example). However, while a lot of work has been done on men and their place in 20th century secular popular music, including recent works on Ghanaian hiplife by authors such as Osumare (2012) and Shipley (2013) much less attention has been paid to women musicians and their works. Women's entrance and sustenance in the industry, and the kinds of songs they sing are yet to be significantly analyzed from either an individual or socio-cultural context. Neither has there been any systematic analysis of changes in the themes addressed by women over the years. We hope that this brief essay will provide a window, albeit a small one, into this neglected area.

Methodology

This chapter is born out of research carried out as part of a larger, multi-country project exploring *Pathways to Women's Empowerment,* under the auspices of The Centre for Gender Studies and Advocacy (CEGENSA) at the University of Ghana. The particular project that this chapter was originally inspired from is titled "Changing Representations of Women in Popular Music" in which the principal researchers, Adomako Ampofo and Asiedu, examine changing representations of women in popular songs and suggest how alternative, more empowering representations can be promoted. Over 250 songs covering the 1930s to 2009 were collected, transcribed, and are being translated. Two workshops were conducted with musicians, radio DJs and others associated with the music industry to allow scholars and practitioners to engage on the subject of women's representations in music. Focus group discussions were held with taxi drivers and students, two groups who are avid music consumers. Finally, a song competition was held to encourage alternative representations of women in popular music in Ghana. The wining songs were then launched on various electronic and print media.

While this chapter alludes to findings from the WE-RPC study by Adomako Ampofo and Asiedu, it focuses primarily on data from the first author's M.Phil. fieldwork for which she interviewed music producers and ten Ghanaian female musicians. Space will not allow us to refer to this entire data set and so here we focus primarily on interviews held with three of the women musicians, Awurama Badu, Akosua Agyepong, and Belinda Nana Akua Amoah, aka Mzbel, representing careers that stretch from the 1980s, a period that saw an influx of women onto the contemporary music scene, to the early post-millennium years.

Awurama Badu, aged 70 at the time of the interview in 2011, became well known in the 1980s for her now classic song *Medofo Adaada Me*, lit., "my lover had deceived me." Like many women musicians of her era, she was a member of a predominantly male band. Born into a family of musicians, Awurama Badu wanted to sing from an early age. After her secondary school education she went to work as a nursing assistant, married and had all her (four) children before joining the police force. Awurama Badu was recruited into the police force as a typist but when she later found out that the police band wanted new members, she auditioned and was selected. Eventually combining her work as a typist and band member proved too much for her and she eventually quit the police service to be a full time musician although she continued to play with the police band. Although Awurama Badu has not composed any new songs in many years, she still performs her old songs, which appeal to a wide audience.

Akosua Agyepong started singing professionally after she graduated from secondary school in 1990. She came to the public's attention not only because she was very attractive, as many women performers are, but she presented a rather afrocentric image and had a fairly good education having recently graduated from one of the more prestigious all-girl high schools. Akosua married Nat Brew, aka Amandziba, a well-known Ghanaian musician and together with Rex Omar they formed the trio Nakorex, which released and performed several hit songs, mainly highlife music. Akosua and Amandziba eventually divorced and she vanished from the music scene for many years. She later had a religious conversion, married a pastor and when she resurfaced on the music scene in 2000 it was with a gospel album. She now runs a television show *Girls, Girls*, meant to encourage young women to lead wholesome lives, and is a regular judge on reality TV music competitions. She also opened a restaurant in 1996, has acted in at least two movies. At the time of her interview in 2011, she was working on a new album.

Belinda Nana Akua Amoah (Mzbel) literally burst onto the music scene in 2000 with her hit song *Awoso me*, lit., "it moved me". Her name has become synonymous with controversy, partly because her songs and music videos have overt sexual overtones in terms of lyrics and dance movements. However, the controversy surrounding her has not been limited to her music. In 2005, during a concert at one of Ghana's universities, Mzbel was sexually harassed as a group of young men pulled her off stage, tore off her clothes and allegedly fondled her breasts and crotch. Barely a year later, in 2006, she was attacked by armed robbers, and it was alleged that she, along with some of her female dancers, was raped—although she herself denied the rape story. Then in 2011, she had an unfortunate encounter with the police. It was reported that she had physically attacked a police officer who had tried to book her for a traffic offence. The reaction of the public to these incidents was largely judgmental and negative. Indeed, there were many who thought that she deserved what had happened to her for parading as a sexual icon in. In an interview with her (May, 2012) she noted that the reactions of the general public to her ordeals affected her psychologically and almost caused her to give up her music career.

Music Consumers Perceptions of Women in the Music Industry
Women musicians have had to, and continue to deal with perceptions of their immorality and irresponsiblity. In a soceity where female professional autonomy is a historical fact, it is also true that being a wife, and especially a good motherhood, is even more valued, and both roles demand that a woman be morally upright. Yet women muscians are viewed as being sexually immoral, and prone to heavy drinking and

drug abuse. Indeed, the only kind of women who are spared from this stereotype are gospel musicians. This probably accounts, at least in part, for the large numbers of women musicians who have carved their niche in gospel music (Collins 2002).

Even today, this fear of being branded as "loose" has become an albatross around the necks of many women who want to be musicians in Ghana. Repeatedly, women have had to endure such branding once they decide to become secular musicians. In an interview with Awurama Badu, she confirmed that when she decided to become a musician, some women in her hometown asked her mother why she had "allowed" her daughter to enter such a profession. The women were only placated when Awurama's mother pointed out that Awurama already had four children, was separated from her husband and was therefore "idle."

When after high school Akosua Agyepong wanted to make music her profession she had to petition a renowned musician, Nana Ampadu, to talk to her parents on her behalf so they would "allow" her to sing. Apparently according to her parents musicians and more so women musicians were " wayward people and not respected". Indeed, Akosua herself admitted that the music industry is a difficult place for a woman, and conceded that she had been successful because she had a male mentor, a seasoned musician—Nana Ampadu—and she was married to one of the big names in the music industry, Nat Brew, himself a musician.

In a 2012 interview on TV Africa, a local station, Mzbel, in answer to a question, answered that she did not intend to get married. When she was probed further, she said "I won't marry, if it happens yes; it is not part of my plans." Considering the controversies surrounding Mzbel, one wonders whether her answer underlines the point made earlier that no one will "embrace her as a bride" or whether her response is just her way of saying to a society that has constructed her as morally loose, "watch me, if this is who you say I am, then this is who I will be." Over and over again women musicians are confronted with similar negative representations and they feel the need to prove to society that although they are musicians they are not promiscuous, and that they fitting role models for yount women. This compulsion to prove one's purity is an ordeal that male musicians can escape from. Indeed, male musicians are normally viewed as "bad boys", but in a romanticized way that enhances their masculinity and sexual appeal.

People also think that women musicians do not have much formal education and that they are therefore unable to find a "real" job. One might have expected these perceptions to have been something of the past and that today woman musicians would be respected as professionals, esepcially since many have studied up to the tertiary level even before entering the profession. Unfortunately, a University degree does not protect a woman from such perceptions, and people believe that even if a woman is not (yet) morally loose, it is only a matter of time for her to become promiscuous, addicted to drugs or an alcoholic. According to one producer interviewed, until women musicians get mentors, the industry will gradually eat them up. Indeed, if a woman wants to maintain her good name in the music industry in Ghana then she should proably become a gospel musician. These negative stereotypes keeps many talented young woman away and thus deprives the society of enjoying their talents.

Women and the Songs They Sing

According to Wright most of the themes addressed in songs performed by women are "common feminine identifiable ideas (community and family for example; 1995: 32)." Although the author does not explain what he means by "feminine ideas" it is obvious from the examples he gives that issues that women sing about fit societal expectations for them. Not surprisingly, since contemporary Ghanaian highlife focuses heavily on romantic love and sexual innuendos (Collins 2002; Adomako Ampofo & Asiedu 2012), our ongoing survey of the songs that form a part of our larger study reveals that a major theme for both women and men is love. However, it is the way in which these issues are approached and narrated by women that is interesting. Mostly women reflect on the beauty of love, the fact that they are looking for someone to love, and disappointment in love. Disappointment in love is one thing that women have sung about since they first learnt to sing and yet this is an ageless theme that never lacks an audience. The first author attended a musical concert organized by the police band at the National Theater. Awurama Badu was invited to sing and just when she appeared to be about to conclude her performance, one of the band members walked up to her and whispered something in her ears. Awurama then started singing her hit song, *Medofo adaada me*. The whole theater came alive and only after she had performed this number could she end her segment of the show. *Medofo adaada me* is a classic example of a women's seemingly eternal cry of being sorely disappointed in love. The woman tells us that:

> *Medofo adaadaa me [a aa]*
> > my lover has deceived me [a aa]
> *Odo adaadaa me [oo]*
> > my lover has deceived me [oo]
> *Medofo agya me awerehow aa*
> > my lover has left me in sorrow
> *Agyegye mea koku me*
> > he has led me to death

In subsequent lines of the song, the woman narrates her ordeal: how she had started life with her husband and they struggled together until they gained wealth. Now when it should have been time for them to enjoy the fruits of their labor together, this ungrateful husband has sent her packing.

Awurama, confirmed the fact that although she had many other hit songs, live audiences always requested for this song to be performed. She also revealed that one woman almost drunk and cried herself to death when she first performed this song in a club at Adabraka, a suburb of Accra, apparently the song reminded her of a disappointment in a romantic relationship.

Akosua Agyepong's classic *Frema* also embodies the pain of a woman dying from unrequited love. She sings:

> *Ao Frema*
> > What is this love I have met (2x)
> > Some love can be deadly.
> *Ao Kwame ei*
> > If you really love me
> *Let me hear from you*
> > Otherwise the next time you hear from me
> > It will be at my funeral.

In this song, the love of the woman for her lover is so intense that the singer wonders if the lover has used magic to bewitch her into loving him. This lover is described as understanding and protecting his woman. She loves him with all her heart and all she expects is for him to love her in return, and yet she is apprehensive, uncertain and afraid of his silences. This apprehension is perhaps justified when one is reminded of the heartbreak which has been experienced by the woman in Awurama's *Medofo adaadaa me*.

Akosua Agyepong's song *Me yɛ Obaa* (lit. I am woman) which praises the awesome beauty and preciousness of God's female creation, also advises women to be decent, respectable, modest, and "expensive" (i.e. not give themselves cheap to any man) in order to win true love (see Appendix). Her song praises and affirms womanhood, she sings of a woman comfortable with her gender identity; and she affirms a fellowship of women: "We are women, God created us as women, He created us well." There is a sense of pride in these proclamations. The song, however, progresses into a passionate moralizing narrative of how women should relate to men, first of all imploring women, especially young women like herself to listen to their parents and be obedient to them. This immediately places her narrative onto a trajectory of traditional norms and values which younger people are to take care to adhere to. Once she has found her true love, she must remain faithful to him, no matter what, for this will earn her the man's trust and proper care. Thus, women derive their value from their relationship with men. In order to do so, they must be careful not to go outside the norms of society's dictates for decent women. Though Akosua presents women as having the power of choice, they really cannot choose to go outside society's norms. They can only choose that which society has sanctioned.

However, today's generation of successful secular singers seem to reject this model and bring greater agency into their lyrics; they sing about what they want from relationships and indicate the power of what they also give. Mzbel's first hit song, which was also a love song, is quite radical when compared to the love songs of Awurama Badu and Akosua Agyapong. Mzbel sings of physical pleasure a woman's power in the relationship. In the song *Awoso me*, lit. *"it has shaken me"*, the woman advises her lover not to cry because what she is doing is sweet. The chorus runs:

> *You are crying because of this sweet thing...*
> *Give it me, push it in, burn me*
> *I can't go, it has shaken me.*

The sexually suggestive lyrics immediately established Mzbel as a "bad girl". This is something the musician herself finds fascinating. She argues that male musicians have been singing about sexual pleasure without censure, indeed to acclaim, and yet she has been branded for addressing the same themes because she is a woman. Her subsequent songs have not departed much from similar themes and the music videos that accompany these songs are as notorious as the lyrics themselves.

An early hit by another post-millennium artist, Becca, who made her musical debut in 2005, bears remarking on. She became a household name with the release of her song *You lied to me*. In the song, the woman chides:

> *You lied to me (ee)*
> *You betrayed my trust*
> *You broke my heart*
> *(Yei yei) , oh baby boy,*
> *Hey a, you lied to me!*

This song tells the usual story of a cheating man, who was also an opportunist, and the woman's resultant broken heart. As usual, the woman gives her all but wakes up to the grim realization that the man was cheating on her. However, unlike earlier generations of women who "stood by" or "waited for" their man, in this song Becca will not tolerate being made a fool of. In the end she tells the man; "no more money from your honey" and sends him packing. She also does not sit pining and hoping for his redemption and tells him : "you can run, you cry, you can give me the whole world" but it is over. Although the song's lyrics are mainly in English, with a few Twi lines, it is loved by people across the social spectrum as they can related to this no-good man getting what he deserves. In one of the project workshops that was held with persons from the music industry, a DJ reported how popular *You Lied To Me* was and that he frequently was requested to play it by listeners, both female and male, with stories of being cheated-upon. They seemed to take strength, he noted, from the fact that in her song Becca did not crumble or wait for the no-good lover, but had the strength to give him the boot. Adomako Ampofo and Asiedu (2011), assert that cultural products such as popular songs are a reflection of the society and its values.
Sad love belongs to the repertoire of human experiences, which will always have an audience. However, it may be that the particular ways in which Ghanaian society is gendered provides women less space to negotiate within romantic relationships. In a society where it is the man who typically initiates and ends a relationship, and where polygyny is tolerated, it is understandable that women are mostly the ones with the heartache. It is, however, interesting to pay attention to how such

issues are addressed across generations. Songs from the 1980's and 1990's depict women as totally disappointed when a man proves to be unfaithful, unreliable, or if there is a break up. The situation of the woman becomes more complex when we consider the fact that many are providers and that while it is easy for a man to initiate another love affair or marriage, the woman is expected to wait for a suitor to come her way and this may be complicated if she happens to have children from the previous relationship. However, the younger generation of women musicians, even though they still sing about disappointments in love, demand greater accountability from their men. Unlike Akosua Agyepong who places the entire burden of being a "good" girl and thus winning a "good man", today's woman looks for equality in the relationship and is willing to take the initiative to end an unfruitful relationship.

Apart from their preoccupation with love, women also sing about issues of social concern, as Akosua Agyepong put it, they are "social commentators and advisors" (Agyepong 2011). Women have sung and continue to sing about issues such as marital conflicts, motherhood, morality, family planning, AIDS and gender-based violence. Another hit song by Mzbel, *16yrs* is about an underage girl who warns a potential sex offender that she would report him to her parents if he touched her wrongly or tries to sexually abuse her, for she is only "16 years". Although this song was received with mixed feelings, mainly because of the so-called sexually provocative dance moves of the music video, the song addresses the a topical and pertinent issue. Herself a victim of sexual harassment, it reminds perpetrators that women and even girls are aware of the law and will not hesitate to seek redress if they are sexually violated.

Trajectories
The trajectories of the three women selected for this study are each interesting in their own ways. Awaruma Badu's career started with the police band and she eventually became one of the most popular women musicians. However, she has disappeared into obscurity, a fact which she herself stressed in her interview. She noted that as women age, as they lose the physical attractiveness of youth with its sex appeal, they are not given the same platform provided aging male musicians. In the words of another older woman musician, they are expected to be at home "helping with the grandchildren." Akosua Agyepong started as a solo

artiste, faded from the music scene for some years, and then re-emerged having rebranded herself as a gospel artiste—though not quite given her forays into film and reality TV, something other female gospel artistes are not known for. Mzbel's story is a little different. She still performs as a (secular) musician, is the unmarried mother of a ten-year-old son, and continues to court controversy.

Perhaps one of the most distinct differences between male and female artists in Ghana lies in their professional trajectories. The interviews with the women musicians revealed that their professional careers are shorter than men's. This can be attributed to several factors: some place a hold, or even abandon their professional lives to attend to the duties of motherhood and raising the next generation. This may be particularly salient for women musicians as marriage and motherhood become pathways to gain social acceptance—in a society that sees them as irresponsible and morally loose, marriage and motherhood represent maturity and responsibility. Even when they return to their work as musicians after childbirth, women often find that the responsibilities of juggling life as a wife, mother and professional musician are too arduous and therefore many let go of their music careers. Theirs is a profession not only with long hours, late nights, and travel, but it also involves all of these in the company of men who are typically not their partners. All three women discussed in this chapter complained that combining women's reproductive roles with a profession in the music industry is a very difficult task.

The privileging of women's reproductive over their professional roles could also account for the fact that women are less successful, and have a shorter professional career in the industry than the men. Virtually free of reproductive and domestic responsibilities, men are able to tour the country and other parts of the world promoting their music. Most of the male artistes also have agents and managers, and hence access to the resources needed to promote their songs, which thus enjoy more airplay. Further, the entire music industry from producer to engineer is virtually run by men, making it more difficult for women to establish non-sexual relationships to their advantage. One of the women musicians interviewed confirmed that as a woman in the music industry you often get propositioned by men in the industry, partly because men, as members of their societies, themselves believe that women in the industry are sexually available. This woman went on to confirm our speculation that women sometimes have to offer more than their qualifications before they can get a producer. Women who refuse such offers have to travel the hard road to get their albums produced. They move from one producer to the other and sometimes the frustration discourages some from following their dreams of becoming musicians. Further, women, even though they might sell more records and have more fans are not perceived as "musicians" nor are they seen as serious competition by the men in the industry. In fact the idea that a woman musician could have a larger fan base than a man of similar ilk is simply viewed as ridiculous by some Ghanaians because according to some music lovers, women do not have as much talent as men and the only reason a woman musician can have a significant male fan base will be because of her body, clothes and dance moves.

Gender socialization includes overt practices such as nubility rites and the division of labor, as well as more covert forms such as through proverbs, songs and even visual art like sculptures (Adomako Ampofo and Boateng, 2007; Agadjanian, 2002; Miescher, 2007). Thus, assigned roles and responsibilities are inculcated into the individuals and these are carried from childhood to adulthood and played out in all aspects of life. Men and women therefore grow up with clear ideas about appropriate gender roles. There is not much fluidity and individual attempts to have a more nuanced gender identity are frequently fraught with difficulties and resistances (Achebe, 2003). Thus women can be professional musicians, only they cannot be professional musicians in the same ways that men are—they should be asexual, pure, motherly, and maintain a solid family life. At the same time today's viewing audience does not necessarily want an asexual performer. The differences between men's and women's status in the music industry are thus not a function of men's greater creativity but rather a result of gender ascribed roles and spaces in society. Women's entry into the industry therefore means that negative perceptions about them are therefore included in the price they have to pay for being allowed to play.

In a society where sex and sexuality are not typically discussed overtly, publicly, or between the sexes, the society is uncomfortable and perhaps unable to deal with the sexuality or sex appeal of women musicians in the context of their professionalism and they remain objectified. Although some Ghanaians are comfortable watching foreign artistes who would be described by Ghanaian standards as "naked" their "own women" must be "decently" clothed, and this is not only the view of men. One 26-year-old female respondent, "we are uncomfortable seeing women wear something short, it's like you are copying the west and showing your body. In our culture, we cannot accept that." However, when respondents are asked to explain what they mean by "culture" they are unable to articulate this. As researchers, what we make of such observations is that people are comfortable watching non-Ghanaian artistes because they see these women as distant, located in the outer spaces of their own cultural parameters, and thus unable to directly affect their so called cherished "culture". On the other hand, Ghanaian women musicians are part of the Ghanaian social structure and have a higher tendency to affect it or even pollute it. And Ghanaians want to hold on to the mirage of a pure, authentic culture.

Carving a space as a serious professional in a predominantly masculine field also means singing about issues that are considered feminine. We argue that this accounts for the fact that women sing about issues such as love and other social ills and less about issues such as politics. After all they are the mothers and automatically the caretakers of the community with the responsibility of being "the sentinels of morality and tradition" and they must therefore be "calm and deal with the mounting social strife" (Wright, 1995). These expectations are played out, albeit not in the same ways, in the lives of the three women discussed in this chapter. Opposition from family and the public is a case in point. While the older two women experienced family opposition, the third and younger woman also suffers from societal stigmatization for being too "sexy." Parents' apprehension that daughters will be tagged as social deviants remains and it is intriguing that over their cumulative 30 year careers perceptions and stereotypes of secular female musicians have not undergone major transformations even as their own careers have evolved. Interestingly though, if they can survive the industry, then as they age, women almost become absolved of these negative perceptions, perhaps because they are no longer as active or sexualized. Indeed, both Awurama Badu and Akosua Agyapong echoed sentiments indicating that older women in the industry should see themselves as societal commentators who "must carry respect and it's one of the best and major things a woman needs to do and that younger musicians should learn these from the older ones" (Agyepong, personal interview 2011). Carving a niche in gospel music provides some respite as well. It spares women the rod of stigmatization associated with women in the secular sector although a critical look at these types of music shows that women still raise and sing about some of the same issues that secular artists sing about albeit with a splash of God in the lyrics.

Do Women Do Songs as Men Do?

This paper discussed ways in which women musicians sing and survive in the music industry. We suggest that women's trajectories as musicians are marred by negative perceptions about their morality. Although marriage and motherhood may help redeem their image, these two institutions also happen to be one of the major factors that curtail their professional lives. Although their gendered experiences may not differ markedly from women in other professions, Ghanaian women musicians are unique in that we interact with them every day on our radios, IPods, computers, phones and televisions and on various occasions such as parties, weddings, child naming ceremonies, and funerals. They are therefore subject to public exposure and scrutiny. While they all sing about love, younger women express more agency and make stronger demands of their lovers in the songs. It is surely time that Ghanaian society learns to accept the fact that gender spaces are more fluid. If not, Ghanaian women musicians will continue to contend with the difficult task of balancing both a career (as musician) and a social role (as morally upright, wife and mother) under perpetual social scrutiny.

References

Achebe, Nwando. 2003. "And She Became a Man: King Ahebi Ugbabe in the History of the Enugu- Ezike, Northern Igboland, 1880-1948." In *Men and Masculinities in Modern Africa*. Ed. by Lindsay, Lisa and Stephan Miescher. Portsmouth: Heinemann.

Ampofo, Akosua Adomako and John Boateng. 2007. "Multiple Meaning of Manhood Among Boys in Ghana." In *From Boys to Men*. Ed. by Shefer, K. et. al. Cape Town: UCT Press.

___.2009. "Becoming an Adult: The Training of Children in Ghana." In *Knowledge Transmission in Ghana*: Research Review Supplement 19.

Ampofo, Akosua Adomako and Awo Asiedu. 2012. "Changing Representations of Women in Ghanaian Popular Music: Marrying Research and Advocacy." *Current Sociology* 60: 258-279.

Aidoo, Agnes Akosua. 1985. "Women in the History and Culture of Ghana." *Research Review* 1 (1).

Arhin, Kwame. 1983. "The Political and Military Role of Akan Women." In *Female and Male in West Africa*. Ed. by Christine Oppong. London: George Allen, 92-98.

Asante-Darko Nimrod and Sjaak Van Der Geest. 1983. "Male Chauvinism: Men and Women in Ghanaian Highlife Songs." In *Female and Male in West Africa*. Ed. by Christine Oppong. London: George Allen.

Asiedu, Awo and Akosua Adomako Ampofo. 2012. "Towards Alternative Representations of Women in African Cultural Products." In *Essays In Honour of Ama Ata Aidoo at 70; A Reader in African Cultural Studies*. Ed. by Ann Adams. Oxfordshire: Ayebia Clarke Publishing Ltd., 219-230.

Collins, John. 2003. "Ghanaian Women Enter into Popular Entertainment." *Humanities Review Journal* (3): 1-10.

Evans, G. 1981. The Organization of Music of African Women. ML 350.EVI, Pamplet box (African Studies Library, University of Ghana).

Mhiripiri, Nhamo Anthony. 2011. "Welcome Singing Sungura Queens': Cultural Studies and the Promotion of Female Musicians in a Zimbabwean Male-Dominated Music Genre." *Muziki* 8:1. Accessed on the 7th September, 2011 from http://www.tandfonline.com/loi/rmuz20.

Osumare, Halifu. 2012. *The Hiplife in Ghana: West African Indigenization of Hip-Hop*. New York: Palgrave.

Quan-Baffour. Kofi Poku. 2009. "Ritual Songs for Girls' Nubility Rites at Bono Takyiman, Ghana." *Muziki,6:1*. Accessed on the 7th September, 2011 from http://www.tandfonline.com/loi/rmuz20.

Shipley, Jesse Weaver. 2013. *Living the Hiplife: Celebrity and Entrepreneurship in Ghanaian Popular Music*. Duke University Press.

Sutherland-Addy, Esi and Aminata Diaw. Eds. 2005. *Women Writing Africa: West Africa and the Sahel. The Women Writing Africa Project. Vol. 2*. New York: The Feminist Press at the City University of New York.

Wright, Owen. 1995. "Popular Music in Ghana: The Demonctratization of the Culture." *African Diaspora Collections* 4:1.

Appendix

Me ye Obaa – Akosua Agyepong (1990)

Me yɛ ɔbaa 3x
   I am a woman
Agya onyame bɔ me baa
   God made me a woman
Ɔbɔɔ me yie
   He created me very well (He did it well)

Yɛ yɛ ɛmbaa 3x
   We are women
Agya onyame bɔ yɛn mmaa
   God created us as women
Ɔbɔɔ me yie
   He created us well

Me nuanom mmaa me srɛ mo
   My fellow women, I plead with you
Mon tie m'asɛm mma me
   Listen to what I have to say
Mɛ hunu biribi ɛsɛ sɛ me ka ho asɛm
   I have seen something I must talk about
Ya yaa yaw
   (bitterly?) painfully?
Mesrɛ yɛ mmaa yi
   I plead with our/us women
Titiriw ɛmmayewa yi
   especially those of you here
Aba baa wa ɔte sɛ me
   Young women just like myself
Yɛn bɔ mmɔde sɛ
   (let us try as much as possible)
   Let us make the effort
Die ɛdi kan no
   First of all
Yɛ bɛ aso tie, ama y'awofuo no
   Let us listen to our parents
   (be obedient to our parents)
Afei nso momma yɛn kora yɛn ho yie
   Let us also carry/keep ourselves
   well/properly
Afie nso momma yɛn sua yɛn ho yo
   Also let us learn about/from each other/
   ourselves well
Ama yɛn mmɛɛma yi nso
   So that these our men will also
Wodi obuo ama yɛn
   they will respect us/give us respect
Dea wo wɔ seisei no nso
   What you now have also

Mo nhwɛ no yiye
   Take good care if it
Me ma yɛn nhenyɛ ntaadie ɛmma yɛn ho ndeda hɔ
   Let us not wear clothes which indecently
   expose us/ that leave us exposed

Ama mmɛma yi
   So the(se)/ men
Aka no asɛm
   don't talk about it

Yɛ wɔ ɔdɔ aa
   If we have love
Ɛnsɛ sɛ yɛ bɔ no dokomi
   we don't have to cheapen it/ make noise
   about it?
Yɛ wɔ ɔdɔ a yɛ ma ne buo ɛnyɛ den kakra
   Let us make our love a bit expensive
Na me kyerɛ sɛ
   What I mean is that
Yɛn kyerɛ yɛn ho, ɛnkeyrɛ mmɛɛma
   Let us play hard to get? Let us show off
   to the men?
Anaasɛ yɛ dɔ no, na yɛn tɔn no aboɔden
   in other words, let us make our love
   expensive/let us sell our love at
   a high price
N'ɛmom ɛsɛ sɛ yɛ hwɛ yɛn ho yie ooh
   But, it is important that we take care/
   be careful
Wo ne Kwadwo nam nnɛ kyena na ɛyɛ Yaw
   You are with Kwadwo and tomorrow
   you are with Yaw
Wo ne Kwame nam nnɛ ade kye aa na wowɔ Kwasi nkyɛn
   Today you are with Kwame and tomorrow
   you are with Kwasi
Mmɛɛma nso hyɛsɛ ebia awadie
   And these men, some may be married
Wo mu bia na ho aa, w'awofo nim no
   and your parents do not know any of them
Ɔkyena wo bɛ hwɛ, nyinsɛn n'aba yi
   Before you are aware, you are pregnant
Kwadwo se ɛnyɛ ɔnoa, Yaw nso anngye
   Kwadwo says he is not responsible and
   Yaw also denies responsibility
Kwame se ɛnyɛ ɔnoa, Kwasi nso anngye oh
   Kwame says he is not responsible and
   Kwasi will also not accept it ooh
Afei na ato wo adwendwen
   Then you will be at a loss

Wo kɔ yi agu, wo ti anye yiew owuo
    If you attempt to abort it and you are
    not lucky, you could die
Wo bɛ wo nsoa a, wo ba yi mu agya
    If you have the baby, it will not have
    a father
Sɛ ɛba no saa na woanim agusi oh
    When that happens, you will be disgraced
Ɛnso kae sɛ na wo aha wo ban no paa
    Remember that then, you would have
    made life difficult for your child
Ɔbaa nso deɛ bɛɛma bia hu saa
    And as for a woman, when a man
    sees that,
Ommu wo biem oh
    he will not respect you anymore
Ɔbaa nso deɛ, bɛɛma bia hu saa
    As for a woman, once men see that,
W'aware e mu ɛbɛ ye den ama wo oh
    marrying you will become a problem/
    You will have difficulty getting a man
    to marry you.

chorus

Me yɛ ɔbaa 3x
    I am a woman
Agya nyame bɔ yɛn mmaa
    God made us women
Ɔbɔ yɛn yie
    He created us well

Mmaayewa, mmaayewa bebree
    young girls, many young girls
Nim agya nom
    Know no fathers
Enti me nuanom mmaa
    So my fellow women
Yen mbo mɔden sɛɛ
    Let us see to it that
Bɛɛma biaa ɔpɛ sɛ ɔne wo nante biaa
    any man who shows an interest in you
Me se fa to n'anim
    I say, put it to him/tell him
N'onkɔ hu w'awofoɔ
    let him go and see your parents
Ɔdɔ wo nkoaa, dea a, wo kae aa
    If he really loves you, as soon as
    you say it
Ɔne wo bɛkɔ
    He will go with you

Ɛnyɛ ahoɛfɛ
    Its not about beauty
Adanse die aba mu oh
    now this is from experience/
    now you have a witness ?
Afei nso sɛ ɛba no saa deɛ aa
    now if it so happens
Me nua mmaa na w'atena faako
    My sister, be faithful to the man/
    stay at one place
Ama bɛɛma yi de gyidie ee asɔ no nu oh
    so the man can trust you and treat you
    well ooh.

Is a Woman Only Worth the Rib of a Man? : The Place of Women in Zimbabwean Musical Arts, Past and Present

Bridget Chinouriri

Bridget Chinouriri is a senior lecturer in the Department of African Languages and Literature at the University of Zimbabwe. Her research interests include indigenous knowledge systems, musical arts, land, politics and gender studies. She is an ethnomusicologist, a creative writer, a culture consultant, and a scientist. Bridget serves on a number of cultural boards in Zimbabwe. She was one of the fellows at the International Center for African Music and Dance (ICAMD) and obtained her MM in 1998 with Professor Nketia as her advisor. She obtained her PhD from the University of Pretoria in the Republic of South Africa in 2014.

Introduction

Musical arts are not just an exercise in the aesthetics of sound but mediate between the societal systems and the key operators, and also imbue spiritual and moral connotations, control personal and corporate psyche thereby inculcating communal virtues, ethos and aspirations in any society. The term 'indigenous' represents distinctive Shona practices lived and practiced in the pre-colonial milieu. The indigenous Shona milieu, like elsewhere in Africa, depicts Africa's indigenous customs and beliefs which gave a foundation of identity in creativity and performance in society (Nketia 1974). The relationship between men and women is a natural relationship which takes on a character that is mediated by a people's culture. Like any other relationship, it is factual that the relationship between men and women, cross culturally, has never been and cannot be thoroughly perfect but this has been and can be managed through musical arts as a strong medium for conflict resolutions.

In indigenous Africa gender was not a pertinent issue before Western modernism invaded, colonized and deconstructed Africa's worldview and socio-cultural knowledge systems. Naturally, women and men are born with similar intellectual potential in spite of their biological differences. Kgafela (2009) describes gender as different from sexuality as the latter concerns physical and biological differences that distinguish male from female, hence, cultures construct differences in gender. The common value and inherent potential of the indigenous woman was not philosophized or rationalized as only 'worth the rib of a man' as the topic suggests. To the contrary, in indigenous Zimbabwean society men and women had well-defined roles and obligations that were specific and exclusive to their respective genders (Oyyekan Owomoyela 2002:91). This signifies that men and women's relationships were reflective of mutual and complimentary responsibility.

As propounded by the Africana womanism theorist, Hudson-Weems (1993:8): The Africana womanist, focuses on her particular circumstances, and comes from an entirely different perspective, one which embraces the concept of collectivism for the entire family in its overall liberation struggle for survival, thereby resolving the question of her place in the venue of women's issues. Thus, the African woman in indigenous society was family centered unlike her counterpart who has been bombarded by foreign theories such as Black feminism and others. The research shall take recourse to African indigenous cultures in order to find out how Africans resolved their areas of disequilibrium and dissonance in the musical arts long before the white man came. Zimbabwe is a patriarchal society and hence, its indigenous music portrays gender stereotypes: how men and women perceive women in general and musical arts' role in particular within the society. This paper therefore seeks to investigate how Zimbabwe's indigenous and contemporary musical arts represent gender roles and the reaction to any behavior that is perceived acceptable or deviant from the expected roles. Lindsey's (2005:2) description reinforces the above point that:

A role is expected behavior associated with status. Roles are performed according to social norms, shared rules that guide people's behavior in specific situations. Social norms determine the privileges and responsibilities a status possesses. Females and males, mothers and fathers, and daughters and sons are all statuses with different normative role requirements attached to them.

Affirmative Portrayal of Women in Indigenous Societies
In indigenous Africa, as Nzewi and Galane (2005) stipulate, generally the woman was celebrated as the spiritual source or the ritual owner of the man. The man ordered the woman, the woman managed the man. The woman commanded on a regular basis the obedience of the entire family by the authority of her traditional role of processing, cooking and apportioning edible food. It was out of bounds for the man to prepare his own food or interfere with the processing of food. In most indigenous patriarchal societies such as Zimbabwe the man was apportioned the power of traditional governance as he wielded ultimate authority and occupied the highest echelons of influence relative to women. On the other hand, women likewise also wielded the decisive power in domains specified for them to the extent that even powerful men could not challenge. Women could successfully influence political, religious and other societal pertinent issues but they were not allowed to openly make decisions--only in private with their husbands or elders of the society.

The indigenous society, to a greater extent, encouraged and perpetuated individuality of performance of people who had outstanding innate aptitude in musical arts, regardless of their gender. Nevertheless, the community regulated the public performance and remained the ultimate custodian of quality and decent performances. The exceptionally talented women in musical arts were accommodated and celebrated by their society. This was rationalized as 'individuality within conformity' of societal norms and values (Nzewi 2009:59). The talented woman was not only an exponent of the musical arts but an invaluable asset and member of the society able to function in other expected aspects of life in the given society. This was a social norm which fulfilled a societal need that would benefit the general human community and environment.

Women in general were the first teachers of musical arts in African indigenous societies and this commenced from conception to beyond the grave. For example, indigenous African practice was that a healthy pregnant mother was encouraged to participate fully in musical arts activities for the purpose of pre-natal sensitization of the fetus to the structured movements of the culture (Nzewi 2009). Women composed lullabies or cradle songs sung to help send and lull babies to sleep (Bebey 1976). Some music composed by women for their own social roles and their popularity would transcend the whole community. Women also managed to control social ills and provide conflict resolutions in their societies through musical arts. They could manage tensions in a polygamous marriage by singing songs with hidden social innuendoes about ill-treatment from the first wife or petty jealousies in polygamous marriages. For example, the song

Jari mukaranga:

Kumutengera jari mukaranga koiniwo
Ndini ndakaubvisa munhamo yemugota
Tikarimaminda yedu tikadyara mbesa dzedu
Tikatenga mombe dzedu
Tikavaka musha vedu
Zvino hauchandida, waunza mumwe mukadzi,
Wamutengrea jari, ko ini rangu riripi?

> *Now you buy your new wife a new quilt what about me?*
> *Remember I bailed you out from being a bachelor*
> *We had our farm and we planted our field*
> *We built our home*
> *But today a new quilt for the new wife, where is mine?*

The above song was sung by the unjustly treated first wife in a polygamous marriage. She bemoaned the ill-treatment that she got from the husband yet she was his first love. *Jari* is a quilt and *mukaranga* is a second wife in a polygamous marriage. The young and new wife is being showered with new gifts by the husband to the chagrin of the first wife. The song would be sung in the presence of other people who could intervene and correct the domestic ill if need be. With such a backdrop, affirming expressions among the Shona of Zimbabwe such as *musha mukadzi* (an ideal home should have a woman) were societal nuances which hailed and promoted the functional role that women played in any homestead in keeping, maintaining and monitoring everything and everyone in the home.

Negative Portrayal of Women in Indigenous Societies.
In order to do justice in this scholarly inquiry, the researcher is cognizant of the other idiomatic expressions and less affirming expressions which attacked and degraded the persona of the woman thus killing and paralyzing the inherent creative force. As stated earlier, Shona indigenous society was not a perfect society. On the other hand, verbal and non-verbal expressions were found in everyday communication, which inflicted low-self esteem and an inferiority complex on the woman and girl child. For example, the Shona maxim, *mukadzi anoridza mbira anobika sadza mbodza* (a woman who plays mbira cooks raw *sadza*). *Sadza* is the staple food in Zimbabwe. The mbira was a traditional religious instrument. This maxim implied that sometimes the women were not supposed to cross boundaries from the domestic/family sphere of cooking into the male's creative sphere of playing *mbira*. Such a mindset resulted in the gendering of musical instruments and performance in some instances. Makwenda (2001:18) avers that Shona women were excluded from playing the *mbira* instrument in sacred ceremonies, especially when menstruating, as they were considered unclean. Women were not allowed the daunting task of playing musical instruments, especially religious ones such as the *mbira dzavadzimu (the mbira of the ancestors)*, a traditional religious instrument of the Shona people. The role of women musicians in spiritual and recreational music has been primarily limited to singing and dancing because most musical instruments were shrouded by myths that made them impossible for women to play. In Zimbabwe, the *mbira* instrument was regarded as a sacred instrument which women were not allowed to touch especially when pregnant, menstruating or breastfeeding, as they were considered to be unclean. The Shona people used the *mbira* instrument in the *bira*

ceremony. A *bira* is a religious ceremony in which family members come together to call on and inquire upon a common ancestry for help and guidance. The term *bira* is derived from the verb *-kupira* which means propitiating. But it was within the same Shona society that pregnant women had to toil in the fields without exceptions as society understood that *nhumbu haisi mumaoko* meant that the pregnancy was not in one's hands, therefore one must work like everyone else.

The Shona and Ndebele societies in Zimbabwe have been patriarchal as have most African societies since the pre-industrial period. Men have been dominating and leading women in most aspects of life as women acted and lived as subordinates. This social theory was created by the society and anyone who turned against this was then defined as uncultured and uncouth. There were some socio-cultural considerations and symbols that were attached to women and musical instruments as mentioned above. For example, according to indigenous lore, the drum was said to be useless if a woman saw it before the drum maker finished making it. It was also believed that a woman would not conceive if she were to place a drum between her legs, a posture done when plays drums. Some scholars have argued that some of these rules and regulations which seemed to infringe women's rights were just a social mechanism of controlling and instilling good behavior in the society. So for example, women were not allowed to place the drum between their legs as a way of encouraging women to sit in a proper and dignified posture.

In games such as playhouse *(mahumbwe)*, children learn and practice the different roles of men and women in the society. These differences in roles are also highlighted in music. Women, however, have always been allowed to play complementary roles to men in the sense that they urged them on for a high quality music performance. Musical instruments had been cordoned off from women through a litany of prohibitive myths and taboos. For instance, in religious ceremonies, men would spend the night playing *mbira*, *ngoma* (drum) and *hosho* (shakers) while women were limited to ancillary roles of singing, handclapping, ululating and dancing. Wilson S. G notes that:

Despite pressure to change, folks in the hinterlands, off the worn paths of acculturation, have somewhat maintained their traditional values. In Saharan Africa, Berber women sit and play the skinned-calabash drum, as do the Peulhs of Sene-Gambia. Still, over here, the idea of women treading in the territory of drumming is frightening to some men. They were taught that men and only men were to be drummers. Men play, women dance: simple. Why?

But in religious ceremonies, no one would dare stop a woman appointed by the spiritual forces to play important roles, even the daunting task of playing the sacred *mbira* instrument. Women were not allowed to beat the drum as beating the drum is likened to beating the husband, and if a woman put a drum between her legs to play it the end result would be that her husband would die. Those women who were afforded the rare opportunity to play drums were those with special roles such as spirit mediums.

Nevertheless, the accolades given to women was something that had meaning in a family where the father played his part as the head of the woman. Though the woman had the ability to administer in the family, she could not represent the father figure or vice versa. Both the woman and the man complimented each other which stabilized the family unit as the social fabric or microcosm of the community and enhanced the God-given inherent creative talent.

The Contemporary Woman Viewed as 'A Mere Rib'

According to Laurent Aubert (2007:3), it is no secret that the proliferation of modern Western civilization and its ideals all over the world provoked deep and irreversible distresses with consequences that have affected each and every domain of culture. Aubert argues that it is factual that modern woman has had to suffer society's harsh whip more than her indigenous counterpart because of social effects from societies other than her own. In contemporary society, the modern-day gender palaver whose historical evolution of the Western notion of modernism generated human and social stresses that have disrupted family bonding and complimentary roles in general and musical arts in particular (Nzewi and Galane 2005).

Modern religions imposed the illogical dogma that the 'woman is only worth the rib of a man' (Nzewi and Galane 2005). This religious dogma which the researcher is fully convinced that the advocates did not fully understand and comprehend helped them to consolidate and perpetuate dominion over the faith-silenced woman in general and the musical arts woman practitioner in particular. When religions such as Christianity (which this researcher has wholeheartedly accepted and adopted as a lifestyle) were introduced to the Africans by former colonial powers, the religions were 'half baked', hence the evidence of several conflicting Church doctrines, yet the manual is the same holy book, the Bible. In line with the above scope that 'woman is only worth the rib of a man', Aschwanden (1989:26) authenticates the same creed that:

The Shona Karanga say men have God's figure--God took clay and water from the earth's belly and shaped a figure. He told himself "this creature must be like me, because when I go it will take my place' he made man and gave him the power to rule and be the strength of procreation. *Mwari* took what was left of the clay and formed a woman.

The above statement by Aschwanden could have been influenced by the introduction of Western civilizations which denotes that women always play second fiddle to men. Nevertheless, the researcher regards the Western exported debate on gender in Africa largely as an attention-grabber whose design is to hoodwink African women and men thereby initiating non-existent wars and causing avoidable animosity between them with the hope of destroying the communalistic and cohesive social fabric which was the hallmark of indigenous culture itself. It is unquestionably clear that colonization disfigured and disoriented the African people and the propagation of their musical arts. It is by closely studying the painful history of Africa and the stale mockery of the African indigenous musical arts that there is understanding of the dilemma and crisis contemporary Africa is in today. But how long shall there be continual lament and regret over the colonial humiliation and degradation caused by Africa's colonizers? Griffiths (2009) quoted by Matereke (2009:83) reinforces the notion that some of the wounds that Africa is suffering now could to some extend be self-inflicted wounds of today's political graft, corruption, poor economic policies and so forth. This may be factual to an extent because some of the challenges that women musicians suffer are inflicted by today's society though the unhealed wounds of the colonial past must always be remembered as the major variant. The debate remains unabated.

The Western woman, unlike her African counterpart, has been a victim of such oppression in her own environment, hence, the battle cry for women's emancipation and status-building and, thus, the creation of Black and White feministic theories from the West. In Africa, Black feminism does not describe the plight of black women, but both the black man and woman have been victims of oppression of western civilizations. Nzewi and Galane (2005: 72) chronicles how the subtle, marginalized, suppressed Western woman eventually began to query the unjust gender status quo in her own society. The oppressed Western woman began to export and impose the social, cultural and gender problems plaguing the West on Africa's secure mental civilization and cultural practices. The African territory, which was already politically, mentally and economically conquered by the Western man, became a testing ground for the Western woman. History has questioned the stance taken by the West of preaching peace, equality and freedom in the name of gender to former women and men captives in Africa. In such a status quo gender should not be taken as a trusted tool with which to solve men and women's imperfections, as it is riddled with crises and dilemmas. As Hudson-Weems (the founder of Africana womanism theory) argues, White women first learned to speak in public and began to formulate a philosophy of feminism to manifest basic rights and place in society yet Africana women had learned and practiced these things centuries ago from traditions in the motherland (2004:26).

Due to the effects of Western civilizations, the family unit in Africa became disintegrated and violated and the idea of communalism has been replaced by individualism. In Shona contemporary society, woman's integrity and family role as a mother/nurturer is still violated, even at the level of the family, which was respected and honored in indigenous lore. Mother-blaming is in large part a reflection of society's general tendency to degrade or undervalue women. For example, if a child is ill-mannered among the Shona today, expressions such as *kufanana nekwakaenda mombe* meaning the child's mischief resembles those of his maternal side (yet this is a patriarchal society) are often used. On the other hand, if the child behaves well, the father proudly and arrogantly calls him *mwana wangu*, 'my child', if ill-mannered *mwana wako,* 'your child', meaning the child belongs to the mother. Letty Cottin Pogrein (1980) quoted by Caplan (1985:51) has traced this in the everyday language of her society and discovered that it is said, "a nasty man isn't nasty in his own right but he is a son of a bitch." Such expressions reflects badly on the person of the mother. Little (1973: 6) aptly sums up the role of the typical African woman by saying:

What kind of creature, after all is that African woman? She lives under a wide variety of conditions, pagan, Christian and Moslem, and exhibits outwardly, at least, an appearance ranging from submissiveness to complete self-assurance and confidence in manner. We can say without much fear of contradiction that in African society the greater part of woman's role is ascribed rather than achieved.

While Albert (1963:180) clearly typifies the African woman when he describes that, "...unlike a man, a *Rundikazi* woman of Burundi in public does not speak, nor does she look you in the eyes." She is the modest and obedient wife of her husband and the mother of her children. The dilemma for the woman musician is that if her society dictates and demeans how she is supposed to behave, if she cannot speak in public, how can she be able to stand and sing in public, let alone face the audience if she is not supposed to look them in the eye? But the indigenous African woman has long practiced and learned these behaviors centuries ago, as clarified by Hudson-Weems (2004). Such prescriptions have marginalized women's credibility as possessing creative God-given talents. To the contrary, Hudson-Weems (2004:1) clearly defines what she calls 'Africana womanism' as something that emerged from the acknowledgement of a long-standing authentic agenda for that group of women of African descent who needed only to be properly named and officially defined according to their own unique historical and cultural matrix, one that would reflect the co-existence of men and women in a concerted struggle for the survival of their entire family. Hudson-Weems (2004:36) concludes that Africana womanism is an ideology created and designed for all women of African descent and is grounded in African culture as it focuses on the unique experiences, struggles, needs and desires of Africana women.

The Contemporary Woman Musician

The proliferation of modern Western civilization which has been perpetuated through colonialism, missionary work, industrialization and technological advancement has not only marginalized indigenous music, but has also negatively impacted musical practice, performance and dissemination. The Zimbabwean constitution states that men and women are equal in all spheres of life but in theory this has been propounded but in practice inequality still persists in different platforms of life including the musical arts. To some extent the indigenous woman wielded power in her society but because of the drastic changes in African economies, social and political relations the power of the contemporary woman is slowly fading away. The concept of equality between men and women disappeared due to the advent of foreign forces on the continent. For instance, Cawthorne (1999:59) chronicles that missionaries expelled spirit mediums for Jesus Christ, traditional healers and mid-wives in child bearing were replaced by western educated doctors and hospitals, and the role of women as educators in storytelling and in folk tales was replaced by missionary schools. Thus, the woman was stripped off her virtue as a mother, educator, healer, nurturer and so forth which she had used through the medium of musical arts. Ajai (1982:78) quoted in Hudson-Weems (2004) elaborates that:

In traditional African societies there was much less scope than now for discrimination between the sexes as there was no opportunity for a greater gulf between man and woman. I am not suggesting that there was always full participation of women on a completely equal basis, but neither was there the completely subservient role which some of our men would like us to accept today. The dependence of women was brought to Africa in part, like so many other 'benefits' of Western civilization, by Europeans, the colonial administrators and the missionaries. When education was introduced, it was initially for boys only. This was the case with higher education and jobs in government and business. If girls were permitted to get on the ladder at all, it was always several rungs below their brothers. In all this of course, our colonial masters were simply reproducing the system they had operated in Europe.

The effects of urbanization and the development of technology has made the musical arts a commodity which can be manipulated, sold and bought as well as accessed in privacy. The establishment of communications media, technology, and commercialization of musical arts as a commodity has had far reaching effects which has been accelerated by the processes of change. Contrary to indigenous milieu systems, musical arts have become commercial commodities that circulate in demographic markets in the contemporary society

(Connel and Gibson 2003). Creativity in the musical arts in the contemporary society has led to the concern whether the creativity fits in or not into societal expectations and sanctions. In music production and consumption women and men face social, institutional, moral, political and economic constraints. Women by virtue of their gender are restricted in terms of their entry into the popular music arena. Popular music in many African cultural contests has been viewed as sites of social deviance Ntarangwi (1999). This ideology characterizes the popular music industry to date with some of its practitioners actively living up to these stereo types. Women tend to suffer the societal harsh whip than their male counterparts because as Ntarangwi (1999) avers that the urban space, where mostly popular music is patronized historically, these have been marked as male's territory and sphere of influence Ntarangwi (1999).

The modern woman musical arts practitioner has often been subjected to the marketing strategies and gimmicks of male managers and bandleaders and in the process ripped off in so many ways. As Zindi (1997:68) points out: 'the majority of women who sing are used as backing vocalists and dancers by male artists'. Thus, some women are expected to fulfill sexually gratifying entertainment roles within the bands and performance venues. Those who performed on stage accompanied by western instruments such as the guitar are labeled as 'cheap' and 'loose' girls. The women are usually placed in a derisory role as they are described as sex objects. The issue of playing instruments maybe a daunting task for female musicians today because the playing of musical instruments had been genderized in the indigenous societies. Though some women today who are strong willed are now learning to play musical instruments in music colleges and universities that offer music as a subject or course.

The success or failure of women musicians in African cultures seems to be intimately tied to marriage that is the quintessential arena where male control is still strongly dominant (Ntarangwi 1999). Because of societal expectations, normally, the status of a married woman is regarded highly than that of a single woman. In indigenous societies, the husband-wife relationship was so strong as it was the basis of survival of the family and the entire community. Because of forces of change it has been a great challenge for married women musical arts practitioners to excel in their creativity as they sometimes failed to juggle and balance the needs of the family, husband and business. Thus most talented women stop performing once they get married. Marriage is a sacred institution in Africa which is as old as history is revered and is supposed to be a setting of companionship and complimentary where true and unconditional love exists.

Insofar as music and dance is taken as any other forms of art, many men still find it unacceptable for their wives to perform in public places such as bars and open air entertainment joints. It is this conservatism that almost grounded *Mambokadzi* dance group following a marriage-induced dancer exodus (*The Standard* 2011). The group has so far lost six members after they married and were told by their husbands that they could not continue their dancing careers. Although most of the men fell for the women as they gyrated on stage, when they married these women they felt it was improper to let them continue with their work after marriage.

To the assertive woman who lives against all odds success mostly comes with a price tag as she may need to forego marriage and family responsibility and face the repercussions. For most women, who have made it in musical arts today, a large percentage of them are either single, single moms or divorced. This has had repercussions on the children raised and the men in most homes have become endangered species, which is contrary to indigenous lore and to Africana Womanism theory. Yet a family is the basic unit and the initial primary institution of socialization. It is within a family that children learn the values and expectations of their given society. Even with the changes that came with colonization, family remains in Africa the microcosm of society particularly for women who are socialized to see marriage as the culminating event of their lives (Cawthorne 1999).

In Zimbabwean musical arts most talented women have had to relinquish their talent and rather have a preference to the comfort of their married status. To those women musicians who dare pursue their talents society and family shun them resulting in no social security provided by family thus the women musical arts practitioners may be exposed to dangers of the society such as drugs and the menacing HIV/AIDS. On the other hand the selfishness of the modern society has predisposed musicians in general in pursuit of self enrichment and aggrandizement to such an extent that they are ready to do anything regardless of how it affects them and society at large. This self-centered attitude is destroying the moral psyche of the contemporary musician. Thus lots of successful artistes get addicted to dangerous, mental and physiological health impairing substances in order to attain and sustain a particular lifestyle and social profile (Nzewi 2007).

The patriarchal power that reigns in many African societies is abused by men who inflict pain on the rights of women through sexual exploitation, violence and marginalization in musical arts. Hope Rusike, an accomplished *mbira* player and songstress in Zimbabwe, has described how she has disastrously tried relationships and failed due to time demands and a fledging career that requires her attention. Rute Mbangwa, a sensational jazz artist, feels she may have marriage problems because men want women who they can manipulate. Benita Tarupiwa, a *mbira* player and singer, sums it up by saying her first 'husband' is her *'mbira'* and that her future husband has to be content with playing second fiddle to the instrument (Interviewed by Mawondo 2011).

There are other women on the Zimbabwe local musical arts scene who have managed to transcend public accusations of prostitution to gain credible positions within the industry (Impey 1990). Some have been successful because of the support of their families first, and secondly, through sheer confidence on their part. For example, women such as Olivia Charamba, Stella Chiweshe, and Prudence Katomeni-Mbofana have made greater strides in tapping their musical arts potential. Makwenda (2005:23) states that some women musicians of the 1960s and 70s such as Lina Mataka, Eveyln Juba, and Victoria Chingate became successful because they had the full support of their husbands. Stella Chiweshe, a great *mbira* maestro both in Zimbabwe and internationally, has attributed her success to a sense of self-worth and self-confidence as she describes that:

> I counted the number of fingers on a man's hands and saw five, I counted the number of fingers on my hand they are also five so I said to myself what the hell, if a man can play *mbira*, I can too. (Makwenda 2009: 3).

However, the other side of the coin presents another scenario where there are a few enlightened husbands who support their wives' talents in Zimbabwe. The challenge that arises is when inexperienced husbands become administrators and band managers for their wives. Due to their lack of experience in the industry, husbands may contribute to the demise of their wives 'talents. Plaxedes Wenyika, a once renowned urban groove artist, saw her career vanish after engaging her husband Nika Joka as her manager. Amanda Sagonda, a once promising gospel artist, has also ssen her career diminish after marrying Mr. Machimbira, who become her manager. Industry inexperience and the failure to separate domestic and work related issues have contributed to the demise of the musical careers of many women.

Women's Bodies in Musical Arts
Physical beauty has been considered an important aspect of women musician's attraction, especially secular musical artists. As Chari (2008:98) contends, the accentuation of a woman's looks and body parts such as thighs, breasts, legs and backside against their personalities, suggests that they are valued more for their physical appearance than their intellect, attitude or behavior. This has had adverse effects on the persona of the modern woman artist who now inevitably clamors for skin bleaching creams, makeup, and revealing clothing to increase their monetary gains from fans. In a music band, many women dancers or vocalists can easily be identified by their revealing apparel. Ntarangwi (1999) aptly describes a scenario in *Rhumba* music where women dress to accentuate their body structure, adorn garments that exaggerate hip movements and expose thighs, while their male counterparts are engaged in what Thomas Deve (1993.94:19) (quoted by Ntarangwi 1999) calls the 'dance of designer labels', where men display the latest fashion trends in men's clothing to their fans. The woman's body inevitably has become a subject to be sung about and to be displayed to lure male fans and musicians often appropriate these physical images as part of their music creation and entertainment. For example, Calisto Nyamhute's popular song called "Special Meat" refers to beautiful women whose beauty is measured by outward appearance which contradicts the indigenous beauty lore which is a culmination of beauty of body, spirit and mind.

Such behavior has earned talented women numerous demeaning, devaluing and derogatory names such as husbandless, unattached, unmarriageable women, single women, ladies of easy familiarity, snobbish, fortune seekers and others. Some modern women artists have diminished social image as a result of what is considered loose and irresponsible lifestyles. The modern woman is often despised by the same audience which patronizes her musical arts, while another fan base describes women as 'objects of adoration' or 'playthings 'because of the unusually 'plastic' beauty they adorn. Sandra Ndebele is a great Ndebele dancer whose music career has been shrouded by controversy. Ndebele has been openly attacked in pages of the press and criticized in the streets because people think her sexually explicit dancing antics are too suggestive and her attire too revealing for their comfort. According to a survey, ninety-eight percent of the audience that patronizes Ndebele's music in night clubs are mostly men, and to this effect, the women folk have scorned her with unprintable Shona expletives. Female fans interviewed felt that female musicians are threats and husband snatchers but this stance was aimed mostly at secular musicians such as Ndebele. Ndebele has been condemned because of her gyrating dance movements which is common with secular musicians. The sexy dance movements and revealing attire is not perceived as mere entertainment but as a way of attracting men. The choice of venues which are frequented by the same males make it even harder for female fans. Society has failed to distinguish the life of the musician on stage from a personal life offstage. In Dudu Manhenga's, a jazz artist's, words:

> "It is as if no-one expects you to go home after the show because immediately afterwards males want to find out where you will be putting up for the night and whether they could join you" (Mawondo: 2011).

On the other hand while today's parents are supportive of their daughter's musical careers, they have reservations pertaining to the content, style of performance, genre, venues and times of performances. As a result, it seems this has inadvertently driven a number of young women artists to gospel music, even if it was not their genre of music, because of its perceived decency and social approval. Rute Mbangwa, a renowned jazz artist, began as a traditional dancer with a children's performing arts workshop but she had to sneak out for rehearsals and shows as her guardians felt it was pagan. However, the same guardians would always book her for praise and worship sessions within their local Seventh Day Adventist church every Saturday. When Dudu Manhenga diverted from the sanctioned gospel band to pursue a career in secular music, her father was most unhappy and even said that she was going to die of HIV and AIDS (interview Mawondo: 2011).

In contemporary Africa, urbanization has resulted in rural-urban migration, which has resulted in the disintegration of the family and some cultural traits which has affected how music making is organized. The people in the urban areas have begun to live a new life, a new culture, a popular kind of music different from the indigenous lifestyle. Society is changing and the girl child now has the same opportunities as the boy child as there is a realization that the only differences are biological. Zimbabwe is experiencing the rise of talented women musicians, instrument players and renowned dancers. The electronic media has had its share in promoting women musicians. One of the radio stations, Radio Zimbabwe has a slot every Thursday from three to four o'clock where music by women is showcased in a programme *Voimba Vanhukadzi* (Now Women Sing).

Women Musicians

Stella Rambisai Chiweshe is one of Zimbabwe's celebrated *mbira* divas who grew up in an area dominated by the Roman Catholic Church where the *mbira* instrument was frowned upon as pagan. The *mbira dzavadzimu* was a sacred instrument used by the Shona people of Zimbabwe to call on the spirit of their ancestors in ceremonies called "*bira.*" In these traditional ceremonies the repetitive, chiming melodies and rhythms of the *mbira* combine with the *hosho* (gourd rattles), singing, and sometimes drumming (on the *ngoma*), to inspire the ancestors to offer advice and guidance through a spirit medium. Chiweshe has been instrumental together with other musicians either male or female in the rejuvenation of the nationalistic spirit of Zimbabwe as they helped to decolonize and redefine African heritages and identities following the demise of colonialism. Chiweshe unapologetically represents the new crop of women musicians who rose against all odds in order to realize potential and talent. In the music realm, defiant *mbira* music was played during the war of liberation and the sound of it symbolized the need to uproot the vestiges of colonialism in Zimbabwe. This is the same music genre that Chiweshe took upon herself to popularize both home and abroad. She has been a true ambassador of Zimbabwe traditional music and has been a cultural archive in which society reads its history through her rich texts and to this end, Chiweshe was the first woman artist to be honored in a musical tradition that has been male dominated to a considerable extent. In spite of this success, Chiweshe has faced challenges. Chiweshe endured years of frustration before her serious desire to play *mbira* caught the attention of her uncle, who broke the social norms and taught her the instrument. Chiweshe learned the instrument in 1966 and that was the troubled beginnings that gave birth to the maestro she is today.

Chiweshe says women were as opposed to the idea as the men. As *mbira* playing was entirely within the male domain, Chiweshe spent a lot of her time surrounded by men, which led the women in her village to look on her as being "loose," as she states herself. "Men played *mbira*, and for me to play *mbira* meant that I had to sit with men on either side of me. It made the women very uncomfortable." But, without reservation, Chiweshe remains steadfast that what she went through, her pioneering force at that time, has made her stronger in other areas in her life as well. Certainly she broke significant new ground for the likes of her daughter Virginia Mukwesha, Chiwoniso, daughter of celebrated *mbira* player, the late Dumisani Maraire, and countless other female musicians in Zimbabwe today who juggle the burdens of the traditional female role with a need to perform and be heard.

During a distinguished career in the music industry spanning over thirty-five years, she has excelled in the promotion and development of the traditional *mbira* genre. She struggled to survive as a 'girl child' within a colonial environment and also against all odds of her society's traditional customs and beliefs. She has managed to strike a balance between being a mother, wife and musician. The sad thing is that Chiweshe lives abroad and her music is better known, appreciated and patronized by foreigners. Apart from being a woman in a male dominated sphere of *mbira* players, Chiweshe's musical career has spanned over thirty-five years of *mbira* playing and she has released more than twenty singles. Chiweshe's band is comprised of *mbira* players, marimba, bass guitars, drums and percussion players.

Sandra Ndebele aka 'Sandy'
Ndebele has been surrounded by controversy and has been given derogatory names by her fans with some name tagging her as the 'Madonna of Zimbabwe' because of her sexually explicit dances. Ndebele has been openly attacked in the pages of the press and criticized in the streets because people think that her dancing is too suggestive and her attire too revealing.

Despite all of the vilification, in 2011 Ndebele married her long-time boyfriend Sibindi in church amidst pomp and fanfare. Tichawangana interviewing Ndebele on the eve of her wedding writes, "I wanted to find out if she would still perform after she got married. 'Yes, I will. Nothing else changes,'" was the response. Ndebele has five albums to her name and is expected to launch another. Asked on the challenges of motherhood Ndebele said, "'I am not finished yet, actually giving birth is something normal and it just takes a few months before one fully recovers. So in other words, I am still the real Sandy whom people used to know, nothing really changes.'" She admits that her career has been a subject of debate in different sectors of society but says that has only helped her to steadily climb the ladder of success as she managed to fight her way out of the mess, (newsdzezimbabwe August 7, 2011). Posting comments on the internet after Ndebele's wedding, many fans had mixed feelings about her new marriage. Some approved it while others scoffed, much like the fan who wrote that *'chirega kutamba sehure wava muroora wekwa Sibindi'* (now stop gyrating like a prostitute as you are now a daughter in law of the Sibindi family.) Sometimes society is harsh and judgemental and fails to demarcate between the person as an artist and the person as an ordinary person.

Women Dancing Groups
In recent years Zimbabwe has witnessed a mushrooming of women dancing groups such as *Mambokadzi, Amavitikazi, Girls La Musica* and others. These groups have become supporting acts to established male dominated groups such as the *sungura* maestro Alick Macheso. Women dance groups have been used by established groups to attract more fans, especially male fans. As Ntarangwi (1999:36) elaborates, these groups are usually appendages of men and their duties often entail the support of well-established male headed bands. The dancers must generate sexually provocative dances for (male) fans. The venues where this music is often played are places such as night clubs and beer halls. The fans and audiences name call and verbally bash these dancers after their performances. Hope Rusike, the Afro fusion songstress, laments:

> "Generally the levels of respect can be improved for both female and male musicians at home. The unfair part, not just in Zimbabwe, is that when they do wrong, or when someone says they have done wrong, women are judged by society a lot more harshly than men. Unfortunately, when they do well they are not praised more than men."

Although dance is much like other forms of art, many men still find it unacceptable for their wives to perform in public places such as bars or open air entertainment establishments, writes Godwin Muzari (*The Standard* 2009). Group founder and director Enisia Mashusha said the marriage exodus that took place in her band affected the group immensely and that she considered quitting at some point. In some instances, men forbade their wives from dancing. But this was not always the case—*Mambokadzi* has two married dancers who have pursued the art beyond their matrimonial vows.

Hlengiwe Dube and Angela Mupariwa say their husbands have been supportive in their endeavors and encouraged them to remain at *Mambokadzi*. "My husband has no problem with me remaining at the group," Mupariwa said. "We met when I was already with *Mambokadzi* and our marriage did not change anything. We were blessed with our first baby last year and I only took a four-month maternity leave but now I am back with the group."

Dancers, particularly female dancers, face neglect and abuse by a public who regard them as sexually immoral people instead of professionals pursuing careers. It is in line with this development that some promoters exploit dancing group members, capitalize on them and underpay the dancers, while some dancers opt to engage in sex in return for money. Arpers Mapimhidze, the President of the Dance Association of Zimbabwe (DAZ) said that there are many challenges which dancers are facing, hence the realization for the need to form an association that would address such loopholes. "We have so many challenges and I am happy we formed this association in a bid to address such aspects, so our task now is to send messages out to the promoters so that they realize the importance of dancers here in Zimbabwe," said the DAZ president. DAZ was formed on the 13th of October 2010 to address the abuse encountered by dancers, especially women in the industry (newsdzezimbabwe April 2011).

Conclusion
While there may be need for dialogue between the sexes to change attitudes, it is not the business of the West, to dictate what, when, how and where to implant dialogue nor to arbitrate, uninvited, in Africa's family affairs. African traditions and cultures have evolved through inherent self-regulatory dynamics which are capable of

effecting harmony and mutual accommodation of the sexes. The integrity of the modern woman artist has often been subverted by her quest for economic motivations and commercial orientation. Yet the indigenous counterpart has remained, to a large extent, the soul and conscience of the entire community. Women's integrity has been important to her and has been appropriately recognized and respected by society. While major steps have been taken toward creating gender equity in Zimbabwe, there is still a need for pro-active actions where women and men work as a unit to undo poor societal attitudes and restructure gendered relationships (Hudson-Weems 2004:21). As a way forward, without reinventing pre-existing wheels, one could move expediently towards resolving the problems of human survival through family cohesiveness, which African womanism most certainly offers.

References

Aschwanden, Herbert. 1989. *Karanga Mythology*. Zimbabwe: Mambo Press.

Boltz, Kerstin. 2001. *Women as Artists in Contemporary Zimbabwe*. Bayreuth: Stuttgartt Krygsheiz Publishing.

Caplan, Paula J. 1985. *The Myth Of Women's Masochism*. New York: E.P Dutton.

Chari, Tendal. 2008. "Representation of Women in Male Produced "Urban Grooves" Music in Zimbabwe." *Journal of Music Research in Africa* 5 (1): 92-110.

Cawthorne, Maya. 1999. "The Third Chimurenga." In *Africa in Reflections on Gender Issues*. Ed. by Patricia McFadden. Harare, Zimbabwe: SAPES Trust, Ltd.

Connel, John. 2003. *Sound Tracks: Popular Music, Identity and Place*. London and New York: Routledge.

Dube, Caleb. 1996. "The Changing Contexts of African Music Performance in Zimbabwe." *Journal of the University of Zimbabwe* 23 (2).

Green, Lucy. 1997. *Music, Gender, Education*. Cambridge: Cambridge University Press.

Hudson-Weems, Clenora. 1993. *Africana Womanism: Reclaiming Ourselves*. Troy, Michigan: Bedford Publishers.

___. 2004. *African Womanist Literary Theory*. Trenton, NJ: Africa World Press.

Impey, Angela. 1989. "Women in the Music Industry in Zimbabwe." Paper presented at the Eighth Symposium on Ethnomusicology, Music Department of Durban Westville, South Africa, August 30 –September 2.

___. 1990. "Women in the Music Industry in Zimbabwe." Paper presented at the Symposium on Afro-musicology, Windhoek Arts Academy, Namibia. August, 23-26.

Kgafela, Nono. 2009. "Images of Women in Botswana's Modern Traditional Music." *NAWA* 3 (1).

Koskoff, Ellen. 1989. *Women and Music in Cross-cultural Perspective*. Urbana and Chicago: University of Illinois Press.

Makwenda, Joyce Jenje. 2001. *Zimbabwe Adding Their Own Beats*. Gweru: Mambo Press.

___. 2005. *Zimbabwe Township Music*. Harare: Storytime.

___. 2010. " Allow Women to Learn Musical Instruments." *The Herald*. February 2.

Manuel, Peter Lamarche. 1988. *Popular Music of the Non-Western World: An Introductory Survey*. New York: Oxford University Press.

Mashiri, Pedzisai. 2000. "Street Remarks, Address Rights and the Urban Female: Socio-linguistics Politics of Gender in Harare." *Zambezia* 27 (1).

Matereke, Kudzai. 2009. "Discipline and Punish: Inscribing the Body and its Metaphors in Zimbabwe's Postcolonial Crisis." *ARAS* 30(1) June.

Mawondo, G. 2011. *An Investigation into the Impact of Gender on Women's Musical Performances in Contemporary Zimbabwean Society: A Case of Harare*. Unpublished Bachelor of Music degree in Ethnomusicology.

Ntarangwi, Mwenda. 1999. "Musical Practice as a Gender Experience: Examples from Kenya and Zimbabwe." In *Africa in Reflections on Gender Issues*. Ed. by Patricia McFadden. Harare, Zimbabwe: SAPES Trust, Ltd.

Nketia, J. H. K. 1974. *The Music of Africa*. New York: W.W. Norton and Company.

Nzewi, Meki. 1991. *Musical Practice and Creativity: An African Traditional Perspective*. Bayreuth: Iwalewa-Haus, University of Bayreuth.

Nzewi, Meki. & Selo Galane. 2005. "Music is a Woman." In *Gender and Sexuality in South Africa*. Ed. by Walton Christ and Muller Stephanus. Stellenbosch: SUN ePReSS.

Owomoyela, Oyekan. 2002. *Culture and Customs of Zimbabwe*. London: Greenwood Press.

Schmidt, Elizabeth. 1992. *Peasants, Traders and Wives: Shona Women in the History of Zimbabwe, 1870-1939*. Portsmouth, NH: Heineman.

Vambe, Maurice Taonezvi. 2001. *Orality and Cultural Identities in Zimbabwe*. Gweru, Zimbabwe: Mambo Press.

Zindi, Fred. 1985. "The Rise of African Female Musicians." *SAPEM* 9 (10).

Zindi, Fred. 1997. *Music YeZimbabwe*. Gweru: Mambo Press.

Zindi, Fred. 2003. *Music Work Book: Zimbabwe Versus the World*. Harare: Zindsc Publications.

Other References
The Standard, 27 June 2009.
Jealous Husbands Break the Fabric of Mambokadzi
http://newsdzezimbabwe.wordpress.com/2011/04/01 We are not prostitutes-zim-dancers.

http://www.the Zimbabwean.co.uk/entertainment/music-and –dance/54561/ women judged harshly.

http://www.zimbojam.com/music-a-dance/dance-news/2184 sandra Ndebele gets her dream wedding.

7

Craig P. Woodson
George P. Hagan

EMBRACING DONDOLOGY— ESTABLISHING A VISION

J.H. Kwabena Nketia Festschrift

Applied Ethnomusicology: My Lifelong Exploration and Expression as a Dondologist

Craig P. Woodson

Craig Woodson is an applied ethnomusicologist with a PhD from UCLA. His company, Ethnomusic, Inc., is a World Music education consultancy specializing in the development of programs and instruments for young people.
In 1977, Professor Nketia invited him to head the Musical Instrument Technology Workshop at the Kwame Nkrumah University of Science and Technology in Kumase, Ghana.
He has performed with the Ghana National Symphony Orchestra, the Los Angeles Philharmonic, and the Kronos Quartet in venues including the Kennedy Center, Carnegie Hall and Lincoln Center. He is author and director of the Roots of Rhythm, a world drumming curriculum for the non-profit Percussion Marketing Council.

Background

My career formed from early connections to the fields of musical performance, instrument technology, and music education. As the son of a musician mother and an engineer father, my world of music began through a passion for technology and artistic expression. As a budding drummer in orchestra at 9 years old, I was fascinated by the buzz of snares on the snare drum and how bouncing the sticks could magnify that effect. My father drove me to the best private teacher in the area, an orchestral percussionist in Louisville, Kentucky. Several years later in Los Angeles, my studies turned to jazz.

In 1957 as an eighth grader, my middle school band teacher, Larry Bellis, invited me to learn how to wrap or 'tuck' a skin around a hoop to make a snare drum head--the inexpensive alternative to buying one. This began my lifelong passion for musical instrument technology. Continuing with drum repair in high school, by age 17 I had also begun teaching and making a living as a musician, primarily on the jazz drum set. Unlike most other instruments, the drum set or 'kit' required building every time it was taken down and re-assembled at a performance. This ritual added to my interest in how instruments were constructed. At that time as a youth music camp counselor, I was asked to arrange a 'creative' piece for the band; my choice was to have the group playing on homemade instruments. It was my first foray into making simple instruments, something that would evolve into a large portion of my professional life.

My introduction to non-European music came as I performed with a show band at a private party in the exclusive Trousdale Estates of Hollywood, California in 1962. The performers during our break were a belly dancer and drummer in a Middle Eastern tradition, both in full costume. I was mesmerized; this was not what one saw in the movies, but a magical reality. It was not until several years later that I was to become very close friends with these two master performers, Leona Wood, dancer, and her husband, Phillip Harland, musician, two of the three founders of the renowned Los Angeles-based AMAN Folk Ensemble.

World Music Study And Performance

After three years at Santa Monica City College, in 1964 I transferred to the University of California at Los Angeles (UCLA). Music education was my major with the tentative goal of becoming a band director. On weekends I performed jazz and pop music with many Los Angeles area musicians, including Stuart Brotman, a string bass player and expert in jazz, blues, and folk music. He introduced me to odd meters such as 7/8, 10/8 and 11/8 from Eastern European countries, the Middle East and Jewish music. I had a basic foundation in 5/4 from Dave Brubeck's 'Take Five' which was a national hit in 1961. This piece would be remembered in Ghana twenty years later in 1984 when I was asked to sit in with a hotel band in Accra, Ghana. They chose 'Take Five' probably to see if I knew my own cultural drumming.

Stuart Brotman encouraged me in three ways: world music performance, simple instrument making, and the blues. Knowing that I could play odd meters, Stuart, now my UCLA roommate, recommended me to perform in an 'ethnic' movie which required playing the Tupan, an Eastern European bass drum; this was my first professional experience outside of the Western tradition. Being a creative thinker, Stuart also was an expert at making music out of anything around the house and appreciated that I could do the same. In the mid-1960's Stuart and I performed as the house band at the Ash Grove, an important Los Angeles venue where many noted blues and folk musicians performed. This club was my introduction to the actual practice of world music of the day.

During the 1960's my father, Professor Thomas Woodson, taught in UCLA's Engineering Department and worked in Brazil on a joint university project in the rural northeast. In his book *Design Engineering*, he constantly referred to the term 'appropriate technology,' in the case of Brazil how using local materials and other resources could assist in accomplishing difficult engineering tasks. This concept was to become the foundation for much of how I approached instrument making with young people and my later work in the drum business.

Dondo Introduction

After transferring to the Music Department at UCLA in 1964, a fellow student, Frank Berberich, invited me to attend the student Ghanaian drumming and dance group that met in the Gamelan Room at the University's new Institute for Ethnomusicology. Entering the room for a trial practice, I immediately recognized one of the instructors, Phil Harland, from his performance two years ago. Phil was assisting instructor Robert Ayitee, an Ewe master drummer from Ghana, who had been hired by the Institute through Professor Nketia. This meeting began my decades-long friendship with Phil and my several years of work with Ayitee. They both appreciated that I was an accomplished percussionist. While many of the students, including Jim Koetting, were excellent musicians, only Dave Garcia and I had played drums professionally. My contact with Prof. Nketia was minimal at this time. (see Appendix, Figure 1).

The drum that immediately caught my attention was the Dondo (Donno, pl. or used here Dondos), the Asante pressure drum, also called a 'talking drum, armpit drum, or squeeze drum.' The Gamelan Room itself was a glorious, hands-on museum of world musical instruments where we were actually encouraged to learn and perform, taught by some of the world's master musicians. I felt quite humbled when I had difficulty playing some of the simplest introductory percussion parts in this Ghanaian group. Furthermore, I had not taken hand drumming very seriously in my studies, but Dave Garcia, a professional conga/bongo drummer, was very generous in giving me catch-up lessons[1]. I continued taking this weekly class as a music education major along with the traditional typical Eurocentric music classes. After graduating with a BA in music (1966), I began graduate studies with ethnomusicology as my focus with great interest in African music.

In 1967 my performance career changed gears when I was invited to play and record with an experimental rock band called the United States of America. This experience expanded to become part of my later professional work in rock and world music[2]. In 1968 I took my first African music seminar with Professor Nketia on his second visit to UCLA. By this time, I had been performing in the student Ghanaian ensemble for several years and Professor Nketia had taken note of my dedication to the music of Ghana. In the summer of 1969, I met master drummer and dancer Kwasi Badu, after he finished a U.S. tour with the National Dance Ensemble of Ghana. That year he replaced Robert Ayitee at UCLA who had gone back to Ghana.

First Meeting with Professor Nketia

My first meeting with Professor Nketia outside of UCLA was when he and I went to pick up Kwasi at the airport as he arrived for his work at the University. Badu would become my close friend, teacher, and co-worker over the next 25 years until his death in 1995. Professor Nketia would become my mentor, friend, the Chairman of my Ph.D. dissertation committee, and the person who directed my work in Ghana (1977, 1979-81 and 1984). Badu spoke almost no English, which I found out when he stayed at my parents' home for his first few days in Los Angeles. It was also the first time that I heard Twi between Ghanaians at full speed, and I remember that it sounded like drumming and it felt like being in Ghana.

Dondology

If Dondology can be defined as the scientific study of the Dondo, then this tribute to Professor Nketia can begin with a brief description of the traditional instrument. I will follow this with details of how I have developed this instrument over the past forty-five years as an Applied Dondologist.

Dondo Parts. Important Dondo parts and their names as discussed in this paper are as follows (see Appendix, Figure 2).

Traditional Materials. The drum body is traditionally carved from a single piece of *tweneboa kodia* (Akan name); the botanical name is *cordia millenii*. The drumheads are goat skin and the stick comes from, for example, the *ofema* bush. The tension cords are typically twisted pieces of goatskin, and the loops are often made from small animal intestine (gut). The spacer hoops are wrapped flat strips of rattan, which are themselves again wrapped radially (like a radial tire) with dried, tall 'elephant' grass.

Dondo History and Types. This instrument has wide distribution in West Africa, and in other regions of Africa under many names[3]. The focus here is on the Dondo that is used in the Asante region of Ghana, being absorbed into this cultural area from military interaction with the northern Mamprusi people (see Appendix, Figures 3A-E).

Dondo Repair. During this ten-year period as a performer in UCLA's African ensemble drums occasionally broke and while some were easy fixes, like broken tension cords, others like drumheads required considerable skill to repair. With my interest in the technology of drums, I began to look at creative ways of repairing the instruments other than the traditional techniques, that is, with 'appropriate technology.' One of my first repairs was substituting nylon polyfilament cord to repair broken leather tension cords on the Dondo. My first drumhead replacement experiment was on the Nigerian Dundun. This version of the hourglass drum had a particularly thin drumhead and as a consequence broke very easily. Mylar plastic drumheads made by the Remo drumhead company were the immediate solution for a quick fix. In order to mount this head I bent a piece of aluminum channel into a circle as a counter hoop in order to grab the metal 'flesh hoop' of the Remo head. I also added some silicon rubber inside center of the drumhead to help with the bass tone (see Appendix, Figure 3D, note discolored area in the head's middle).

My second Dondo experiment which followed soon after included changes to drumhead and the body (see Figure 3E in Appendix).

Dondo Science and Technology. There are many unique scientific and technological features to the Dondo which I had not known in my study of European percussion. Thirteen of some significant ones are as follows:

1. **Venturi Effect**. The hourglass shape emphasizes the Venturi effect (in a constricted column of air, forced airflow will increase in velocity)[4]. This principle increases the efficiency of how the two drumheads interact. There are many variations of sizes depending on the region of Africa from a long and narrow body to short and wide (around 12" to over 25"). The bowls vary in shape as well. The wider the bowl the greater the bass tone and visa versa.
2. **Coupling**. The drumheads act as a coupled frequency, that is, when one drumhead is struck on this type of double-headed drum, the other head instantly reacts. This coupling is enhanced by the Venturi effect as the air velocity is increased through the tube when one drum head is struck.
3. **Collar**. In order to have a deep bass tone on the hourglass type of pressure drum, there needs to be a 'collar' or a shallow drop from the bearing edge to the flesh hoop. In other words the skin has to be loose

enough to lower the pitch; otherwise the tessitura will be restricted to a narrow, upper range.

4. **Hooked Stick**. The Dondo is struck with a hooked stick at almost a right angle mainly for the purpose of initiating the Venturi effect and coupled frequency. This stroke exerts great force near the center of the head where it is loosest. If the stick accidentally hits near the bearing edge where the tension is greatest, the skin can easily break.

5. **Variable Pitch**. The Dondo is one of the few membranophones that is capable of producing a definite pitch. While the normal modes of vibration of a circular drumhead are non-harmonic, the Dondo has a definite harmonic pitch probably because the Venturi effect assists the membrane's fundamental mode of vibration.

Another unique feature of this type of pressure drum's tone is that the tension of the drumheads can be varied over a range of 1.5 octaves in a fraction of a second. This flexible capability enables the performer to produce even microtones if needed. Considering that the Dondo can be used as a 'talking drum,' the instrument can produce the six notes in the normal Akan speech mode.

6. **Underarm Pressure Drum**. The drumhead's tension is changed by pressure on cords squeezed under the arm. To have the Dondo's widest pitch range requires that the drumhead be completely slackened until there is no tone; only a dull 'thud' should sound when the drum is held up and stuck away from the body. As soon as the drum goes under the arm, the correct tuning would yield the lowest tone when struck. This procedure is how one is assured that the drum is properly adjusted.

7. **Drumhead Thickness**. In order to get the required sound of the relatively small drumhead diameter, each of the two skins has to be thin and should be the same thickness. Hitting the drum correctly, of course, requires great care since it is quite easy to break the skin especially near the bearing edge.

8. **Spacer Ring Flesh Hoop**. The Asante Dondo has a significantly narrow waist which provides the Venturi effect as well as room to squeeze the drum as it is being tightened. However, the addition of a flat spacer ring adds extra distance enabling a greater usable space for

squeezing. This type of spacer is unique to the Asante Dondo. Other similar drums have a longer waist or a wider opening at each end requiring narrower spacer rings, more in the form of a tube. Significantly the Dondo's spacer ring, which is made of rattan, needs to be rapped a second time, in a radial way, to hold the rattan in place. The skin is sewn on to this ring with twisted gut cord, and loops are positioned for attaching the tension cords (see Appendix, Figure 6A).

9. **Modifier**. For some versions of this drum, seeds, pebbles or even bones of ancestors are placed inside, or a gut snare is stretched across the one or both drumheads. In some traditions these objects are considered to be the 'voice' or spirit of the instrument and are required before the drum is to be played. This sound modifier is not typically used with the Asante Dondo.

10. **Loaded Head**. On some versions of this hourglass pressure drum, a paste or other weight is added to the center of the drumhead. This 'loads' the drumhead and helps emphasize the bass tone, especially needed on smaller diameter drumheads.

11. **Skin vs. Plastic Drumhead**. Skin drumheads provide the ideal flexibility for tension variations on the Dondo. Mylar plastic is considerably stiffer and while very strong and almost 100% water resistant, it is not as flexible as animal skin. As a result, drumming on Mylar produces much higher overtones. The microscopic crisscross fiber structure of the skin is the key, providing the necessary flexibility for more of the bass tone to be activated. Because the molecular structure of Mylar is less flexible, its rigid nature results in greater activation of the higher overtones. Loading Mylar in the middle of the drumhead with a weighted paste helps activate the bass tone.

12. **Tuning**. When tightening the Dondo, the drum is placed horizontally between one's knees and each cord is pulled tight (like tightening a shoelace from the bottom up) to insure the collar is at about one-half inch from the bearing edge. The tie cord around the drum's waist is then pulled tight, to keep the collar in the correct position.

13. **Playing Technique**. The drumhead is struck near the center with a rebound stroke or a damped or muted stroke. In the first case, the

beater's head is on the drum as short a time as possible, whereas the second type requires the drumstick to stay on the drumhead at least momentarily. A glissando up on this variable pitch drum only occurs when raising the drumhead tension (pitch) by squeezing the cords; for a glissando lowering the pitch, the head needs to be repeatedly struck as the tension cords are released. Since the drumhead needs to be quite thin for the best tone, great care needs to be taken not to hit too hard and too near the bearing edge, the area of highest tension and the easiest place to break the head. The primary control of sound is with pressure on the cords, with very rapid squeezes and releases of the tension. These actions produce rapid pitch variations, akin to a vibrato effect, a particularly important requirement of the Asante Dondo sound. Badu described the squeeze under one's arm as trying to squeeze a circle with a triangle. Proper squeezing requires the elbow to be pressed back, the drum pulled up into the armpit, and the cords stretched out with the thumb near the waist (see Kwasi Badu in Appendix, Figure 8).

14. **Talking Drum**. The Dondo is one of the instruments used to communicate through the Ghanaian tone language. As such there are typically six tone levels required, but this can be reduced to a minimum of three and even two, low and high. The combination of rhythm and pitch variation produces understandable Twi. Badu said that the name 'Dondo' was spoken on the drum (onomatopoetically), 'Don-' with a low tone and '-do' with a high tone.

Aluminum, Fiberglass, Cardboard Dondos. My fascination with the unique Dondo drumhead and body technology, and my desire to have one of my own, inspired me to make one with available materials, again using appropriate technology. I noticed that the shape of the upper portion of the hourglass Dondo was the same as lamp shades in the Institute's world instrument display cabinets. I found similar fixtures in a surplus metal store along with an aluminum tube, then had the parts welded together; a specialized Heliarc weld was required for aluminum (see Figure 3E in Appendix).

Using the drumhead tension system of the large Nigerian Dundun (Figure 3D in Appendix), my first synthetic Dondo took shape. Unfortunately the drumhead thickness and flexibility did not match the size of the drum's opening, so it did not work as expected. The experiment did, however, provide proof to me that this particular type of small, variable pitched, double-headed hourglass shaped drum required a very thin and flexible drumhead (see Figure 3E in Appendix).

1970
First Field Work: Europe and Morocco. As my interest in ethnomusicology grew, it was important to conduct field work, prompting me to visit musical instrument collections in European museums and do field research in Marrakech, Morocco in the summer of 1970. My early fascination with the buzz of a snare drum drew me to the Bendir, a single-headed frame drum with a simple, single cord snare system-- possibly one of the progenitors of the modern European snare drum. In Marrakech, I interviewed, filmed and performed with market place performers, and fell in love with field work[5].

Dundun in London Store. On my return to the U.S. through London, I happened upon a music store that had a Nigerian Dundun that was made by a Nigerian company called Afrikadabra. The drum body looked like wood but it was made with a Fiberglas and polyester resin. The drumheads were skin and the tension cords leather as on the traditional Dundun. It was housed in a felt lined case--modeled after one for a violin. If this were not impressive enough, it had an internal microphone and jack that were attached with an audio cable to a large amplifier and a 'wah-wah' pedal for changing the timbre. This instrument was shockingly unique in my experience and was a great inspiration.

Ethnomusic, Inc.
1971-73
Dondo Plugs and Molds. Having already experimented with non-traditional materials, I wanted to try the Fiberglas approach myself. Back in California, a friend in the plastics business showed me how to make an hourglass shape out of Fiberglas and resin. This involved several steps:

1. Determining the correct model on which to base the body shape. This I did by measuring instruments in the UCLA Gamelan Room collection.
2. Making a solid wooden 'plug' in the shape of a Dondo by turning a solid piece of wood on a lathe. I did this first with two pieces glued together.
3. Making a Fiberglas mold in two parts; inside this hard shell was a softer silicon rubber interface that reflected the wooden surface of the plug (see Figure 4 in Appendix).

I turned the hourglass plug on a lathe in stages. As soon as the medium size worked I made two other sizes larger and smaller and an even smaller toy size. Experiments involved various drum bodies including both Fiberglas and cardboard tubes attached together with Fiberglas. The least expensive was a small Dondo made with a cardboard tube, marketed as a toy[6] (see Figure 5E in Appendix).

Dondo Drumhead Experiments. I conducted considerable experimentation on Dondo drumheads because of their unique spacer ring, the cord tension system and the difficulty of re-stringing a drum when the head needed replacing. The initial idea was to duplicate the original design but use nylon rather than animal skin for the tension cords, keeping the drumhead itself skin. This was culturally less intrusive but the breaking problem remained. The loop sewn through the drumhead was still an inefficient system for restringing a drum when heads broke (see Figures 5B and 6A in Appendix). The loop problem was solved with a metal hook system with what are called 'double headed tacks,' resembling long legged staples. At first these were bent manually to make the hook, later with a specially designed rig for mass production (see Figures 5A, C in Appendix). While this hook system made the drum easier to restring, the skin drumhead was still easy to break and was susceptible to various weather conditions. As a result, the next idea was to use a Mylar plastic drumhead along with the bent hooks; this would solve both problems. With the plastic head, the sound was not as deep as the skin drumhead but the two largest technical lacing problems were solved (see Figures 5C, D in Appendix).

Leather cords on the traditional Dondo were susceptible to breakage. The first idea, to replace them with round nylon polyfilament, was too rough on a person's uncovered arm as the cords were squeezed. The next idea was to use a flat 'parachute' cord, which was strong enough but had too much flexibility. Eventually a thicker round cord was used.

Making the traditional spacer ring was too labor intensive and had to be redesigned for mass production. The initial idea to cut them out of pressboard was too time consuming so a die was purchased to cut them out of thin plywood. The tacks were hammered or pressed through the head during assembly. This became the final production model (see Figures 5C and 6B in Appendix). These major changes in the drumhead design resulted in twelve U.S. patents being awarded to me and my company, Ethnomusic, Inc., in 1976. The patents involved sandwiching the drumhead in between two pre-cut rings and stapling them together. The hooks were then sent through the ring and bent with a rig, all in one operation (see Figure 6B in Appendix).

The rings had two different inside diameters: the smaller inside diameter was to set the proper distance for squeezing (Lower Spacer Ring); the larger inside diameter allowed for a collar which was needed for the bass tone (Upper Spacer Ring). This meant that the collar would be closer to the bearing edge, not a problem for the sound (see Figure 6 in Appendix).

Dondo Stick Experiments. The Dondo also required a specialized hooked stick, which I developed over several years beginning with a duplication of the traditional version and ending with a reinforced metal version with a pre-bent aluminum angle (see Figure 7 in Appendix).

The Drum Industry

The Drum Industry and Remo. In 1970, a percussionist friend, Dave Levine, introduced me to his boss, Remo Belli, president of Remo, Inc., a world-renowned drumhead company. This was the beginning of my long personal and professional association with David and Remo. Belli had revolutionized the drum industry by introducing plastic Mylar 'film' drumheads in 1957; his contributions continued later including to world drumming and music therapy. Dave and I stayed in touch and re-connected on a large project for the percussion industry in 2004.

1973-76
Ethnomusic, Inc. Completing my master's degree included accurate real-time transcriptions of drum solos by jazz drummer Tony Williams. This work used the Melograph Model C, an early sound printing device pioneered at the Institute of Ethnomusicology. By the time I earned my master's in 1973, I had adjusted my career goal to combining ethnomusicology with music education in a business. With this in mind, I wanted to apply my studies to provide world music solutions to educators. This led to formation of my company, Ethnomusic, Inc. a business model that would produce instruments and educational materials for students, educators and professional musicians based on music from around the world. After almost 10 years of studying and performing various types of world music as a professional drummer and at UCLA, I saw that there was a need for the production of

world musical instruments and educational material for educators and professionals. I wanted to use my understanding and appreciation of world musical cultures to benefit society by turning theory into practice. My first public project was the production of a concert in 1974 that featured two contrasting cultures, Cuban and South Indian. This production experience led me later to conduct much larger events that involved audience participation.

African Percussion EXperience (APEX). After several years of work and experimentation with technology, I had developed a product and the company Ethnomusic, Inc. which became incorporated in Los Angeles in 1976. From my experience as a teacher, it seemed that educational kits would offer an introduction to understanding world music. I began with the African instrument that I knew the best, the Dondo. The first kit was called APEX, the African Percussion EXperience--how to play the Dondo and Adawia bell parts for Adowa music. It consisted of three sizes of Dondos, a booklet with background and transcriptions, and audio tapes in regular and slow speeds performed by Kwasi Badu. I wrote the transcriptions in both the Time Unit Box System (TUBS), designed by Phil Harland (mentioned earlier), and in western notation for those both with and without musical training. The wavy line shows the subtle and very fast squeeze patterns required for playing the master Dondo part (see Figure 8 in Appendix).

By 1976, I had secured my twelve U.S. utility patents on drumhead design and manufacturing technique. I began production and marketed this educational package at the main music industry show called NAMM, the International Music Products Association. Being the first of its kind on the market, sales of music kits increased rapidly and I moved the operation out of my garage and back yard into to a nearby manufacturing facility in Venice, California.

In the fall of 1977 as sales were increasing, Prof. Nketia, saw my progress on manufacturing Ghanaian instruments in APEX, and invited me to Ghana for a one-month review of an instrument-making research project in Kumasi, at the Center for Cultural Studies (CCS), at the University of Science and Technology (UST). This was an offer I could not turn down, and I knew that my life was about to change in an unexpected and miraculous way.

To Ghana
1977-1978
Preparation for Ghana. At the conclusion of this one-month trip across Ghana, I wrote a paper summarizing what I felt could be done to improve this research project which would begin the production of prototypes of African instruments for Ghanaian schools. After reading this document, Prof. Nketia offered me a position as Senior Research Fellow at UST at CCS to direct the research project. Later named the Musical Instrument Technology Workshop (MITW), this research and development facility was a unique project that promised to be an unparalleled opportunity to help build music education in Ghana and potentially elsewhere in West Africa. As such it was to become a tremendously positive, life-changing experience. After some consideration, I accepted, but it required that I now had to put my company plans on hold.

Nketia suggested that I complete my Ph.D. using research during my work at the Centre. From 1978-1979, I completed my coursework at UCLA, filled remaining orders for Ethnomusic, and packed for a stay of two to three years in Ghana.

1979-85
Musical Instrument Technology Workshop. In November 1979, I moved to Kumasi, Ghana with my wife, and began work as Senior Research Fellow and Director of MITW. The four primary tasks were all in line with what I had done to develop my company, Ethnomusic: (1) conduct research on instruments and musical traditions that have been neglected and were in danger of disappearing; (2) identify master musicians and instrument makers to help with the project; (3) develop prototypes for African sets of instruments (that would be used in over 5,000 schools in that country); and (4) begin prototype production for testing (at sites around Ghana). This research continued for two years and extended to all areas of Ghana. The primary method was again to use appropriate technology, using locally available tools and materials for our purpose of "increasing cultural awareness," a major goal of the research according to Prof. Nketia. By 1981, MITW had achieved its initial goals, and I returned to California to complete my doctoral dissertation on the art and technology of the Asante Atumpan drums[7]. In November 1983, with the Ph.D. completed, I returned to Ghana as Acting Director of the Center for Cultural Studies as well as Director of MITW. During this trip, I provided leadership training that would enable

the Workshop to continue after my scheduled departure in December 1984. The MITW has now operated successfully over the past several decades and currently produces drums and other instruments for sale from their showroom (see Figure 9 in Appendix).

Ethnomusic Consultancy
1985-89

Refocus Ethnomusic, Inc.. Back in California in early 1985, I realized that over the decade since beginning Ethnomusic, other companies, both large and small, had begun producing or importing world musical instruments for the U.S. market, including African hourglass drums like the Dondo. As a result I re-evaluated the current need in world music education and decided to change the company's focus from manufacturing to world music educational consultancy. I felt that there was a need to have young people in the United States benefit from making their own instruments as I had seen children do in Ghana. It seemed that teachers would also benefit from these hands-on activities for the many multi-disciplinary lessons they provided including science, history, social studies, language arts, art, and music. This approach would put inexpensive and good sounding instruments from around the world in the hands of young people for both classroom and home use, especially those who could not afford them.

Prior to 1985, making simple instruments had been only a secondary interest of mine, but now with over 20 years experience in instrument design both in the U.S. and Africa, I had a new challenge: use appropriate technology at the simplest level for children to have immediate access to world music. This new approach required designing a wide range of instruments, all age-appropriate technologies that could be completed by students ages five and up; some were designed only for older students and adults. Some of my most successful instruments have been 'composites' or several-in-one ideas. For example, the Drumpet, consists of an African drum, European trumpet, South American scraper, Asian flute, and Middle Eastern zither, all made with recycled materials[8].

School Programs. There were several ways to market this approach: (1) hands-on student workshops, (2) assembly presentations, and (3) teacher and parent workshops. Arts organizations had been developing outreach programs to schools since the early 1970's; I had previously worked with a few of them.

- In 1985, I auditioned for a newer, larger program at the Music Center of Los Angeles County. 'Music Center on Tour' sent visual and performing teaching artists into hundreds of schools to do assemblies and workshops. These events were paid for by state or parent funding. I began with two programs both featuring a homemade version of the Dondo. A World Orchestra You Can Build - on making twelve simple musical instruments from five major world cultures
- Adowa: African Drumming and Dancing from Ghana - on how to make simple drums, play authentic drums, and dance Adowa

A description of Adowa by John Mitchell in the Los Angeles Times (1988) states,

> "...As part of his performance, Woodson introduced several examples of African drums to his audience. He demonstrated how drums are made with an instrument resembling a common garden hoe. He even brought some homemade drums fashioned from empty water bottles and coffee cans..."[1]

Homemade Drums. As with all instrument designs for these presentations, I based my ideas on authentic instruments and if possible on how children made instruments around the world. The homemade drum Ghanaian children called a Dondo was typically made from a small, empty evaporated milk can that they covered (for drumheads) with dried latex rubber extracted from a rubber tree. In addition children might dye the rubber several colors for decoration and even sell them in the market. Because these particular cans were quite shallow, one could squeeze both drumheads with one hand changing the pitch; hence, children called it a 'Dondo.' The wrapping technique that Ghanaian children used was what I call the 'star pattern'. While this design works it does build up more tape material in the middle, leaving thinner areas near the bearing edge, and this is where a drumhead can easily break. The extra tape in the middle did, however, load (add weight to) the head giving it a relatively low register. Seeing the creative minds and enterprising nature of Ghanaian youths was a great inspiration.
I realized that such hands-on experiences were often eliminated from educational curricula in America. These lessons were all valuable when I began designing homemade drums with newer materials.

My exploration to design a new and simple drumhead was inspired by the Remo company's 1981 drumhead made out of bullet-proof Kevlar. The idea of a vertical and horizontal weave in combination with the Ghanaian use of stretchable strips of sticky material, gave me the idea for making a simple drumhead with tape. Two-inch wide Polyvinyl Chloride (PVC) tape was very strong, easily available, inexpensive, and the thinner version was easy to stretch. What made this material extremely useful for drumheads was that when stretched across a drum body and was stuck to the body's outside wall, the tape held its tension. Its attributes made it ideal for a new simple and effective drumhead for homemade drums. These ideas all began in the early 1980's but became my focus after 1985.

Many years later during a teacher workshop, I learned from science teacher, Dr. Joe Wesney that the reason the tape was strong was because of its molecular structure; it is made of molecule chains that easily stretch. Furthermore he stated that the tape breaks easily because with a slight jab from a sharp object (pen or pencil) the chains "unzip." Fortunately, a drum beater is not sharp and the tape can withstand the force. The key to making this material work effectively as a strong drumhead was to crisscross the tape in what I called the 'tic-tac-toe' or weave pattern (an easy pattern for children to remember—also the way most cloth is made). Thus when the woven pattern is stretched over any hollow tube or other shape, the tape will stick to the side and the drumhead will remain tightened.

The first drum I tried was taping over a tin coffee can as children had done in Ghana; it worked. This was also very successful over a picture frame to make the Adufe, resembling a double-headed square drum found in the Middle East and on the Iberian Peninsula.[9] This wrapping technique can also be used to make a single-headed version of the rectangular drum, such as the Tamalen in Ghana.

Homemade Dondo. After the tape idea proved successful on cans and frames, I tried it on a Dondo. Over many years this homemade pressure drum idea evolved into more efficient versions each time getting closer to the authentic Dondo sound. The first successful homemade Dondo- -and still the easiest to make--is made with two #10 cans (a typical #10 coffee can is found in school or restaurant kitchens), two embroidery hoops, PVC tape, and strapping tape (with strings inside), along with a dowel stick for the beater. I used this Dondo in my World Orchestra student assembly (see Figure 10A in Appendix).

I first experimented with the homemade hourglass-shaped Dondo in 1999 by connecting two clay flower pots end to end. This required carefully hammering out the bottoms of each pot and gluing them together at the base allowing air to flow between the heads. The drumheads were attached with crisscrossed tape over a tube bent into a circle. This Dondo was designed for my school assembly called 'To Mars with Music in 2030.' The assembly's content was based on my participation in an educational video for the National Aeronautics and Space Administration in 1999 that showed young people how the Arts might be taken to Mars on a future trip. I used the clay pots because this material would be plentiful on the Red Planet. In 2006, I designed a more authentic sounding Dondo for upper grade students and teachers. This drum used two plastic flower pots, a piece of PVC tube, and the same drumhead as the first two Dondos.

1989-99

Relocating in Ohio. Deciding to raise my young family in a rural setting, I moved to Ohio in 1989 and set up business in Chagrin Falls, near Cleveland. My school assemblies continued with frequent trips to Los Angeles, but expanded in the Midwest. I began teaching college courses that focused on instrument making.

Play-Along Concerts. In 1991, through my promotion of instrument making courses for teachers, I was invited to design a set of simple instruments to be used in an educational 'play-along' concert with the Cleveland Orchestra. This was the first of many such events with major orchestras around the U.S. and in Europe; each audience member made instruments and played along with the orchestra on one or more pieces as a part of the concert. Using homemade instruments in a concert setting had now become part of my profession, an interest that had begun over 40 years earlier as a teenager[10].

Remo Consultancy. My earlier friendship with Remo Belli and his company also became a business relationship after showing him some of my ideas in the late 1980's. I was hired as a consultant and began working on some of their prototype drums including goblet (djembe/doumbek) and hourglass (Dondo) types based on African designs.

The most recent project is a craft for making drums (see Figure 12B in Appendix).

While I had allowed my earlier drum patents to expire, the ideas were still not being used in the music industry. Remo Belli took note of this and developed a related product called Sound Shapes (SS). These drums used several of my ideas, for example, sandwiching a Mylar film drumhead between two flat rings stapling them in place. Along with his own Pre-Tensioning System (PTS) -- a technique for tightening drumheads in the manufacturing process -- the whole new line of SS drums was formed.

2001-2003
Based on my 1960's work in rock music, I was hired as Senior Director of Education at the Rock and Roll Hall of Fame and Museum in Cleveland, Ohio. In developing children's programs on rock history, I used the Dondo as an example of Hip Hop's roots to speech rhythm in Africa. While at the Rock Hall I remained a Remo consultant, helping to develop their new Nigerian Dundun (see Figure 5D in Appendix).

2004-2011
Roots of Rhythm and NAMM. In 2004, I was invited to write a world drumming curriculum called Roots of Rhythm (ROR) for the non-profit Percussion Marketing Council (PMC) by my longtime friend and PMC associate, David Levine. This free online curriculum was jointly sponsored with the International House of Blues Foundation (IHOBF), under Executive Director, Susan Jauron. As one of the sixteen chapters, I chose the Dondo to represent a drum capable of speech rhythm, this featuring Adowa music. The complete package includes authentic recordings from the Smithsonian collection and Dondo transcriptions of Badu.

The PMC and IHOBF need was for multi-disciplinary content to be taught in workshops for non-music teachers; ROR contained instrument making projects including the homemade Dondo. This work was possible with the support of NAMM Foundation, the non-profit part of NAMM, the International Music Products Association. In 2010 I was appointed Director ROR for PMC, and continue to present ROR teacher workshops around the country and overseas (see Figure 10A in Appendix).

Making a Half Dondo. As my work with students and teachers increased, it involved events requiring traveling around the US and overseas. To make a Dondo more easily for such travel and to reduce the cost, I changed the drum to half size with one head; this type of drum is similar to one found among the Hausa in Nigeria[11] (see Figure 10B in Appendix).

Humanitarian Work

In Iraq. In 2008 and 2009 I traveled with music therapist Christine Stevens to conduct drumming and drum making workshops in northeastern Iraq. One of the drums I made was the Dondo, first instructing adults who in turn taught children to make their own drums (see Figure 11A in Appendix).

In Java. In 2009, I joined a team of American artists for a three-week UCLA/U.S. State Department program in Yogyakarta, Java in Indonesia. My contribution was to bring drumming and instrument making to earthquake victims in the Bantul region and to work with teachers and artists (see Figure 11B in Appendix).

Drums of Humanity. As a result of my work and collaboration with Stevens, I along with Dr. Irina Shiyanovskaya, a physicist, began a 501(c)(3) non-profit organization called Drums of Humanity in 2009. With funds raised though this NGO there will be greater opportunities to bring music and instrument making to those recovering from war and natural disaster.

Continuation

In spring 2011 I met with Professor Nketia during his trip to Chicago, Illinois to discuss ways to further the MITW project connecting recent Remo drumhead technology with traditional Ghanaian drums. I presented him with several adaptations of various types of Remo drumheads for use as a new instrument-making craft, and on a variety of wooden Ghanaian drums from MITW (see Figure 12 in Appendix).

Conclusion

Applied Dondology. My own study and performance of music changed profoundly when the music of Ghana and the Dondo came into my life, all through Professor Nketia and his passion for African music, ethnomusicology, scholarship, and education. My goal of reconnecting people to their cultural heritage, and providing opportunities for musical expression through the making of simple musical instruments for a more peaceful world, is directly linked to his influence. I have offered my story as partial evidence of the profound influence that Kwabena Nketia has had on so many lives around the world, directly and indirectly. My musical evolution, coming first from ignorance of African music, to an appreciation at UCLA, to awe of master musicians, study and travel in Ghana, to fieldwork, research, and experimentation, to building a company based on drumming in Ghana, to educational outreach with Kwasi Badu, and to recent humanitarian work, all has a direct link back to this inspirational man, whom I consider my African father. *Meda wo ase.*

Endnotes

1: My image of African drumming to that time had come mainly from stereotypical adventure or Tarzanesque movies of the 1950's.

2: Since several of the other members of the band had been UCLA students and had considerable exposure to world music through the Institute, we were able to incorporate such global resources in our compositions. My sound experiments included making my own electronically amplified drums with piezo electric crystals as pick ups for the vibrations.

3: A few of the other names for the hourglass pressure or squeeze drum: kalangu (Hausa of Nigeria), *kanango, dundun, iyalu* (Yoruba of Nigeria), *hutamba* (Sierra Leone), and *dawura, ntremu, nonka* (Ghana), see Figures A-C.

4: G. B. Venturi (1746-1822) physicist found that a short tube with a constricted, throat-like passage increases the velocity and lowers the pressure of a fluid conveyed through it (from *Webster's New World Dictionary of the American Language*, World Publishing Co. Cleveland, Ohio 1962, p. 1617).

5: This field research became the basis of my paper for *Selected Reports in Ethnomusicology* (1974). In this paper I also used the real-time notation system that I had developed for my master's thesis on jazz drummer, Tony Williams. I would later use variations of this system for transcriptions of the Dondo and the Atumpan (my Ph.D. dissertation).

6: While a professor at Harvey Mudd Engineering College in Pomona, California, my father, Professor Thomas Woodson, had students conducta marketing study of this drum as an undergraduate project in the local area (1976-77). Students presented the results in a paper at the end of the term. This was part of his efforts to get educators and industry more connected at the undergraduate level.

7: A review of MITW can be found in my article titled, 'Appropriate Technology in the Construction of Traditional African Musical Instruments in Ghana." published in *Studies in African Music, Selected Reports in Ethnomusicology*, (Volume 5, 1984, UCLA).

9: Tens of thousands of the Drumpets have been made by young people and adults around the world. Since the 1970's I have designed over 300 instrument making projects for use by young people and adults. (more information is at www.EthnomusicInc.com).

10: More detailed descriptions of how these drums can be made with tape are found in Dr. Woodson's online curriculum that I wrote for the Percussion Marketing Council, for free download at www.RootsofRhythm.net.

11: Concert venues included the Royal Festival Hall in London, Dorothy Chandler Pavilion in Los Angeles, Brooklyn Academy of Music, and Carnegie Hall. This included international play-along concerts with the Kronos Quartet.

12: During a conversation with Ghanaian master drummer Obo Addy, in November 2011, he recalled this seeing the traditional half hourglass drum of the Hausa people, which I had seen in the 1960's at UCLA.

Appendix

Figure 1: UCLA Ethnomusicology Dance Festival 1968
L to R: Phil Harland, Jim Koetting, Dave Garcia, Author
Performing Brekete (Leona Wood is off stage)
Photographer is unknown.

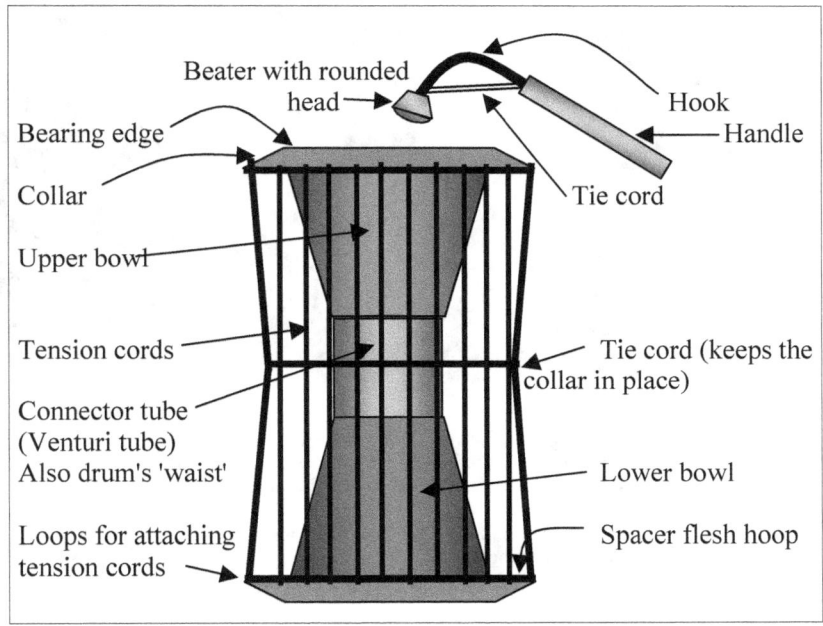

Figure 2: Dondo Part Names

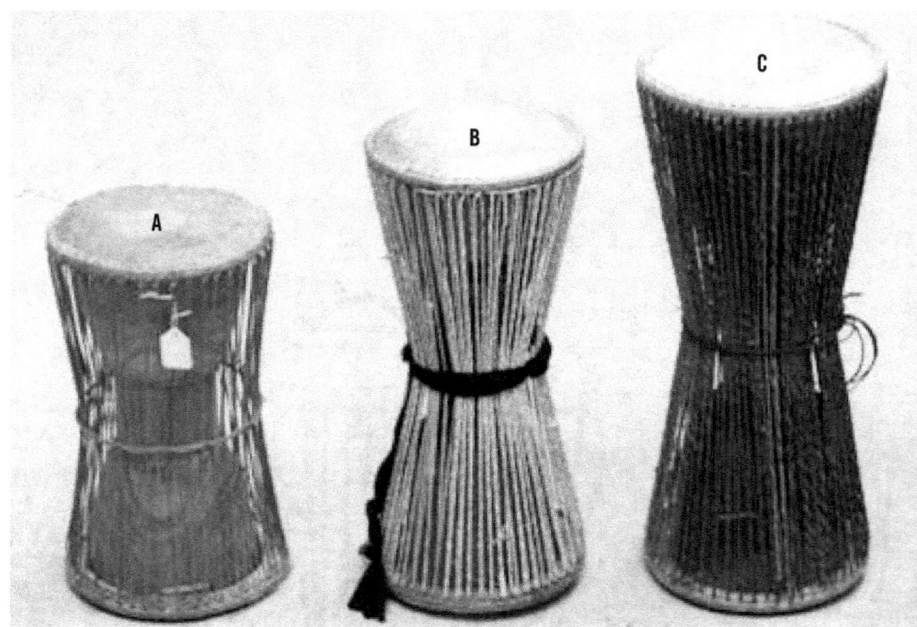

Figure 3 A–E: Three Traditional Asante Dondo, New Tension and Drumhead System on Dundun and Dondo (1967-68)
A. Dawuro **B.** Ntremu **C.** Nonka **D.** Nigerian Dundun
E. Ghanaian Dondo
Small, Medium, Large, Mylar Drum Head, Mylar Drum Head
Traditional Wood Body, Aluminum Body

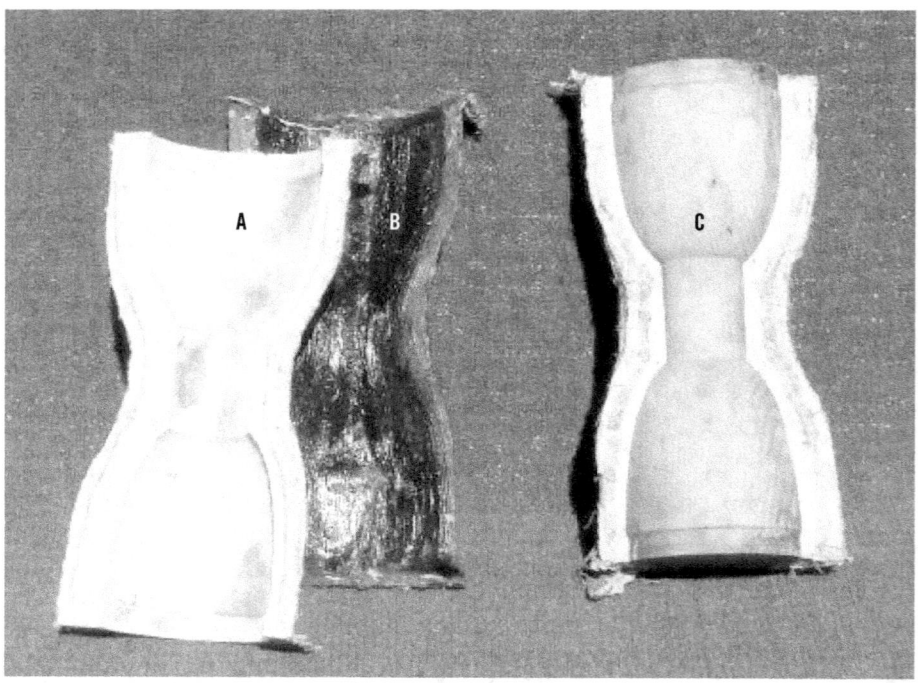

Figure 4: Dondo Molds and Plug (1972-1977)
A. Interior White Silicon Rubber Mold to Get the Wood Grain Effect
B. Exterior Black Fiberglas Mold to Support the Rubber Mold
C. Solid Wood 'Plug' or Master Dondo Shape of the Body

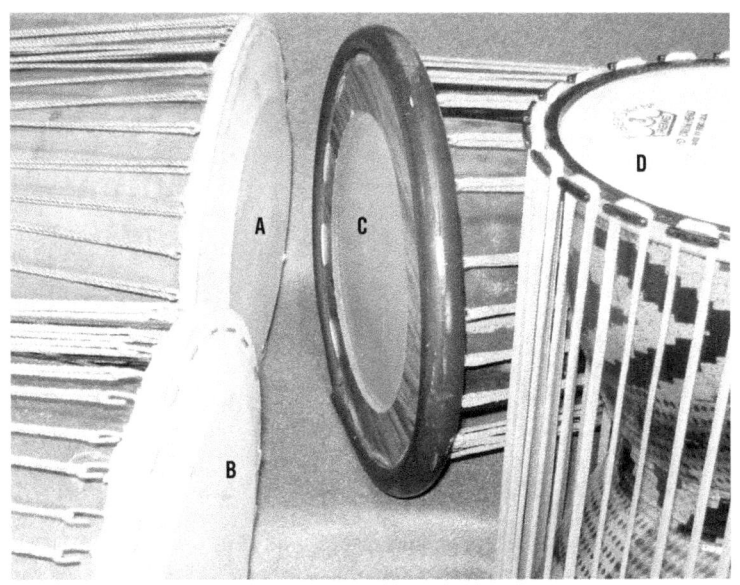
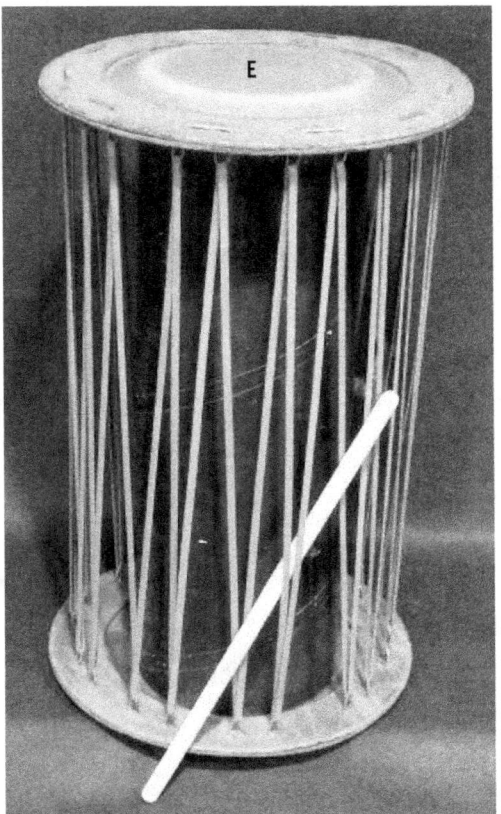

Figure 5
APEX Dondo Tension Systems
A. Narrow Staple J-Hooks with Calfskin Head
B. Nylon Loops Sewn On with Calfskin Head
C. Wide Staple J-Hooks with Split Tube Cover on Mylar Head
D. Remo T-Hooks based on Woodson Design
E. Woodson cylindrical Toy Dondo with Wide Staple J-Hook

Figure 6 Traditional and Woodson Patented Dondo Drumhead System (Side View)

A. Traditional Spacer Ring System

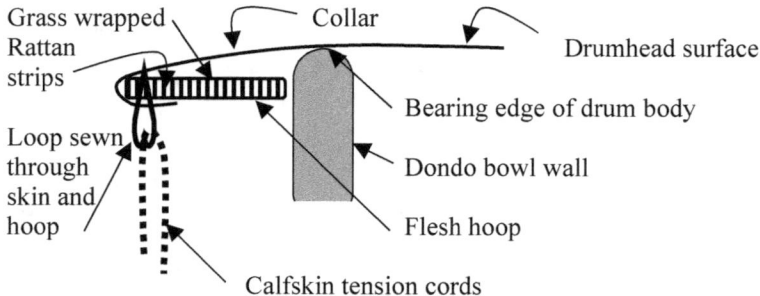

B. Woodson Patented Spacer Ring System (1975)

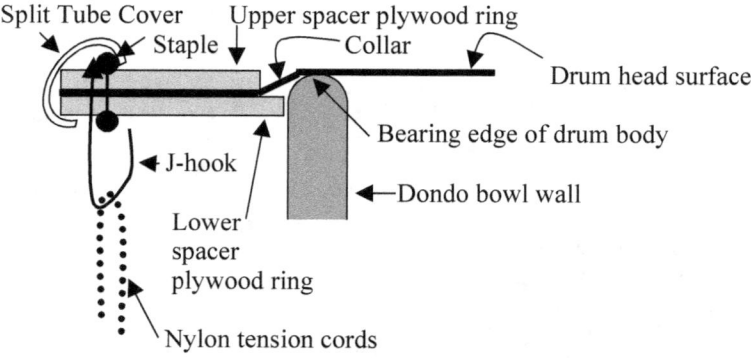

Figure 6: Traditional and Woodson Patented Dondo Drumhead System (Side View)

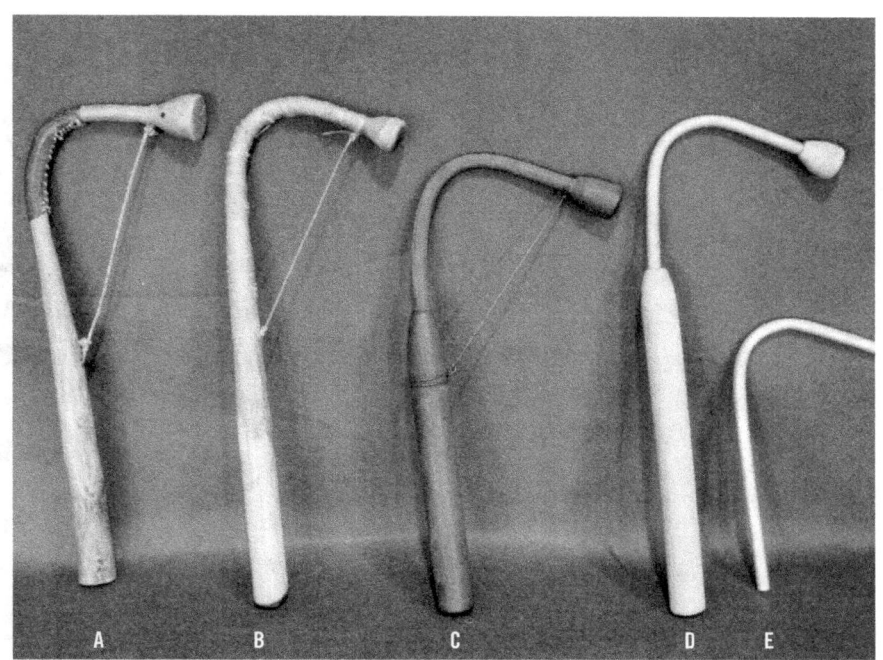

Figure 7: Woodson Dondo Sticks/Nkonta
A. Traditional Nkonta with Leather Reinforced Hook (1966)
B. One Piece Rattan Nkonta with Fiberglas Reinforced Hook (1972)
C. Three Piece Wood Nkonta with Rattan Hook (1974)
D. Three Piece Wood Nkonta with Wood Handle and Beater and Aluminum Hook (1976)
E. Aluminum Hook before Assembly

A. Nonka, B. Ntremu, C. Dawuro, D. Adawia (Lg.)   Author with Kwasi Badu (1975)
E. Adawia (Sm.), F. Booklet, G. Tape Cassette

Figure 8: Africa Percussion Experience (APEX)

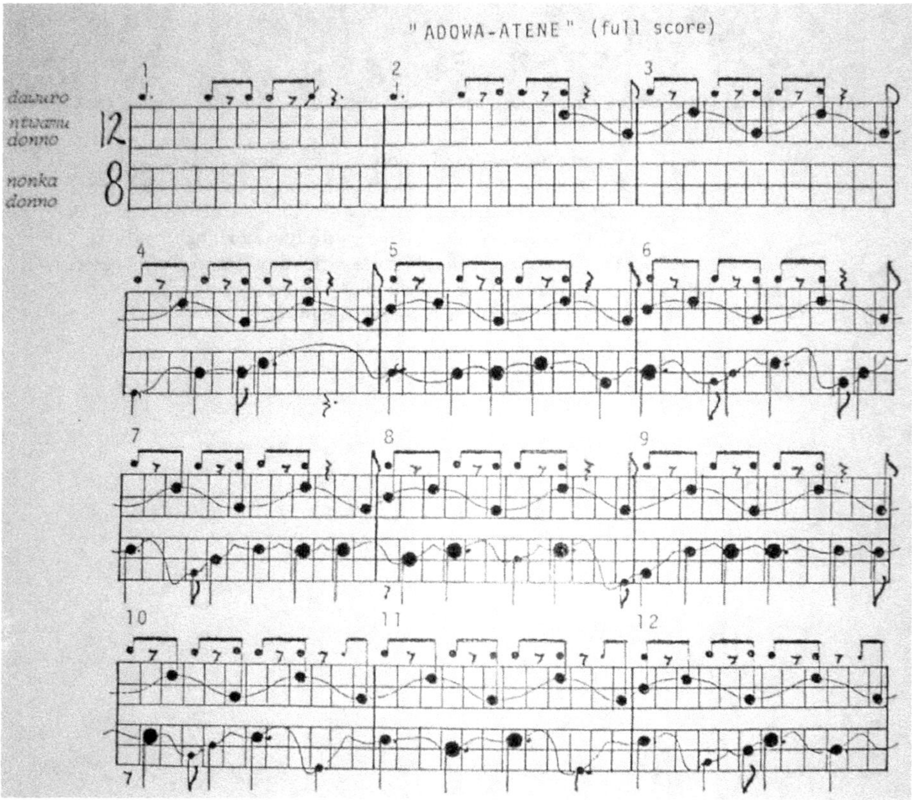

All parts are played by Kwasi Badu. Nonka is the master drum part.
The wavy lines represent the squeeze patterns.

Figure 9: Musical Instrument Technology Workshop Showroom 2011

1. Tape two coffee cans together (open at both ends). 2. Wrap PVC tape around hoop in crisscross pattern keeping collar in place. 3. Tape two heads together loosely with strapping tape. 4. Tape end of stick for beater.

A. Full-Size Homemade Dondo

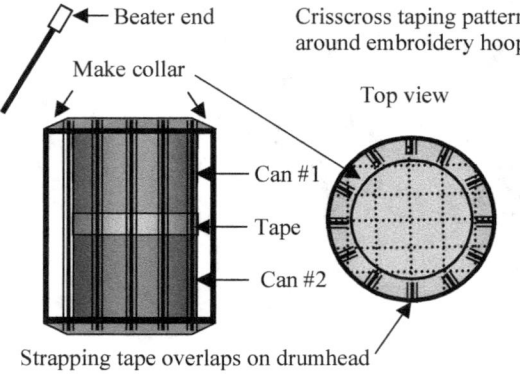

Teachers playing homemade Dondo in Roots of Rhythm workshop

B. Half-Size Homemade Dondo

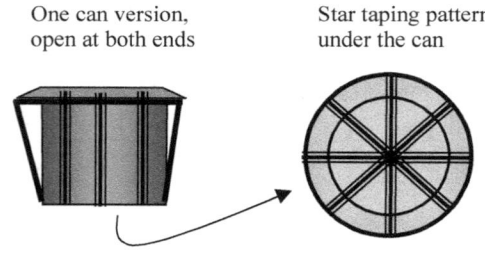

Students making homemade half Dondo in a workshop

Figure 10: Making and Playing Homemade Dondos

Figure 11:
Humanitarian Use of Dondo Making

Dondo Making in Darbandikhan, Iraq.

Teachers in Yogyakarta, Java

Figure 12: Prof. Nketia with Author 2011 in Chicago, Discussing MITW and Remo Drumheads on Traditional Drum Shells.
Photograph by Author's son, Theo Woodson

Prototype Dondo Craft with Remo Sound Shape

Dondology: Music, Mind And Matter

George P. Hagan

George P. Hagan taught for many years at the University of Ghana, Legon. He is the former director of the Institute of African Studies at the same institution, and the former chairman of the Ghana National Commission on Culture. He is a social anthropologist with several publications, including his co-edited volume with Irene K. Odotei, *The King Returns: Enstoolment of Asantehene Otumfuo Osei Tutu II and the Ayikesee (Great Funeral) of Otumfuo Opoku Ware II* (2002); *Divided We Stand: A Study of Social Change Among the Effutu of Coastal Ghana* (2000); *Nkrumah's Leadership Style: An Assessment From a Cultural Perspective* (1985); *Culture and Development* (1978); and *Black Civilization and Philosophy: The Akan Tradition of Philosophy* (1977).

Introduction

In his life-long academic work on music in African cultures, which he crowned with his historic professorial inaugural, subtitled 'Dondology Revisited', J. H. Kwabena Nketia defined the subject, substance, methodology and scope of the study of music and music-making in African communities and made *Dondology*, African ethnomusicology, a systematic, multidisciplinary, interdisciplinary and relevant academic subject world-wide.[1] Besides bringing traditional African music into the mainstream of intellectual discourse, Nketia's publications provide important and insightful material for the study of African history, mythology, literature, poetry, dance, drama, aesthetics, cultural anthropology, religion and philosophy, creating a wealth of knowledge on African societies and cultures. As a non-musicologist, I here wish to attempt to celebrate this monumental intellectual legacy by looking at how *Dondology* enhances the study of African cultures in relation to the fundamental questions of African philosophy.

In his prodigious and authoritative writings on music-making in African communities, Nketia characterizes music as a vital part of African community life, and indicates that, as a creative activity, music-making is pervasive, multifunctional and multi-contextual and reaches the depths of lived experience in all communities. Nketia further points out that, while music is performed as an extraneous, incidental accompaniment to some formal and informal events, in others music constitutes an intrinsic and essential part of the character and purpose of what occurs (*The Music of Africa*, 1974). In this regard, though Nketia does not assert this categorically, it might be inferred from his statements on the import, uses and impact of music in individual and community life that cradle songs, initiation songs, play songs, courtship and love songs, wedding songs, hunting songs, work songs, war songs, praise songs, religious songs, funeral songs and dirges, do not only add meaning, entertainment or embroidery to events, more importantly, they energize, drive and direct the course of events to an expected existential end. For example, commenting on the Ghanaian Frafra people's practice of weeding with the accompaniment of music, Nketia wrote:

> This has a remarkable effect on the speed as well as the efficiency of grass cutting, for rhythmic movements that are properly organized on some regular basis appear to be less fatiguing than movements in which exertion and release of effort do not form an ordered sequence (1972:28,29).

This comment, made from an outsider's perspective, suggests that music might definitely have some effect on such banal practical activities of life as soothing a child to sleep, enchanting and seducing a lady, rowing a boat or cutting a field of grass or, indeed, influencing the outcome of a football match, even if belief in the efficacy of music in sublime activities such as festivals, rites of transition and worship be treated as folklore. The issue here is that, in both the profane and sacred uses of music, we are confronted with the urgent need to obtain the insider's view and understanding of the import and impact of music on events and entities in terms of African beliefs and concept of reality.[2]

In the mind of the African, music has some direct and inexorable impact on objects, events and processes at several interrelated levels. At one level, music impacts on individual and collective consciousness and states of mind and changes individual and collective moods, attitudes and emotions in tune with the nature, functions and contexts of events. Music also stimulates and intensifies human interactions and collective experience to the extent of generating strong collective sentiments in groups to overcome individual sentiments of fear, pain, doubt, shame and anxiety. In this way, music mediates the relationship between the mind and the human body, giving the mind greater control over the body and over individual physical and emotional responses to situations and events. Traditional war songs condition fighters to overcome fear and endure physical pain. Work music concentrates minds and improves coordination and efficiency. The influence of music on mental and physical health and general wellbeing of members of a community is well known and well documented.

At another level, music reaches out to the supernatural, mediates the relationship between humans and spirits and brings individuals and communities into communion with their divinities. Nketia notes that the Konkomba lute player performs for himself when he wants to be in close communion with his god, as does the Gabon ritual expert who plays the *wombi* chordophone (1972: 23). I am also informed that the Builsa of Ghana use the castanet to invite their deities to support them when in personal danger. More generally, when seeking supernatural assistance, African communities employ singing, drumming and dancing either to attract deities to possess individuals or to transport some individuals into higher spiritual realms to experience ecstasy and trance and come out with revelations. Through music the gods reveal their presence and their personal identities and come not only to play, but also to reveal to communities some hidden moral infringements, the actions needed to restore the moral health of a community or the impact of forthcoming events. Such revelations serve to elevate and purify community moral consciousness, reaffirm the basis of moral community and prepare communities to deal with uncertainties in life. Music bridges the human and the divine.

At yet another level, it is African belief that music mediates interactions between humans and the physical universe and impacts on weather conditions and the rhythms of the seasons. Some African communities use music to stop rainfall or create rainfall; and some employ music to regulate the eco-system and regularize the seasons. It is widely held that music can influence plant and animal life and increase or reduce the yield of the earth. In several cultures, a ban is placed on drumming and noise-making at the beginning of annual planting seasons, as noise can destroy newly germinating crops. The ban is lifted to usher in a festive season of harvest celebrations and thanksgiving.

Finally, in African reality music can transmit to and act on inert matter and change their attributes. Sound and music can degrade or destroy physical entities, as in the classic case of the fall of the walls of Jericho in the Good Book, or invest physical entities such as stones, pieces of iron, corpses, and pieces of wood, with superior properties like vibrations, auto-mobility and sentience. In many African cultures music is performed to make corpses dance or make effigies shake and move. In a nutshell, in the way African cultures construct reality, music touches all things, penetrates all things, transforms all things and unifies all things: music is vital in human existence both in relation to the spiritual world and in relation to the world of physical nature. And this is the basis of the intensive and pervasive presence of music in African life everywhere. It is perhaps in the realization of the importance of including African beliefs in the study of music-making in African cultures that Nketia proposes that to study a musical instrument, an item of material culture, it should be viewed "from a historical perspective, in terms of origin and development, or from a cultural perspective, in terms of social uses, functions and the beliefs and values associated with them" (Music of Africa: 68). Beliefs and values are critical ingredients of music in social contexts, and their relevance to the study of musical instruments should logically extend to the study of the music produced by both instruments and the human voice.[3] it is with such deeply held beliefs about musical instruments and the sound of music that African communities rationalize, if not justify, the moral and religious imperatives of music-making in African communities.

Thus, beyond, and in addition to the concerns of ethnomusicologists and the questions that ethnomusicology investigates about music-making in African societies, we need to ask: What do Africans consider the intrinsic nature or essence of music that, in all contexts and concerns of life, they consider music to have some efficacy and definite effect, or indeed, to be imperative? What is the intrinsic substance or being of music that it touches so many chords and varieties of being and drives all transitions and transformations? These questions, arising out of African beliefs, would move the boundaries of African ethnomusicology to encompass, on the one hand, the study of African perception of music, as a creative product of mind and matter, and, on the other, the study of the impact of music on the human mind or states of consciousness, and on the physical environment and gross matter. The title of this paper springs from these issues.

My thesis is that African musical cultures have their own remarkably similar conceptualization of being (ontology) as well as of the nature and genesis of musical knowledge (epistemology). These fundamental beliefs serve to explain the intrinsic nature of sound and music and how music impacts on all types of being. The purpose of this paper is to direct attention to the fundamental ideas surrounding music in the life of the African and reveal a host of interesting ethnological data about music-making in Africa which ethnomusicology might possibly ignore. Exploring the ontological and epistemological ideas around the practice of music should close the loop on the understanding of the power and functions of music in the life of African communities.

The material evidence on the ontological and epistemological foundations of music-making in African cultures are copious; but it is more patent, explicit and easier to access in some cultures than in others. To indicate the entry point of my personal exploration of the ontology and epistemology of African music-making, the first part of the paper presents and interprets the Ghanaian traditional drum text with which the Akan drummer opens formal performances. The drum text offers a statement on the Akan and, indeed, a widespread African concept of being and indicates the cosmic origins of music.

The second part of the paper explores the epistemological questions the drum text raises. The drummer repeatedly implores the physical components of the drum for knowledge. A musical culture depends on all kinds of knowledge – technical, musical, historical, moral and social. The text leads us to enquire what kind of knowledge a music maker requires from the world of nature to be able to produce music. This leads into philosophical speculation on what nature contributes to a people's musical culture. The third part of the paper gives a brief summary and some recommendations.

Part One: The Ontology of African Music – the Akan Statement

The Akan drummer, *Odomankoma* K*yerema,* (the Divine Drummer) opens his performance on all formal occasions with this tribute to the drum and the entities with which the drum is made:

>   Spirit of the Cedar tree,
>   The Creator's drummer announces,
>   That he has made himself arise
>   As the cock crowed at dawn,
>   We are addressing you, and you will understand.
>
>   Spirit of the Elephant,
>   The Creator's drummer announces,
>   That he has started from his sleep,
>   He has roused himself at early dawn.
>
>   (Spirit of) the fibre, *Ampasakyi*
>   Where art thou?
>
>   We are addressing you,
>   And you will understand
>   O Pegs (made from) the stumps of the *Afema* tree,
>   Where is it that you are?
>   We are addressing you,
>   And you will understand.
>
>   Earth, while I am alive,
>   I depend on you.
>   Earth that receives dead bodies,

> The Creators drummer says,
> From wherever he went,
> He has roused himself.

He has roused himself (Rattray, 1927; 1954; 1969; Busia, 1954, 1960; and Nketia, 1963). The drummer concludes these verses with the refrain: "I am seeking for knowledge; let me know."[4]

Why does the drummer salute the spirit of the cedar tree, of the elephant, the pegs, the drum strings, the drum stick and the entire earth before making his salutations to the chief and his audience? And why does the drummer address the request and a plea to them, "I am learning, help me to know."?

Though neither R.S. Rattray nor K.A. Busia, who collected and highlighted the drum text, gives any traditional exegesis of the text, their comments make it clear that the spirits addressed here are identified not as entities occupying the components of the drum, but as the subliminal essences of the materials. Rattray wrote:

> At the national festivals, the *adae*, which are really in a sense funeral customs, it is the spirit of the tree, the spirit of the fiber, and the spirit of the elephant that go to the making of the composite drums, which are honoured equally with the names of the dead kings, and have pronounced over them the lament for the dead (1954: 186).

While the drummer gives reverence "equally" to the spirits of component parts of the drum as he gives the names of the kings, thus underscoring the Akan and African view that all existents have spirit (*sunsum*), unlike the kings whose spirits are identified by their distinct names as unique individual beings, it is not to a particular spirit of an individual tree, an individual fiber or an identified elephant that the drummer addresses the communication: the drummer directs his salutations to the generic spirits which give the types of entities their general character and properties.[5]

The difference between the generic spirit of things and an individual spirit, such as a god inhabiting a tree, comes out in ritual offerings to trees which are abodes of a resident spirit. Rattray observed:

> The tree is in this instance nothing more than a shrine in which some spirit, quite different from the tree spirit, had come to rest, in spite of, or ignoring, the other spirit already in possession, i.e. the spirit of the tree itself (Ibid: 5).

The concept of the species spirit or *sunsum* here is not unlike the concept of the Platonic Forms: all objects of the same kind have the same *sunsum*. The many drums that use these materials as components attribute the performance capability of the drum to the universal essences of the elephant, the trees, the pegs, etc; and it is these that the drummer addresses. In elaborating this concept of spirit, what emerges in Akan thought is that *sunsum* is a common active substratum of all existents and what accounts for being and becoming. Busia wrote:

> The Earth too has spiritual power. It is her spirit that makes the plants grow; she has the power of fertility. She is not a deity, for she has no priests or priestesses, and does not divine (1954: p.195).

In African cultural beliefs, "nothing is quite inert; there is a force or power in everything which can be known, and 'personalization' is very much a matter of more or less" (John Beattie: 1964, 224). It is this spiritual power or potency inherent in all existents, which we associate with musical objects and music, and which accounts for the taboos and regulatory norms which surround them, that some ethnologists have described as 'the mystical attribute of music'. In the drum salutation, therefore, the *kyerema* declares that he relies on the spiritual power (*tumi*, Akan) of the components of the drum produced by the earth for the efficient and reliable performance of his drums. That the imprecations and salutations are not by word of mouth, but through the drum, suggests that the sounds from the drums constitute a vehicle of communication with the spiritual substratum of the diverse entities. The drummer communicates with all cosmic entities through their *sunsum*.

The Drum as a Potent Spiritual Entity

Configured and constructed out of a variety of objects, a drum is more than the sum of its physical parts. It is a distinct entity: it has its own identity, properties and qualities; and it has its own intrinsic spiritual essence. Each drum of a kind thus has its own taboos or rules about who plays them, when, where and in relation to what.

Rattray observed:

> We have seen in Ashanti how the roots and leaves of many 'powerful' trees are taken as subsidiary ingredients which contribute to the making of a shrine for a god, and how certain other plants are employed because of their particular spiritual potency (ibid, p7).

The drum, however, does not become a shrine for a particular spirit to occupy it. A drum has its own inherent spiritual force.
In African traditions, therefore, the construction of a musical instrument is a creative process that involves not only the manipulation of the gross physical objects – the tools, wood and animal skins and other things, to bring into being a new physical entity; it involves a confrontation and conflict of spiritual forces out of which emerges a distinct subliminal force. The process of creating a musical instrument is thus hedged about with ritual rules and observances. The maker of the Akan drum traditionally pours a libation to his materials and his tools to ensure that they might not break or harm him.[6] The final product of the creative process receives an offering of libation or an egg or blood – a clear indication of reverence to a new spiritual being. Traditionally, "a newly made pair of *fontomfrom* drums may have a dog sacrificed upon them" (Rattray, ibid: 285).

The Lovedu, in whose culture drums had a special place, counted drums as "great *digoma*, objects or activities in which power is concentrated" (Krige and Krige, 1956:166): "Though made by men and women, there is something almost supernatural about a *goma*" and its manufacture is called 'giving birth to' (*hu dwala digoma*)"; and this was fraught with danger. Of their sacred drums, *digomana*, "it is said that their maker 'will see them with his eyes but never hear them with his ears'. He was put to death when he finished the work" (ibid: 129). Of the major traditional drums of the Ibo of Nigeria, Amaury Talbot wrote:

> The chief instrument is the great Ikoro wooden drum....The maker of it and his wife, if he had one, were usually sacrificed when the instrument was finished, but in the Owerri region a slave was generally offered up instead"(1926:814,815).

The killing of the drum maker, which is practiced in several cultures, might be interpreted in several ways. From one perspective, it suggests that the maker creates an entity of such great intrinsic power that his own life is extinguished by his product. From the representational perspective, the drum becomes a transcendent collective representation of the community spirit; and were its maker to live, he would have to be considered a higher power than the drum. And could the power of national institutions like the Golden Stool of the Asante have the same force, if the myth of their divine origins were replaced with historic narratives about who might have produced them. In some cultures, the maker of the drum was, for this reason, a non-indigene wood-worker enticed with promises of security and rewards to carve the drum, only to be killed after he had produced the drum. Once fashioned, or procured, musical instruments, of which drums were the largest and most important, occupied a special place in and impacted on the lives of their creators, their players and their communities. Some cultures, the Akan and Baganda among them, recognized the individuality of some drums and gave them 'personal' names and honorific titles and appellations. The Fanti-Akan gave some drums names like *Kyin* Kofi, *Kyin Daadze*.

With the taboos that tradition associated with certain instruments, an intimate relationship developed between performers and their instruments, which was both sentimental and spiritual. When the Akan drummer is offered a drink of water or gin, he would first give some to his drums. Just as he needs restoration, they too need restoration to be able to perform well and avoid mishaps. By that same token, the drum protected the drummer by the rule that the *kyerema* cannot be executed. Among the Fanti, the major taboo for a *kyerema* is that he should never carry or fire a gun: in war, the *kyerema* always had a contingent of men to protect him.[7]

The Opposites in Nature

In many African belief systems, every entity or force, property, quality or relationship has its opposite. As an Akan proverb says: "Good and Evil are twins, between them there is no boundary; but they are incompatible." And so the entire furniture of the universe is ordered by the alignment of complementary opposites - male and female, left and right, east and west, north and south, good and evil, sacred and profane, truth and falsehood, etc. This conceptual frame pervades the domain of human activity and reflects in the arrangement of entities in music-making.[8]

The major Akan drums like the *etwie, fontomforom*, and *kete* have gender attributes: they are made and played male or female. Thus, we have male and female *Atumpan* drums, male and female *Bommaa* drums, male and female *Akukuadwo* drums, and male and female *Etwie* drums. The distinction between male and female drums does not lie in size, shape, or mode of construction. Though some female drums show two large breasts and some male drums may show phallic symbols, such gender tokens are not necessary features of African drums. Generally, it is by sound or tones that male and female drums are distinguished: male drums usually have deeper tones compared with their feminine counterparts. The Akan *dawuru* is an instrument with male and female parts which are played together.

Male and female drums are played together in a way that indicates that they are in dialogue and mutual interaction. The music of a drum ensemble is the output of male and female instruments; and it is a synthesis between the opposite high and low tones. When one drummer performs on the male and female drums, he stands behind them, with the male on his left and the female on his right. To the audience, the male is right and the female left. The symbolic inversion in the position avoids a situation whereby the drummer would have his back to his audience – a gross abuse in African cultures. All these indicate the extent to which awareness of the cosmic order informs musical culture in Africa. The Divine Drummer has to align himself with the cosmic order of entities in the universe.

The Spiritual Power of Sound and Music

African traditions consider the sounds that humans and musical instruments produce to be imbued with spiritual power and energy. The Kriges observed of Lovedu drums: "Not only are drums gods, but their sound is thought to be very pleasing to the *zwidajani*, those ancestral spirits who, when the drums are sounded, come and sing and dance" (1956:127). Because of the inherent spiritual energy of sounds produced from musical instruments, especially the drum, music can stimulate activity in other beings. Music can stir (Kenyan-Akan) the human spirit, strengthen, purify, protect and prolong it; and music can transmit spiritual force from one entity into another. Rev. Roscoe wrote of the Baganda royal drums:

When the special drum, *Kaula,* had a new skin put on it, not only was a cow killed for the skin, and its blood run into the drum, but a man was also killed by decapitation, and his blood run into it, so that, when the drum was beaten, it was supposed to add fresh life and vigour to the King from the life of the slain man (1965: 27, 28).

By this very token, sounds, and, especially, the throbbing of drums, can diminish and degrade the life and character of entities. And this gives existential power and value to silence in the life of the African. Bradbury recognized this intrinsic spiritual power of music by observing of Ibo songs that "many of the songs have both the character and force of prayers and as such they are an important part of the rituals" (1973:198/199. Needless to say, it is not only ritual or religious songs that have this spiritual force: even songs for play and entertainment, praise songs, courting songs, work songs, marching songs and war songs, have, to different degrees, spiritual power not different from ritual songs; and this idea is central and fundamental to the understanding of the place of music in African spirituality.

Because a song is alive as a spiritual entity, every song takes its place in living space and community consciousness with its name, identity, power and moral character. Songs are performed only by specified individuals or groups of performers, at certain times, places and within defined contexts. They are performed in open social space or confined to specific circumscribed ritual or political spaces and contexts. Many songs are context specific. Outside those contexts they can unleash negative spiritual forces. Given their spiritual power, a song can engender conflict or help establish togetherness. Indeed a song can strengthen bonds of internal cohesion and be also offensive to outsiders and, thus, negative in a wider social space.

Songs might be classified as low or high in social standing – belonging to the common classes, to royalty or to the religious. Songs may be classified along gender or generation lines and may be restricted to prescribed gender or age groups. However, since as living entities songs have their own life careers, a song can undergo change in its social identity and place over time. A ritual song, a war song or a royal music may, over time, come to be performed out of context and be performed for the entertainment of all social groups, while a play song or a palm-wine bar song may become a religious song or a song performed only for royalty. Further, the intrinsic power and energy of a song may wax and wane over time; and a song can thus have a long life-span or be short-lived. Some songs die at birth. But for some songs there occurs life after death: some songs are resurrected, or experience revival of life, long after they are considered dead.

For a song to survive and thrive in community space, it has to be strongly planted and kept alive in another space – in the memory or collective consciousness of a community. The idea that music has to survive in mind-space struck me from an experience I had. An ensemble of drum and horn blowers started playing to usher the guest of honour and other invited guests to a public function; but they would not stop playing for the function to begin. When I enquired why they were being so recalcitrant, the leader told me if they did not play all the verses of their rendition, the song would "leave their minds (*Obe fi hen tsir mu*)." By not refreshing the life and integrity of the song as a mental entity, it can disappear from memory. In cultures without writing, continuity and frequency of performance assures the longevity of a song.

In this regard, a song is also kept alive by the sense of ownership that attaches to it. In many communities, the person who creates a song is honoured and rewarded. In many Ibo communities, "The composer of a new tune or dance is greatly honoured, and in most places any person or club which wishes to use it must obtain his permission and usually give him a present" (Talbort 1926: 808). A piece of music represents wealth and can thus change the identity and station of a composer or a player in a community. The collective ownership or patronage of a song or the appropriation of a song for political or ritual use might help the survival of a song.

Above all this, such is the power of music that, though an individual or a group of people may claim to possess a song, ultimately a song can be said to possess a people. An Akan proverb says: "when you purchase a chicken you purchase constant irritation; when you purchase *kente* you purchase your master or owner (*wo wura*). When a song takes up space in a people's deepest consciousness and binds them to ideals, values, sentiments, attitudes and actions that define and direct them, it limits their freedom and haunts them. Indeed, like the *Akom* song, other kinds of song - *asafo* songs and play songs (wrestling songs, for example) can produce trancelike states in individuals and groups and make them behave out of character, manifesting the finest decorum or the roughest behavior.

Part Two: The Epistemology of African Music – Music, Knowledge and Perception of External World

What kind of knowledge does the Akan drummer seek when he implores the spirits of the elephant, the *tweneboa kodua* tree, the pegs and the twines and the Earth or Nature, as a whole, for knowledge? In many African cultures, musical instruments constitute a 'knowledge, information and communication medium'. The drum, the horn and the kora communicate knowledge of a people's history, their ethos, norms and beliefs, their ideals community values, corporate identity and character. They instruct about a community's social and political groups, their functions and constitutions. They impart proverbial wisdom. Among the Lovedu, when the heir to the throne is receiving instruction in the use of rain-making medicines before the demise of the ruling chief, she must be sitting on the smallest but the most powerful of the four sacred *digomana* drums, the main instruments for making rain and regularizing the seasons (Krige and Krigge 1956:127). This symbolic act establishes the connection between the knowledge for rain-making rituals and the power of the sacred drums. The drums can impart knowledge, so to speak.

Nketia explains that the Akan drummer strives to maintain the forms of the past and to acquire the skill and knowledge of those before him, and makes this public declaration:

> Drummer Opon Agyei Kyekyeku,
> The drummer is drumming on the talking drums.
> The Creator's Drummer is playing on the talking drums.
> Fair Opoku says he is about to play on the talking drums.
>
> Fair Opoku says he is kneeling before you;
> He prays you he is about to drum on the talking drums.
> When he drums, let him drum smoothly and steadily, without faltering.
>
> I am learning let me succeed (1963:175).

The drummer seeks from acknowledged masters the knowledge that human instruction can give him. If so, pleading with the spirits of the elephant, the tree and other entities in the drum for knowledge, would seem to suggest that besides that knowledge to be acquired from master drummers, the world of nature can furnish some other kind of knowledge relevant to music-making. What information or knowledge do the components of the drum or the spirits of the elephant, the tree, the pegs and the fiber hold that is essential to music production or the composition of sound texts? More widely, what knowledge do the things in the universe hold for which the drummer pleads "I am learning, help me to know"? What knowledge or information can entities in nature impart to the drummer without which music-making becomes impossible? We are here constrained to speculate.

Our sense of reality – of entities, space and time and movement of objects, is closely linked to our perception and knowledge of the external world through sound. In the physical world, sound transmits information about the mass, positions, or direction and force of movements of objects; and the changes in our sound environment give information about the passage of time. Sounds from the natural world provide humans information and guide for many activities, and also for our safety. Imploring nature for information can mean this; and this relates to music-making in an interesting way, as I shall explain later. But what knowledge can the materials of the drum give us?

The amazing range of materials that African cultures employ to make music perhaps indicates that every entity has potential sound-making capabilities, or can, in combination with other entities, contribute to producing some sound or a particular variety of sound. Africans make music using water, sand, seeds, shells, bones, horns, skins, hair, trunks, stones, pebbles, metals, glass, etc. And to all these might be directed the plea, "We are addressing you; let us know". The growth of a community's musical culture in terms of the range of instruments, the variety of sounds and the richness of variety of music, would depend on the knowledge that a community gathers about objects in their environment and the sounds that they can produce. In a community's accumulation of knowledge about entities in its physical environment, knowledge of the characteristic or identifying sounds of entities constitutes one of the foundations of their musical culture and technology. The sound-making property of entities and the qualities of the sounds that entities emit out of their intrinsic nature or being might be one kind of knowledge that entities in the universe can give.

The sound that each entity produces is unique to its nature. Conversely, the sound that an entity makes often identifies what kind of thing it is. This means two things. First, the sound that one type of entity emits another kind cannot emit; and the sound that one particular instance of an existence can make, we consider all other examples of that type of material as capable of producing. The sounds that elephant skins emit are distinct from the sounds that sheepskins or leopard skins emit. And we expect every individual elephant skin to produce what sounds elephant skins produce. A leopard skin or an antelope skin would give their own distinctive sounds when struck or rubbed. Similarly, the sound that the wood of an *odum* tree can give differs from the sound that a *hyedua* tree can issue. Xylophone makers prefer certain types of wood to others. And the xylophone maker takes it that any instance of a type of wood would give the same range of sounds as any other particular piece of wood of the same species.[9]

Second, the sound that a piece of skin emits can indicate whether there are flaws or defects in it. The same applies to a piece of iron, brass, a shell or a piece of bamboo. The sound that a type of entity emits is so intrinsic to its nature and being that it provides the measure for assessing the integrity and quality of particular pieces of that type of material– whether a piece of wood or metal of a particular kind is damaged or adulterated, or undamaged, 'sound' and fit for purpose. This idea is expressed in the proverb, "*Ahwene pa nkasa*. (Quality beads do not make noise)." In crafting a musical instrument, the craftsman seeks to harness and bring out of a chosen material the best sound that the particular kind of material can produce either by itself or in combination with other objects. Harnessing or shaping an entity to make it issue the characteristic sounds it emits involves human genius and creativity. The process demands knowledge of the properties of things, but also the technical knowledge and skills of craftsmanship without which the desired or pristine sounds cannot be brought out of a material. A musical instrument thus represents a product of mind-matter interaction: The design and craftsmanship derive from the mind; but materials determine the design and construction that bring out of them the best sounds.

In this connection, the producer and the player of a musical instrument expect that instruments of the same kind would generally be expected to produce the same kind of sound. Nketia points out, however, that musical instruments of the same material and construction may nevertheless not sound perfectly the same. Each would have its own particular distinctive sound, giving them their uniqueness and individuality.

Natural Sounds as a Resource for Music-Making
A musical culture is founded on, or requires, yet another kind of essential knowledge from the world of nature: physical nature gives to a people the variety of sounds that they employ in their music-making. This kind of knowledge has logical and existential priority over the knowledge of the sound-making potential of materials or existents. Without first perceiving or hearing particular kinds of sounds, humans cannot invent instruments to produce such sounds. The sounds and tunes we perceive in our ecological and cultural space constitute the material, the sense data, that the composer requires to produce music; and an environment and a culture create an array of sounds as a musical resource for making music. The dominant sounds of different environments make for differences discernible in the musical cultures and music compositions of nations. The sounds of winds, thunder and lightning, the drizzle and the torrential rain; the ocean waves and the surf; and sounds of birds, insects and other animals are embodied in the music of many cultures. It is difficult to conceive of sounds in a piece of music that humans do not receive or perceive from the external world. But it is the sounds within a particular ecological and cultural environment that the composer's mind selects and weaves together to create a song. Composition of music involves the weaving of perceived or known sounds, tunes and rhythms together to meet standards of aesthetic appeal in a musical culture.

Direct imitations of sounds produced by entities in nature occur in the art of music-making the world over. However, the crafting of instruments to produce a particular kind of sound in nature may not be common. This is why this beautiful description of the *etwie* drum, one of the important drums in Akan royal instrumental ensemble is of significance:

...the *etwie*, or leopard drum, is carried over the shoulder. It is covered with the skin of a leopard. The tense membrane of this drum is made of a skin rubbed down until it is thin as a sheet of paper. The drummer does not beat the face of the drum: he rubs the end of his bent drum-stick backwards and forwards across its surface, when it emits a sound exactly like a snarling leopard (Rattray, ibid: 282).

It was an art of genius to produce the *etwie* drum; but it was more ingenious to develop the technique for producing the snarl; and I am informed that the snarling sound can be produced by drums made with other skins. Thus the technique is the real source of the snarl, not the leopard skin. Rattray notes that the *etwie* drum taboos blood; it may be smeared with eggs-- a symbolic break from the leopard. In ancient times, Asante warriors used the *etwie* to scare their enemies away. According to Nketia, a royal drum called *oburukuwa* acquired its name from imitating a bird of that name. And though not much has been researched about horns and flutes and lutes, rattles etc. in this regard, the sounds they produce more immediately imitate natural sounds of elephants, bulls, cats, dogs, birds, rattle-snakes, monkeys and hyenas than any drums can produce.

The bull-roarer or whizzing stick, which the Bushmen use has lost any symbolical significance which it may have, and is used mainly for attracting bees on account of the similarity of its sound to that of the buzzing of these insects (Musical Instruments of Native Races of South Africa: 272). Considering the fear that elephants are said to have of bees, it is conceivable that the Bushmen might have used the instrument to drive away elephants. In the many instances of the use of instruments to imitate sounds in nature, humans seek to control nature – to drive away danger or to attract and catch a prey – all for survival and sustenance of life. In the human struggle for life, sounds are a powerful instrument for controlling nature and human behavior; and this makes sound an appropriate symbol of power.

The use of human voices and of various instruments to reproduce the sounds of creatures in the wild for protection (by frightening off dangerous animals and scaring humans), for hunting (by attracting prey) and for play would have given rise to the ceremonial and ritual uses of sound in early human communities alongside sketches of animals and plants. The belief in the inherent efficacy of imitative sound and visual representations in controlling nature would have conveyed to humans a sense of great power over visible and invisible entities. To peoples who live close to nature there is reason to access nature for knowledge and for power.

This then is the interpretation we might offer for the tribute that the Akan drummer pays to the universe as the source of the knowledge. If the sounds a people use in their music have their origins in the external world, this should justify the African belief in the cosmic or divine origins of music. When the *kyerema* implores all things in the universe, "I am learning; enable me to know", it is clear that he cannot create, except with the sounds and rhythms that the senses perceive from the outside world; and he cannot reproduce these sounds except by using the material resources of the universe. The Drummer is addressed as *Odomankoma Kyerema* – the Divine Drummer, perhaps because he harvests and selects, puts together, garnishes and transmits to humanity what sounds and rhythms the Creator, *Odomankoma Boadee* put into the world of nature from the timeless past (*Firi tete*: Akan).

Part Three: Summary and Recommendations

The study of African beliefs about musical instruments and music is an important dimension of African Ethnomusicology. The beliefs embodied in the Akan drum text have helped to uncover African responses to the fundamental questions of being and perception in respect of music. The text posits that all musical instruments are spiritual in being and the sounds and music they produce have spiritual potency that impacts all beings and transforms them.

The text also can be understood to respond to the sources of musical knowledge. The great variety of things that Africans use to produce music shows that music derives from the core being of things and communicates to the core being of things, every entity producing a characteristic range of sounds or tunes. On account of this, one form of knowledge that a culture requires to make music derives from identifying the sound making properties of things. And this connects the music of a culture to the physical environment and ecology of a community. A community's ecological niche constitutes a culture's musical resource. It is this resource that produces the materials for fashioning the instruments for music-making.

What guides the selection, fashioning and use of material things for making music is another kind of resource of the external world. Fundamentally and ultimately, humans need to perceive and appreciate sounds to be able to compose music and fashion material objects into instruments to produce a musical composition. It is the sounds, tunes and rhythms of external physical nature that a community and its creative people employ to produce music. Humans compose music with sound percepts from their environment – the sounds of winds and birds and plants – and they with imitate these sounds with our voices and with the sounds produced by physical entities in their environment to produce these sounds to make music. The Akan drum text forever reminds us of these two profound sources of knowledge about music-making and justifies the claim that music is a gift from *Odomankoma*, the Creator, mediated by the human mind – especially the mind and creative consciousness of the music-maker.

Kwabena Nketia has enlarged our knowledge of music-making in Africa and left a vast recording of music in African communities. What should complement this is a museum of musical instruments and, indeed, of all natural objects that communities use to produce sounds. Together with such objects, we need a museum of environmental sounds, that is, the sounds that Africans hear in our physical environment and ecological niches. This would provide the connection that the African sees between his life and music and their divine origins. And this would help us to immortalize Kwabena Nketia as the Divine Drummer, *Odomankoma Kyerema*.

Endnotes

1: 'Dondology' is a term of ridicule and contempt which some academia in Legon gave to the course on African music and dance when it was first introduced into the academic curriculum of the University of Ghana at the Institute of African Studies. This negativity made the professorial inaugural of Nketia an occasion of great enlightenment about the sophisticated, complex interdisciplinary character of African ethnomusicology.

2: Though the idea that the African has a definition of reality that enables people to consider witchcraft, magic and sorcery real is well known, discourse on subliminal forces as relates to normal human activities is mainly related to African religious and ritual life. That mind-set however influences the African in all activities from love, through work, to war. And music reveals its prevalence in all domains.

3: Nketia has done much to bring this out in his many publications, starting with *Funeral Dirges of the Akan People*, 1955. The subject however needs more focused and systematic research.

4: The importance of this text is that it is an institutional statement, universal, formal, and transmitted from generation to generation. It connects the mind of the drummer and his audience to both the physical and the spiritual world.

5: When a wood carver is about to cut down a tree he makes a sacrifice of a chicken, and in this case addresses the spirit of the individual tree: "I am about to cut you; do not let the iron cut me, and do not let me suffer in health" (Rattray: ibid: 185, 186). He does not speak to the generic spirit.

6: As a cultural practice the Akan pours libation to begin every activity. And the libation recognizes that there is danger in the strife between good and evil in every situation.

7: Every kind of drum has its taboos. But the *Kyerema*, who is immune from capital punishment, together with the court crier and the executioner cannot stop drumming in the battle situation and fire a gun: the moment the drum goes silent there would be confusion and disorder.

8: There is extensive ethnographic literature on the theme of symbolic dualism. The emphasis here is that for the African the metaphor expresses the reality of the dialectic as a cosmic force.

9: In the Upper West region of Ghana the traditional xylophone producers prefer to use the wood of a tree found near a river, in a particular place. The same type of wood harvested elsewhere is considered not suitable for the xylophones.

References

Beattie, John. 1946. *Other Cultures*. London: Cohen and West.

Bradbury, R.E. 1973. *Benin Studies*. Ed. by Peter Morton-Williams. London: Oxford University Press.

Busia, K. A. 1960. "The Ashanti." In *African Worlds*. Ed. by Daryll Forde. London: Oxford University Press.

Hammond-Tooke W.D., ed. *The Bantu-Speaking Peoples of Southern Africa*. London and Boston: Routledge and Kegan Paul.

Johnson, Samuel Rev. 1921. (Rep. 1937, 1956, 1957, 1960). *The History of the Yorubas From the Earliest British Protectorate*. Ed. by Dr. O. Johnson. London: G. Routledge & Sons, Ltd.

Kirby, Percival R. 1959. "The Musical Practices of the Native Races of South Africa." In *Bantu Speaking Tribes Of South Africa: an Ethnological Survey*. Ed. by Isaac Schapera. London: Routledge and Kegan Paul Ltd.

Krige, E.J and Krige J, D. 1960. "The Lovedu of the Transvaal." In *African Worlds*. Ed. by Daryll Forde. London: Oxford University Press.

___. 1956. (Fourth Impression). *The Realm of a Rain-Queen*. London: Oxford University Press.

Nketia, Kwabena J. H. 1955. *Funeral Dirges of the Akan People*. London: Achimota.

___.1963. *Drumming in Akan Communities of Ghana*. Edinburgh and London: University of Ghana and Thomas Nelson and Sons. Ltd.

___.1970. *Ethnomusicology in Ghana: An Inaugural Lecture." Delivered on 20th Nov, 1969 at as the University of Ghana, Legon*. Accra, Ghana: University Press.

___.1974. *The Music of Africa*. New York: W. W. Norton and Co.

___.1984. "The Juncture of the Social and the Musical: The Methodology of Cultural Analysis." *The World of Music* 23 (2):22-35.

Rattray, R.S. 1954. (Second Impression). *Religion & Art in Ashanti*. London: Oxford University Press.

Roscoe, John Rev. 1963. (Second Edition). *The Baganda An Account of their Native Customs and Beliefs*. London: Frank Cass and Co., Ltd.

Talbot, Amaury P. 1926. "The Peoples of Southern Nigeria: A Sketch of Their History, Ethnology and Languages, With An Abstract of the 1921 Census." London: Humphrey Milford Oxford University Press.

8

Patience A. Kwakwa
Mitchel Strumpf
Jesse D. Ruskin
Godwin K. Adjei
Paul W. Schauert
Sylvanus K. Kuwor

EXPERIENCING AND ARCHIVING THE VISION

J.H. Kwabena Nketia Festschrift

Kwabena Nketia and The Creative Arts: The Genesis of the School of Music and Drama, and the Formation of the Ghana Dance Ensemble

Patience A. Kwakwa

Patience A. Kwakwa studied at the Julliard School of Music in New York and at UCLA where she earned her BA in dance. In 1974, while teaching, she earned her MA in African Studies from the University of Ghana. As one of the pioneers of the music, dance and drama programs in Ghana in 1962, she studied under both Professors Nketia and the late Manwere Opoku. She has lectured in several institutions including SUNY Brockport, the Interlochen Arts Academy in the US, Simon Fraiser in Vancouver, Canada, Jos and Ahmadu Bello in Nigeria. She has done research on African dance forms in Ghana and Northern Nigeria. In 1989 she received the ECRAG Award for her contribution to the development of dance. She retired from the University of Ghana in 2010 and soon after taught for a year at Ashesi University in Accra.

The School Of Music And Drama And The New Awakening

Three events led to the establishment of the School of Music and Drama:
- The New Awakening
- The name change from the University College of the Gold Coast to the University of Ghana free from colonial attachments
- The establishment of the Institute of African Studies

The New Awakening

Much has been written about the activities of colonialists and missionaries on the African continent before independence and their impact on the African way of life. Many people including the elite, even though they may not have accepted totally the developments that took place, abandoned much of their own cultural heritage. They would be indifferent to traditional social and political gatherings, such as traditional marriage ceremonies, funerals, or durbars. If there was a compelling reason for their attendance they would wear western clothing instead of their African attire. They were often missing at music and dance programmes offered in the traditional settings. English was the language they spoke.

Towards the end of the nineteenth century, a certain awareness began to grow among groups of people at various levels of Ghanaian society. These groups were concerned about the prospect of losing their identity and self-respect as a result of cultural neglect. Around the same time a "movement of cultural awakening had also began which used traditional cultural expressions as a basis for creating consciousness of identity and leverage for building a united front in the fight for independence" (Nketia 1993: 30). It encouraged the literate community to wear their traditional attire in the tradition of the "Gone Fante Movement" of the late 1890s of which Kobina Sekyi was the prime mover. During the high tide of imperialism in the early decades of the twentieth century, those ideas resonated with African nationalists like Mensah Sarbah, Pixley Seme and others (interview, Professor Addo-Fenning, July 7, 2011). Indeed from the mid-19th century onwards Kwesi K. Pra recalls that "people saw the emergence of a westernized African anti-colonial nationalism gestation" (Bankie 2001: Foreword).

Kwame Nkrumah himself talked about *African personality.* In line with Pan-African thought he wanted Africans to appreciate their culture and do things the African way. He wanted Africans to prove to the world, especially the West, that Africa was capable of managing its own affairs. With this idea in mind, Nkrumah wanted to see an "African opinion" develop in Africa (interview, Professor Addo-Fenning, July, 2011). According to Lamelle, "the initial thrust of the Pan-African movement was to restore to the black man his identity and dignity by glorifying the African past to enable him fight for his freedom … Hence they managed to bring the movement to the African soil" (Lemeile 1992: 7).

President Nkrumah was not alone. Earlier Pan Africanists such as W.E.B. Dubois, Marcus Garvey, and Henry Sylvester Williams, a Trinidadian, favored Africans developing their own things instead of copying others, especially the West (Lamelle1992: 7). Meanwhile, the late Professor Kofi Abrefa Busia (later, Prime Minister of Ghana), then head of the Sociology Department of the University College of the Gold Coast, had employed a research fellow and, single-handedly, he was "researching into traditional music and related practices, documenting and analyzing the material for future use intended to fill a vacuum he had perhaps anticipated" (July 1987: 91). This research fellow was Kwabena Nketia. In July's words, "he was in the mainstream of the renaissance of traditional arts and culture in Ghana" (July 1987: 92). Nketia was at the time away on a Rockefeller - funded tour of some higher institutions in the United States of America.The situation needed to change. But how? And in what way or ways? For President Nkrumah the solution lay in establishing a new university, a university with a different structure from the one established before independence, a university which would incorporate programs in Africanism in its curriculum (Nkrumah's speeches: Nov. 25th, 1961: Legon). African studies was high on the agenda and according to the Eminent Historian, Professor Addo-Fenning, "it was a very big thing" (conversation with Addo-Fenning July 2011).

Nkrumah had on few occasions denounced the institutions of higher learning as designed to suit the colonial order. He regarded the products as reflecting the ideas and values of the colonial powers. "… ivory towers lacking the sympathy of the people" (Nkrumah's Speeches: Nov. 25th 1961: 157).

An international commission was set up in 1960 to review the programs and the status of the University College of the Gold Coast (UGCC) then in affiliation with the University of London to upgrade it to full university. The University of Ghana (UG) was to become independent (Nketia 1998: 311).

Thomas Hogkin, a highly respected academic, was brought from Britain to serve as Secretary to the Commission. The late Nana Nketsia IV, then Omanhene (Paramount Chief) of Esikado in the Central Region and Minister Plenipotentiary in Dr. Nkrumah's government, was Assistant Secretary. Dr. Hogkin and Nana Nketsia IV worked together as Secretaries to the Commission. To make sure that the provisions in the commission's report were implemented, Nkrumah appointed Nana Nketsia IV Interim Vice-Chancellor for a two year period, while a search was made for a substantive Vice-Chancellor (Nketia, 1998: 313). The recommendations of the international commission included the establishment of an Institute of African Studies (IAS) in an independent University of Ghana. Meanwhile, Nketia had returned from his Rockefeller-funded tour of some top universities in the United States of America in 1960. According to Nketia, the tour had been arranged by Mr. Robert July, author of *An African Voice*.

The tour of the United States had brought Nketia into close contact with world class scholars in their various fields. He learned that: "What most of the scholars had in common was commitment to studies that integrated music, society and culture" (Nketia, 1998: 31). During his tour, Nketia met and studied under Henry Cowell, a composer whose interest "was in fusion of western and non-western music" at Columbia University; Charles Seeger and Mantle Hood, who were said to be founding members of ethnomusicology at the University of California, Los Angeles. UCLA's ethnomusicology program included the study and performance of non-western music; composers and experts on dance at the Juilliard School of Music in New York; the renowned professor of anthropology, Melville J. Herskovits, and musicologist Alan P. Merriam, both from Northwestern University. He also met scholars like George Herzog, Miecysiaw Kolinski, David P. McAllester and Willard Rhodes. He had studied some of the works of these people so it was a delight to see them in the flesh and hear them speak. He audited their courses. Nketia describes the tour as more than beneficial (Nketia 1998: 31). Indeed it was a milestone in his life. He was returning home with new ideas and new methods of composition. In Robert July's words "Nketia was ideally grounded to develop a wide range of musical activities that would encourage research, teaching and creative composition in the music of Africa."(July 1987: 93)

Establishment of the Institute of African Studies (IAS)

Back at home Nketia got to know that he had been declared *persona non grata* in the Department of Sociology. In his absence, Professor Busia had left and the new head of the Department seemed to have decided unilaterally that drums (artifacts?) did not belong to the Sociology Department and had looked for a room in the Archaeology Department to store Nketia's belongings. But as the wise saying goes, when one door closes another opens. Nketia a firm believer in this adage, did not fret nor shout at the top of his voice.

In 1961, shortly after his return home, the IAS was founded as a semi-autonomous and post graduate unit within the University of Ghana and Thomas Hogkin, who had been brought down as Secretary to the International Committee, was made its first director. He chose Nketia, whose work he was acquainted with, to be his Deputy. Because of its importance to him personally, President Nkrumah inaugurated the IAS himself. When IAS was established few people were selected to do a two-year MA course in African Studies. According to Prof. George Panyin Hagan, a pioneer student of IAS, eight (8) students were selected -four (4) Ghanaian, two (2) American, one (1) British and one (1) German and they were all required to audit Music and Related Arts courses which Nketia had mounted (Interview: Prof. Hagan, August 23, 2011). Nketia mentions that people did not have a coherent body of knowledge to teach and, therefore, handbooks had to be prepared and some lecturers were transferred to IAS. Professor Ivor Wilks for example was transferred from the Department of Philosophy to IAS because of his interest in oral history. Mr. Edmond Francis Collins remained in the Philosophy Department but he worked closely with Professor Ivor Wilks at IAS (Nketia, interview May 24, 2010).

And What Expertise Did Nketia Bring to the Newly Founded IAS?

Since 1949 Nketia had been writing and publishing books and articles, poems and stories. He had composed songs. He had been giving lectures and writing articles for journals and the local papers. At the Presbyterian

Training College (PTC) he had earned his Teacher's Certificate 'A' and his writings and compositions had qualified him for scholarship to the University of London's School of Oriental and African Studies to study Linguistics and Phonetics with Professors Ida Ward and J.R. Firth. While there he had audited Professor Firth's graduate and advanced linguistic courses. These courses provided Nketia with the theoretical tools to analyze traditional poetry such as *apae*, traditional songs as well as the language of the drums. He had also earned his first degree in Music, English and History at Trinity College of Music and Birbeck College. For three years he taught the Royal Cadets Twi and what he wrote on Akan phonetics was used to teach students. Nketia added that the authorities there had wanted him to work on his doctorate degree but the government of Ghana thought he had already spent five years outside. He was asked to come back home (Nketia interview May 17, 2011).

In the Sociology Department, his degree, numerous publications and compositions qualified him for the position of a Research Fellow. Professor Kofi Abrefa Busia saw his potential and prepared him for his future positions (Nketia 1998: 308-310). He not only equipped Nketia with the necessary tools but also assigned to him a team of research/field assistants, which included a competent technician from the Ghana Broadcasting Corporation (GBC). In a period of ten years, says Nketia "I researched into and gathered concrete knowledge and data on music and related courses in several communities ... I would do my own transcription and I would analyze, classify and interpret evidence ... When I got an idea I would write and publish it ... Prof. Busia would also encourage me to attend conferences whenever there was the opportunity to do so" (interview Nketia: May 10, 2011;). In the Sociology Department Nketia audited Professor Busia's own courses to broaden his own critical and analytical perspective. He also published the papers he read at conferences.[9]

After the study tour of the USA, Nketia had gained not only the requisite education but also the experience and international recognition. Thorsen sums it up when he writes: "by the 1950s Nketia took on a leading role as a scholar. He focused on all-embracing analytical studies, proliferated as a role model for major part of African scholarship" (Thorsen 2004: 201). This was the expertise Nketia brought to bear on his work at IAS.

President Nkrumah founded the Academy of Arts and Sciences of which Nketia is a founding member. He says that when Nkrumah saw his curriculum vitae prepared by A. L. Adu, he was so impressed that when Dr. Hogkin left he gave him the post of Director, IAS (interview Nketia:May24, 2010). Nketia was poised to move IAS forward, to unfold the plans he had kept for so long and to experiment with his ideas not only in a theoretical but also in a practical manner. "It was time to move into the visual dimensions of music ... There must also be performance and new compositions" (July, 1987: 93-94).

Soon Nketia began collaborating with the US universities he had visited and with some of the eminent professors he had met. Two master-drummers, Kwasi Badu and Robert Ayittey were sent to assist with musicological work at UCLA while another drummer Abraham Adzinya was sent to Wesleyan University for the same purpose. Kakraba Lobi was later sent to Japan. Nketia's globalization of African music had begun. In the pages that follow, the focus is on how Nketia worked with IAS; how he merged Nkrumah's vision with his own; how he translated that vision into concrete achievements; his recruitment of individuals to assist him in the creative experiment; and the impact of his initiatives on Ghana, Africa and the world at large.

The Genesis of the School of Music and Drama
Shortly after he became Deputy Director of IAS, Nketia created a new unit within the IAS, "The School of Music and Drama." Why? Nketia explains:

> Ethnomusicology has both a theoretical and a practical side. Over 15 years I had been engaged in the theoretical and not the practical aspect of music, which is visible and helps to give meaning to the theoretical work. At IAS, I had mounted a Higher Diploma course in Music and Related Arts – music with dance, drama, visual arts, poetry, praise poetry etc., but it was still academic. All the four students who enrolled in the course had a diploma in western music. Besides, they had to write thesis and sit for examinations. It was still not visible and so the creative part of my research was looking for an avenue for expression. So with the creation of the School, I had an outlet a creative outlet I must say. The School of Music and Drama can thus be seen as an institution for realizing Music and

> Related Arts in practical terms... when I wrote to Dr. Nkrumah to set up the School of Music and Drama, he agreed. Nana Kobina Nketsia took the letter to him and it was signed and approved (interview Nketia: July 8, 2011).

When asked why dance was not included in the title, Nketia responded thus: music and dance are one in the performance of music. Earlier, in an interview with Robert July in 1987, he stated: "No African ethnomusicology program can afford to neglect the visual aspects of this music which influences its conception as well as its interpretation and function." (July 1987: 94). It is because of specialization that they are separated (interview Nketia: July 8, 2011).

The school was established in 1962 with a small budget from the Institute of Arts and Culture, the outfit of Nana Kobina Nketsia and funds from the IAS. Indeed the setting up of the school had been approved much earlier before IAS was established (interview Nketia: May 18, 2011). In his speech at the opening of the School of Music and Drama, President Nkrumah charged the researchers:

> Your research must stimulate creative activity ... I hope that the School of Music and Drama will provide this institute with an outlet for creative work ... There should be development of new forms of music, dance and drama and a close link with the National Theatre to express the ideas and aspirations of our people ... This should lead to new strides in our cultural development (Nkrumah's Opening Speech, 25th November, 1963).

Here, Nkrumah is speaking of a national theatre movement which will bring together all the practices of the different ethnic groups to promote unity and social cohesion (Nketia 1965: 48). Nketia believed that Nkrumah was interested in things that led to performance and progress that is why he supported the works of Beryl Karikari, Saka Acquaye, Ajax Bukana, among others. Nketia was convinced that he fitted into Nkrumah's vision. He was confident that the experiment would succeed. This is what he said to Robert July in 1987: "Ghanaians love their culture, with genuine love and appreciation for the arts (developed through education at all levels) and the basic human attraction to music, the urge to dance for aesthetic enjoyment was there as strong as ever, it just needed to be nurtured and guided" (July 1987: 95).

Nketia's creative life did not start with the establishment of the School of Music and Drama. It began when he was a young boy attending school in Asante Mampong. In 2002, E.A. Akrofi, quoting DjeDje and Carter, wrote in his book: "Throughout primary and middle school, Nketia showed exceptional talent and sensitivity in music, dance, poetry, and dramatic arts." (Akrofi 2002: 3). Nketia himself tells a story about how he decided to study at the Presbyterian Training College (PTC), Akropong and adds that he wanted to compose songs as well as play the piano. In an interview, he told the writer that composition was his first interest, and that it was Busia who got him interested in academic work. True to his word, when he became a teacher at PTC he composed songs and taught them to the students. *Onyame Mma N'asuafo* was the first song Nketia composed as a teacher at PTC.
It was a marching song which all the students loved and would sing as they marched to assembly each morning. He also composed *Y'agoro Yi* and taught it to all the houses for competition. He wrote a book *Akanfo Nwom Bi* and learnt to play the piano and the harmonium. While at the sociology department he continued to compose songs, write poems, books and even a play, *Ananwoma* and a fiction, *Kwabena Amoa*. Again he and Busia set up a "folk society" to enable students of the university campus to look at their culture and examine it. At IAS, he mounted a course in Music and Related Arts. Thinking that it lacked practical content he would bring Opoku from Kumasi on Fridays to teach dance. Palm wine was served on this occasion (Nketia interview, September 7, 2011). These reflect the importance Nketia attached to the practical aspect of preserving culture. Indeed, it was a priority. Nketia himself had said that musicology had both a theoretical and a practical side; so that the establishment of the school after he became deputy director of IAS could not be seen as surprising. The part in him that was creatively inclined was yearning to express itself.

For Nketia, "the preservation of the arts of Ghana were not to be done through speaking and writing about them ... There was the need to keep them alive in performance programs." (Akrofi 2002: 102). In the School of Music and Drama practical artistic production and performances could be undertaken and institutionalized. This would give him the opportunity to practice to the full his brand of ethnomusicology which Akin Euba describes as exemplifying the concept of "creative ethnomusicology" (Euba 1993: 16); as well as carry out Nkrumah's mandate. The school would be his center for the creative arts; a center for individual initiatives. It would thus serve as a developmental institution "to fill the vacuum he had anticipated" (July 1987: 92). Nketia's music and creative arts would also expand.

Onset of the Experiment

The launch of the project led to an unusual development on the campus of the premier university. Drummers now became a part of the congregation. Nketia vividly recalls an incident which prompted a student to write to Kwapong, then pro-vice-chancellor of the university about the invasion of the university campus by "dondology." This did not worry Nketia. He continued with his experiment because, as he said, "the impression of the University, especially the School, everywhere was good." The involvement of Nketia himself and Opoku and his students in state ceremonies made many more people aware of the experiment going on. In his inaugural titled "Dondology Re-defined" in 1973, Nketia was asking African intellectuals to recognize the development of the performing arts so that people begin to look at Legon through the window of the arts (interview Nketia May 19, 2011). Indeed it was during Nketia's tenure that foreign students especially Americans began trouping in to Legon to study.

Recruitment and Programs

Recruiting staff was not a very easy task, for in those days there were very few people trained in these new areas. Somehow, Nketia knew whom he was going to select.

Music

For music, his choice was his mentor, Ephraim Amu, a pioneer musicologist who, among other things, had developed a system, of transcription, analysis of rhythms and pedagogies" (July 1987: 85-90). He was teaching at Kumasi Technical College, Nketia had met him while he was a teacher at PTC, Akropong (Akrofi 2002: 8). As soon as he retired Nketia gave him a senior research fellowship appointment at the School of Music and Drama with a clear mandate to teach compositions to the students of music, pass on his experience as a composer and music educator and continue with that which he was already involved (Amu 1993: 21). He prepared materials for the school, composed his music and wrote his songs in the two languages he spoke fluently, Twi and Ewe, and taught it to his students both Ghanaian and foreign alike and they all sang in these two languages happily (July 1987: 89). Shortly after he had been employed, Amu raised an all-male student choir supported by flute and drum orchestra and toured the entire country with the students.

The big chance came when in 1969, Amu and his students represented the University of Ghana at an all-Universities choral concert at the Lincoln Center for the Performing Arts in New York City and other University campuses in the United States of America. The tour was very successful and in 1972, Amu confided in Professor Anquandah, Archaeology Department, that it was one of the proudest moments of his life when the Lincoln Center audience gave the school's choir a standing ovation (Amu 1993: Vol. 1: 22). Meanwhile Nketia was also teaching in the music department. Through political contacts teachers were brought also from other countries to assist with teaching. The music program had taken off but its content was more western oriented than African. However, the students appreciated the course offerings because of their background. Later, some of Nketia's Music and Related Arts students in the Institute of African Studies after graduating joined the staff at the department: Ben Anin, Simeon Asiamah and N.Z. Nayo and Nissio Fiagbedzi. Nketia had a very high regard for Amu. He described him "as a very strong personality. He would look everywhere for the bamboo and cut it for his flute, *attenteben* (interview Nketia April 7, 2011).

Drama
When Nketia mounted his course on Music and Related Arts at the IAS he brought in Efua Sutherland to assist him with the program. Together, they taught Drama in African Societies. Sutherland was already highly accomplished in the arts. Among many things, she had founded the Ghana Writers' Society and had launched the *Ɔkyeame*. She developed playwriting to create a body of dramatic literature written by Ghanaians for Ghanaians. These were not available to Ghanaians. She also wrote short plays based on stories of Kwaku Ananse (the trickster in Akan folk tales), created new things from the old and staged them. Thus she too was in tune with Nkrumah's vision. While at the Institute she continued with the numerous projects she had begun and though she and Nketia decided that the course in Music and Related Arts was too

academic, they saw it as laying the foundation for study in African arts. Sutherland had succeeded in building a studio where her short plays could be staged. The studio, popularly known as the Drama Studio, was inaugurated by President Nkrumah. From that time on it served as the focus of the activities of students of drama. There they studied their academic subjects, rehearsed and performed their plays. Later, Ama Atta Aidoo, from the English Department, and Sandy Arkhurst and Allan Tamakloe, from the school, became her assistants. Ama Atta Aidoo had already written *Dilemma of a Ghost* (Interview Martin Owusu: August 24, 2011).

The drama studio was built where the National Theatre now stands. It was pulled down to make way for the National Theatre and through negotiations between the Chinese who were building the theatre and Muhammed Ibn Ben Abdallah who was the head of the National Commission on Culture, the Drama Studio was reproduced in its original form on the Legon campus to serve the entire university community. It has now been renamed Efua Sutherland Drama Studio.

Staging dance, music, and drama on the Western stage was a new development in Ghana. Hence, someone with that expertise was sought. Joe de Graft who had been trained in Western drama was brought from Kumasi where he was teaching to assist with teaching and play production in the Drama Department. He was also a playwright and an actor and he handled all of the theory and technical courses in theater. According to Martin Owusu, one of de Graft's devoted students, "Joe employed western techniques to promote their African cultural value... His approach to drama was global to enable students to be functional everywhere." The diploma program in Drama included the following: Drama in African Societies, which was taught by Nketia; Analysis and Interpretation, Theatre History, Directing and Production, Acting, Stage Design and later, Sophia Lokko joined the staff to teach Drama in Education (interview Martin Owusu August 24, 2011).

Sandy Arkhurst and his cohorts were the pioneer students of drama in 1962, and they had to enroll in the certificate course for one year. When the second batch of students, including Martin Owusu, came a year later, they joined Sandy Arkhurst's group to begin the diploma course. They did not have to go through the certificate program because they were trained teachers. Martin Owusu recalls that Nketia went to the Ministry of Education to negotiate with the authorities for them to grant the group who were trained teachers study leave with pay (interview Martin Owusu: August 24, 2011).

Both Sutherland and de Graft wrote plays that were directed by de Graft but it was Sandy Arkhurst who brought audiences to the studio. As director of the Drama Studio, Arkhurst explored ways of educating the audience in a way that would make them enjoy the plays that were staged at the studio and, again, it was Nketia who provided the funds he requested for this exercise (interview Sandy Arkhurst August 22, 2011). Martin Owusu and his cohorts, on the other hand, returned to secondary schools after graduation and taught drama, organized drama groups and established schools' drama festivals, thus popularizing drama. No wonder enrollment in the Theatre Department has always been higher than that of Music or Dance. Some of the graduates pursued further studies and returned to teach at the school. These include AsieduYirenkyi and Sandy Arkhurst.

The Dance Program
Nketia's vision for dance was in line with that of Nkrumah. The former wanted to interview and recruit young people to be trained first, to perform their own traditional dances (old forms) as well as the traditional dances of other ethnic groups in Ghana, West Africa and elsewhere; second, they were expected to be able to create new forms based on the old repertory, so that simultaneously with acquiring expertise in the old forms, the dancers would make creative additions to them and even create new forms. Creativity was to be apparent to an audience as a dancer performed. Nketia refers to such dancers as "creative performers" – dancers who add to what they perform artistically (Nketia, in Skinner 1965: 591). Third, the trained dancers were expected to take up assistantships in schools after completion of their course in order to pass on skills and knowledge to generations after them. In other words, Nketia's vision was to create experts or experienced dancers, who could perform several repertories, compose new ones as well as teach the dances they had learnt to young ones. They were expected to talk about the dances also. Consequently, the dance program was not to be only practical; it was also to have a theoretical component. Nketia's goal was three-fold, preservation, performance/aesthetic and educational. Each of these was important to Nketia. This indeed was in line with Nkrumah's concept of national

cohesion, which sought to explore the development of dance as a visible manifestation of his concept of African personality (July 1987: 101).

Nketia did not have to look far for a helper to achieve his three-point objective. Mawere Opoku and Nketia had been close friends for a very long time and the relationship had been very good. Earlier, Nketia had invited Opoku to come on weekends to IAS to teach dance at the university, on which occasions palm wine would be served. Opoku himself had begun a similar program at the Kumasi Cultural Centre. He was a perfect candidate. Nketia offered him a full-time appointment as research associate. His mandate was clear; to build the dance section within the school and set up a dance ensemble.

In the latter part of 1962, twelve students - six males and six females were recruited in the dance section of the School of Music and Drama to begin the program in dance. These had emerged victorious after an audition which followed an advert. They had been chosen because they were young. They were secondary school (high school) leavers and they had aptitude for dance; though their academic background was not high, Nketia and Opoku felt that they could be encouraged and assisted to upgrade themselves while they were at Legon. Indeed, it was necessary that dance students were recruited young because of the subject itself and the nature of the training dancers go through. It was quite rigorous and if casualties in the classroom and rehearsals were to be avoided, then older people who might have tighter muscles and very firm bones would not be recruited. Because they were dealing with a performance art, it was thought that younger people would be artistically more pleasing to watch on stage.

During the audition, which followed an advert the young ones were asked to dance 'solo' to highlife music, Nketia and Opoku looked for the following among other things in the individual: firmness of body, poise, carriage or comportment, response to musical rhythm, clarity of movement, facial and body expression.

When the twelve had been selected, they were enrolled in a two-year certificate program. There were no boarding facilities for students of dance at the university. Students would come from their respective homes for classes which began very early in the morning, whether or not there had been a performance the previous evening. There was nothing like normal closing hours for dance students. Students went through a daily routine of going to classes, both theory and practical followed by rehearsals and sometimes a performance as well. Later, Nketia and Opoku got them to be housed in two rented premises in Madina, one for the young men and the other for the girls. Madina at the time was quite bushy and the students felt isolated.

Together, Opoku and Nketia prepared the syllabus for dance in line with those of conservatories abroad. It began with a two-year certificate in dance as a prerequisite for the 3-year diploma. The certificate incorporated theory and practical subjects: english, french, anatomy, laban notation, the role and meaning of dance in our cultures, and repertory and performance. English, French and anatomy were taught by lecturers who had been invited from the university community. Mawere Opoku taught "The Role and Meaning of Dance in Traditional Society" and laban notation. He also taught or supervised all practical lessons as well as rehearsals in the evenings, maintaining discipline at all times. Nketia was also present during class as well as rehearsal hours. Both Nketia and Opoku would attend performances with the group. Needless to say the program was painstaking and Opoku was demanding in his expectations. No student dared flout any rule or regulation.

The theory lessons were held in the Russian-built 'temporary' and pre-fabricated structures around the quadrangle opposite the old IAS parking lot; while the practical lessons took place in the open, as is the custom in the villages, on the grass inside the quadrangle. Experts in dance and drumming were recruited from various localities as demonstrators. Initially, few local artistes from various regions of Ghana were employed. M. S. Grace Nuamah, a most graceful woman, popularly known as Auntie Grace and Kwasi Badu, a master-drummer from the Asantehene's court, were brought from Kumasi for Akan dances; Seth Ladzekpo, a fine and calm young man, was later joined by his uncle, Husunu Afadi, a noble looking man and a disciplinarian from Anyako in the Volta Region, for Ewe dances; Iddrisu Dagomba a fantastic *donno* player, from the Northern Region for Dagbamba dances and Mr. Asmah, a master-drummer, quiet elderly but jovial, from the Western Region for Nzema/Ahanta dances. Later, there came a host of drummers and dance demonstrators who were employed on part-time basis. Others were brought in as and when their services were required. But generally, Opoku and his students would travel to the localities to learn the dances through participation with the indigenous themselves. Back at base, Legon, Opoku would begin rehearsals of the dances and his choreographic work. As it is done in traditional setting, students were required to dance bare-footed. It is interesting to note that forty-nine years after the inception of the school some of the students are still dancing bare-footed in the quadrangle, especially in the evenings, due to lack of space.

While the certificate course was going on, the students of dance were also being mobilized to form a troupe to perform at state functions. Nketia, Opoku and students alike took part in celebrations of state. This made many more people aware of the on-going experiment. In early 1964 the "University Dance Group" as it was initially called, was formed and the group toured several cities in Ghana. The people's response was enthusiastic. The awareness had been raised about our culture; from now on attitudes would change. Enrollment in the dance section would increase.

The two-year certificate program which began in 1962 ended in the latter part of 1964. By September 1964, Nketia and Opoku had succeeded in securing scholarships from the Institute of International Education (IIE), an educational body in the United States, for two students who had taken part in the certificate program. They were to leave Ghana immediately for New York City to further their education at the Juilliard School of Music, the prestigious institution which both Nketia and Opoku had earlier attended. Having completed all course work and other requirements in the certificate programme they were issued with their certificates. At Juilliard, the school's authorities, Martha Hill, then head of the Department of Dance, and June Dunbar, the administrator, viewed the certificate as equivalent to the 'A' Level School Certificate at the time. After a short performance-audition had been conducted, the two Ghanaian students were admitted to the B.A. program because of the certificate and their high level of performance of African dances.

Back at home in Legon, some of the students who had earned their certificates enrolled in the three-year diploma program but they continued to perform as members of the University Dance Group with the rest of the students who were not taking part in the diploma program. These and the newly admitted students to the certificate and diploma from 1964 to 1967 became the founding members of the Ghana Dance Ensemble when it was inaugurated in 1967 at the University of Ghana. Nketia became its director and Mawere Opoku its artistic director. Nii Yartey recalls that those who wanted to continue with the diploma program were made associate members. They could join the performances of the Ensemble whenever they were needed (interview Nii Yartey, August 23, 2011). In 1966 the two students transferred to University of California, Los Angeles (UCLA) and by September 1969 they had both returned to Legon to assist with teaching in the dance section.

Nketia, Mawere Opoku and the Dance
Opoku was senior lecturer in art at The College of Technology in Kumasi when he met Nketia. "He had specialised in sculpture, and more particularly, on wood engraving" at Achimota College (July 1987: 97). Opoku was older and therefore tended to see Nketia as his younger brother. They had a good relationship which spanned several decades. They were two different people in terms of personality and taste. Asked how they managed to get along for so long, Nketia's response was: "Bertie will talk and I will listen." They, however, shared a similar background in terms of descent, upbringing, creativity and interests. Both descended from families which held chieftaincy titles and they had been exposed to traditional and court education in their respective homes from infancy. They had received training in "traditional lore and etiquette and were both sensitive to cultural and aesthetic inheritances expressed in terms of linguistic symbolism, religious or communal ceremonies, and particularly the dance which occupied such a central position in African social and cultural life" (July 1987: 97).

Opoku and Nketia were also in London together during World War Two, the big brother holding the hands of the younger brother, leading him to shops where he could purchase warm clothing and, also, to dance performances. Like Nketia, Opoku had received a Western education. He had also received Rockefeller funding to study and work with dance experts in the United States. Opoku studied modern dance with Martha Graham. He studied composition and laban notation at the Juilliard School of Music in New York which enabled him to direct the dance program single-handedly as well as set up the ensemble. While studying in New York, he worked with and assisted

Agnes de Mille with her choreographic work, *Kwamina*.

Though a teacher of art at Kumasi, Opoku concentrated his attention on dance once he was employed full time at IAS. The two would go on field trips together, each one holding his recording machine, and they would discuss issues. Nketia and Opoku worked in close collaboration with one another.

Nketia states: "I admired Opoku very much; firstly, he had love for the dance and he enjoyed the choreography even more; secondly, he had tremendous capacity to analyze movement." Nketia attributes this to Opoku's training as an artist. "Art proved to be very good in its application," … "as an artist Opoku was imbued with a very special kind of professionalism. The discipline in art, lines, connections, relationships, etc. all gave his work a quality which was almost intuitive… at that time the concept of looking at movement and studying movement structure was new… Just as he would put on canvas what was in his mind, so would he establish the form, context, and movement as he choreographed." Besides, he continues, "Opoku had an eye for movement, timing, use of space" and, one would add, design, dynamics and rhythm. "He worked with intuition and he had a way of acquiring steps." This, Nketia believes, was a family trait. "He succeeded because he came from a family which appreciated creativity and artistic excellence"(interview Nketia June 7, 2011).

Opoku's work reflected discipline. He would look at a body before assigning it movements, for the Akan observer is not just satisfied with the dancer's movements being correct; they must suit the performer as well. Often an observer who is pleased with a dancer's artistry would remark: *asa no fata wo* (literally: the dance suits you). To this effect, Opoku would sketch figures on a notepad as he designed the dance. This helped him in making selection of dancers for roles. Sometimes, dancers would be peeved when they were not given the roles they thought they deserved.

Certainly Opoku faced problems in this re-contextualization exercise. He had to see his work in terms of theater conventions. How for example, does one transform a dance that is performed for hours in its own original setting in a locality into a two-hour performance on the proscenium stage? Again, traditional dancers generally face the drummers when they perform. They are also close in terms of space. To produce this in the theatre would be to have dancers turn their backs or side to the paying audience, depending on where you place the drummers. Then, there were solo dances which employed subtle movements. How does the audience observe dancers from afar and appreciate the subtle gestures they make? There were also complaints that the dances were linear in design. These were a few of the problems that confronted Opoku.

He relied on his training in choreography to solve some of these problems. Sometimes, he used measures such as exaggeration of an original gesture or movement, modification, rhythm change, space directions, dynamics, formation and inclusion of extra dancers if the dance was originally solo. One observes this in dances such as *Togo Atsia* and *kete*. Opoku was very effective and he would always go back to seek the reaction of experts from the cultures to which the dances belonged. For both Nketia and Opoku, feedback from the people, especially those in the localities, was very important. In 1987, Nketia had this to say to July, "Whatever we do, we must send back to the community for all categories of people to enjoy." It will be "an outreach to children and adults to refresh their memories of the traditional arts of Africa, to offer the opportunity of participation as performers or observers." (July 1987:94) Feedback was good especially in the initial stages.

There was no doubt that the experiment in dance was successful. The local people were overwhelmed the first time they saw the dancers perform. Nkrumah and Nana Nketsia IV believed in what Opoku and Nketia were doing and therefore were willing to support them with funds. They gave them money for the establishment of the school and for the auditioning.

In March 1964, the university dance group was sent to Malawi to participate in its independence celebrations and the group came first in the competition that was organized there. The visit was so successful that, back at home, Nketia recalls, a letter appreciating the creative experiment had been sent to requesting him at the same time to set up the dance ensemble. A great impact has been made, not only in Ghana, but in another African country. Nketia and Opoku had done what Nkrumah wanted and "it was time to move on with the dance" Nii Yartey recalled.

It was obvious that the emphasis was going to be on dance.

The dance ensemble was unique in the sense that, in recruiting dancers, Opoku and Nketia looked for young people who had aptitude for dance and not those with high academic backgrounds, but who could be trained to have higher academic qualifications. Physically it worked well. The approach was practical but also theoretical. There was commitment for studying the dance forms. In the experiments of other African countries there was not a school for learning the dance forms. In Ghana, it was important to project unity and diversity of the African personality through dance (July 1987: 98). Later, in 1967, after the ensemble had been inaugurated, it went on tour of the United States and below is one of the reviews it received. It is narrated by Robert July:

> A critic was impressed by what he saw as "the classic character of performances, purity of movement, elegance and stance, the combination of physical dexterity with eremony ... The accent was upon decorum, graciousness, regal behavior ... earthiness, physical force ..., even in the swiftest most emotional moments, the contours of classism were maintained" (July 1989:102).

Nketia's objective had been met. The company had succeeded in preserving the character of traditional dance and music while reshaping them for theatrical presentation before non-participating audience. Here, one may observe Nketia's creative input. The songs, whether they were composed or transcribed were selected to suit particular dance pieces. *Twɛntwɛnko and Ɔwankyiasa,* sung in the Akan ceremonial and *Laa le me loo* sung in "lamentation for freedom fighters", for example, combined with the dances perfectly to bring out their inherent emotional content. The audience could not help but be touched "spiritually and esthetically."

When Opoku had finished his work, he had this to say:

> "We have tried ... to work out a form of presentation which highlights and clarifies essential forms of the dance without destroying their basic movements and styles, their emotional, symbolic and cultural values or their vitality and vigor ... We have tried to use ... the comments and criticisms of experts in

our villages ... We have tried to see our dances with Ghanaian eyes and not with the eyes of Hollywood or the squinted eyes of the amateur dance anthropologist ... We have insisted not only on correctness of movement but also, on the quality of movement ... we have followed the warning that a dance form which does not recreate ... stagnates and dies" (July 1987: 102).

Opoku made a great impact in Africa and many countries outside, but because he did not write much; his legacy may not be clearly seen, but his impact on Africa is felt. Everywhere in Europe and America there are dancers and drummers teaching. Many have earned higher degrees and are drawing good salaries. The dance ensemble became a model for others. Nketia told the writer that on one occasion after the dance ensemble had performed at a university ceremony, Alex Kwapong, then vice-chancellor of the University of Ghana, referred to Opoku who was then a senior research fellow, as "Professor". In Nketia's words, "Opoku became a professor by acclamation" (Nketia interview: May 19, 2011).

Impact
Nketia's impact has been duly acknowledged by scholars. Thorsen writes: "Nketia's experiment in the 1960s was partly responsible for interdisciplinary studies emerging with the growth of institutes for Music and Music Research all over the African continent" (Thorsen 2004: 201). Nketia's vision helped to develop the arts. It became a guiding principle for others to follow. He created awareness among Ghanaians and other Africans of the importance of their culture – language, mode of dressing, traditional practices of music, dance and drama; visual arts, food etc. He prepared people to make the transition from the traditional to the contemporary environment. Today educated chiefs and traditional leaders have no inhibitions in dressing appropriately on important traditional festive occasions. This generated pride in people and increased cultural awareness. Young men began to wear Joromi shirts while the elderly brought out their Kente cloths. On the shelves in people's living rooms were displayed lots of artifacts made in Ghana. Radio stations began using vernacular in discussions involving culture as a sign of the new awareness of the value of African culture. The new interest generated attracted many African Americans to Ghana and other African countries in search of their roots and identity. PANAFEST is perhaps the greatest tribute to the initiatives

of President Nkrumah, Nketia, Nana Nketsia IV, Ephraim Amu, Mawere Opoku, Efua Sutherland, Joe de Graft and others. The study of the performing arts was a novelty on a Ghanaian university campus modeled on Oxford and Cambridge. By bringing them into the open and performing them on stage in the theatre, Nketia gave them a wider national appeal and invested them with political significance. The study of dance brought out the multi-dimensional nature of dance, music, art, drama, spectacle, poetry, etc. This created greater political impression and attracted more attention.

The school and, especially the ensemble, became models for other African countries. Products of the school who had completed their three year diploma were considered for admission in universities in the US, the UK, and other parts of the world for graduate study. Skilled personnel, both literate and illiterate were invited to assist with ethnomusicological studies elsewhere. Others set up on their own to render services to those who needed them, thereby creating employment for many. Wherever they went they were successful. For those who remained at home, some went to teach other subjects in second cycle schools because dance was not offered in the schools. Others were absorbed by governmental agencies of arts and culture to help in the development and preservation of our national heritage.

The pioneer students of drama—Martin Owusu, Kofi Yirenkyi, Kofi Mends, Ernest Abequaye—went back to teach in secondary schools, and formed drama societies to popularize drama. In this way they built on the foundations laid by Nketia. Those who travelled outside the country returned to assist with teaching, play production and directing at the school, as was the case in music. In the words of a pioneer student of IAS, George Panyin Hagan, "Nketia's own international standing with certain international centers, helped to make the School of Music, and Drama intellectual centre of excellence" (interview George Hagan: August 23, 2011). People from all over the world have over the years come to study the performing arts of Ghana. The school's example was emulated in other universities on the African continent and quite a few of the heads of department have received training in Ghana.

Nketia's participation in the African Negroes Festival in Dakar, and

FESTAC '77, as well as his musicological activities in other parts of Africa gave his work a Pan-African perspective (Nketia in Thorsen 2004: 203). Nketia's comment on the importance of cultural identity is worth noting: "I spread what is African but wherever I go people take whatever they want from it. The problem with us in Ghana is that we are prone to the colonial idea that ours is inferior and theirs is superior. The idea is that one should make use of a model. You take from it what you want and add to yours but you do not throw yours away. I have not lost my identity" (interview Nketia June 23, 2011).

Problems
No doubt there were problems that Nketia confronted. He recalls: "The program had to face implications of social change: new habits of listening, new communities of taste, new concepts of performance, new models of presentation and new perspectives in performer/observer relationship ... After independence in 1957 it became necessary for me to cover all forms of music and music making, both traditional and contemporary." (Nketia, 1998: 28). Another major problem was the lack of specialized scholars, suitable infrastructure and weak intra-African cooperation (Nketia in Thorsen, 2004: 201). Again, following the overthrow of Dr. Kwame Nkrumah, resources dried up.

In the dance program, the abandonment of plans to use diplomates to form the ensemble created a problem. The problem was beyond Nketia's ability to solve as at the time, dance, unlike drama or music, was not taught in basic and secondary schools. Consequently the majority of those who applied to join the ensemble did not have a western educational background.

Lessons
The keys to Nketia's phenomenal academic success were diligence and commitment. Nketia promoted music through diligent research. At PTC, Akropong, he worked very hard. He would walk from Akropong to Larteh to visit Otto Boateng and to listen to his music because he liked his music. In London University and at the Department of Sociology, Legon, he audited courses that he considered relevant to his field of study. Nketia had a vision which he kept in focus throughout. This is a trait necessary for any great achievement. Also, the people he employed in the early stages of his work were visionaries. They had initiatives of their

own and shared these with their students. He recognized the necessity to train people to sustain his ideas and bring them to fruition.

Nketia maintains a daily work routine. He does not allow any opportunity to pass him by. He does not think or worry about extraneous problems. He only thinks and worries about music. Nketia recognizes that his accomplishments are not for himself or Ghanaians alone. It is a legacy to the whole world.

On July 8, 2011 a very interesting conversation ensued between Nketia and someone on the other side of the telephone line. This person was urging Nketia to take action against someone who was exploiting his works for financial gain. This writer was not eavesdropping as she was sitting next to him. Here is Nketia's response to the caller:

> *"Wotwa ɔkwan a obi fa so"* [if you create a path anyone can use it] so that if anyone takes my material and sells it, I will not say anything.
>
> *ɔmfa, mede kyɛ no* (he can take it, I give it to him as a gift)
> I do not want quarrels or enemies. I have been like this for fifty years by His Grace. *Medeɛ m'awie.* (I have finished my work).
> *nea me yɛɛ nyinaa me yɛ de maa ɔman* (whatever I did, I did it for the nation).
>
> *Mensɔ manso biaraano* (I do not encourage litigation).
> At this time in my life I am not a policeman to worry about criminals. *Me honhom mpɛ* (my spirit abhors such a thing).
>
> *Metwerɛ adanse kronkron de hyɛ Nyame animuonyam.*
>
> *Nyɛ sɛmede pɛsika.* (I wrote the truth to glorify God and not for monetary gains).
>
> *Onipa beyɛɛ bi na w'ameyɛ ne nyinaa.* (No man can perfectly manifest his blueprint in this life).

Fascinating! But this is Nketia at his selfless best.
On this day Nketia advised:

"We must innovate based on our experiences and we must move with the community for them to gain trust in us – in order words, let the community understand what we do. We miss a certain rapport which we had. For this, colonialism and social change are responsible. What we should think of now is how to integrate as a people. We do so only at school, church, youth camp etc. There is differentiation wherever we go. Contemporary contexts must create linkages beyond church groups, youth camps, schools etc."

References

Adinku, W. Ofotsu. 1994. *African Dance Education in Ghana*. Accra: Ghana Universities Press.

Agawu, Kofi. 2000. "The Legacy of Ephraim Amu." Paper delivered for the Ephraim Amu Memorial Lecture at the National Theatre, Accra, Ghana.

Akrofi, E.A. 2002. *Sharing Knowledge and Experience: A Profile of Kwabena Nketia, Scholar and Music Educator*. Accra, Ghana: Afram Publications.

Amu-Ephraim. 1993. *Amu Choral Works. Vol. 1, New Collection*. Accra: Waterville Publishing House.

Andre, Naomi. 1999. "Nketia, J.H. Kwabena." In *The International Dictionary of Black Composers*. Ed. by Samuel Floyd. Chicago; London: Fitzroy Dearborn.

Bankie, B.F., ed. 2001. *Globalising Africans Towards the 7th Pan-African Congress*. Capetown: The Centre for the Advanced Studies of Africa Society.

Curriculum Vitae of J.H. KwabenaNketia.

DjeDje, Jacqueline C. and Carter, W.G., eds. 1989. *African Musicology: Current Trends: A Festschrift Presented to J. H. Kwabena Nketia*. Los Angeles: African Studies Center and African Arts Magazine.

Euba, Akin. 1988. *Essays on Music in Africa*. Bayreuth, West Germany: IWALEWA-Haus, Universität Bayreuth.

July, Robert W. 1987. *An African Voice: The Role of the Humanities in African Independence*. Durham: Duke University Press.

Lemelle, Sidney J. and Ife Nii-Owoo. 1992. *Pan-Africanism for Beginners*. New York and London: Readers and Writers.

Mathew, Fr. George C. and Francis Carmel. 2011. "God's Word." *Daily Reflections*. St. Pauls, Mumbai and Vaigrai, Tamil Nadu, India.

Nketia, J.H.K. 1949. *AkanfooNnwom Bi*. London: Oxford University Press.

___. 1955. *Funeral Dirges of the Akan People*. London: Achimota.

___. 1962. "The Problem of Meaning in African Music" *Ethnomusicology: Journal of the Society for Ethnomusicology* 6(i): 107, January.

___. 1963. *Folk Songs of Ghana*. London: Oxford University Press.

___. 1965. *Music, Dance and Drama: A Review of the Performing Arts of Ghana*. Tema, Ghana: Ghana Information Services.

___. 1968; *Our Drums and Drummers*. Accra: Ghana Publishing House.

___. 1970. "Ethnomusicology in Ghana" An Inaugural Lecture delivered on 20th November, 1969 at the University of Ghana, Legon. Accra, Ghana: Universities Press.

___. 1984. "The Aesthetic in Ethnomusicological Studies." *The World of Music* 26(1): 3-28.

___. 1995. *National Development and the Arts of Africa*. Accra, Legon: International Center for African Music and Dance.

___. 1998. "The Challenge of Cultural Preservation in a Dynamic Social Environment." Paper read at the National Festival of Arts (NAFAC'98) Symposium, International Center for African Music and Dance. Accra, Legon.

Nkrumah, Kwame. 1961. "Flower of Learning." Speech on his installation as Chancellor of the University of Ghana and of University of Science and Technology, Nov. 24th 1961.

Obeng, Samuel. 1979. *Selected Speeches of Kwame Nkrumah*. *Volume 2*. Accra, Ghana: Afram.

Skinner Elliot, P., ed. 1965. *Peoples and Cultures of Africa*. Garden City, New York: Double Day/National History Press.

Stig-Magnus Thorsen. 2004. *Sounds of Change – Social and Political Features of Music in Africa*. Stockholm: Swedish International Development Cooperation Agency.

Stone, Ruth, ed. 1997. *The Garland Encyclopedia of World Music, Vol. 1*.Garland Publishers: New York, 28-32.

"The Musician of 1956" – Daily Graphic, January 2, 1957.

Professor J. H. Kwabena Nketia: Ethnomusicologist and Educator

Mitchel Strumpf

Mitchel Strumpf is the academic director of the Dhow Countries Music Academy in Zanzibar. Since 1968, Strumpf has taught and has been involved with establishing new music programs in African universities in Ghana, Nigeria, Malawi, Zimbabwe, and Tanzania. His current academic interests include developing methods and materials for teaching African music traditions in the schools and African music history. For many years he served as director of the Malawi Choral Workshop (1985-1996) and the coordinator of the Ethnomusicology Symposium of the University of Dar es Salaam in Tanzania from 2007-2013.

As a humanist, Professor J. H. Kwabena Nketia has devoted his life to the study of African music traditions, focusing his attention on the human values and concerns of the people making and employing such music and on the creation of African music compositions, old and new. In addition, however, as an educator having started his career in teaching in 1942, he has also dedicated much of his efforts to assisting others to research, understand and perform the music, dance, and theater and language traditions of Africa. This paper focuses on Nketia as a scholar strongly interested in using his knowledge and experience to help others grow intellectually, culturally and spiritually. It focuses on Nketia's searching for and studying African music traditions not only to fill libraries' shelves and archives' cases with written information and recorded sounds and videos, respectively, but also to enable knowledge, listening and music -making experiences for African and all other people interested in knowing more about the music cultures of African people.

Concerning Nketia the educator, this paper builds on a statement he made in 1975:5 in his Foreword to *Notes on Education and Research in African Music No. 2* where he finds fault in the then current activities of the more 'formal' music education in Ghana failing to promote "meaningful", scholarly involvement of people with Ghanaian music traditions. He puts forward that,

> Anyone who observes music lessons in our schools or examines the syllabuses in current use cannot fail to notice the somewhat lowly position that African music still occupies. Not only does one find little originality in the approach to the teaching of the subject, but also much of what is presented does not appear to offer the kind of challenge that would stimulate further exploration of the techniques and materials of this music outside the classroom, or encourage meaningful participation in traditional music as a form of community experience.

In the current paper, I recall my association with Professor Nketia over the years as Nketia articulated various concerns within the broad area of music education. These remembrances include a time in the late 1960s when the "Prof." enthusiastically encouraged me to write a method course for students of the University of Ghana and elsewhere to study

Lobi-Dagarti xylophone music traditions; a period also in the late 1960s sharing Nketia's excitement with establishing factory facilities for the making of quality *atenteben* bamboo flutes and various Ghanaian drums so that schools all across Ghana could offer children music-making experiences in the classrooms; and in 1997 seeing Professor Nketia's devotion to developing quality, effective music education materials when he told participants participating in a UNESCO-sponsored Music Education conference in Zomba, Malawi about his asking his grandchildren, "What did you do in your music class today?", and they responded, "We talked about 'crotchets and stuff.'" For Nketia, 'talking about crotchets and stuff' was then, as it is still today, certainly not enough to provide a child with information and experiences to enjoy and perform the music of his or her culture.

This paper observes ways the professional interests of Professor Nketia have opened up to the topic of education in and through music within his realm of ethnomusicological thought in a good number of ways. In doing this, the paper centers attention on Nketia's studies on musical enculturation and musical training and on his interests in music curriculum development and the development of music teaching materials (teachers' guides, text books, music-instrument provision, etc. for the schools and other learning places).

Nketia on Musical Enculturation
The field of ethnomusicology has included within its confines the study of *musical enculturation*, the process that leads individuals to embrace the music traditions of their culture as something truly belonging to them. It is most often an effortless form of music education; a process of absorption that takes place when an individual, fascinated by a musical sound or musical structure, desires more exposure and association with that sound or structure.

In his important work *The Music of Africa* (1974:60), Nketia comments on the significance of 'musical enculturation', seeing it as being similar to language learning, a common process of human development. He suggests that, "The African mother sings to her child and introduces him to many aspects of his music right from the cradle...Participation in children's games and stories incorporating songs enables him to learn to sing in the style of his culture, just as he learns to speak its language."

Nketia (1974:21) emphasizes that it is community sharing, and community living, in general, in Africa that allows and encourages musical enculturation to take place so effectively. He suggests that it is the musical activities within the community that help young people move forward in the process of enculturation, in grasping the musical sounds that quickly become a part of their being. The basis for music making and music appreciating, he puts forward

> ...is usually the community, those members of the ethnic group who share a common habitat (such as a group of homesteads, a village, a town, or a section of a town) and who live some kind of corporate life based on common institutions, common local traditions, and common beliefs and values.

Community cultural sharing in African cultures, compared to the more individual or small-unit cultural sharing, i.e., family sharing, in the Western world, Nketia sees as providing greater strength in the strong enculturation of African people to the feelings and understanding of their music backgrounds.

With community cultural sharing being prominent in African cultures, he points out in his article Music Education in Africa and the West: We Can Learn from Each Other (1970:48), music teachers are more often than not a part of the community, more often highly experienced with performance practices, and more passionate about passing on the musical, as well as many other traditions of the community to their students. He states that for the teacher, coming from within the community, "Our task as educators...is not only to impart knowledge and skills or nurture creativity in children, but also to contribute to the development of the personality of the child who lives his life both as an individual and as a member of social groups."

Although most musical enculturation and 'traditional' training in African music is informal, that is to say a friend showing another friend how to play an instrument or an unstructured, casual observation of a respected performer doing something one has interest to imitate, there are circumstances as musically-inclined individuals grow older and live within their cultural community, when association with a music instructor ('trainer'), a master musician perhaps, may become necessary.

Nketia on Training Students in African Music Traditions
Focus of the Curriculum

'Music training', considered here as purposefully-carried-out efforts of teachers and students to acquire music knowledge through musical experiences, has been focused upon by Nketia in a good number of articles and book chapters (1954, 1967, 1971, 1974, 1975, 1978). He (1954) discusses music 'training' in a traditional setting through one example from the formal training of an Akan chieftaincy's musician. Learning through observation is more or less satisfactory to achieve good performance skills for the secondary drummers of the Asantehene's court drum ensemble, however, Nketia states, for the master drummers, it is apparent that more thorough, rigorous lessons from an instructor are required. Nketia (1954:40) describes such training as follows:

> Instruction was not always on drums; sometimes it was on boards, bamboo or short branches of raffia palm. Instructors spoke rhythms – sometimes in intelligible utterances, sometimes in nonsense syllables, especially if there happened to be some unwanted person about. Sometimes rhythms were tapped behind the shoulder blades of a pupil to give him some idea of the distribution of the sequence of drum beats to the hands. This training sometimes extended over years for boys, during which rhythms were memorized and techniques mastered.

Praising the benefits and appropriateness of traditional music training, Nketia also sees the "apparent weaknesses" of such training in Africa, and elaborates on this a bit, saying that such music training "...seems to be an infrequent expedient in some societies;" "Musical apprenticeship... is not a highly developed institution...," "...the very organization of traditional music tends to impose limitations on the extent of the knowledge acquired by individuals (for example). While women may be familiar with the music of heroic associations, for example, we would expect to find a better knowledge of this music among men."

"In spite of its apparent weaknesses," Nketia (1974:63-64) often comes back to his more inner feeling that "...the traditional system (of music training) seemed to work well in the past." (In some cases there were religious sanctions to support it. It insured that there were enough specialists who could perform on their own or give the required leadership).

While the community orientation in African culture in the past was the way of life, Nketia (1970:54), as a realist, finds it clear that from the changes that have already taken place affecting African culture by the impact with the West, "...musical life that depends solely on informal processes of enculturation for its survival cannot endure the pressures of the modern world. In a community-oriented music education program for contemporary Africa, therefore, it is necessary that the learning process be systematized on some formal basis."

With such "systemized," "formal" music education activity, Nketia (1999:8) emphasizes the need, and thus pleads for curriculum developers to include in the new curricula for music training the spirit, significance, function, value and presentation practices of music within the framework of their culture. He expresses the need of African music 'trainers' to facilitate the establishment of a strong African music foundation within an African educational system. This, he suggests (1996), may be done through developing effective training materials strongly based on African musical understanding. So too, he continually emphasizes that African music training must be based on African music teaching/learning pedagogical principles including, "...the careful selection of (African) musics for performance and listening...as well as attention to the processes by which music is taught/transmitted and received/learned within (African) cultures, and how best the processes can be preserved or at least partially retained in classrooms" (Campbell 2010: 39).

Even from his first paper that focused on music training, "Music Education in African Schools: A Review of the Position in Ghana," Nketia (1966:231) warns against music training in Africa having a centre of attention on materials and pedagogy not meaningful within an African community's musical context. He writes:

> As music is traditionally practiced in African communities as an integral part of social life, there is the danger that musical activities in the classroom – an artificially created musical situation – may be unrelated to experience in society. There is the danger

that the teacher might treat music merely as an object of instruction rather than as something vital, alive and part of experience.

Nketia makes historical observations, describing an early view expressed by colonial observers, William Ward as one example, on the importance of Western music to Ghanaian music training. Ward (and sadly too many other Western scholars of an earlier time) strongly felt that African music traditions had little musical quality until they started incorporating Western musical understanding and performance training. Nketia (1963:1) wrote that, "...Ward (1927), the historian and musician, who played an important role in Ghanaian music education in the 1930's...believed that "if it (African music making) could learn from European modern developments in form and harmony, African music should grow into an art more magnificent than the world has yet seen" (223).

Nketia (1974:18), however, also quotes an additional, albeit a bit compromising, early perspective from Reginald Forsythe, 13 years after Ward's more Euro-focused comments (1940:174-175), that suggested that:

> African children should be taught African music alongside with European music. Only in this way can we expect to create an African school of composition, which will necessarily have to be a fusion of African and European idioms. Of course, all this rests with individual genius, but I look forward to the day when great works by African composers, works stamped with that originality and depth that is Africa's will be heard in the concert halls of the world.

Discussing this cross-cultural quagmire that was evident especially in the period immediately after the colonial era, Nketia (1966:232) suggests that in the mid-1960s in Africa there was "undue prestige... [given to] foreign cultures at the expense of corresponding indigenous forms. This is particularly noticeable in music education...." To be worthwhile training for an African student, Nketia (239) says, the curriculum for music learning,

> ... must be preceded by a search for a clear definition of aims and objectives so that music education in post-

colonial Africa does not continue as a mere extension
of missionary or colonial educational aims but
something based on how contemporary Africans see
music education in relation to their society....

By 1988 Nketia expressed the importance of an 'intercultural approach' to music education, suggesting benefits from music education for intercultural understanding, perhaps of greater need at that time than in earlier periods when African people were more isolated from the rest of the world "...The intercultural approach" he wrote:

...offers the greatest and most flexible scope for
developing varied programmes in music education, for
it can be applied to any set of musical cultures—those
within one's own immediate environment, those with
which one is frequently confronted by the media, the
music of societies about whom one's pupils may have
read or heard in their social studies lessons and so on
(1988:101).

Focus on Teachers, Teaching Materials and Music Instruments in the Schools

Nketia saw the difficulties of advancing a quality music curriculum that could promote the study of African music traditions in the schools of Africa as being primarily a lack of trained teachers with clear African music culture/performance backgrounds. In addition, there was very limited availability of appropriate and quality teaching materials and a lack of traditional music instruments for performing African music traditions. It was also clear that music instrument makers, seriously declining in numbers as generations had less and less need for these instruments for cultural music making, could not produce the instruments in sufficient quantity to supply the needs of effective school music programs.

In the traditional setting the music instructor has to have a vast, in-depth knowledge of the music tradition(s) being taught. The techniques of the music making as well as the cultural details, including aesthetic considerations that accompany the musical sounds are important areas of skills and conceptual knowledge that the instructor must possess. Nketia makes it clear that the trainer in the traditional setting has to be both a teacher of the music tradition, as well as a teacher of other aspects of cultural thought, and puts forward that,

> Because music making is so much a part of community life, the primary objective of music training, where given, is to prepare the individual for his musical roles in community life –his role as an individualist, a lead singer, or a member of a chorus...There are very clear expectations of the breadth of knowledge required of those who take on leading roles. Any individual must be acquainted with the range of individual items which constitute the standard repertoire used on important occasions...he must be able to express himself fully and intellectually in the language and idioms of the music of his culture (1975:13).

As a major challenge, Nketia (1966) notes that to achieve such training in the academic setting of a formal African primary or secondary school, it is necessary to have teacher training in such areas of knowledge. In most cases, such training is not part of the music-teacher training in African teacher training college today, and the music teacher, in all too many cases in Africa, is handicapped as:

> (1) he has no indigenous tradition of music pedagogy of a systematic nature to guide him; he is himself a product of acculturation and his training may show a bias of a type which may now be his task to eradicate from the educational system; (2) the material he needs is not always available...(3) he has not cultivated a broad outlook in music or widened his horizon to include the music of other African cultures...He feels that the gap between music in the classroom and music in the community can be bridged if the study of music education is combined with the study of ethnomusicology in music teacher education programmes in Ghana and sub-Saharan Africa (Akrofi 2002:152 articulating Nketia's (1966) writing).

While early published attempts had been made in Ghana and elsewhere in Africa to provide teaching materials to be used in the schools (see for example Amu "How to Study African Rhythm" in the *Teachers' Journal* of the Gold Coast (1933:154-157) and Nketia's classroom-oriented *Our Drums and Drummers* (1968)), little appropriate 'method-course' materials were written that observed African pedagogical principles for the study of African music making. In this light, in 1969, Professor Nketia encouraged me, then a researcher/teacher at the Institute of African Studies, University of Ghana, to study with Mr. Kakraba Lobi, renowned Lobi-Dagarti musician with the Ghana Dance Ensemble, and analyze methods for learning/teaching the Lobi-Dagarti xylophone (*gyile*). Arrangements were also made for me to visit north-western Ghana to study the music of the *gyile* as an expression of Lobi-Dagarti culture and to purchase five Lobi-Dagarti xylophones for teaching purposes at the University of Ghana. *Ghanaian Xylophone Studies* (Strumpf. 1970) was the successful outcome of this venture and, through Nketia's enthusiasm for using this material with Ghanaian and well as non-Ghanaian music learners, the method course became a prototype for other similar attempts (see Wiggins 1989).

As the computer age erupted and combined with the use of recordings to learn African music traditions, new educational possibilities using computer-oriented teaching evolved. Nketia (1997) suggested in the Foreword to *African Drum Music* by Kongo Zabana that:

> As opportunities for learning to understand and appreciate drumming in contemporary contexts through (community, well respected music teachers teaching with the tried and true cultural methods) are no longer as frequent as they used to be, there is need for recordings that will enable interested individuals to listen to the performance of particular drum pieces over and over again and absorb some of their essential characteristics. Analytical recordings which allow one to listen to each drum separately and in combination with another instrument can, to some extent, also help to clarify this complexity as they enable the listener to figure out the constituents of the patterns that are played....Just as transcription of traditional songs provide source materials for music education, so may the scores of drum music be used in a similar manner – as *aide memoire* for learners, as source for rhythmic exercises, as materials that may be set to nonsense syllables and performed as spoken drum texts as it is customary in traditional practice. It is with these and other uses in mind that the International Centre for African Music and Dance at the University of Ghana

has embarked on this project aimed at making African drum music accessible to a wider public in the form of musical scores, audio and video recordings.

In the late 1960s, Nketia focused much attention on championing the development of mass-produced, African musical instruments to satisfy the performance needs of the growing number of students in music classrooms in Africa and other parts of the world. Together with his former teacher and later colleague Dr. Ephraim Amu, then Head of Music in the School of Music and Dance of the Institute of African Studies, who had collected, composed and transcribed music of the *atenteben* bamboo flute tradition of southern Ghanaian ethnic groups, Nketia pursued processes to make *atenteben* flutes in large numbers yet still keeping the tonality and quality of the traditional flute as well as its ability to perform the music traditions as used in southern Ghana. A successful 'factory' for this was set up within the space of the Institute of African Studies on the University campus and soon thereafter local school authorities were buying exceptionally good quality *atenteben* flutes and establishing large flute ensembles in their schools to play well-researched, Ghanaian music traditions. This success was repeated soon thereafter with a careful study of the manufacturing of the *donno*, hour-glass drum and later the *gyile*, north-western Ghanaian xylophone.

The preparation of teacher-guide materials was the next music education focus Nketia offered his attention to. In 1997, together with other prominent African musicians, ethnomusicologists and educators from many corners of the continent at a UNESCO-sponsored conference I organized at the University of Malawi in Zomba, Malawi, Nketia served to facilitate the writing of *A Guide for the Preparation of Primary School African Music Teaching Manuals*. This valuable 'guide' was distributed to schools across Africa and has served to help develop effective teaching materials for music classes in many African countries.

As the legacy of Nketia the ethnomusicologist is appropriately affirmed over and over again, his great contribution to the study of education in and through music in Africa and other parts of the world and his writings and actions to promote fitting, effective, high-quality music education in the schools of Africa should also be noted with similar dynamic accolades. For Nketia, it is clear: music education of the highest quality in African schools is a right of all children. His life-long work to help provide this quality music education certainly cannot be disputed.

References

Akrofi, Eric. 2002. *Sharing Knowledge and Experience: A Profile of Kwabena Nketia: Scholar and Music Educator.* Accra: Afram Publications, Ltd.

Amu, Ephraim. 1933. "How to Study African Rhythm." In *The Teachers' Journal of the Gold Coast,* 154-157.

Campbell, Patricia Shehan. 2010. "World Music Pedagogy for Musicians Who Teach." In *Readings in Ethnomusicology: A Collection of Papers Presented at Ethnomusicology Symposium 2010.* Ed. by Strumpf, Mitchel and Imani Sanga. Dar es Salaam, Tanzania: Department of Fine and Performing Arts, University of Dar es Salaam.

Forsythe, Reginald. 1940. "Review of William F. Ward's *Music: A Handbook for African Teachers* (London, 1939)." In Overseas Education XI (3): 174-175.

Nketia, J. H. Kwabena. 1954. "The Role of the Drummer in Akan Society." *African Music* 1: 34-43.

___. 1963. *African Music in Ghana*. Chicago: Northwestern University Press.

___. 1966. "Music Education in African Schools: A Review of the Position in Ghana." In *International Seminar on Teacher Education in Music*. Ann Arbor: University of Michigan, 231-243.

___. 1967. "The Place of Authentic Folk Music in Education." *Music Educators Journal* 54 (3): 40-42, 129-133.

___. 1968. *Our Drums and Drummers*. Accra: Ghana Publishing House.

___. 1970. "Music Education in Africa and the West: We Can Learn From Each Other." *Music Educators Journal.* 57 (3): 48-55. November.

___. 1971. "The Objectives of Music Education in Contemporary Africa." *Papers of Lusaka Music Education Conference*. Legon, Ghana: Institute of African Studies.

___. 1974. *The Music of Africa*. New York: W. W. Norton and Company.

___. 1975. "Foreword." In *Notes on Education and Research in African Music No. 2*. Legon, Ghana: Institute of African *Studies*, University of Ghana.

___. 1978. New Perspectives in Music Education. *International Music Education*. Canberra, Australia: *(ISME) Yearbook* 5: 104-111.

___. 1988. "Exploring Intercultural Dimensions of Music Education: A World View of Music in Education." *Proceedings of the 18th World Conference of the International Society for Music Education*. Canberra, Australia: ISME: 96-106.

___. 1997. "Foreword." In *African Drum Music*. Ed. by Kongo Zabana. Accra, Ghana: Afram Publishing, Ltd.

___, ed. 1999. "A Guide for the Preparation of Primary School African Music." *Teaching Manuals*. Accra: Afram Publications, Ltd.

Strumpf, Mitchel. 1970. *Ghanaian Xylophone Studies*. Legon, Ghana: Institute of African Studies.

Ward, W. E. F. 1927. "Music in the Gold Coast." *Gold Coast Review* 3 (2) 199-223.

___. 1934. "Music in Gold Coast Education." *Gold Coast Education* 5 (2) 64-71.

Biographical Writing and Individual Creativity in African Musicology

Jesse D. Ruskin

Jesse Ruskin's research addresses musical creativity and cultural entrepreneurship among Yorùbá musicians in Nigeria and the United States. He also works in the areas of audiovisual archiving, biographical methods, and Cambodian popular music. Ruskin's work has appeared in *Ethnomusicology*, *Black Music Research Journal*, *Ethnomusicology Review*, and the *Los Angeles Times*. He was editor-in-chief of the *Pacific Review of Ethnomusicology* from 2006-2008. Ruskin holds an M.A. and PhD in ethnomusicology from UCLA and a B.A. in sociology/music from Tufts University.

This essay developed out of a bibliography that I compiled on biographical writing in African musicology. I was struck by how sizeable this literature is and what a significant place it occupies in the field. Inspired by Professor Nketia's masterful historiographical essays "Perspectives on African Musicology" (1986) and "The Scholarly Study of African Music" (1998), I reviewed the literature for historical and thematic links. This process revealed both a clearer picture of African musicologists' tendency toward biographical research and a new lens through which to view the more general disciplinary move in ethnomusicology towards individual-centered studies. The essay addresses four questions: 1) What are the general issues surrounding biographical writing in ethnomusicology? 2) What historical factors or intellectual trends underlie the focus on individuals in African musicology? 3) What are the general features of biographical literature in African musicology? 4) Finally, I ask how biographical writing in African musicology relates to broader trends in ethnomusicology.

Over the past two decades, ethnomusicologists have begun to place individual musical experience at the locus of ethnographic inquiry. This peaked in musical ethnography during the late 1980s to early 90s and has remained a consistent feature ever since. It also grew as a theoretical concern during this time. Tim Rice's 1987 model for ethnomusicology brought individual creativity into conversation with more familiar questions about the historical and social dimensions of musical practice. In a theoretical move in 2001 towards "an ethnomusicology of the individual," Jonathan Stock identifies several factors underlying the rise in biographical writing in ethnomusicology, including the recognition of individuality within the musical communities we study; the reflexive turn in the social sciences; and theories of culture that account for individual variation and agency. Work by Mark Slobin (1993) and Rice (2003) suggests that we might also consider globalization and the deterritorialization of cultures impetuses for the study of individual musicians.

Some of the seminal works in modern American ethnomusicology, such as Paul Berliner's *The Soul of Mira* (1978), John Miller Chernoff's *African Rhythm and African Sensibility* (1979), and Charles Keil's *Tiv Song* (1979), incorporate the life histories and perspectives of individual African musicians. Veit Erlmann (1989:32) argues that this literature posed a challenge to anthropology because it "brought to light a surprising measure of autonomy exercised by composers and musicians beyond the normative patterns of cultural behavior and highlighted the fact that African performance is more than a system of collective adaptation." Indeed, by the 1980s, the anthropological convention of anonymity was no longer the rule in Africanist ethnomusicology, and African composition no longer reduced to "quasi-mystical acts of communal creativity" (Blacking 1989:17). During this decade, three anthropologically-trained ethnomusicologists, Chris Waterman (1982), John Blacking (1989), and Veit Erlmann (1989), would all make significant arguments about the importance of acknowledging individual experience, agency, and creativity in the study of African music. Similarly, recent work in ethnomusicology (e.g. Ballantine 1996; DjeDje 2008; Erlmann 1991, 1996, 1999; Taylor 1997; Turino 2000) demonstrates a growing interest in the worldviews and creative procedures of individual African musicians and composers, and their roles as representatives and interpreters of cultural tradition.[2]

In African musicology, a field that overlaps yet is partially distinct from ethnomusicology, this trend was prefigured by the development of scholarly interest in individual musicians during the post-independence period of the 1960s and 1970s (see Nketia 1998:41-47). During this era, many African musicologists maintained a focus on musical tradition as the product of individual artistry and innovation. In doing so, the tenor of scholarship shifted from the anthropological preoccupation with "culture" toward an emphasis on "cultural development." The focus on individual creativity was identified as a major trend in African musicology by the late 1980s (DjeDje & Carter 1989a: 41-42), and a recent survey of periodical articles indicates that this focus has become even more prominent since the 1980s (DjeDje 2005:276).

The term "African musicology," introduced by Klaus Wachsmann in 1966, and later refined by Nketia and DjeDje (1984) and Nketia (1986, 1998), designates an approach to the study of African music that is both "scholarly and humanistic." It is an orientation that encourages African subspecialties within musicology, fosters equal collaboration between African and Western scholars, and marries theory and practice in service of the scholarly, creative, and development needs of post-independence African societies. African musicology, as Nketia (1986, 1998) and Nketia and DjeDje (1984) suggest, emerged from both Western and African streams of scholarship during the transitional periods of African nationalism and independence. It was a time when Western music scholars were reorienting their theories and methods to acknowledge African agency as artists and interpreters, and a time when African music scholars were rediscovering and redirecting their own musical and national histories. While African intellectuals and artists have long played an active role in the scholarly study of African music, it was not until the postcolonial period of institutional development that African scholars gained international recognition (Nketia 1998), and not until the early 1980s, as Professor DjeDje has said, that African musicology emerged as a field. For the purposes of this essay, I follow Nketia and DjeDje (1984) in treating African musicology as a scholarly <u>orientation</u> that draws on multiple disciplines, rather than a distinct discipline <u>per se</u>. Indeed, one of the most passionate advocates of African musicology, Akin Euba, was trained in both composition and ethnomusicology. From the start, a defining feature of African musicology has been its attention to the artistic development, creative processes, and repertoire of individual musicians. My hypothesis is that there are five interrelated reasons for this rise in attention to the individual musician in African musicology, all of which are set against the history of colonialism and independence, the challenges of nationalism, and the development of postcolonial cultural institutions: 1) Europeanization and the emergence of iconic figures in concert and modern church music; 2) government patronage and the development of postcolonial cultural institutions; 3) the confluence of nationalist ideologies and new perspectives among Western scholars; 4) curricular development and the canonization of "black composers"; and 5) urbanization, mass-mediation, and the emergence of popular music stars. These intellectual-historical moments have been well documented by Nketia (1986, 1995, 1998), Omibiyi (1979), and Omojola (1994, 1995), among others. My goal in this essay is to consider ways in which these factors relate specifically to the development of biographical writing in African musicology. I base my argument on cases drawn primarily from Ghana and Nigeria, as the majority of individual-centered studies concern musicians from these two countries.

The first factor in the growth of biographical writing is the emergence of an elite class of artists and innovators in African concert and popular musics. The intensive cultural contact brought about by European missions and colonization, as well as the first waves of African cultural nationalism that emerged as a response to it in the late 19th century (Nketia 1998:17-26; Omibiyi 1979:75) had profound effects on African musical cultures. The development of Western concert music in Nigeria during the 1880s fostered new ideas of musical individuality and distinction, as exemplified in Robert Coker, a composer trained in Germany who was often referred to as the "Mozart of Africa" (Omojola 1994:534; see also Omibiyi 1979:76-78). Europeans, of course, did not introduce the idea of individual creativity to the continent, but they did bring a particular notion of musical exceptionality with which African musicians and intellectuals had to contend. Those formally trained in Europe, especially, were challenged to make their education relevant to the needs and aspirations of their communities and nations.

The 1890s saw an influx of Europeans to Lagos, and with it an increasing awareness among formally educated Nigerian musicians as to the cultural effects of colonization. Nigerian church composers such as Emmanual Sowande and the Reverend J.J. Ransome Kuti, both of whom were trained in Western musical systems, responded to the European presence by experimenting with vernacular approaches to composition. By the turn of the twentieth century, Mosunmola Omibiyi (1979:77) writes, these individuals "began to distinguish themselves in the use of traditional music in liturgy." Modern church music, the product of subsequent composers such as Ikoli Harcourt-Whyte in Nigeria (Achinivu 1979; Omojola 1995:34-37) and Ephraim Amu in Ghana (Nketia 1998:22-26; Omojola 1995:149-164), offered a context where creative use of indigenous musical resources became itself a marker of musical individuality, an expression of cultural pride, and a service to the community. This would inspire future generations of artist-intellectuals, such as Akin Euba and J. H. Kwabena Nketia, who would become known not only for their musical exceptionality, but also for their role as "spokespeople" for their communities and, in some cases, as icons of resistance to cultural imperialism (DjeDje and Carter 1989a:39-40). As such, many of the aforementioned musicians and their protégées would themselves become the subjects of fascinating biographical and musicological studies (e.g. Achinivu 1979; Agawu 1984; Agyemang 1988; Akrofi 2002; Alaja-Browne 1981; M. Amu 1988; Njoku 1998) and the inspiration for volumes of collected essays in their names (DjeDje 2005; DjeDje and Carter 1989; Omibiyi-Obidike 2001; Omojola and Dor 2005; Tse Kimberlin and Euba 2005).

A second factor in the rise of biographical writing is the effect of government patronage and institutional development in the arts.

African musicology, as Nketia (1986, 1995, 1998) suggests, emerged during the era of cultural nationalism that followed independence in Nigeria and Ghana. It was a period in which governmental policy was aimed at forging national and pan-African arts and cultural institutions. Nketia (1995:14) elucidates the outcomes of this "governmental intervention in the status of traditional music and dance." The decade of the 1960s was, in Nigeria and Ghana, a time of state supported institution building, which saw the creation of local, national, and university-based departments, councils, commissions, and ministries of culture. This was the defining moment when "musicology came to be accepted, as both an academic discipline and something that could be of practical value to cultural development" (Nketia 1998:38). These developments led to the growth of a class of "academic musicians" (Omibiyi 1979:80), such as Fela Sowande, who would find their professional homes in the university, and a subsequent generation, including Ayo Bankole, whose creative work would be profoundly influenced by their academic training in historical musicology and ethnomusicology (Euba 1977:106, 1988:87). These academicians would become not only internationally renowned researchers and interpreters of African music, but also the subjects of study by their own students and followers. Writing by academic musicians tends to concern the artistic contributions of peers and predecessors in church and art music (e.g. Euba 1977, 1988; Nketia 1993; Sowande 1966; Omojola 1994, 1995, 1998, 2009; Uzoigwe 1978, 1992) and reflections on one's own creative work —what Akin Euba has termed "automusicology" (e.g. Euba n.d., 1999, 2005a, 2005b; Dor 2005; Uzoigwe 2005).[3] This subset of literature shows academic musicians' commitment to understanding and cultivating the unique creative and scholarly legacies of their teachers. More broadly, such biographical and autobiographical writing demonstrates an understanding of scholarship and creative practice as being mutually constitutive – one being crucial to the sustenance of the other.

As well as cultivating academic musicians, the cultural institutions that flourished during the era of independence sought the services of "traditionalists," providing them with newfound mobility (Nketia 1995:14). University music and theatre programs and national performance troupes linked these local artists into cosmopolitan musician networks, and afforded them the opportunity to travel and interpret their art to wider audiences. This mobility encouraged musical innovation and invited collaboration between traditional artists and academics, leading to studies of individuals and studies based on the expertise of these individuals. Significant academic studies of traditional musicians include Ampene (2005), Aning (1989), Dor (2000), Euba (1990), and Nayo (1964, 1969). Like academic musicians, many traditionalists became recognized both for their musical prowess and their skills at interpreting for foreign audiences (Campbell 2005; Kubik 1974; Locke and Lunna 1990; Locke and Agbeli 1992; Noss 2002). Regarding the expanding roles of traditional musicians, DjeDje and Carter (1989a:39) write, "not only did traditional performers and composers begin to receive acknowledgement for their contributions, but certain individuals of African descent...began to be looked upon as innovators and spokespersons for the larger community because of their research experiences." African musicians and academicians were no longer seen as the objects of Western gaze, but rather as subjects and agents, "active in the study and destiny of their musical traditions."

A third and related proposition is the resurgence of interest in indigenous African culture by African and Western intellectuals during the eras of nationalism and independence, and with it an interest in individual creativity as an engine of cultural continuity. This may be explained in part by the impact of nationalist ideologies on African intellectuals and a simultaneous shift in orientation among Western scholars of African music, both of which saw cultural development as a necessary corollary to the political transition from colonialism to independence. Senghor's Negritude and Nkrumah's notion of African personality were influential on postcolonial creative arts and African music scholarship, each supporting national cultural policies and spectacles that would encourage both the recovery of African material heritage and the search for essential characteristics and principles of "Africanness" (Nketia 1995; Wachsmann 1966). They were, in this respect, simultaneously excavating and (re)inventing the cultural roots of political solidarity.

Parallel to the revival of interest in traditional African arts among African intellectuals of the 1950s and 60s, Western intellectuals and collectors such as Hugh Tracey began to recognize that their preservationist instincts might be of value to the interests of Africans as well. The *Journal of the African Music Society*, the publication of the organization which Tracey helped found in 1947, was a landmark of

African musicology—bringing together scholarship by Western and African scholars in the service of African cultural development (albeit conceived from a Western viewpoint). Nketia's (1998:51-54) description of Tracey's work suggests a point of articulation between Western scholarship and African cultural nationalism. A deep engagement in South African life led Tracey to "view African music primarily as an artistic heritage to be shared, preserved, and promoted" (51). Tracey's commitment to documentation, dissemination, and development aligned him more with the pragmatic goals of African cultural revivalism than with the theoretical interests of American anthropologists such as Alan Merriam. Furthermore, Tracey's interest in maintaining creative continuity—through uncovering "the disciplines and foundations of African artistry for future generations to build on" (Nketia 1998:53; Tracy 1963:5)—would later be echoed in Akin Euba's notion of "creative ethnomusicology," which called for more attention to the artistic implications of scholarly research (Euba 1989, 2001). It is not surprising, then, that the confluence of Tracey's ideas with ideologies of cultural nationalism is reflected in an increasing scholarly interest in the "creative artist" and individual creativity.

For African and Western scholars alike, the artistry and innovations of individual musicians proved fertile ground for demonstrating the inherent logic and value of African music, and afforded clues about its creative procedures and its potentials as a resource for national cultural development. The goal of Tracey's African Music Society, as his journal editorial of 1961 states, was to affirm the "validity" of "indigenous musical standards," and through this, to "prove that Africans can be both culturally distinctive as well as territorially independent" (Tracey 1961:5). Following up this editorial in 1962, Tracey links African political change to cultural development by arguing for the social value of the "creative artist." He writes that "it is _not_ enough to stir up patriotic fervour...unless that same zeal blossoms into a deeper appreciation off the intrinsic qualities of the most sensitive and articulate members of any society...and in Africa, above all, its poets, composers, and folk musicians." It is to these individuals, he suggests, "that all politicians must look for the qualitative assessment of the success or failure of their activities" (Tracey 1962:5).

Wachsmann is more explicit about the connection between cultural nationalism and musical biography in his 1966 article on Negritude and

African music scholarship. "In Africa in most recent times," he writes, "biographies of local musicians have begun to appear and the anonymity that hitherto surrounded these men may soon be a thing of the past." He proceeds to link the interests of ethnomusicology and those of the Negritude movement by arguing that the emergent genre of African music biography would afford unprecedented knowledge of the individual creative mind and of "the stimuli that make musicians want to create music" (1966:15). What he suggests here is that Negritude's interest in the reclamation and re-presentation of African cultural heritage, especially in its literary forms, would be served by scholarship that attended to African musical creativity as simultaneously rooted and innovative—the creative engagement of individual musicians with their changing environment.

At the time of Wachsmann's publication, there were only a handful of published studies focused on individual African musicians. These included Hugh Tracey's (1948) study of Chopi music as told through the lens of two prominent Chopi composers; Andrew Tracey's (1961) participatory study of the mbira tuning and performance practices of Jege A. Tapera; David Rycroft's (1961/62) analysis of Mwenda Jean Bosco's innovative guitar style; Nicholas Nayo's (1964) thesis on the life and works of Ewe *hesino* (composer/poet/singer) Vinorkor Akakpo Akpalu; and Fela Sowande's (1966) review of Nigerian music history, which gives special acknowledgement to the pioneers of African art music. Each of these works, in its own way, seeks to demonstrate the artistic value, structural logic, historical significance, and adaptive flexibility of African music by examining the articulation of, to recall Erlmann (1989:31), individual creative autonomy and broader cultural patterns. Topics, themes, and issues that arise from these writings include individual artistry and artistic uniqueness; the articulation of individual choices with normative rules and patterns; transcription and analysis of repertoire; and individual innovation and exceptionality. Indeed, by the end of the 1960s the "anonymity" that Wachsmann saw in scholarly representations of African music was no longer the rule, and individual-focused studies proliferated in the following decades. A fourth reason for the increase in individual-centered studies is the development of postcolonial curricula in African schools and universities, and with it the perceived need to generate literature on African composers and their work (Achinivu 1979:12; Nketia 1998:46). Achinivu (ibid.) suggests that the lack of biographical material on

African artists explains the exclusion of African music from many African colleges and universities prior to the 1970s. Furthermore, he ties the need for music biography to the interests of cultural development by quoting at length the comments of South African trombonist Jonas Gwangwa, who argues that "to retain the African heritage, we have to start to study some of the black composers, the African composers, see how they go about their music" (Achinivu 1979:11-12). This literature began to emerge in the 1970s and blossomed in the 80s. While Nayo (1968) and Abdulkadir (1975) produced dissertations on traditional musicians, Achinivu's (1979) study of Ikoli Harcourt-White and Uzoigwe's (1978) dissertation on Akin Euba would be the first book-length treatments of "neo-African" composers and their work. Mosunmola Omibiyi's (1979) article on the Nigerian music scene would be among the first after Sowande's (1966) to examine modern African music history through a biographical lens, and Eileen Southern's (1976) brief biography and dialogue with Fela Sowande would provide an illuminating look at the artistic development and worldview of one of Nigeria's most revered composers. The 1980s would see a proliferation of book-length studies on African composers, including Alaja-Browne's (1981) thesis on Ayo Bankole; Misonu Amu's (1988) thesis on her father, Ephraim Amu; and Fred Agyemang's (1988) biography of the same composer. A number of articles on such individuals would also be produced during this decade, including Kofi Agawu's study of Ephraim Amu's musical style (1984, 1987) and cultural vision (1987); Ben Aning's (1989) article on the compositions and stylistic innovations of xylophonist Kakraba Lobi; DjeDje and Carter's (1989b) "biobibliographic" tribute to J.H.K. Nketia; and Akin Euba's (1988) discussion of Ayo Bankole as an exemplar of "modern African art music." In addition to generating academic interest in "neo-African idioms" and composers, Akin Euba (1999:74) notes that postcolonial curricular development can generate individual talent and expression in ways not possible in traditional contexts.

A fifth factor in the growth of biographical writing is the historical confluence of urbanization and the mass-mediation of African music, exemplified in the explosion of popular radio and the growth of the recording industry in mid twentieth-century Africa. "African radio stations," Nketia (1998:46) writes, "did not broadcast programs of traditional and contemporary music without mentioning the names of individual artists, bandleaders, or composers, while record companies, promoters, and managers often focused attention on artists and ensembles." In the case of *juju* music in Nigeria, Chris Waterman (1990:95) suggests that this electronic mass mediation was in part responsible for the "efflorescence of local substyles," a development "grounded in the efforts of musicians to create distinctive "sounds" or "systems" that might attract the attention of talent scouts from recording companies and appeal to members of their own communities." Although juju's primary milieu was live performance, some individual juju innovators, such as I.K. Dairo and King Sunny Ade, became "stars" not only by being the clients of powerful elites, but also by the exposure afforded them by radio and television appearances and their access to the recording industry (Waterman 1990:100-116). It should be noted, however, that with the "discovery" and promotion of local musicians by academics and record companies, and with the efforts of local musicians to simultaneously "modernize and indigenize" their arts for maximum appeal (ibid.:101-102), the line between what constitutes a "popular" or "traditional" musician has blurred. More appropriate, perhaps, would be to subsume popular musicians within Kubik's (1974) category of "neo-traditional" or Euba's (1999) notion of the "neo-African." In any case, studies of such artists span the decades after independence, including Rycroft's (1961/62) study of Bosco's guitar repertoire; Kubik's (1974) short monograph on the Kachamba Brothers Band, a group with whom he performed, toured, and recorded; Omibiyi's (1983) article on Bobby Benson, the "father of Nigerian popular music"; Erlmann's (1989, 1996) and Ballantine's (1996) intensive studies of the life history, philosophy, and creative procedures of *isicathamiya* star Joseph Shabalala; and, more recently, Thomas Turino's (2000) monograph on popular music stars in Zimbabwe.

Conclusion

Biographical writing in African musicology, to put it simply, can be viewed in terms of several underlying contexts: the emergence of contemporary musical environments in which individuality is expected and valued, as well as an increasing awareness of how individuality operates in traditional contexts; the development of institutions that support the dialogue of research and creativity; and the convergence of preservationist and nationalist ideas about the social significance of the creative artist. If this appears to be a somewhat deterministic argument, my intentions are quite different. The essay is, at heart, an intellectual history of the values and commitments that are evident in

African musicology's biographical literature: the presence of individual personality in communal expression; pragmatism in scholarship and composition; and the social relevance of the creative musician. It is, in other words, about the domains where African scholars and musicians exercise agency within the constraints of their historical circumstances. The vast majority of biographical writing in African musicology deals with art composers and popular musicians, especially those who were innovators in the use of indigenous musical resources. Studies of traditional musicians occupy a significant place as well. Regionally speaking, Nigerian, Ghanaian, and South African artists dominate the literature, but there are significant studies that concern other areas. In this corpus of biographical writing, narrative approaches are diverse. They include the periodized life and works model derived from historical musicology; selective analysis of individual style or creative strategies; dialogues between author and musician; single-voiced or monologic biography, and autobiography (or automusicology). A theme suggested by much of this writing is *cultural mediation*—meaning the ideological groundings, social strategies, artistic resources, and creative procedures through which artists negotiate the European "encounter." Such studies approach culture contact not only as a discourse of coercion and resistance, but also as one of creative possibilities.

Biographical literature in African musicology deals primarily with what Nketia (1995:1) would call the "contemporary contexts" of African music, environments of change in which individual innovations and interests have moved to the foreground. "Unlike traditional arts that are closely integrated because of their community orientation," Nketia (1995:14-15) writes, contemporary arts are evolving separately in a mileu of change in which the focus is on individual creativity." It should be noted that the apparent increase in artistic individualism has been of concern to some such as Francis Bebey ([1969] 1975:104), who see the community orientation of musicians as crucial to the survival of African arts.[4] It is this very "milieu of change," however, that has allowed scholars to see that individual artistry and innovation are just as much a part of the traditional arts as they are of the contemporary, and, furthermore, that community orientation is also a part of the contemporary. In other words, the interests of artistic communities and creative individuals, as well as the traditional and contemporary forms of expression on which they rely, are not necessarily divergent; they intersect in mutually dependent ways (see Dor 2004 for an Anlo Ewe case study). More useful than the tradition/modernity dichotomy is the examination of how communities and individuals differently "negotiate continuity and change" (Waterman 1990:16) using the social networks, technologies, and cultural resources available to them. Accordingly, Christopher Waterman's work on popular music centers much of its analysis on the lives and work of key figures in popular music, who he terms "culture brokers." The collapsing of the tradition/modernity binary into more fluid and strategic terms is also a feature of studies of African art composers (Dor 2005; Euba 1988).

This fluidity is what Kubik (1974) implies with his concept of the "neo-traditional" and what Euba (1988, 1999) suggests with his notions of "interculturalism" and "neo-African idioms and contexts." Tradition and innovation, from this perspective, exist not in separate spheres, but in a cyclic relationship where "today's innovations will...in future become traditions in their own right" (Euba 1999:75). Euba asks, for example, if the function of the juju singer is substantially different from that of the Yoruba praise singer. Rather than trying to ascertain which one is more traditional or authentic, and categorizing them on this basis, Euba suggests that it is more useful to examine musicians in terms of their creative responses to shifting social conditions (Euba 1999:69). In the field of art music as well, Euba (1988) sees the binary opposition of the indigenous and modern as highly problematic. For Euba, indigenization and modernization in African art music exist in a dialectic—the indigenous *is* modern in the sense that it contains all of the material and conceptual resources necessary for the creation of new concert music, and conversely, the modern *is* indigenous to the degree that it is conceived using those resources (1988:93-94). More recently, Ghanaian composer George Worlasi Kwasi Dor (2005) argues in similar fashion that indigenization, the "revitalization" of the past in the present, was a crucial aspect of the development of African choral music. He observes processes of assimilation and resistance in the compositional practices of Amu, Blege, and himself, from the perspective that the musical encounter of Africa and Europe cannot be explained only in historical and political terms as a monolithic clash of cultures and their musical forms. Musical syncretism is recast as the creative strategies of particular actors who create new music, identities, and solidarities through the strategic use of multiple cultural resources: "More attention," he argues, "should be paid to composers' innovative drives, creative ingenuity, and quest for meaning in relation to their choices from a fountain of resources, both African and Western" (Dor 2005:447).

There are parallels here to the issues associated with biographical writing in ethnomusicology, including the recognition that musical individuality is often the norm, the understanding that researchers are participants in the worlds they study, and the reevaluation of analytical concepts to account for individual agency. The difference is that African musicologists tend to approach these issues with reference to practical concerns of composition, performance, and repertory preservation. Culture is seen as more than a concept to be refined; it is also something to be tested, developed, and maintained through creative practice.

Endnotes

1: Earlier versions of this essay were presented at the 2008 Annual Meeting of the Society for Ethnomusicology, October 27, Middletown, Connecticut; and at the 2011 Two-Day International Conference in Honor of Emeritus Professor J. H. Kwabena Nketia, September 23, University of Ghana, Legon. Travel to Ghana was made possible by a grant from the UCLA Herb Alpert School of Music Student Opportunity Fund. Special thanks to Jacqueline Cogdell DjeDje, George Worlasi Kwasi Dor, and Kathleen Van Buren for their helpful feedback at various stages of this project.

2: I am not arguing that anthropology previously ignored the individual, but rather suggesting that a critique of "anthropological anonymity" was central to arguments justifying the study of individual African musicians.

3: While Akin Euba (2005b) developed the concept of "automusicology" as a means of bridging scholarship and creative practice, I would argue that T.K.E. Phillips' book *Yoruba Music* (1953) anticipated this approach. It is among the first automusicological works in the sense that Phillips used his own experience as a composer to formulate his theories of Yoruba pentatonicism and rhythm, and to understand the possibilities and limitations of combining Yoruba and church musics.

4: Thanks to Kathleen Van Buren for drawing my attention to Bebey's view on this subject.

References

Abdulkadir, Dandatti. 1975. "The Role of An Oral Singer in Hausa/Fulani Society: A Case Study of Mamman Shata." PhD. dissertation, Indiana University.

Achinivu, A. Kanu. 1979. *Ikoli Harcourt Whyte: The Man and his Music: A Case of Musical Acculturation in Nigeria.* Hamburg: Karl Dieter Wagner.

Agawu, Kofi V. 1984. "The Impact of Language on Musical Composition in Ghana: An Introduction to the Musical Style of Ephraim Amu." *Ethnomusicology* 28(1): 37-73.

___. 1987. "Conversation with Ephraim Amu: The Making of a Composer." *The Black Perspective in Music* 15(1): 50-63.

Agyemang, Fred. 1988. *Amu the African: A Study in Vision and Courage.* Accra, Ghana: Asempa Publishers, Christian Council of Ghana.

Akrofi, Eric A. 2002. *Sharing Knowledge and Experience: A Profile of Kwabena Nketia, Scholar and Music Educator.* Accra, Ghana: Afram Publications.

Alaja-Browne, Afolabi. 1981. *Ayo Bankole.* Master's thesis, University of Pittsburgh, PA.

___. 1985. *Juju Music: A Study of its Style and Social History.* PhD. dissertation, University of Pittsburgh, PA.

Ampene, Kwasi. 2005. *Female Song Tradition and the Akan of Ghana: The Creative Process in Nnwonkoro.* SOAS Musicology Series. Aldershot, Hampshire, England, and Burlington, VT: Ashgate.

Amu, Misonu. 1988. *Stylistic and Textual Sources of A Contemporary Ghanaian Art Music Composer: A Case Study: Dr. Ephraim Amu.* Master's thesis, University of Ghana, Legon.

Aning, Ben A. 1989. "Kakraba Lobi: Master Xylophonist of Ghana." In *African Musicology: Current Trends Vol. 1.* Ed. by Jacqueline Cogdell DjeDje and William G. Carter. Atlanta/Los Angeles: African Studies Association, 93-110.

Ballantine, Christopher. 1996. "Joseph Shabalala: Chronicles of an African Composer." *British Journal of Ethnomusicology* 5:1-38.

Bebey, Francis. (1969) 1975. *African Music: A People's Art.* Translated by Josephine Bennett. Westport, CT: Lawrence Hill & Co.

Berliner, Paul. (1978) 1993. *The Soul of Mbira.* Chicago: University of Chicago Press.

Blacking, John. 1989. "Challenging the Myth of 'Ethnic Music': First Performances of a New Song in an African Oral Tradition, 1961.'" *Yearbook for Traditional Music* 21:17-24.

Campbell, Corinna. 2005. *Gyil Music of the Dagarti People: Learning, Performing, and Representing a Musical Culture*. Master's thesis, Bowling Green State University, Ohio.

Chernoff, John Miller. 1979. *African Rhythm and African Sensibility: Aesthetics and Social Action in African Musical Idioms*. Chicago: University of Chicago Press.

DjeDje, Jacqueline Cogdell. 2005. "African Musicology: Current State of Research and Future Directions." In *Multiple Interpretations of Dynamics of Creativity and Knowledge in African Music Traditions: A Festschrift in Honor of Akin Euba on the Occaison of His 70th Birthday*. Ed. by Bode Omojola and George Dor. Richmond, CA: Music Research Institute Press, 267-299.

___. 2008. *Fiddling in West Africa: Touching the Spirit in Fulbe, Hausa, and Dagbamba Cultures*. Bloomington: Indiana University Press.

DjeDje, Jacqueline Cogdell, and William G. Carter. 1989a. "Introduction: African Musicology: An Assessment of the Field." In *African Musicology: Current Trends Vol. 1*. Ed. by Jacqueline Cogdell DjeDje and William G. Carter. Atlanta/Los Angeles: African Studies Association, 39-44.

___. 1989b. "J.H. Kwabena Nketia: A Biobibliographic Portrait." In *African Musicology: Current Trends Vol. 1*. Ed. by Jacqueline Cogdell DjeDje and William G. Carter. Atlanta/Los Angeles: African Studies Association, 3-29.

Dor, George Worlasi Kwasi. 1992. "Trends and Stylistic Traits in the Art Composition of Ephraim Amu, N.Z. Nayo, and J.H.K. Nketia: A Theoretical Perspective." M.Phil. thesis, University of Ghana, Legon.

___. 2000. "Tonal Resources and Compositional Processes of Ewe Traditional Vocal Music." PhD. dissertation, University of Pittsburgh.

___. 2004. "Communal Creativity and Song Ownership in Anlo Ewe Musical Practice: The Case of Havolu." *Ethnomusicology* 48(1).

___. 2005. "Uses of Indigenous Music Genres in Ghanaian Choral Art Music: Perspectives from the Works of Amu, Blege, and Dor." *Ethnomusicology* 49(3).

___. 1991. *African Stars: Studies in Black South African Performance*. Chicago: University of Chicago Press.

___. 1996. *Nightsong: Performance, Power, and Practice in South Africa*. Chicago: University of Chicago Press.

___. 1999. *Music, Modernity, and the Global Imagination: South Africa and the West*. Oxford: Oxford University Press.

Erlmann, Veit. 1989. "A Conversation with Joseph Shabalala of Ladysmith Black Mambazo: Aspects of African Performers' Life Stories." *The World of Music* 31(9):31-58.

Euba, Akin. 1977. "Obituary – Ayo Bankole (1935-76)." *Nigerian Music Review* 1.

___. 1988. "Ayo Bankole: A View of Modern African Art Music Through The Works of a Nigerian Composer." In *Essays on Music in Africa Vol. 1*. Ed. by Akin Euba. Bayreuth: Bayreuth African Studies and IWALEWA-Haus, 87-118.

___. 1990. *Yoruba Drumming: The Dundun Tradition*. Bayreuth, Germany: E. Breitinger, Bayreuth University.

___. 1999. "African Traditional Musical Instruments in Neo-African Idioms and Contexts." *In Turn Up the Volume! A Celebration of African Music*. Ed. by Jacqueline Cogdell DjeDje. Los Angeles: UCLA Fowler Museum of Cultural History, 68-77.

___. 2001. "Issues in Africanist Musicology: Do We Need Ethnomusicology in Africa?" In *Proceeding of the Forum for Revitalizing African Music Studies in Higher Education*. Ann Arbor, MI: The U.S. Secretariat of the International Center for African Music and Dance, The International Institute, University of Michigan, 137-139.

___. 2005a. "Themes from Chaka No.1: A Pianistic Realization of African Polyrhythm." In *Towards An African Pianism: Keyboard Music of Africa and the Diaspora Vol. 1*. Ed. by Cynthia Tse Kimberlin and Akin Euba. Point Richmond, CA: MRI Press, 113-122.

___. 2005b. "A Theory of Automusicology and Its Application to Themes from Chaka No. 2." Paper Presented at the Second International Symposium on the Music of Africa, Princeton University, December 9.

___. (n.d.). "Yoruba Religious Arts, Secularization and Modern Music Theatre." Unpublished paper.

Keil, Charles. 1979. *Tiv Song: The Sociology of Art in a Classless Society*. Chicago: University of Chicago Press.

Kubik, Gerhard. 1974. *The Kachamba Brothers' Band: A Study of Neo-Traditional Music in Malawi (Zambia Papers 9)*. Manchester: Manchester University Press.

Locke, David, featuring Abubakari Lunna. 1990. *Drum Damba: Talking Drum Lessons*. Crown Point, IN: White Cliffs Media Co.

Locke, David, featuring Godwin Agbeli. 1992. *Kpegisu: A War Drum of the Ewe*. Tempe, AZ: White Cliffs Media Co.

Nayo, Nicholas Zinzendorf. 1964. *Akpalu and His Songs: A Study of the Man and His Music*. African Music Diploma thesis, University of Ghana.

___. 1969. "Akpalu and His Songs." *Papers in African Studies*. Legon: Accra 3: 24-34.

Njoku, J.A. 1998. "Art Composed Music in Africa." In *Garland Vol. 1 (Africa)*. Ed. by Ruth M. Stone. New York: Garland, 232-53.

Nketia, J. H. Kwabena. 1986. "Perspectives on African Musicology." In *Africa and the West: The Legacies of Empire*. Ed. by Isaac James Mowoe and Richard Bjornson. Westport, CT: Greenwood Press, 215-253.

___. 1993. "Introduction: The Historical and Stylistic Background of the Music of Ephraim Amu." In *Amu Choral Works, Vol. 1*. Ed. by Ephraim Amu. Accra: Waterville Publishing House and Presbyterian Press, 7-23

___. 1995. "National Development and the Performing Arts of Africa." Unpublished Paper.

___. 1998. "The Scholarly Study of African Music." In *Garland Encyclopedia of World Music, Vol. 1 (Africa)*. Ed. by Ruth M. Stone. New York: Garland, 13-73.

Nketia, J. H. Kwabena and Jacqueline Cogdell DjeDje. 1984. "Introduction: Trends in African Musicology." In *Selected Reports in Ethnomusicology, Vol. V: Studies in African Music*, ix-xx. Los Angeles: Ethnomusicology Publications, Dept. of Music, University of California.

Noss, Kathleen Jenabu. 2002. *African Musicians, Musics, and Metaphors Across Space*. Master's thesis, University of California, Los Angeles.

Omibiyi, Mosunmola. 1979. "Nigerian Musicians and Composers." *Nigeria Magazine* 128-129:75-88.

___. 1983. "Bobby Benson: The Entertainer Musician." *Nigeria Magazine* 147:18-27.

Omibiyi-Obidike, M.A. Ed. 2001. *African Art Music in Nigeria: Fela Sowande Memorial*. Lagos: Stirling-Horden.

Omojola, Bode. 1994. "Contemporary Art Music in Nigeria: An Introductory Work on the Life and Works of Ayo Bankole." *Africa* 64(4).

___. 1995. *Nigerian Art Music with an Introductory Study of Ghanaian Art Music*. Ibadan, Nigeria: IFRA.

___. 1998. "Style in Modern Nigerian Art Music: The Pioneering Works of Fela Sowande." *Africa* 68(4):455-483.

___. 2009. *The Music of Fela Sowande: Encounters, African Identity, and Creative Ethnomusicology*. Point Richmond, CA: MRI Press.

Omojola, Bode, and George Worlasi Kwasi Dor, eds. 2005. *Multiple Interpretations of Dynamics of Creativity and Knowledge in African Music Traditions: A Festschrift in Honor of Akin Euba on the Occasion of His 70th Birthday*. Point Richmond, CA: MRI Press.

Phillips, T.K.E. 1953. *Yoruba Music: Fusion of Speech and Music*. Johannesburg: African Music Society.

Rice, Timothy. 1987. "Towards a Remodeling of Ethnomusicology." *Ethnomusicology* 31(3):469-88.

———. 2003. "Time, Place, and Metaphor in Musical Experience and Ethnography." *Ethnomusicology* 47(2):151-79.

Rycroft, David. 1961-2. "The Guitar Improvisation of Muenda J. Bosco" (Parts I and II). *African Music* 2(4):81-98; 3(1):86-102.

Slobin, Mark. 1993. *Subcultural Sounds: Micromusics of the West*. Hanover, NH: University Press of New England.

Southern, Eileen, and Fela Sowande. 1976. "Conversation with Fela Sowande, High Priest of Music." *The Black Perspective in Music* 4(1):90-104.

Sowande, Fela. 1966. "Nigerian Music and Musicians: Then and Now." *Composer* 19:25-34.

Stock, Jonathan P.J. 2001. "Toward an Ethnomusicology of the Individual, or Biographical Writing in Ethnomusicology." *The World of Music* 43(1):5-19.

Taylor, Timothy D. 1997. *Global Pop: World Music, World Markets*. New York and London: Routledge.

Tracey, Andrew. 1961. "Mbira Music of Jege A. Tepera." *African Music* 2(4):44-63.

Tracey, Hugh. [1948] 1970. *Chopi Musicians: Their Music, Poetry, and Instruments*. London: Oxford University Press.

———. 1961. "Editorial." *African Music* 2(4):5.

———. 1962. "Editorial." *African Music* 3(1):5.

———. 1963. "Editorial." *African Music* 3(2):5.

Tse Kimberlin, Cynthia, and Akin Euba. Eds. 2005. *Towards An African Pianism: Keyboard Music of Africa and the Diaspora Vol. 1*. Point Richmond, CA: MRI Press.

Turino, Thomas. 2000. *Nationalists, Cosmopolitans, and Popular Music in Zimbabwe*. Chicago and London: University of Chicago Press.

Uzoigwe, Joshua. 1978. *Akin Euba: An Introduction to the Life and Music of a Nigerian Composer*. Masters thesis, University of Lagos.

———. 1992. *Akin Euba: An Introduction to the Life and Music of a Nigerian Composer*. Bayreuth: Eckhard Breitinger.

———. 2005. "African Pianism: The Problem of Tonality and Atonality." In *Towards An African Pianism: Keyboard Music of Africa and the Diaspora Vol. 1*. Ed. by Cynthia Tse Kimberlin and Akin Euba. Point Richmond, CA: MRI Press, 103-111.

Wachsmann, Klaus P. 1966. "Negritude in Music." *Composer* 19:12-16.

Waterman, Christopher A. 1982. "'I'm a Leader, Not a Boss': Social Identity and Popular Music in Ibadan, Nigeria." *Ethnomusicology* 26(1).

———. 1990. *Jùjú: A Social History and Ethnography of an African Popular Music*. Chicago: University of Chicago Press.

Kwabena Nketia and the Genesis of Archival Collections at the Institute of African Studies

Godwin K. Adjei

Godwin K. Adjei is an ethnomusicologist, research fellow, and head of the Music and Dance Section in the Institute of African Studies at the University of Ghana-Legon. He has worked extensively in the Akan chieftaincy institution. His research interests include court music and chieftaincy, political commentary in traditional and modern genres, heritage studies, music and gender, youth sub-cultures, and the analysis of transformational techniques in music.
His article, "Reducing Male Monopoly of State Drumming in Ghana: The Axim Experience" (2007) appears in the *Research Review* (IAS, University of Ghana, Legon). A joint publication, "Music and the Challenge of Democracy," is forthcoming in the *Journal of Intra-African Studies* (Ibadan, Nigeria).

IAS Audio-Visual Archive and Nketia

In this paper, I will present the history of the audio-visual archive of the Institute of African Studies (IAS). I begin with the following rhetorical questions. (1). How did Nketia come by the idea of setting up an audio-visual archive? (2). How did he manage to get resources to support this idea? What were some of the challenges he encountered in the setting up of the archive?

Nketia started his archival collections in 1952 in the Department of Sociology then headed by the late Professor K. A. Busia, a research fellow and lecturer in African Studies. When Nketia was appointed a research fellow in 1952, one of the expectations of Kofi Abrefa Busia, the professor and head of the Department of Sociology had of him was that, "he would develop African materials and theoretical perspectives to a level that would permit the establishment of a separate department for courses in African Music and related arts at the degree level at the University of Ghana" (Djedje: 1989). His job description however did not include the development of an archive of recordings of African music or he would have functioned like other professional collectors like Hugh Tracey of South Africa. He was to do research into language, music, dance and folklore.

He served in the Department of Sociology for ten years and was the first to join the (IAS) as a senior research fellow when it was established by Nkrumah in 1962. Soon afterwards Nketia was appointed an associate professor and deputy director, and later became director of the IAS at the end of his third year succeeding Thomas Hodgkin. He was simultaneously also the director of the School of Music and Drama and the Ghana Dance Ensemble of which Mawere Opoku served as artistic director (ibid).

The archival collections which originated in the Department of Sociology moved with Nketia to the IAS when he was appointed to the institute, where he was fortunate to have enough space to set it up properly as an archive. Later he directed Mary Seavoy, his graduate assistant from UCLA, who was by then doing her field research in Ghana, to re-catalogue the collection, using the Library of Congress Cataloging system at the UCLA archive.

With time, a few colleagues and visitors deposited materials when the Archive opened up but this did not make them co-founders. Additionally he received recordings from the UNESCO collection and other sources as well as individuals. Such voluntary gifts are normal when an archive is formally set up so one can thus say that the Archive benefitted from individuals and institutions from the personal reputation of Nketia in Ghana and abroad. This is what Nketia personally has to say about his research and the setting up of the archive:

> The recordings go back to 1952 when I was appointed Research Fellow in African Studies in the Sociology Department (then headed by Professor K. A. Busia). I sustained the field recording program in the Institute of African Studies when I was appointed Professor and Director, and set up the collection as an Archive in the Institute with the help of a graduate student of mine at UCLA (where I also held a tenured Professorship) who came to catalogue them according to the system used at the Library of Congress. I expanded the archival holdings with new field and commercial recordings when I set up the International Centre for African Music and Dance in Legon with the assistance of the Ford Foundation (Nketia: 2010).

Challenges

Though Nketia succeeded in setting up the audio-visual archives for the Institute and the University in general, his effort to get this facility established did not go without challenges. Six years after his appointment as a Research Fellow at the department of sociology, Nketia was awarded a Rockefeller Foundation Fellowship to travel abroad for one year from 1958 to 1959. On his return to Ghana however, he learnt that the archival collections and musical instruments, particularly drums that he left in his office before his travel had been transferred from the Sociology department and damped at the Archeology department. This was because Cynthia Heron, an American sociologist who replaced Kofi Abrefa requested to use his office space in which the aforementioned materials and equipments had been kept. In consequence of this, Nketia had to automatically re-locate to the Archaeology department after his foreign tour. Luckily, around the same time, Peter L. Shirnnie, the then head of Archaeology department was also brainstorming to establish an

American model of African studies in the form of just an office which was to serve as the base for all the researchers of the department. This move by Shirnnie coincidentally, met with Nkrumah's vision and practical plans of changing the face of the University and which led to the establishment of the Institute of African Studies in 1961 and commissioned in 1962.

The establishment of the Institute was to serve as a boost to the development of Music and the related arts which in fact was the prime objective of Nketia. Hence, without any hesitation, Nketia capitalized on the new development by relocating this time round, from the Archaeology department with all his accumulated archival materials and drums to the newly established Institute where he was enthusiastically welcomed by its first director, Thomas Hodgkin. Though the treatment meted out to Nketia at the Sociology department while he was away on his one year tour abroad could be described as a bitter pill, he did not allow it to frustrate him in any way. As a stalwart in his field of study who knew what he was about, he remained resolute and very hopeful, even though his own colleagues around him did not understand his line of academic pursuit.

Nketia and the Concept of Audio-Visual Archive
Nketia started his field collection from the period of his appointment at the Sociology department in 1952, but the idea of archival set up did not occur to him until his one year travel abroad through Rockefeller Foundation Fellowship. In fact it was during the tour that Nketia got the exposure to the work of archival institutions and their relevance to academic endeavors such as the management of field records. In addition to formal courses, the Rockefeller Foundation Fellowship arranged a number of visits and cultural experiences for Nketia so that he could meet and interact with some of the ethnomusicologists whose works he had read and a few other American composers. He met Milton Babbitt and Mieczyslaw Kolinski in New York, visited Indiana University, Bloomington, where he had interesting discussions with George Herzorg and saw the Archive of Traditional Music. His tour took him to the University of Illinois at Urbana, principally to see the School of Music and its Percussion Ensemble, and the laboratory of Harry Patch. He was sent to Princeton to meet Roger Sessions and then to the Institute of Ethnomusicology at UCLA where he had what he describes as "a delightful two weeks with Mantle Hood" (Djedje: 1989).

The most outstanding of Nketia's visits abroad in respect of the setting up of the Institute of African Studies archives is the visit to the archive of traditional Music at Indiana University. The visit in no small way equipped him with an initial knowledge about an archive and this is what urged him to place more premium on his field collections which he later re-organized as the core material to establish the IAS archive.

Sources of Financial and Technical Support
A major set-back to research in most African universities is lack of financial and technical support. Because of this problem, researchers in these universities who are expected to go to the field for data are often found tied to their offices, because their salaries which can be described as stipends cannot carry them through. Though financial and technical support has been the bane of most researchers, Nketia's situation was quite unique and unprecedented. To a very large extent, Nketia's encounter with Prof. Kofi Busia at the Sociology department at the prime of his academic carrier could be described as a timely intervention to the rapid development and growth in his academic pursuit. Because of Busia's interest in Nketia's work, he arranged for the latter to have the departmental car with a driver, a research assistant, a tape recorder, and a technician to assist him in the field with recordings and photography when he discussed his plan of action with him. In addition to the equipments and other logistics, Nketia was also given adequate financial support to carry him through his field research. This support which can be described as a divine academic intervention in no small way propelled Nketia on to accomplish such an academic excellence which is also reflected in the setting up of the IAS archive.

Holdings of the Audio-Visual Archive
The audio-visual archive is a joint archive of I.A.S and the International Centre for African Music and Dance (ICAMD) which contains field recordings on audio format collected in the 1950s to 1970s, from the Old Institute of African Studies (I.A.S) Sound Archive. The archive contains materials made up of a broad range of musical traditions found in Ghana, including Ga, Akan, Dagaare, Frafra, Sisala, Lobi, Fante, Ewe traditional music etc., as well as recordings of live performances of Ghanaian popular music and recordings of endangered languages (1998: 8). With time, the audio-visual Archive's holdings have been expanded with new field and commercial recordings on both audio and video format from ICAMD archive. These materials are mostly

indigenous music and dance forms. Programs comprising selected funerals of royals, ordinary individuals and personalities, traditional festivals and national festivals such as Pan- African Historical theatre Festival (PANAFEST), and Emancipation day celebration. Other materials in the archive are data on music, rituals, interviews on selected musicians and dancers of the older generation as well as young musicians and dancers (Judith: 2010).

Patronage

The materials in the audio-visual archive are used by music and dance lecturers and students of the university and all other tertiary institutions in the country. It also serves as the research centre for many international scholars and researchers. The archive's stock is approximately six thousand, i.e. the materials are deposited on mediums such as: compact disc, reel-to-reel, digital audio tapes (DAT), audio cassettes, vinyl discs (LPs), mini-DV tapes, VHS, Hi-8 and video tapes etc. The Archive is indeed a "Treasure House" as well as a potential National Cultural resource. It is indeed a fact that the collection of Audio materials in the ICAMD/I.A.S. Archive dates back to the early 1950s, and the process was actually initiated by Emeritus Professor J.H. Nketia. Generally speaking, the materials represent the largest and most authentic and unique forms of Ghanaian traditional music that cannot be found anywhere else in Africa and the world as a whole. About ninety percent (90%) of these materials are on 1900 reel-to-reel tapes. The archive has further been expanded with the acquisition of commercial recordings as well as field recordings on audio and video formats between the 1980s and 2010.

Donations

Items donated so far include the Mary Seavoy collection of field tapes, records, videos, slides, photographs, audio and video recordings of traditional Music and dance of Malawi, Venda, obtained through the good offices of Mitchel Strumpf and Gustav Twerefoo respectively, the GILLBT recordings of church music in Traditional singing styles donated by Paul Neely, field recordings he made at Nandom and Sisaala, Lambusie and parts of Burkina Faso, DAT copies and videos donated by Trevor Wiggins of Dartington College of Arts (UK), a cassette dubbing of Rattray's cylinder recordings of *atumpan, bragoro* (puberty songs) made in the 1920's donated by British Sound Archive, video version of a silent film at the Smithsonian Institution made in the 1920's, by Herskovits in

Asokore in Ghana deposited by Catherine Cole, then a visiting Fulbright student. A major donation made to the center consists of copies of field recordings and other materials compiled by Leo Sarkissian, Honorary Fellow of ICAMD and producer of Voice of America's Time in Africa. As the field recordings were made on large reel to reel tapes, arrangements have been made for them to be transferred to cassettes before they are shipped to the center. The center has received recorded materials from the UNESCO Collection, Tervuren Museum and colleagues in Zimbabwe, and Solomon Mbabi-Katana, a retired African musicologist in Uganda who has extensive field recordings of music in East Africa he made with a grant from the Rockefeller Foundation, brought them along when he came into residence in March 1998 for a semester as a senior fellow so that copies could be made for the Centre's archive while he worked on a couple of his writing projects.

Donations of equipment have also been received. Professor Lester Monts donated a professional still camera and a Sony audio cassette recorder to the center during one of his visits, while Swartmore College donated a DAT recorder, hI-8 Video Camera and computer software (Life forms) through Professor Sharon Friedler of the Department of Music and Dance (1998).

Stock of Audio Collection
1. Contemporary Highlife, Old Highlife, Contemporary Local Gospel, Old Gospel, Concert Parties, Folk Music, Music from Across the World including both religious and traditional music (Commercial Tapes). ***Number of items**=940*
2. Compact discs of Traditional/folk/religious etc. Music from Africa and the rest of the world. ***Number of Items** = 152*
3. Unpublished field works donated by Dominik Phefferoen (Compact Discs format). ***Number of Items** = 17*
4. Compact Discs of Highlife, traditional and folk music from Ghana. ***Number of items** = 97*
5. Compact Discs of Gospel Music from Ghana. ***Number of Items** = 30*
6. Miscellaneous CDs. ***Number of items** = 58*
7. Special collection from Dr. Fiagbedzi (Field work, Cassettes Format) ***Number of Items** = 177*
8. Hip-life Cassettes. ***Number of Items** = 8*
9. Field works of traditional music on analogue cassettes (Catalogued) ***Number of Items** 622*

10. Field works on analogue cassettes (In the cataloguing process). **Number of Items** = 120
11. Digital Audio Tapes (DAT) of Field works. **Number of Items** = 272
12. Vinyl Discs (LPs) of old highlife music, folk music from some African countries etc. **Number of Items** = 1,100
13. Reel to Reel tapes. **Number of Items** = 1900

Video Collections
1. Video's of field works On VHS format. **Number of Items** = 53
2. Documentaries (Commercial Videos) – On VHS Format **Number of Items** = 73
3. Research recordings on Hi-8 and Video 8 (In the cataloguing process) **Number of Items** = 120
4. Research recordings on Hi-8 and Video 8 Formats (Catalogued) **Number of Items** = 28
5. Research works on Mini-DV. **Number of Items** = 19
6. Video materials deposited in the Archive by Dominik Phyfferoen on VHS Format. **Number of Items** = 13
7. DVD materials and notes accompaniment deposited by Dominik Phyfferoen

Challenges

Though the Archives of Recorded Sound at the Institute of African Studies is on a much smaller scale, Agawu sees it as a valuable resource made up of recordings dating back to the 1950's but which has been underused until Wolfgang Bender and his team managed to copy the entire collection and had it deposited at the Johannes Gutenberg University in Mainz, Germany (Agawu 2003:34). Like most educational institutions in Africa, particularly in the West African sub-region, the audio-visual archive is also weighed down with problems. A summary of the problems of the archives by Kofi Agawu is as follows:

> While it is gratifying to see Mainz built its collection of material on African Music for use by scholars from around the world, it is sad to note that, once again, activity on the African continent has more or less been declared impossible. Certainly working in Mainz is from the point of view of creature comforts and accessibility easier than working at

Legon, where the archivist may not be seen for days, where the playback equipment, although visibly displayed, does not work, and where a request for a copy of this or that recording may be greeted by suspicion that the scholar is going to make money with it (Agawu 2003).

Though this problem as has been pointed out by Agawu used to engulf the archive some years ago, the working environment has now changed for the better. The archive is now being manned by a trained archivist who can be located for assistance twenty four hours a day. As a result, patronage of the place has improved very considerably.

Digitization (Data Migration)

About eighty percent of the materials in the archive are in analog format. We are now in the 'digital' world; therefore the issue of converting these analogue materials onto a digital format is very crucial. As has been pointed out already, the role of the audiovisual archive is to ensure the safety and longevity of the materials. It is therefore highly important materials in the archive are migrated onto the latest technologies so that it remains accessible to future generations.

The necessity for collecting materials from the past and organizing them in archives so that we in the contemporary times may use them in our studies is very crucial. The past is always relevant to the present, informing our views, answering our questions and pointing us in the right direction. At the same time, contemporary insights assist us to reacquaint ourselves with past documentation and see in it for the first time as it were, implications hitherto unseen or unappreciated. Archives are an essential means of examining the past.

Acquisition of Materials

Over the years, the materials in the AV archive have been acquired through the following means:

1. Field trips
2. Gifts and donations of field and commercial recordings by affiliates of ICAMD/IAS
3. Purchase of new Commercial recordings (Hip-life/Highlife) on audio tapes and CDs.

For the past three years, very minimal additions have been made to the archive's stock. Scholars who visit the archive prefer to tap information and do not leave copies of their research. It is indeed very important to make mention of Dominik Phyferoen an archivist and ethnomusicologist from Belgium who deposits about seventy percent of his research work in the archive after each of his research visits.

Play-back/Back-up Copies
With the exception of the Reel-to-reel which have copies stored on Digital Audio Tapes (DAT), all other materials in the archive have single copies each and the need to have play back copies on each material is very important. Secondly, since all the materials are stored in one location and do not have copies elsewhere within the university or outside the university, in case of disaster, all these valuable materials will be lost.

Space
The archive staff and users are always battling with space. Since there isn't much space, the archivist in charge cannot deal with multiple requests at a time. Therefore one can only use the archive by appointment. Given the experience in research and my plans to undertake further research, I would most strongly support any request for additional Institutional funding to ensure that the Archives of the IAS keep pace with the reception and processing of documents and related materials vital to keeping alive our connections. Distribution of Archives Alan Lomax in 1968 described Africa as "the best recorded of continents, yet if one compares the modest holdings of schools, universities, independent archives, and radio stations on the continent to their counterparts in Europe and America, one finds that there is simply no comparison. Published discographies and videographies confirm that, as with books and articles, the majority of ethnographic recordings are found outside the continent (Agawu 2003: 33). There are however a few exceptions like the remarkable collections of recordings of traditional African music of the International library of African Music (ILAM) in Rhodestown, South Africa begun by Hugh Tracey in 1954. Though Agawu describes the Archives of Recorded Sound at the Institute of African studies as being on a smaller scale, he goes ahead to also describe it as a valuable and fantastic resource that needs to be maintained and improved upon by all and sundry.

Budget Consideration

The Audio Visual Archive possesses an invaluable wealth of recorded musical and dance traditions which need to be kept alive, and managing and maintaining the AV Archive is very expensive. For instance the cost of Audio visual products and resources keep on increasing more than expected and at the same time, changes in technology also renders equipment obsolete. Magnetic media needs to be refreshed, digitized and migrated to avoid decay. Currently, a greater number of playback machines are broken down and the need to replace them is very urgent. For example: Only one television which is about 18years old is connected to the VCR and the other playback machines, at times it (the T.V) has to be slapped before anything can be viewed on it. The reel-to-reel tapes which were collected by Prof. Nketia in the 1950s cannot be accessed because the player is down and new ones cannot be traced on the market. Mini-DV, Hi-8 and Video-8 tapes can hardly be accessed because there is lack of funding to purchase the players.

Only one Pentium 4 Dell computer has been assigned to the Archive, and this single computer performs all the core functions of the archive. It is used as music player for archive users, for cataloguing, to burn music on CD, typing of official things and to retrieve materials from the Internet. Meanwhile Pentium 4 Dell is not the ideal computer for an archive of this sort. The archive needs about three computers to perform different tasks outlined above; preferably one G5 apple computer for editing or making video files and two Dell Computers for other purposes.

Donation of recorded field documents by Fellows of the Institute and the entire university community should be considered a priority. Furthermore, scholars from the global world who are aware of such a facility at the Institute are encouraged to also make further donations either in cash or in kind to support the running of the place. Failure to maintain such a valuable asset bequeathed to us by our legendary Professor, J. H. Kwabena Nketia we must know will not be taken kindly by posterity. As a matter of fact, Nketia's singular effort with regard to the establishment of an archive at the Institute of African Studies goes a very long way to confirm the symbolic statement that, "he is a man of many parts" and it is important that we continue to be proud of him for his outstanding work as a scholar and music educator of such rare distinction.

Acknowledgments

My sincere gratitude goes to the renowned ethnomusicologist and composer, Professor Kwabena Nketia, for his assistance in the tracing of the origin of the audio-visual archives of the institute. I am also grateful to Mrs. Judith Opoku-Boateng, the present archivist, for providing me with a comprehensive update on the state of the audio-visual archives long before the international conference.

References

(n.d.). Retrieved from www.unesco.org/webworld/wirerpt/wirenglish/chap14/.pdf.

Agawu, Kofi. 2003. *Representing African Music*. New York and London: Routledge.

Cohen, Marilyn and Jasper Addo. 1998. Accra: International Centre for African Music and Dance.

Djedje, Jacqueline Cogdell and William G. Carter, eds. 1989. *African Musicology: Current Trends, Vol. I*. of A Festschrift Presented to J.H. Kwabena Nketia. Los Angeles: UCLA African Studies Center/ African Arts Magazine and Crossroads Press/ African Studies Association.

Kunst, J. 1959. *Ethnomusicology: A Study of its Nature, its Problems, Methods, and Personalities to Which is Added a Bibliography* (3rd ed.). The Hague: Martinus Nijhof.

Nettle, Bruno. 1983. *The Study of Ethnomusicology: Twenty-Nine Issues and Concepts*. Urbana: University of Illinois Press.

___. 1964. *Theory and Method in Ethnomusicology*. Glencoe: The Free Press.

Opoku, N. J. 2010. *Annual Report on IAS Archive*. Accra, Legon: Institute of African Studies, Music and Dance.

Nketia, Nationalism, and the Ghana Dance Ensemble

Paul W. Schauert

Paul Schauert is a lecturer at Oakland University. He holds a PhD in ethnomusicology from Indiana University. Since 2004, he has been working intermittently with Ghana's National Dance Ensembles. He has presented at numerous international conferences, including the SEM, ASA, and CORD. He has published articles in *Africa Today*, *Ghana Studies Journal*, and *Transactions of the Historical Society of Ghana*. Additional articles of Schauert appear in the edited volume, *Over the Edge: Pushing Boundaries of Folklore and Ethnomusicology*; two entries for the *Dictionary of African Biography*; and numerous reviews in the *Journal of Folklore Research and African Music*.

On a bright Friday morning in September of 2011 in the courtyard of the Institute of African Studies at the University of Ghana (Legon), as scholars from around the globe gathered for a conference paying tribute to Professor J.H. Kwabena Nketia, the elegant and noble sounds of Akan court drumming filled the air, welcoming the attendees. Singing, dancing, and drumming the praises of the emeritus professor, an ensemble of artists performed the Asante royal music of Kete and Fontomfrom, certainly befitting the academic royalty that was being honored that day. After the large booming Fontomfrom drums had sounded their last appellation, keeping with Asante royal custom, a group of *mnensuon* horn blowers trumpeted loudly, signaling the arrival of Nketia. With regal Kente cloth draped around him, a humble and elated Nketia, grinning broadly, was led into the conference hall by the horn blowers in a slow stately procession. Once inside, he met with a *seprewa* (small harp) player, who continued to laud the professor with poetic lyrical proverbs in Akan/Twi (Nketia's mother tongue).

Appropriately, performing these various praises that day were members of the Ghana Dance Ensemble (GDE), the national company that Nketia himself had founded nearly five decades earlier at the very university where the conference was held. The ensemble's performance not only acted as a fitting tribute to Nketia, but also demonstrated the enduring legacy and relevance of this troupe. While there has been much written about the GDE (cf. Adinku 2000; Fabian 1996; Hirt-Manheimer 2004; Opoku 1967; Schauert 2011; Schramm 2000; et. al) which has covered an array of issues ranging from representation to creative process, power, and the performance of political ideology, given the nature of this publication, here I instead concentrate on chronicling Nketia's involvement with this organization; in so doing, I illustrate that not only was he instrumental in its founding and early years, but has continued to have a significant impact on its trajectory and practices. Consequently, departing from much of the writing about Nketia's career, which primarily focuses on his work as a scholar, educator and composer, this article highlights his role as an African/Ghananian nationalist.

Cultural Re-Awakening: Nkrumah, Nketia, and African Personality

Seizing on a weakened Europe and the increasing global recognition of universal human rights following the devastation of WWII, African states began to more fervently agitate for independence in the 1950s. While each played distinct but often complimentary roles, both Kwame Nkrumah and Nketia were caught in this sweeping push for political autonomy, sharing the belief that local cultural traditions should be mobilized to build a national consciousness. While Nketia remained firmly planted in cultural activities, Nkrumah's role was more explicitly political. Nevertheless, when Nkrumah became head of government business in 1951, his policies were guided by his identity as a 'cultural nationalist,' recognizing the arts as a valuable mechanism to propagate an ideology of African Personality[1] and further his Pan-African agenda. His approach to government helped usher in a period of cultural re-awakening in Ghana, wherein indigenous traditions that had once been suppressed by colonial powers received a new level of state support to buttress their new role as instruments of nationalism. Although, during the early 1950s, Nketia was not heavily involved in affairs of the state, concentrating instead on teaching and publications, as we will see, he would later prove vital in providing the artistic resources that Nkrumah required to enact his vision of cultural nationalism (i.e., African Personality and Pan-Africanism).

As sites where knowledge of these local traditions could be brought, stored, and disseminated, Nkrumah found public – government-subsidized – educational institutions (particular higher education) to be productive domains to foster national unity in a drive towards independence. Nkrumah, in other words, viewed his educational policy as the "centerpiece of his cultural policy and aim of the development of African personality" (Hagan 1991: 5). Therefore, to ensure that schools (primary through college) were in line with his vision of nationalism, Nkrumah's government, in 1951, assumed full responsibility for educational policy. Nkrumah instituted policies that would encourage the development of a space where Africans of all nationalities could be re-educated in an African-centered and socialist manner in order to produce freedom fighters and liberators of colonial oppression.

In particular, Nkrumah continually emphasized the role of higher education, asserting the need for change at the University of Ghana

(Legon), because while this institution was based in Africa, prior to independence, it was headed by Europeans and included faculty and staff comprised primarily of Western scholars. It is not surprising then that during the colonial period only marginal attention was given to teaching Africans about Africa at Legon. Despite its Western character, Nkrumah insisted that the University "relate its activities to the needs and the interests of the nation, and the well-being of the people" (Haizel 1991: 71). During the University's early years, this mandate proved difficult to institute.

The sociology department, chaired by a Ghanaian Kofi Busia, however, offered opportunities for a more local voice to emerge at Legon, countering Western hegemony by bringing into focus the aims of African Personality. In its efforts to achieve a full expression of Nkrumah's vision, in 1952, the sociology department hired Kwabena Nketia, a then promising young scholar who had previously studied with the revered Ephraim Amu. As a research fellow, Nketia was charged with the task of collecting and analyzing a variety of African languages, music, dance, and folklore. This repository of materials subsequently became the basis for a new Africa-centric model of cultural education in Ghana that served to revitalize local traditional arts and practices.

Nketia, at this time, also actively promoted local culture through organizations apart from the University. In June of 1955, Nketia became a founding member of the Arts Council of the Gold Coast.[2] Under the direction of Philip Gbeho, a leading scholar and Ewe master drummer, this body was responsible for promoting African arts activities. One of the primary ways it accomplished this was through its initiation of the National Theatre Movement (NTM). After independence in 1957, Nkrumah charged the newly renamed Arts Council of Ghana with the task of increasing the scope of the NTM; as such, Nketia recalled, "[It] gave birth to many new performing arts groups across the country," and it was "fast stimulating" a new awareness of theatre based on indigenous traditions (Nketia quoted in Botwe-Asamoah 2005: 160). Overall, this movement sought to "emphasize the underlying unity of the nation and the equal importance of the contributions which can be made by her people in every region" (NAG/RG3/7/33: 66). Hence, the goals of this organization were directly in line with Nkrumah's objectives regarding African Personality and Pan-Africanism. Yet, to ensure that this organization would carry out his political ideas, Nkrumah made himself president of the Arts Council in December of 1958. Working with key members of the Council, including Nketia, Nkrumah established a myriad of performing groups in every region; these groups included drama, dance, music, choral, and orchestral ensembles, which performed in numerous state-sponsored festivals (cf. Botwe-Asamoah 2005: 163-67).

Although this panoply of ensembles implicitly performed on behalf of the nation, none did so explicitly; earlier in 1958, after witnessing the dance performance for the Independence Day celebrations, Nkrumah decided that Ghana needed a singular performance troupe that would represent the nation and accompany state functions, furthering the "cultural emancipation of Ghana and Africa" (Adinku 1994: 6). This idea would have to wait a few years before it could be brought to fruition. Fortunately, events at Legon proved to make this vision possible.

Back at the university, where Nketia tirelessly labored to keep ethnomusicology alive, while Ghana was establishing its newfound freedom significant changes were beginning to take hold as Ghanaians assumed leadership roles at this institution. Most notably, to ensure that its direction aligned with his ideological principles, Nkrumah appointed himself chancellor in 1961. This appointment paved the way for the establishment of the Institute of African Studies (IAS),[3] which increased the overall African presence at Legon. At the Institute's inauguration Nkrumah remarked that,

> One essential function of the institute must surely be to study the history, culture and institutions, language and arts of Ghana and of Africa in new African-centered ways – in entire freedom from the propositions and presuppositions of the colonial epoch...by the work of this institute, we must re-assess and assert the glories and achievements of our African past and inspire our generation, and succeeding generations, with a vision of a better future(1963: 14).

In short, Nkrumah viewed the Institute of African Studies as an ideal place to foster African Personality. Although the IAS was initially directed by Thomas Hodgkins, it was under the direct supervision of Nkrumah, who chose Nketia to direct its School of Music, Dance, and Drama (founded in 1962). Nketia was an obvious choice for this task not only for his work and reputation as a scholar, educator, and composer,

but also for his alignment with Nkrumah's ideological objectives. Nketia agreed with Nkrumah,
stating that,

> The concept of African Personality was meant to be at once liberating and creative, bringing into focus *African alternatives to Western values* and *institutions* that had been imposed upon subject peoples by colonialism. It was important to combat the claim to the universality of Western culture...[and] to put forward an African alternative that would assert a valid African civilization, both at home and abroad (Nketia quoted in July and Benson 1982: 71; emphasis mine).

Like Nkrumah, Nketia asserted the need to create an African-centered approach to revitalizing indigenous traditions in order to overcome racism and colonial oppression in an attempt to firmly establish Ghana as a nation. Nketia also shared Nkrumah's desire to institute practices that would influence a large group of individuals, stating that, "It is certainly my hope that in the creative arts there will be interaction between the narrow circle of intellectuals and the community at large, so that the gap between past and present, between the traditional and the contemporary can be bridged, creating social solidarity and national unity" (Nketia 1959: 2). Serving such objectives, in October of 1962, Nketia, with the aid of a subsidy from the Ministry of Culture, in his administrative capacity at Legon founded the Ghana Dance Ensemble as the IAS' performance demonstration group. Not forsaking his duties as a founding member of the Arts Council, this troupe subsequently became the "nucleus" of the National Theatre Movement, and a vital way to project African Personality and Pan-Africanism within Ghana and abroad. Arguing that the GDE be housed at the University, Nketia merged his artistic and educational objectives. When asked about this decision he recalled:

> At the time there were really no other African dance companies that the GDE was based on. There was the Guinea Ballet, but they were commercializing the dance. We didn't want to do that here. We wanted to connect the ensemble to education. That's why we located it at the University. This makes the GDE unique.[4] No other dance company has this sort of relationship with a university or education in general (Nketia 2005).

Moreover, in creating such a configuration, Nketia furthered his conviction that, "A national theatre movement must be backed by a training institution such as an academy or school of music...Such a school could be a centre for building up the artistic fragments, in which ethnic groups specialize, into larger wholes for wider audiences" (Nketia 1964: 92).

Nketia's insistence that the GDE be connected to education allowed the ensemble to have far-reaching effects. William Adinku, a member of the GDE since its founding, writes that, "the beginning of dance education in [Ghana] was linked to the formation of the Company [GDE]" (1994: 5). The ensemble was part of a larger aim that sought to educate Ghanaians about their national heritage. It was the intention of Nketia that participants would be trained in traditional music and dance, so they could then go out to teach in Ghana's public school system. To serve this end, initially (unless individuals were specifically employed as music and dance instructors because they had special expertise in traditional culture) those who intended to become members of the GDE had to simultaneously enroll in the dance diploma program offered by the University at Legon (cf. Adinku 1994). With these credentials, many (former) GDE members have taught music and dance throughout the public school system in Ghana and beyond.

Nketia's decision to attach the GDE to education and its institutions was informed by the lessons he had learned from observing other national dance companies. He noted that, "Many countries eager to build national dance ensembles overnight have usually created an amorphous group of people drawn from different regions, each of whom can only do a particular dance and nothing else. The result has sometimes been just a flash in the pan and nothing of lasting value" (Nketia 1967). While many other (African) national ensembles have fallen by the wayside, due, at least in part, to its firm grounding in education that Nketia ensured, the GDE has persisted, contributing to his (and Nkrumah's) enduring legacy. Moreover, as this discussion will soon show, Nketia's method of training – teaching artists to perform more than just their own familiar local community dances – encouraged a sharing of culture that contributed to the solidification of unity in a diverse nation.

A Dancing Cadre and Going Beyond Ethnicity

While the Ghana Dance Ensemble was linked to education and the University, it was under government subvention, requiring the GDE to simultaneously fulfill a duty as a political instrument of nationalism. Therefore, it was important that those involved in the organization aligned with the political objectives of African Personality and Pan-Africanism. When Nkrumah asked Nketia for a recommendation for a person to run the day-to-day activities of the GDE, Nketia did not hesitate to offer Mawere Opoku, who became the ensemble's first artistic director in 1962. Nketia chose Opoku not only for his expert knowledge of indigenous traditions, but also for his nationalistic ideologies. While both sides of Opoku's family were Asante chiefs, ensuring that Opoku had received special training in traditional lore and etiquette, including dance, he also shared Nketia's (and Nkrumah's) nationalist orientation. Enacting such an ideology, during the 1950s, Opoku gained a reputation as an excellent organizer and performer of indigenous Ghanaian art forms through his leadership of a dance troupe at the Asante Cultural Centre – a civic enterprise founded by his cousin Alex Kyerematen; while this group performed mostly Asante dances for Akan dignitaries, it also performed dances of other ethnic groups in a type of proto-national mosaic. It was through this ensemble's performances that Nketia first became aware of Opoku. Subsequently, Opoku's approach to the GDE was to "unify the [ethnic diversity of Ghana]... through the dance forms, thereby underscoring Nkrumah's drive for a unified nation and a unitary government" (Opoku quoted in Botwe-Asamoah 2005: 200). Moreover, Opoku understood his role as a civic duty, becoming an artistic public mouthpiece for Nkrumah's political philosophies. In all, Nkrumah, Nketia, and Opoku, along with the staff of the GDE, acted as a 'dancing cadre', which worked to bring to light a full expression of African Personality and Pan-Africanism.

Nketia and his dancing cadre were called upon to address one of the fundamental challenges of achieving these nationalist objectives: fostering unity among a diverse group of citizens. Although Ghana had attained sovereignty, in order to maintain stability and identity as a nation, its citizens needed to adopt the pluralism that comprised their bourgeoning nation. The complex demarcations of various 'ethnic' groups on a map produced from the 1960 census, illustrates the staggering diversity that Nketia and the GDE worked to display and unite through music and dance (see Figure 1).[5] Brought together through the arbitrary borders left by a colonial legacy, independence and the emergence of the nation created a new juxtaposition of these ethno-linguistic groups with which Ghanaians were forced to grapple. Such a configuration brought about inter-ethnic/regional tensions, evidenced by numerous anti-Nkrumah groups such as the Asante-based National Liberation Movement, the Northern People's Party, the Togolese Congress, the Muslim Association Party, and the Ga Shifimo Kpee. These divisions were evident in the early years of the dance ensemble, as Nketia recalled, "Right at the beginning of independence the ethnicity was very strong, even though we were bringing things from various places. People would identify with a particular group, and as soon as they come and begin to dance they are shouting and so forth" (2005).

Included in a host of politico-cultural state projects, the GDE was one particularly visible way the Ghanaian government worked to encourage its citizens to appreciate the diversity of their nation. Nketia, in particular, was charged with discovering a way to accomplish this task through the dance ensemble. To implement this national agenda, after conferring with Opoku, Nketia decided to recruit specialists in several regions to teach a range of dances to young students from various ethnic backgrounds. When asked about the GDE's recruitment process, Nketia remarked that, "we were trying to go beyond ethnicity…we are all involved in things that cut across ethnicity, and that cutting across ethnicity is the national thing" (2005). This approach to the dance ensemble is perhaps seemingly unsurprising given the state's call to promote 'unity in diversity', however, other national dance companies in Africa relied heavily on the dominant demographic group as emblematic of the whole nation.[6] Nketia could have certainly gone this route, using the majority Akan ethnic group (of which he was a part) to represent all of Ghana. But as a person who was committed to the ideals of African Personality, Nketia elected instead to take a more equitable and inclusive approach. With such an approach – sharing a diverse array of cultural experiences/expressions – he predicted that individuals would become familiar with the traditions of their African/Ghanaian neighbors, resulting in national solidarity.

To facilitate a unification of diversity, Nketia ensured that the staff of the GDE would consist of an ethnically varied body of individuals drawn from several regions of Ghana. Nketia, along with staff of the GDE (notably Opoku), was personally responsible for scouting artistic talent in Accra in addition to relying on his years of research throughout Ghana and continuing field studies during the ensemble's early years; such ethnographic work enabled the troupe to draw upon a wide range of the most reputable cultural experts. According to William Adinku, a member of the ensemble since its inception, Nketia recruited staff from Ga, Ashanti, Ewe, and Dagbani language groups, who each taught and performed their respective traditions (2000: 132).[7] Given the diversity of staff, it is not surprising then that the ensemble's repertoire was expansive, including dances from majority and minority ethnic groups. In this way, author Kofi Botwe-Asomoah states, "The repertoire of the GDE and its performance represented the highest expression of African Personality that Nkrumah envisioned" (2005: 208).[8]

Nketia's decision to incorporate a plethora of local traditions and require each new member to learn this entire repertoire, encouraged performers to embody these diverse cultural practices and the pluralism of their nation. When asked about how this approach to representation related to the larger aims of nationalism, Nketia stated that, "the object [of the GDE] was to ensure that whatever constitutes the national heritage is shared, and that you had a model of what we thought the nation could profit from in terms of making use of what all the culture groups had to offer in a national context" (2005). Regarding how this objective actually played out in the early days of the ensemble, he remarked, "In terms of our concept of a national culture we were beginning to integrate...We had Dagomba drummers playing Ashanti dances, and Ewe playing Akan and so forth...so Gideon (a regional specialist employed by the GDE), an Ewe drummer, became an expert Adowa (Akan dance) drummer" (2005).

The GDE subsequently displayed their abilities to cross such ethnic divisions. As Nketia recalled, "We [the GDE] went to Christian village, which was close by [to Accra], and had an Ewe community. Our dancers danced [Ewe dances] with them...and they [the villagers] would make comments. They liked it, and pointed to the ones they liked best. Sometimes the dancers were not even Ewe" (2005). I have collected a plethora of examples in which dancers were attributed the ethnic identity of the dance they were performing despite self-identification with a different ethnic group. For example, a senior Ewe dancer in the ensemble, Wisdom Agbadenu, stated that after a GDE performance of the northern Dagbamba dance called Bamaaya, an audience member came up to him and greeted him in Dagbani. The audience member, who was from the northern region, was shocked to learn that Wisdom was an Ewe, and rewarded the dancer with 10,000 cedis (about one U.S. dollar) and a handshake (Agbedanu 2005). Similarly, Nketia remarked that when Gideon Alorwoyie (cf. Davis 1994), an Ewe master drummer employed by the GDE, played Asante dances for an Akan community, the "teacher of this [Akan] tradition" preferred Gideon's drumming to that found in the local community (2005).

In all, going 'beyond ethnicity', performers convincingly performed the traditions of their neighbors, embodying national unity, encouraging audiences to do the same. While in the very early days following independence, as Nketia noted, audiences largely only cheered when their own ethnic dances were performed, "a couple of years later Ghanaians were getting used to the things from various places, so that you find when the Agbadza [an Ewe] dance comes on, the Asante, all of them are clapping. So we were beginning to appreciate the differences which became part of the composite" (2005). Consequently, by forming, guiding, and promoting the GDE, as part of a dancing cadre, Nketia was crucial in the overall nation-building process within Ghana during the early post-independence period.

Because nationalism is an ongoing phenomenon, requiring individuals to continually confront and come to terms with the diversity of their country, the type of boundary crossing that Nketia cultivated in the 1960s has persisted into more recent years. As one dancer told me in 2007:

> [The] dance ensemble has…really changed my life, because at first I always think about my ethnic background. I don't respect anybody's tradition. When I came to the dance ensemble I always fight with them and say my festival is the best. But when I got to know about other people's festivals I said 'oh so there are festivals like that.' Because, when I came to the dance ensemble, I only knew about my own festival, and I was not the type to go out. When I first came I thought about that, but now I think everybody is one. I respect other traditions now as a whole. I respect each and everyone's ideas. I feel like I am a part of all Ghana (Agyette 2007).

Through the course of fieldwork, I collected numerous similar stories of individuals recounting their experiences of going beyond ethnicity. Thus, Nketia's (and Nkrumah's) legacy of performing and promoting 'unity in diversity' persists, informing the lives of participants in Ghana's national ensembles.

Not only did Nketia urge the GDE and its audiences to go beyond ethnicity, but, in line with Nkrumah's Pan-African political agenda, he also directed them to go 'beyond Ghana.' Speaking about his experience in the GDE during Nkrumah's presidency, Emmanuel Duodu remembered, "In those days this ethnic group is superior to that. Nkrumah tried to kill that kind of tribalism and nepotism. And, whether you are Nigerian or Malian, you are the same people. And, the dance ensemble projected this" (2007). One of the ways the ensemble projected this sentiment was by incorporating a number of pieces from outside Ghana. A book about the GDE published in the 1960s, for instance, lists a Nigerian dance called Ijaw, while the Dahomey Dance Suite I and Dahomey Dance Variations listed therein, are both from Togo. Additionally, I have found pictures from the 1960s of the dance ensemble performing "Togo Atsia."

Furthering this Pan-Africanist objective, Nketia was also instrumental in the organization and administration of the ensemble's travels abroad. In July 1964, Nkrumah commissioned the GDE to represent Ghana at Malawi's Independence celebration, which was the ensemble's first performance outside of Ghana (Adinku 2000: 133). The following year, Nkrumah, a leader who adopted many socialist ideas, sent the ensemble on a three-month tour of Eastern Europe including Czechoslovakia, East Germany, Hungary, the U.S.S.R., and Poland as part of his "Moscow-oriented foreign policy" (Adinku 2000: 133). The ensemble later represented Ghana at the first World Festival of Negro Arts in Dakar in April 1966. Over the years, particularly in the 1960s, Nketia played a crucial role in assuring that the ensemble continued to disseminate African Personality throughout the world on numerous international tours,[9] affirming and strengthening bonds with Africans in the European, American, and Asian diasporas.

Authenticity and Authentication

Although the GDE was founded in 1962, it was not officially inaugurated, or "outdoored" as Nketia remarked,[10] until 1967 at the University of Ghana in Legon. On this occasion, Nketia gave a speech in which he told the audience:

> We have approached our task [of establishing a national dance ensemble] as a creative experiment. We have tried not only to learn and teach the dances as they are done in the villages, but also face the problem of presentation in the new context of the theatre, to work out a form of presentation which highlights and clarifies the *essential* forms of the dances without destroying their basic movements and styles, their emotional, spiritual and cultural values or their vitality and vigor. In this respect, we have tried to use as our yardstick the comments and criticisms of experts in our villages and towns who helped us all along to spot and crystallize the *essential* qualities that are looked for in our dances (1967; emphasis mine).

Nketia's remarks alluded to his keen awareness of the issues of authenticity and authentication, which are inherent to the GDE as dances are transformed from community events to national spectacles. In other words, Nketia predicted that as familiar local cultural expressions underwent a process of modification − adapting them for the stage − audiences would likely question the validity of these altered forms. And, he knew that if audiences − primarily Ghanaian citizens − doubted the validity of these forms, this skepticism could easily translate into criticisms about the project of nationalism as a whole, jeopardizing the future stability and solidarity of Ghana as well as the legitimacy of its government. Hence, as Nketia remarked, "It was very important to ensure that the [dance] movements [used in the GDE] were correct, and that the dancers who were trained could dance in the village and be judged authentic" (2005). To ensure that the GDE's dances remained closely linked to local practices, Nketia relied on his extensive field study of nearly every region in Ghana, primarily conducted between 1952 and 1961. Subsequently, Nketia continued to encourage research that informed and 'grounded' the GDE. As Opoku stated:

> I must say in his [Nketia's] capacity as director he provided me and my aides with all the necessary facilities that enabled me to choreograph some of the dances currently in use in this country...Nketia as director of the Institute used his contacts

and his standing as an academic of repute to secure funding for projects. Land Rovers and recording equipment and funds were at the disposal of all staff for collecting materials from all over the country (quoted in Vieta 1999: 448).

This research, coupled with the expertise of Opoku and the GDE staff, provided a firm basis for the confidence that the ensemble's representations would be judged favorably by various Ghanaian communities.

Nketia was also insistent that the ensemble make frequent sojourns to observe local dance practices in their idiomatic cultural context. For example, according to Adinku, "They [the GDE] visited the Manhiya Palace of the Asantehene Sir Nana Osei Agyeman Prempeh, who made it possible for them to be exposed to the Kete dance and music. Members also visited Asante-Mampong, Sekondi, Krobo Odumasi, Akropong-Akupim, Winneba, Kpong and Anyako to observe dances..." (2000: 133). Overwhelmingly, the GDE has been lauded for its performances, implicitly authenticating the ensemble. Affirming its legitimacy, founding member and former GDE director E.A. Duodu remarked, "If you go to statistics, I would say that 90-95% of Ghanaians would not ascribe to criticism. Because everywhere we go, local audiences accepted it wholeheartedly. If you go to Asante and you do Adowa, they are excited" (2007). Such a positive response would not have been possible without the solid grounding in Nketia's (and Opoku's) research along with his careful recruitment of reputable local experts.

Yet, as Duodu comments imply, the GDE was not without its detractors; as he continues, however, "Those who criticized that [the dances] had been adulterated are few people. A few intellectuals, because they have learned to criticize" (2007). One of the most notorious criticisms, against which Nketia (and Opoku) had to defend, came from dance scholar Drid Williams who came to Ghana in 1967. After witnessing dances in 'village' contexts, she began to criticize the ensemble, noting the minute discrepancies between their repertoire and its community-based counterparts (cf. Williams 1997). As Nketia recalled, "[Williams] had some anthropological training and started making a loud noise about, oh this is really not the authentic. You know because they [the GDE] are not carrying the drums on their head and so forth" (2005). He defended Opoku and the ensemble by stating that the goal of the ensemble from its outset, "was not to present an anthropological specimen. It was to create an art" (Nketia 2005). After all, as he stated in his inaugural address: "The Ghana Dance Ensemble stands for tradition. But it also stands for creativity." Answering Williams' claim that the GDE's dances are "fairly worthless" (1997), he explained that, "The dances don't lose meaning in the new context. That was the old way of thinking about it, sentimental perhaps. The dances acquire another meaning in the context in which it is being performed. And for us the national meaning is extremely important" (Nketia 2005). Nketia's remarks critique Williams' objectivist and outmoded views of authenticity; he notes that she was locked into an "old way of thinking" – eternally searching for the elusive origins of culture rather than recognizing its inherent construction and subsequently attempting to understand these re-inventions (cf. Bendix 1997; Hobsbawm and Ranger 1983).

Despite such reproach, the GDE has acted as a "felt authentic grounding" (cf. van de Port 2004) for individuals, giving them a basis for their belief that the 'essence' of culture has been preserved by the ensemble. Participants' confidence in this conviction is due in large part to the activities and reputation of Nketia. As one dancer put it, "They [the GDE] do it the real way...They [Opoku and Nketia] did the research. They went to the villages and brought it here" (Agyette 2007). Another reiterated, "Nketia and Opoku had done the research. [They] were professors at the University. They do the right movements. I trust them" (Agyari 2006). Consequently, for decades, including the time of my own fieldwork, the GDE has not only been a source of 'authentic grounding' for members of the ensemble itself, but also for numerous local amateur groups in Ghana who come and peer in the ensemble's rehearsal hall to "steal" movements and music (Diku 2005). These so called 'amateur' artists have, like their professional counterparts in the GDE, repeatedly pointed to the research of Nketia (as well as Opoku and Adinku) as the basis for their belief that what they were acquiring was 'authentic.' In this way, Nketia continues to have a considerable effect on the reputation of the GDE.

The National Theatre Controversy
In early 1986, President J.J. Rawlings of Ghana traveled to Asia where, in an effort to strengthen diplomatic relations, he signed an agreement

stating that the Chinese would build a national theatre in Accra.[11] This political action had a profound impact on the trajectory of the GDE. With these plans in motion, Ghanaian cultural officials, primarily Dr. Mohammed Ben Abdallah who had been instrumental in both persuading Rawlings to build a theatre (instead of a soccer stadium) and bringing the Chinese on board, proposed to relocate the GDE to the newly constructed National Theatre where the ensemble would become its resident dance company. This proposal was highly controversial, sparking a vigorous debate that pitted Abdallah and his cohorts against Nketia and others who advocated that the GDE remain at the University of Ghana. On the one hand, Abdallah, along with his friend Francis Nii-Yartey who had been the artistic director of the GDE since succeeding Opoku in 1976, argued that the new National Theatre would be the appropriate place to develop dance in Ghana. As Nii-Yartey explained:

> For the first time we [Ghanaians] had a national theatre, and I could do my work. And I started producing, creating dance-drama, dance-theatre more correctly. I need a big space. I needed to move forward. So I took it as an opportunity...The University to me was inimical to the development of the arts (2006).

Nii-Yartey has also noted that he was frustrated with the University's bureaucratic system, and has commented that his University colleagues did not share his expansive artistic vision, alluding to his perception of the Legon faculty as too conservative regarding the arts (2006).

Echoing these sentiments, Dr. Abdallah has stated that:

> On the Legon campus, there was also a problem with space, that there was a conflict all the time between [the] Dance Ensemble and the rest of the School of Performing Arts, always vying for rehearsal space. Facilities at the Theatre here alone help the national companies to be able to *fulfill their potential*... We assumed it was obvious...You don't have a national theatre and then put your professional national companies somewhere else, especially in our case where *the National Theatre is the best*

equipped for what they are doing. A lot of work has gone into providing for the dance company, for example, one of the most modern dance studios in Africa (Abdallah quoted in Yankah 1993: 23; emphasis mine).

Abdallah was also an advocate of Nii-Yartey's artistic vision for the development of contemporary Ghanaian dance; as he told me, "he [Nii-Yartey] probably was one of the few people who really understood the role of dance in national development, and the need for the development of African dance. These are two very important things" (2007). Citing physical, pragmatic, and ideological obstacles at Legon, which, in their estimation, hindered the "development" of dance in Ghana, Abdallah and Nii-Yartey continued to fight to bring the GDE to the National Theatre throughout the 1980s.

Fearing that, if moved, the GDE would lose sight of its educational objectives, Nketia, Opoku, and University officials strongly advocated for the retention of the ensemble at Legon. An anonymous memo submitted on behalf of the University dated July 1, 1986 addresses the commissioner (presumably Abdallah), outlining the basic tenets of the argument for the ensemble's retention at Legon. This document states that, "Events have proved the University is the right training ground for our genuine Ghana dance culture and its presentation as seen by dance troupes throughout the country" (1986: 3). Noting that the link to education was paramount to the "Founding Father of the Ensemble [Nketia]," subsequently the memo points to the GDE's vital role in teaching University students about their national heritage.

In addition to this educational objective, those that preferred the GDE to remain at Legon cited additional benefits to this institutional connection. This affiliation, Nketia argued, would guarantee that research could be conducted and transferred directly to the GDE, thus presumably ensuring that the cultural traditions represented on stage would closely resemble those practices found in local communities. Supporting this position, University officials included an appendix to the memo, again invoking Nketia, pointing to his inaugural speech in which he suggests that, "The training [of the GDE] could not have been devised effective[ly] without previous research into music and dance. And it is in this regard that the link with the Institute of African Studies [at the University] has proved beneficial" (1986: 2). In other words,

Nketia and others of similar mind regarded the GDE's link to the University as a way to ensure the authenticity of the ensemble and its repertoire. Along these lines, the memo goes on to argue that previous dance ensembles in Ghana disappeared because "they did not present *genuine* Ghanaian dances. The danger is that the Ensemble, uprooted from its home and the University's aura may either fade away or present dances which do not reflect our *Grass-root* dances" (1986: 3; emphasis mine).[12] As such, the above statement consequently reveals that many at the University, including Nketia and Opoku, feared that if the GDE was removed from this institution the authenticity of Ghana's national culture would be in jeopardy.

After a thorough debate between these opposing factions, a law was passed, which eventually led to the bifurcation of the GDE. In 1990, PNDCL 238 repealed Law 232 establishing the Commission on Culture (COC) with Abdallah as chairman. Among other responsibilities, this law solidified the COC's direct control over the National Theatre, which included the Ghana Dance Ensemble as one of its resident companies (cf. Botchwey 1993). Without stating it directly, the law urged the GDE to move to the new Theatre. However, as Nii-Yartey noted, "the University said we don't regard the law" (2006). And, as author Krista Fabian wrote, "Opoku and Nketia, standing firm in their belief that the company must be linked to an educational institution, refused to move, in spite of the lure of financial rewards" (1996: 11). Nii-Yartey, on the other hand, was eager to relocate the GDE to the National Theatre. He told me that, "I'm a good citizen, so I had to regard the law. And, I wanted to develop so bad" (Nii-Yartey 2006). After further negotiations, eventually a compromise was reached wherein the government agreed to allow those who wanted to stay at the University to do so. According to interviews, about half of the thirty members decided to stay at Legon, while the other half chose to leave for the National Theatre.

Although pragmatic concerns such as job security and salary weighed heavily on the minds of GDE members, ideology and personal loyalties, particularly to Nketia (and Opoku) also played a role in this decision making process. When asked why he remained at Legon during the split, the most senior drummer of the GDE at the time of the separation, Foli Adadae remarked, "Opoku and Nketia were like my fathers; they treated me like their own child" (Adadae 2006). Many other (former) members cited their loyalty to Nketia, Opoku, and their commitment to the continuity of tradition and education as reasons for their decision to stay at the University. Thus, not only was Nketia a significant presence in the discussion leading to the split, but his reputation and clout convinced participants to remain at the University despite government pressure. In all, while the new Theatre ensemble (eventually renamed the National Dance Company of Ghana) focused its attention on the production of elaborate dance-dramas and African contemporary dance, Nketia, and his cohorts, succeeded in maintaining the GDE's link to education.

Conclusion

After founding the Ghana Dance Ensemble and setting its ideological course, over its nearly five-decade lifespan, Nketia has remained a significant figure in shaping its direction and identity. Anchoring the GDE firmly in the political objectives of cultural nationalism, Nketia helped produce a dancing cadre that continues to disseminate African Personality and Pan-Africanism throughout Ghana and the world. Employing an inclusive recruitment and representational strategy that harnessed the diversity of Ghana, Nketia and the GDE have encouraged individuals to 'go beyond' ethnicity as well as transcend national boundaries. Simultaneously, Nketia's careful and comprehensive research coupled with his insistence that the GDE's dances be verified by local cultural experts (i.e., chiefs and elders) and his defense against the ensemble's detractors has served to authenticate the group's repertoire and cement its legitimacy. Lastly, perhaps Nketia's most profound impact on the nature and trajectory of the Ghana Dance Ensemble was his insistence that it be attached to an institution of higher learning, a partnership which he defended vigorously when it came under threat by government mandate. While many national ensembles in Africa have come and gone, Nketia created a lasting legacy by firmly rooting the GDE in education.

Endnotes

1: According to Nkrumah, "African personality is merely a term expressing cultural and social bonds which unite Africans and peoples of African descent. It is a concept of the African nation, and is not associated with a particular state, language, religion, political system or color of the skin. For those who project it, it expresses identification not only with African historical past, but with the struggle of the African people in the African Revolution to liberate and unify the continent and to build a just society" (1973: 205).

2: Nketia was chairman of the Arts Council of Ghana from 1976-1979 (cf. Akrofi 2002).

3: Kofi Busia had proposed the institute in 1960. However, his idea met with the stiff resistance of the Eurocentric administration that inhabited the University at that time.

4: Indeed, although there has been much written about national dance ensembles (Castaldi 2006; Hagedorn 2001; Kaschl 2003; Shay 2002; et. al), none has been linked so directly with a state educational system as the GDE.

5: Data according to the 1960 census: Akan (Twi, Fante, Nzema) 44.1%; Mole-Dagbani (incl. Dagarte, Frafra, Kusasi, Dagomba, Mosi) 15.9%; Ewe 13%; Ga-Adangbe 8.3%; Guan 3.7%; Gurma 3.5%; Grusi 2.2%; Yoruba 1.6%; Mande 1.4%; Hausa 0.9%; Central Togo Tribes 0.8%; Tem 0.7% (Gil, Aryee, Ghansah 1964: xxxiii-xxxiv).

6: Castaldi, for instance, writes about the "Wolofization" and "Mandification" of national ensembles in Senegal (2006).

7: The staff of the GDE initially included Mustafa Tettey Addy (Ga-Adangbe), Hunusu Afadi (Anlo-Ewe), Iddrisu Alhassan (Dagbamba), J Asmah (Ahantan), Kwesi Badu (Asante), John K. Bennisan (Togo-Ewe), Osei Bonsu (Asante), Kodzo Ganyo (Togo-Ewe), and Seth Kobla Ladzekpo (Anlo-Ewe) (cf. Adinku 2000).

8: A book published on the GDE in the mid-1960s, attests to the efforts made by the GDE staff to represent diversity. It states that the ensemble's repertoire consisted of twenty-three Ghanaian dances – six Asante (Akan), nine Ewe, five Dagbamba/Hausa, one Lobi, one Nzema, and one Ga (196?: 25-26).

9: These include, in chronological order: Britain 1968, Mexico Olympic Games 1968, Nigeria 1968, Italy 1968, Paris 1968, New York 1968, U.S. 1969, USSR 1969, Germany in 1970 and 1974, Jamaica 1977, Germany 1979 and 1980, Italy in 1980, Paris 1981, Yugoslavia 1981, Paris 1983, U.K. 1984, London in 1985, New Delhi and Bombay, India in 1987, Guyana and New York in 1988, Canada, Germany, Holland, Nigeria, Switzerland, Tokyo, Zimbabwe and U.K. in 1989, Germany in 1994, Osaka, Japan and Korea in 1995. Additionally, the *Spectator* includes reports on the GDE's participation in "Dance/Africa" in Chicago in 1996, "Images of Africa" in Copenhagen, Denmark in 1997, and tours of Indonesia and U.K. in 1995, Denmark in 1999, London in 1999, and Jamaica in 2003. Through personal conversations I also learned that the GDE (Legon) had toured Malawi in 2006, and the NDC had performed in India during the Ghana @ 50 celebrations (March, 2007).

10: In his speech entitled "A Bold Experiment," which he gave in 1967 at Legon, Nketia referred to the inauguration of the ensemble as its "outdooring." An outdooring is a celebration wherein, a few weeks after a baby's birth it is presented to the community.

11: At least since 1959, Nketia and the Arts Council of Ghana were agitating for building a national theatre in central Accra (Ghana Natl. Archives, RG3/7/59). This plea continued to gain momentum throughout the 1960s with the advent of the National Theatre Movement. Architectural plans were commissioned and can be found in the National Archives of Ghana. However, as Nketia told me, the theatre proposed by the Arts Council was never built.

12: I interpret the use of the terms such as "genuine" and "grass-roots" here as synonymous with "authentic" (cf. Handler and Linnekin 1984).

References

Abdallah, Mohammed Ben. 2007. Interview by author. Digital recording. April 25. Legon, Ghana.

Adadae, Foli. 2006. Interview by author. Digital recording. July 11. Accra, Ghana.
Adinku, William. 1994. *African Dance Education in Ghana*. Accra: Ghana Universities Press.

___. 2000. "The Early Years of the Ghana Dance Ensemble." In *Fontomfrom: Contemporary Ghanaian Literature, Theatre and Film*. Ed. by Kofi Anyidoho and James Givvs. Atlanta: Rodopi, 131-135.

Agbedanu, Wisdom. 2005. Interview by author. Digital recording. August 9. Legon, Ghana.

Agyari, Solomon Atagi. 2007. Interview by author. Digital recording. May 9. Accra, Ghana.

Agyete, Leslie. 2007. Interview by author. Digital recording. August 17. Legon, Ghana.

Akrofi, Eric A. 2002. *Sharing Knowledge and Experience: A Profile of Kwabena Nketia Scholar and Music Educator*. Accra: Afram.

Bendix, Regina. 1997. *In Search of Authenticity: The Formation of Folklore Studies*. Madison: University of Wisconsin Press.

Botchwey, Judith. 1993. "A Descriptive List of the General Records Relating to the Arts Council in the National Archives of Ghana, 1954-1982." Diploma, University of Ghana, Legon.

Botwe-Asamoah, Kwame. 2005. *Kwame Nkrumah's Politico-Cultural Thought and Policies: An African-Centered Paradigm for the Second Phase of the African Revolution*. New York: Routledge.

Castaldi, Francesca. 2006. *Choreographies of African Identities: Negritude, Dance, and the National Ballet of Senegal*. Urbana: University of Illinois Press.

Davis, Arthur L. 1994. *Midawo Gideon Foli Alorwoyie: The Life and Music of a West African Drummer*. PhD. dissertation, University of Illinois.

Diku, Willie. 2005. Interview by author. Digital recording. July 26. Legon, Ghana.

Duodu, E. Ampofo. 2007. Interview by author. Digital recording. June 27. Legon, Ghana.

Fabian, Krista N. 1996. "Professional Dance in Ghanaian Society: The Development and Direction of the Ghana Dance Ensemble." Diploma, University of Ghana.

Ghana Dance Ensemble Office Files. July 1, 1986. University Memo. "The Ghana Dance Ensemble."

Gil, B., A.F. Aryee, and D.K. Ghansah. 1964. *1960 Population Census of Ghana: Special Report 'E': Tribes in Ghana*. Accra: Census Office.

Hagan, George. 1991. "Nkrumah's Cultural Policy." In: *The Life and Work of Kwame Nkrumah*. Ed. by Kwame Arhin. Accra: SEDCO, 3-26.

Hagedorn, Katherine. 2001. *Divine Utterances: The Performance of Afro-Cuban Santeria*. Washington D.C.: Smithsonian Institution Press.

Haizel, E.A. 1991. "Education in Ghana, 1951-1966." In: *The Life and Work of Kwame Nkrumah*. Ed. by Kwame Arhin. Accra: SEDCO, 53-81.

Handler, Richard and Jocelyn Linnekin. 1984. "Tradition, Genuine or Spurious?" *Journal of American Folklore* 97(385): 273-290.

Hirt-Manheimer, Isaac. 2004. *Understanding "Fast Agbekor": A History of Ghana's National Dance Company and an Analysis of Its Repertory*. M.A. Thesis, Wesleyan University.

Hobsbawm, Eric and Terrance Ranger. 1983. *The Invention of Tradition*. Cambridge: Cambridge University Press.

July, Robert and Peter Benson, eds. 1982. *African Cultural and Intellectual Leaders and the Development of the New African Nations.* New York: The Rockefeller Foundation.

Kaschl, Elke. 2003. *Dance and Authenticity in Israel and Palestine: Performing the Nation.* Leiden: Brill. National Archives of Ghana Document. RG3/7/33.

___. "The Function and Constitution of a National Theatre." RG3/7/59.

Nii-Yartey, Francis. 2006. Interview by author. Digital recording. August 6. Legon, Ghana.

Nketia, J.H. Kwabena. 1959. "The Creative Arts and the Community." Lecture, Symposium on Building an Intellectual Community in Ghana. University of Ghana, Legon: Nov. 25, 1959.

___. 1964. "National Theatre Movements and the African Image." *The Pan-Africanist Review* 1(2): 88-93.

___. (1967)1993. "A Bold Experiment." In *International Reviews of the Ghana Dance Ensemble*, Ed. by A.M. Opoku. Legon: University of Ghana Press, 12-14.

___. 2005. Interview by author. Digital recording. August 18. Legon, Ghana.

Nkrumah, Kwame. (1963)1992. *The African Genius.* Speech delivered at the Institute of African Studies, October 25, 1963. As cited in: Handbook of the 30th Anniversary Celebration of the Institute of African Studies and School of Performing Arts. Accra: University of Ghana, 12-21.

___. 1973. *Revolutionary Path.* New York: International Publishers.

Opoku, A.M. 1967. *The Ghana Dance Ensemble.* Accra: Pierian Press.

Schauert, Paul. 2007. "A Performing National Archive: Power and Preservation in the Ghana Dance Ensemble." *Transactions of the Historical Society of Ghana* 10: 171-181.

-----. 2011. *Staging Nationalism: Performance, Power, and Representation in Ghana's State Dance Ensembles.* PhD. dissertation, Indiana University.

Schramm, Katharina. 2000. "Dancing the Nation: Ghanaische Kulturpolitik im Spannungsfeld zwischen Nation und globaler Herausforderung." *Spektrum* 74.

Shay, Anthony. 2002. *Choreographic Politics: State Folk Dance Companies, Representation, and Power.* Middletown, CT: Wesleyan University Press.

Van de Port, Mattijs. 2004. "Registers of Incontestability: The Quest for Authenticity in Academia and Beyond." *Etnofoor* 17(1,2): 7-22.

Vieta, Kojo T. 1999. *The Flagbearers of Ghana: Profiles of One Hundred Distinguished Ghanaians, Vol. 1.* Accra: Ena Publications.

Williams, Drid. 1997. "Traditional Danced Spaces. Concepts of *Deixis* and the Staging of Non-Western Dances." In *Tanzkunst, Ritual und Buehne: Begegnungen zwischen Kulturen.* Ed. by S. Schmiderer and M. Nürnberger. Frankfurt am Main: IKO Verlag fuer inter-kulturelle Kommunikation, 255-263.

Yankah, Kwesi. 1993. "Mohammed Ben Abdallah: Is He Killing the Arts?" *Uhuru* 6: 21-25.

Representation: My Africanist Perspective

Sylvanus K. Kuwor

Sylvanus K. Kuwor is a lecturer in Dance Studies in the School of Performing Arts at the University of Ghana, Legon. He holds a PhD in dance and anthropology from the University of Roehampton-London. His expertise is in ethnochoreology, the anthropological investigation of dance through ethnography and history, dance performance, and aesthetics and criticism. He is a visiting lecturer at the Norwegian University of Science and Technology in Trondheim and the University of Roehampton in London, United Kingdom.

Introduction

The issue of representation still dominates the central stage of twenty-first century scholarship after many scholars have shared their thoughts on the concept from their various ideological perspectives in recent years. This essay discusses the influence of these perspectives on representing 'African arts' with my interest located in the context of building a theoretical framework within which scholars must operate in making statements about 'African Dance' and its related art forms. The formation and operations of the Ghana Dance Ensemble out of Nkrumah's concept of Cultural Emancipation produced many dance companies including Adzido Pan-African Dance Ensemble that operated in the United Kingdom for twenty years (1984-2004) under British funding. Questions about how these companies are represented locally and internationally lead to many issues this paper intends to address.

Existing and Emerging Perspectives

Cultural theorist, Stuart Hall examines representation through language as the center of the process of producing meaning. His book, "Cultural Representation and Signifying Practice" (1997) discusses semiotic and discursive approaches to representation. Semiotic approach deals with how language produces meaning (its poetics) whereas the discursive approach deals more with the effects and consequences of representation (its politics). Hall's study explores representation as a signifying practice in a rich diversity of social contexts and institutional sites, including the use of photography in the construction of national identity and culture; the poetics and politics of exhibiting other cultures in ethnographic museums; fantasies of the radicalized other in popular media, film, and image; the construction of masculine identities in discourses of consumer culture and advertising; and the gendering of narratives in television soap operas.

Looking at representation through dance, the dancer, choreographer and scholar Anthony Shay also uses cultural studies and social sciences including sociology and anthropology to create a work that cuts across the many disciplines involved to interrogate state-sponsored folk dance. His book "Choreographic Politics" (2002) is the first book to address the topic of such ensembles, their institution and organization. It examines the repertoires, performances and choreographic strategies, artistic directors and choreographers of these companies within the political, social, gendered and national contexts in which each company was created. Including a look at the music and costumes, the book captures all these theatrical elements and discusses how various companies employed them in designing their choreographic pieces in order to represent the national identity their states wanted to promote. Shay's work simply defines representation as the power of describing others.

Brenda Dixon-Gottschild, an African American dance professor, explored this issue through a personalized cultural study into what she called 'excavation of Africanist presence in performance.' Her book, *The Black Dancing Body* (2003) interrogates the black dancing body through personal experiences, critical analysis of visual and print documentation and also through the view points of twenty-four different contemporary dance practitioners including Trisha Brown, Bill T. Jones, Shelley Washington and Ralph Lemon, representing a variety of dance eras, idioms and traditions. As a person of African lineage, her research on this concept often considered as very sensitive due to the fact that it touches much on racism, blackness and also the somewhat essentialist terms 'Africanist' and 'Europeanist.' Her work fully articulates the representational elements of a black body in a performance. She cites one of the popular Balanchine ballets- 'The Four Temperaments' which "utilizes Africanist characteristics such as kicking rather than placing the leg extensions; allowing the pelvis to be pulled of centre; flexing the hands and feet; letting the energy determine the form rather than the traditional ballet convention of letting form and the vertical aligned spine dictate the outlay of energy" (Dixon-Gottschild 2003:21).

Her discourse also makes reference to the work of Kwame Anthony Appiah, an established scholar who called for an abandonment of the very concept of race, arguing that it is a biologically meaningless term that confuses socially constructed decent systems and prejudice with biological heredity. Dixon-Gottschild rejects this call with much stronger arguments to suggest that the theory of Appiah is worthless and concludes with the suggestion that: "we need to apply genetic theory from a different perspective to utilize it from a non-radicalized starting point" (Dixon-Gottschild 2003:5). Indeed her groundbreaking work full of thought provoking arguments also reveals a spark of controversy with naked contradictions which clearly positions her theories and her entire reasoning in the face of many reviewers as a carefully designed polemical prose with deliberate awareness that her arguments will be challenged.

The work of an African American dance scholar, Thomas F. DeFrantz titled *Dancing Many Drums* (2002) is another scholarly work that explores the representational elements of African American dance and the influence it has had on American and world culture over the years. His approach uses a collection of essays on African American dance history, theory and practice to re-evaluate the terms 'Black' and 'African American' as both racial and dance categories.

Reopening the Debate

In reopening the debate on the issue of representation, I would like to look at the term with my 'Africanist' eye in order to put it in the right perspective with a special reference to the current controversy surrounding how Africa is being represented by Western scholars. Africanism in this context is not limited to only Africans who are devoted enough to promote and protect traditional and cultural values of their continent. There are also non-Africans who in their research journey may be sympathetic to African arts. These scholars are also called Africanists. However, my Africanist background stemmed from birth through training to practice with full immersion into the cultural values of Ewe people in Ghana.

Representation may be defined as the act of description, portrayal or imagining of an image, scenario or place. It could be referred to as an act of placing something to stand for or as an embodiment of a certain thing. Based on this definition, representation may be considered as any image, be it in films, art or the media, used as an equivalent or a substitute for something else. Hence, the act of dancing or dance making can be regarded as a significant form of representation. In view of the fact that the words 'Africa' and 'Black' have long been associated with barbarism and demeaning undertones that both insult and undermine black people's intelligence, their humanness and their humanity as Nelson Mbulaheni, the African linguistic expert argues, African arts and literature today find themselves attempting to hold a positive mirror up to the black people of the world, aiming to rectify the negative portrayal of black Africans by the Western world for years (Mbulaheni, 2008).

These issues surrounding the term 'blackness' in relation to arts have been in the public domain over the past four decades with human right and anti-racial activists, artists and other stake holders engaging in several public debates to find a suitable meaning that may possibly attach some positive perception to the term. Dance scholar, Christy Adair, in 2007 reopened the debate on the term 'blackness' using the experience of Phoenix Dance Company in the United Kingdom as a perfect replica of black arts companies that have experienced the stigma that has been attached to blackness over these years. Her book, *Dancing The Black Question* (2007) examines the formation and development of Phoenix Dance Company from 1981 to 2001 using an interdisciplinary approach which involves cultural studies, postcolonial theories, dance studies, political science and anthropology to raise questions about dance history, dance structures, critical response and cultural identity.

Discussing the company's first six years of existence which begins with the founding members who were described (by Senior in Judd 1997-98:32) as 'the group of five young black men who changed the face of British contemporary dance when they founded Phoenix in 1982', Christy Adair poses a big question to this description as to whether it was the true reflection of the company. By asking this question, I believe she was wondering why this had not given a positive representation to the company in British media all those years. In her view, answers to this single question in contrast to interviews she conducted produced many perceptions of Phoenix thereby making the history and legacy of the company a complex one over which a number of people have a sense of ownership (Adair 2007).

Indeed Adair's research reveals among other factors the marginalization confronting black dance at the time which stemmed from the unfair representation of black artists as one of their major setbacks. She cites few books that fully documented work of White British and American artists and deliberately ignored the important contribution of black British artists and African American artists. Walter Sorell's 'Dance in Its Time', (1981); Edward Thorpe's 'Black Dance', (1990) were among those cited. Although Adair's focus is on contemporary dance, her research crosses all borders to borrow elements from other dance forms including traditional African dance for the enhancement of her work given that contemporary dance has the flexibility and provides room for creativity. Representation as a tool has been used to analyse and portray layers and complexities of meaning perhaps with the intention of allowing the viewer to look deeper than the surface, obtain a fuller understanding and unpack all the elements of the story and its connotations. However, sometimes this tool is used by choreographers, dancers, writers and visual artists to simplify meanings in order to spread ideas or agendas as efficiently as possible amongst audiences.

My emerging research informs my thinking that the issue of representation can only be fully dealt with by exploring every aspect of the term from a pure and non-radicalized perspective. The current conflict between African indigenous scholars and their international/Western counterparts over who is more qualified to represent the arts of Africa is a clear indication of two racial forces of antagonism working against each other. In as much as it has an impact on representation, it is very important to look at the root of racism and this could be attributed to a number of factors under the transatlantic slavery that witnessed the transportation of able bodies from Africa to Americas and Europe for over three hundred years. Carolyn Fluehr-Lobban reminds us that "although race as a concept developed in the West during the Enlightenment, it was spread to many parts of the non-West world through international commerce, including slave trade and, later colonial conquest and administration-which have used it as effective tool of social division" (Fuehr-Lobban 2006: 4).

While it is very important for all humankind to mobilize forces globally in a collective fight against any form of racism, it is equally very important to be aware that any individual or a group of individuals that attempts to fight a monster called racism with the sole purpose of claiming superiority over the other race is potentially racist. Martin Luther King Junior made a valid point when he said: 'A doctrine of black supremacy is as evil as a doctrine of white supremacy' (Scott King 1987: 19).

As an African, born and raised in Africa, my training and practice in traditional African dance formed over three decades is enough to suggest an absolutely new perspective in representing the arts of Africa. My background as a practitioner in both Africa and Europe all these years has given me the opportunity to experience the art form both in its native soil and on the proscenium stage, an experience capable of moving one's perception from convergence thoughts to divergence thinking.

The Holistic Nature of African Dance

Given that the African continent consists of fifty-four different nations, each with diverse ethnic groups and their various unique cultural practices such as music, dance, language, storytelling, moonlight games, food, occupations, fashion, design and accessories, names and philosophical sayings, revealing the holistic nature of African arts as a shared tradition of the people, and as such, can never be represented effectively by a single individual. Furthermore, to engage in the representational elements of African dance, one must spend a considerable amount of time to learn and understand the art form as well as the purpose it serves in the various African communities. Understanding the functions of African dance requires an understanding of an African conception of dance and African philosophy of life. For example, Professor Mawere Opoku, a renowned African choreographer defines African dance as 'a language or a mode of expression that manifests from the heart, using movements and gestures which have their counterparts in our everyday activities, to express special and real life experiences' (Opoku 1966:19).

Although Opoku's definition might not perfectly fit in that continental characterization, there are some elements which many African dances share. For example, the polycentric nature of the African dancing body allows movements to be concentrated in a portion of the body, be it the torso, hips, legs, arms, hands, feet and even the toes. Secondly, these separate regions of the body are recognized and utilized either individually or simultaneously depending on the dance type, rather than moving as one limited unit. Above all, African dance does not exist without its music—usually characterized by drumming, singing and the accompaniment of other percussive instruments such as bells, shakers, clappers, whistles and others. Considering the above elements, how can this holistic art form be represented effectively through the various media available to us in today's world of technological advancement without a firsthand look at its practical component?

Although Stuart Hall and other Western cultural theorists have developed a strong theoretical foundation regarding representation, Western conventions alone cannot be used to fully represent the arts of Africa. This is not to say that these conventions are totally irrelevant in African dance scholarship. Contrary to the views of both African indigenous scholars and their Western counterparts on representation of the African arts which currently generates conflict between them creating barriers to the development of the art form, I have a different perception.

My Africanist perspective proposes a holistic approach involving integration of vocal and instrumental sounds with body movements and gestures, visual imagery and the various traditional African sensory modalities in the arts making process to locate dance and its related art forms in socio-cultural frameworks adaptable to scholars, practitioners and teachers as observed by Amegago (2011). For this approach to be complete, it must touch both the conceptual and practical elements of the art form in a collaborative process involving both native African scholars and their Western counterparts who are able to spend a considerable amount of time to experience the art form in its native soil.

Colonialism, Nationalism and Political Interference
Dance needs a theoretical framework within which its practitioners and scholars must operate effectively, but unfortunately Africa has not yet developed its own structure. John Miller Chernoff, an American ethnomusicologist, identifies this huge gap in his experience as an ethnographer in Africa. He notes: "Two major gaps in the academic study of African music; these are the lack of unifying framework for evaluating the information collected about African music and the lack of theoretical perspective for integrating musical analysis with social analysis" (Chernoff, 1979: 29). The creation of these gaps could be attributed to the fact that the power of oral tradition has been used over the years and also the over-reliance on this single ancient institution in propagating the art form.

Another contributing factor has been colonization where Africans were led to rebel against their own culture. In Ghana for instance, the colonial era (1860–1957) was characterised by negative attitudes towards the music and dance practice. Colonizers regarded Ghanaian dance/arts as barbarism, heathenism and primitive (Agawu 1995; Bebey 1975; Nketia 1974). However, after independence from British colonial rule in 1957, the first president of Ghana, Dr. Kwame Nkrumah, proposed the concept of cultural emancipation. In fact, in his independence speech Nkrumah declared 'the independence of Ghana is meaningless unless it is linked to the total liberation of the African continent' (Nkrumah, 1957). This declaration saw many African leaders declaring support for the Ghanaian leader and soliciting his support in pursuance of the said ambition. The product of his concept of cultural emancipation metamorphosed into the establishment of the Institute of African Studies at the University of Ghana, Legon. This institute was tasked with the responsibility of research and documentation of Ghanaian/African heritage. In 1962 this institution gave birth to The Ghana Dance Ensemble through a process described by Anthony Shay (2002) as folklorization; and this became a post- independence dance company led by two prominent Ghanaian music and dance scholars J.H.K. Nketia and Mawere Opoku.

Nketia was among ten distinguished African personalities who were awarded by The Pan African Society for Musical Arts Education (PASMAE) in Ghana on December 10, 2010 for their meritorious contributions to the development of indigenous African Music and Arts. In a speech, Nketia reaffirmed:

> "Our educational system is still in transition from its colonial beginnings as far as its African content and orientation is concerned. Our country still has some way to go in making cultural studies programmes in schools true to life for all Ghanaian school children by not presenting them only as cultural displays or as elements of antiquated cultures of their forebears about which they learn in the classroom with no proper relation to the experience they are supposed to encapsulate" (GNA, Dec. 10, 2010).

It is very important to acknowledge the fact that people are represented, in part, according to how they represent themselves. Formation of the Ghana Dance Ensemble was holistically done with much input from the custodians of the various art forms in all the regions of Ghana. However, what Anthony Shay described as 'parallel tradition' in his book *Choreographic Politics* (2002) was visible throughout their entire repertoire as theatricalization was used to transform the various dances from a community participatory activity into a stage performance designed for audience although those choreographic designs were in direct violation of the traditional norms that see dance as a shared tradition of the people.

Despite the above challenge, the company started touring nationally and internationally exhibiting the unique cultural heritage of Ghana. Therefore, the Ghana Dance Ensemble, in this context, was used to gather the various local community cultures into what can only be described as a 'national culture' of Ghana. This system provided the dancers opportunities to learn and perform dances that were not necessarily from their own communities.

Scholars have shared their thoughts on the formation of the Ghana Dance Ensemble (Adinku, 1994; Nketia, 1977; Schramm, 2000). While Adinku considers the national dance company as a repertory troupe experimenting with traditional dances and their models in new development, Nketia and Schramm see it as a new cultural movement that ideally contributes to the creation of national identity. Other African countries began to follow the trend by forming such post independence dance companies to represent their national identity on the international stage. 'Heart Beat of Africa' was one such group from Uganda, East Africa. Anthropologists, Judith Lynne Hanna and William John Hanna described the emergence of such groups as a renaissance of African culture. They wrote:

> "The appearance of Uganda's 'Heart beat of Africa' a national troupe of dancers and musicians at Expo '67 attracted international attention to this East African country's attempt to preserve valued elements of ethnic cultures, enhance its national pride and future and project its image from the outside world" (1968).

Unfortunately, th political climate in Africa interfered with the progress of such renaissance groups, making it very difficult if not impossible for them to achieve their main aim of representing the identity of their various countries. In the case of Uganda, Idi Amin's regime (1971 – 1979) negatively affected the arts in general leading to the eventual collapse of Heart Beat of Africa as most of the artists either went into exile or abandoned their craft for fear of losing their lives. In Ghana, although the arts had suffered at the hands of politicians who consistently refused to fund cultural programmes over the years leading to public agitation, a proper cultural policy was drafted and launched in 2004 to take care of the arts and the entire culture. Ghana now has in each of its ten regions a very important institution called the Centre for National Culture operated by the National Commission on Culture (The Arts Council of Ghana) where the author of this paper has worked as a cultural officer for five years.

In developing a theoretical framework for African dance, there is the need to use some Western conventions. This will require a proper collaboration between Western Scholars and their African counterparts to provide the opportunity for both groups of scholars to experience the art form on its native soil. A few Western scholars have attempted this approach by doing ethnographic studies but could not succeed due to the fact that their works focused on only the musical aspects of the art form. Burns (2009); Jones (1954); Chernoff (1979); Koetting (1970) and Locke (1982) are good examples. Locke studied the music of Ewe people in Ghana and his background as performer reflected in his approach emphasizing both descriptive and analytical methods. Chernoff, a social scientist on the other hand, observed the musical types of Dagombas and the Ewes with a combination of his learning experience and the aesthetics of his acculturative experience in Ghana that emphasizes his approach as more descriptive than analytical.

Burns is a Mexican -American ethnomusicologist who spent ten years in studying a small Ghanaian community in West Africa. During this period he learned and mastered the music, dance and language of a section of the Ewe people who live in a small town in the Volta Region of Ghana called Dzodze. His recent work *Female Voices from an Ewe Dance-drumming Community in Ghana* (2009) with a DVD documentary could be regarded as a starting point of what I call a holistic approach to the study and representation of the arts of Africa. His work brings a clear distinction between researching through thorough ethnographic study on one hand; and relying on mere stage productions and making one's own judgements on the other hand. Clearly, his work could be described as the most satisfying one among the lot listed above simply because he concentrated on a small group in an Ewe community.

Burns has done ground-breaking work in the field of African dance but I would consider myself a passive reader if I did not point out the conflicts and confusions that were consistently occurring in his discourse. For example, his ability to speak Ewe language deceived him to believe he could translate Ewe philosophical sayings as though they were English expressions, and in the process, there were many perplexities. Clearly, all of the above studies reveal a common problem that stems from a general lack of a holistic approach, as stated in Koetting's research, which was first identified by Anku (1997). He states:

> To analyse the patterns of a drum ensemble piece individually is to miss the main characteristic of the music, which is the totality of sound produced by the interrelation of the various parts. This is particularly true in viewing the relation between the master drum and the rest of the ensemble [....] what is needed is a comprehensive analysis that can encompass similarities and differences as components of the whole.... A deeper probe of the music involving such detail as the precise beginnings of master drum patterns, possible verbal meanings in subgroup or individual supporting patterns, and dance associations—would have to be made before any trustworthy conclusions could be reached (1970, 139).

Interestingly, Koetting's point does mention dance associations but fails to touch on the dance component of the art form.

The Need for Paradigm Change
The main setbacks to achieving a holistic collaboration include lack of trust on the part of the custodians of the art form, perhaps understandable given the inequality they suffered during the slavery and colonization of African people. To free ourselves from this entanglement, there is the need for a paradigm shift regarding what has been mentally constructed over the years. To advance my argument further, it is necessary to look at the word paradigm in the proper context. It is very easy to misuse, abuse, misunderstand or even hate the word paradigm if much care is not taken. Paradigm is a way of thinking, perceiving, communicating and viewing the world; therefore, it can be called a worldview or a mindset. It is part of the human cognitive domain that the bearers are not aware of due to the fact that it functions at a subconscious level. In the context of this essay, paradigm includes theories, principles, values, beliefs and doctrines. Psychologically speaking, it is the rigid tacit infrastructure of ideas that shapes not only our thinking but also our perception of the world.

Scientifically, it constitutes the immune system of our mind against new ideas which might be dangerous. However if it prevents the take up of any new idea, then I am afraid it is more dangerous.

Africans at home and in the Diaspora can be misled by paradigms to assume some sort of supreme power regarding representing the arts of Africa. Interestingly, some of these 'powerful Africans' have not been in touch with the art form and cannot identify its key elements. It is also possible to find several African indigenous scholars who are totally missing on the 'stage' due to the fact that they lack the practical training in the art form. The Ghanaian famous musicologist, Dr. Dartey Kumordzie remarked in a telephone interview: "There is a very limited number of African music and dance practitioners who double as scholars, and these are the right paint brushes that can put Africa on the global canvas. Therefore, we have a collective responsibility of creating a conducive environment which will motivate people in society for the purpose of transferring their skills into the younger generations" (2010).

A perfect example of such combined scholar-practitioner is Modesto Amegago, a Ghanaian music and dance scholar who uses an integrated approach in his teaching practices of African music and dance in North America. In an article titled "Integrated Approach to Teaching African Dance and Music: Challenges and Prospects", Amegago discusses his experiences of using this approach focusing on the method of designing integrated courses, the strategies of teaching, learning, assessing and evaluating these courses and the challenges posed to this approach as a response to the needs and demands of some institutions. Justifying this approach, he writes: "Such an approach is geared towards reintegrating the various aspects of African Performing Arts which are now modelled under separate areas such as music, dance, drama and visual arts in most contemporary arts educational institutions" (Amegago 2007). The Ghanaian dance academic in a telephone interview referred to representation as a multidimensional process and pointed to the holistic technique as the appropriate approach to represent African arts.

The core point from the already established Western conventions here is centered on **concept** and **meaning** as the significant elements of representation which need, in this case, to be communicated artistically through dance. However, these elements are naturally the embodiment of the culture of a given people/society. As an African traditional dance practitioner, I would look at culture in this context as the accumulated practices and experiences of a people in a given geophysical environment through time and causation. In other words, culture is the totality of the knowledge system of a people relating to every aspect of life. It is however, dynamic and in constant flux.

The dynamism of African culture is guided by its underlying bedrock of metaphysical elements such as insight into principles and mechanisms of social life, cosmogony, music, movement, language, philosophy, religion, customs and beliefs, symbolism and visual arts; all of which constitute a holistic art form known as dance, and was originally stored in a repository called oral tradition. For example, Ghanaian ethnic groups have a number of good values such as good moral living, and respect for the elderly, all of which are stored in their songs, dance movements and drum languages simply to serve as guiding principles which also provide room for innovation in future developments. Scholars of African music and dance have acknowledged the effectiveness of the power of this oral tradition and expressed their thoughts on the challenges facing its sustainability. Doris Green, an African American notator writes: "When keepers of African oral tradition die, they literally take libraries of African Music and Dance into the grave where it is entombed and lost to the world forever" (Green, 1998).

By looking at representation as a surrogate will lead to questions such as, what is it a surrogate for? How close is the surrogate to the 'original' thing? What attributes of the original does it capture? What attributes of the original does it omit and so on? In representing African arts, one would have to seek answers to the above questions and the most satisfying method is to experience the practical element of it in its native soil. Anthony Shay notes: 'An artistic director or choreographer can learn dances by using a number of methods. By far the most satisfying is fieldwork in which the individual goes to the place where the dance is natively performed' (2002: 43). This, in Africa will lead to the development of deeper sense of understanding of the art form as a spontaneous emanation of the people. Therefore, the best way of representing Africa is to look at both ontological and epistemological approaches to its holistic art form. This herculean task must be carried out collectively.

On Friday, 17th September, 2010, a conference was organized at the University Roehampton in London for staff and postgraduate students on 'The Idea of University'. A hundred and twenty years after his death, John Henry Newman's concept of university still remains a fresh challenge for the twenty-first century scholars. In fulfillment of Newman's (1854) notion of enlarging the mind to experience other disciplines in order to acquire knowledge and skills in other areas apart from one's own field of specialisation, I decided to hold an African drumming and dance session for the participants at the conference. (This was not pre-planned.) In her conference report, Professor Tina Beattie wrote: " A real highlight of the day was when Kwashie conducted an impromptu drumming session during the lunch break, and the drums talked among themselves with their own particular blend of eloquence, humour and intelligence" (Beattie 2010). While it is important to note here that Beattie reported the true picture of the session, it is equally important to state here that in Africa, the word impromptu would not be needed due to the spontaneous nature of the African arts.

Royce Anya Peterson, a renowned ballerina and anthropologist who utilizes a comparative, cross-cultural and cross-temporal approach to study issues of artistry, virtuosity and interpretation in performance made a distinction between 'knowing something by the doing of it and knowing something by thinking about it' (Royce 2004: 228). The holistic technique can only work perfectly by looking at the African arts with an interdisciplinary approach that is capable of touching its sociological, political, anthropological, musical, historical and cultural dimensions. In addition, representing this holistic art form in the modern globalized world of creativity and innovation must adopt flexible tools to make room for adjustments, modifications and negotiations in order to serve multicultural needs of society.

Returning to the point of using dance as a tool for representation in relation to the above point captures the thoughts of Alessandra Royo to reaffirm the notion that dance representation is based on classifications which are not meant to reflect a definitive order of things but are conceived as flexible tools of understanding. "Representing dance is not about capturing its authentic essence but about transformation. Documentation of dance is about capturing and transforming, through interpretation fragments of the dance experience" (Royo 1997). This gives us the awareness that dance representation cannot produce anything called original or authentic.

Until this holistic approach is used collectively to develop theoretical framework, African dance can be aesthetically appealing to its audience but its concept and meaning with all other representational elements will still be totally missing in contemporary scholarship. Speaking from my own Africanist point of view, our own paradigms can mislead us to believe that apart from the Africans, no other scholars are needed to engage in constructing appropriate framework within which statements could be made about the African arts. It is impossible to view one's own self completely without using a mirror. This reminds me of the Ewe wise saying that: "*Nunya Adzidoe, asi metune o.*"(Knowledge is like the trunk of a baobab tree that a single person's arms cannot encompass).

Clifford Geertz, a highly influential American anthropologist, made a good point about the best way of looking at an art as viewing it in its own terms and thinking about our own reactions. I am of the view that by viewing African arts in its own terms will lead us to study and know the people as well as their thoughts being expressed in the arts. Geertz also proposed a theory of art as a cultural system (1983) in which the response to aesthetics is both intellectual and emotional or rooted in one's feelings. "These feelings in turn are seen as rooted in culture itself manifested in the varied expressions of religion, morality, science, commerce, technology, politics, amusements, law and even in the societal organisation of everyday practical existence" (Geertz 1983). I would not hesitate to consider Geertzian theory as a vital part of a foundation upon which African theoretical framework could be built.

It is rather unfortunate that Western stereotypes of Africa have been used to represent the African arts leading to the ignorance of its vital elements such as good values, principles and mechanisms of social life. The term stereotype, deals with the received common idea or convention that will standardize image or conception of a type of a person or people. Generally, stereotypes that are directed towards people are often not polite and can be considered as very derogatory. In her book, *Dancing The Black Question*, Christy Addair describes 'Adzido Pan African Dance Ensemble' as "an African ensemble of twenty-eight dancers, funded by the arts council that had become the example of Black British dance that was promoted and that reinforced stereotypes of black arts" (Adair 2007: 98).

This description put me at a total loss considering the fact that her polemical narrative deserves a high level of prestige in both professional and academic dance circles. I began to pursue Adair with many specific questions in order to fully understand her position and this led me to an article written in a British newspaper 'The Observer' by Jann Parry. She writes "Adzido is a company in search of identity. After losing its way doing traditional African dances, it has turned to black South African choreographers for a contemporary urban image. Adzido, relaunched, has still to determine where it's going and what it's for" (The Observer, 11 July 2004). In order to respond appropriately to the above review, I deem it necessary to give an overview of Adzido.

Adzido Pan-African Dance Ensemble

The formation of Adzido recalls a group of dancers and musicians who made a journey from Ghana into the United Kingdom in 1974 with the name 'Sankofa'. The main purpose of this group was to perform Ghanaian dances as a way of promoting the cultural heritage of Ghana. While some members of Sankofa made their way back to Ghana after a successful British tour, others decided to stay to become cultural ambassadors due to the enthusiasm and prestige with which their performances were received.

But these cultural ambassadors could not continue their work without some setbacks including lack of funding as well as opposition and humiliation they received from British society. In an interview, George Fiawoo, one of these Ghanaian cultural ambassadors, stated clearly that in going about their usual practice to perform Ghanaian dance in schools in the early days, they thought it wise and culturally appropriate to wear African costumes. Their costumes rather became objects of mockery as even students were making the most derogatory statements about them such as; "Look at the black monkeys; here they come again in their pyjamas" (Fiawoo 2010).

It was during this period that British authorities decided not to encourage the development of ethnic minority arts with a general claim that efforts to do so would bring division. A comprehensive report written to the Arts Council of Britain by Naseem Khan in 1976 titled, *The Arts Britain Ignores* strongly disagrees with British authorities and fully articulates the need to encourage the ethnic minority arts in Britain arguing that the introduction of ethnic minority arts provided the opportunity of seeing, learning and experiencing fresh cultural forms, thereby creating multi-racial society, a vital aspect which is worth fostering and promoting (Khan 1976).

Felix Cobbson, a Ghanaian teacher working in the United Kingdom who had already started teaching African Drumming in a secondary school in Harlow tried to mobilize these Ghanaian cultural ambassadors into his dance group but unfortunately this move did not materialize. According to Khan's report, Cobbson had already trained and presented on stage young native British dancers in West African dance, a performance which became the talk of town with the fascinating element pointing to the fact that there was not a single African or West Indian in what was described as a 'competently performed piece' (1976:7). Indeed, the work of these Ghanaian cultural ambassadors became popular as they kept traveling the length and breadth of the country in teaching the Ghanaian dance repertory such as Kpalongo, Adowa, Gahu, Gota, Bima, Atsiagbekor, to mention a few.

In 1984, George Dzikunu mobilized these Ghanaian artists and Adzido was formed as a black dance company that survived in the United Kingdom for two decades. A black dance company in this context refers to a dance group that has its root in the African cultural idioms and continues to represent, reflect and advance the cultural heritage of black people. Discussing this dance group in an African cultural and philosophical context primarily requires insight into the meaning and significance of its name. The name 'Adzido' in Ewe language (in the Volta Region of Ghana), refers to the baobab tree. This name was taken from the Ewe wise saying stated earlier that goes; *Nunya Adzidoe, asi metune o*. (Knowledge is like the trunk of a baobab tree, that a single person's arms cannot encompass it).

In fact, the baobab is among the largest and longest-lived trees on earth. It survives prolonged droughts by storing water in its massive, fibrous, sponge-like trunk which can be up to thirty to sixty feet in diameter. That trunk can be hollowed out to make a shelter, or cut into water containers. When in leaf, the Baobab produces an edible fruit that has the highest concentration of Vitamin C of any plant. The leaves themselves are rich in Vitamin A and the shade of those leaves and branches provide a relatively cool refuge for other living things in the sub-Saharan heat. Therefore the baobab tree is a symbol of endurance, conservation, creativity, greatness, ingenuity and dialogue.

Adzido's early performances were Ghanaian dances that are usually to signify a rite of passage or another form of celebration such as a child moving into adulthood, a marriage or to signify love. One example is 'Tokoe', a puberty dance of the Dangbe people in the Greater Accra Region of Ghana. Later, their performances transformed into what could be described as classical African tribal dance adapted for stage performance in a form of moulding traditional dances around selected themes and poetry.

In the 1970s and early 80s, much of the funding for the minority arts came through social rather than artistic sources. Hilary Carty writes: "Adzido was initially under the auspices of the Manpower Services Commission while the majority of groups received small pockets of funding from Local Authority Social Services and Education budgets rather than artistic ones" (Carty 2007). Looking at the nature of their funding, the groups were not motivated enough to expand their artistic work in order to create and reach audiences beyond the then small community outreach environment. Adzido's first full-length piece was 'Coming Home', with about twenty dancers and musicians telling the story of the son of an African chief who returns home to Africa from the West and discovers he has forgotten his tribal dances. This show was performed at Sadler's Wells Theatre of London in 1988. Certainly, Adzido's expansion from a small community size through national to continental/international status put the company in the limelight for support and encouragement thereby attaining Arts Council Funding from 1991.

In terms of representation, Adzido began with the traditional dances from Ghana in four different categories: war dances, cult dances, social dances and royal dances. The company later expanded its repertoire to include dances from West African countries such as the Adzogbo from Benin, Atsia from Togo, Wango from Senegal, Wale from Guinea and the rest with which they fully exhibited artistically onstage the cultural diversity of the West African sub-region. George Dzikunu, who had been the artistic director of the company until 2000, used his initiatives to bring music and dance artists from all over the African continent to work with the company. This move saw a significant development of the company with further expansion of their repertoire to cover dances from many parts of the African continent. The membership increased up to twenty-eight dancers and musicians, who began embracing a rounded production format basically showcasing different types of African traditional dances. In 2004, the company folded following the withdrawal of their funding by the British Council.

As a dancer, master drummer and general practitioner of a range of dance forms from the West African sub region, my practice in multicultural Britain in more than two hundred schools over the last six years has been received with much enthusiasm and prestige due to the basic foundation laid by Adzido. Many dance practitioners and scholars have made reference to Adzido from different ideological perspectives in their works. Anthropologist and dance scholar, Andree Grau, in a comprehensive piece titled *Dance and The Shifting Sands of Multiculturalism* describes Adzido's stage works as 'exuberant performances' that were enjoyed by their audiences (Grau 2008). Hilary Carty, a dancer and arts administrator, writes "Adzido sought to mould the traditional dances around a theme or poetry, creating a more epic style with a company of over 30 dancers and musicians" (Carty 2007: 19).

The review in the Observer Newspaper presents a few questions for Jann Parry, and these include whether or not she has ever watched the full repertory of Adzido; her knowledge and understanding of African traditional dance; the criteria she used in assessing the company to arrive at this suggestion and finally the rationale behind her judgement. Perhaps the provision of specific answers to these questions will lead the critical reader to believe that Jann Parry's article is not a deliberate attempt to stereotype Adzido in British media. Although I am disappointed at the high level of attention given to the concept of race by twenty-first century scholarship, I can understand why scholars such as Brenda Dixon-Gottschild do not want to do away with the concept of race. Carolyn Fluehr-Lobban in her book, *Race and Racism* (2006) examines the foundations of race in American society. She offers a simple and accessible explanation of the biology of race and a cross-cultural perspective on the social context of race, color-coding, ethnicity and ethnocentrism. In a world where race is a factor in almost every society and its politics, her research finds abundant evidence that race is a dynamic, changing concept; and that it is a cultural concept rather than a biological 'fact.'

Conclusion

Having identified such factors that challenge effective representation of African arts including, the use of wrong technique by non-Africans; the neglect of African arts by its owners as a result of slavery and colonialism; the marginalization the practitioners of African dance face even in their own home soil; and lack of well-developed African frameworks, this essay reminds us that we must not forget that race and racism are two different concepts. The two are not the same. Race may be a biological inheritance (although most socialists would disagree with this notion) while racism is an ideology belonging to the realm of cultural construction and of power politics. We cannot do away with different groups of people, but we can easily wipe out a mental construct called racism without losing anything from our various cultures. Therefore, scholars who still argue and cite lack of place to dump the concept as the only reason they cannot do away with racism; my collaborative holistic approach prepares a befitting grave as a burial place for it.

In conclusion, I consider the point made by the established Ghanaian philosopher, Kwame Anthony Appiah that "the description of someone else's folk philosophy, without any serious analysis of its concepts or any critical reflection on how understanding the world with those concepts allow us to appreciate what may not be appreciated in other conceptual schemes, is surely a mere curiosity" (Appiah 1992: 94). Appiah is of the view that analyzing African philosophy in Western contexts tends to be problematic. In as much as this is still a problem in twenty-first century scholarship, my argument emphasizes the point that an attempt to resolve it must consider the guiding principles of African cultures such as the distinctive factors in the face of globalization and multiculturalism of today's technological world. In view of this, I argue that considering the multi-dimensional nature of representation, African dance analysis must employ an interdisciplinary framework—historical, sociological, anthropological, cultural and musical—using a holistic approach that combines both the practical and conceptual elements of the art form as well as African multi-sensory modalities.

References

Adair, Christy. 2007. *Dancing The Black Question*. London: Dance Books.

Agawu, Kofi. 1995. *African Rhythm: A Northern Ewe Perspective*. Cambridge: Cambridge University Press.

Amegago, Modesto M. 2011. *An African Music and Dance Curriculum Model: Performing Arts in Education*. Durham, N.C.: Carolina Academic Press.

___. 2007. "Integrated Approach to Teaching African Dance." *African Journal for Physial, Health Education, Recreation and Dance (AJPHERD)*. 13(3): 231-240 September.

Appiah, Kofi A. 1992. *In My Father's House. Africa in the Philosophy of Culture*. New York: Oxford University Press.

Asante, K. W. Ed. 1996: *African Dance; An Artistic, Historical and Philosophical Inquiry*. New Jersey: Africa World Press.

Bebey, Francis. 1975. *African Music- A People's Art*. New York: Lawrence Hill Books.

Burns, James. 2009. *Female Voices from An Ewe Dance-Drumming Community*. Surrey: Ashgate Publishing Limited.

Chernoff, John Miller. 1979. *African Rhythm and African Sensibility-Aesthetics and Social Action in African Musical Idioms*. Chicago: University of Chicago Press.

DeFrantz, Thomas F., ed. 2002. *Dancing Many Drums*. Madison, Wisconsin: University of Wisconsin Press.

Fraleigh, Sondra Horton and Penelope Hanstein. Eds. 1999. *Researching Dance: Evolving Modes of Inquiry*. London: Dance Books, Ltd.

Geertz, Clifford. 1983. *Local Knowledge: Further Essays in Interpretive Anthropology*. New York: Basic Books Inc.

Gottschild, B. 2003. *The Black Dancing Body*. New York: Palgrave Macmillan.

Hall, Stuart. 1997. *Representation: Cultural Representations and Signifying Practice*. Milton Kynes: The Open University.

King, Coretta Scott. 1987. *The Words of Martin Luther King, Jr*. New York: New Market Press.

Loomba, Ania. 2005. *Colonialism/Post Colonialism*. London: Routledge.

Nketia, J. H. K. 1970. *African Gods and Music*. Accra: University of Ghana, Legon.

Obeng, Samuel. 1997. *Selected Speeches of Kwame Nkrumah Vol.1*. Accra: Afram.

Opoku, A. M. 1966. *Choreography and the African Dance*. Accra: University of Ghana, Legon.

Royce, Anya Peterson. 2004. *Anthropology of Performing Arts; Artistry, Virtuosity and Interpretation in Cross-Cultural Perspective*. Walnuk Creek, CA: Alta Mira Press.

Shay, Anthony. 2002. *Choreographic Politics*. Middletown. CT: Wesleyan University Press.

Stone, Ruth. 1998. *Africa, The Garland Encyclopaedia of World Music*. New York. Garland Publishing, Inc.

23–24 September 2011

Two-Day
International Conference
University of Ghana
Institute of African Studies

The conference was the first
event of the Intellectual and
Cultural Heritage Festival Series.

MEMORIES

Dearest Prof. Yɛda wo ase!